Sources Of
American Spirituality

Isaac T. Hecker
The Diary
ROMANTIC RELIGION
IN ANTE-BELLUM AMERICA

Edited by John Farina

PAULIST PRESS
New York ◆ Mahwah

Library of Congress Cataloging-in-Publication Data

Hecker, Isaac Thomas, 1819–1888.
    Isaac Hecker: the diary.

    (Sources of American spirituality)
    Includes bibliographies and index.
    1. Hecker, Isaac Thomas, 1819–1888—Correspondence.
2. Paulist Fathers—United States—Correspondence.
3. Converts, Catholic—United States—Correspondence.
I. Farina, John.   II. Title.   III. Series.
BX4705.H4A3   1988   271′.79   [B]   88-15267
ISBN 0-8091-0391-5

Published by Paulist Press
997 Macarthur Boulevard
Mahwah, N.J. 07430

Printed and bound in the United States of America

CONTENTS

PREFACE   1

GENERAL INTRODUCTION   3

EDITORIAL PROCEDURES   79

TEXT OF THE DIARY   87

NOTES TO THE DIARY   327

LIST OF EMENDATIONS EXPLAINED   380

LIST OF EMENDATIONS   381

BIBLIOGRAPHY   429

INDICES   443

PREFACE

The many different pieces of this book require some explanation. The book contains Isaac Thomas Hecker's writings and my own. I have spent a good deal of ink describing Hecker's. Hence, all that is needed here is a road map to mine.

I have written two types of introductions: individual introductions to each of the six volumes of the diary and one general introduction. In the introductions to the volumes, I highlight the main themes of the volume under discussion and trace the basic outlines of Hecker's activity during the time he is writing. For that reason, I spend little time in the general introduction dealing with the volume-by-volume development of the diary and with biographical facts about Hecker. In the general introduction, my main concern is to present an interpretation of the cultural developments of the 1840s and to set the diary in the context of those events. There I argue for the importance of the diary and for the significance of Hecker's attempts to express his American, Romantic, Catholic experience.

To the text of the diary I have added many notes, which have the same goal as the introductions and indeed are supplements to them. The bibliography is a list of all sources given in the notes and introductions, plus those I used as background material.

The text of the diary is a complete, critical edition. It represents the first such edition of this previously unpublished document. The Editorial Procedures section explains the philosophy and method used to create the new edition. The List of Emendations that follows the text gives the original manuscript reading and the details of every change made.

The publication of this work in *The Sources of American Spirituality* series is appropriate indeed. It was the study of Hecker's thought that originally inspired me to conceive of the series back in 1982. Hecker was one

1

of the great champions of indigenous religious expression; hence, I feel confident he would approve of the scope and goals of the *Sources*. It is, therefore, particularly appropriate that this work should be published during the centennial year of his death.

There are of course many people to thank. I am grateful to the Paulist Fathers for their support during the years, especially that of Frs. Lawrence McDonnell, William Dewan, Joseph Gallagher, and Kevin Lynch. To my able assistants I owe a real debt. Georgia Mandakas worked diligently on the text, and Thomas Hur was an indefatigable assistant with the notes and introductions. Helen Curran, Robert Sirico, and Cynthia Funk each played lesser, but much appreciated, roles. Patrick Kennerly provided valuable help with proofreading. To my colleagues and Robert Emmett Curran, Joseph Chinnici, and Christopher Kaufmann I am thankful for expert criticism. Roger Sorrentino also offered valuable advice. My wife Paula did the copyediting. I am also thankful to the staff of the Library of Congress, especially Bruce Martin, and to the charming collection of mavericks and sages who populated the alcoves of the main reading room for their presence.

GENERAL INTRODUCTION

CHAPTER 1

THE CHALLENGE OF THE DIARY

With hundreds of books being written on the history of the United States every year, why should one spend time reading a text from the last century that was not even intended for publication? Why should one struggle with the fledgling prose of a man in his early twenties who had little formal education and had not, by the time of his first diary entries, mastered the mechanics of the English language? These are serious questions that confront anyone dealing with unpublished materials that were clearly written for private use. Yet, some of the very qualities that make this piece problematic give it a unique status as a source about the role that religion played in the culture of the antebellum United States. In this document, the times are reflected in an immediate, often uncritical manner. Furthermore, they are reflected through the person of one wholly absorbed by questions of ultimate meaning. The religious quest is—in its most primitive, most essential mode—the story of the person trying to find meaning in the universe. That universe includes all that he experiences, internally and externally. How those experiences are interpreted, how they are bound together, is the stuff of religious expression. Hence to view that process through the genre of a personal diary is advantageous, because it is a genre that is closer to immediate experience than published writings. Seen in this way, this document sheds an unusually revealing light on the interplay of the secular and the sacred in America during the 1840s. Its importance lies in its character as an attempt to create a symbolic language to express a new form of religious experience that never had existed before with quite the same self-consciousness and definition. That experience is best described as American, Romantic, and Catholic.

Along with a handful of converts from the 1840s, Isaac Thomas Hecker (1819–1888) attempted this new language, bringing to his effort an unusually keen sensibility that afforded him a vivid, rapturous awareness of the religious dimension in himself and in the world around him. Although some Catholic prelates like Martin John Spalding and John Hughes reflected the impact of the Romantic mood and of the American experience on their religious thought, the fuller expression of this new hybrid experience was reserved for a small group of individuals of the 1840s. Although it is not my purpose to trace in detail the little-known dimensions of that movement, what follows will in fact deal with its main stream in which Hecker constantly swam.

It was Hecker whose voice—perhaps one should say whose heart— gave the movement its finest affective religious expression. That expression began right with the earliest extant fragments of his diary, dating back to the final months of 1842, and continued throughout the document, often struggling under the burden of educational lapses, pulling itself up slowly during the course of two and one-half years and at times bursting through with originality and vigor.

Biography

Isaac Hecker was born in New York City on December 18, 1819. His mother, Caroline Friend Hecker, and father, John Hecker, were natives of Germany. Isaac was the youngest of five children. One, Henry, died as an infant. His two older brothers John, Jr., and George, were joined by a sister, Elizabeth. Mrs. Hecker was the controlling influence in the home, especially after 1823 when her husband's brass foundry business failed. After that time, Isaac's father became a shadowy figure, present and regarded lovingly, but having little influence on family affairs. At one point Isaac addressed him in a letter, urging him to overcome an unnamed bad habit. Clearly, by the time Isaac started writing, John was, for whatever reason, a broken man. John, Jr., who had learned the baking business from his maternal uncle Christopher Schwab, decided after the failure of his father's business to open a bakery. George and Isaac became partners in an enterprise that began with a small shop on Rutgers Street. A combination of hard work and ingenuity caused the business to prosper. By the year in which the diary begins the Hecker Brothers had four locations in Manhattan, plus a recently completed flour mill at the corner of Cherry and Pike Streets. George and John were well on their way to becoming millionaires.

Among the many and varied influences on Isaac's intellectual development prior to his first extant writing in 1842, the most important was his experience of Methodism—the religion of his mother—which he encountered in the lively Forsyth Street Church. In that setting he had imparted to him ideas about the importance of community in the fostering of faith, about the reality of Christ and the nearness of his Spirit, and about the signs of the times that made his nation and his age special. He also experimented with the progressive Unitarianism of Orville Dewey whose Church of the Messiah on Broadway was the scene of the proclamation of a gospel of human ability, progress, and practical application of religion to everyday life. Even the radical ideas of Joseph Smith captured his attention in the person of Mormon evangelist Parley Parker Pratt whom he met when Pratt was in New York publishing a book on Mormonism in 1837.

Isaac had had little formal schooling and since age 13 had been working, first in jobs for Methodist magazines and then as a partner in the baking business. By 1842 he was anxious to get a more formal education, and his hopes were boosted by a visit to the family home by Orestes Brownson. Brownson was in town to deliver a lecture series for the Loco-Foco party on the relation between religion and democracy. The Hecker brothers had become heavily involved with that party and the cause of Jacksonian political reform. John, Jr., who remained active in New York politics his whole life, at one time running for mayor, was a leader of the group. Brownson, upon meeting Isaac in 1842 and hearing of his desire to study, suggested that he visit him at his home in Chelsea and then consider spending a time of study at Brook Farm. Isaac was excited by the idea and received the loving, if somewhat skeptical, approval of his family who liberally supplied him with funds for his trip and education. That pattern of support was to continue, especially in the person of George, Isaac's closest friend throughout his life. One year after Isaac, George converted to Catholicism and remained a faithful, extremely generous supporter of his brother's ministry.[1]

The diary begins during the transition period when Isaac is away from home for the first time to pursue an education while his brothers are busily and successfully laboring. He remains at Brook Farm from April to September 1843, during which time he spends two weeks at Fruitlands. After that he returns home to New York and takes up part-time work with the family business and enrolls in the Cornelius Institute in New York to study classical languages, with an eye toward the ministry. He goes off again to continue that study with George Bradford in Concord in April 1844. During his month there he stays at the home of Henry David Thoreau as a boarder. His decision to enter the Catholic church causes him to return home, where he stays for the remainder of the time of diary writing, until July 1845.

What happened after the period covered by the diary is of course the main reason why we look to the writings of Hecker in the first place. The story of his work as a Redemptorist missionary, as the founder and superior of a new congregation—the Missionary Society of St. Paul the Apostle—his work as a journalist and his efforts at Vatican I and later in Europe as an advocate of worldwide spiritual renewal has been told elsewhere. Anyone familiar with it will see the ways in which his thought in the diary was the basis for what followed.[2] Doubtless it developed and matured, but the beginnings are here. Walter Elliott himself, in organizing the Hecker papers after his mentor's death in 1888, wrote on the cover of the final volume of the diary: "The germs of nearly all his later ideas are contained here." If the style of the piece is understood and its purpose grasped, the later musings of Hecker, especially when he returns to diary writing in the 1870s while chronic leukemia is ravaging his body and threatening to break his spirit, appear as part of a larger story of growth. Anyone who would understand the mature Hecker fully must grapple with the early diary.

Given this, I have made an effort throughout to view the diary in its own times, to understand it as part of antebellum American culture. This approach will enlighten those who would see in Hecker only what pertains to the Americanist controversy. That controversy began after his death, and as such, to impose its world view on the earliest writings of Hecker done over half a century earlier would be anachronistic. Furthermore, as William Portier has suggested, it was precisely such a failure to deal with Hecker on his own terms that fueled the fires of the controversy in the first place.[3] As I shall show in chapter 2, the unwillingness to see Hecker's diary as a part of the culture that spawned it was the single most important reason why Elliott's *Life of Father Hecker* became the target of the anti-Americanist Charles Maignen's attack in *Le Père Hecker, Est-il un Saint?*

Form, Style, and Scope of the Diary

The diary is written in six bound notebooks, each having retained all of its leaves. There are three separate fragments. The first, Fragment A-D, is a folio written on all four sides. I have designated it Fragment A-D to indicate the number of pages, four, pages A-D. It is dated at the top "42," which of course must signify 1842, but the month is uncertain. We know, however, that it was not until the fall of 1842 that Hecker began attending seriously to introspection, study, and reading, so it is very likely that the fragment is from that time.

The second, Fragment E-H, is a folio dated January 10, 1843, on the first page, with no other dates elsewhere. The third, Fragment I-L, contains the date "3d Feb.," which is in all likelihood, February 1843. It contains two more dated entries from February 4 and 5 and one undated, preceding the February 3 entry. It is an incomplete entry, the only one in the diary.

The first bound volume of the diary is the largest of the six books. It contains a pencil-written, partial index on the first leaf, followed by an undated dedicatory prayer, after which comes the first dated entry of April 15, 1843. At the top of the page is written "Brook Farm." The final entry is May 20, 1843.

Volume 2 likewise contains a partial index in the front cover and opens with the heading "Concord, Mass., May 30th 1844. Thursday." The final entry is dated July 23, 1844. Volume 3 follows the same pattern and is dated from New York on July 25, 1844, to August 28, 1844.

The fourth volume is different both in form and content from all the others. It begins with an explanation that it will be used to "record the many smaller venial sins which beset my path," and in fact, it is just that—a prolonged examination of conscience. It reflects one aspect of his new-found Catholic piety and lacks the speculative charm of the other books. It was written between September 9, 1844, and January 1, 1845. One could argue that it should not be part of the diary because of its distinct form. It, however, was written about his internal states and in content, if not in form, resembles the rest of the diary that was clearly written during the same time. It has always been handed down with the diary, as part of the same fond. For those reasons it is included here and designated Volume 4.

During part of the time he was writing Volume 4, he was keeping another book, which in style and content is much like the earlier diary volumes. It is different, however, in that it has only one date, December 1844, at the beginning and another, June 28, 1844, at the end. The style is more continuous than other volumes, but only slightly so; it is still full of aphorisms and undeveloped ideas as are the other diary volumes. Although the diurnal entry style is absent, I have included it as Volume 5 for the same reasons I did Volume 4. The final volume is dated from January 20, 1845, to July 28, 1845, and, like earlier volumes, contains dated entries.[4]

As Toby Tanner so gracefully reminded us, the New England Renaissance was characterized by an effort on the part of writers to get back to the fresh, original, childlike moment of perception. That first moment of awe, that instant when the horizon in all its immensity pops into view, that wonder was the goal rather than the analytical exercise in which judgment is the most valued faculty. As Thomas Carlyle said in his memorable words which every Transcendentalist found echoing in his heart: "Wonder is the basis of Worship: the reign of wonder is perennial, indestructible in Man."[5] This wonder engendered an inclination to see all of nature, indeed all of existence as a whole, to take it all in uncritically, thrilled by its power, its beauty, its potential.

Certainly, as appealing as Tanner's characterization is, there are exceptions to the rule he lays down. There were at least two types of minds among New England prophets of the movement called by many simply the Newness. One was indeed the wonderer Tanner describes; the other, however, exercised far more the critical faculties. Indeed his critique of the present order was what motivated him and gave his prose a starting point. If in the first category one would put Emerson, Thoreau, and Alcott, in the second one must name characters whom posterity has not regarded as highly, but who were in their own day as important: men like Theodore Parker, Orestes Brownson, William Henry Channing, and George Ripley.

Hecker learned how to write in the company of Transcendentalists of both types. Raised in a German-American home by parents born in Germany, he could read and speak his parents' tongue in addition to English. He had had no long periods of formal schooling in either language, however, and when he moves away from home to go to Brook Farm to study in April 1843, that lack is painfully evident. His difficulties with the written language go beyond the common inconsistencies of antebellum American prose. He simply does not have a clue on how to spell, as he complains in the diary itself, nor any firm sense of grammar. Hence his use of punctuation and his capitalization are erratic. The first sections of the diary are especially rough, using spaces—irregular spaces—in the place of periods and commas. At Brook Farm, however, he is reading widely. He studies the articles of his friend and mentor Orestes Brownson, whose prose teaches him something about consistency, logic, and argumentation. He reads articles in the *Dial* from which he gleans a scattering of literary criticism by authors like Ripley and Charles Dana. He also peruses the indecipherable efforts of Alcott and the radical reform articles of Charles Lane. But he is most interested in fiction and attracted instinctively to the reign of wonder.

His background makes the writings of the German Romantic novelists most compelling. He reads Goethe's *Die Leiden des jungen Werthers, Dichtung und Wahrheit,* and *Die Wahlverwandtschaften.* But it is Jean Paul Richter that draws him most strongly. An early fragment of the diary reveals just how much he liked the German Rousseau. He tells us that he has just read through Richter's *Heperus, Siebankas, Titan,* and his autobiography, *Wahrheit aus Jean Pauls Leben.* That means over 3000 closely printed pages. Not surprisingly they had their effect. Hecker not only uses scenes from Richter for his own imaginative flights, he emulates the style. That style, as far as any in the Romantic period, presaged the modern psychological novel with its focus on the consciousness of the individual, its disregard for traditional formulations of plot, and its sense of being unfettered by cause and effect, and chronology. It also carried with it a bathetic quality that has made it eminently forgettable for most contemporary readers. When Hecker tries his hand at a Richter fantasy, the product is a good deal less refined, devoid of classical imagery, limited to one character and one theme, lacking the finesse of his hero.

There is one thing, however, that it does not lack. From the first page there is an intensity that burns through all of the imperfections of form. He is the wonderer, the youth suddenly becoming aware of others, of the problems of vocation, of God, but most importantly of his own consciousness.

That awareness is shocking at times, troubling and perplexing. It sends him off groaning with discomfort. At other times it is thrilling and it makes him laugh and sing and shout inside. And there are times, especially later in the piece, when it is comforting, when he can rest in the consciousness of his own being, confident that God is near and that the world is a friendly place. Although the forms are often imperfect, the cadence—the voice—is strong and clear. It is his heart that comes through the blemishes of style and captivates us with its humanity, its strangeness, and above all its intensity.

Throughout, the diary is an exploration of his internal states. It is a place for emotional experimentation where he can try out a feeling, test a conviction, prove a hunch. As such it has a tentative, meandering quality. When struggling with the church question in the spring of 1844, for example, one day he is writing that the church "meets all my needs." The next he is penning the conviction that it does not answer to his innermost sensibilities. Or, when he is studying at Brook Farm we read that to engage in his family's baking business is to do "the Devil's work," only to hear him announce a few weeks later that he is on his way home to New York to work with his brothers.

The diary is primarily about himself. We do find a few choice descriptions of Brownson, a famous critique of the Transcendentalists as cold-blooded aestheticians, and a number of discussions of his readings. But they are not the thrust of the document. Rather, we have a portrait of the self, seeking to understand itself. All that it sees around it, it filters through the prism of its own awareness. Three great intertwined questions dominate the text and set the context for the self's explorations: Who am I? What should I do with my life? and What role does religion play in my life? In this sense the diary is an exercise in autobiography more than it is a commentary on the times. Certainly it is not full-fledged autobiography as in a presentation of a retrospective account of a whole life (or a significant part of a life) written as avowed truth by the person who lived the life.[6] Yet it does share aspects of that genre, not only in its subject and focus, but in its preoccupation with questions of truth and meaning. G. Thomas Couser argued that American autobiographers tend to assume the role of prophet, incorporating didactic, hortatory impulses, conflating personal and communal history, and creating exemplary patterns of behavior.[7] While the full range of those characteristics appears only in undeveloped forms later in the late 1850s when Hecker writes two apologetical works, the diary does deal repeatedly with questions of truth, whether they are about the validity of his own sentiments, the origin of the church, or the type of work he should do. For even though the focus of the piece is the self, that is not its goal. Its end is the relating of the self to truth in a proper manner. We are not presented here with a solipsistic fantasy, but rather with the quest of the individual seeking full realization of his potential, always ultimately concerned with his relation to the whole. The person finds meaning by entering into his own subjectivity, but then the relation of the subject to the object, the Me to the Not-Me, must constantly be addressed. Once he discovers that the Catholic church plays an essential role in that relation, he is ready to proclaim that truth. It is at that point, late in the diary after his conversion, that the prophetic element emerges in force, even though it had been hinted at before.

So then the diary is about Hecker's self, but as we have intimated, it is an expansive, transcendent self. It is a self that asks questions common to youth and deals with the basic religious questions, and in that sense its story reaches over the century to our own time.

To watch the story unfold in all its richness, however, requires a detailed examination of the cultural context. Seen as an isolated bit of writing, its significance is minor, and one would be hard pressed to say why it should command our attention. Yet, if we view it as a reflection of the culture of the early 1840s, it shows us a great deal about the interface of society and religion in antebellum America. Because its author was associated with some of the best minds in the American Renaissance and because he was shaped by large-scale forces that were transforming a nation, and indeed were altering the world, this piece is a diamond in the rough that in a proper setting is more valuable than one might imagine at first glance.

CHAPTER 2

THE USES OF THE EARLY DIARY[8]

Although the diary has never been published, it has had a rather influential career. Since the early 1890s when Walter Elliott uncovered it among Hecker's personal papers as he gathered materials for the first biography of the Paulist founder, the early diary has functioned as the major source of information on Hecker's formative years.

Two of the most famous and controversial studies of Hecker are no exception to this: Elliott's *Life of Father Hecker* published in New York in 1891 and in a French translation in Paris in 1897, and Charles Maignen's famous attack on the French edition of the *Life: Études sur l'Américanisme. Le Père Hecker, Est-il un Saint?* published in 1898 in Paris and Rome and in an English edition in London.[9] In both of these works—whose importance in the Americanist controversy has been clearly illustrated—the early diary functioned as the main source for establishing an interpretive model for Hecker's life and thought.[10] Elliott led the way with this approach and, not without good reason, stressed the continuity between the understanding and experience of the interior life—or, to use a more contemporary term, the spirituality—of the young Hecker and the mature Paulist superior. But he did so in a manner that invited Maignen's stinging critique and total rejection of his interpretation of Hecker's spirituality.

When Maignen wrote his work in 1898 he did so to respond to what he described as "the grave evil and imminent peril to which the Church seemed . . . to be exposed."[11] That "evil" was, of course, the attempt on the part of American and European churchmen to promote the progressive ideas that came to be described as Americanism. The French edition of Elliott's *Life* had become a focal point of these new ideas in France, and with this there had arisen a tendency to view Hecker as the prophet of a new enlightened Catholicism in which the antagonism between the church and the modern society would be diminished. The Paulist founder was the model of the modern Catholic; in the words of one of the leaders of the movement, Archbishop John Ireland, he was "the flower of the American priesthood—the type that we wish to see reproduced among us in the wildest proportions." This tendency Maignen described as an attempt to present Hecker as a saint, as the bearer of a "new mysticism, of a supernatural light risen west of our world."[12]

Although clothed in bitter sarcasm, Maignen's position is partially correct. Ireland in his preface to the American edition and Abbé Félix Klein in his preface to the French edition both look to Hecker as a special model. Klein, in particular, does call attention to Hecker's keen insights about the modern soul's relation with God; and clearly Klein, Ireland, and indeed Elliott himself believe and wish to represent that Hecker was the recipient of God's valid inspirations.

Maignen, however, tries quickly to push the Americanizers, as he labels them, beyond this important, but by no means unique, claim. By labeling Hecker's ideas "a new mysticism" in the opening pages of his book, he makes a statement that none of the Americanizers or Elliott would have wished to make, especially since for Maignen this new mysticism is at its core heretical and even diabolical. To understand how Maignen supports such a startling claim requires a study of his method.

Maignen takes as his sole source of information about Hecker the French edition of Elliott's *Life*. He quotes profusely from Elliott's text and even is careful to cite the page numbers. When he quotes Hecker, he does so accurately, at least in a literal sense. He, nevertheless, generally ignores Elliott's glosses and evaluates Hecker's words according to his own agenda. He further ignores Elliott's attempts to contextualize the quotations from Hecker and is ignorant of the settings of the various selections in the original documents.

A second major methodological principle Maignen employs is to use the statements of the young Hecker as a paradigm for understanding his thought throughout his life. While on the surface this may sound like nothing more than the historical method, it is, in the hands of a skillful, vitriolic polemicist, a formidable weapon. With this weapon he inflicts his most damaging blows. In his preface there is a sophistical, or perhaps just sarcastic, attempt at exonerating himself from any charge of mishandling history: "Without confounding the epochs and attributing to the priest what was written by the layman and the Protestant, we have pointed out in the former more than one feature of resemblance with the latter."[13] But in fact he does "confound the epochs" and attribute to the priest the spirituality that is contained primarily in one source: the early diary.

Maignen is able to do this readily because he is given an opening by Elliott himself, an opening not mitigated by the editor of the French edition. Elliott makes a point of insisting on the relation between Hecker's early spirituality and that of his maturity. He speaks of the "unity and consistency of his interior experiences from first to last." The diary is portrayed by Elliott as the single most important proof of this. He even goes so far as to say that it is one of the best statements of Hecker's spirituality: "No records have been discovered of his interior life which are at all compatible in fulness. . . . "[14]

Although this last statement is, from an archival standpoint, true, it is linked by Elliott with two other tendencies, which when combined leave the diary material presented in the *Life* open to the kind of attacks Maignen makes. The first is Elliott's insistence on viewing the diary in an unhistorical manner. In other words, he emphasizes that Hecker's statements on the interior life, which he cites at length in chapters VI through XII of the *Life,* were not influenced by the people, events, and ideas of Hecker's youth. He is rather emphatic on this: "They might have been written," he writes of Hecker's words, "in a desert for all evidence they give of any specific influence produced on him by personal contact with others." Elliott believes, and expects the reader to also, that Hecker was the beneficiary of extraordinary supernatural graces, that God was leading him in the way of infused contemplation. By adducing lengthy segments from the early diary Elliott hopes that the reader will readily see the unusual work of God. He had been surprised to learn of the diary's existence shortly after Hecker's death. His excitement caused him to assume that his readers would be struck by "the unexpectedly strong witness they [the writings] bear to the wholly interior and mystical experience of the man . . . to the real and objective character of that leading."[15]

This unhistorical approach is supplemented by an uncritical approach. Elliott tries admirably to present Hecker's ideas as free as possible from his own interpretation. He attempts to introduce the reader into the edifice of Hecker's writings by means of his limited commentaries, which he hopes will serve as "hinges and latches of that edifice's doors." For every one word of his, he promises in the preface, one will find three of Fr. Hecker's; and he is not far off in his estimates.[16] Ironically, however, this method does not entirely work, certainly not for a critic like Maignen who would not have appreciated Hecker under any circumstances, but also for anyone who is not willing or able to recognize the supernatural graces that Elliott sees so clearly.

Hence the diary is presented *in toto* as a valuable mystical tract. Elliott makes no attempt to suppress more bizarre sections of the diary. Maignen is able to read such statements as "good works are a hindrance to the gate of heaven." "I direct your pen, speech, thought, and affections though you know it not sensibly." He reads of strange angelic apparitions and ghoulish nightmares, of ascetic extravagances and of antinomian flights of fancy. All are presented under the favorable glow of Elliott's pietistical affection.[17]

Maignen, like a lion moving in on its prey, picks up Elliott's offer to see the unity in Hecker's mystical life. He is further encouraged by the placement of a chapter on Hecker as "the mystic and the philosopher" before chapters dealing with his entry into the church. Maignen avidly seizes this and makes the early diary the primary source for his understanding of Hecker's Catholic spirituality. Having done this, it is a simple matter to demonstrate that Hecker, although the recipient of inspirations that Maignen agrees were "truly supernatural," was "often deceived" and stopped on his way to holiness by "the illusions of an unbalanced imagination—perhaps even by diabolical influences."[18]

The tendency so evident in Maignen to misinterpret the diary is not, unfortunately, the sole domain of the anti-Americanists. In an otherwise very able book, Ann Rose in her recent *Transcendentalism as a Social Movement,* befuddled by the bits and pieces of information about Hecker that she received—essentially from the diary—describes Hecker as the victim of a great upheaval caused by the conflict between the values of the trade nexus out of which he came and those of the Transcendental social reform movements. Although doubtless such a conflict did exist, it did not cause the kind of catastrophic psychic dislocations that Rose imagines. Freud replaces the keepers of the ancien régime as the Grand Inquisitor; Hecker is described as having "nervous fits," hearing "disembodied voices," and suffering from "an unidentified sexual disorder for which others advised marriage but which convinced him always to remain celibate."[19]

There have, of course, been more friendly uses of the diary over the years. Clara Endicott Sears in her *Fruitlands* has a chapter containing a number of long quotes from the diary that present Hecker's impressions of Fruitlands straightforwardly. In addition, all the contemporary works, starting with Vincent Holden's *The Early Years of Isaac Thomas Hecker* and extending through David O'Brien's upcoming work, rely heavily on the diary.

Given this history of use, it becomes all the more important to understand the diary as part and parcel of the age in which it was produced, to see it not only as a record of the inner life of a young man but also as a reflection of antebellum American culture.

CHAPTER 3

UNION AND LIBERTY IN ANTEBELLUM AMERICA

If in fact, as Michel de Certeau has argued, culture is the language of spirituality, then it is reasonable to assume that the ideas of the culture of a given time and place will in some way shape the spirituality of those living in that time and place. Culture provides the symbolic systems, the tools of thought and expression that give form to the ephemeral experience of the human with the ultimate reality.[20]

The culture of antebellum America fostered two controlling symbols, taken from the realm of political science, that functioned to give shape and direction to broad segments of the society. They were the ideas of union and liberty.

In the 1840s the United States was still a young nation. Its constitution was barely a half-century old, and a generation was still alive that had firsthand memories of Washington, Franklin, and Jefferson. Throughout the period, the quest for national union preoccupied the populace. It had crescendoed over the two preceding decades. During the 1820s the interest in national politics grew, fueled by the entrance of six new states between 1816 and 1821. In 1828 the percentage of Americans voting in national elections more than doubled from the previous election. The broadening of the franchise meant that the common man, regardless of the amount of property he owned or his religious affiliation, could participate in elections. By 1832 the Washington caucus system of choosing candidates had been replaced with a method of national nominations. In every state except Delaware and South Carolina popular election of the representatives to the electoral college became law. Between 1828 and 1848 the number of active voters increased by over 250 percent.

Union was at once an ideal to strive for and a symbol of a present sense of nationhood. It was raised as a banner by those who sought to promote a new sense of unity against those who saw independence of local governments and of individuals as the more important value. Thus, when in 1829 Senator Robert V. Heyne argued for the rights of the states to nullify federally imposed tariffs, Daniel Webster of New Hampshire could respond to the assertion with the famous slogan: "Liberty and Union, now and forever, one and inseparable." President Andrew Jackson himself, in responding to South Carolina's challenge in the nullification controversy, evoked the imagery of the sacred Union—"that Union which, coeval with our political existence, led our fathers, without any other ties to unite them than those of patriotism and common cause, through a sanguinary struggle to a glorious independence; the sacred Union, hitherto inviolate, which perfected by our happy Constitution, has brought us, by the favor of Heaven, to a state of prosperity at home and high consideration abroad, rarely, if ever, equaled in the history of nations."[21]

Here is the sacralization of the concept of union that was common in the Jacksonian era. Union is interpreted as a divine gift, not merely as a political expedient. It, moreover, constitutes the nation in an essential way and is the cause of the country's prosperity, which is of course interpreted as the greatest the world has ever seen. Union is linked with the written Constitution. The distinction between the Constitution as a means and the Union as an end is blurred as the two are merged. The Constitution then shares in the sacralization of the concept of the Union; it becomes a specially inspired document which is to be venerated as containing all the answers to the nation's internal political problems.

Over against this there were those who would emphasize the other element of the American Holy: independence. Among the most eloquent to raise the banner of liberty in their fight for independence and local autonomy was the man whom Brownson considered the finest statesman of his age, John C. Calhoun. "Our Union—next to our Liberty, the most dear," he would assert against the arguments of Webster and even of his President, Andrew Jackson. The Revolutionary War was still a powerful memory, especially to those older families with eighteenth-century American beginnings. Not even the staunchest Unionist would wish to be seen as limiting liberty, so strong was the attraction of that idea. The struggle between the values of liberty and union was played out repeatedly whether the question was tariffs, admission of Texas to the Union, the national bank, or slavery. Indeed, it was the failure to produce a viable balance between those two values that led at length to the wholesale carnage and destruction of the Civil War.

In the religious realm this same battle was being fought, albeit with different tactics and weapons. At their heart the issues were the same. In the one camp were those who favored liberty. This insistence on liberty took various forms in various traditions. For the Methodist it meant freedom from the restrictions of the Calvinist doctrine of double predestination and liberty from the Anglican and Episcopal forms of polity that limited the ministry to an educated, male, churchly caste. For Charles G. Finney it meant liberty from the old theories—still vigorously defended by Princeton's Charles Hodge—of how God sent times of renewal to his church when it suited his sovereign purposes, and freedom to develop new measures that made the most of human ability and capitalized on the opportunities of the present. For many of the lay trustees of the Catholic parishes it meant freedom to control in some measure the future directions of their own churches and to retain some say about how their hard-earned money was spent. For the radical reformer John Humphrey Noyes it meant freedom from traditional notions of morality between the sexes, the room to live out free love like the angels who neither take nor are given in marriage. For Horace Bushnell, sitting in the land of steady habits, it meant the freedom to rethink the relation between nature and the supernatural and to move from his Congregationalist past to a present inspired by his reading of the new German theology of Schleiermacher.

But over against this tendency was the other demiurge of the age, the quest for union. So it was within the Catholic communion that efforts were made to create forms and structures that would unite the disparate forms of devotions into groups whose worship could join harmoniously with that of the universal church. The ubiquitous emphasis on discipline in the church, as reflected in the Plenary Councils of Baltimore, had as its objective effecting a greater and more perfect union. The appeals of a John Hughes to the papacy as the symbol of a united Catholic culture or the attempts of a Martin John Spalding to present a picture of the church joined to a suffering and victorious Christ shared a sense of the importance of union.

Among Protestants there was a widespread dissatisfaction with the divided, divisive nature of the church. Movements that stressed church union were numerous. There was the Church Union of 1803 joining Presbyterians and Congregationalists, the efforts of Lutheran Samuel S. Smucker to promote an "apostolic Protestantism" that would unite American Christians, and the work of Mercersburg theologians John W. Nevin and Phillip Schaff to forge a catholic evangelicalism. More to the margins of the society there were the efforts of Alexander Campbell to restore the original purity and union of the church through his restorationist, Disciples of Christ movement and the novel attempts of Joseph Smith to declare a new chapter in the age of the church by reestablishing an apostolic order in the Latter Day Saints.

The religionists who stressed union would often venerate a sacred document as a symbol of and a means to union, in much the same way as Americans venerated the Constitution. Thus the Mormons would look to the Book of Mormon and the Campbellites to the New Testament that in its simplicity portrayed a unified Christian church. Often the two great urges toward union and liberty were joined in one movement, or even in one person. Just as often the balance between them was imperfect, and led to count-less contradictions and ambiguities.

These two notions of union and liberty played a major role in the two movements that, more than any others, provided the cultural and intellec-tual contexts for the diary. The Oxford movement in America, centered in New York, Hecker's home, emphasized the notion of union. Transcenden-talism, centered in his temporary abodes in West Roxbury, Harvard, and Concord, Massachusetts, stressed liberty. Together those movements worked to bring him into contact with the fundamental urges of the emerg-ing American nation and with some of the leading thinkers in America at the time. Those two movements were, as we shall see, diverse and in many ways dissimilar. They shared, however, a Romantic impulse that accounted for the fact that many like Hecker, Charles King Newcomb, Sarah Stearns, and Sophia Ripley, while they were at Brook Farm, closely followed the development of the movement in Oxford and New York.

CHAPTER 4

THE ROMANTIC MILIEU: TRANSCENDENTALISM
AND THE OXFORD MOVEMENT IN AMERICA

Illustrating the common ground on which Transcendentalism and the Oxford movement in America attracted the attention of the young Hecker requires an understanding of the Romantic movement that shaped them. It was the cast given each movement by the Romantic impulse that not only drew Hecker, but enabled him ultimately to reconcile the conflicting forces within them.

Arthur Lovejoy warned, with good reason, that the extension of the term "Romantic" beyond its use to describe a particular literary movement in Germany is doomed to become so general as to be meaningless.[22] There is also another danger. Romanticism in Germany took on some different shapes than did movements in the United States commonly referred to as "Romantic." Looking to the Middle Ages and antiquity for inspiration, for example, may have had an escapist motivation in Germany. In America that same thing was part of an effort to reconstruct the social order of the day and create a new and better future; it was engaging the present, not fleeing from it. Certainly one must be careful when speaking generally about "Ro-mantic" traits.

Nevertheless, it is hard to gainsay the fact that during the first quarter of the nineteenth century an intellectual movement—perhaps it is better, along with Sydney Ahlstrom, to call it a mood—emerged throughout west-

ern Europe that had an effect on antebellum American culture and that had
certain identifiable characteristics. Although the essence of that mood cannot be exhaustively defined in a few words, it seems plain that a certain
sympathy of spirit did exist among the literature, art, philosophy, and theology of the age that began around 1781 and continued until the second half
of the 1840s.

Among the better recent efforts to describe the sentiment is that of
Thomas F. O'Meara. Writing of the Romantic age, he says: "This period
. . . proved to be not a brilliant coda to the Enlightenment but a transition
to a different world. . . . Romanticism offered not reason but intuition, not
mathematics but electricity and chemistry, not only republican society but
the freedom of the solitary hero, not reasoned plan but turbulent nature."[23]
To those characteristics could be added a new emphasis on history as the
queen of the sciences and with this a concern for process and evolution over
the categories of being and staticity. Feelings and intuition were given a
heightened value in the idealistic, antimechanistic systems of the Romantics. And everywhere the term "spirit" appeared as a fitting symbol of the
age that rejected the vision of *l'homo machine* for a vision of man as Prometheus—the sharer of the divine flame that illumined his being and called
it to actualize its awesome potential.

Other aspects of the impulse are brought out well in the 1810 book *On
Germany* by Germaine de Staël. She praised the new art as "modern, national, popular, grown from the soil, from religion and the prevailing social
institutions." Throughout she emphasized the particular over the universal,
the popular over the elitist, the sentimental over the rational, the original
over the conventional, and the modern over the classical.[24]

If the seeds of the movement could be found in Jean-Jacques Rousseau's *Émile,* it was, however, on German soil where they took root. In
1781 Kant launched his Copernican revolution in philosophy with the *Critique of Pure Reason* that attributed to the mind a new power and importance. "The object (as object of the senses) must conform to the
constitutions of our faculty of intuition," he wrote, and a whole generation
of German philosophers took note and developed grand metaphysical systems. Hegel supplied the inspiration for Protestant theologians Friedrich
Schleiermacher and Augustus Neander, while Friedrich Schelling did the
same for a growing movement among the Catholic theologians of Tübingen.

In Great Britain, Samuel Taylor Coleridge's *Aids to Reflection* posited
the famous distinction between Reason and Understanding that was to have
a major effect on American religion via James Marsh's 1829 edition.
Thomas Carlyle gave poetic expression to the idea of the movement and
inspired American bards like Thoreau and Whitman. France, though the

center of Enlightenment thought, also felt the force of the new thinking, with François René de Chateaubriand, Joseph de Maistre, and Félicité de Lamennais, who, along with Jean-Baptiste Lacordaire and Charles de Montalembert, attempted to incorporate the new emphases in their thought. Among the French, however, it was Victor Cousin who had the greatest impact on antebellum American religion after his introduction to American readers by Orestes Brownson in the 1830s.

Such cataloging of the major characteristics and personalities of the Romantic impulse, as necessary as it is, is no substitute for attempting to see just how the mood influenced Hecker in the writing of the diary. The Oxford movement in America and Transcendentalism, which we have mentioned as the Romantic representatives of the drives toward union and liberty, when studied give the best available clues to the process by which the Romantic impulse shaped the writing of the diary.

The Oxford Movement in America

Writing back in 1939 in an article on the Oxford movement in America, E. Ryan was at pains to show that it was not simply an extension of the movement in England and that it had a certain inner dynamism of its own.[25] The article is useful in pointing out that the efforts to recover elements of the High Church tradition among American Episcopalians did predate the start of the Oxford movement, which Newman placed at the publication of John Kelbe's "National Apostasy" in July 1833. Shortly after the formation of the Protestant Episcopal church in 1789 an Anglo-Catholic movement began that stressed the use of Catholic forms of church decoration such as altars, sanctuary lamps, and vestments. Connecticut was one of the strongholds of the High Church movement, but with the coming of John Henry Hobart as bishop of New York, the center of the Anglo-Catholic thrust shifted. From 1811 until his death in 1830 Hobart did much to stir sympathy for Catholic tradition among friends like Mrs. Elizabeth Bayley Seton (whom he, nevertheless tried to dissuade from actually becoming a Roman Catholic) and at the school he helped shape—the General Theological Seminary, founded in 1817 in New York and moved to its present location in the Chelsea section of the city in 1820.[26]

That there was considerable interest in the Catholic side of Anglicanism in America before 1833, nevertheless, should not obscure the obvious fact that the Oxford movement in England was the spark that lit the gathered kindling and turned it into a blaze. There was no original thinking about the themes raised by the movement on this side of the Atlantic. Neither were there scholars of the stature of Newman or Pusey here, and clearly the American Tractarians made their every move in response to the Oxford leadership. The struggle between the high churchmen and the low church-men was likewise in its essence the same in America as in Oxford. The Low Church or Evangelical party had considerable strength in the Episcopal church of the 1840s, especially outside of Chelsea, and was constantly wary of efforts to move beyond the carefully structured *via media* that it so prized. The symbol of this *via media* was the Thirty-nine Articles, crafted to be a careful blend of Protestant and Catholic theology.

The fears of the Low Church party were confirmed when in 1841 one of the leaders of the Oxford movement, John Henry Newman, published *Tract 90*. In that famous piece he argued for a Catholic interpretation of the Thirty-nine Articles that moved well to the Rome-ward side of the equation. *Tract 90* was condemned by Newman's bishops, and that condemnation, along with the decision of the church to establish the Jerusalem bishopric, set him moving fast down the path to Rome.

At General the tract had a major effect on some, among whom was future Paulist Clarence Walworth. Walworth, in his history of the move-ment, described number 90 as "making a hit" among the Anglo-Catholics at the seminary.[27] He, future *Freeman's Journal* editor James McMaster, and Arthur Carey were among those students who looked to Oxford to bathe in a new splendor the truths that they believed were—though neglected—part of their tradition. Carey's ordination to the priesthood was objected to by the Low churchmen, who were able to press him on his opinions in the ordination examination held in June of 1843. Carey was asked whether he would become a Catholic priest if he could, whether he believed in the doc-trine of Transubstantiation, what his views were on justification, and his opinion of the Thirty-nine Articles. Despite a good deal of haggling among the examiners, Carey was exonerated and ordained on July 2.

The situation at the seminary that Walworth called "a little Oxford on this side of the Atlantic" came to a head in the fall of 1843. With the or-dination of Carey, the president of General, Bishop Benjamin T. Onder-donk, became the object of an Evangelical backlash. Worried by what they saw not only in New York but also in Oxford, in Ireland with O'Connell's movement, and in the successionist controversy in Scotland, the Evangel-icals decided to rid their church of the Roman menace. Their assault against Onderdonk drew wide-scale attention. Onderdonk's subsequent condem-nation, along with the conversion of Newman, did much to push the Amer-ican Tractarians out of the Episcopal church. Walworth converted in May 1845; McMaster the next month.

The appeal of the movement is well captured by a statement of Wal-worth's. He conceded that some called the new movement Romish, others superstitious, a return to religious darkness and barbarism. But for him it was "a spirit of reform, and return to true doctrine and genuine piety." The movement was "a spirit of reform."[28] What better choice could he have made to capture the Romantic sentiment that lay behind the Tractarian phenomenon. It was seen as a vehicle of new life, as a matter of primary importance. In no sense was it merely an academic debate over the intention of the authors of the Thirty-nine Articles or the validity of Anglican orders. All those issues were debated in the most civil manner, but behind them lay the heartfelt commitment of the interlocutors. It was consciously a reform movement with a spirit of urgency and a sense of mission. Like so many of the reform movements of the 1840s, it drew on a Romantic sense of history as revelation, in this case, of the more perfect will of God for the church. It sensed the beginning of a new moment and the obligation to respond to it in heroic fashion, even if that meant radically altering the present structures. Thus Onderdonk could found Nashotah House in Wisconsin, which Walworth dubbed "A Protestant Cîteaux," and Walworth and McMaster could leave the church of their fathers and join a little-known order of German missionary priests.

As they had in American Catholicism, so too did the times promote crisis in the Anglican communion. The formation of the Protestant Episcopal church independent of the mother country brought with it the challenge of forming a distinctive church that was truly American, yet Anglican. How could that be done so as to distinguish it from the burgeoning Evangelical denominations and yet maintain an appropriate autonomy from Europe? Even more central in Walworth's view was the tension that was caused by the disunity of the Protestant Episcopal church. Made hungry by the age's quest for union, men like Walworth looked in vain at the confused array of options in the church and likened it to a P.T. Barnum menagerie in which a "group of various animals, by nature most hostile to each other, shut up in one cage and obliged per force to keep peace." The force that held together that "happy family" in England was either the large and powerful Catholic church or the monarchy which together, each in its own way, kept the inhabitants by necessity ostensibly peaceful.[29] But here in the United States there was no "royal Barnum" or powerful adversary to keep the peace, and the result was chaos. More than that Anglicanism was artificial. The Romantic impulse that surged through the nature mysticism of a Blake, the penchant for organic categories that made its way into the thought of a Schleiermacher and ran through the novels of Richter was unable to be satisfied with such an artificial synthesis as the *via media*.

The Oxford movement, whether in England or New York, stressed the unitive, synthetic elements of the Romantic mood. Walworth's talk about "returning to true doctrine" picks this up. The movement spurred new study of the fathers and of the councils of the church. It gave impetus to the new science of the history of dogma and, through the efforts of Newman, made one of the century's most successful attempts to come to grips with a realization of the importance of the historical, critical approach as applied to the truths of revelation. Though it spoke of a return, it was progressive, not retrogressive, in its orientation, looking to the future and aware of the church's role in the new age. This was true especially in the reform-minded United States. It took its strength from a sense of returning not to the dead letter but to the life-giving source, in this case, the creeds of the ecumenical councils and the teachings of the Fathers. The way to find true doctrine was not through endless debate in the menagerie yard: it was by returning to the life of the church, which was its mystical essence. As Brownson found his questions about truth best answered by a theory of Life by Communion, so too the American Tractarians had the sense that the divine life had been passed down through the Apostles to the Church and that it was sustained now by the Spirit.

Thus it is no surprise that the third element that Walworth listed was "a spirit of true piety." The interest in ritualism, the fascination with liturgical patterns, vestments, devotions, and relics all spoke of the movement's openness to the affective side of religion. At its heart was a revolt, a revolt against the mechanistic age of industrialism with its dehumanizing rhythms and ways. The longing for true piety permeated the movement. Newman's celebrated *Tract 90* was preceded by John Keble's *Tract 89: On the Mysticism Attributed to the Early Fathers of the Church.* It was an effort to establish the exact nature of that mysticism and to examine the first principles upon which it was based. That examination was prompted by the belief that many of those assumptions were more accurate than those upon which contemporary society was built. Keble, with not so subtle irony, contrasts his sympathetic view of mysticism with the current attitude: "Mysticism implies a sort of confusion between physical and moral, visible and spiritual agency, most abhorrent to the minds of those, who pique themselves on having thoroughly clear ideas, and on their power of distinctly analyzing effects into their proper causes, whether in matter or in mind." Again mysticism conveys something initially and altogether remote from common sense and practical utility, which he thought were "the very idols of this age."[30] What a wonderful indictment of the enlightened age of industrialism! How thoroughly he despises it, how effectively does he strike the same note that made the essays of Emerson ring. In the midst of a patient, scholarly discussion he is able to cast a spell that charms the readers, calling them back to an encounter not with a dead tradition, but with the primordial source of life and truth whose providence guides nations and individuals and whose worship is meet and right.

This was the Oxford movement that Hecker encountered in his New York home. While it is unclear just how he became involved, what is certain is that by the time he started writing letters in late 1842, he and his brothers were following events in the movement both in Britain and especially in Chelsea with great interest. They were reading and rereading the *Tracts for the Times,* although we do not know which ones exactly. His brother John was friendly with Bishop Onderdonk and joined the Episcopal church in March of 1843, definitely affected by the movement. John went on to become a prominent Episcopalian, purchasing *The Churchman* magazine in 1857. We also know that when Isaac came back from Brook Farm in the fall of 1843, he visited Benjamin I. Haight, professor of pastoral theology at General and rector of the Puseyite All Saints' Church in New York. He also visited Bishop Samuel Seabury around that same time. He seems to have known Arthur Carey as well, whose death he laments in a letter to his family.[31]

But even if we had none of this evidence, his writings themselves would betray his involvement. Isaac was thoroughly acquainted with the basic dimensions of the movement, even in the opening pages of the diary. His early prayer that God lead him "into his holy church" is clearly not inspired by his childhood Methodism or by any definite knowledge of the Roman Catholic church in America. His reading of the catechism of the Council of Trent, which he begins in 1843, is also evidence of the Oxford spirit. It was the teachings of that Council that were the nub of the dispute between the *via media* men and the Tractarians. Arthur Carey was grilled at his ordination exam on his opinion of the teachings of that Council.

Likewise, another of Hecker's favorite books of that time, J.A. Moehler's *Symbolism,* was a popular book in Chelsea. The long 1838 work of the Tübingen Romantic Catholic theologian attempts "the scientific exposition of the doctrinal differences among the various religious parties opposed to each other."[32] The book was an irenic presentation that got to the heart of the differences among the Christian churches. Its sensibilities were that of the Romantic yearning for a spirit of true piety. Consider Moehler's concluding remarks on Swedenborg, whom he viewed, in the final analysis, as far beyond the pale of Christian truth. He tried, nevertheless, to understand the man's great appeal. He argued that Swedenborg, as outrageous as his beliefs were, was able to become popular precisely because the age was starved by rationalism and sought true spirituality: "Our age is doomed to witness the desolate spectacle of a most joyless languor, and impotence of the spiritual life, by the side of the most exaggerated and sickly excitement of the same; and, if we do not, with a living spiritual feeling, return to the doctrine of the church, we will soon see the most wretched fanaticism obtain the same ascendancy. . . . "[33] During his examination of Catholic doctrine Walworth demanded and finally got a copy of *Symbolism* from a reluctant Catholic bookseller in New York who wanted to give him the same old here-

we-go-again, four marks of the church classic, Milner's *End of Controversy*. Moehler's book delighted both him and McMaster and sped them
along to Rome.[34]

The image of the church that Moehler presented resonated with the
new stress on the developmental philosophy of consciousness and with the
overriding organic metaphor:

> The church is the eternal, visible form of a holy, living power of
> love, which the Holy Spirit imparts. The church is the body be-
> longing to the spirit of believers, a spirit that forms itself from
> inward out. . . . Tradition runs through all the periods of the
> church and is alive at every moment. The incarnational expres-
> sion of the Holy Spirit gives life to the collectivity of the faith-
> ful.[35]

All of that love of the ideal notion of the church, so characteristic of
the Oxford movement, finds its way into Hecker's diary. Consider just a
few examples. When at Brook Farm, in his first record of conversations
with members of the community, he says that he, Ripley, and Dana had a
discussion on the church "which was not all-together uninteresting to
them" (April 15, 1843). The next day he visits the Catholic church at West
Roxbury to attend Easter services and is impressed. Later on April 18 he is
pondering the questions of apostolic succession, tradition, and infallibility.
On May 10 he is speaking of the church in terms of an organic extension
of the very life of Christ. And on November 14 he talks at length about the
church as the means through which Christ communes with humanity. That
early concern for Oxford-oriented questions only accelerates as he reaches
the spring of 1844, having returned home to New York. The second volume
of the diary tells the story of his final resolution of those questions about
the church that he had begun asking in 1842. When he decides that he must
enter the church, he determines that it must either be the Episcopal or the
Catholic, and for some time cannot decide which.

It was the Oxford movement that set the agenda for Hecker's thinking
about the church question. It presented him with an idealistic sense of the
church as a living body, drawing together in itself the wisdom of the past,
the hopes of the future, and the energies of the present age. The church for
Hecker, as for Moehler, was the visible form of the divine life of Christ
imparted by the Holy Spirit. Such a vision of the church was not—as we
shall see later—one that he received from the immigrant Catholic church.
Its agenda of providing corporate identity for an embattled minority was
foreign to him. Its pugnacious spirit, its efforts to bring order and regularity
to the administrations of the church, and its ever-present ethnic flavor found

no sympathy in him. When during 1843 and the first half of 1844 he was trying very hard to become a Catholic, it was his perception of those things that held him back. He complained about the "foreign character" of the Catholic church in this country, he bemoaned the lack of awareness among the Jesuit clergy at Holy Cross. In all of it he was sympathized with and goaded on by Brownson, whose mind kept driving him toward the church but whose cultural sensibilities were repulsed by the hoards of Irish immigrants that crowded the churches.

Transcendentalism

There is another factor that holds Hecker back from becoming a Catholic that plays a major role in the diary. It is a concern that takes nourishment from another stream within the Romantic current and finds form in another movement in American culture. Liberty: Was there an American of the 1840s who did not prize it? Could Hecker as the youngest partner of a successful, independent business and member of the Equal Rights party in New York that promoted opposition to Monster Monopoly, paper money, and banks not think of independence? So it was that when Isaac turned to the study of matters of religion and philosophy in late 1842 he was ready to respond to the songs of freedom that many in American religion were singing.

In going to Brook Farm in April of 1843, he was traveling into the heartland of Transcendentalism, which, in matters of religion, was the great antebellum champion of liberty. "Transcendentalism" is most often used to name a diverse cultural movement which began in 1836 in New England and ran its course for the next decade and a half. Despite this diversity, the emphasis on liberty runs the range of Transcendentalist thought. An article that appeared in the October 1841 issue of the *Dial* entitled, "The Original Idea of Brook Farm" captures that free spirit well: "The church of Christ's idea, world-embracing, can be founded on nothing short of faith in the universal man, as he comes out of the hands of the Creator, with no law over his liberty, but the Eternal Ideas that lie at the foundation of his Being."[36]

Writing in the 1960s, George Hochfield detected this thrust in his depiction of Transcendentalism as "an attempt to complete in the world of thought what the American revolution had begun in the world of action."[37] The extension of that revolution to the inner sphere meant constructing a new theological anthropology that had as its goal not merely a new American but a new, universal human. This was to be brought about by linking two elements. Reason, stripped of its enslavement to sense perceptions and able to consider consciousness itself as a reliable source of religious insight, was the first. This concept of reason was not entirely devoid of the enlightened appreciation of the power of reason, which was at the heart of the democratic ideal. It retained the core of that notion but pushed back its boundaries to include the data of consciousness as well. To that new sense of reason was linked the Romantic organic metaphor which interpreted the world in categories of growth, change, interdependence, and development. This combination proved potent and created a vision of the person as enabled by powers of reason to change the world and called to do so by the inevitable progress of history to which he was organically linked. In religion this democratic revolt meant that the individual's rights and powers to know God were emphasized. By attending to the intuitions of his nature and by using his gift of reason the person could realize his union with God, and could do godlike things to improve the world. A phrase from the early Brownson sums it up. When speaking of America he said: "Here, if anywhere on earth, may the philosopher experiment on human nature and demonstrate what man has it in him to be, when and where he has the freedom and the means to be himself."

This democratization of religion, this—in Hochfield's words, enshrining of the democratic Adam—brought with it of necessity a new understanding of the relationship between the secular and the sacred. It pushed back and expanded the perimeters of the sacred sphere. Certainly any charge that religion in America was ever limited to the churchly sphere would be grossly inaccurate. Surely, the very conception of a heavenly city set on a hill was one that denied such a delimiting of the influence of religion in the secular affairs of the nation. Indeed, the most widely promulgated tradition in the formative days of the Republic—the Reformed tradition—spoke eloquently of the sovereignty of God, which meant that he was Lord over all of human affairs. But Transcendentalism, as a revolt against the social systems of its day, attempted to deny the institutional church's rights to set those limits. It did this by severing the bonds among the church and revelation and individual salvation. It was the individual, by force of his very nature and by means of attending to his consciousness, who would determine where the sacred was to be found: not priest, not creed, not congregation. That is the common theme that runs through the writings of radicals like Theodore Parker in his *The Permanent and Transient in Christianity* and more moderates like George Ripley. Ripley is a good example, because even with as much respect as he had for the church—his wife became a Catholic and he saw Catholicism as one of the most effective social associations in history—he still could not consider joining, or even admitting of its necessity. To do so would be to give up the liberty that he and others had won in rebelling against the Unitarian establishment, which in fact had already moved far to the left of orthodoxy in its views—but not far enough for a new generation.

This attempt to assert the liberty of the individual to know and experience God suggests a certain mystical dimension to the religion of the Transcendentalists. It caused Frederick Ives Carpenter to view the Transcendental movement as essentially religious, inspired more by what he calls "the religious sentiment" than by the Kantian reason. For him the movement was "primarily a reassertion of the mystical basis of all religion" against the rationalism of Unitarianism and the pessimism of Calvinism.[38] Defining "mysticism" is doubtless an even more daunting task than attempting to delimit "Transcendentalism." Using a definition such as Andrew Louth's that speaks of mysticism as "the supposed essence of religion, or God consciousness that precedes from any particular dogmatic framework" captures some of what Alcott and Lane were about. Evelyn Underhill likewise speaks of mysticism in a manner that makes the term suitable for use in this context. Mysticism, she says, is "the expression of the innate tendency of the human spirit towards complete harmony with the transcendental order."[39]

Using definitions like those it is clear that the attempts of the followers of the Newness in New England of the 1840s did incorporate certain mystical emphases into their experience. When in August of 1843 Hecker went from Brook Farm to the Fruitlands community in Harvard, Massachusetts, he was moving into the center of interest in mysticism in New England. Apparently, he was not unaware of this. Upon his meeting of the Fruitlanders he writes to his family that he has met members of the school of the "spiritualists or mystics." As the first volume of the diary makes clear, the weeks that Hecker spent at Fruitlands had a significant effect on him. It was at Fruitlands that he was introduced to contemplative tradition and to the apophatic dimensions of spirituality. It is important then to understand the spiritual vision of the Fruitlanders.

Fruitlands was the creation of Bronson Alcott and Charles Lane. Born in Connecticut in 1799, Alcott could easily lay claim to a number of superlatives among the Transcendentalists of the 1840s. He was regarded as the best conversationalist, the worst writer, the most effusive, the least responsible of any of the major figures. He was, despite his quirkiness, a leader in the movement. His advocacy of new ideas in education made his Temple School, which he ran in Boston between 1834 and 1836, a notoriety. During that time he published his most coherent and successful book, *Conversations with Children on the Gospels.* He was an original member of the Transcendental Club and was a contributor to the *Dial* as well as the author of his most nebulous achievement, *Orphic Sayings.*

His function as member of the school of mystics is best revealed, however, by his love for and promulgation of Platonism. His first acquaintance with Plato dated back to the summer of 1833 when he read Thomas Taylor's translations of Plato's *Cratylus, Phaedo, Parmenides,* and *Timaeus.* During this same time he also discovered the writings of Proclus and Plotinus, again in Taylor translations. He saw in those writings the much needed corrective to contemporary intellectual life. Decrying the commitment of his age to a dead materialism that limited the world to sensations produced by the five external senses, he looked to Platonism to revive awareness of the invisible, ideal realm. The effect of his age's pattern of thought on religion was ominous: "It shuts God from the universe, and carried to its legitimate issues, results in Pantheism—building up on an inconceivable basis the whole fabric of religion, which it must assume is independent of man and nature. It makes of exterior nature a self-existent substance and sees not in the laws and vicissitudes of things the movement of Spirit." But Platonism saved Alcott from this fate, sweeping away the dross of Enlightened bondage to the material realm: "I see clearly what before was obscured by the gloss of exterior matter: Spirit all in all—matter its form and shadow."[40] This vision of the all-pervasive nature of Spirit was one that Alcott was never able to get from Christianity. It is no surprise if one remembers that the major Christian denominations that vied for Protestant Alcott's attention may be divided—albeit somewhat simplistically—into three camps. In the one was the orthodox Reformed establishment, which by the 1840s had certainly gone through major changes since the days of its great spokesmen in New England like the Mathers. It had seen the attempts of Jonathan Edwards and his school to interpret the degrees of Dort in the light of new ideas of Locke, and it had in the 1830s witnessed the far more radical challenge of Nathaniel William Taylor to the doctrines of absolute predestination and the impotency of the will. Yet the tradition remained an advocate of human depravity and the absolute sovereignty of God, which left little room for ideas about the capacity of humans to participate in the revelatory process and their ability to be inspired and to participate in the divine life by reason of their nature. Though intellectually rigorous, the tradition for many like Alcott was unwilling even to ask the questions that interested him. It was in the business of defending traditional doctrines and interpretations of Scripture and revelation. He, on the other hand, was focused on the Newness.

The second choice Alcott had was the revivalists. While there were many differences among the itinerant Methodists, the Baptists, and the followers of Charles G. Finney, they shared in common an emotionalism and an emphasis on personal experience, the power of the will, and the nearness of God to everyday life that Alcott would have appreciated. But they did this, by and large, at a cost to the intellectual life. The anti-intellectualism, the oversimplification, the sensationalism—none of these would appeal to as arcane a thinker as Alcott.

The third option was Unitarianism. Here in the likes of Andrews Norton and in any good graduate of Harvard Divinity School the intellectual side was well developed—perhaps too much so, with an overreliance on reason and sense data. Doubtless it is this religion, more than any other that Alcott had in mind when he decried the "dead and corrupt mass of material elements," that had become the subject of religion. His attraction to the reformed wing of Unitarianism, which gave birth to the Newness, was just that, an attraction, a groping after a fresh alternative. Plato gave him the intellectual keys he needed to open the door to a different world—a world of ancient Greek mysticism that was at once satisfying to the intellect and deep enough to touch the chords of sentiment in his soul. Platonism also was attractive in that it was metaphysical. It presented a grand theory of all being; it excluded nothing; it totally redrew the lines of demarcation between the sacred and secular in a way that Alcott found compelling.

Thus sensitized to the spiritual nature of being, he was able to go back to Christianity and glean from it new insights. As George Mills Harper has pointed out, he attempted with the enthusiasm of a prophet a synthesis of Christianity and Platonism.[41] Christianity remained for Alcott the great religion of the heart whose doctrines of mercy and compassion were unparalleled as guides for society and outlines for virtue. What was missing, however, was the mysticism of knowing, which he discovered in the Platonic tradition. That tradition, as expressed best in Plotinus, had as its object union with the divinity. Such union was to be attained through a process of enlightenment that freed the individual from the shadows of illusion and showed him the ultimate ideal nature of reality that lay behind the multitude of forms in the material world. That realization and the ensuing perception of the union of all things is achieved in the process of contemplation—of seeing rightly through the forms to the essence of things. Plotinus views contemplation as the highest end of life; all things are "striving after contemplation, looking to this as their one end." An element that differentiates Plotinean mysticism from its Christian counterpart is that this moment of vision requires no special grace. No mediator, no Savior is needed. This was one of the reasons why it appealed to Alcott and other Transcendentalists who increasingly were eager to see enlightenment and revelation as the products of nature, not of grace.

Alcott's knowledge of Platonism received a boost when in 1842 he journeyed to England. There he met a small group of the disciples of James P. Greaves (1777–1842), an English reformer deeply interested in Platonism, who had recently died and left behind one of the best libraries on Platonic philosophy in English. When he returned to Boston with the library, its arrival was duly noted in the *Dial* that described it as "amounting to about a thousand volumes, containing undoubtedly a richer collection of mystical writers than any other library in this country."[42] Indeed the library was a treasure trove of English editions of Platonic philosophy containing works by Plato, Plotinus, Porphyry, Proclus, Xenophon, and Jamblichus. But it was also more than that, for it contained numerous volumes of Christian mysticism. Protestants like Jacob Boehme, William Law, Edward Taylor, George Herbert, and Sebastian Frank; Catholics like Julian of Norwich, Brigitta of Sweden, François de Sales, Roberto Bellarmino, Thomas a Kempis, and François Fénelon; plus the Quietists Madame Guyon, and Miguel de Molinos. It also contained the works of occultists like Jane Lead, K. Digbey, H.C. Agrippa, and Eastern tomes like *The Laws of Menu*. Thus to the Platonic emphases were added, in a most eclectic and disordered fashion, ideas from a whole range of Western and Eastern mysticism.

The Eastern component is particularly interesting. The Fruitlanders, along with their friends in Concord, were reading some of the earliest English translations of the great books of the East. The world of the East had been opened to English readers since the late 1780s when Sir William Homes and Sir Charles Wilkins translated works like *Menu* and the *Bhagavadgita*. By 1836 all of the major works were available. Alcott, along with Emerson and Thoreau, had read *Menu,* Confucius, and Zoroaster. Thoreau's comment in *Walden* that "the pure Walden water is mingled with the sacred water of the Ganges" is an apt metaphor. Eastern concepts were in fact mingled with the New England mind so that it is hard to distinguish which part came from where.

The other leading light at Fruitlands was Charles Lane. He illustrates another distinctive element of the mysticism of the Fruitlanders: its asceticism. Lane was born in Great Britain and had around the time he met Greaves left his job as an accountant to devote himself to reform. More than Alcott he was aware of the social dimensions of the Newness and wanted a radical social as well as spiritual reform. His radicalness fit well into his ascetical character. He preached a doctrine of self-denial as the means for opening the soul to the influences of the Love Spirit. The self-denial meant no private property, no partaking of the slave trade by wearing cotton clothing, and no eating of animal products. It meant fasting and practicing detachment from alluring persons and things. Diligent and earnest, he contributed virtually all of his personal wealth to start Fruitlands. When it failed, he moved with his young son to the Shaker community in nearby Harvard. Lane made Fruitlands a place of ascetical practices. Alcott, though more indulgent, joined in and brought his family along, as we know from his daughter Louisa May's account of morning cold showers.

The Transcendental mysticism of the Fruitlanders, as I have characterized it, sprung from a desire to assert the freedom of the individual soul to know God, to be in touch with the vital principle, to contemplate divinity.

But as a mystical thrust it had as its end the thing that we have seen worked as liberty's antithesis in the dialectic of the age: union. Plotinus states the relationship between contemplation and union most effectively. For him "the object contemplated becomes progressively a more and more intimate possession of the contemplating beings, more and more one with them."[43]

This mystical link between liberty and union was reflected in the wider movement also. As one reviewer put it, people were "dimly groping after the point of union between the supernatural and the rational." The *Christian Examiner* ran an article on St. Teresa of Avila and one on Fénelon by William Ellery Channing. The March 1841 issue carried an article on the life of Bernard of Clairvaux in which the author praised Bernard as a "mystic living in an age tending to rationalism. His was a life in which "contemplation was preferred before action." The September 1837 issue ran a series of articles in which it dealt favorably with the Catholic mystics for their synthetic, unifying tendencies.[44]

Coming to Brook Farm had created a crisis for Hecker, precisely because it put him in the stronghold of liberty just at the time when his involvement with the Oxford movement in America was moving him toward a position that stressed unity. The presence of this mystical interest in union helped mitigate that conflict, as did the social theories of the reformers to which we turn next.

CHAPTER 5

THE SOCIAL DIMENSION

Transcendentalists and Transcendentalists

Hecker's struggle to reconcile the demands of liberty and union was aided by the fact that while he moved in the Transcendentalist circles he encountered even among those prophets of freedom a concern for synthetic social structures. But the willingness to enter into communitarian efforts, as well as the conviction that they were expedient means of reform, were manifested to different degrees among Transcendentalists, so much so that it is possible to divide them roughly into solitary and communitarian camps, based on their attitude toward the importance of the community in the process of self-realization and social renewal.

Emerson's Transcendentalism was typical of the thought of those I am calling the solitary Transcendentalists. It was characterized by a belief in the godlike capacities of human nature, a commitment to self-culture as the necessary and sufficient means to perfection, and a denial of the role of the church, or any other institution, in personal or societal salvation.

There is another division of followers of the Newness that cuts across the lines of the first, that between Christian and non-Christian, or more precisely that between those holding traditional understandings of Christ and the church and those who did not. Among the Transcendentalists there were those who attempted to blend a belief in the basic tenets of the Newness with a faith in Christ, and even in the church. Among them there were men like James Marsh, Caleb Sprague Henry, and Frederick Henry Hedge.[45] There were also many—like Charles Lane—who held the Emersonian line about human nature that denied the necessity of Christ and the church for salvation. In between the Marshes and the Lanes were many whose faith in Christ and the church stopped short of the flat denials of Emerson but was far more unorthodox than that of Marsh.

In fact many of those in the communitarian camp rejected traditional understandings of Christ and the church, but were captivated by visions of a unified humanity. For them society must be reformed, and the reform could not be merely individualistic. In the favorite saying of the American Fourierists that was flown on every one of their mastheads: "Our evils are social . . . and only a social reform can eradicate them."[46] These souls grouped themselves together, convinced that the creation of reformed societies was crucial. Though they were unorthodox in regard to their Christology and ecclesiology they came to places like Brook Farm and Fruitlands. In their number may be named George Ripley, founder of Brook Farm and original member of the Transcendentalist Club whose 1836 debates on miracles with Andrews Norton were crucial in the development of the Transcendentalist movement. So motivated by the social question was Ripley that he led the community he had founded to become a Fourier Phalanx in 1844.

It was to these communitarian Transcendentalists that Hecker was attracted, as we have seen. It was no accident that Hecker never had much to do with Emerson. They knew one another, and Hecker did spend a little time traveling with him and visiting him, but he clearly did not like the man. He became the inspiration for the famous description of the Transcendentalist that occurs in the entry for June 13, 1844:

> A transcendentalist is one who has a keen sight but little warmth of heart. Fine conceits but destitute of the rich glow of Love. He is *en rapport* with the spiritual world, unconscious of the celestial one. He is all nerve and no blood, colorless. He talks of self reliance but fears to trust himself to Love but is always on the lookout for some new facts. His nerves are always tightly stretched like the string of a bow; his life is all effort. In a short period they lose their tone. Behold him sitting on a chair! He is not sitting but braced upon its angles as if his bones were of iron

and his nerves of steel. . . . He prefers talking about Love to possessing it, as he prefers Socrates to Jesus. Nature is his church and he is his own God.

Whenever Hecker speaks of the "transcendentalist" he means one who follows Emerson's thoughts on Christ and the church. He was aware of the presence of people like James Marsh and Caleb Sprague Henry who held more orthodox Christologies and ecclesiologies, but they were not the pure Transcendentalists, and their efforts to blend elements of the Newness with traditional Christian understandings never received from him the attention one might expect they would have.

It is, rather, this attraction to the social dimension among many of his new Transcendentalist friends that captivated him and had a great deal to do with Hecker's ultimate attraction to Catholicism.

The Communitarian Movement in the 1840s

The 1840s in the United States saw an explosion of communitarian sentiment. Whereas in all the years prior to 1840 a total of only thirteen communitarian experiments had been started in the U.S., in just four years between 1840 and 1844 a total of thirty-six were formed.[47] In the most comprehensive study to date of the phenomenon, Arthur Bestor classifies the communities into five different groups. There were the foreign language sectarians, like the Catholic community founded in 1843 in Warren County, Pennsylvania, the Peace-Union or *Friedens-Verein;* the backwoods utopias like the Bethel community in Missouri; the religious communities like the Mennonites; the Owenite communities, of which seven were founded between 1825–27; and the Fourier Phalanxes, no fewer than nineteen of which were formed during the first four years of the 1840s.

Writing in the 1870s John Humphrey Noyes, founder of the Oneida Community, in his *History of American Socialisms,* argued that there was a connection among the seemingly diverse movements of the day. They shared the main idea of "the enlargement of the home—the extension of the family union beyond the little man and wife circle to large corporations." He also noted a similarity between the religious revivals of the twenties, thirties, and forties and the communitarians. Essentially the revivals prepared the way for the social experiments, in that they made people aware of a more perfect order of society and filled them with faith that such an order was possible. These movements together raised the hopes of the nation for a future in which a more perfect union of society where both the spiritual regeneration promised by the revivalists and the social restructuring offered by the communitarians would be made one.[48]

Noyes was himself one of the leaders of the communitarian reforms, and as such, his contention that there was a rapport among the diverse groups is noteworthy. Bestor, in looking at the data, concluded that Noyes was right.[49] Hence Robert Owen was conversant with the Shakers and with the Rappites whose colony at New Harmony, Indiana, he purchased as the site of his own experiment. He also knew of earlier attempts, like the Jesuits' *reducciones* in Paraguay. The Brook Farmers not only knew the Shakers in nearby Harvard but also were familiar with the Zoar community, the Hernhuters, the Moravians, and the Rappites. At the height of the communitarian craze in the forties, twenty-four new communities were founded in the states of Massachusetts, New York, and Ohio, and exactly half were within thirty miles of a preexisting colony of Shakers or German sectarians.[50]

The communitarians shared common hopes and visions because they were responding to common problems, the problems created by the new industrialism. Eighteen-nineteen, the date of Hecker's birth, was a year of economic depression caused when the Second Bank of the United States became overextended in its issuance of notes. The opening up of the Western frontier and the expansion of the cotton industry in the Southwest, however, quickly offset the momentary panic caused by the stumbling of the new, unproved banking system. The boom that followed saw the expansion of a new kind of industrial system in the U.S. It had begun in 1813 when Francis Cabot Lowell organized the Boston Manufacturing Company, bringing together wealthy Boston capitalists. Their idea was to commit large amounts of capital to the development of self-contained manufactories of a scale hitherto unknown in America. Their first project was the creation of an industrial town at the confluence of the Concord and Merrimac rivers. Lowell, as the new site was called, was America's first company town. Its creators boasted about its neat streets, its bucolic touches of lawns and flower gardens, its lightsome factory buildings, the clean and comfortable boarding houses for the factory operatives, and the presence of churches and even a library. To the town flocked bevies of young women from the farms and small shops of the entire river valley region. The girls were paid more than what many of them could make elsewhere, between $3.00 and $4.00 per week. The industrious ladies found time after their thirteen-hour days to engage in literary pastimes, represented in their paper, the *Lowell Offering,* which contained poetry, short stories, and letters written by workers.

The success of the Lowell enterprise encouraged the Boston Manufacturing Company to expand. Between 1821 and 1830 the Boston group opened nine new companies in Massachusetts and southern New Hampshire, each devoted to turning the South's cotton, bought cheap, into textiles which, because of the efficient scale of production, they could sell at very competitive prices in the U.S., Europe, and even China. With the manufactories came new associated corporations, real estate development companies, insurance companies, banks, and water power companies. By 1840 the Transcendentalist mecca of Concord was surrounded by burgeoning industrial towns like Lynn, Framingham, and Nashua. The fifteen families of the Boston Manufacturing Company controlled forty percent of the state's bank capital, thirty percent of railroad mileage, and twenty percent of cotton manufacturing.

Yet this success had another side. It left in its wake the transformation of older social systems and values. It was a revolution that changed the way people worked, where they lived, how they related to one another, and certainly how they thought. The town of Lynn is an example. At the turn of the century Lynn had become a center of shoe manufacturing. The industry, however, was based on small family-owned shops in which family members and perhaps one or two employees worked in ten foot buildings adjacent to their dwellings. There the master taught his trade to his apprentice. A person learned how to make a shoe, every part of it, and how to see it through to completion. The shop owner would buy his supplies from small merchants, produce his shoes, and then sell them, often loading his work into a wagon and traveling to Boston shops. But with the induction of large-scale capital around the time that the Boston group was developing Lowell, a new class of industrialists emerged who bought labor and treated it as another commodity necessary to the production process. The society was split into those who purchased labor and those who sold it. With the large-scale manufactories, the ten-footers were closed; the work place and the home were separated, and the master-apprentice system scrapped. Now the worker needed only to attend to one item in the production process. The final product was the result of a corporate effort, but the effort was largely that of machines; men were their attendants, their operatives. The close-knit culture of the past was replaced with one of disunion. The day was divided into closely-kept hours. The labor was parceled out and delimited carefully. Under the traditional system work was only one element that people shared. They shared a common place, often a common religion, a common history. Now that was all changed, all broken apart.[51]

With the uprooting of old structures came the need to create new ones that would order behavior. The mill owners were ingenious in their promotions of the values of industry, decency, and honesty. Groups like the Society for the Promotion of Industry, Frugality, and Temperance were formed. Often religion proved the perfect device for extending the type of social control over the operatives that would be in the best interests of the owners. Thus, the Methodist Benjamin Franklin Newell, a lay minister of

Lynn, saw his religion as a means to help him succeed in the factory system, not as a basis upon which to criticize the values of the owners. In his journal he could thank God for aiding him through the long hours of exhausting work without ever quitting.[52] The company rules that the operatives had to follow required that they attend church services every week. What is more, this fusion of the self-interest and greed of the owners with religiously backed values of righteous living was genuinely believed by many of the capitalists themselves.

Yet while religion mollified and pacified some, it engendered in others a rage against the injustices of the new industrial order. Theodore Parker was one thus incensed. In his "Thoughts on Labor," written for the Transcendentalist magazine, the *Dial,* he decried the state of society that resulted in the laborer being forced to tarry for twelve to sixteen hours of the day, with little time left for the cultivation of the mind and soul. He blasted the system that could allow the capitalist to profit at the cost of another's labor and denounced the unfettered greed that lay behind it all: "But as yet we are slaves. The senses overlay the soul. . . . The class of Mouths oppresses the class of Hands, for the strongest and most cunning of the latter are continually pressing into the ranks of the former." Emerson, in his essay, "Man, the Reformer," written for the same forum, offered his own critique of a society in which materialism reigns over idealism and crudely denies it any say in the matters of life. William Batchelder Greene excoriated the usurious banking system in his *Equality.* Orestes Brownson likewise found fault with the new industrial order and spoke against it in articles like "The Present State of Society." He surveyed the problems of unemployment caused by overproduction, of poor working conditions, of poverty and want, and laid them all at the feet of what he saw as the salient characteristic of the new industrialism: Mammonism.[53]

This conviction that materialism was the essential evil behind the new industrialism was at the heart of the social theory of the Transcendentalists. In this regard the movement was a revolt, not only against certain ways of thinking within the Unitarian church, but in fact against the major transformations rocking antebellum America. It was a revolt that attempted to strike a blow to the roots of the emerging evil, for true to their New England Puritan heritage, the advocates of the Newness saw instinctively that the problem was not with the machines themselves, but with the hearts of the men and women that employed them. What was their stress on self-culture but a response to the anticulture of the industrial age? As intellectuals they criticized the philosophy of Locke as being at the heart of the problem, and the historians of ideas have been always willing to see in that the origin of the revolt. But in a frontier society of highly mobile people it is not the ideas contained in century-and-one-half-old treatises that cause revolts. It is the breaking up of families, the relocation of workers, the advent of seventy-eight hour weeks spent doing the same task under the whirl and din of a steam-driven master that change the way people think.

The remedy to the materialism of the industrial age was a new awareness of the spirit. That theme runs throughout the literature of the Newness from the radical Theodore Parker, to the visionary Alcott, to the poetic Thoreau, to the practical Ripley. It was spirit that could free us from the bondage to things that the captains of industry were eager to uphold and that the established churches in their coldness and insensitivity to sentiment and intuition were unwittingly contributing to. It was the things of the spirit that the society had to encourage, and appropriately the table of contents to the first edition of the *Dial* reflects that emphasis. John Sullivan Dwight wrote "The Religion of Beauty." Parker wrote "The Divine Presence in Nature and in the Soul." Thoreau wrote "Sympathy," and Alcott his "Orphic Sayings." To the machine they opposed Nature; to efficiency, Beauty; and to *deus ex machina,* God as living Spirit. The age spoke of the division of labor, and they of the unity of life, of the correspondence between the material and the spiritual. Industrialism presented man with a mechanical mate unlike him and unable to respond to his most human actions. A God conceived of as remote either as the sovereign Lord whose ways are not our ways or as the Enlightenment version of God-the-Great-Watch-Maker would not do for those who rejected that match. God had to be a God like us, whose essence, whose Spirit, was one with us.[54]

What the age needed, then, was a greater awareness of the spiritual dimension. In calling for it the Transcendentalists often looked to the past for models. With the Romantics they looked to the ancient societies of Egypt and of the Far East. They looked to the ancient Greeks. And they also looked to the Middle Ages. But, as was the case with the American Tractarians, the peering back was not in the final analysis retrogressive, for they hoped not for a return to the past but for a new age in which the best of the past and present would be synthesized. They believed that Providence was moving history forward to a better tomorrow. Brownson ends his *New Views* appropriately with a chapter on progress. It is God's "richest gift." It is the mark of every living thing. Seen in that light even the evils of the present were but a means of aiding progress itself. Brownson the prophet then could look to an age in which spiritualism and materialism will be reconciled, in which "industry will become holy."[55]

The new synthetic age that many hoped for was also an age in which science and religion would work hand in hand in providing a picture of the universe. An article by Harvard professor Louis Agassiz captures well this hope. The scientist, Agassiz explained to an audience of New York surgeons in 1847, must not think he is finished when he has examined particular events in great detail. He must go beyond those isolated data and aim at synthesis. He must try to see the grand design. In doing so his greatest aid is the human soul that is endowed with an ability to emulate its creator in this regard. "We have within ourselves," he said, "that which assures us of a participation in the Divine Nature; and it is a peculiar characteristic of man to be able to rise in that way above material nature and to understand intellectual existences."[56]

The revolt against industrialism, the hope for a new synthetic age, the emphasis on spirituality, and the faith in science as an aide all come together in the communitarian movement that in 1843 and 1844 was to have the greatest impact on Transcendentalism: Fourierism.

Fourierism

Charles Fourier (1772–1837) was a French philosopher and social utopian who never visited America. Beginning in 1808 with the publication of *Théorie des quatre mouvements et des destinées générales,* he devoted his life to promoting his theories of reform. While lecturing and writing he supported himself by his work as a traveling salesman and accounts clerk and by a small family annuity. In 1832, three years after the publication of his most accessible work, *Le Nouveau Monde industriel et sociétaire,* he and a small group of followers attempted to create the first Phalanx at Condé-sur-Vesgre, but the community ended in failure before all of the buildings could even be completed.

Fourier's unimpressive temporal achievements were matched by a dubious literary heritage. His works have a bizarre quality reflected in the numerous indecipherable tables, the prolix analogical charts, and cryptic pagination. With characteristic French boldness they announce the discovery of the theories that govern the social relations of all humanity. They contain a vision of a world in which all human passions will harmoniously be given virtually unlimited expression. So wild are his ideas on the free expression of sexuality that some twentieth century commentators have labeled them "the fantasy of a traveling salesman who spent restless lonely nights in grubby provincial hotels."[57] How is it that the thoughts of such a man could influence sophisticated New Englanders like George Ripley and William Henry Channing? The answer in part lies in the person of Albert Brisbane, but beyond that it rests in the particular condition of the communitarian reform movement in New England during 1843 and 1844.

Brisbane (1809–1890) was a native of upstate New York, who in his young adulthood spent time in France, where he came into contact with the thought of Fourier. In 1840 he published an explanation of the Frenchman's theories entitled *The Social Destiny of Man, or Association and Reorgan-*

ization of Industry. It was followed by a pamphlet summary, "Pamphlet on Association, A Concise Exposition of the Doctrine of Association," which had a wide circulation. Brisbane was a forceful and articulate young man who promoted the new ideas tirelessly. He wished to be referred to as an "American Associationist" rather than a "Fourierist," thereby emphasizing the ongoing, progressive nature of the movement. He skillfully muted the more controversial aspects of Fourier's thought, especially the ideas on sex, and pitched his writings as a scientific body of theories that related perfectly to the very issues with which the communitarians were struggling. His success lay in the fact that there were a number of common concerns among the critics of the new industrialism that they, in effect, had no good answers for. Their solutions were tentative, experimental. The presence of a large body of relevant ideas, comprehensive in scope, complicated enough to bear careful scrutiny, and claiming to be universally applicable, was appealing. Most who adapted the ideas did just that—they picked and chose their way through the arcane mass of ideas and used what helped.

Among Brisbane's early converts was none other than Horace Greeley, who in the 1840s was one of the nation's most powerful newspapermen. He dedicated a whole front page column of his *New York Tribune* to Associationism, thereby giving Brisbane and the movement a huge and influential forum. By July 1842 Margaret Fuller had decided to publish Emerson's article, "Fourierism and the Socialists." Of even greater significance for the Associationists than the *Dial*'s interest was the patronage of the nephew of William Ellery Channing, William Henry Channing. Channing had gone to New York in the fall of 1843 to start a monthly journal dedicated to advancing the cause of reform called *The Present*. In the first issue of September 1843, he wrote an article on Fourier in which he noted that the ideas of the Frenchman, thanks to the efforts of Brisbane, were now beginning to receive in America the attention they deserved. "Few who have paid Fourier the respect he merits," he wrote, "will deny that he has cast light, much needed and timely, upon the darkest problems." Although he wished to maintain a certain critical distance, Channing admired the boldness of the Frenchman's thought. He urged his readers to try his ideas and test them against their own experiences. He was well aware that interest in the topic of association was "all but universal" in American society. "Every day brings tidings of some new movement of those who are roused by a great hope to leave accustomed spheres of business, wonted social circles, the old mill rounds where for years they have been grinding saw dust for bread, and to enlist in these raw militia of social reformers."[58]

Channing was right about the widespread interest. A sign of it was the conventions held in 1843 and 1844. On September 25, 1843, in Pittsburgh the Western Fourier Convention was held, which culminated with a "Proclamation to the People of the West.'' The meeting of the Friends of Social Reform in New England was held in Boston on December 26–27, 1843. The objectives of the meeting were to bring together those interested in social reform and confer over possible strategies and shared action. They shared concern over ''tyranny of capital, chattel slavery, and earth repugnant industry.'' They also were united by their common admiration for Fourierism. To it they would look, as a convention, for solutions to their problems. The Friends of Social Reform were headed up, predictably enough, by people who were either already in communities, or those who were involved in the political reform associations in the large industrial centers. The roster of leaders lists three from the Northampton Association community, one from Brook Farm, five from Lynn, one from Lowell, and seven from Boston.[59]

The actual event, at least in the eyes of Channing, lived up to expectations. He characterized it as nothing less than the mark of the commencement of a new era in the history of New England. He saw it as a great river of reform that was fed by the Christian spirit of the sons of the Pilgrims, wearied by polemics and eager to substitute radical justice for superficial alleviation of wrongs. It was nourished also by the other single issue reform movements of the day like abolition, temperance, and women's rights. The political climate of the day also contributed to the popularity of the movement. The protection of the capitalist behind laws of incorporation, the establishment of a new banking system that favored capital over labor, and the struggles between the Northern and Southern states over the extension of slavery into the new states and territories all called out for action. From the time of the original call for the conference to its opening, support had grown to include men like George Ripley and Charles Dana, along with Adin Ballou, and members of the Hopedale community.

The conference adopted three resolutions that bristled with a sense of urgency, optimism, and radical, non-violent enthusiasm. The first proclaimed the common belief that the reform movement was one with the larger sentiments of Christian brotherhood, liberty, and peaceful reform. It stated the conference's opposition to the social injustice of the present system of ''moneyed feudalism.'' The second gave unmitigated support to the theories of Fourier. The third urged that Associationist societies be formed throughout the country and that publications like *The Present* be supported to promulgate the message.

One of the first groups to take that advice was Brook Farm itself. Buoyed by the conference, the members voted in January to become a Phalanx (as Fourier's visionary communities were called) and issued a new constitution reorganizing the community along strict Fourierist principles. The movement continued its spread, with over nineteen Phalanxes being formed by 1844. When the Associationists met in conference in New York on April 6–8, 1844, to celebrate the birthday of Fourier, the movement was at its height. The convention, which met in Clinton Hall, was addressed by its president, George Ripley, its vice-presidents Horace Greeley and William Channing, and by Hecker's old Brook Farm roommate, Charles Dana.[60]

There were specific aspects of the Associationist movement that made it appealing to the Transcendentalists Channing, Ripley, and Dana. The first was its reform orientation, which is pervasive in the excerpts from the writings of the movement that we have already seen. The Associationists made a direct appeal to the American Revolution as a basis for their movement. They were called to continue the work of the Revolution, which had been betrayed by the selfish interests of capital. The freedom which had been won was in danger of being usurped by the industrialist and his greed. "We have political liberty," wrote *The Phalanx*, "but not industrial liberty . . . for the laboring masses are the living machines of Capital and the slaves of Repugnant industry."[61] In this emphasis on freedom the Associationists tapped that powerful urge in American life and linked it with their overriding concern for unity.

The second was its faith in progress and in the perfectibility of humanity. To this was joined a belief in the coming of a new age in which the discord and sufferings of the present order would be replaced by harmony and synthesis. This millennialistic hope shared certain similarities to the millennialism of another popular voice of the 1840s, revivalist Charles G. Finney, who spoke of an age of justice and harmony that would precede the Second Coming of Christ and that would be brought about by the grace of God and the work of believers in spreading the Kingdom of God. Fourier and his disciples in this country were able to capture the primordial hope for a better tomorrow in much the same way. Listen to Fourier: "The present age is going to be the spectator of a scene which can take place but once on each globe; the passage from social incoherence to social combination and harmony; it is the most brilliant effort of universal movement which can take place in the universe."[62] Fourier's writings are replete with this theme. The age of industrial incoherence in which labor is opposed to capital, men are opposed to women, slaves are opposed to masters, spirit is opposed to matter is passing away, and all that one needs to do is see the new order—the real, universal order, the stages of which Fourier has devised—and all will be well.

Among those theories was the theory of passional attraction. It stated that the attractions of the passions are what govern people's behavior and that to fight against that reality is vain. Those passions, however, are not irrational, mysterious libidinous forces, but rather they are rational, knowable, and predictable. The key to good government, then, is to create a so-

ciety in which those passions are in harmony. At this point Fourier became
very specific, if not more than a little abstruse. But it was that specificity
that made his ideas appealing.

There was also a very real sense of the historical necessity of the new
movement. It was a new age, or as Madame Gatti De Gamond's article in
The Present put it, a third dispensation. The first had been that of the family;
the second, that of the nation. Now the unity that they strove for imperfectly
was about to be attained in the final dispensation, the universal dispensation: "Man is one, and he hath one great heart." The third age would be
complete: "Unity in labor, unity in stock or capital, unity in science, unity
in art, unity in government, unity in enjoyment."[63]

This conception of union was appealing to the Transcendentalists because it was a union that enabled them to keep their most valued possession:
spirit. Especially in its American version, Fourierism bent over backwards
to show that it was not opposed to religion, but in fact had the religious
sentiment at its heart as the greatest passion into which all the other passions
flowed. That claim was disputed by many, but Brisbane, and most eloquently Channing, argued strenuously that Christianity and Associationism
were in no way opposed. Channing's magazine was replete with religious
imagery, as one might expect from a Harvard-trained Unitarian minister
with one of New England's best theological pedigrees. The social reform
he sought was seen in terms of biblical categories. Justice was the justice
of the LORD who defends the poor and meek. He constantly appealed to
the virtues of holiness, truthfulness, and humility. Articles had names like
"Heaven Upon Earth," and "Christian Song of the Middle Ages." His aim
in publishing the magazine was nothing less than "to advance the Reign of
Heaven on Earth," "to call our fidelity to the Divine Guidance in this land
of promise, to which Providence led our fathers in the fullness of time."
Channing, the student of his famous uncle, saw himself as being faithful to
the same call that motivated his ancestors.

It was that spirituality, blended with a practical scheme which could
result in action, that appealed to men like Channing and Ripley. Channing,
interestingly enough, went out of his way to criticize the reform efforts of
the Fruitlands mystics, after Alcott and Lane—along with Hecker—visited
him in New York in September 1843. Channing styles them "the Essenes
of New England" and criticizes their ascetical orientation as disrespectful
of the body and of Nature. He disavows their mysticism and opts instead
for a life of action based on reason but conscious of the beauties of nature
and art.[64]

There was one more reason that Fourierism appealed to them. We have
noted that the Transcendentalist reformers were not retrogressive. They
took elements of the past and blended them with what they thought would

be the new waves of the future. This gave them a certain respect for parts of modern society, one of which was science. As we have seen with Agassiz, they fought the positivistic interpretation of the new science and believed that they could blend their intuitionalist approach with it. Hence the theories of people like Swedenborg, himself a scientist, who put forth his findings on the spiritual world in the same factual manner that he used in writing geological reports on the mines of Sweden, appealed. Fourier was very much in the same mode as Swedenborg—though less enchanted by the occult—as Channing, for example, realized explicitly. The Frenchman spoke of having "discovered" the theories of passional attraction, the combined order, the series of groups, and he meant that quite literally. He openly compared himself to Newton and Leibniz and often placed his theories next to theirs. His American propagandists picked up on this quite successfully. Brisbane's *The Phalanx* was subtitled the *Journal of Social Science*. This scientific tint gave the theories an appealing hue. They were perfect for experimentalists. Presented as theories, they could be tested and tried without requiring first a fanatical abandonment of critical reason. The only authority they had was the authority of science—they would have to be verified through experience. That left the Yankee Associationists free to modify, and free to appeal to their own private judgment, which was capable of testing the tenets of the theory.

Associationism and Catholicism

The interest in Associationism in New England had the effect of creating an appetite for models of social organization that would meet the needs of the present. As we have mentioned, the communitarians were aware of other social experiments, as they were of other pre-industrial ages that were free of the tyranny of capital. With the European Romantics they looked to the Middle Ages as one such time. It functioned as the symbol of a synthetic age in which spirit and matter resided in harmony, with considerations of the soul having precedence over those of the body. I say that the Middle Ages functioned as a symbol, because they were seen as the representation of an ideal, more than as an actual period about which much was known. That vision of an age thus ordered is captured in the poem by Ellery Channing (William Ellery Channing II), "Christian Song of the Middle Ages," which his relative William Henry cherished and published in his magazine:

Like waving vine the hard stone bends
Into cathedrals soft and free,
An angel every coping tends,
The fretwork blesses sacredly.[65]

There was interest also in the Catholic religion of that age. Samuel Ward translated Dante for the *Dial,* and Sophia Ripley became a devotee of the great Italian poet. William Betchelder Greene wrote on St. Augustine for *The Present.* Channing himself did pieces on *La Madonna di San Sista.* James Walker praised Catholicism for its unifying tendencies in *The Christian Examiner.* The Associationists took specific interest in Catholicism, in some part due to the fact that their founder was at least nominally a French Catholic. An article by William Henry Channing in the Brook Farm publication *The Harbinger* entitled "The Catholics and Associationists" makes clear that although he does not agree with some of the peculiar teachings of the church, it is "the most successful attempt in the history of the world to bring the race into unity," and as such should be regarded with respect and sympathy by Associationists.[66]

For some, though, any effort to link Catholicism and Fourierism was mistaken. Brownson, though not yet a Catholic, took the lead in advancing this idea. In the April 1844 number of the *Brownson Quarterly Review,* the habitual critic included a discussion of Fourierism in the first of a two-part essay on the role of the church in social reform, called "No Church, No Reform." In that essay he argues that the power to save humanity is not indigenous to the race. "Man is not sufficient for his own redemption." The power must come from a great force, God in Christ. It must, further, be embodied, not pure ineffable spirit but God manifest in the flesh. For him "either Christ is embodied or there is no redeemer." Pure theory alone will not do, neither will mere human institutions. His critique of Fourierism becomes more detailed in "Church Unity and Social Amelioration," which appeared in the next number of the *Review* and had more to do with Fourierism, since Brownson had just read the proceedings from the Associationist Conference held in New York that spring. Fourier's ideas about harmonizing human passions according to the laws of passional attraction Brownson denounces as nothing more than Epicureanism. Though Fourier talks of selflessness, his system is ultimately selfish, since it gives no real way for people to escape their own selfish tendencies. The references to Christ and the church that Fourierists make he dismisses as merely symbolic. "Christ is the ideal of perfect manhood"; the church is merely the house that man builds for God. Fourierism is based on a relativistic philosophy that disregards the truth claims of Christ. It is another example of the "miserable eclectism" of the age that reads all, collects and accepts all, and comprehends nothing.[67]

The response of the Associationists to this was quick and forceful. In the July 13 issue of *The Phalanx* Brisbane and his staff took on Brownson directly, quoting the relevant section of "Church Unity and Social Amelioration" in its entirety. They felt that they had been deeply wronged by

Brownson. They could not imagine that he had ever studied their writings and thought his statements utterly false and libelous. They rejected his claim that Associationism is essentially selfish, arguing that the end of life is harmonic destiny, which is to be achieved in place of the cursed subversive destiny of the present age in which all of man's attractions and faculties are in disarray. To achieve that primordial order, self-sacrifice is involved. Indeed an emphasis on the selfishness of the industrial order is ubiquitous in their writings. Secondly they rejected Brownson's claim that they were antireligious. They did this by reprinting the Associationist Convention's "Address to the People of the United States" that was published in the April 6, 1844 *New York Tribune*. That address was written by New York Associationist leader Parke Godwin and had as its main purpose to refute the accusation that Associationism was antireligious and anti-Christian. It explicitly stated the belief on the part of the Associationists in the inspired nature of the Bible, in the divinity of Christ, in the Kingdom of God. It maintained that the basis of reform is religious. Although all that is needed for a more perfect human society is contained in the Scriptures, the means to bring it about in the present day are not. They must evolve with time. They must utilize the science of the day and carry on the work of redemption to the present. This the theories of Fourier do. They are to be taken as theories, not as religious doctrines. The Associationists even insisted on not being called Fourierists, for they believed the insights needed were in a state of development and required experimentation and perfecting.

There is little doubt that Brownson did not really study the Associationists but instead used the convention as the occasion for comments that he wished to make about the need for the Church in human society. He was in this case at his bombastic worst and largely merited the label "bigoted scribe" attached to him by his angry opponents. What was narrow was not his conclusion: "no church, no reform," for that as a statement of faith in the unique redemptive powers of Christ and in the role of the Church must in some version be the confession of all Christians. It was, rather, his failure to see the Associationists in anything but a negative light that was tendentious. He gave them no credit for criticizing the injustices of the industrial order. No credit for their synthetic view of society. No credit for compassion for the oppressed.

But despite this, there was some truth in his critique that got to the philosophical heart of the matter while ignoring all the psychological elements, with the result of totally enraging his opponents. He perceived that, though they may have believed in Christ and in many cases even been church members, the scope and thrust of the reform was toward a new age in which the present institutions—including the religious ones—would be replaced. This he judged to be a chimera, precisely because he had come to believe that the saving power of Christ must have been embodied in an institution directly and at the time of Jesus, and that that institution must have existed continuously since then, or there could be no real way for it to affect the present.

Brownson at this time was quickly moving toward the Catholic church, and the U.S. Catholic press was not unaware of his trajectory. A December 9, 1843 article in the *Boston Pilot* gave an account of Brownson's lecture on "The Unity and Catholicity of the Church Essential to Reform," which he had given in Boston earlier that month. The article reported his views— which were similar to what he said in his *Review* later—and essentially endorsed his views on Fourierism and welcomed his conclusions. An earlier piece in the June 1843 *Catholic Herald* had done essentially the same with another statement of his on Associationism.

Brownson's conceptualization of the Catholic church as an alternative to Associationism was one that the bishop of New York, John Hughes, had come to on his own from quite a different direction. By far the most active American Catholic thinker on social questions of the early 1840s, Hughes had a feel for the problems that the new industrialism was causing, especially for the poor immigrants who were often exploited by the system. The main points of Hughes's presentation were that society was an organic whole in which persons were bound together by fundamental ties. The valuing of the worth of human nature, as redeemed in Christ, should be the most important consideration of a political economy. Without the salvation of Christ, no redemption is possible, for man is lost in selfishness and sin. "The grace of Christ is the capital renovating the power of the soul, and enabling her to enter into the commerce of charity, with God and the neighbor for its objects, and by which treasures, in the language of Scripture, may be laid up in heaven."[68]

In Catholicism these truths are reflected. They were subverted by Protestantism, which, with its doctrine of justification by faith alone, made good works of no value and vitiated the sense of corporate responsibility that was the hallmark of the Catholic Middle Ages. The new industrialism grew out of the Protestant ethic of *sola fide* and the individualism it engendered. What was needed was a reform that would "bring temporal interests into harmony with spiritual—infuse some portion of the attributes of God, justice and mercy into the minds and hearts of princes, of legislators, of nobles, of landlords, yea, if possible of capitalists. . . . "[69] Indeed Hughes was a dogged spokesman for these views. He saw the hunger of the times for an alternative. He saw the work of the Associationists (which he regarded much the same way as Brownson did) and of the other communitarians. He saw the Loco-Focos and the incipient efforts at unionization. And he saw the weakness of Protestantism on the social question.

Indeed, there is no doubt that Brownson and, in his wake, Hecker, were impressed by the views of Hughes on the social question. The great difference between Hughes and the Fourierist was that Hughes represented an ancient institution with a long record of social amelioration; the Fourierist, on the other hand, had a theory and little else. Catholicism loomed as a model of an alternative society that in the view of its advocates had preserved the synthesis of the Middle Ages and contained in it a perfect blend of spirit and matter. The whole quest for union that was so strong in Hecker had to find a concrete expression. When he saw his mentor Brownson, who had experimented with voluntary organizations such as his Church of the Future that had sought to bring about a version of unity but failed badly, turn vigorously toward Catholicism, he followed quickly.

CHAPTER 6

CATHOLICS IN THE 1840S

What did the Catholic church in the United States that Hecker began moving toward in late 1842 look like?

Like so much else in his native land, the Catholic church was in a state of transformation. What had been a small minority community, content to live as polite citizens and good "Catholic Christians" according to the enlightened views of their urbane spokesmen like John Carroll and Jean Cheverus, was being changed by what happened daily at the docks of Boston and New York. There a steady stream of Catholic immigrants, largely from Ireland and Germany, stepped off the ships onto their new homeland. They came, in most cases, to start over again, and often that meant starting from scratch. But although they had left behind them family, friends, and possessions, they did not, by and large, leave behind their faith with its multitude of national styles and expressions. The immigrant church that would dominate the next seven decades was emerging with all of its size and all of its problems. Whereas in 1815 there had been only 100,000 Catholics in the United States, by 1865 there would be over three and one-half million. The Catholic community would go from being a loosely knit minority living on the margins of Protestant America to being the largest denomination in America, centrally organized around a powerful episcopate, boasting a growing middle class and new-found political muscle.

The United States Catholic church of the 1840s was not only in a state of transition, it was in a state of tension as well. It was inevitable that so vast a change in the demographics of the church would lead to conflicts both within its own ranks and with the non-Catholic culture that surrounded it. The internal tensions were predictable enough; one national group attempted to promote its own welfare to the chagrin of another. There were also the struggles over Catholic support of public schools and battles over control of church property in which local parishes attempting to follow a congregational model of church ownership found themselves outgunned by the maneuvers of bishops intent on stamping out what they considered to be a Protestant practice. And behind all this were the debates over how and at what pace Catholics should leave behind the ways of their homelands and adopt the culture of their new land, a culture that some found far too tinged with anti-Catholic principles.

But the internal battles of this time, as real as they were, were over-shadowed by the larger war. In 1843, the year that Hecker began his diary, the American Republican party was formed and became dominant in two of the most important cities of the nation: New York and Philadelphia. A year later it was reorganized into the Native American party that devoted itself to promoting the concept of an America controlled by "native," that is, Protestant, Americans. The party built on a long tradition of bigotry that had always been part of a culture shaped by the most anti-Catholic segment of the Reformation. Eighteen thirty-six, the year that Emerson published *Nature,* also saw the debut of a classic of hate literature, Maria Monk's *Awful Disclosures of the Hotel Dieu Nunnery in Montreal.* The book implanted in the imagination of anti-Catholic America pornographic stories of priest-nun affairs, and murdered babies buried in convent cellars. Two years earlier the Ursuline convent in Charlestown had been burned by an angry mob, and the great scientist, inventor, and bigot, Samuel F.B. Morse, had uncovered a plot to bring America under Roman control that he published in his *Foreign Conspiracy Against the Liberties of the United States.* In that same year hatred turned into bloodshed in Philadelphia. A meeting of the American Republican party erupted into an orgy of destruction in Philadelphia's Irish Kensington district in May. For the next week the riots raged, resulting in the destruction of thirty homes, two churches, the diocesan seminary, and a 5000-volume library of the Augustinian priests. All Catholic worship was suspended for a time until an uneasy truce was reached. In July trouble started again when a heavily armed anti-Catholic mob found a cache of muskets hidden in St. Philip Neri's Church. A battle ensued between the Irishmen and the rioters that lasted the night and left fourteen dead and fifty wounded.[70] Beyond the acts of mob violence, the political rhetoric and hate-mongering literature there was the daily prejudice and persecution that kept Catholics, especially Irish Catholics, from obtaining much-needed employment.

That kind of pressure was certain to have an effect. One thing it did was to virtually preoccupy the literary activity of American Catholics. The pages of the Catholic newspapers and magazines like Philadelphia's *Cath-*

olic Herald, New York's *Freeman's Journal,* Boston's *Pilot,* or Baltimore's *United States Catholic Magazine* are dominated by the consciousness of persecution and prejudice. The pages are filled with excerpts from Protestant publications that are dissected and rebuffed. Statements of public officials or Protestant clergy are monitored and taken to task at every opportunity. Events in the political and cultural life of the nation are seen in terms of the broad Protestant-Catholic confrontation. Constantly the truth of Catholicism is portrayed in no uncertain terms and contrasted with the deficiencies of Protestantism. The leaders of the church were likewise preoccupied, and their statements fill the pages of these publications, more often than not portraying triumphantly the glories of Catholicism. Taken as a whole this is a highly politicized literature in which the real issues of major social conflict are ever present. Sometimes they are submerged in a discussion of elements of Catholic piety like devotion to Mary, or sacred relics, or the use of the sacrament of penance. Other times they are imbedded in a presentation of a bit of history about the Spanish Inquisition, Nestorianism, or the Middle Ages. And often they are more obviously part of stories about Millerism, the Anxious Bench, or the burning of St. Augustine's Church; but always they are present, shaping, coloring virtually everything.[71]

The dioceses of New York and Boston in which Hecker lived during the years of his diary certainly evidenced these larger trends. New York's position as the center of American commerce in 1842 did much to enhance the prestige and importance of the Catholic church there. It was in that year, from which date Hecker's earliest writings, that John Hughes assumed duties as the bishop of New York. For the next twenty-two years he would rule his domain with savvy, skill, and an iron hand. At the beginning of the decade of the 1840s there had been only eighty to ninety thousand Catholics out of the city's population of 313,000. They were concentrated in ten churches, many of them on the East Side. By 1865 there were over 300,000, nearly one-half of the city's population. Although there were Catholics from France, Italy, and a host of other nations living in New York, the Irish and the Germans were by far the two largest groups. The German immigration had gone into high gear after the War of 1812 and was swelling during the 1840s to its peak, reached in 1855. In Hecker's own Lower East Side lived one out of every two of the city's Germans during the forties. The Irish immigration was staggering. Many of the 700,000 Irish that entered the country during the 1840s came through New York. Often the city was only a temporary residence for them before moving out, perhaps to work on a canal or help build a railroad that was stretching westward over the vast continent. Peter Knights in his study of the population trends of Boston during this period found that six in ten inhabitants of the city remained less than a decade, and New York Catholics, as Dolan has shown, had a similar rate of mobility.[72]

Confronted with the problem of ministering to disparate scores of immigrants, many of whom were inactive church members, Bishop Hughes, like his counterparts throughout the country, chose to stress the elements that would bring a sense of unity to the Catholic community. Those bonds of union were fostered by appeal to the universality of the faith, as expressed in its tridentine formulation. The catechism was more than a guide to perfection, it was a practical handbook for Catholic living. Certainly the threat of nativism caused Catholics to stick together and emphasize what they held in common. The real tensions that existed between the Irish and the Germans were counterbalanced by a stress on the universality of doctrine and by an emphasis on the great symbol of the church's oneness: the pope.

Boston, like New York, was a great port city into which streamed thousands of Catholic immigrants during the 1840s. Historically the city had been the center of the Puritan establishment, which still formed the intellectual foundation of the city. That the religion of Rome should have a hard time establishing itself in the rocky New England soil is no surprise. The short and dubious career of Father Claudius de la Poterie in the late 1780s did little to help the Catholic cause. But with the sensational conversion of John Thayer, Congregationalist minister and member of an old New England family, new life was infused in the small Boston Catholic community. The coming of the first bishop, Jean Cheverus, in 1810 set the stage for organized ministry, and Cheverus, like Carroll, was a highly cultured soul who was able to fit in with the city's upper class quite comfortably, all the more so because of his refined French background that made his Catholicism easy to accept.

During Hecker's days of soul searching in New England, the diocese was under the control of Bishop Benedict Joseph Fenwick, a Maryland-born Jesuit, whose episcopacy lasted from 1825–1846. Despite growing opposition that erupted in 1834 with the burning of the Ursuline convent in Charlestown, Fenwick was able to organize the huge diocese, creating new parishes and an impressive array of social and educational ministries. Fenwick had an enormously positive effect on Hecker when Hecker visited him in Boston in 1844 to inquire about the faith. "I love Bishop Fenwick as a father," he told Brownson. Indeed, Fenwick was a father to some of the most important converts in antebellum America. In addition to Hecker, he had a positive effect on bringing Episcopal priest Virgil Barber and his family into the church in 1818. He also helped Brownson along at a crucial stage in his conversion and dedicated a large part of his *Memoirs to Serve for the Future* to the story of the conversion of John Thayer.[73]

Catholic Response to the Romantic Mood

How did the American Catholic church of the 1840s toward which Hecker found himself drawn respond to the Romantic impulses that were inspiring him? It is extremely difficult, given the diversity of the Romantic impulse, to answer this question in any definitive fashion. There are, however, a number of clues that provide examples particularly apt for the Hecker story.

In a recent work Patrick Carey has argued that although the nineteenth-century American Catholic community was slow to register the Romantic impulse, a response did occur beginning in 1829 and lasting throughout the 1880s. He rightly sees the Romantic ingredients in the ecclesiology and apologetics of John Hughes and Martin John Spalding and in the piety of the day.

Yet what is most germane for our story is the highly selective manner of that appropriation. In studying it, the vivid character of Hecker's far more thorough appropriation of the Romantic impulse becomes clear. The response of the American Catholic community of the 1840s to the Romantic mood may be seen by first examining the thought of two of its most vocal leaders, John Hughes and Martin John Spalding, and then by looking at ways in which the devotional revival of the forties and fifties used Romantic themes. Lastly we shall trace the direct response of American Catholics to the two manifestations of the Romantic mood in America with which we have been concerned, the Oxford movement in America and Transcendentalism.

As we have noticed in chapter 5, New York's John Hughes stressed a theology of incarnation that saw the church as an organic extension in time of the very life of Christ. He spoke of the necessity of Catholicism for society and presented the church as the guarantor of culture. Hence the Incarnation for him was "the great idea of the great lever which Christianity presented for the elevation of the human race."[74] He presented Catholicism as the mirror image of Protestantism, contrasting Catholic unity with Protestant disunity, its infallibility—as symbolized by its teaching authority—with Protestantism's free-for-all of private opinion, its visible, sacramental presence with Protestantism's rejection of external worship, and its reliance on the rich tradition of the ages with Protestantism's thin trust in *sola scriptura*. It was the vision of the church as a great organic extension of the divine life into the present that doubtless gave Hughes's apologetic a Romantic hue. But also his conception of the synthetic nature of the relationship between Christ and culture and his insistence on the ultimate unity of all life were not at all dissimilar to the same stress in Brownson.

Yet in the final analysis, Hughes would distance himself from much of what was part of the Romantic impulse. There was an abhorrence of intuitive, subjectivistic emphases, a lack of any sense of the function of the individual in the process of revelation, and a limited appreciation for the role of sentiment in religion that spoke eloquently of the need for compassion but little of the feeling of holiness. In fact he emphasized a static view of truth—the only movement of history that counted was that which broke down the decadent social structures of a Protestant culture and moved humanity back to the Catholic solution. Joseph Chinnici's characterization of Hughes's thought as a kind of "resurgent Counter-Reformation Catholicism" contains much truth. Perhaps his role as a leader of an embattled minority robbed him of the luxury to be a muse. Dagger John was in the final analysis a fighter, not a poet.[75]

Martin John Spalding, bishop of Louisville, and later archbishop of Baltimore, became a great friend of Hecker's after the founding of the Paulist order in 1858. They worked together at the First Vatican Council, and in the 1870s Spalding named him his literary executor. That friendship is a clue to the affinity that both had to a type of Catholicism that would be in touch with the world around it and able to respond to the questions and needs of the people. Among the Catholic American prelates of the antebellum period, Spalding was the most interested in history. He was deeply influenced by the work of Johannes Baptist Palma, a professor of ecclesiastical history at the Urban College in Rome, who published his *Praelectiones Historiae Ecclesiasticae* between 1838 and 1840. Spalding wrote broadly on aspects of the church's history in the Medieval and Modern periods. He looked at history as a process through which Providence brought about the will of God. Hence in studying it one could find the clues to the meaning of the present and future, since it was all part of a meaningful, purposeful process. In this sense he had a good deal in common with the Oxford divines and with the many Romantics who studied the Middle Ages. He saw Catholicism as destined by Providence to be the regenerator of Western civilization. God was moving all of history on to a fuller realization of the aspiration for divinity of the human soul. Movements of the day that stressed human dignity and social amelioration were providentially moving society closer to the church. In his essay on the "Influence of Catholicity on Civil Liberty" he made the point clear: "Can it be that Catholicity, which saved Europe from barbarism and a foreign Mohammedan despotism, which in every age has been the advocate of free principles, and the mother of heroes and of republic . . . is the enemy of free principles? We must blot out the facts of history, before we can come to any such conclusion! If history is at all to be relied on, we must conclude that the influence of the Catholic Church has been favorable to civil liberty."[76]

Another way in which he evidences a touch of the Romantic mood is his style. Though not drowned in the bathos of a Faber, he does evoke emotional, fanciful images that place before their reader's imagination a vivid picture of, say, the suffering, crucified Christ surrounded by his mother and disciples. The reader is invited to enter into the scene and to unite his own suffering with that of Mary and Christ.

But Spalding's purpose in analyzing history or in evoking certain sentiments was, in the final analysis, apologetical. His *Miscellanea,* which contains long works on history, when viewed as a whole, is essentially an apologetical work that uses history as proof of the rightness of Catholic claims. There is no self-conscious appropriation of any of the style of the Romantics. Spalding is an interlocutor in the enlightened, and indeed in the classical, sense. His writings proceed from one argument to another, patiently presenting the evidence of the past in support of his case. Yes, he did borrow some of the Romantic sense of Providence and nostalgia about the Middle Ages, but it was all in the service of the defense of Catholic doctrine and the institution of the church.

A similar picture of a highly selective appropriation of Romantic sensibilities may be seen in the devotional revival that began shaping Catholic piety in the 1840s. Thomas Wangler's study of liturgical calendars, devotional manuals, rituals, church architecture, and decoration has reconstructed a picture of part of that rich life in Boston. The 1840s in Boston were part of a transition from the Neo-Classical period in Catholic piety that had begun during the last decade of the eighteenth century. The new Romantic trend that was emerging was by mid-century full blown. It was part of a larger devotional revolution that was affecting all of American Catholicism. Encouraged by the papacy and by orders like the Redemptorists and the Jesuits, devotionalism spread among the people. Veneration of Mary became an increasingly important component of Catholic piety, with the definition of the dogma of the Immaculate Conception occurring in 1854 and the proclamation of the feast of the Immaculate Heart of Mary. Sodalities proliferated, and the entire month of May was devoted to Our Lady. Devotion to other saints, each with his or her own special intention, grew as well. The sentimental, subjective feelings of piety were stressed, as devotions like the Sacred Heart, which focused attention on the seat of feelings and emotions, became popular. Related to this was a tendency to champion the virtue of innocence as seen in devotions to women saints and to the Holy Infant Jesus.

In addition to these characteristics, the era was marked by a Gothic revival in church architecture. Churches were to emphasize the transcendent form of the Middle Ages. The irregular, mysterious line of high Gothic replaced the straight, plain shapes of the Neo-Classical age. Church decoration greatly proliferated, with every attempt being made to make interiors symbols of heaven. The liturgy, diverted by the popularity of devotions, shifted its focus from Christ and the Communion of Saints to an uncertain center.[77]

This shift had been propelled by the emergence of a new industry: the publication of devotional manuals. The growth of the Catholic middle class brought with it the ability to support a growing Catholic publishing industry, as men like J.D. Sadlier of New York and John Murphy of Baltimore tried to match the success of Protestants like Charles Scribner and the Harper brothers. The proliferation of devotional manuals that contained within their pages the concern for personal salvation, the emphasis on sentiment, ritual, and "feminine" traits of docility and submissiveness had, as Ann Taves has shown, begun in force in the 1840s.[78]

Students of this devotional movement have seen in it elements of the Romantic mood, and not without good reason. The personalism of the devotional religion along with its stress on sentiment certainly were part of a Romantic style. Furthermore, the network of sodalities and confraternities that emerged created social networks that were attempts to deal with the problem of relating the individual with his unique range of emotional responses, thoughts, and feelings to the society, in this case the church. Furthermore, they were efforts at promoting a sense of communion between the living church militant and the mystical church triumphant. This effort to unite the mystical and the concrete, the ideal and the real, was a constant Romantic quest.

Yet I would argue that a closer look at the way in which the mood influenced the Catholic revival reveals another dimension. The appropriation of Romantic themes that was reflected in the new styles of church architecture and the new devotionalism was a hybrid of Romantic, Enlightenment, and traditional Counter-Reformation themes that stopped far short of any kind of thorough implementation of Romantic emphases to such a degree that the term "Romantic" may not at all be the best description.

It is true, for example, that church decoration took on more elaborate Gothic and Baroque forms, but a look at one of the 1840s' most influential books on church decoration, James Meagher's *Teaching the Truth by Signs and Ceremonies,* indicates that something else was involved. Although Schelling's Bruno would have been thrilled by the title's implication that truth and beauty are intimately related, the contents of the book are dominated by a concern for reason that suggests far more the Age of the Enlightenment than the Age of the *Critique of Pure Reason.* The chapter titles alone tell the story. Chapter one: "Reason Leads Us On." Chapter two: "Reasons for the Church and Its Parts." This is followed by "Reasons for Things in the Church,'' and ''Reasons for Having Latin.'' Any sense of reason in the Coleridgian usage is absent here.[79]

When we analyze the devotionalism that marked the Catholic revival of the forties and fifties we see that it too was an attempt to incorporate in a highly selective manner certain Romantic sensibilities and by its very structure to exclude others that would be in conflict with traditional Counter-Reformation Catholicism. Devotions had clearly defined ecclesiastical dimensions. It was the bishops and priests who told the laity how to be devout. Devotionalism gave not just an encouragement to pray to a saint, but the text of the prayers themselves, the time to say them, the place to say them, the effects of saying them. The Dionysian spirit, the sense of revolt against the efforts of the *Aufklarung* to order all of life in the best of all possible worlds, is totally lacking from the devotional revival.

The ''Romantic'' spirituality of devotionalism portrays none of the unbridled emotion and pathos so crucial to the mood. We see instead a genteel romanticism of purity and childlikeness. Purity derives from an absence of contact with a defiling world, not from a pure state of nature. Hughes was right in line with the shapers of the new devotionalism in his insistence on the corrupt state of human nature. Yet for the Romantics—stretching back to their harbinger Jean-Jacques Rousseau—nature was not the place where humanity was corrupted but the ground from which it learned of passion, power, individual rights, and the importance of the subject in the process of revelation.

In addition, the important emphasis on development and evolution that was the bedrock of the great dialectic philosophies of the age is not to be found in devotionalism, nor is any concern for the religions of the East, nor the national characteristics of the races, nor any interest in the new sciences.

The connection between the growing ultramontanism of this period and the attempt of devotionalism to control and delimit the Romantic spirit is as evident as it is noteworthy. True, the papacy for Hughes and Spalding was a symbol of the unity of the faith in the midst of a disintegrating culture. But ultramontanism also had another side that made it more than a Romantic quest for the new synthetic order. It also meant the centralization of power, the organization of the religious life under a neatly defined chain of command. The efforts of men like Hughes, Fenwick, and Spalding to stamp out lay trusteeism and to promote strong discipline in their dioceses were part of the same trend and owed as much to the will to power as they did to a quixotic longing for the culture of Christendom. Napoleon was a Romantic hero, but he was admired by Romantics for his defiance of Fate and his ability to shape his own destiny, not for his subjugation of the peoples. The appeal of the princely ruler, the leader as Providential Man, was a Romantic

theme that ultramontanism and the related episcopal authoritarianism exploited and often misshaped not only in the hands of Hughes but in those
of De Boland and Manning as well.

In fact devotionalism, by attempting to control the Romantic spirit,
was, I would argue, a distortion of it that left the forms, but stripped them
of their pathos and their animating power. It selectively removed the elements that would not serve the goals of the institutional church—the self-
reliance, the rebellion, the reliance on intuition—but left those that would—
the effeminate virtues of piety, purity, and submission. Thus stripped of its
soul, sentiment became sentimentality, passion became bathos, self-reliance became personalism, and loyalty to the intuitive perception of truth
became submission to the church's hierarchy. Like so much else in the immigrant church, devotionalism became a way of building Catholic identity
in the midst of an unfriendly environment. It concentrated on changing people's minds but not on changing the structures that shaped their thinking.
Toward those it bred acceptance. It gave individuals hope, it opened new
outlets for growth, but only within a tightly controlled system.

Response of the Catholic Community to the Oxford Movement and Transcendentalism

A further sense of the Catholic community to which Hecker was drawn
can be obtained from an analysis of the ways in which it responded to the
two movements that did so much to shape his sympathies: the Oxford movement in America and Transcendentalism.

The Oxford movement provided American Catholics with a spectacle
that was a welcome sight for their sore eyes. They rightly perceived, despite
the disclaimers and intricate twists of logic by Oxford divines and Episcopalian professors, that the movement represented a disaffection on the
part of a prestigious group from Protestantism into their own camp. That
men of such culture and intellectual refinement as Newman, Pusey, and
Keble would look their way was heartening to a group of embattled American Catholics that was often stereotyped by the behavior of their most un-
cultured, rough-hewn segment. The movement captured the attention of the
Catholic press. An analysis of the contents of the *Catholic Herald,* the *Freeman's Journal,* and the *United States Catholic Magazine* for the years
1843–44 shows just how popular the movement was. In the *Catholic Herald*
there were no fewer than fifty articles on the Oxford movement. In the *Freeman's Journal* there were fifteen, and in the *United States Catholic Magazine* there were eight.

Among the most penetrating responses to the Oxford movement in
America were those of Francis P. Kenrick, bishop of Philadelphia from

1830–1851 and later archbishop of Baltimore, and his brother Peter R. Kenrick, archbishop of St. Louis. Peter Kenrick published in 1841 *The Validity of Anglican Orders Examined* that studied the nub of the question.[80] But it was his brother who played the larger part in responding to the Oxford movement. In the opinion of one of his biographers, Francis Kenrick's most significant effort on behalf of the national church was his attempt to foster the Oxford movement in America and to bring its adherents into the Catholic church.[81]

In 1841 Kenrick issued an appeal to Episcopalians "inviting them to follow up to its legitimate consequences the movement toward the Catholic church which had begun in England."[82] The work was occasioned by Newman's 1841 "Catholicus" letters to *The Times* of London, which were later published in the Tamworth Reading Room. That same year Kenrick published his *Letter on Christian Union* in which he defended the primacy of the pope, and *The Catholic Doctrine on Justification,* which took its raison d'être from the abandonment of *sola fide* by the Oxford divines the year before. The tome on justification is cautious. It blends a joy over the turn of the Oxford divines toward Catholic principles with a certain frustration over the slowness of Anglicans to follow through on their convictions. Kenrick is genuinely miffed at the persistence of anti-Catholic prejudices, especially the attacks on the papacy that he sees in America. He is thoroughly aware of developments within the Episcopal church in the U.S. and is ready to do whatever he can to aid. His offers were rebuffed by both low churchmen and high churchmen like the Episcopal bishop of Vermont, John Henry Hopkins, which accounts for the slightly defensive tone of Kenrick's piece. Yet he is sensitive to "a yearning after Catholic unity, and a wearisomeness of the endless divisions, which under the name of Religion, disfigure and disgrace Christianity."[83]

Despite Kenrick's sympathy, his responses to the Oxford people in this country are, for the most part, exercises in the traditional style of apologetics as found in the leading text of the day, John Milner's *End of Controversy.* There is little appeal to sentiment and emotion, little evocation of an idyllic Middle Ages, and little attempt to embellish the symbol of union with allusions to organic and progressive categories. The Romantic inspirations of the movement seem to be of little interest to him. Certainly he does not reflect a Kantian awareness of the subject as the starting point for an apologetic. Nor does he wish to interject his personal feelings into the discussion.

In 1841 Kenrick was cautiously hopeful but not hopeful enough to extricate himself from the mindset of an embattled leader of an oft-despised group of immigrants whose presence was causing major social and economic readjustments along the Main Line that were to boil over in bloody anti-Catholic riots in 1844. After that time Kenrick was not as sanguine and when in 1855 he returned briefly to the subject in a rebuttal to a new book by his old debating partner Bishop Hopkins, his tone, as well as Hopkins's, was far more ascerbic and curt than it had been in the early forties.

That mindset of confrontation and persecution also influenced the response to the movement by Bishop John Hughes, in whose diocese the Oxford movement in America made its greatest gains. Hughes saw the movement, as had Kenrick, essentially as a vindication of Catholic doctrine and as proof of the errors of Protestantism. But Hughes, more than any of his fellow Catholic prelates of the 1840s, was tuned into the social implications of religion, as we have seen. Accordingly, he looked at the Oxford Movement in the context of industrial England and saw there its origin. The movement was due to a dissatisfaction with the Protestant doctrine of justification by faith alone. As we saw in chapter 5, he believed that that teaching had vitiated the basis for charitable social works; it "has chilled every generous emotion of self-sacrifice and Christian heroism, which the charities of the Christian religion are wont to excite in the human breast. . . ."[84] Hughes saw among the Oxford reformers the feelings under the surface of their writings that were struggling for direction. That direction, he felt, could only be supplied by the Catholic church. Hughes the social critic, more than Francis Kenrick the theologian, sympathizes with the pathos of the movement because he sees it as more than an intellectual phenomenon. But like Kenrick, Hughes sees an opportunity to denigrate Protestantism and exalt traditional Catholic doctrine. Hughes's critique of the social order owes nothing to the Oxford Tractarians; they are merely proofs for his long-established position, just as for Kenrick they are proofs of the rightness of his views on justification.

A similar tone characterizes the *United States Catholic Magazine*'s articles on the Oxford movement in America that it ran in its 1843 editions. In the April number, three articles deal with the movement directly or with the issues raised by it. The first is a review by an English convert from Methodism of a book by Walter F. Hook, an Anglican priest who was the object of Francis Kenrick's overtures two years previously. This book argues for the validity of Anglican orders. The reviewer vigorously and rudely attacks Hook's claims. Hook labors hard to "wash out the blot of Protestantism from the [Anglican] church" but finds it like an attempt "to wash a negro white."

The article is followed by a piece that defends the validity of Catholic orders. To that is added a description of the ceremonies of Holy Week at Rome, which comes the closest of any of the articles to catching, however briefly, the Romantic fascination with the beauty of the Middle Ages. The intelligence section of the magazine is filled with excerpts from newspapers and journals on Puseyism. An article from the *Christian Advocate and Journal,* the paper for which Hecker worked as a young lad, is excerpted with great glee. The article is an alarmist report about the rapid spread in England of "the Man of Sin." From the *Mélanges Religieux* is taken a report of a conference in Manchester on the question of what is the true church, after which ten members of the audience stood and renounced Protestantism and declared their allegiance to the Catholic church. In the domestic intelligence section, an excerpt from the Episcopal *New York Evangelist* elicits the comment that it is "a consoling evidence that, however boldly some writers may protest against the influence of the Oxford Movement, in exhibiting the truth of Catholicity, its religious investigations are attended, even in this country, with a near approximation to the ancient church, and sometimes with an open avowal of her truth and divine origin." That last response is enlightening, for it shows that for the editors of the *United States Catholic Magazine,* the Oxford movement in America was in fact a consolation that they, the persecuted minority that they were, were in fact right. In that regard the responses of Kenrick and Hughes, though more refined, agreed. To the immigrant church consolation was far more important than any nebulous sympathies with the impulses that lay behind the movement.

The one major figure who was in part an exception to this was Martin John Spalding. His response to the Oxford movement shared with those of Francis Kenrick and John Hughes the view that it was a vindication of Catholic truth. Like them Spalding was bothered tremendously by the efforts of those who were sympathetic to the movement but bitterly anti-Roman. He devoted a good deal of ink to refuting their accusations about points of Catholic doctrine. He was, however, more of a scholar of church history than any of his episcopal counterparts in New York and Philadelphia, and that gave him a certain appreciation of the movement that was lacking in Hughes, and even in Kenrick. He was willing to see it as more than another proof of the church. Spalding thought that the movement had exercised a "beneficial influence" on the religious mind of the age. It had awakened inquiry on the "great and all important" question of the church and aroused the attention of many to the evils of sectarianism and to the importance of religious unity. Furthermore it had eloquently set forth, in a "new and more favorable light," many of the distinctive doctrines of Catholicity and stimulated inquiry into the principles and institutions of the ancient church, kindling in the hearts of many Protestants a new fervor to explore the hidden treasures of Christian antiquity and improving our knowledge of the church fathers. Also it had been the means for leading many "ingenious and learned" Protestants to the church. Not only did he have an appreciation of the positive effects of the movement on patrology and church history, but he also sensed the value of a fresh presentation of the ancient Catholic faith.

To this he added a certain admiration for the men of the Oxford movement, respecting no doubt their learning and, in the case of the converts, their self-sacrifice. Yet in the final analysis, Spalding's purposes were apologetical, and he would not waste such an opportunity as the Oxford movement. In this regard he was part of the larger Catholic response, although much of what he said stands in contrast to it as a minority voice.

Transcendentalism

Over against the wide-scale response to the Oxford movement in America, the response of Catholics to the movement known as Transcendentalism was miniscule. An analysis of the same Catholic publications that were so filled with articles on Oxford turns up not a single article on the subject for the years 1843–44. Moreover, one searches the works of spokesmen like Hughes, Spalding, and the Kenricks almost in vain for any comments. Hughes, in the introduction to Antoine Martinet's *Religion in Society* (New York: Sadlier, 1850) shows a blindness to the differences between the Associationists and Transcendentalists by lumping them together as promoters of social reforms based on the principle of self-interest—the very notion against which page after page of the Fourierist magazine *The Phalanx* is devoted.[85] Spalding likewise in the corpus of writings collected in *Miscellanea* only makes a few passing references to it that also lump it together with Fourierism and relegate it to the abyss of modern infidelity.[86]

Two exceptions—which do not alter in any significant way the picture painted above—were the bishops that influenced Hecker the most during his conversion period: Fenwick and McCloskey, who at least in their personal responses to Hecker—as related in the most summarial way in the diary and contemporary letters by Hecker—convinced him of a certain sympathy for the processes of thought that had led him to them.

The reason for this cool response was that Transcendentalism was, as we have illustrated, emphasizing the urge of liberty and was, as such, of little use to a community bent on establishing unity. The fact that there might be something good in the impulses that lay behind the movement seems to have never entered the mind of the Catholic mainstream as evidenced by its periodicals and the publications of its bishops. By confusing the solitary and communitarian influences in Transcendentalism the Catholic community missed an opportunity to attract the sympathetic hearts of many who were looking for new, more synthetic models.

Despite this there was a class of individuals drawn to Catholicism from the midst of the Romantic currents that the United States church tried hard to ignore.

CHAPTER 7

THE CATHOLIC CONVERT MOVEMENT

AMONG THE TRANSCENDENTALISTS

Despite the ignorance of Transcendentalism by the American Catholic church of the 1840s, the option of blending the love of freedom with the desire for unity in the Catholic church was one that attracted a number of individuals associated with Transcendentalism during 1843 and 1844. Their motivation came more from developments in the secular culture of the age, the Oxford movement in America, and within Transcendentalism itself than from the immigrant Catholic church. As we have suggested, the strongest attraction to Catholicism was among the communitarians and Association-ists, and the members of the Oxford movement in America. In chapter 4 we studied the motivation of converts from American Tractarianism, men like Clarence Walworth and James McMaster. It remains to look more closely at the small group of Transcendentalist converts and Catholic sympathizers in whose circle Hecker traveled.

At least four people who were intimately involved in the Fourierist life of Brook Farm went from Associationism to full membership in the church. Unfortunately the story of that little group is shrouded in the shadows of incomplete knowledge, due to the lack of ample primary sources. Never-theless, the outlines of the story can be discerned. There was Sarah Stearns, the niece of Sophia Dana Ripley, who was one of the original members of Brook Farm and a member during the Fourierist days. Stories of her going off to Mass at the Catholic church in West Roxbury have filtered down. After the breakup of Brook Farm she converted and entered a convent (which one seems unknown). There was George Leach, one of the original members of Brook Farm. In the year that Hecker arrived there, Leach and his wife left to open a Grahamite Hotel in Boston. He became deeply in-terested in the Associationist cause and was part of the group who in De-cember 1843 issued the "Call to the Friends of Social Reform in New England." That interest in a unitive society led him to the Catholic church by 1850. Hecker stayed at a Grahamite hotel—which may have been Leach's—during his spring 1844 visit to Boston, just prior to his conver-sion. There was also James Kay, Jr., a Philadelphia native, who came to Brook Farm in 1844 after it had become a Phalanx. He was a prosperous businessman who had been one of the leaders of the Associationist move-ment in Philadelphia. We know that by 1845 he had converted and was writing sympathetic letters to Hecker.[87]

The best known member of this obscure group was the wife of the founder of Brook Farm, Sophia Dana Ripley. The product of two Boston

Brahmin families, the Willards and the Danas, she was a refined, well-educated lady and a distinguished linguist, excelling especially in Italian. In George Ripley she found a noble mate, and together they were in the vanguard of Transcendental reform. At Brook Farm she taught Italian and French and worked on some of the earliest American translations of Dante, and is likely responsible for the interest in the great Italian poet that Hecker showed during his Brook Farm days. In the spring of 1844 when Hecker was on his way home from Concord during a time when he was ready to make his final decision for Catholicism, he visited George and Sophia Ripley at Brook Farm and shared with them his new convictions. Sophia listened attentively and sympathetically, and Hecker at the time suspected that she might be moving toward Rome herself. In fact she was. By 1846 she had accepted the faith privately, but refrained from public profession because of the effect she thought it might have on the tottering Brook Farm Phalanx. A year later she was received into the church. During the years of the Ripleys' residence in New York when George worked as a literary critic, at first in the most pecuniary and finally with the most comfortable situations, his wife was busy with Catholic charities. Her greatest work was with the poor children of Randolf's Island and with the city's ladies of the evening. She was one of the main patrons of the Sisters of the Good Shepherd and worked tirelessly to get them established as a religious community with the grudging consent of Bishop Hughes. In 1861 she died of cancer.

During her New York Catholic years her confessor was none other than Fr. Hecker, who was until 1857 a Redemptorist and later the pastor of the Paulist mother church, St. Paul the Apostle, on Ninth Avenue at Fifty-Ninth Street. A year after her death in 1861 he wrote a tribute to her which gives us an insight into her spirituality: "Her attachment to the Catholic Church was very deep. She did not enter it for any passing excitement. . . . " He relates how she not only accepted the full range of Catholic doctrine, but also embraced the liturgical life of the church as well.[88]

In addition to those who actually converted there were those who came to prize aspects of Catholic thought and practice. Again they were all communitarians. Sophia's husband George, for instance, was more than tolerant of his wife's faith. He wrote to Fr. Hecker during the 1860s, advising him to consider giving a mission in Concord and assuring him of his support and his conviction that it would do a number of people much good.[89] In 1848 he published a warm account of his attendance at a Christmas Mass that inspired him, despite his ultra-Protestant background.[90] Hecker told the story of how Ripley had, during one of his conversations with him, asked him whether he would be willing to minister to him on his deathbed, if he should desire it. In 1880 Ripley did call the priest when he was dying in New York. Hecker, himself enfeebled by illness, did not receive the message—which he says Ripley sent five times—until it was too late. Ripley had lost consciousness by the time Hecker arrived.[91]

Charles King Newcomb was another who never did make it all the way to Rome, in his case due in part to the opposition of his friend Margaret Fuller (before her Italian sojourn) and his mother. Newcomb is best remembered for his contribution to the *Dial*, ''The Two Dolans.'' One year younger than Hecker, he went to Brook Farm at its inception in 1841 and remained there four years. His interest in Catholicism was part of a larger mystical orientation that won him the reputation for odd, introverted behavior at the Farm.[92] His room was filled with crosses and pictures of saints. He could be heard chanting litanies in the middle of the night and talked often of contemplation and mystical reveries. It was his writing, however, that won him the most attention. Emerson especially became his admirer and friend. He encouraged him to complete the ''Two Dolans'' manuscript and urged Margaret Fuller to publish it in the *Dial*. Deeply influenced by Richter, his prose had a certain dreamlike quality about it. Emerson worked hard with him to add some order to his text that was characterized by poor spelling and atrocious grammar. Yet for Emerson it was a work of genius, full of the universe.

Before coming to Brook Farm in 1841, Newcomb attended the Episcopal seminary at Alexandria, Virginia, but left before ordination, disgusted with the sectarian nature of Episcopalianism. Then in 1838 he spent some time in New York studying Catholicism with an unknown professor. His commonplace books from this time are full of materials from church rituals and from the writings of Catholic mystics.

His love of Richter and his mystical bent make it very odd that Hecker never mentions him in the whole of the diary. They seemed like natural soulmates.[93]

There are also the stories of Brook Farmer Nathaniel Hawthorne becoming very sympathetic to Catholicism after leaving the Farm and going to Rome, the venue for his novel *The Marble Faun*. His daughter Rose and her husband were received into Catholicism at the Paulist church in New York. After leaving her husband she became Mother Alphonsa, the foundress of a community of nuns given to work with the incurably ill. William Henry Channing also had Catholic sympathies. Hecker said of him in 1844 that his heart was Catholic, though his mind still was stuck in Protestantism. His articles in *The Harbinger* on ''The Catholics and the Associationists'' and ''Unity in Catholicity in the Church'' confirm Hecker's insight.[94] According to Sophia Ripley, Channing's wife Julia almost converted.[95]

We have already seen that some Transcendentalists, though thoroughly committed to liberty, felt that they had to find new unitive structures and that the social reform movement, especially in its Associationist phase, gave them what they hoped would be a way to reconstruct a unitive society without sacrificing their individual freedom. Those like Channing who looked to Catholicism with sympathy, but never converted, were content to see the church simply as a model. Those that actually entered the church from among the Transcendentalist ranks felt a need to convert. Why?

Georgiana Bruce Kirby in her recollections of her Brook Farm days was intrigued by the same question. She had no firm answer but suggested that some might have sought comfort after the disappointment following the failure of Brook Farm. Others, she thought, found Catholicism the ultimate Newness, a radical departure with their past life that answered to their new tastes for universalism. Still others, she conjectured, were simply impressionistic souls who found the romance of the ancient faith irresistible.[96] Ann Rose in speculating on Sophia Ripley's conversion suggests that it was partially the result of the ambiguous status of women in the reform movement. The church provided her with a community outside of the home, where she could freely share her sympathies without the constant chores of home life, or the domestic labors of taking care of star-struck male boarders at Brook Farm.[97]

All of these are plausible and, I think, insightful. But they are not the reasons that are reported by the converts themselves, at least in the limited number of such reports that are extant. In those the motives are twofold: a desire for association with a universal body that represents a unitive culture, and a conscious need for the grace of Christ that flows through the Church's spiritual ministry. Sophia Ripley came to see that all her relations with others were "those of the intellect and imagination, and not warm heart ties." She felt that she did not love anyone as she should.[98] As Hecker said of her motives: "It was her deep felt want of the assistance of God's grace and her profound conviction that the Church was the dispenser of that grace that, in spite of every worldly consideration, led her to enter its fold."[99]

It was certainly the same with the convert who along with Hecker gave the clearest explanation of his conversion, Orestes Brownson. Brownson, though never a Brook Farmer, certainly was moved by the same winds that blew through West Roxbury. The difference between Brownson and the Brook Farmers was that he was always, it seemed, one step ahead of them in his religious thinking. He had taken up the call to universal reform through the institution of new synthetic structures back in the late 1830s. He had read Benjamin Constant and Pierre Leroux before any of the New Englanders and by 1844 had clear ideas about what he could and could not accept from their thinking. By that time he had in fact come to the unswerving belief: "no church, no reform"; no reform of society and no reform of his own heart, which, as hard as it might be to imagine, was a concern of the vociferous controversialist. It was not, as the Transcendentalists claimed, by merely coming into a moral harmony with Christ that people were saved. They were saved rather "by Christ himself, by his being formed in them, the wisdom of God and the power of God, and through his indwelling Spirit. . . . "[100] That conviction motivated his attack on Fourierism and left him only to decide what was the true church. He struggled with Anglicanism, concluding, with some help from the Tractarians but largely on his own, that the Anglican claims were illegitimate. His was an organic sense of grace, not as intellectual suasion or moral model, but as life itself. It was that life, and the perception that it was contained in the church in a unique way because Christ had infused it into his church at Pentecost, that made the crucial difference between the Catholic admirers and the Catholic converts.

It was this that Brownson drove home to Hecker in a June 6, 1844 letter. If he really desired personal holiness he must put himself under the direction of the church, Brownson told him. "You can obtain it only through the grace of God, and the grace of God only through its appointed channels." Hecker had to struggle hard to accept that, because he felt his individuality would be lost in the church and because he often felt that nothing more was needed than his contemplative communion with Spirit. It was a real struggle because he was drawn to both poles. When he came to accept that the Spirit that led him interiorly was the Spirit of Christ that animated the church, he was ready to be converted. But oddly enough, as volumes 1 and 2 of the diary show, that idea was present before he actually converted. What held him back until June 1844 was the same thing that keeps many "ideal" Catholics today from ever entering the church. He was not much attracted to the people who filled the pews. His reasons for being drawn to the church had little to do with much of the agenda of the immigrant church. The local parish was never his focus before or after his conversion. It was the universal scope that was his concern. He never was interested in providing children with education, nor would he have dreamed of offering ethnic groups social societies to preserve their national customs. His was not the mindset of a persecuted member of a minority. Unity, but not conformity, was his goal; freedom, not authority, his method. As we have seen, the Romantic impulses that had moved him to the door of the church were muted within its structures. But there was one area in which the immigrant church did appeal: in the very elements that were crucial to Sophia Ripley and Brownson—its emphasis on unity and the need for the grace of Christ as mediated by the church. Those, in the final analysis, were the most important considerations for Hecker.

Brownson actually shared a similar problem. He did not think much of the Irish approach to religion and he knew that it dominated the American church. As Hecker's response to Brownson's chiding in his June 6, 1844 letter shows, it was only after Hecker heard that Brownson was going to convert that he made his decision to enter the church. After that he moved faster and preceded Brownson in, but that was a physical, not an intellectual movement. Brownson was Hecker's hero of culture. If he could endure the immigrant church and see in it the holy, catholic, and apostolic faith, so could Hecker.

CONCLUSION

HECKER'S ACHIEVEMENT

Seen against the background of U.S. antebellum culture, Hecker's achievement, even as it appears in the inchoate and immature forms of the diary, emerges more clearly. The achievement was an attempt, by no means entirely successful, but nevertheless significant, to develop a new language of religious experience that was American, Romantic, and Catholic.

I say first that he attempted to develop a new language. I do not by this mean that he put forth any formal linguistic theory as did, for example, the Hungarian Charles Kraitsir in the 1830s. I mean simply that he attempted to express a new phenomenon for which there was no precedent in American thought, and that that caused him to search for a new mode of expression. There were others of his time who were likewise trying to give expression to that phenomenon, many of whom we have already met. But there were none in America who significantly preceded Hecker, and none whose attempts were any more successful. He was in the first generation of Catholic Americans who had been formed by the Romantic impulse.

The Romantic revolt against the sensism of the Enlightenment and the materialism of the Industrial Revolution developed as part of its reassertion of the primacy of the spiritual a conviction that the new mode of seeing the world as "in-breathed" with spirit required a new way to communicate that vision as well. In America the Transcendentalists had been made very much aware of that by the book that the first meeting of the Transcendentalist Club had discussed, James Marsh's edition of Samuel Taylor Coleridge's *Aids to Reflection*. In his preface, Marsh called attention to Coleridge's distinction between Reason and Understanding. He believed that it was of major importance because by its careful delineation it gave expression to certain spiritual realities that the language of Lockean philosophy was unable to express. The Understanding was the power that ordered the perception of the senses and performed rational operations with the data that the five senses supplied from the external, physical world. The Reason, on the other hand, was the power to intuit, to respond to sentiment, to discern spiritual things. The current age was dominated by the Understanding, but the perception of spiritual realities called for the powers of the Reason. It was then Coleridge's new language that gave opportunities to better express the place of the sacred to make people perceive that there was more in the depths of their minds worth exploring than that which the Empiricists led them to think. As Philip Gura concludes in his excellent analysis of Marsh: ''The idealistic philosophy Marsh helped introduce through his sponsorship of Coleridge and the Cambridge Platonists lent itself to a variety of constructions in psychology and philology; and because of this, Marsh went far toward providing his contemporaries with a new vocabulary for dealing with the philosophical and theological complexity of the nineteenth century, a vocabulary which, though ''scientifically'' precise, found a place for words that displayed man's capacity for dreaming.''[101]

Horace Bushnell, the Hartford Congregationalist minister, took the process one step further. When he was a young student at Yale in the early 1820s he found himself without the language to properly express the religious sentiments that were coursing through his sensitive heart and mind. He set himself to finding such a language, and when he discovered *Aids to Reflection* it engrossed him for a full six months. He tried in his own writing to find new expressions that would more accurately give voice to the complex, new experiences of God that he was having. His efforts bore fruit in his 1848 masterpiece *God in Christ*. He explained how he was interested in language chiefly ''as regards its signification, or the power and capacity of word, taken as vehicles of thought and spiritual truth.''[102]

His study led him to conclude that words were signs and images of the truth, not its absolute equivalents. Humanity's comprehension of spiritual things, likewise, could only be ''analogies, signs, shadows.''[103] He was, nevertheless, not a relativist; he believed in the immutability of truth, but was highly aware of the changing, imperfect nature of human attempts to express it. Hence what was needed was not the development of a rationalistic faith at the expense of the Coleridgean Reason, but a cultivation of ''the perceptive power in spiritual life, an unction of the Holy One . . . an immediate, experiential knowledge of God.''[104]

Both Bushnell and Marsh remained practicing Christians. Indeed it was the vitality of their spiritual experiences that led them to search for fuller modes of expression than those afforded by their traditions. With many of the Transcendentalists this was not the case, as we have seen. They went the route of radically developing the ideas broached by Coleridge, Marsh, and Bushnell and came to view Christ himself as pure symbol with no necessary objective reality.

Hecker, of course, did not even move as far in that direction as did Bushnell. Yet he shared Bushnell's and Marsh's problem. Inspired by the new currents of thought and taken up by the complexity of an age in which the old forms of life and thought were giving way, he was at first unable to express them adequately. In the first entry of the diary, his apprehension is clear: "I have not yet attained the power to speak it. It rests in me yet undeveloped." Upon going off from home to study, the complexities of his young life had begun to crowd in upon him. He was raised to work in business, but he began to become aware of the negative aspects of the current economic order. He began to call it the devil's work, a demonic system opposed to the highest aspirations of humanity. He had been disrupted from his course as a son of an avid Methodist mother by the Oxford movement in America. But the disruption was minor compared to the ideas of the Newness that spoke of intuitive religion that needed no churchly expression whatsoever. The struggles between the competing forces needed voice that old ways of thinking and speaking could not supply.

He became aware of the changing, creative aspect of his comprehension and expression of experience. Prophecy, both as proclamation of the truth and as foreseeing of the future, became a favorite theme. There was something—he did not know what to call it, especially at the beginning of the diary—that was coming, that was going to change things dramatically: "It is a hidden force energy power. . . . It wants exposition. . . . It will put on a new face features countenance upon the individuals of Men. It will be a truth of an unknown force in the life of Man. It will be in a sense a new Creation unfolding a new law of his being." We see developing in this passage a sense of the future that was so intimately linked with the need to create a new tomorrow. It is an unfolding of "a new law of his being"— an organic, natural, quintessentially human thing, a spiritual, living thing, not a mechanical, artificial mode—that he looked for. His experimental efforts to give it voice are obvious. He searches for the right word. He pursues one line of thought to try its effectiveness and then abandons it in the next entry or even in the next paragraph, leaving plenty of room for the Charles Maignens of the world to find demons lurking in between. But the direction is always clear. No it is not linear; it backs and circles about, yet its motivation, its will is strong and constant. Give expression to this new life within. Find a way to do this. Let the spirit within break through: " . . . the Soul has increased disproportionately to its powers of activity hence it would burst its integuments its enclosure and rush out of its entombment in matter & Time into ethereal Eternity. . . . "[105]

The next step in his quest for expression led him to investigate the contemplative dimension with the help of the Fruitlands mystics and their library. Dipping into the Quietists and the Vedas and Gita he developed a desire to overcome the inadequacies of his language by moving beyond speech altogether. On August 16, 1843, he writes: "I feel daily I am tending more and more to Quietism; being less willful and more peaceful." He talks of being "silent to the world."[106] "Be silent and let thy silence speak," he advises himself on that same day. The move toward an apophatic mysticism was accompanied by an increased confidence in his method of attending to the inward Spirit. With it came a willingness to accept the passive dimensions of the spiritual life, to faithfully wait for God's leading, and beyond that an effort, at least, not to care about outward actions, to be indifferent to all but the will of the Spirit.

He, nevertheless, could not rest entirely content with that approach, since he was part of an age of action, of empire building and conquering continents. Ultimately he must be a doer and a proclaimer. His effort then to find a voice continued. He grew in his awareness of the aesthetic dimension of religious experience, helped by his reading of Richter and Schelling and by his acquaintance with Brook Farmers like musician John Dwight Sullivan, linguist and critic Charles Dana, and soulmates George and Burrill Curtis. The aesthetic had two main elements: an association of God with beauty and a stress on categories of seeing as basic to religious experience. An entry from December 14, 1843, illustrates this well:

> Lord let me see more of Thee. Open thou more of my vision. Give me a purer heart. . . . Oh Lord I feel this is but the struggle of my soul to see Thee more completely and help Thou it in its attempts. Thy beauty Thy loveliness oh God is beyond our finite vision far above our expression.

The religious person was a poet. Genius, he insisted often in his correspondence with George Curtis, was religious in its essence. Beauty lay in the correspondence of forms with the eternal essence. He wrote in a May 14, 1844 entry that sums up his thought and ironically shows us how right he was when he said that his vision was superior to his powers of expression: "He who lives in the closest accord with nature in the completest harmony with all the laws of God is the most poetic natured man; in other words, the most godlike natured man is the beautifullest."

One of the other ways in which he gave expression to that new language was in his pain. From the earliest entries to the last volume, the diary is a book to which he turns when there is no one else who will understand. Often it is in times of perplexity that he comes. The style that he learned from his reading of the Romantic novelists and poets served him well. It enabled him to pour out the feelings of alienation, the bouts with grief, the horrors of doubt and indecision. It gave him ways to experiment with new ideas, new feelings. Fortunately no pious scribe has gotten to the diaries of Father Hecker. With the exception of some isolated, childish attempts to efface the record of his encounters with his heart throb Almira Barlow, he himself left things substantively as he wrote them. We, therefore, have an emotional record of the moment, one that constantly is talking about a critical reaction to his surroundings. His sentiments repeatedly are dialoguing with his surroundings. In the diary we hear only his voice. The other voice, that of his surroundings, is largely silent (which is why I have gone to such effort to present the part of the cultural context).

His constant effort to find a new voice continued yielding fruit after his conversion in June of 1844. Given a new confidence in his beliefs, and given, suddenly as it were, a rich set of external practices, his writing is less desperate, less pathetic. Nevertheless he carries his efforts forward as a Catholic. He does not simply adopt the vocabulary of the Church's catechism or even the words of his Bishops McCloskey or Hughes. As Mary Lyons has shown so well in her dissertation, he takes with him much of his Transcendental rhetoric.[107] The morning on which he is baptized his diary entry is full not of segments from the tridentine rite of Baptism but of musings on somnambulism, dreams, and a declaration: "The true being of man is mystical. We say that we know not what man is. The stones with which the streets are paved, which we walk upon, we feel a mystic union with. Matter seems not to be a hindrance to spiritual perception, rather it is the form in which the spiritual is cognizable."[108] Yes, that was why he could enter the church, because he believed that the spiritual could take form in the matter of the church. But his concerns, as this entry shows, were still with the spirit, not with the matter. His efforts to incorporate his Romantic sensibilities with his Catholic faith continue throughout volumes 3, 5, and 6 of the diary.

Given this, the question arises, Was Hecker really Catholic? There have been some, like Edgar Alexander, who have argued strenuously against the program of blending Romanticism and Catholicism. For him Romanticism's emphasis on subjective experience bears only a superficial resemblance to the Catholic view of what he calls "objective ontologism." Romantic pantheism is opposed to objective Catholic theism. The subjective aestheticism and occasionalism of Romanticism is set against the realism of Catholicism. To the Romantic subjectivistic glorification and deification of the ego is opposed the ontological definiteness and theological security of the Catholic within an objective order of existence. The anti-Protestantism and concern for the Middle Ages that was so much a part of the Romantic impulse he sees as retrogressive escapism, pseudo-Catholic at heart.[109]

As tempting as it is to dismiss this as Neo-Scholastic sour grapes offered by a disgruntled maidservant at the banquet of modernity, the critique does highlight aspects of Romanticism that are in tension with some traditional Catholic understandings of the person, the church, and salvation. There is no doubt that the 1840s saw manifestations of the Romantic impulse that did in fact do all the things of which Alexander accuses it. His main burden is to show how in the hands of men like De Maistre and Adam Mueller the Romantic impulse was made the basis for a ''pseudo-theological'' justification of the totalitarian state, a use to which the Nazis put it as well. He is right to call attention to the dark side of Romanticism, the side that in Germany led to the egotism of Fichte and in America to the somewhat glib efforts of Emerson to redefine the nature of revelation and to relegate Christ to symbol.

But it must be remembered that the Romantic impulse was a variegated phenomenon that expressed itself in different ways at different times. To dismiss it, en masse, as ''pseudo-Catholic'' is to ignore the efforts not only of Hecker and Brownson in America, but of many Catholics in the Old World who responded to the Romantic impulse. In England there were Newman, Faber, and Manning; in Italy, Rosmini and Bosco; and in France, Lacordaire. In Germany there were three generations of German Catholic theologians from 1789 to 1848 who, taking their inspiration from Friedrich Schelling, attempted to rethink Catholic theology in the context of the currents of the age.

Writers such as Friedrich Schlegel and Johann Adam Moehler were Catholic Romantics whose works Hecker read before his conversion. After becoming a Catholic, he studied the theological writings of Johann Joseph Gorres, Johann Sebastian Drey, and J.M. Sailer. Their agenda, as Thomas O'Meara has shown, was to rethink subjectivity and revelation in the light of the new age. Mindful of the dangers of individualism to which the Reformation had made Catholic theology extremely sensitive, they, nevertheless, joined the Romantic revolt against the Enlightenment's materialism and accepted the subjective starting point for metaphysics. But they strove to articulate an objective idealism that did not relegate the objective world to a reflection of one's own face in the bottom of a well. In regard to revelation, they attempted to see the world as an organic whole, instinct with God's life. Nature was the medium through which revelation could occur. How to do that and yet avoid pantheism and naturalism was the burden of those Catholic thinkers.[110]

It is not necessary here to discuss just how the German school formulated its positions, for in the final analysis, it would be difficult to show—beyond what we have already seen—any direct relationship between them and the undisciplined diary musings of Hecker. What is clear is that both they and Hecker responded to similar forces within the culture of the day and attempted similar solutions to the problems they faced. In this regard he may be seen as an American manifestation of a larger historical moment in the epic of nineteenth century thought.

Yet he can rightly be called Catholic, not only because of the continuity between his thought and that of the other Romantic Catholic thinkers. If one means by being Catholic that one accepts the faith of the church and abides by its practice and discipline, then certainly he was. It is remarkable that once he converted, he never uttered a word of disagreement over doctrine or practice. This not only was the case in his diary but in the entire corpus of his Catholic works. Rather than criticize Catholicism, he becomes one of its most energetic defenders in the nineteenth century. He clearly broke, as we have repeatedly seen, with those Transcendentalists who had no need for Christ. His devotion to the Redeemer was deep and almost as pervasive as his love of the Spirit. It was linked with a fidelity to the church and a conviction of its necessity both for the saving of the individual and the society. His missionary work, as well as his writing and pastoring, all reflected these convictions. They were attempts to value both the ideal and the reality of the church—the excellence of its tradition, the truth of its doctrine. There was, after his conversion, no serious complaining about the sad state of the actual Catholic church in America. When he did express a criticism, it was in the context of offering a remedy, which more often than not was simply a call to the Spirit, a testimony to the other dimension. The problem was never that the tradition had neglected that spiritual dimension, but rather that the present age had—not the church of the age, mind you, just the age, the society at large. Because of that, Catholics might be tempted to forget as well.

The other way in which he was Catholic is in his prizing of the universal nature of the church. What drew him to Catholicism continued to intrigue him. It was the synthetic society of the new age, but unlike the dreams of the Fourierists, it was here and now, visible and concrete. Coming into communion with it was an integrating experience for him. His diary entries begin to glow with the peace of assurance. The components of his life appear more neatly joined together. He rested, but still sought more; he was confident, yet still curious; he was enthralled with the richness of his inner life and found a banquet for his soul in the rites of the church.

That his attempt to give new expression to his religious experience should be in many ways so crude when compared to that of a Drey or a Gorres is in a certain sense appropriate. He was the product of a developing culture, whose finest schools were a long way from Jena and Tübingen indeed. The manifestations of the Romantic mood in American religion, even the best of them, were unrefined and coarse compared to their European counterparts. Bushnell pales next to Schleiermacher; Marsh is a shadow standing before the light of Coleridge; and Brownson's polemics are as harsh as the blows of his blacksmith's hammer when compared to Moehler's. Add to this the fact that Hecker did not have even the best education that his country could offer him, and the point becomes all the clearer.

It is not, however, for sophistication that one should look to Hecker or, for that matter, to any product of nineteenth century American intellectual life. It is rather to the freshness, the primitive energy of his experience that one should be open. Though he lacked the philosophical depth of Brownson, the fineness of expression of those admirers of Catholicism like Hawthorne, Lowell, and Newcomb, and the social consciousness of another admirer, William Henry Channing, Hecker gave the movement to express an American, Romantic, Catholic spirituality its most sustained effort. His voice, as rough and unrefined as it was, issued from a heart that was tuned in to the mystical dimension to a rare degree. As a littérateur, as a theologian, as a philosopher, he was an amateur of mediocre abilities. As a seer, however, he was gifted.

Hecker's Romantic, Catholic, American voice, speaking out of the whirl of the cultural upheaval of the 1840s, gave form to the complexity and suffering of the times. As he wandered between two ages, one dead, the other seemingly powerless to be born, he caught a vision of what America could be and what Catholicism really was, and he tried to tell of it for the rest of his life. The diary presented here is the first, and in many ways the freshest and most invigorating, of his many attempts.

NOTES

1. At the time of his death in the 1880s, he left an estate of over two million dollars. One of his checkbooks from the 1870s is extant and reveals just how generous he was. The majority of the entries, which include checks to pay business expenses, are to Catholic charitable enterprises in New York.

2. See the works of Walter Elliott, Vincent Holden, and John Farina in the bibliography. In *An American Experience of God,* chapters I-III, I devoted a great deal of time to an examination of the early influences on Hecker's development. Given that, there is no need to repeat it here.

3. See William Portier's "Isaac Hecker and Testem Benevolentiae" in John Farina, ed., *Hecker Studies* (New York: Paulist Press, 1983), pp. 11–48.

4. Walter Elliott gave these parts of the diary different titles, which he wrote on their covers along with short signed notes about their contents. Through volume 4, I follow his numbering, but after that he calls my volume 5 the "first part of the last part," and my volume 6 "the Fifth Part." In the interest of clarity, I have chosen to call the two parts volume 5 and volume 6, respectively. There is no extant Elliott transcription of my volume 5, as there is for the other volumes.

5. "Transcribed Thoughts of Professor Tuefelsdrockh," in Toby Tanner, *The Reign of Wonder* (Cambridge: Cambridge University Press, 1965).

6. See Barrett John Mandel, "The Autobiographer's Art," *Journal of Aesthetics and Art Criticism* 27 (1968):217.

7. *American Autobiography: The Prophetic Mode* (Amherst: University of Massachusetts Press, 1979), p. 1.

8. Part of this section is taken from my article, "The Uses of the Early Diary of Isaac Hecker," *U.S. Catholic Historian* 3 (Spring 1984): 279–93.

9. All references to Elliott are from the 1891 Columbus Press edition. Those to Maignen are from the 1898 Burns and Oates English edition.

10. For bibliographic material on Americanism and a current discussion of the role of Hecker's thought in the controversy see Joseph P. Chinnici, *Living Stones* (in press), chapter V; William L. Portier, "Providential Nation: An Historical-Theological Study of Isaac Hecker's Americanism" (Ph.D. dissertation, University of St. Michael's College, 1980) and *Isaac Hecker and the First Vatican Council* (Babylon: Edwin Mellon Press, 1986).

11. Maignen, p. xxi.

12. Elliott, p. xvii; Maignen, p. 3.

13. Maignen, p. xxiii.

14. Elliott, pp. 57, 58.

15. Ibid., 57 and 67.

16. Ibid., p. iii.

17. Maignen, pp. 16 and 22.

18. Ibid., p. 12.

19. Ann Rose, *Transcendentalism as a Social Movement* (New Haven: Yale University Press, 1981), p. 129.

20. See Michel de Certeau, *La Fable Mystique* (Paris: Éditions Gallimard, 1982).

21. A Proclamation of the People of South Carolina, in James D. Richardson, ed., *Messages and Papers of the Presidents, vol II,* (Washington, D.C.: Government Printing Office, 1896), p. 641.

22. Arthur O. Lovejoy, *Essays in the History of Ideas* (Baltimore: Johns Hopkins University Press, 1948), pp. 228–53.

23. Thomas F. O'Meara, *Romantic Idealism and Roman Catholicism* (Notre Dame: University of Notre Dame Press, 1982), p. 1.

24. See Eugene Weber, *Europe Since 1715* (New York: Norton, 1972), p. 280.

25. "The Oxford Movement in the United States," *Catholic Historical Review* 19 (April 1933): 33–39.

26. See Sister Mary A. Kwitchen, *James Alphonsus McMaster* (Washington: Catholic University of America Press, 1949), pp. 21–52.

27. Clarence Walworth, *The Oxford Movement in America,* (New York: The Catholic Book Exchange, 1895), p. 8.

28. Ibid.

29. Ibid., pp. 39–40.

30. John Keble, *The Tracts for the Times #89: On the Mysticism Attributed to the Early Fathers of the Church* (London: James Parker, 1868), p. 3.

31. Hecker to family, May 23, 1844.

32. *Symbolism,* trans. James Robertson, 5th ed. (London: Gibbings, 1906), p. 1.

33. Ibid., p. 476.

34. Walworth, p. 96.

35. J.A. Moehler, *Die Einheit in der Kirche* (Mainz, 1825), in O'Meara, p. 149.

36. In John Humphrey Noyes, *The History of American Socialisms* (Philadelphia: Lippincott, 1870); reprint (New York: Dover, 1966), p. 112.

37. George Hochfield, ed., *Selected Writings of the American Transcendentalists* (New York: New American Library, 1966), p. x.

38. Frederick Ives Carpenter, *Emerson Handbook* (New York: Hendrick's House, 1953), p. 26.

39. See Karl Rahner, "Religious Enthusiasm and the Experience of Grace," in *Theological Investigations* 16 (Baltimore: Helicon, 1967), p. 47; Andrew Louth, s.v. "Mysticism," in *Westminster Dictionary of Spirituality* (Philadelphia: Westminster, 1984); Evelyn Underhill, *Mysticism* (London: Mathuen, 1911), part 1, chapter 1.

40. Odell Shepherd, ed., *The Journals of Bronson Alcott* (Boston: Little Brown, 1938), p. 36, in Kathleen Raine and George Harper, eds., *Thomas Taylor The Platonist* (Princeton: Princeton University Press, 1969), p. 60. Cf. pp. 49–89.

41. *Thomas Taylor The Platonist,* op. cit. Looking back at his efforts in the 1840s Alcott recalled: "Plato and Christ interpreted each other and the mind of mankind" (Odell Shepherd, ed., *The Journals of Bronson Alcott* [Boston: Little Brown, 1938], p. 23). Entry for March 28, 1850.

42. In Shepherd, *Pedlar's Progress,* p. 338, from the *Dial.*

43. Plotinus in *The Essence of Plotinus,* comp. Grace Turnbull (New York: Oxford, 1934) pp. 113–14.

44. Review of James F. Clarke's translation of *Revelation of Specimens of Religion, Christian Examiner* 30 (March 1841): 363; "Life of St. Bernard of Clairvaux," *Christian Examiner* 30 (March 1841): 1 f.; James Walker, "Reaction in Favor of the Roman Catholics," *Christian Examiner* 23 (September 1837): 1 f.

45. See Ronald V. Wells, *Three Christian Transcendentalists* (New York: Columbia University Press, 1943).

46. See *The Phalanx or Journal of Social Science Devoted to the Cause of Association or a Social Reform and the Elevation of the Human Race* 1 (October 5, 1843):1.

47. Arthur E. Bestor, *Backwoods Utopias* (Philadelphia: University of Pennsylvania Press, 1950), p. 243.

48. Noyes, pp. 25–26.

49. Bestor, p. 47.

50. Ibid., p. 58.

51. See Alan Dawley, *Class and Community: The Industrial Revolution in Lynn* (Cambridge: Harvard University Press, 1976).

52. Ibid., pp. 34–36.

53. "The Present State of Society," in Henry Brownson, ed., *The Works of Orestes A. Brownson,* vol IV (Detroit: H.F. Brownson, 1900), p. 436.

54. *The Dial* 1 (July 1840).

55. *New Views,* pp. 47, 48, in *Works,* op. cit.

56. In Bode, ed., *American Life in the 1840s* (Garden City: Anchor, 1967) p. 126.

57. Frank Manuel, *The Prophets of Paris* (Cambridge, Mass.: Harvard, 1962), p. 262, in M.C. Spencer, *Charles Fourier* (Boston: Twayne, 1981), p. 13.

58. *The Present,* pp. 28–29.

59. "A Call to the Friends of Social Reform in New England," in *The Present,* 1 (December 15, 1843): 208.

60. See *New York Tribune,* April 5, 6, 1844.

61. 1 (Oct. 5, 1843): 1.

62. From the *Theory of the Four Movements and General Destinies* in *The Phalanx* 1 (Nov. 4, 1843): 27.

63. Madame Gatti de Gammond, "The Third Dispensation," *The Present* 1 (Nov. 15, 1843): 110–11.

64. *The Present* 1 (Sept. 1843): 71.

65. *The Present* 1 (November 1843): 136.

66. *The Harbinger* 39 (July 25, 1846): 102–04. In the mind of their enemies like William Brownlow there was also a relation between the political reform movements of the Democratic Loco-Focos and Catholicism, one which was ominous in its implications and threatened to spread the specter of the Vatican over this free land. See William G. Brownlow, *A Political Register* (Jonesborough, TN: Jonesborough Whig, 1844).

67. Orestes Brownson, "Church Unity and Social Amelioration," *Brownson Quarterly Review* (August 1844): 517–18.

68. John Hughes, *Introduction to an Inquiry,* pp. xvi–xvii.

69. "The Science of Political Economy," in Lawrence Kehoe, ed., *The Complete Works of the Most Reverend John D. Hughes,* vol 1 (New York: Catholic Publication Society, 1864), p. 21.

70. See James Hennesey, *American Catholics* (New York: Oxford University Press, 1981), pp. 120–22.

71. See for example the index to the *Catholic Herald* for 1843.

72. Peter Knights, *The Plain People of Boston* (New York: Oxford University Press, 1971); Jay P. Dolan, *The Immigrant Church* (Baltimore: Johns Hopkins University Press, 1975).

73. On Fenwick, see Robert Emmett Curran's superb contribution to the Sources of American Spirituality series, *American Jesuit Spirituality: The Maryland Tradition* (New York: Paulist Press, 1988).

74. Lawrence Kehoe, ed., *The Complete Works of the Most Reverend John D. Hughes,* vol 1 (New York: Catholic Publication Society, 1864), p. 354, in Pat-

rick Carey, *American Catholic Religious Thought* (New York: Paulist, 1987), p. 19.

75. Joseph Chinnici, "John Hughes: Power, Poverty, and Persecution in the Immigrant Community," in *Living Stones* (in press).

76. *Miscelleanea* (Louisville: Webb, Gill, Levering, 1855), p. 150.

77. See "Catholic Religious Life in Boston in the Era of Cardinal O'Connell," in Robert Sullivan and James O'Toole, eds., *Catholic Boston: Studies in Religion and Community, 1870–1970* (Boston: Northeastern University Press, 1986).

78. See Ann Taves, *Household of Faith* (South Bend, IN: University of Notre Dame Press, 1986).

79. James Meagher, *Teaching the Truth by Signs and Ceremonies* (New York: Russell Brothers, 1882).

80. Peter Kenrick, *The Validity of Anglican Orders Examined* (Philadelphia: Cummiskey, 1841).

81. Hugh J. Nolan, *The Most Reverend Francis Patrick Kenrick, Third Bishop of Philadelphia* (Philadelphia: American Catholic Historical Society of Philadelphia, 1948), p. 380.

82. Francis Kenrick, *Letter on Christian Union Addressed to the Bishops of the Protestant Episcopal Church in the United States* (Philadelphia: Cummiskey, 1841), in Nolan, p. 373.

83. Francis Kenrick, *The Catholic Doctrine of Justification* (Philadelphia: Cummiskey, 1841), p. 8.

84. "Introduction by the Rt. Rev. Bishop Hughes to Mr. Livingston's Book on Imputation," in Kehoe, ed., *The Complete Works of the Most Rev. John Hughes,* vol. 1 (New York: The American News Company, 1864), p. 44.

85. In *Complete Works,* vol. II (New York: American News Company), pp. 787–90. On the transformation of the Romantic mood, cf. Virgil Nemoianu, *The Taming of Romanticism* (Cambridge, MA., Harvard, 1984).

86. Martin John Spalding, "The Spirit of the Age," in *Miscellanea* (Louisville: Webb, Gill, and Levering, 1855), p. 391.

87. See James Kay, Jr., to Hecker, March 24, 1845.

88. "Tribute to Mrs. George Ripley," Paulist Fathers Archives (hereafter, PFA), n.d. but c.1862.

89. George Ripley to Hecker, as January 12, 1863, PFA.

90. "A Christmas Mass," *The Harbinger* 7 (January 1, 1848): 69.

91. "A Tribute to Mrs. George Ripley," op. cit.

92. See Joel Myerson, *The New England Transcendentalists and the Dial* (Cranbury, NJ: Associated University Press, 1969), p. 181.

93. Ibid., pp. 182–85; Joel Myerson, ed., *The Transcendentalists* (New York: MLA, 1984) pp. 214–15. The most complete secondary source is Judith K. Johnson, ed., *The Journals of Charles King Newcomb* (Providence: Brown University Press, 1946).

94. "The Catholics and the Associationists," *The Harbinger* 3 (July 25, 1846): 102–04 and 3 (September 5, 1846): 193–95; "Unity in Catholicity in the Church," 2 (May 16, 1846): 365–67.

95. Sophia Ripley to Charlotte Dana, Oct. 29, 1849, in Rose, p. 197.

96. *Years of Experience* (New York, 1887), reprint (New York: AMS, 1971), pp. 182–83.

97. Rose, p. 196.

98. Sophia Ripley to Charlotte Dana, March 1843, in Rose, p. 196.

99. Tribute to Mrs. George Ripley, op. cit.

100. "No Church, No Reform," in *Works,* vol. 4, pp. 500–01.

101. *The Wisdom of Words* (Middletown, Conn.: Wesleyan University Press, 1981), p. 49.

102. *God in Christ,* pp. 10–11.

103. *God in Christ,* p. 78; Gura, p. 65.

104. *God in Christ,* pp. 91–93.

105. Fragment A–D, n.d.

106. July 26, 1843.

107. Mary E. Lyons, "A Rhetoric for American Catholicism: The Transcendental Voice of Isaac T. Hecker (Ph.D. dissertation, University of California at Berkeley, 1983).

108. August 2, 1844.

109. Edgar Alexander, "Catholicism and German Romanticism," in Joseph Moody, ed., *Church and Society* (New York: Arts, 1953).

110. See O'Meara, op. cit.

EDITORIAL PROCEDURES

The manuscript of the diary presents a number of challenging problems to the contemporary reader. Although it was never intended for publication, there is some evidence of Hecker going back over portions of the text at a later time and correcting them. Nevertheless, the final product is rough, and one is confronted with the tension between the goals of rendering a literal transcription faithful to the original, on the one hand, and producing a readable text, on the other. Throughout I have tipped toward the side of faithfulness to the original. That goal has, at times, been compromised in the interest of readability, but every emendation made has been recorded in the List of Emendations (LOE), which appears as an appendix to the text. The following points sum up the methodology employed.

1. The goal of this edition is a critical text that follows the original as closely as possible and allows the reconstruction of the original manuscript.

2. The syntax, punctuation, and spelling of the original manuscript are retained except in the cases where, in the editor's judgment, serious confusion would result. In such cases, changes have been made and the manuscript reading given in the LOE.

3. Interlineations are incorporated in the text. The manuscript reading is given in the LOE.

4. Parts of the manuscript text contain no terminal punctuation. Where there is an apparent end of a sentence followed by a word beginning with a capital letter, a space is inserted between the two apparent sentences.

79

5. Cancelled material is included in angle brackets (⟨⟩) in the text only when it is deemed significant. In cases where it has been omitted, the manuscript reading is given in the LOE. Where the cancelled material is clearly legible, Roman type is used within the angle brackets; where it is conjectural, italics, are used. Where the cancelled material is unclear, a missing letter is indicated by a dot in angle brackets ⟨.⟩; a missing word by a dash ⟨-⟩.

6. All ampersands are rendered as etc. Ampersand c (&c) in all cases is rendered etc.

INTRODUCTION TO VOLUME 1

The first volume of the early diary spans a period of sixteen months—
from around January 10, 1842, to May 23, 1844. It is the longest of the six
books, comprising some 42 percent of the total diary and documenting what
doubtless was the most tumultuous period of Hecker's young life. Between
its leaves, as it were, we see flash before us four venues: Brook Farm, Fruitlands, Concord, and New York City. Just prior to the beginning of the book,
Hecker was a young man deeply interested in religious questions who, with
his brothers in New York, kept abreast of developments in the American
Oxford movement, centered at New York's General Theological Seminary.
Reading the Tracts for Our Times and J.A. Moehler's Symbolism had set
him thinking about the question of the church, dissatisfied as he was with
his mother's Methodism and convinced that movements toward unity
among Christians were providential. In the fall of 1842 a change had come
over Isaac that riveted his attention on questions of his own identity. Propelled by a desire to attain through intellectual means the kind of upward
social mobility that his brothers were bent on gaining economically, he went
off to Brownson's Chelsea home, and after a brief stay enrolled at West
Roxbury's Brook Farm as a student.

His first encounters with the Newness made him "laugh and cry" as
he read the massive novels of Jean Paul Richter and Goethe, the essays of
George Ripley, the articles of Brownson, the philosophy of Leroux, and the
criticism of Schlegel. That encounter set off a profound process of reeval-
uation that threw him at times into confusion and lifted him at other moments to mystic heights. The two major struggles that emerge in this volume
center on the question of his vocation and the issue of church affiliation.
Both rage virtually non-stop throughout the book.

His stay at Brook Farm began on January 10, 1843. During his eight months there he lived comfortably, first working part-time as the community baker, then rooming with Charles Dana and devoting himself full-time to study. He met the winsome Curtis brothers—George and Burrill—plus Ida Russell, Georgiana Bruce, and his heartthrob Almira Barlow. He also came to know and esteem George and Sophia Ripley and John S. Dwight, and with these friends he corresponded briskly after leaving the Farm in August. There he also met the visitors who came to muse, Ralph Waldo Emerson, Henry David Thoreau, Charles Lane, and Bronson Alcott.

Lane and Alcott held a special appeal, and the three weeks in July that Hecker spent with them at their fledgling Fruitlands community was of great significance in his inner journey. There the contemplative seed that had begun sprouting in his soul blossomed under the encouragement of the founders and the other members—Samuel Bower, Sam Larned, Abraham Everett, and Joseph Palmer—whom Hecker rightly referred to as the "spiritualist or mystic school."

But a dissatisfaction with Alcott's rather heavy-handed attempts to solicit contributions for his community from the youngest member of a prosperous baking company repelled Hecker and sent him packing from Fruitlands on July 24. From there he returned to Brook Farm, after a visit on route to the Shaker community in Harvard. He remained at Brook Farm until August 13. By then he was convinced that he should try living with his family, blending his desire for intellectual and spiritual cultivation with involvement in the family business. His concern with social reform motivated him to work to change the way in which the company treated its employees and to aid, in small and simple ways, his family. His time at home was divided between work, study, and political activity. Though his desire to cultivate his interior life was the controlling force during this time, he involved himself, along with his brothers, in the campaign of John C. Calhoun.

Upon returning home he had once again come into the orb that had influenced him so in the latter part of the previous year. Interest in the Oxford movement that was shaking New York Episcopalianism and was converting John Hecker was still the primary religious focus of the Hecker home. There was also politics, encouraged by the future New York mayoral candidate John—and the Calhoun candidacy fostered big plans and grand hopes. Both those forces brought Isaac back into closer touch with the one who had influenced him most decisively earlier in the year: Brownson. Attending the Fourier Convention in April 1844 in New York provided a climactic setting in which his own views became clearer as his move toward the church accelerated. The no-churchism of the Transcendentalists and the Fourierists, as appealing as it was at times, was ultimately rejected. No church, no reform, he concluded with Brownson. The necessity of Christ *as Mediator, giver of grace to raise a fallen humanity, was held as more important than the free-spirited inspirations of the Fruitlands mystics or the sophisticated theories of the Associationists. Convinced that he must give himself to the full-time service of the church, he went to Concord to study Latin and Greek with George Bradford. It was there, living at the home of Thoreau, studying languages and reading the mystical writings of Eriugena, the Victorines, Eckhart, and Pseudo-Dionysius that the final entries in this volume were made. When in the third week of May he left Concord for a short vacation to Boston, he was struggling with the question of which was the true church and leaning heavily toward Rome.*

The Diary

I have just read through *Siebankas. Hesperus. Titan.* of Richter and his life published in Boston.[2] I am conscious of an influence which prevents me from speaking of the character of him and his writings at present but the influence of these words has tended to feed the flame of my present life which is marked with the coldness of Carls letter to Albano, the Phantasie of Schoppe and the love of pure Love of Albano. This is the outside of my *spirituelle*. This is my form of the activity of my mind and in reading Carls letter, Schoppes apostrophe of himself, it was like tearing out my spirit because I have not attained the power to speak it. It rests in me yet undeveloped. In reading these it was like tearing it out by pieces and caused a kind of suffocation a gasping for life. But this being the phenomenon doubtless it will change and become past   But the hidden object, the noumena (it cannot be called object for it is uncontemplatable) which to me is the only reality, for me is only touched upon in a few words *"Denn etwas hoheres als das ewigen den All-Ersten. den Gott."*[3] It is truly in the sense *Leben* (Life) is commonly understood. It is behind, it is not the *scheinen* as he says but the *sein,* not appearance but the is, the Cause. The love of its development lies deep deep in the dark unfathomable inexplicable being Man. It is the unspeakable inexpressible terrible something a serious reality to him who is conscious of its attempts to realise its self. It is not the shine of something but it would come out. It is the Cause of appearence. It is something wanting an object yet not an object for it would act its self out without object; it would be its own subject and object   Ye may talk about impossibilities visions dreams & transcendentelism tho it all amounts to words words miserable not to say innocent ignorent twaddle. It is not as unmeaning something or as might be said the Soul has increased disproportionaly to its power of activity hence it would burst its integuments its enclosure and rush out of its entombement in matter & Time into ethereal Eternity that it may breathe and become a living AM. It is not unknown. Many have so considered it that by letting day light in that it may creep out through the creatures apertures instigated by unmanly despicable weakness of an effeminate nature dishonorable to humanity and the noble Gift[4]   It is not by fear despair or Suicide that it finds utterance nor by whimpering Wertherism.[5] It is a reality a truth not a shine a spectre. It would have deep hearty utterance in this life in the Present in this world of Time & Space. It is a pressing Truth and if faithfull to it it will find its utterance in a voice unusual and perhaps unpalateable but terrible to stirring up Mens Souls to struggle strife Life. It is the would-be-spoken. Has Brownson spoken the word "Communion"? He has spoken in this word the Ideal the Contemplated. He has read the invisible letters marked upon the forehead of Time Future. His nature has preceded the development of its race hence is it that he heralds the future and he remains an isolation an inexplicable to his times. Hence the charge of Change   Change ignorently confounding Progress Progress with Change. But he can leave as others have done the labors of his life to be interpreted by an age of Purer Hearts ernest elavated spiritual and a more Religious Catholic Future than the Present without fear of being unappreciated as a great mind Reverenced as the father of a new light Loved as a Man and be looked upon as the greatest Reality of his Age[6]   Yet to me Communion is not the word   I can accept it and feel a void. It expresses the want of the times but this is not want which I am speaking of. It is a hidden force energy power which communion cannot satisfy. It wants explosition for when it does come it will not be by measure. It will put on a new face features countenance upon the Individuals of Men. It will be a truth of an unknown force in the life of Man. It will be in a sense a new Creation a development of a deeper life   A new dispensation unfolding a new law of his being

[FRAGMENT E-H]

Jan 10 1843

Could I but reveal myself unto myself? What shall I say? Is life dear to me   No. is my friends dear to me I could suffer and die if needs be for them but yet have none of the old attachment that I had for them   I would clasp all to my heart love all for their Humanity but not as Relations or Individuals   I feel as life is too much for me. It is indiscribable painfull for me to live and rather than to go through the ordeal of living I would prefer leaving this life. My spirit shrinks from contact with those that surround me. There is none that I can commune with. It is only by unuttered prayer that my bosom is unburthened. Riches I have given up. What pleasure can I receive any more I would love but alas who will receive it. My being is full of life but to whom shall I speak? Who understandeth my speech   Lord I am alone in the midst of Men. My heart is overflowing and I am a prey unto myself. Oh give me utterance that my soul can pour out its burthens. What am I now away from my home? When I think of turning back to my old life my spirit leaves my body. What shall I do? How can I work but in and by the spirit that controls? And how can I stand before others. Lord if I am to be any thing I am of all unfit for the task. How shall

I do   Who shall I cry to for help but he that has given me life and planted in me this spirit? Unto thee then do I cry from the depths of my soul for lights to suffer; so give me rather death. In my present form here am I amidst others. Why must I suffer so? Wherefore am I here? If there is any thing that is for me to do why this darkness all around me   I would not no I ask not to be happy   I will forego all kinds of hopes which I always had a presentiment   I must do which young men are prone to picture in their minds of my age if only I could have a ray of light on my present condition. My love of all wordly things are gone. They are past without gratification. My mind has been clear and why now this state of lonliness   I labored for Riches but renounced them   Friendship is gone   Love in its accustomed sense is gone and here I am left alone and I would cry with all my soul and heart what shall I do? Who will be unto me now a friend a Comforter? Will it be said Christ? Alas in this I drink too deeply. And how shall it get utterance? If this had utterance then I might live again but I am unworthy of it   I have no faith. Say greave not the spirit   I do not grieve it but it will kill me. Why choose such a vessel as I. I cannot go backwards neither would I if I could. Neither can I go forwards hence I would be glad if I was taken from this life in my present state as I am. O Lord receive me   Yet would I do my duty here establish thy Kingdom here and which I pray O Lord open thou my eyes to see the path thou wouldst have me to walk in. Thy spirit has led me in all my present judgments but I have not looked unto thee for light which I hope I may have the faith to ask in the right spirit so as I can receive thy blessing of wisdom

11th

Last evening Mr Brownson received a letter from home to an answer to his which he sent accompanying the one I sent—which was the 1st that I had partially opened my mind to my family—he sent unbeknowingly to me in which they ask his advice in my going to Brook Farm in answer to which he advises them to consent to my going etc.[7] I am now more settled than I have been for some time and hope I shall at BF find things agreeable. It is my intention to study the French & music   I hope and pray that I may be studious and not wasteful of my time & oh I hope of all things my *life* will be continued which I now have other than this or its progress would be death and I would rather be taken from this stage of action than loose it   True life is one continuous prayer one unceasing aspiration after the holy   I have no conception of a life insensible to that which is not above lofty   I would not take it on myself to say I have been ''born again'' but I know that I have passed from death to life and that things below have no hold upon me further than they lead to things above[8]   It is not a moral restraint that I have over myself but it is a change a conversion of my whole being that I have not need of restraint. Temptations yet beset me but of a different kind not sensual but I am led to be untrue to my life. If I am not on my guard I become cold   May I always be humble meek prayerfull and be open to all new light love and life   God is always giving but we turn our backs and will not receive   He is always near to those that seek him and the riches of his mercy Love & wisdom is showered upon those who seek him diligently with a penitent humble and childlike heart. Who can fathom the blessings of God? It is infinite in its source and its kind. How shall I speak of him who has not the love of God who sees not his Goodness mercy love & Wisdom? Alas he that is without God has nothing but that which is an injury a curse to his soul. The peace of God passeth all understanding. Oh how full of it were the apostles but to God I raise my feeble voice for all that he is done and that even now in these days he has brought to light the Gospel again. This does my soul confess to itself   Who can measure the depths of Christs suffering? Alone in the World having that which would give them life everlasting a heaven to them who would receive it yet despised spit upon and rejected of Men. Oh how sweet must it have been to his soul when he found even one who received even a portion of that precious gift which he came to the world to bestow. Well could he say Father forgive them they know not what they do? He would give them life but they would not receive. He would save them but they rejected him. He loved them and they despised him alas alas   Who has measured in a small degree the Love of Christ and yet denies his superiority over Man   His Love Goodness mercy are unbounded   Oh Lord may I daily come in closer & closer communion with Thy son Jesus Christ

[FRAGMENT I-L][9]

at least that which in I can live or else it will terminate in that which I do not myself fully believe but cannot help saying it—Death   I am tossed about on the sea of Life without knowing which way to steer or direct my steps. The Transcendentalist would say thou art doing thy greatest work when thou dost not know that thou art consciously doing anything   To this I can only say I do not believe it   I may be in that state when the tide of my life is on an ebb not knowing which way it will run which perhaps is the most critical period of ones life but it is not a period of positive action but just before the positive action commences. This may be true but alas how long is this period to last? May not the ship strike on a rock and be dashed in to peices. This heaving of the billows of Life who is able to stand untouched unmoved Oh that the dawn of Day would break upon my soul that I might see unto what I was born   Man perhaps never can see his destiny and in this sense. I do not hope for to see only what I want is that I may live in any one direction. Not that I shall see where or whence this direction will lead me to but that I may walk in the road and leave the end for the end

What judgment is formed of me in this community I know not but evidently I am not one of their spirits. The tone of their speech to me is different   Mr Hecker is pronounced in tone different from the tone they address others   I dont know but that I will be unable to become one of the Community. In their Life it is clear that they commune with different kind of objects from what I do hence their life is different and my speech is not understood or else misunderstood   I have not as yet spoken to one person who I could hold conversation freely with. It seemed to be a labor to talk.[10]

Night.

To day I feel returning the condition of mind which I had when I left home. If it should drive me from here I do not know where I shall go but as it has so far directed my steps and that in a way to me most agreeable I trust it will. If I am to move from here it will continue to do the same in the future   In to thy hands oh Lord I commit myself and thou doeth with me as seemeth good in thy sight. But grant oh Lord thy spirit to me that I may be willing to do thy will and not strive against it. Give me power that I may walk in thy direction and teach me how to pray that I may receive thy blessing for without thee I am worse than nothing. And oh keep me from sinking in a low sense of thy Power Goodness & Willingness to help those that call on thee in sincerity   Lord give me the sense to feel thy presence allways

3d Feb

My life in this last 9 months appears to me as a dream in which I am bound   I cannot go back to my old Life. If I should return home in this life I do not see how I can live there everything is so contrary to it   Oh Lord I pray keep me not in suspense. Lead me on to what this is tending to. Keep me not in suspense for even here is not my life. It is only a temporary resting place perhaps an intermediary place suitable for my condition at present. Let me look back for a moment and see how I have come to my present condition & place. Leaving out the cause of my inability to work the first condition I found myself in was that to labor I was unable.[11] My family supposed that if I could labor it would restore me which was true in the sense they understood restoration   I tried it but my spirit overpowered me & I was forced to leave it   The Dr he had no effect upon me because he understood not me   I made a visit to O A Brownsons for 3 weeks off & on   I found myself better and worse in the old sense of considering it. I then came here. I commenced after a few days to labor here and by my

labor which caused me for a time to have an appetite for a different kind of
food from which I was Tabu. I was getting back fast to my former old state
until I became depressed and heavy in mind & body   I should have been
taken sick had I not changed my diet & having done so my labor I fear in
a short time will have to cease. My new state will become predominating
again which now I feel working on me gradually. There is no escape from
it and from here whence shall I go? When the time comes doubtless I will
find a place. A way will be made open as there has been even up to this
time. My future is dark before me   I feel myself acting in the midst of
beings but alone unconnected & solitary   Who is me   What have I
been   What relation have I to others   Why is my past to my present like
another person   Why have I lost the sense of Relationship to my kindred
relatives   Why have I lost my old memory   Why can I not study   Who
is it that my conversation is held with when I am in half waking state as I
often find myself   Why is it that I feel an influence drawing me out of the
life of this world and those around me   How can I live unless there is a
new way opened to me or go into my old state which would be death   Oh
who can I find in my state to sympathize with   Prayer is a relief, but alas
I feel the want of a person to commune with   Why is it that I cannot find
any one to converse in my spirit which I have but only can I converse when
I speak from their spirit

4th.

Am I to be seperated from those that are around me? Oh what must I
feel in my bosom? It is impossible that I can ever return back into my old
state and who shall I find to commune with   Alas all is to me a Dream my
past & present   I am floating about like air. Oh I am seperated. There is
something that attracts my spirit off Where is it going to. What is this working in me   Oh Lord raise me up from this world for I am becoming un-
suited for it   I exist not in this Life   I commune not with Man nor in
what I do does my spirit enter. It is only in thee that I find communion   Oh
Lord grant that this may be uninterrupted and that I may drink deeper &
deeper in thy spirit

5th

Could we but look behind this world of sense and flesh what strange
sights we would see. Could we see the wheals which work the panoramic
activity of Man   How we would wonder at our life. The activity of Man
is a show of the spirits   I live in this age on this planet. Why have I a
sphere a destiny to fill out which can only be done on this planet & at this
Time and amidst the environments of the present

VOLUME I

Oh Almighty Gracious Father who gavest me life willt thou bless and graciously lead me in the study I am about to undertake   Give me always bounteously of thy spirit and direct me in the true path in which I ought to go that I may inherit eternal life   Oh Father without thou directing my footsteps I will be lost   Oh willt thou teach me humility kindness and childlike confidence in thee   For what am I Lord without thee? Unto whom can I put my trust if it is not in thee? Didst thou not give me being all all that I have   Lord I feel that it is in me not in thee that which prevents my being better than I am   Oh Lord help help me   Look down graciously upon me oh all ye saints pray for me   Ye that are in heaven intercede and plead for me   Oh guard me from the snares of sin from Pride ambition self-confidence and in what I am about to undertake willt Thou Father give my thy spirit that I may judge those things I may read with candor impartiality without prejudice bias or blindness   Willt thou give me the spirit of industry perseverance enlighten my understanding purify my affections and make all my desires holy   Oh Father I feel that I am in thy hands that thou leadest me   Oh may I become an instrument of thine in doing much good   Lord I am weak nothing nothing oh Lord and in thy hands commit I my spirit. Do with me oh Lord as seemth good in thy sights   I feel willing to leave all for thee nay Lord I have nothing to leave for in thee I find every thing yea more   Finally oh Lord lead me to thy Holy Church which I now am seeking for by the aid I hope of thy holy spirit. Willt thou lead me in the road by which I may come into Thy fold even as it seemth good to thee. Amen[12]

BROOK FARM 1843

Morning

April, Saturday. 15. After having made a visit for a fortnight to my home I returned here on Thursday to stay the summer with the object of studying   I have felt that my visit had the effect of keeping me back or it may be perhaps even that I have receded from the state in which I was in before I started but I hope & trust that in a few days by fasting and prayer I will be able to be where I was & continue to improve. If I cast a glance upon a few years of my past life it appears to me mysteriously incomprehensible where I am now   I confess sincerely that altho I never have labored for it still something always in me dreamed of it   Once when I was lying on the floor my mother said to my brother John without anything previously being spoken on the subject she said suddenly in a kind of uncon-

scious speech "John let Isaac go to College and study"   These words
whent through me like liquid fire. He made some evasive reply and there
it ended. Altho this always has been the secret desire of my heart from my
youth to study I never felt inclined to open my mind to any one on the subject and now I find after a long time that I have been lead here as strangely
as possible[13]

Afternoon

After having said a lesson in French I went with ⟨— —⟩ a walking in
the woods. My time was spent very pleasantly. The scenery was beautiful.
The Gothic formed woods which was very striking. The beautiful green
pine trees and the moss of various tints covering the ground the heavens
with the clouds the sun bursting through them at intervals with the silence
and shadey mystery of the woods above all a soul susceptible of love and
beauty gave to all such enchantment and my heart filled with love that I felt
guilty of enjoyment. At tea we had a chat upon the Church: Ripley, Dana
& others that I can perceive that it is a topic which is not alltogether un-*in-*
teresting to them

Monday. 17.

Yesterday I whent to the Catholic Church west Roxbury; it was Easter
Sunday. The services of the Church were to me very impressively
affecting   The altar piece was Christs rising from the tomb. This was the
subject matter of the Priests sermon. In the midst of it as he was preaching
he turned and pointed to the painting with a few touching remarks turning
all eyes towards it which made his remark doubly affective   How inspiring it must be to the Priest when he is preaching to see around him the Saviour the godly company of Martyrs Saints and Fathers   There may be
objections of having Paintings & sculpture in the Church but I confess that
I never enter a place where there is either but I feel an awe a invisible influence which strikes me mute   I would sit in silence covering my head.
It is if there is a sanctified atmosphere filling the place which fills my soul
when I enter as if I were in an holy temple. Thou standest in a holy place   I
would say a hard word a heavy foot step makes me shudder as if infidels
were desecrating the place   I stand dumb speechless in a magical atmosphere that runs through my whole being scarcely daring to lift up my eyes
for fearing of being struck senseless. A perfect stillness comes over my soul
and it is as it were soaring on the bosom of clouds.[14]

Tues.

If this book is not agoing to be the revelation of my thoughts what is
it good for? For what purpose is it written with these characters? Why this

time wasted misspent? Are the emotions of my heart the deep thoughts of my soul to remain enclosed in itself? Nay why should I not speak when my soul is full overflowing with Love Life   If I cannot speak out from my soul to others shall I not speak purely to myself? What is the hindrance? Nay why should there be any? So let me speak

The afternoon of yesterday a ⟨Lady⟩ (Mrs. Barlow) came in to my room and we entered into a conversation a—communion. Before I have had intimate conversation with her and from the reports I have heard of her I was influenced to keep my self at a certain distance so that instead of being ⟨the motive⟩ body it is vice-versa. Instead of I *dissait aller* to ⟨her she put forth her love openly to me⟩   But to understand what the effect the reports that I had heard had upon my mind I will transcribe it after I have written our yesterdays conversation—no   I will not write down this interview I will scratch out the name which I have written above[15]

Aftern

I confess that either the Church is not sufficient for my wants or I have not seen it in its Glory. The latter I hope it may be. (What makes me spell so bad   I have to alter every few words knowing before that they are wrongly spelt)   I want not to say it but I must confess It fills me no more   I contemplate it   I look at it. *Comprehend* it   It does not lead me to aspire   I do not feel as if it had some thing to give or what it has to give is not that which my soul is aching for   I know what can be said against this. That I know not what the Church has untill I commune with it—become one of its members and that it satisfies natures greater than mine   That it is the true life of the world; out of it there is no true spiri-tuality—that before I can judge rightly I must have a life equal in purity and elavation to it and much more might be said But after all what is it? The Catholic shows up the Anglican, the Anglican the corruption and even their want of unity. the Protestant the Presbyterian claim their mission at the ex-pense of consistency and good logic   The decrees of Trent are explained by the Catechism which has not equal authority under the Catholic church. One Dr holds we must pray to the Pictures. Others hold that they are a means of exciting holy emotions. In one that Mary intercedes for us; another that she has authority over Christ and commands for us ₋ One would think Christ is willing and had no need of Marys intercessions. The whole fact is I suppose if there is anything in Successions Tradition Infallibility Church organism and Form it is in the Catholic Church and our bussiness will be to be done with this controversy and call a oecumenical Council which shall settle these matters according to the Bible Tradition and the light of the Church[16]

My soul is so disquite   My heart aches   It is as if my soul is weeping continually   Alas what is all this Tears flow from my eyes
involuntarily   My soul is greived for what. Yesterday, as I was praying
the thought flashed across my mind   Where is God? Is he not here? Why
prayest thou as if He is at a great distance from thee   Where canst thou
place him. Think of it. Where canst thou place him. What locality? Is he
not here in thy midst. Is his presence not nearest thee   Oh think of it. God
is here. His presence is allways, universal and nearest   Am I impious to
say that the language used in scripture for Christ's expresses the thoughts
of my soul   Oh could we but understand that the Kingdom of Heaven is
always *at hand* to the discerner   And God calls upon all to Repent for ye
shall not all disappear until it shall open   This generation shall not pass
away[17]

The empirical condition of Eternity is Time, of Immensity is Space.
Or rather perhaps we are only able to perceive Eternity in Time, Immensity
in Space which are (Time & Space) their limitation or their phenomena or
actuality their acts or facts. Every reality is a monad a one—unity. There
may be monads who develope or who fullfill their destiny in other worlds
beside this one on which we are actualizing ourselves. There is no monad
seperate from all others. No cause *ohne* phenomena   Or as the english
perfectly expresses the thought: There is no cause with-out phenomena.
Cause is in shining throughout phenomena. Life is the action of one monad
drawing by its superior intelligence-love-power the lesser monads to itsself
in order to fullfill its destiny unconsciously perhaps the most of its time but
often perceptively. It is not to say that these lesser monads are perverted
from their destiny by this acton on the part of their superiors. Man is attracted to the Earth—why? because he can only fullfill his being destiny
here which is a conjoint activity a mutual support.[18] The Earth gives him
support and he beautifies it in return. He may even think that he does not
aid it in its destiny but it has a destiny and he being here is evidence of it
and while he supposes he is acting out his own destiny he is acting with
conjointly the whole universe. Hence when Man fell the whole universe was
brought into travail and bondage and when its Redeemer was crucified the
whole universe convulsed and is now waiting groaning for the time of its
deliverance   Hence is All—one bound indossulibly together

I wanted to continue this and attempt to show that in our life we go
under a series of changes through the successive development of each etc.

I am rather unstudied   I feel that I never can return back to my old
life that I would rather become an associate here than go back. Still after

all I might return because if I should return I would present such a different aspect to those around me for I am changed. It would make my world so different that I might live as agreeable there as here   I am in an impersonal state. Oh heaven I am thankfull to thee that Thou didst last evening teach me such an importen salutary lesson   Oh how thankfull gratefull I am   Oh I am conscious that there is something nay someone who does protect me from falling enticed by evil desires that keep me from their power or action   Two nights have I awaked or have been awakened and I saw some one and no sooner would I attempt to utter than it would be gone   But last night I had a dream which was all importent to my present circumstances and doubtless to my future happiness   How can I doubt these things   Say what may be said still for all these have to me a reality a practicel good bearing upon my life   They are impressive instructors whose teachings given in such a real manner that they influence would I or not   Real pictures of the future as actual nay more so than my present activity. If I should not follow them I am alltogether to blame   I cannot have such adviser upon Earth. None could impress me so strongly with such peculiar effect and at the precise time most needed   Where my naturel strength is not strong enough I find there comes foreign aid to my assistence. Is the Lord instructing me for anything. I had six months ago three or more dreams which had a very great effect upon my character; they changed it   They were the embodiment of my present in a great degree. Last evening's was a warning embodiment of a false activity and its consequence which will preserve under God's assistence my falling. Oh I feel now much better from its influence   I see by it where I am. It has made me purer and hallowed me more   Oh how thankfull I ought to be   It is of an impearchable worth. Who could do this for me but some good spirit. Oh how wonderfull do we live.[19]

Noon.

The Catholic Church alone seems to satisfy my wants my faith life soul. These may be baseless fabrics chimeras dire anthrophormophagi[20] or what you please   I may be laboring under a delusion; any thing you please   Yet my soul is catholic and that faith answers responds to my soul in its religious aspirations and its longings   I have not wished to make myself catholic but it answers to the wants of my soul. It answers on all sides. It is so rich full. One is in harmony all over   In unison with heaven the present living in the naturel body and the past who have changed. There is a solidarity between them through the Church. I do not feel controversial. My soul is fullfilled, argue not, come and taste, try & see; heaven will make us all aggree. There is no controversy in heaven. To know you must come and try. To know if you are wrong you must see or be in the right. I want to progress in life not waste my time in going back. Others may bark at my eating if they please and if that nourishes them well and good; it will not do for me. I shall not bark back in return but press forward. The simple fact is I want to live every moment. And I cannot by barking   I want something positive living, nourishing. I negate only by affirming. All other is death   No croaker but a liver.

Tues. Evening

This morning I was in a very low state of life lost allmost into the flesh   I was cold dreary and had fallen in a identity of in or with my body. At noon I returned to myself was filled again and now live continuously flowing on   Oh would that my life were one continuous flowing stream of my present living   I have done little in study these few days back but feel that I have lived very much   My soul has been in my speech this afternoon and my heart has been serene calm overflowing with life and I feel now filled   What is a hindrence to me I suppose is contemplating any certain amount of study which I ought to have accomplished looking to it as an end   Why should I not be satisfied when my life is living growing   Did Christ the Apostles study languages   If I have the life is not that the end

"A mans transgressions partake of the character of his company" Confucius.[21]

Fri.

What shall I say   Am I wrong   Should I submit and give myself up to that which does not engage my whole being. The Church is not to me the great object of life. I am now out of it in the common meaning   I am not subject to its ordinances. What shall I say?. Is it not an evidence of a truer life that I am not able to foresee the future   Is not the true way for me to go in that wherein I feel that I exist   Is it not best for me to live my own nature than attempt to mold it like some object   Is not our own existence more than the existence in the world. I read an extract from Heine upon Schelling which affected me more than any thing I have read for six months   I read it this morning   The Church says S in substance was 1st Petrine then Pauline and must be love embracing John like. Peter, Catholicism; Paul—Luther—Protestansm; John–*venir etre*. The statement struck me and responded to my own dim intuitions   Catholicism is solidarity   Protestansm is individuality What we want and are tending to is the unity of them both which Johns spirit does and in each individual   We want neither the authority of History or of the Individual, Infallibility or Reason but both combined in Life. Neither Precedent or opinion but Being   Neither a written or a preaching Gospel but a living one.

First seek the Kingdom of God then all things will be added. I will give unto you the spirit of truth which shall lead you into all truth.

Religion Christ is the foundation of all usefull practicel knowledge. Of what use is the knowledge of physiology to a parent who has no sympathy for its offspring   Would the cannibel be prevented from shedding the blood of his fellowmen by knowing the flesh of animals is the same as Mans Would the knowledge of *materia medica* make one benevolent if he should see one in distress on the road side. Are the wisest brightest of mankind the best. Is not true wisdom holiness. Does not wordly knowledge puff a man up. Should we do or attempt any thing from any other motive than a Christian one. Does not science advance by the motives that Christianity inspires the individual the love of Humanity—Is not it the germ from which civilization springs   Do we attribute sufficient influence to it for our Scientific artistic and other branches of knowledge.

The Sun Moon Planets Stars Man Animels Vegatabels Minerals are all invisibly connected together are a Unit. The Universe is a Monad   The Universe is the comprehension of our vision subjectively.[22]

It is only through Christ we can see the Love and Goodness & wisdom of God. He is to us what the microscope is to the Astronomer, with this difference: He exalts purifies us that our subject becomes the power to see. The microscope is a medium through which the boundaries of our vision are enlarged but is only passive   Christ is an active Mediator who begets us if we will and gives us power to see by becoming one with him

May 3d Wed.

The best sermon upon Christianity is a Christian. The greatest mystery of human life is that we can see ourselves active which is in other words self consciousness. Fear and Hope, Past and Future, Memory and the Ideal, Subject and Object are correlative thoughts   They exist together and cease simultaneously also   Time and Space in the same manner. How stands the case with me at present? It is as it were   I am living in a world wherein I find none around me in. I find no one to meet me   Are we not created to find such a response to ourselves   Can it be possible   No we were not given this aching longing seeking intimation without object. What a panoramic scene the world displays in which we see ourselves as a part ha ha. It is sometimes a gay joyfull hopefull picture and then then a deep serious sincere terrible intense tableau. We look all of us upon the world as suits our moods assimilating to ourselves only such kind of food as nourishes our dispositions and no doubt there is variety of nourishment in the world to suit every variety of disposition   Every personality individualises the world to

himself not subjectively but truly objectively   When we look we always
see something taking the collective sights of all. We shall find the true
centre. All the radai meet in the centre. Every individual ought perhaps to
be satisfied with the beings character what he is   For it is a very importent
truth of Fourier that attractions are in proportion to their destiny: Fear in
proportion to hope; Pain in proportion to Pleasure; Strength in proportion
to destiny etc.[23] But this is mysterious that we know all this. "And Man
has become as one of us"   We are all Dead. Ah mystic doest thou show
thyself in this shape. But now being dead will we receive life and immortality (for I imagine immortality the solidarity of life that is to say the union
of the two lives here & heaven) through Jesus Christ the Son of the living
God and loose "the knowledge of good and evil." "For as in Adam all
died so shall ye all be made alive through Christ" The effect of the fall was
literally the knowledge of good and evil   God knows no evil and when
we become one with him by the mediator we shall regain our previous
state   Knowledge is the effect of sin. And perhaps destined to correct
itsself   Consciousness and knowledge go together. Spontaneity and Life
are one. Knowledge is no gain for it gives nothing   It can only know what
has been given through spontaneity. Spontaneity is unity one; knowledge
is a division of being   If Adam had not been seperated he would not doubtless have sinned   The woman that thou gavest to me said unto me eat and
I did eat. Still through the seed of the woman, which will be the union restored, is the serpent to be bruised.

Thur.

The real effect of the theory of the Church is to isolate ourselves from
the outward world withdraw from its enjoyments and live a life of sacrifice
of the passions   This is one statement. Another would be this; All these
things can and should be enjoyed but in a higher purer a more exalted state
of being than is the present ordinary state of our minds   The only opposition to them is when the soul becomes sensual and falls into their arms
and becomes lost to higher and more spiritual objects   Then there is the
life of the Man of Wealth of Pleasure the Scholer, the Divine etc. all of
which have their pleasures and griefs   Stop. Why need I try to peirce in
the future All is so dark before me impenetrable darkness. I live it appears
in the centre. Nothing appears to take hold of my soul or it seekes nothing:
where it is I feel or know not. I meet with no one around me. I would that
I could feel that some one lived in the same world that I now do. There is
something cloudy that seperates us. I cannot speak from my real being to
them. There is no recognition between us. It is when I speak to them as if
a burden accumulated around me and oppressed me and I feel like making
an effort to throw it off and speak out from the deep consciousness that I

feel but I cannot utter in their presence. If I do my thoughts and feelings return to me unrecognised without they being perceived   I feel oppressed. I feel continually a dark irresistible desire to give vent to the oppressive sensation in my bosom that it may escape take its Liberty and fly into the ethereal bosom of the clouds. Will I ever meet with that one which the windows of our souls will open simultaneously?

Baptism is the outward sign of the inward immersion of being into another state of life which the person passes through in becoming a christian. Conversion then immersion; the whole being plunged into a new state, atmosphere. He breathes a new life. He is born into the Kingdom of God wherein if he is faithfull he shall receive the gifts promised unto the saints. Baptism is the speech of the new birth   It is the word of conversion   This immersing the soul in a more interior state, the profound truth & meaning, the words of John. Its significant expression and much more is a matter demanding much reflection

Fri. [5]

Man is a being. Being he is before we can take cognizance of him. We are only able to cognize him as an Activity in some direction   For all Activity is qualified by some qualities which are elementary. We know him as transcendental as Action Cognition Sentiment indissoluble one (Leroux)[24] or Phrenologically as Propensities Intellect Sentiments. deeper than this we have not been able to penetrate in his nature   All we can say is That Man is being of triune developement of A. C. S. which again are divided into division innumerable   The gratification of which is called happiness   It his destiny to act. Act he must. Life is integral.

Mon. [8]

I intended to continue the former and show that life was the gratification of our faculties their satisfaction and thats all stript of its poetry.

On Friday night I saw a red fiery glaring eyed coper coloured skined singuler dressed fiend. In stretching to grasp and grapple with it I awoke setting up in bed with my arms extended[25]

On Saturday night I awoke in saying the World is like a flower bush which bears beautifull flowers; he that attempts to pluck one pricks his finger with a thorn. To day I wrote 2 letters one to my home the other to Mr Martin Last Sunday I heard O.A.B.[26]

Wed. [10]

This morning I awoke with this thought impressed upon my mind   Life is like a Knot in the wood   There is a continued series of circles proceeding from the intense consolidated centre until the outer ones

are lost into the extremity to sight   So is it with life   How much of it is
of this superficial outward circle wherein our centre does scarcely
enter   How little do we speak from the centre of life   We exist for the
most part in the superficial circles   It is not often that we are in the centre
of our being. It is only by times. I feel now conscious that I have this fortnight back been gradually floating towards the superficies   This present
consciousness of it is evidence that I have been arrested and I pray my heavenly Father to give me strength that I may live more in that "eternal life"
brought to light in his only true Son Jesus Christ of Nazareth in whom Grace
& Truth dwelt fully, Who was the Word and to us a Witness being the Word
made manifest in the Flesh. How true is it that he that looseth all things in
the sense of the world receives tenfold in Christ   It appears to me that
Christ never lived dwelt in his accidents but in the Eternal life, The Father,
as He said; and until we become conscious of this continually we have come
short of the high *calling* in Christ Jesus. Woman what have I to do with
thee! This is the depth of Life. He that hath an ear let him understand. Happiness or indefinite or infinite Progress is not the law or end of our being
but Eternal Life in which there is no happiness progress or pleasure but existence. God is not subject to accidents. Man cannot be God in the absolute
sense but I conceive he can attain to his highest conception of him   Is not
the faculty of Conception an part of his Soul. Is not a Conception an act of
the Soul   In a sense then Man is what he conceives. Conception is to the
Head what action is to the Heart—a fact a reality an immortal act destined
to exist for all Eternity   It may be said that we cannot get out of the sphere
of accidents for every fact of life is an accident every action every thought.
This may be true in a certain sense that is to say if we mean to be without
accidents, because abstract all of Mans actions and you leave him unexist-
ing; but he does not live in the accidents   He is not subject to them. When
they wish to command, he replies. "Woman what have I to do with thee"
They are really accidents to him   He has no autobiography to write. He
lives. Thinkest. Thou God writes. This is his writing: the whole
Creation   He proceeds. He is not reflective. To Him there is nothing Old
or New   So is it with him who is one with the Father. There is nothing
spoken that shall be lost. There is nothing hid that shall not be revealed is
the correlative   Men are seeking for Christ but know it not. The Christians
never looses himself. It is not this thing or that thing he is anxious to build
up. Is not God all powerfull   They all have a temporary value nay do they
not become letts and hindrances. He is in his Father and does he loose himself in his Creations. Possess thyself. How much in two words!! Understood
rightly they are enough

    What I have said here is it not in direct opposition to the Establishment
of a Church   I confess it is so. When I reflect that Christ has not plainly

spoken of one I have no assignable reason why he should not have so done. But has not the Church sprung literally from his life hence been founded by him even if it has not his life in its fullness it still has more than the world has or can give   Has it not been the channel through which his life has been continued through the past unto this our time   Blot out the Church; have we any conceivable method through which we might have any connection with the life which he brought into the World. None other but a perpetual Generation of Messiahs equal to him. Equal to him or else it would benefit us more to fall back upon his life. That we have not had a Generation of Messiahs as some pretend is historically true, for the Holy Divine men of the Past we find in the Church and they confess they are indebted to Christ in and through the Church for their Life. Is it a question which we shall believe: those holy men or our philosophers? I think not. Or if we stand upon the same platform with Christ as some of our moderns pretend why is it that none of us have not in a very great degree arrived at the fullness of Love & Truth as Christ. And even the best exampels they can show for a shadow of proof of their hypotheses confess Christ was the media of their Life. How is this? This is against them. Can they deny it. Nay the glaring fact stares them in the face daily of our weakness   If we have immediate communion with God as Christ had it confessedly does not amount to much for the bright examples of history are in opposition to their case. These men that rail so bitterly against the Church what are they   Are they better than the Church for that is the apparent assumption   Is the cause they advocate Holier Higher than that of the Church? This they appear to assume   If it is it ought correspondingly effect upon them a superior life of Disinterestedness and love to that of the Church. Is it so? How stands the case. Show me thy works and I will show thee thy faith. Ye Messiahs, Martyrs, Saints of this Unchurch Theory where are ye crucified stoned burnt spilling your blood like water for your noble cause. Alas for poor human nature! What are the sacrifices that your Priests have to undergo. Poverty? Ah no except from necessity   Do they give up the pleasure of Wife and all the joy of Domestic Bliss? Nay alas no such sacrifice as this does their cause inspire. Why talk then about thy superiors in virtue Disinterestedness and zeal. Shall we charge ye with depraved and blind restless hearts of rash heedless wayward and want of true sympathetic minds superficial unhistorical illusive philosophy   Nay, Nay, tho ye are Pharisees we leave it to Heaven and the future to judge. That philosophy which is unhistorical is inhumane cold unloving irreligious and a solemn lie[27]

Fri 12

Warum can der mensch nicht sein ohne Leben. Why can we not be without living is a question which at times recurs to my mind which is perhaps in other words the state which my soul desires. Would be to my present as not being.

Eveng.

I am setting by my table with the window up the moon shining through it in the room   The evening is beautifull   The light of the moon has a marked effect upon me. It stirs me   I feel eager wild audacious restless and awakened   I am conscious that it plays an importent part in the different states of my mind.

Tues.

Life appears to be a perpetual struggle between the heavenly and the wordly.

Here at B.F. I become acquainted with persons who have moved in a higher rank in society than I have been and persons of good education fine talents all of which have an improving influence upon me   And I meet with those who I can speak and feel to a great degree that I am understood and my feelings responded to. In N.Y. I am alone in the midst of people. I do not feel their presence   I am not in any internal sense in rapport with them living in myself in the inner world.[28]

I suppose the reason why I do not now in my present state feel disposed to connect myself with any being and rather would avoid a person whom I felt conscious I might or would Love is that I feel my life is in a rapid progress and that my choice now would not be a permanent one. For when I reflect upon the choice that I would have made time back (if there had not been something deeply secret in my being which prevented me) would be to me now I am a afraid very unsatisfactory   I feel conscious there could not have been a change or growth mutually equally because the nature of some are not capable of much growth and I mistrust wether there would not as often happens been a inequality hence a disharmony a unhappiness.

To be required to accept your past is most unpleasant. Perhaps the society with which I was surrounded did not afford me a being which unified with mine own. And I have faith that there are spiritual Laws which lie beneath all this outward frame work of sight and sense which will if rightly believed in and trusted will lead to the goal of eternal life harmony of being and union with God. So I accept my being led here   Am I superstitious or egoistical in believing this   This is no doubt a disputed territory. What is superstition? Have we any objective rule to compare our faith with it which would give us the knowledge of our superstition. How much of to day was miraculous and superstitious to the past. I confess I have no rule or measure to judge the faith of any Man. The past is always the state of Infancy. The present is a eternal youth aspiring after manhood, hopeing wistfully, intensely desiring, listfully listening, dimly seeing the bright joy-full star of hope in the future artfully beckoning him to move rapidly on while his strong heart beats with enthusiasm and glowing joy. The Past is Dead. Wish me not the Dead from the grave for that would be death reen-acted but now let them go to bright heaven living a life of love sweet joy and peace   Oh were our wishes in harmony with heaven how changed would be the scenes of our life. What is now sorrow would be turned into joy and life would give us a more exquisite pleasure that I fear it would intoxicate with its sweet joys   This accordence would be music which the Angels now only hear too delicate for beings such as we now are   Listen! Has thou not heard in some of thy bright moments a strain from heavens Angelic Choirs. Oh yes in our sleep the Angels have whispered such rich music. The soul being passive such times we then can hear that the pleasure does not leave us when passion and thought take their accustomed course   Doest thou not feel that there is all around thee a music so sweet heard only by God & his angels   Oh Man were thy soul more pure what a world would open to all thy senses   There would be no moment of thy existence but would be filled with the music of love   ''And the Prophet said in that day my eyes were opened''   And behold what he *saw*. He saw it   Could we but hear. The word of the Lord is evermore speaking   Alas where is the one that can hear. Where are our Isiahs Ezekeials & Jeremiahs   Ha ha thou old shrunken visaged black hollow eyed doubt! Hast thou passed like a black cloud over Mens' souls making them blind deaf and dumb   Ah ha doest thou shudder   I chant thy requiem and Prophets Poets and Seers shall again rise   I see them a coming   Great heaven Earth again shall be a Paradise and God converse with Men.

Wed. [17]

About 10 months ago or perhaps 7 or 8 I saw (I cannot say I dreamt for it was quite different from dreaming as I thought. I was seated on the side of my bed) a beautifull angelic pure being and myself standing along side of her feeling a most heavenly pure joy and it was as if it were that our bodies were luminous and they gave forth a moonlike light which I felt sprung from the joy that we experienced   We were unclothed pure and unconscious of anything but pure love and joy and I felt as if we had always lived together and that our motions actions feelings & thoughts came from one centre and when I looked towards her I saw no bold outline of form but an angelic something I cannot describe but in angelic shape and image. It was this picture that has left such an indelible impression upon my mind, and for some time afterwards I continued to feel the same influence and do now at times so that the actual around me has lost its hold on me   In my state previous to this vision I should have been married ere this for there are those I have since seen would have met the demands of my mind. But now this vision continually hovers oer me and prevents me from its beauty of accepting any else   For I am charmed by its influence and I am conscious that if I should accept any thing else I should loose the life which would be the only existence wherein I could say I live.[29]

Wed.

I shall purchase some apples to day and eat light food at least for a time being so inclined   My soul feels like praying continually to heaven. When ever I feel as I now do I have less inclination to eat and especially heavy gross food

June. 1st Wed.

In the World one cannot live a spiritual life because it requires so much labor to support one in food & clothing that he looses his inward eternal life for the material and life in time. Here at B. F. if one has to sustain himself here without having any other means to aid him he must employ his strength and life to that degree that he has not time for the culture of his Spiritual   I cannot return home as it was without loosing my spiritual life   I cannot remain here and support myself without subjecting myself to the same conditions   These are my conclusions   Here I cannot expect that they can or will be willing to sacrifice much of their present expenses for food and clothing for the sake of gaining time for spiritual culture nor do I see how I can at home live with my relatives and have that time which my spiritual life requires   For the only way that I can see that I can have sufficient time for my spiritual culture is to give up the external taste for fine clothing and variety of food   Simple durable clothing simple and nutrative diet are the only means I know of by which I can have time for Spiritual Culture   I would prefer adopting the life of the monastery to that of the external world. The advantages for my being are greater   The harmony of the two is the full and perfect existence. But the spiritual should always be preserved at the expense of the other which is contrary to the tendency of the World and perhaps even here   I would prefer going hungry in body than in soul   I am not speaking against either for I believe in the fullness of life in all its wants being fully supplied But the kingdom of God is to me more than that of this World   I would be Plato in Love, Zeno in selfstrength and Epicures in Estheticks   But if I have to sacrifice either then let Epicures go altho I am fully sensible of the importence to our Culture of all the external beauty which we possibly can surround ourselves with   But Humanity and myself are first then comes the Material Universe[30]

June. 5th Evening

I have returned again into my interior[31]   Ah what is life to me; it offers nothing   Is this our destiny to live a life of Sin or not exist   Why was I made with all these susceptibilities. Great heaven   I cannot see into these things. What meaneth this. Religion does not satisfy me either in its Catholic or Protestant phase   I feel inwardly cramped in. I must retire alone in solitude for a time. On the 1st I had a beautifull dream   It made me much more lovelier. On the 3rd I had a dream ah I shudder to think of it   Oh how hor*rid;* it is too horrid. Away oh hell fiend   Oh may I not be so inflicted again. I am now I know not where. Lost. A void is in me. All is nothing around me. I would let out this void. I feel an eagerness. Oh how hollow are all things. I feel as if I had no Soul. Oh what mockery is in me. Let the All tumble into darkness what then. Oh what is dancing around me. A bird is singing in the night. Why have I no sympathy with those around me. Why is all life to me as nothing as humbug as a farce.

June. 12.

What are all these complaints perplexities and wailings; wherefore all this   Should I not be above all these whimperings. Why lie lost in these? Is there nothing nobler higher which my soul lives in. I would that I could find something in which I could engage my mind in or my soul would be interested in. To be above all this is to be in something that is the rub of it. I sometimes feel empty a mere an atomy without heart or Soul   I would make vent for the void I feel in me. And my consciousness of being is in the absence of being. Why write these down   would it not be better to chew these all up in silent and digest them inwardly.

Aftern.

At times I feel an impulse to cry out what wouldst thou have me to do. What shall I do. I would shout up in the empty vault of heaven ha aha! Why plaguest thou me so   Great heaven what wouldst thou have me to do. Give me an answer unless Thou wouldst have me consumed by inward fire drying up the living liquid of life. Would thou have me to give up all. I have   I have no dreams to realize I want nothing have nothing and am willing to die in any way starve give up now yes even now   Yes come now this moment I'l embrace thee death come come   What ties I have are few. Those can be cut with a groan   Ha ha the world is nothing to me. What care I if I go? What is around me may be beautifull to others but to me it is not so   Ha ha what care I if I go? Come death come now I have nothing here that binds me so hurrah, let us laugh and go. Resign thyself to be nothing & shut up thy book. Ha ha ha ha.

Living is madness. Lies are unrealities. A sane man never lies.

I am. I am not are correlatives. The expression of love and grief is one. In the writings of the most spiritual religious writers are to be found the strongest and deepest irreligious sceptical thoughts. Catholicism is the strongest argument against the authority of the Bible. To them it is a shadow. When we give up God we find him. Christianity and Atheism are correlatives. Religion consists not in the object which is worshipped. A man may be religious and an atheist. I mean an atheist in the common opinion of others. Christ was a blasphemer to the Jews. It is singuler that he that lives in the eternal life in uttering the highest truths apparently utters the greatest paradoxes to those that hear him. Is not this Jesus the carpenter the son of Mary. Men are Gods perverted that is sons of God. I and my Father are one. Ye in me I in ye and one with the father. Greater works than I do shall ye do. Do these words not teach that Christ was not in a peculiar more one with God than we might become and if so where is and what becomes of the trinity. Christ was a Carpenter says Mark. Either we are more than we are or capable of more than we are aware of or the circumstances of Christ his words and his nature are strangely incomprehensible. Man has unconscious strength that he is not aware of. He is more than he dreams of. The brightest example of manhood is Christ. I feel that. I should perish if I wrote these thoughts in an irreligious undevout irreverent sceptical spirit. But I do not know what it is; when I speak from my deepest life which is always the most religious it would be blasphemy to the religious, truth in words to the Rationalist   The Religious would accept my spirit perhaps the Rationalist my words. The Rationalist appears to me soulless; the Religious without depth or clear perception. Rationalism in a sense is to *me* a dark unconscious expression of a deeper Religious life. He is not dead he sleepeth. And He cried with a loud voice Lazarus come forth. Oh I am a mystic   I am afraid to others. A deeper penetration a inperception what does it not unfold explain. Oh how many mysteries are uttered innocently unknowingly. Does the Lion know its beauty strength and purpose. Oh Man what are *thou?* We play a part in the Universe it is well perhaps we are not aware of. Does not the Widow in India bear witness that matches are made in heaven on the funeral pile. Where is there faith like this? Ah they are heathens too. Did not Pythagoras bear testimony to the thought Before Abraham was I am. Are we not to explain the mysteries of each other. Did not Christ astonish the Jews with his understanding all the Scriptures as he did and was for his life was deeper under all that he *e*xplained   If person would hear m̧e I should like to read for them a infidel tract for Religious exercise. In a certain state of mind which a sect of the Mohammedans produce by dancing music etc. they eat poisonous reptiles and other fatal things with eagerness and without injury or harm   To be an infidel Man must dethrone God. Man *is* and if he should destroy all that is external from him he would still have to believe in his own reality. Rationalism is the strongest argument in favor of Christianity

June. 16.

I have to stand upon my realities. I could sham flatter and be believed but I cannot, will not, and shall not. I can suffer bear pain and anguish of soul that is something but I cannot bear to be nothing a vacuity. Thou hast written to me thy thoughts and feelings. I have said nothing. I will be still. I can suffer on all sides let even death come. I can accept to be less than I am. I did not expect this. But I will be still, silent.

June 19.

It is my intention to start for Harvard this afternoon to Mr Alcott & Lanes household to see and observe their manner of living and to feel what sort of men they are. I will perhaps be much effected by them for I am led to them from a deep eternal life   I go not from external and outward inclinations. This life that has led me I know not what to say about it   It is not a question of trust or distrust of will or inclination. Sometimes I think that I ought to try and struggle once more against it and see if I cannot subject it   At other times I feel that I ought to have faith and be led   If I attempt to struggle once more against it it would reduce me as it has done heretofore and for me to continue as it does it will lead me from my Parents Brothers and Sister Bussiness wealth my former hopes Dreams and life. What shall I do? This is a deep perplexity to me. I am going to Alcotts because my spirit leads me there. Some persons would advise me to give up all trouble and throw myself upon this life let it lead where it would. Others would advise me not to think of such a thing and that it is visionary and a dream to return to bussiness and my friends. What shall I do. There is some one who could give me advice in whom I would have confidence in because of his plain undisguised truth to me and who would put me to rest and peace. He would be a father a person who I could lean and rest upon his bosom who would sympathize with and comfort me. There is such a one   I feel it   I am conscious of it but who or where I cannot tell. May I find him   Oh Lord. Lord forgive me my sins and save me from all errors and lead me in the path that thou wouldst have me to go   Is there no one who I can go to that may open my eyes that I may see. Oh Lord direct me. And if thou directest me now give me faith in thy means. I am Oh Father one of thy children; thou knowest all that I do   My heart is open to Thy inspection. Do not let me suffer for thou art tender compassionate and full of love. Let me see; open thou my eyes, and grant that I may hear thy voice more distinctly

June. 24.

I returned last evening from Alcott's or Fruitland as they have named it. There is a deeper life there than there is here. There is much here which are good beneficial to my character   Here it is more outward   There it is inner. It would be to me a great sacrifice to leave here. Much of their speech is of the same character that I feel but I must stop   I do not feel like writing altho my mind is full and much worried. I wrote a letter to my home this morning. The last one I wrote has not been answered; for its answer I look with patience and anxiety for it was written different from what I have written

Two paths apparently are open to my view which to follow is the question. One road is to live in the world in bussiness and make life as aggreeable and as happy as possible; accept all things with the least possible evil a sort of computation of interest. The other road is to leave all be self denying, upturn all my former views of life and go in the blind world of chaos of life and live on   The fact is I can do nothing while there is such a deep I do not know what to call it in me. I believe all things and doubt all things. Accept all and doubt all   Absolute faith absolute scepticism. Prayer and Doubt. What can I do. What shall I do. Tell me it is weak to ask such questions to go and do   But the fact stares me in the face. What is all? After you have did all you could what then. I believe I could do this: get a farm and some friends who I love and live on simple externals in all respects food clothing dwellings etc. etc. My brothers are hard at work at home   I am here a doing nothing   I have been accustomed to work from my youth and here I am doing nothing   I am doing nothing. Nay can I not be still; work out some plan of action in which I can engage either here or at home   Yes let me write as if I know what I would or could do.
Dear Relatives

Let me tell you what my spirit leads me to do and how it would do it. I would return home for the purpose of basing our bussiness on Christian Love in its universal and deepest sense   I would sacrifice all that I have in the attempt to do it and that too daily   I would not say that it could be done absolutely   I do not believe that it can be but I would do it as near as possible   I would commence by reforming our diet then our clothes then furniture and cast off all all luxuries by which I mean all in the minutest as well as the largest of things which we now use in any manner or shape which we can do without, without reference to the caprice or fashion of the World   One fundamental principle in bussiness with us I would commence immediately; there should be no accounts kept and this should extend its self as far as possible   And to conclude this in one sentence without further talk. Do all that can be done.[32]

Solomon said after he had tasted all the joys of the world "Vanity of vanities all is vanity"   I my Friend who have scarcely tasted any of the pleasures of the world would say with Solomon. All is vanity   I see nothing around me in which I can work   All are vanities shadows; beneath all there is nothing; they are clouds vain phantasies   I would great God what is all this for. Why torment and pain so. Why is all this action a profanity to me ah and even holiness what is it. Oh I am dumb. My soul is inarticulate. There is in me that which I would pour out. Ah why is it that the noblest actions of humanity speak not to my soul. All life is inadequate but not in the sense of the world   I would joyfully be silent obscure dead to all the world if this alone which is in me had life   I ask not for name riches external conditions of delight or splendor   No the meanest of all would be heaven to me if this inward impulse had action lived out   But no I am imprisoned in spirit. What imprisons? What *is* imprisoned? Who can tell? You say Good adviser you must accept things as they are—be content to be—have faith in God—work that which thy hands findeth to do—. Good but it is taken for granted we know what things are which is the question   And *what* to be. "Be content to be"   Be what! That is *the* question. "Have faith in God." Yes. But how and what. Work. Yes. How like others? But this is not work to me; it is death; it is no work; nay worse it is sin hence damnation and I am not ready to go to hell yet friend. I would rather beat my head against the wall die in the battle than accept plasticly indolently punily the slow lingering annihilation of my soul. Acept things as they are. But I cannot and thus it is that I am in a state I cannot. Your work gives *me* no activity no action *I* am not *in* the work you set before *me*. It is dead lifeless work for me   And starve if I must is better than do the profane the sacreligious labor you place before me. It is better to die outright than to live a slow lingering torturing death. Your work is to me the Devils work which is unwork, self destruction. I want Gods living work to do. My labor must be a sermon and every motion of my body a word every act a sentence. My work must be devotional. I must feel that I am worshipping   It must be music Love Prayer holy to me   My field must be the Kingdom of God. Christ must reign in all. That I do must be Christ in me doing and *not me*. My life must be poetical divine and my action pictures beautifull paintings. Head Heart and Hands must be in trinity in one; they must tone in one accord. Music must flow in—all and all—ways from my being. My work must be work of inspiration and aspiration   My Heart cannot be in heaven when my head and hands are in hell. I must feel that I am building up Christs kingdom in all that I do. Do not that which in I feel Christ is not. Grieve not the spirit. It is to give Christ room for action in my heart soul and body is my desire my aim purpose being   I deny Christ every act that I do which is not done with and from his spirit. My object of life is to live out the Christ-all-loving spirit. Any other life is no-life. My soul must be *in*-formed after the pattern of Christ. I must feel I am acting out the will of God hence establshing the Kingdom of God upon earth. It is not he that goeth to church says his prayers sings psalms praises God says Lord Lord who is in God and establishing his Kingdom. No. It is he that is doing it. The Earth is to be his Kingdom and your prayers must be deeds and your actions must be music ascending to heaven in the sweet-est divinest tones. God must be planted. The Church must be the Kingdom of God in its fullness. All things must be done holely. Unholy things must pass away and die. To be unchristian in action is a deeper blasphemy than to be unchristian in mere words. It is a much deeper crime as it is to imagine a thing and to do it.[33]

The Kingdom of God is right-doing. Then will come to pass as the prophet Isaiah has said "For ye shall go out with joy and be led forth with peace: the mountains and the hills shall break forth before you into singing, and all the trees of the field shall clap their hands." "Instead of the thorn shall come up the fir tree, and instead of the brier shall come up the myrtle tree: and it shall be to the Lord for a name, for an everlasting sign that shall not be cut off." Is the Lords Prayer never to be filled? If he prayed in vain, who of us need expect an answer. "Thy Kingdom come upon Earth as it is in heaven"

Are we Christians if we act not in the spirit which Christ acted. Shall we say what shall we do? Follow the spirit of Christ which is in you "unless ye are reprobates ye have it in you" wherever however and withsoever it lead you. Be ye faithfull as I am said Jesus. Love one another as I have Loved you. Take up your cross and follow him. Leave all if the spirit leades you to leave all. Do whatever it leades you to do. There will not be any lack of action. Let him be all in all. Let your indwelling be filled with all-loving-Christ-spirit. Care not for the world give up wealth friends those that you love the opinions of all be willing to be despised spit trodden down crucified without murmur in love in God. Be silent and let thy silence speak. For this end came I into the world   Father I thank thee that thou hast glorified thy-self in me. Now art thou manifest. The end of the world is at hand. It is fullfilled. The Kingdom of God is begun. Darkness will no more spread over the land and the cloud will be roled up like a scroll and vanish into Light. God will be all in all even as it was in the beginning is now and shall be forevermore.

Tues 27 Evening.

I have been given this evening advice the same as has been given to me first by the Dr who first attended me, next by my dearest friend, and this evening by a man who now resides here.

Wed morning

Rather than follow this advice I would die   I should be miserable all my life nay death before this   These men appear to me as naturel men but not in the life I am in They are older have more experience and more judgment than I have perhaps but from the point of view which their judgment is formed their advice does not appear to be the council for me. I never can or will save my health or life by such means. If such is the only remedy then unremedied must I remain. But this is not the cause that they suppose of my present state of mind. It is deeper higher and oh God thou knowest what it is. Willt Thou give me hope strength and guidence[34]

In a sketch of the life of Shelly I read that he Coleridge and Southey at a period of their life when they were young they contemplated purchasing on the Banks of the Susquehanna a piece of ground to live in community to live out that life of love which inspired them   The impulse the divinity was not aged enough in them; they became Poets prophets of it   They saw it in the future; they sung of it in their poetic strains. Byron died in work. Carlyle in his last work Past & Present in his last Chapters prophecies still bolder than the former and in inspiring thoughts. In reading his book—the last chapters it is an echo of my own Soul. "To make some nook of Gods creation a little fruitfuller, better more worthy of God; to make some human hearts a little wiser, manfuller, happier,—more blessed, less accursed! It is work for a God." So writes on the last page of the Book.[35] This is to me prophecy. In this idea I now am; in it is to me my future   I have left home bussiness friends prospective wealth all for this life. How to realize it I know not and this is my trouble my pain perplexitie   I cannot accept this place; it is not self denying sacrificing enough for me; it does not attempt enough for me; it is too much like society   It is not based upon the universal-love-principle. It is not Christ like enough for me. I have discussed enough with my Brothers at home about so regulating our bussiness and it does not amount to much. To go to Alcotts to try it there is possible. Here I now am. My Brother I expect on here soon. If he does not come I shall have a talk with Mr Ripley and if he does not meet me for I shall tell him my wants and the reason of my leaving him   I want to sacrifice more to live more for others than what they do here. If I am not met I shall make up my mind to try Mr Alcotts   It may be a good experience for me to go there at any rate   My life I feel is devoted to this object   All that I have life and all is in this for in this I live and have my being

Thursday. 28

To day I live in the now in the present which is a moment. All around me the past; now and to be are what to me. Time is no more. A stillness is in me which nothing can penetrate. Persons, Friends, all are to me as what I know not. I have no sense of anything; where I am, no emotion, thoughts, no sense of my flesh, no hunger, or whant. I feel one, and still not one, with all things. Never more distinct from others still never less personality. I feel lost and found at the same moment. Am and am not. Being and not being.

Friday 29.

Last evening I had no real sleep   My mind was incessantly active not dreaming but conversing in a purer a higher state, it was freer easier in its activity. I cannot recollect much what I spoke or conversed about   I saw as I thought my Sister dead   I did not weep or despond. It appears I was fully conscious of her future existence. I awoke in saying we do not die, death is the leaving the gross heavy particles which we have assimilated in our present manner of existence. Which struck me that death was not a law of our being but a violation of our beings law. This violation unharmony and violent seperation takes place because we are not pure holy, pure in body, holy in mind. Christ came to redeem us from Sin and death and that we are progressively advancing toward that end, when here will be Heaven. And now Eternity.[36]

I do not know what to say. Am I led by something higher to the life which I am tending to or know   Sometimes I think it is most proper for me to attempt to return home accept things as they are live a life like others and as good or as much better as possible. If I can find a being with whom I feel I can live happy I would accept such a one and give up my life which now leads me. This would be the prudent and rational course my friends would say but this is not appears mine. I am here is one evidence that it is not mine. Second that which has led me here I struggled against as much as laid in my power until I became weak sick and confined to my bed; farther I could not go. They tell me if I was married it would not be so with me. I will not dispute this altho I do not believe it. But my good friends that is the difficulty—to marry is to me impossible. You tell me this is unnaturel. Yes my brethen this *may* be unnaturel; how shall I be naturel   Must I commit that which in my sight is a crime which I feel would make me miserable and be death to my soul. But this is foolish and onesided in you; you are wrong minded   You will loose your health your youthfull joy and the pleasure which God has by human laws designed you to enjoyed   You should give up these thoughts and feelings of yours and be like those around you. Yes my kind friends, this advice from you I accept with love from your kindness towards me. But alas I feel your advice come from such a source that I cannot receive it.

July. 5th.

My brother George has been here.[37] He staid 3 days. He told me that he had talked with my brother John often on living a life which is higher nobler more self denying than what he had done. It appears from his conversation since I have left home they have been impressed with a deeper and higher spirit. To me it is of much interest how I shall act, what I shall do. I have decided to make a visit to Fruitland. To leave this place is to me a great sacrifice. I have been much refined in being here. I have no one to whom I can go to for advice. To go to Fruitland. To stay here. To purchase a place for myself. Or to go home. These are questions which I feel the want of some friend to consult with. If I wish to be self-denying one might say at home is the best the largest field for my activity. This may be true in one sense. But is it best to go where there is the most difficulties to overcome. Would it not be best to plant the tree in the best soil where it may grow the most in every direction. At home to be sure if I have the strength to succeed I may perhaps do the most good and it may be the widest sphere of activity for me. But there are many difficulties which have such a direct influence upon one to injure to blight all high noble sentiments that I fear to encounter them and I am not sure it is my place. I feel also at present, a hesitency, in going to F. Perhaps it would be best for me not to speculate on the future but go and look to Him who is above for a wise direction in all that concerns my life. Sacrifices must be made. I must look for them accept them in a meek, humble willing spirit.

July 7th.

I go to Mr Alcott's next Tuesday if nothing happens. How long I will stay there   How I will like it   And what effect it will have upon me either for good or evil wether I will be interested in them All is to me unknown. I have got made for me 3 pairs of coarse pants & coat. It is my intention to commence work as soon as I get there. I will gradually simplify my dress without any sudden difference altho it would be much easier to mak a radicel and thourough change of all than it is peice by peice. But this will be to me a lesson of patient perseverance. All our difficulties should be looked upon in a light to improve and elevate our minds. I can hardly prevent myself from speaking how much I will miss the company of those whom I love and associate with here. But I must go. I am called with a stronger voice. This is a different trial from what I ever have had. I have had the trial of leaving kindred, but now I have the trial of leaving those I love from affinity. If I wished to live a life of the most gratifying and aggreeable company and amusements I certainly would remain here. Here is refining amusements cultivated persons and one who I have not spoken of who to me it is too much to speak of   One who would give up all for me. Alas him I must leave to go: Who is Isaac Hecker? What is he? Where is he from? Where is he now? Where is he going? What will he be? What of him, then? This is singuler that one can ask these questions of himself and without being able to give a intelligible satisfactory answer to any of them. If this world is not a mystery and all things that are therein is then what is mysterious?

July 12.

Fruitlands—Last evening I arrived here after tea. I whent out in the fields and worked an hour in raking hay with the persons here   We returned and had a conversation of clothing. Some very fine things were said by Mr Alcott & Lane. In most of their thoughts I coincide; nay they are the same which of late have much occupied my mind. Alcott said that the world to Emerson was a lecture room to Brownson a rostrum.

12.

This morning after breakfast there was held in the room a conversation on Friendship and its laws and conditions. Mr Alcott placed Innocence; Larned, thoughtfulness; I, seriousness; Lane, Fidelity.

13.

This morning after Breakfast there was held a conversation on The Highest aim. Mr Alcott said Integrity; I, Harmonic being; Lane, Progressive being; Larned, annihilation of self; Bower, Repulsion of the evil in us. Then there was a confession of the obstacles which prevented us from attaining the highest aim. Mine was the doubt that the light is light not the want of will to follow, or the sight to see.[38]

I cannot understand what it is that leads me, or what I am after. Being is incomprehensible.

What shall I be led to? Is there a being who I may marry which would be the means of opening my eyes? Sometimes I think so, but it appears impossible. Why should others tell me that it is so and will be so in a unconscious way, as Larned did on Sunday last, and as others have before him? Will I be led home? It strikes me these people here Alcott & Lane will be a great deal to me. I do not know but that they will be what I am looking for, or the answer to that in me which is asking. Can I say it   I believe it should be said. Here I cannot end, they are too near me; they are not high enough for to awaken in me a sense of their high superiority which would keep me here to be bettered, to be elevated. They have much very much. I desire the strength of self-denial of Mr. A. And the unselfishness of Mr. Lane in money matters. In these both they are far my superiors. I would learn this from them. I would be meek humble and set at their feet that I might become as they are. They do not understand me but if I am what my consciousness my heart leads me to feel; if I am not deceived, why, I can wait. To be sure wait. Yes, patiently wait. Is not this the first time since I have been here that I have recovered myself? Do I not feel that I have something here to receive, to add to, increase my highest life that I never felt anywhere else. Is this sufficient to keep me here   If I can prophecy I must say no. I feel that it will not fill my capacity. Oh God strengthen my resolution, let me not waver, and continue my life. But I am sinfull. Oh forgive my sins. What shall I do oh Lord that they may be blotted out   Lord could I only blot them out of my memory nothing would be too great or too much. It is dark. I must stop. Heaven protect me.

18.

What is looked for is a full complete expression of the pious spirit of the Age. The Church is it not. The state is it not. Society is it not. Family or individuals are it not. Who and Where shall it be expressed, lived.

I have thought of my family this afternoon the happiness and love with which I might live with them again. To leave them, to think not of returning to them, to live once more with them—can I entertain the idea? Still I cannot conceive how I can live in bussiness and partake of the practices and indulge myself with the food and garmenture of our home and city. To return home if it were possible for me would most probably not only stop my progress but very likely put me back. It is useless for me to speculate on my future. Put dependence on the spirit which leads me. Be faithfull to it and work. Leave results to God. If the question should be asked of me wether I would give up my kindred and Bussiness and follow out this spirit-life, or return and enjoy them both? I could not hesitate a moment for it would not compare; there would not be room for a choice. What I do I must do for it is not I that do it. It is the spirit. The spirit may be what it is; that question I cannot ask nor answer: what it leads me to do will be the only evidence of its character. I feel as impersonal as a stranger to it. I ask: who are you? Where are you going to take me? Why me? Why not someone else? What purpose? Why so dark and obscure? I stand astonished amused to see myself. Alas I cry who am I and what does this mean and am lost in wonder.[39]

21 Sat.

Last evening I had a dream of my mothers death. I felt all the pain and anguish of soul that I should have felt if it had been really so. Alas I thought who is there at home to receive me and I felt the union of our family had been broken up and we were scattered as fragments.

Yesterday after supper a conversation took place between Mr Alcott, Lane and myself. The subject was the position of myself with my family my duty and my position here. Mr Alcott asked me for my first impressions as regards the hindrances which I had seen since my being here. I told him frankly   1.st   His want of frankness 2. His disposition to seperateness rather than win cooperators to the aims in his own mind. 3. His family who prevent his immediate plans of reformation. 4. The place has very little fruit on it which it was and is their desire should and ought to be the principle part of their diet. 5. I feared they had too decided a tendency to literature to writing for the success & immediate prosperity of their object.[40]

My relations with my Relatives are very critical at this period; more so than they ever have been. It is a very important moment. It is the crisis of the state we have in for this year back. How it will terminate I know not. If God gives me strength to be true to the spirit, how far they will at home accord with it is to me very doubtfull. Wether they will sufficiently for me to return or no is questionable is to me deeply interesting and highly importent to my future life. For it will have a great effect upon my future circumstances. I have written a letter to them asking their views of life their aims and I am anxious for their answer. It is not a willful question of returning for it is the spirit which guides me and if it can live there I go back. If not I am governed and I must stay and go where it leads, wherever that may be.

22

I wish to write to my brothers. I feel the great importence and serious results of my own return, my own weakness, and the many difficulties which I will have to encounter. I will attempt to sketch a draft so as to get my ideas somewhat in shape for to be rewritten when I receive a answer to the one I have written:

Dear Brothers:

I am fully impressed with the importence of our rejoining again in actual life. It will I am conscious involve a change and perhaps one in which you would not be a willing cooperator but this I cannot say until we understand each other more fully. I will be as open to you as I am to my own consciousness and declare to you my spirit and the aims to which it wishes to actualize its-self. But first of all let me say that I am as impersonal and distinct to the spirit which is in me as you are. I feel that I am weak feeble instrument through which it expresses itself. It has led me against my will and all the strength and struggle I have had in my power I have exerted against it which has only served to make it more deep & interior. I have been subjugated by it and I must follow. And the question is now with me can the conditions at home be such that I can live there? How useless would it be and how much more sinfull would it be for me to come home knowing that it is not the place for it and that I will be driven away again in a short period. Therefore is it that by declaring each others aims we will be able to see where we stand and what we can do.[41]

Man requires a new birth—the birth of the feminine in him.[42]

The question arises in my mind wether it is necessary for me to require the concurrence of my brothers in the views of life which now appears to demand of me their actualization. Can I not live on simple diet and garmenture without their doing it? Must I needs have their concurrence? Can I not leave results to themselves? If my life is purer than those around me why cannot I trust in its own simple influence? But if their is a great difference of spirit, can we live together? Does not like seek like? In money matters it must certainly be otherwise than it has been; in this we must aggree that there shall not be any accounts kept whatsoever between us let the consequences be what they will. I would rather suffer evil from dependence upon the principle of love than to accept the principles of self to exist between us. I ask my nature demands not a cent above my immediate necessary wants. What they are must be placed upon my own spirit as I would leave to them to judge for themselves. They may demand 10 times more than myself which to me would be happiness to see them use it. And even did I think they used it wrongfully, all the check I would be willing to exert would be that of love and mutual good feelings. I feel conscious if I remain as I now am I shall require but very little for myself, but this would still give me greater happiness that I could have the circumstance of showing to them my love. What little I should require should be spent to the benefit and amelioration and help of others. I would diminish my own wants for this purpose. I can at home live a secluded life. I will go home live longer there be true to the spirit with the help of God and wait until further light and strength. I have lived at home so long and become what I am and it appears to me possible that I may live still longer at home. I feel that at this place I cannot live as I would. This is not the place for my soul. I must try once more my home. What will be the consequence time alone can tell. Thus far have I come I can say at home; whether it will put me backward or make me remain stationary or I will be able to progress when I return must be left to the trial. I will follow the spirit and not the opinions or the approbation of others. Let them say what they will and how they will, it is not their approbation or opinion I am living for. I go and most likely this Wednesday when I intended only to go and make a visit and return. They will I know speak of me differently from what they have which I might avoid by returning and remaining with them some time longer but this I shall not do. I have not neither will I practice any thing for to gain the good opinion of others. I have a life to lead   I am called upon to lead it; the influence of others shall not swerve me from it. They are beings and I am one. My life is not theirs. Theirs not mine. They have been the means of giving me much light upon myself but I feel I would live and progress more in a different atmosphere.

Tues. 24

To morrow I go from here to Boston and from B to Brook Farm and from there I suppose home. I would not be surprised if I should find myself home in two weeks. At home I will live a solitary life. I have always slept with and had the same room with my brother George but I now feel strongly inclined to have a room and bed to myself that I may be alone and solitary.[43] I must be to myself. I will with the help of God and oh how I desire this help live a life seperate from those around me; one obedient to the spirit. What the spirit will lead me to, what it may accomplish in me, I know not, but I will with the help of the spirit be a humble and passive obedient instrument. I feel that I am under its influence that it is it that leads me that I am dead to the old that was in me altho I never was completely without the spirit. There was always a small stream running through my being. Lord I ask not what purpose this is for but only that I may be patient, silent, still, in peace & quiet. Let not the outward tempt me but keep me in the inward life which I have entered. Lord what thou wouldst have me to do is no question with me. It is to be governed by thy spirit wethersoever that leads; whatsoever that tells me to do or to speak is what Thou wouldst have me to do. Lord I feel that I am weak, and am afraid that I will fall into many temptations. Willt Thou give me the humility to confess them and the strength to mend my ways.[44]

Abraham came into my room to speak to me about going to the Tropics for to live a True life. He was led to do it on account of a few words which I have now and then spoken on the subject. I told him my views on the subject and said in conclusion I did not know in what way I might be led but somehow or other from the first I felt there was a sympathy between us. And if the spirit lead me there as the fit place I should go etc. Abraham is the sincerest seriousest persons that I have known.

What a mystery is life! How are we led! Who can tell what to-morrow may bring forth? I will live on live on looking not behind or around me. I am nothing nothing. I have passed into All. I? There is no I. No one, no personality. That is gone. It was but a dream. They expect what was to return home. Their Idea, their memory to be reproduced, but how will they be surprised to find a new being in the place of the old. Alas! Isaac has gone, has fled. I am no Son. No Brother. I will move in their presence like a shadow. They will not be able to speak to me. It will be to them a dream. They will think they have been asleep. I cannot speak to my old associates. I must be alone. My conversation is within. They will be a hindrance. I must avoid them. What have I to do with them? Who are they? They are different beings. They will clasp my hands with a cordial clasp and they will shrink as from the grasp of an electrical rod.

Wed. 25.

This morning I depart from Fruitlands. I have learnt much since I have been here. I have come in contact with some of the most prominent men of this school the spiritualists or mystic. I feel that I could not get much more if I should stay any longer   They did not appear to me to be mystical nor so highly spiritual. But enough. I depart perhaps not to return again.

Farewell Fruitlands Birds Trees Hills mountains, valleys   Farewell Ye Inhabitants Alcott, Lane, Abraham, Bower, Mrs Alcott, and All the Children. May Providence be in and with you. Fare-well in God.[45]

Fri. 27.

I arrived here at B F on Wed   I made the attempt to write a letter to my brethren but could not finish and leave it untill I receive an answer from them. I feel that it is almost needless for me to say what my purpose is and under what conditions I can return home. This place here does not answer to my wants. Fruitlands I cannot say that it does and hence it is my duty to return home and be what I am and let come what will come. Destiny is Providence and who can understand or search out God. what may be the consequences of my going home cannot be said but let them be what they may it is better to meet them and be done with them. Let us meet the face of things: the bolder we march up to them the better. It is foolish it is weakness to put them off. Life is in proportion as we deal with realities; the faster they come and we have the strength to meet them the more we live   And life is the highest gift of God. Who would loose a moment of life? Inspiration should be allways and continous as Eternity. Every moment of un-inspiration is death. Death is not being God-inspired. Alas in the midst of life how much death. The best of Men how little have they lived. It is a lamentable a deplorable fact that out of the 70 years of Mans allotted earth existence he lives at best not really in the highest sense and in which he has the capacity always to live in not 3 out of the 70. Who is there can say he lives an hour daily of divine life. Alas how many is there that even do not so much know scarcely what it is. Living Dead Men. Living like Devils Beasts or Men but Dead to Godliness, to Divinity. Man is not aware of his Godlike capacities. This thing we call Man, what is it? What does it mean. May not Man transcend Humanity. I believe in Metamorphosis not in metapsycosis.[46] It is another word for Progress. Man is undergoing a Metamorphosis continually. He is not the same two moments. Man Thou hast thy creation in thy own hands and the points of alternating are Christ and (not Lucifer for that is light but) Satan the Devil. Men are not fully awakened of the responsibility that rests upon them the deep eternal importence of every act of life even a word a thought. Ideas are the shadows of change. God is the Eternal Stillness without Idea Thought or Sentiment. He is. I am what I am. The was, is & the to be. He that progressess most thinks, feels, & acts, most. He is the most alive. Metamorphosis & Change in the ascendent scale is the meaning of Progress which is growth, advancement, putting forth. It is the centre acting out unfolding its self. Why does Man become a stranger to Man? Is it not because there is a continual Metamorphosis going on & that Friend ceases to commune with Friend and is alienated.[47]

If there is any difference of being, I know of no greater than God & Satan. I would look sooner for a lion to turn a Lamb than satan to become a Saint. What yet remains in the Eternity of our being is unknown to us. We know only so far as we live it out. What a charm, what a curiosity, what a picture is the phenomena of the Soul! Every new thought feeling or act springs from the depths of the Soul, the Unknown, the nearest to God if not him. Man gives being to that which had no being. He creates something where there was nothing. He is a Creator. A God in God. Every Man I meet is an unconscious prophecy to me. I would awaken him to the wonder of his being. He that has and is most sees most in others. Hence Christ said: Greater works than I do shall ye do. Who is a better authority than he who saw all that is in Man. Every human being strikes me as a wonderfull becoming as if a God was struggling for birth in him. He is a imprisoned God. Like the young bird fearfull to venture to fly. Man appears to me not as a body but as a spirit-being, unconsciously giving utterance to God. Spirits doing acting suffering and when I see him labor it is not as a body I see him but as a Angel a Immortel spirit the infinite breath of God.[48]

Sat.

When I return home for I have made up my mind so to do will I not be necessarily must I not be opened to keep the bussiness in a good condition be more employed in it than it will be for my good. It will be said: bussiness will go backwards unless we make greater exertions; we must give more of our time to it; it will not do unless we do so. This is the tendency and temptation of bussiness that it constantly makes greater and greater demands upon your time   And it appears unless you are perpetually progressing you are going backwards. For my own opinion. It appears to me most feasible and the best plan both for the good that might be done for others and for ourselves would be to purchase with what we have a country place. And the simplicity in which we could and of the highest considerations we ought to live would give the opportunity of doing good to others and to the culture of our own souls. For it is not in giving money we help others; nay have not those who have helped the world most always been the poorest in the wordly sense. What had Pythagores, Socrates, and above all what had Christ. was he not the poorest of Men having no place even to lay his head. Oh heaven what have we and are not aware of it? Our fine couches we are as unconscious of as of the air we breathe. Oh God it would be a kind a loving act to strip us of all that we may become conscious of thy great gifts and be gratefull thankfull of thy great-loving-kindness. It is from deprivation self denial that the well of love and gratitude is opened in the pious soul. There is no greater curse then Riches. How hard is it for a rich Man to enter into the Kingdom of God. Riches is the Siren which entices Men to sleep a life-long slumber keeping the Godlike energies in stupor. Hence is it that it is easily perceivable to what end wordly bussiness will and does lead he that engages in it. This cannot be so with me. My soul will do as it has done again if I return; in a short time it will free itself again　　And the only permanent condition of life which appears for me to live in is what I have stated. But still I feel perfectly willing to try and see what a new attempt may bring forth and that as speedily as possible for I have nothing that keeps me from going home now that I will not have in 6 weeks. It is in intense trial that my energies come out and I feel like saying: come on as soon as ye please this moment as well as next week. With God's help I will if you please take a trial with ye Tempters. Let us meet boldy and with mighty valor face to face for if there is then a defeat there will be a defeat, and a Feat in such a rencounter to the victor. It is the old struggle about Mose's body. Let us have it out and be done with it and say Amen. So be it. Being willing to return home still I am not unanxious to hear from my brothers the answer which they have written to my last letter which I have not as yet received but expect this morning in an hour from now. Wether it will be to the purpose is indefinite or a simple request for me to make a visit to talk it over home or a simple reply that they are willing to do all that can be done or perhaps an advice or a vague expression of sentiment without a practicel plan or principle is impossible for me to tell. Still it will be important for the answer what ever it may will be the expression the shine of their minds. Hence its coloring will indicate their state of being which is all that I wish to know but not all that I desire to *be* for I would have them to *be* in God, in his kingdom, filled with The Spirit. It is strange it is more than strange how this life of ours waves to and fro before and after and ever ceasing in a effluence. And life's phenomena is like standing, stational shadows, fixed, immovable in the Pantheon of the Soul's Memory.

The Pantheon of a nation is its best history. Man is known by his reminiscences, his recollections.

Mon. July. 31

I rec'd from my brother John an answer to my letter on Saturday morning after I had written the above. He said in the letter he felt at times the necessity of changing our circumstances and that he is willing to do all that can be done. I have written him a reply which will be sent to him tomorrow morning and with the opinion that I will be at home in 2 weeks. What will be the consequences of my going home, wether I can stay or what I may do or how my life will be led will have to be left to the time when it comes. I expect a letter from my brother George this week or perhaps tomorrow. With the letter to my brother John I have sent one to Mr. Martin which I should like to transcribe but it is unworth the time.[49]

Man is the symbol of all mysteries. Why is it that all things I hear see or feel seem to be instinct with prophecy? That I do not see any more individual personalities, but priests and oracles of God? The age is big with a prophecy which it is in labor to give birth to. All nature animate and inanimate is murmuring a dark prophecy half articulate.

I feel conscious my experience is different now from what it has been. My life is much fuller and every fibre of my being seems teemed with sensitive life. I live wholly in another atmosphere of sentiment & thought from what I have heretofore. Whether this will remain so permanent or still increase dependest upon time to answer. I can find no one who is one with me in my thoughts or experience, who is genial. My nature craves something different from what I have had. Wether I will ever get it depends on Providence.[50] Still I trust I will be true to this longing this aspiration as a God implanted prophecy which will be realized in time. As for instance as I am now I have less real union and sympathy with her and those who I have met much nearer heretofore. It appears their atmosphere is denser, their life is more naturel, in the flesh and instead of meeting them in my highest I can only meet them by coming down into my flesh in my body which it appears to me I am almost unconscious of in that sense. There is not that sense of heaviness dullness fleshiness in me. I feel no naturel desires no impure thoughts nor wanderings of fancy. Still, I feel more intensely and am filled to overflowing with love and desire for union and nearness but no one to meet me where I am and I cannot meet them where I am.

August 1.

I have been much impressed of late with the very great effect the nation and the Family progenitors have on the characters of their offspring. Men talk about universality-impartiality many-sidedness free judgment unbiased opinion etc. when their national and family dispositions is the centre and ground of their being and hence their opinions. It appears they are most themselves when they show these traits of character. They are most naturel and earnest and at home when they speak from this link which binds them to the past. Their hearts are opened and they speak with a glow of eloquence and a peculiar unction that reaches the hearts of others and touches the same chords in the breasts of all who hear them. It is well for Man that he feels that he has in him a part of the past; that he would not be what he is unless there had been a past and to which he feels greatly indebted and which inspires him with deep instinctive reverence when he looks back or when the instinct is awakened in his bosom. Man is in a much greater degree the creature of the past than he gives himself credit for. He reproduces daily the sentiments and thoughts of the dim and almost obscure before. There are certain ideas thoughts aspirations which have not had their fullfillment that run through all Men from the beginning untill now and are continually reproduced. There is a unity of race called Humanity; one Place called Nationality; one Birth called kindred; and one affinity called love and friendship. From all these relations we are greatly influenced   They all make a mark upon the Man.[51]

Aug 2 Wed.

Prophecy is the enunciation of the divine aspiration of the Soul which is the Soul seeing the glorious becoming which is wrapt up in the dim approaching distance. There is the same certainity in Prophecy as there is in Science. The Genius of prophecy has not yet been born (but he is presaged) who shall collate prophecy and make it as certain as Astronomy or any of the exact sciences. Man will reduce the facts of the inward world to the same certainty as he has done in the outward world as soon as the faculties which take cognizance of the inner eternal world are as fully opened as the faculties which take cognizance of the outward world are. The faculties which take cognizance of the outward world are. The faculties which take cognizance of the eternal inner world have not been awakened in only a few of the human race and they have been called to distinguish them Prophets Miracle workers Providential Men Men inspired Seers and Poets   Now this is the privilege of all Men in a greater or less degree just as it is as regards the outward faculties.[52] For when Men were as dark to the outward world as they now are to the inward the Man of Science the Astronomer the Mathematician the founders of the arts were miraculous Men, Gods, and they were deified. What any one Man (and this is a most comfortable and cheering thought) has been or done all may be or do for each Man is a type a pattern of the whole human race And I care not if Men say these miracles or great acts which Men hold to be true and actual are mere aspirations dreams myths   I care not; it is still more glorious for us, for then they are to be done, they are before us, they are in the Coming and these glorious divine prophetic instincts implanted in the human Soul are to be actualized and the Golden Age the dreams of Orpheus the inspired strains of the Hebrew Bards and above all the prophecies of Christ are before us. The divine instincts will be realized as sure as there is a God above that inspires them. It is the glory of God that they should be so. It is his delight. This world must become heaven. This is its Destiny and our destiny under God is to make it so and prophecy is given to encourage and nourish our hopes and feed our joys. That we may say with Job: I know that altho worms shall eat this flesh and my bones become dust yet will I see my Redeemer at the latter day face to face.[53]

The belief in the special guidance of God has been the faith of all deeply religious Men. The evil of this faith is in this when Men are so guided for I will not dispute the fact but only give an explanation of it which appears to me to reconcile it with the regular order of the working of laws established by God. My explanation would be this: it is not a miraculous power specially bestowed upon Man but a higher degree of inspiration than the ordinary, for the ordinary life is inspired and the other is a higher degree of it and this is so as I will explain   The evil is from the contrary opinion and it is this: Instead of Men seeing it is only a higher degree of insight they believe they have a miraculous special gift and that all that they say is infallible whereas it is not so for it is their own individuality raised up in purer state of being and instead of being raised up to reorganize or to found a new Sect or to cause revolutions they should fullfill the old continue it farther and as far as they have been given light to do it. In making or forming sects they reproduce their own individualities with all their errors. So did Luther Swedenborg Wesley men of modern times who were attuned to a greater degree than the mass of their fellows. Their mistake lies in this in their attempting to make of their individual experience Universal ends. No Man does this in the ordinary state; but they being lifted up a little above the Mass they became intoxicated   The only one so far as I have read who has had humility equal to his inspiration, was *Jacob Boehmen.* Luther Calvin Fox Penn Swedenborg Wesley had self in view; selfism is mixed with universalism   None have spoken so pure and universal as Boehmen. He is the most inspired man of Modern times. More Love and Truth he had than all the others put together and less faults than either taken singly.[54]

We should aim after being better: if we be better, we will think, feel, act, and speak, better   It is not knowledge of the head the intellect that gives wisdom or life. Out from the heart springes the issues of life. When we are united to God all the windows of the Soul are opened. But we never can unite ourselves by opening the windows but by our souls being united the windows will be opened. "First seek the Kingdom of God and then all these things will be added." "The Kingdom of God is within you." "Knock and it shall be opened seek and ye shall find." "For he that asketh God will give abundently"

4

The glory of our nature opens with our shame. Joy and pain are twin sisters. Guilt Remorse are copulated with Innocence Peace. Progress is Death. He that loves me most gives me the most pain. Oh Love me not so much I would cry for thou makest me terribly miserable   We are only fully conscious of the real sense of this life in the struggles of death. Life is Death. For Life is living and to live is to flow out to grow to give existence to void to give extense to the intense.

With our Hosannas are mixed Lamentations and vice versa   The Deepest love is the sign of the capacity of the keenest pain & sorrow. Every spiritual act is a birth, and not without pain and bitter anguish of soul is it born. Existence means the pain of Joy and Sadness of Love. Success and Disappointment can and have each killed their equal army of Men. The power which can raise a Man from the Dead can kill, and vice versa. Christ raised the Dead by a word; Peter killed by a word. He that has power to forgive necessarily had the right to condemn. Life is successive births. Being passes through successive circles of being. He that is above sin can forgive & condemn sin & sinners   Light adds not light to light but increases it proportionately; the flame ascends higher like two that love; they both ascend higher from their own love each give but do not loose but increase each other. The union of the two gives birth to that which is greater than them both. Two streams being joined have by their union their rapidity accelerated. The strength of two combined is more than that of two separately. To be conscious of dieing daily is to be conscious of the highest life that is the fullest.

5

Death is but an event a circumstance; it is an act of the Being. Being dies not but death is a fact of life standing in relation to Being as thought sentiment or any other function of the Soul. Being never dies. Death is another added to the already many metamorphoses that the Human Being passes through. To die is an Act of the Soul hence it is always superior to death. Birth and Death are the highest acts of the Human Being. There have been those that have never given Birth as well as those that have never died. We should accept death as we do sleep as a fact of experience as a mode of life as one of the blessings for it is. Every act of Self denial is an act of death and if we fully performed our duty death would be laying off a robe   Transfiguration should be continually going on & when we come to the end of our course we would be prepared as the child is for its birth.

7 Mon.

I have written home that I should start from Boston on next tuesday or wednesday. I feel that my life is one that cannot exist at home. Heretofore I felt it was impossible for me to go back home and at present I am indifferent not knowing how it may turn when I get there. At least whatever turn it may take either that I can stay or that I am led into a different path which ever course it may take it will be one which will be marked through out my life. It is no doubt the period of life when if there is any thing in me it will burst out what ever it may be and manifest itself.

8

He that arranges the Past before his bar and passes judgment upon it that is such a judgment as to condemn it is ungenerous inhumane and is in want of true charity. Maurice in his *Kingdom of Christ* page 305 is guilty in this particular very guilty.[55] I feel that I am a brother a child of the past since what I am the past has made me and I thank God that He has given me a heart to feel and gratefully humbly to acknowledge it   The past I reverence   Thou noble past what suffering pain and ardous labor hast thou done for thy children many who now are as ungratefull as parricides   Parent of my being to thee I shed my tears to thee I offer my heart to thee I bow in deep awe and look up in thy love smiling paternal countenance with clinging embraces of dutifull love do I clasp thee   Oh thou give me the smile of thy encouragement and the bright hopefull glance of thine eyes   The good that is in me thou hast cherished and bestowed unto me; what other is in me thou hast nobly fought against and thou has transmitted the noble courage wherewith thy sons can like their sires fight heroically against the evil   Bless God   God thank, God be good unto thee oh Noble Souls of the Past!

How little we know of Christs ordinary common daily life.

9

Humanity has been and is growing sloly but progressively to a clearer consciousness of the invisible world. A Transfiguration it is sloly passing through.

This morning as soon as I awoke I was impressed with the feeling of deep regret which I will feel in leaving this place.

Yesterday Charles A Dana and myself whent to Newton to see Wm Green who is studying divinity there[56]   I started the question with him wether if Mans self was wholly annihilated put out and he became a perfect temple of the divine spirit, would he not be the same as Christ was, one with God. The more one denies self the language of Christ becomes his language because he has the same mind. Jesus became Christ. His orthodoxy led him to take a different view. We continued the conversation on Hegel Leroux and Pantheism.[57]

It is to me exceedingly oppressive to write as I now do. Continually does myself appear in my writing   I would that my I was holly lost in the sea of the spirit, wholly lost in God.

Man should not think feel or act unless he is inspired to do so. Why is it that we cannot give the mind free play and let it utter itsself on any topic it may be inspired to speak upon. He that has faith all things are possible for faith is an act of the soul and thy faith is the possibility of thy power.

If Men would act from the present inspiration of their souls they would know much more than they do get by reading or by speculating.[58]

No Man in his heart can ask for more than he has. Think of this deeply.

God is just. We have what we ought to have even by our own sense of justice.

It is singular it appears to me that my consciousness of self gradually looses itsself as my life increases and still not singuler for it is only a greater fullness of the life giving spirit which is universal impersonal love.

Mr Dwight below has just struck the piano and awakened in my mind the questions why should not life have a May-day play season? This light joyfull hearted-ness has never been my experience. Will it ever be?[59]

Humanity is constantly enlarging in depth and in breadth. One generation builds upon the other. The present generation is added to the preceding one so Humanity is constantly increasing.

The desire to love and be beloved to have Friends with whom you can commune to enter society in which you do enjoy is it not best to give up these desires to deny & sacrifice them? But it may be said these desires gratified add to life and is it not the question how we shall add not diminish life. But in giving these desires up would not our life be increased by its flowing in a more heavenly direction?

We are feeding the demons daily that are in us by our wicked thoughts and our sinful acts; these are their meats and drinks. Ha ha I make them gasp. Sometimes it makes my heart laugh quite merrily to think of it. When I am hungry and there is something tempting on the table hunger like a serpent comes up in my throat and laps its dry tongue with eagerness for its prey but it returns often chagrined at its discomfiture.

That which tempts us we should deny no matter how innocent it is in itsself. If it tempts, away with it, crucify it untill it tempts no more then partake of it for it is only then you can pertake of it prudently and with true temperance   Eat not when you are hungry for you will be led to eat too much but only taste or take a luncheon that your hunger may be appeased untill a more convenient season.[60]

All our emotions thoughts are caused by some agent acting on us   As by music our sensibility is affected and in us is awakened feelings and thoughts so it is as respect all the senses and the spirituel faculties. Hence we should by all possible means purify refine our organization that we may hear the deliculest the sweetest the stillest sounds and murmuring whispers of the angels even who are in our midst. How much fuller richer would be our life if we were more delicate tender and acuter finer textured. How many exquisite delights nature yields we are not yet aware of. What a world are we surrounded with that none but Holy Men Prophets and Poets have had a glimpse of.

The soul is a plate on which the senses deguerryotypes endelibly the pictures of the outward world. How cautious ought we to be where we look what we hear what we smell feel or taste. And how ought we to exert ourselves that all around should be made Beautifull Musical Fragrant Delightfull and Delicious so that our beings may be awakened to the highest to a divine sense of life without a moments interruption.

Every new relation that one is placed in every new thought sentiment or act that one experiences increases life according to its quality. This reflection strikes me in thinking on my return to my house   Since my departure from home the objects which have affected in all the ways that my being is capable of being affected have been of a much higher order than those that have surrounded me in my past life hence they have improved refined my being. Beautifull scenery fine music cultivated and more than ordinary society intimate friends and some who I love all these have been more to me than what I have had and are more than I will have when I go home and place myself in nearly my old relations. There was a internal change in my being before I departed; there has been quite an effect on me from my association since I have been away so that I am quite different in one sense much farther developed more grown; and where my position, in what relation, this difference will place me at home my curiosity is quite excited to know   Oh heavenly Father will thou give me grace and strength to keep getting better to over come all temptations that may beset my path   Oh Lord awaken me more to the divine capacities thou hast endowed Man with and willt thou make my sight clearer and my hearing delicater that I may see more and more of thy law and hear more and more of thy divine voice of love   Oh may I become more obedient meek Humble like Jesus Christ my master Lord and saving Redeemer to whom and to thee and to the holy spirit my soul is indebted wholly without measure   Oh make my heart more devout; inspire my soul; raise my thoughts and may thy spirit dwell in me in fullness to over flowing. Lord help me to over come all selfwill to crucify self that there may be nothing of the old Man left and that I may be a new Man born begotten in the Lord Jesus Christ who in heaven on the right hand of God giveing help to all those who ask in sincerity and Truth   Oh Lord my heart desires thy assistence in utterable longing it would fly to thee if it had wings and fall at thy feet and ask of thee of that water and meat that would quench and feed indeed unto eternal life. Oh Father why should my heart be so pained after thy loving spirit. Thou hast said ask and it shall be given   Now oh Lord I ask in Jesus's name give unto me more and more of thy loving spirit. Fill my whole being that there may not remain any thing but thy loving kindness   My soul is bowed down before thee oh Lord. Bless and bestow unto me thy gift heavenly Father   Amen[61]

10. Thurs.

There is no such thing as living in Eternity for living necessarily implies succession and succession measured is time. There is no life without motion for life is motion emotion, and motion is succession moving; hence it is in time as in space. What we mean when we speak about living in Eternity or in the All is higher state of being wherein the past seems as so different that all old things have passed and being so full and dassled with the present it seems tho we were out of time & Space whereas it is only a higher purer form of both. Time & Space are the recipients of life.

Was the Spirit of Christ large enough to cause the unity the Brotherhood of Man. Every great Man has his disciples who are one in being disciples of the spirit which was in the Teacher. Is the mission of Christ to redeem the whole race to bring them into the bonds of Charity and love uniting them with God   We cannnot say it is, not until we have lived up to his life. Until then we have no right because we have not the power to know w⟨h⟩ether his spirit will lead and be the final dispensation of our Father to his Children. But we can say we do not know what he has in store for us nor even what he has already given when we have not as yet received in ourselves. How many many joys and rich blessings are waiting for to enter our hearts prevented by our disobedience. Alas we ourselves shut out so many blessings unconsciously   We should pity ourselves more could we see ourselves. With divine capacities still struggling with the animel.[62]

I become so eager that at times I would fain if wings were given me to leave my body and soar up to heaven on the sweet bosom of the clouds. But body and soul are indissolubly united and we are to transfigure the body into a temple a covering worthy of heaven a process slow but a visible progress and a felt difference. We are to etherealise the body or in other words the resurrection is to be accomplished without death on this side of the grave so that death will be swallowed up with life, immortality into being. The barrier between this world and the next—death—is to be thrown down and pass away, and Man stand in the face of heaven in the presence of God in the society of his angels with the fellowship of the Holy Men Prophets Poets and Saints of the past. Amen   Oh God be thou my helper strength and Redeemer   May I live wholly to thee   Give unto me Grace and obedience to Thy spirit   May all self be put away from me that I may enter into the glorious liberty of the sons of the living God: Jehovah. Awaken me   Raise me up   Restore me oh Lord Heavenly king Jesus Christ.

11.

In Man as in God there is a kingdom a darkness a desert which we cannot penetrate   In the I we see something we cannot penetrate, a celestine desert.[63]

Sund. 13

This is the last day that I remain at Brook Farm[64]   It is with no little emotion that I leave. Since I have been here I have become acquainted with some of the best minds in New England   Much very much has my character grown and been influenced in the period I have been here since last January   Many of my dreams and earnest aspirations have been met here. I do not ever anticipate such society and refining amusements again   Miss Frances Auston Elli has been here the 3 days singing occasionally   Mr Dwight and George Curtis[65] have just finished singing with the Piano Beethovens music with "Kennst du das land"[66]

Alas I know not what to say. My heart has such a strong attachment to the people here and the spot.

Where will I be led   I return home like returning to a new world not knowing where I am   Alas what shall I say   My future is dark but with a purpose in it I feel.

Here I sit with pen in hand, book being on the table by which I am sitting, with a light tunic on and a drab velvet scull cap made with the hands of one who has come nearer to my heart than any other human being that I have ever become acquainted with and whose nearness I will feel most when I have left this place   Will I be drawn in the future to any of these persons I have met here   What purpose my destiny is educating me for I know not. Perhaps these are the last words I ever shall write at Brook Farm   My heart is gratefull inexpressibly gratefull to the originator of this place Rev Geo Ripley   How much I have gained by his labor   Oh may I be able to manifest my gratitude to him in a way which will satisfy my heart. To thee I dare say friend Ripley my heart is gratefull to thee from the very source of its life   May heaven lead thee[67]

15

To day I have arrived home   I am thankfull that I am in the state of mind that I am   Much worse I expected to feel   I have written a letter to Geo Curtis to Providence. To-morrow I commence to work. My interior state is quiet peacefull. I feel in the midst of many but as not one with them   I have not met anyone yet   My Dear Mother understands me better than any one else. How far bussiness will interfere with my interior life remains to be seen. Oh Lord help me to keep the resolutions of my heart which are to not let the world enter into my heart but keep it looking towards thee. My heart has been in constant prayerful state since I have been home it is living in its own sanctuary its own temple   God oh Lord preserve it.

Fri. 18.

My mind is in such a state that I have not been conscious of being still since I have been home. It has not found its place its home as yet. It is just like one who is lost not knowing which way to look or to go. Tuesday afternoon I wrote to Geo Curtis   Thursday to Almira.[68] I will continue here patiently waiting to see what will turn up. Last evening I attended a Methodist Love-Feast. In returning I stopped at the ward political meeting[69]

19.

Last Thursday I whent and saw Edward Palmer   He impressed me very much   I loved him. He is to me a beautiful spirit. My spirit is drawn towards him. Shall we come nearer?[70]

Sunday morning   The tolling of the bells makes me feel sad. My heart aches after the smile of thy beaming countenance. Life is a sad earnest purpose   Men may say what they please; life impresses weightily upon he who drinks deep from the source which being flows. "The ground of all great thoughts is sadness"   Never can I remain still fixed to enjoy the now   Ever am I soaring higher and will be until the thread of life is spent (should it break before my aspiration is spent? Thats impossible). Aspiration is as unfathomable as heavens height is unreachable and the thread of thy being is as infinite as life   And life is as infinite as love   And Love as God   And God as stillness for stillness he was before Creation, Life, Motion. Stillness precedes all Godlike thoughts, feelings, acts. Oh holy quiet. Oh peacefull stillness.[71] Oh divine loveliness   How eager how intent is my soul for thee. Alas here in the midst of the busy smothering mass of Men the internal issues of life are shut up by the incessant profane babbling of Men. Oh silent woods wherein devout souls are inspired by thy holy atmosphere. Sanctuaries of God. How much nearer we are to thee oh God when we enter thy own dwelling place consecrated by thy own presence wherein all that brethes breathes Thee. In thy temple we become more and more thee. Our life is increased and we not only grow but are added to from thee and thou art incarnated a new in us. I never enter thy woods without being quickened nor leave them without being inspired with a serene lovefullness purer of heart.[72]

26

Woman was an afterthought with God. An after thought but a divine after thought.

I had yesterday afternoon a conversation with an acquaintance Dr Vethake the author of the two articles in the Pathfinder on "Femality" We are nearer to each other than I had expected. The subject of the difference of sexes has of late been a subject which has occupied my attention very much. I differ in my opinions and sentiments very widely from him. He holds Man is to be more of a Man and Woman is to be more of a Woman so that the two may form a whole. Man is Truth. Woman is Love; and marriage is the union of Truth or wisdom and Love. (He has studied Swedenborg deeply altho he does not speak of him.) The delight of marriage consists in the communion of the two natures. Now I am inclined to think the two sexes should be in the same Individual being. That the same Individual should unite in his own being both sexes.[73] He should be full of grace and truth the same as Jesus Christ. Whose life it was to do the work of His Father. Who had united in him the perfect lovefullness and tenderness of Woman with the wisdom and strength of Man. The manner of his birth has often struck me as a secret mystery. A male being born of a Virgin! What could he be but filled with Femality with Love such as no other being had ever been. He was without spot or wrinkle a perfect pattern of a divine being. The second Adam. The manifestation of a holy, (whole) being. A heretick of the 13teenth century I have just read after the above paragraph maintained, "That at the end of the World both Sexes shall be re-united together in one person and that re-union began in Jesus Christ; and that if Man had continued in the State wherein God had produced him, there would not have been any distinction of sex" (See Bayles article Adam). The unity of both sexes originally, was believed by the Jewish Rabbis. The Revelations of Antionette Bourigon, 1679, is to the same purpose She says "Men think to have been created by God as they are at present, altho it is not true, seeing Sin has disfigured the work of God in them, and instead of Men as they ought to be, they are become Monsters in Nature, divided in two imperfect Sexes, unable to produce their like alone, as trees and plants do, which in that point have more perfection than Man and Woman, incapable to produce themselves, but in conjunction with each other and with Pains and misery" etc. (See Bayles art on Adam)[74]

"Christ the second founder of Humanity without sin" having both natures re-united in him or never having sinned they were never dis-united. Hence he is the giver of true divine life. We find not the slightest trace of any sexual thought or feeling in all the history that is given of Christ. Light and Warmth should be one in the same being. Head and Heart; Understanding and Impulse; must be oned. ''Be ye perfect as your Father in heaven is perfect''   God is one from whom procedeth Love and Wisdom   Adam was before the Woman was formed from his rib in the image of God.

Aug. 29.

My diary has been kept in letters   I have written 3 or 4 within a few days.[75]

I feel that the life here is gradually influencing me more and more. My time for meditating and reading is shortened and the outward engages too much my attention.

Evening

To day I have been strongly impressed of the externality of the life led here in the City. My heart is not here.

Aug 30.

I find that I can live if my past 9 months or more is any evidence on a very simple diet Grains Fruits & nuts. The latter I have just commenced to eat with pure water. The Wheat I have yet ground and made with unleavened bread but as soon as we shall get in a new lot of wheat I shall try it in the grain which will be perhaps this week.[76] I was under much fearfull apprehension that when I should return to the City it would present so many temptations that I should not be able to withstand them and especially the bussiness which I follow being of such which presents temptations every moment. But I feel deeply grateful that so far I had had no reason to be fearfull of my being led away. What yet remains? My Diet is all purchased and all produced by hired labor   My dress I suppose the most of it by Slave Labor. And I cannot say that I am rightly conditioned until all that I eat and drink or wear is produced by *Love*.[77]

Suppose my brothers are willing to go in the Country   would I be willing to go with them   To leave the society here and the many intellectual advantages which a City always gives   And to leave also the opportunity of connecting myself with such society as is at Fruitlands and Brook Farm? These are questions not fancies to be answered. To day I put them; the answers will be forthcoming for I feel they are in me growing out to expression.[78]

Men have fear to utter absurdities. The head is skeptical of the Divine

Oracles of the Heart and she clothes her oracles before she utters them in such a fantastic dress that Men see the words but loose the life the thought.

Evening

I have just received two letters: one from A.B. and the other from Chas Dana. The first was full of interesting incident of Brook Farm and the later from lieber Carl was quite interesting.[79]

Sept. 1

There are two ways which the Spirit may live out itself. One is to leave all these conditions and to purchase a spot of ground and live according to its daily dictates. The other is to make the conditions here as harmonic as possible giveing the men an associative interest in the accumulation of the associative labor. Both schemes require the renunciation of self, of property. Love universal Love is the ruler and only in it can the Spirit find peace or be crowned with the highest happiness.

Sept. 1

Yesterday evening was the first that I tried to eat wheat grain instead of unleavened bread. And I eat it instead of bread for this mornings breakfast.

Is there such a Substance as absolute Substance? Something permanent real idestructible unchangeable? This I am led to ask in thinking what is it that essentially is the *me?* As an absolute substance it cannot be otherwise than a part of God the only absolute substance cause. If it is not an Absolute substance it must be a part of the phenomena of the Absolute substance depending for its continued existence on the cause, absolute cause, of its first appearence. To say that the Me is a cause is to fall in with the opinion of Spinoza for there can be but one Absolute Substance of Cause.[80] To say that the Me is not a Cause you fall in with the Oriental philosophy of a vague phenomanalism. The one is peculiarly northern in its Character; the other piculiarly southern   Or perhaps still a better classification: one is Eastern, the other Western. One is consolidation, the other is Individualism. The Central and the Super ficial. This dualism of thought has been reproduced into our Political system of government and often in its political controversy. One leads to Spiritualism the other to Materialism

2nd

The mystery of Mans being the unawakened Capacities in Man we are not half aware of. But a few of the Race the Prophets Sages and Poets give us but a glimpse of Mans high destiny. Alas that Man should be in the midst of so much on the boarders of such mighty truths and stand as blind and as dumb as a low animal before them.

Baal sometimes but ignorently utters true prophecies. This I am led to say from a remark I heard a man make to day Speaking of Diet. He said "why, what do you intend? At last you will have Men to live on God." We must become God like or Godfull. Live as he lives. Become one with Him until then we are aliens Prodigals until reconciled with our father. Until our wills accord perfectly with his until we can say I and my Father are One, We have not commenced to Be. We must fullfill what the Apostle said and it means much perhaps more than we consciously have imagined   That in God we live and move and have our being.

The relation the connection of Man with God is the highest the divinest and all relations that interfere with this relation should be severed. Question. Does not every other relation interfere with the divine relation?

The deeper and more profound a truth the less proof can you give in its support.

Sept 4th

Life is mysterious. Why should there be a difference in sex? Why cannot men and women speak together love one another and have friendly and intimate intercourse with each other as they have with themselves. Sometimes I think all I can do and the best I can do is to find reason for that which is and further the present without questioning or disputing the legitimacy and usefullness of it.[81]

5th

We often act to be understood by the heart not by the head and when the head speaks of its having understood we deny its understanding. It is the secret sympathy of heart which is the only response that is looked for. Speech is cold profane.

8th

I would die to prove my immortality. Yesterday I purchased three steel engravings from the master pieces of great sculptors. This is the way I would feed my sight and taste rather than in a luxurious table. And to day a sketch of Prometheus bound.[82]

I whent on the evening of the 6th to see the french opera company in the opera of the "Black Domino of Auber".[83] It did not please me as well as some music I have heard but parts of it was very beautifull. The hymns of the Nuns were very sweet. The thought occurred to me that if the Church does not provide for the true wants of Humanity religious gratification She must be still if Men feed them profanely. The Church has not done its duty hence so many secular Societies of Reformation Temperance etc. The Church has provided the means for the salvation of the Soul of the Sinner by spiritual acts such as prayer pennance Eucharist and her 7 Sacraments   She must now provide the terrestrial Sacraments for the Salvation Transfiguration of the body.

8th Evening.

We should constantly strive to actualize the Ideal which we perceive. Do we actualize all the beauty and holiness we perceive then we are not called upon to deny ourselves for we are living on all sides as full far and as high as we have the capacity to perceive   Are we not in this state of being? Then if we are sincere we will give up the lower and unnecessary gratifications for the purpose of the ideal we have in view

9th.

We are called at times to rely on Providence to be according to the world and its wisdom imprudent and reckless. So I am willing to be thought. each one of us has an individual character to act out to realize *under the inspiration of God* and this is the highest the noblest we can do. We are forms differing from one another and if we are acting with the inspiration of the Highest we are doing all that we can do; more the angels do not. What tends to hinder us from realizing the Ideal which our vision sees must be denied be it self Wealth Opinion or Death.[84]

Sept 13.

The Heart says Be all that you can. The Intellect says When you be all that you can what then?

We act all of us like insane; we are possessed and utter the spirit that possesses us.

He that loves with his whole Soul is lost in the infinite love.

Infinite love is the basis of the smallest act of love and when we love with our whole being we are in and one with God

Increase thy love by being truer to that which you hast if thou wouldst be nearer to God.

We draw we are one with the infinite in every act of love we do

To Love is to loose onesself and gain God.

To be all in Love is to be one with God

When the Spirit begets us we are no more. The Spirit is and there is nothing else

We never should speak but let the spirit speak in and through us

There is much debauchery in speaking willfully.

Every act of self is sin is a lie

The *spirit* will lead you into solitude and silence if it has something to teach you

The spirit will lead you into all truth not external things by observation

You must be born again to know the truth; it cannot be inculcated

To educate is to bring forth not to put in. To put in is Death; to flow out is life.[85]

13.

Mr Alcott and Lane left here this morning. They have been with us since last friday   I whent with them to see Mrs Black & Mrs Green and met Wm Chase Mr Thorou Wm Channing and Miss M. Fuller.[86]

15.

This morning I have felt like weeping bitterly constantly.[87]

16

I feel that daily I am tending more and more to Quietism: being less willfull, and more peacefull. What is not spoken from the Spirit is profane and all life is of the Spirit. The nearer we approach God the less personality do we feel conscious of. In approaching God we loose self and find life. For *self*ishness is Sin and Sin is Death. And God is Love and Love is Life. Things around me appear like shadows in a dream. At present I am without hope or sorrow desire or regret remembrance prospect or present. All the accidents of individuality have ceased and I cannot affirm that I am. I ask for nothing but stillness: perfect noiselessness. The things which I do in bussiness are foreign to me and I am in the midst of these circumstances as a Stranger. All I would do is to better the conditions which come under my vision without purpose or plan for the future. I am too sensitive to the noise and confusion and the unpleasant and astringent tones which strike my ear on all sides. Oh that beautifull sweetness of heart whose presence I lightly feel and see like a dim shadow that makes the soul tinged with the richness of melody. Where thou clearer to my vision what discourse of music could life be and poetry its speech.[88]

15.

Reasons for not eating Animal food

It does not feed the Spirit

It stimulates the propensities

It is taking animal life when the other Kingdoms are sufficient and better increment

Slaughter exercises the lower propensities and stimulates them

It is the chief cause of the slavery of the kitchen

It generates in the body the diseases the animals are subject to and encourages in Man their bestiality

Its odour is offensive and its appearence unaesthetick.[89]

16

Jean Paul thou lovely and beautifull soul in the transcripts from thy soul do I find nourishment for my heart, such as no other author has given unto me. Shall we never meet?[90]

24

Sunday afternoon. What shall I say   The human heart is wicked above all things. The enemy of Man is subtle and watchfull beyond conception. Instead of being on the way of goodness I am just finding out the sinfullness of my nature its crookedness its impurity and darkness. I want deep Humility and forgetfullness of Self. I am just emerging out of gross darkness and my sight is but dim so that my iniquities are not wholly plain to my vision. At present I feel as if a week of quiet stillness would be the means of opening still deeper the still flowing fountains of divine life. I would cut myself off from all relations but that of my soul with the presence of the Spirit   All other seems an intrusion wordly and frivolous. The inpouring of the Spirit is checked by so much extraneous attention to other than divine things. In the bustle and noisy confusion its voice remains unheard. I feel that one of my greatest weaknesses because it leads me to much sin is my social feelings. They keep and lead me too often into frivolous conversations away from Silence and in meditation with the Spirit. I have felt lately almost ready to say with Luther that good works are a hindrance to the gate of heaven. Self pride and approbation is so often mixed with them. I feel that there has nothing been spoken against the vain attempt to trust in good works but my soul fully accords with—this is a new a very new experience for me.

24

By practice of our aspirations ideals and visions we convert them into real being.

We should be able to say "Which of you convinceth me of sin" before we are fit to preach to others and our preaching have a practicel effect upon Society.

Did all our effort flow into realizing the teachings of the Spirit we should do much more good and be greater in the sight of God than we are now by so much speaking and writing. But let us be watchfull that the pride of good works does not take place of that of speaking and writing.

By our sins and many wickednesses we are prevented from entering in the promised land and we must die just in sight of it   Instead of being humble willing and self denying in our youth being led by the Spirit of God we keep on in the spirit of the world and give all the substance of our being in its service and when we are nearly worn out we flee to God and die perhaps only in sight of heaven instead of having been one of its inhabitants reliving it upon Earth in the full bloom and flower of our Youthfull joy of life.

It is the realization of the inspiration of God in and through us which is the Dial of our life. All other knowledge is but dross and as Paul says ''dung''. The knowledge of God is all and every thing; it is the knowledge of the mystery and secret of all things. He that knoweth God knoweth all things. Oh let us strive after a closer acquaintence with him a more intimate intercourse a more perfect union a greater confidence and trust in His almighty loving-kindness.

I would not go to Church to hear the Preacher but I would *be* at home what they that go *hear*.

The Lord has been good unto me and my heart is filled with his warm love. Blessed be thou oh God for thou hast given me a taste of thy sweetness   Thou hast awakened in me   Thou hast put into my heart gratitude and thankfullness and an over flowing heart of praise. I would stand still and shout and bless God. It is God in us that believes in God. Without the light of God we should be in total darkness and he is the only source of light.

The more of God that is in us the more we see out of us.

Thy inspiration oh God is love and wisdom   In Thee they are one in unity even as the fire which giveth light and warmth.

Thou art the true eternal food of life and he that has tasted of thee can never be at rest until he is wholly filled with thee. Lord when we are with out thee we are gone lost dead in darkness. It is in and by thy presence we live and move and have our being   Ever more oh Lord increase thy spirit in us until between Thee and us there is no more we or Thee but all in Thou oh Father   Like the fixed light in a crystal which flashes back the light of the Son. So does the soul of Man reflect God. A good life consists in passive as well as active virtues[91]   Oh Lord so fill me with thee that nothing shall be left but thee and *I* be no more   The reason why Men are perplexed and in darkness about their being and the questions which their being often asks is not that they are insoluble but the disposition and spirit in which they are attempted to solve them is so contrary to a state in which they are soluble that appear as hidden mysteries

When we come together to converse we should come to learn each other what good we ought and can do and so mingle the brightness of the light of one with the dimness of the other. Our meetings should be such that we should go away feeling that God had been with us and multiplied us in our blessings. The question should be brother can you teach me the way of the Lord in a more perfect way than in which I tread it so my soul will be increased and God will abide more and more in me   Oh he is my brother my master who leads me to do more and more good and to Love and live more of God. He that does not increase my heart in Love or my mind in true godly wisdom or to do more good than I do is unprofitable and is negatively injurious to me.

Willfullness locks up while willingness unlocks the portal to the divine mysteries of God. I would not attempt to solve a mystery by intellect but by being

28

What is Quietism? Is it not when fully carried out the Brahmanic doctrine of Annihilation of reabsorption into God instead of conversing with God   This incessant activity of Men is most devilish. I would that all Men should be made to stand motionless and still be Men. All relations that we have are evil. And I would overcome death by not coming up to it. Let us go inwards instead of outwards. I will stop writing for this is foolish and springs from a diseased irritation.

17teenth Oct. Evening.

It is sometime since I have written in this Book. All my spare time has been occupied in writing letters to my friends, meditating, feeling, arranging matters with my brothers regarding our relations with each other, and attending to the bussiness. I have had little time to read, and to visit my friends. Since I have written my feelings have become more definite, my thoughts clearer, and more distinct, and my whole mind more systematic. In my letters I have been in writing some of them rather perplexed and found it difficult to write as I wished; this arises I think from a willfullness on my part which ought to be overcome One I wrote to day to Mrs Almira ⟨Bar⟩lowe a ⟨wo⟩man I am deeply attached to in answer to the last I received from him in which he complained of the impersonal tone of my two last to him and was written in a misapprehension of my state of mind towards him   My answer was free from my heart. It came unbidden flowing freely from the fountain of life   My wish was for him to write immediately. How my letter will impress I am a little curious to know.[92] George Curtis in a letter to me his last one speaks of me as one desirous to work upon the m⟨anl⟩y etc. He has totaly misapprehended me in the view he has of my character   This I always felt in his presence   It is as it were we understood each others being but not expression. What turn our friendship will take I leave to time and circumstance to develope.[93]

In relation to the settlement which has been made with my brothers it gives me the opportunity of doing what my Spirit long demanded of me. This afternoon I have been working on their bedroom making it larger and more pleasant for their minds. This is the first movement I have made in ameliorating their condition   What the next step I may be led to take I am unconscious of but hope that God will give me strength and Goodness to continue.

I feel like asking my friends sometimes who am I?

Time is required for the heart to feel and sympathise as well as the head to think and meditate. It is in profound stillness in the depths of silence the heart communes in its depths annihilating both time and space.

Thus would I represent the different movements of the times.

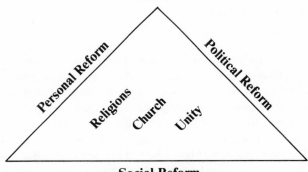

Social Reform

Under these different heads can all the movements of the day be classified. The Church is the centre the Soul of all reform all progress. The formula of the personal reformer is the denial of self, purity and chastity of life. Holiness and oneness with God. Love.

The 2nd Universal brotherhood, Equality in society in rewards of labor.

The third Equality before the state, representation of the whole, reciprocity of intercourse.

The centre, union of the fragmentary parts of the Church, Catholicity, Universal inspiration. Universal development. Harmonic progress. etc. etc.[94]

17.

Last evening I was to see Macready in Hamlet.[95]

18.

I feel this afternoon a deep want in my soul unsatisfied by my circumstances here, the same as was experienced by me last winter when I was led from this place. It is at the very depth of my being. Ah it is deeply stirred. Oh could I utter the aching void I feel within. Could I know what would fill it. Ah, Alas, nothing that can be said no nothing can touch the aching spot. In silence I must remain and let it ache. I would cover myself over with darkness and hide my face from the light. Oh could I call upon the Lord. Could I say Father. Could I feel any relationship.

19

I have attempted three or four times to answer a letter that has been sent to me and for my life I cannot do it. Why I know not but so it is. Since I receid this I have written 3 or 4 since but it appears as if my tongue is still and my heart shut when I put my hand to the paper to write   I will reattempt again this evening with the firm determination to send what ever my pen scribbles off on the paper.

26

Where does the doctrine of self denial stop; where is its end? Does it not end legitimately in the extinction of all thought, the annihilation of all sentiment, the cessation of all activity, the very doctrine of Brahmin. All activity is vicious; creation is damnation and life is synonomous with Sin. To be is answered by it in not being not to be; reabsorption into the original all for the act of separation which was the creation of thee as an individual was sin. Therefore not to be should be thy life purpose   But how not to be is the question which we have to solve? Shall we by creating and creation? Ought we not logically instantly stop all motion be still as a statue motionless as God and so end this life of creating sin. The Christian says to be; the Brahmin not to be   Which is the question? To be, or, not to be? Shall we by an act give up our life and so end the drama of lifes existence? The fact of our existence is a sin and the best and only good act we can do is to undo ourselves and so cease to be[96]

The less we want says Socrates the nearer we shall be to God. To consummate this would be to give the quietus to all wants and so be reabsorbed into him.

28

Sunday. I am restless. Could I but loose myself in something once more. Great heavens could I but utter that aching that void which panes me within. What am I? Where am I going? what is my destiny oh heavens? There is nothing that takes hold of me. I feel no relations with any one   Alone I would wander that I might loose myself in forgetfulness in some distant land.

This week back the old feeling the sudden shocks of life pass o'er me.

I am enveloped in an impenetrable mystery through which I cannot pierce in any direction. On all sides I am hemmed in by a thick mist. Most unnaturel do I feel   Oh could I retire. Good heaven what does this life mean   Am I but some one else? Who am I? What will be the end of me? Ah all is mystery past present future   Oh to be as I have and now am is most miserable. And what to do I know not. Preach resignation; what then what is it? Why not as well preach Action restlessness? I am much what the past has made me; its pregudices faith and opinions are instild in my very being even the family cast runs in my veins I am modified by all that I see   I live not in myself but become a portion of that around me   And free from all this what would I be? Great vital questions agitate my Soul   Practical questions too. Questions which if settled at all must now be settled else time and opportunity will slip through my fingers. How can I dispose of them? To those I would write to my mind will not permit. Should their friendship cease nothing I feel would now be lost for I am now nothing but the sanctuary of nothingness

Nov 1.st

Are we once born of the spirit we shall be led by it in all reforms to do and to abstain from all things which are an hindrance an obstruction to the full and complete harmonious life of the spirit in us   And he who cannot see the enemys of the spirit which he indulges proves only his own blindness consequent on his faithlessness for there is no virtue which the spirit does not teach if we would hear its whispering voice in our hearts. The miser is an outward example of what the Christian should cheerfully do from the spirit of God living within. What does not the miser do for his God Mammon? Should not the Christian be willing to do for his God, Love and Wisdom. Ah would only Christians take the example of the miser in his abstinence in his sacrificing all things to the one object. Do for the establishment of Christs kingdom upon Earth what he does for money.

4th

All things considered under any circumstances could I have more advantages of doing good and opportunity of self culture than I have here in my present position?[97]

One thing here there is too much demand on me for physical action   My heart and head have not their share of time. But when I consider I am at loss to know how we can possibly in any way diminish our bussiness without a still greater demand on us for physical labor in consequence of diminishing it.

Yesterday afternoon I whent alone in my bedroom and I was led to pray and to think what can I do for my friends around me more than what I do.

This morning I arose and prayed and felt determined not to let any outward event disturb my inward life that nothing should ruffle my inward peace and that this day I would live a day of inward life let come what would.[98]

Often I think of my past life and my present life and I feel such a strenght of emotion that I would cry aloud Oh heaven help me from my course. This is not the life I would live and I cannot endure it but Ah alas   How shall I change it?

Oh Lord willt thou guide me and lead me no matter in what pain or distress I may have to pass through to the true path which thou wouldst have me to go in. Oh I thank thee for all that thou hast in any way inflicted me. It has been to me the greatest blessing I could have received. And oh Lord chasten me more for I need it. How shall I live that I may be the best I can be under my conditions? And if these conditions in which I am placed are not the best where shall I go or how shall I change them. Teach me oh Lord and hear my humble prayer.

It is a great blindness of Men that they do not see Christ in the midst of us now leading, teaching, and exhorting us how we should live, and what we shall do. Is he not the life, the Soul, of all Christendom so far as it is better than Heathendom which state we would have been in had it not been for his influence acting on us as it has in time past and present. We are what we are through the medium of Christ the Redeemer. Take away the existence of Christ what would we have been now? Is he not so far as we are better than we would have been without him all in all?[99]

When a higher dispensation of light and love is manifested in a man he of necessity must preach condemnation to those who remain in the state they are in when they have the capacity to be what he is. Hence we have in us the latent capacity to become more than Christians which is doubtfull. He that proves us so must necessarily preach condemnation to us as unbelievers and children of hell for we are in hell compared to him.

5th Sunday afternoon.

'Tis strange that I feel the presence of Mrs Riply so near me as I have for this week back? And it is not alone her nearness to me but her oneness with me her near naturel relationship when I have not heretofore felt this at any time in her presence or otherwise? 'Tis strange and I do not know how to account for it.[100]

Man is in the midst of the spiritual world and through his imagination he communes with its inhabitants.

This morning while Wm Channing was preaching I put my hand before my eyes so that all was obscured from my sight but he preaching then I imagined he was preaching to the spirits and thought of Christs preaching to the spirits in prison. And the scene was so thrilling and affected me so that a profuse sweat came o'er me and violent nervous shocks.

Why it is? What it is? Or how it is that I feel around me the constant presence of invisible beings who affect my sensibility and as it were I converse and commune with in feeling and thought but not in expression who at times so move me that I would escape if by running away from where I am would rid me of their presence for I cannot scarcely remain still where I am. I feel like beating raving and grasping what I know not. Ah it is an unearthly feeling and painfully inflicts my heart. I would escape from it and how I know not. If I remain where I am still, it by collecting its scattered rays burns in my soul so deeply, bringing forth deep sighs groans and at times making me almost utter an unnaturel howl which to repress takes all my energy.[101]

How shall I escape this, get rid of it? Is it by remaining here and so bear and live it out or is it by travelling? The latter disposition of late has often been active in me and whether it will result in that course I know not. From such a cause I was driven last winter from home and what will be the result now is what I know not and which my curiosity would like to now know for did I now know it I would not wait until it came with such power on me as to drive me away as it did before which was painfull and torturing to the extreme. Ah what nervous strength and energy at these times I feel. Do I speak of it to my brothers they have not the same experience and they cannot understand me. My timidity of not wishing to be thought as desiring anything extra on account of my life makes me bear until it is endurable. Hence I am silent so long as it does not speak for itself which extremity might beforehand be prevented were circumstances otherwise but as they are let them be born says strength and resignation united with hope. 'Tis this that is fabled in Prometheus and Laocoon and how well fabled too.[102]

My disposition of late has been to look into the Church matters with more interest than it has for 6 months back. Last evening I made a visit to the Rev Mr Haight and conversed with him for an hour and a half on Church matters[103] We did not differ much nay very little in our opinions. If the Church of Rome had fallen into corruptions in her over warmth the Anglicans have neglected some of her duties by her coldness. And if the Anglican receives the first 5 or 6 Councils as legitimate and rejects the council of Trent as not being a full Council still as an individual I think and feel she did not establish or enjoin anything in those decrees which were not in harmony with the spirit of Christ, Scriptures and Tradition but the anglican thinks she has and hence in his judgment they are unwarrantable and not necessary.

Nov 14.

This afternoon I am very sad and sorry at heart. A sadness which no sympathy touches is on me.

15

How does Jesus commune with Humanity through the Church? Does he now commune with the Church? Was the life given to his immediate disciples by him all that has been given and transmitted to us through the Church or does he now commune with the visible Church? And how? He promised to be with his disciples even unto the end of the world. To send them the Comforter which should lead them into all truth. That he would intercede for us to the Father etc. The Church holds that its Sacraments and forms are the visible means of communing with the invisible   The answer of the Church is that there is an invisible grace imparted to the worthy receiver through the visible forms of the Church; this is her answer. Is it true that such grace is imparted? If it is it will be shown by its fruits. Contrast the Catholic who believes most in the Sacraments and the Quaker who does not believe in them at all in a religious and moral point of view. And certainly if the Sacraments have any beneficial effect it would be shown in contrast by those who totally deny their efficacy with those who religiously believe in them. Now does this contrast show what one would naturally expect to flow from the faith and doctrine of the Sacraments[104]

17

Oh Lord keep me from all wordly ambition; keep my eye singly upon Thee   Oh heavenly parent kind father give me strength to persevere in goodness selfdenial and all holy aspirations   Oh Lord I am weak wavering; willt thou give me power and firmness. Help me oh Lord to control and keep my appetites in subjection. Make me willing to be nothing for Thee. Burn out of me all earthly dross by whatever afflictions are necessary in thy sight. If I am better I know I shall see the work Thou woulds have me to do. It is because of my unworthiness and impurity that I am sorely perplexed and unsettled   Oh Lord according to thy Grace willt Thou aid me in my necessities and lead me aright.

The Lord my shepherd is. He shall my wants supply

Since I am his and he is mine. What can I want beside.

Behold the Lamb of God which taketh away the sins of the World!

Oh Lord give me the power to utter my heart.[105]

Mon 20

Men seize upon an idea become slaves to it judge and estimate all other movements opinions by it making it the catholic standard by which they judge All ideas Men and institutions.

I feel in better health than I ever have both mind and body at the same time having an increased sensitiveness so that the touch of any one I cannot bear.[106] Also I am conscious of a more constant and spiritual communion, feel more vividly and distinctly the infuence and presence, spiritual presence of others.

There are some who cannot understand you by speech others not by writing others not by your mere presence and others by your existence without regard to time or space   These are all stages of progress. The world is in the second state in that of writing and reading. Some individuals are out of it or nearly so are in the third and at time in the last state; but few tho.

The best publication a man can make is that of a pure life.

A man dare touch but should not be touched.

I lay down in my bed with the same feeling as when I awake in the morning. In one I anticipate as much as the other. The event emotions and thoughts in my sleep are to me as much of my real life as my day events etc. Wake and Sleep are two forms of existence; the latter state is full of interest to me and expectation. The two states mutually act upon each other.

Why say I have been thinking, reflecting, on this or that why not say I affirm. Is it because of thy want of faith?

Our grumbling comes much more from an indisposition to do than from a living faith.

Hope, Faith, Wish, are the presentiments of sight the evidences of becoming sight to the senses. They are the presentiments of sight the forerunners of vision. It is by these we *know*.

23

Science is but the realization of the objects seen in faith

All revelation discovery is first through the faculty of faith.

To believe is to see, not with the senses but with the higher faculties of the Soul such as reason imagination Hope etc.

Every faculty may be elevated to the state of prophecy I believe.

These two nights back my venerated and loved Grandfather has appeared to me in my dreams. The first evening he was exceedingly beautiful.[107]

Christ was the true pattern of a Man what a Man should be not in outward acts, visible conduct, but what he should be in spirit in disposition in power and glory. His outward life was affected by the nation in which he was born his parents his country his age and its peculiar virtues and vices   Therefore to copy his outward conduct would be in many respects now to deny him Spiritually; it is to have the same mind in us as was in him that we should aim for.

Reasoning is faith struggling with doubt.

I should like to read a chapter of faith without doubt, it would be a pure flowing stream of Prophecy.

I have doubts of the common notion of immortality because I have a dim insight into a different one and also because my own personality is a mystery to me. In me I feel conscious that my forparents exist, live, and have a part of my being. Much of my existence is their life. In me they realize themselves. And what may I be but they? And the future coming but me? The ideal of the past is now actualized—the ideal of the present will be actualized in the future. Hence the meaning of the word progress. I have the same feelings thoughts and do the same deeds in mind as my progenitors did before me   Am I not them and they me? Does not the mother sympathise in joy sorrow in all the variety of life with her offspring hence live in them and her life is kindred or give let to as the life of her children is? The life of Men is One. What mean we by individuals?

Mond 27 half past 5 o clock in the morning

Great God what is our destiny? What are *we*. Our individuality what is it? Have we an individuality only as united in one or are we separate beings who commenced being when we were born upon this Earth? It is inconceivible that we should have commenced being at the time we were born upon this planet. Who can believe it? How can that have a commencement which has no end and if we did exist before how did we exist? Is our spirit generated the same as our flesh and Adam the parent of all our being. Do not facts prove this. In Adam we all lived and sinned fell. Does not this bear testimony to the fact that our spirits are begotten. Like begets like and many other such common sayings prove the same fact. Does the past live in the present and will the present live in the future? Most assuredly if the present gives birth to the future which it always does for without that there would be no future. As much so as the parent lives in the child. But is the parent lost or does it wholly exist in the child? What is generation? Is the parent any the less for generation? Does it make any difference whether the man is as regards his immortality a parent of 6 children or childless or a celibate? But does not the celibate beget in another form what the parent does? What does the parent beget in children but love wisdom in a word all that is in himself? Does not the celibate beget the same in only a different embodiment? He influences and lives in other Men in all that he influences and his life exists in those objects he has influenced and communed with. But if we influence others do they not equally influence us? If all thats around me is a portion of me is it not equally true that I am a portion of it? Most assuredly. Then I do not loose but gain in being by living. Therefore instead of loosing myself in the objects I commune with I gain and increase my life. Precisely so. But such communion I constantly change my life my being and I am not one moment what I was before hence my *me* is changed my immortality is in my progress (God be blessed) and my identity is in my life and that is in Jesus Christ who brought light and immortality to life. To sum up my immortality is in my identity but identity is only I am I this moment   This is all I can affirm of myself   This is all that needs be affirmed. This gives me progress and immortality whereas if there were no progress or change in the identity Man would make no progress and every change would be a loss instead of a gain as it now is.

Dec. 2. Sat.

My heart these two days back has been filled with love. Oh had I some one to whom I could unbosom myself. There is a some thing which affects my heart invisible and to me strange.

I will not feed my body with impure food. Is it not of infinite more importence that I should not feed my spirit with deeds of impurity? By this I mean my gaining a living by the making and selling such articles as are in my judgment injurious being luxurious and alltogether unnecessary? Should I cease from doing that which is contrary to my spirit—what should I do? I confess the way of duty is not plain to me. Oh Lord enlighten thou my path. My only aim oh Lord is to be guided and to fulfill the Spirit. Nothing oh Lord am I willing to be as I am. I see that thou art all in me and oh God subdue that which remains yet of myself.

Dec 6.

Day before yesterday morning I fasted took a good cold shower bath.

My diet is apples potatoes nuts and unleavened bread. No water scarcely a mouthful a week.

I can scarce keep my heart from writing to Almira this evening. I feel that is near to my heart. What positions will we occupy in the future? I can scarcely think we will be so far apart as we now are.

I feel neither like reading writing or thinking but being perfectly still.

A feeling heart prevents one from being studious.

This thought occurred to me the other day   Mans progress is slow. Why? Because no Man raises himself alone   His life is one with all. Hence he is burthened with their sins; their weight is upon his shoulders and it is only by miraculous power he can rise with all the sins of humanity upon his shoulders. Here in lies the explanation of the truth that Christ took all the sins of humanity upon him and suffered for them on the Cross. The innocent suffered was a sacrifice for the guilty. Oh ungrateful blind hardened humanity The love of Christ should have made thee cry aloud. The heavens should echo your heartful gratitude from the depth of love which you beheld in Christ. Oh what is so ungrateful as the heart of Man. Ah the stones would cry aloud had they but the power to speak. God forgive us if such ingratitude can be forgiven if it is possible love can be so deep so great as our ingratitude. Oh Lord my heart is choked from the utterance of its depth of thankfulness. Oh Dear Christ   Oh sweet Christ   Oh loving Christ   Oh more than brother friend   Oh more than any other being can be   Oh thou Son of God   Oh thou who showed forth the pure love of God. Oh thou inexpressible love   Oh draw me nearer to thee; let me feel more of thy love more of thy purity   Oh baptize me with thy spirit and loosen my tongue that I may speak of thy love to Man   Oh thy love cannot be spoken nor can our hearts feel the greatness of thy love. God what is thy mercy that thou sufferest us to live: Our ingratefulness is too Great to be uttered. Lord I am silent for who can speak in thy presence. Lord Lord   Oh Father   Oh Love Love Loving kindness   My heart would fly away.[108]

Dec 9th.

I cannot say I have made up my mind as yet to live. This is perhaps because I have not found the object of my existence. In ten days I shall have lived 23 years on this earth with my present memory and shall I be left without an object? Shall I live objectless?[109]

It is one of the highest states that a human being can be in is to live without a conscious or perceptible object but with perfect peace and quietness. When the veil shall have been lifted up from our present life by our "new birth" we shall see that he that has lived as the lilies of the valleys grow is most beautifull good & true and that the chronic desire of consciously doing something springs from a partiality a smallness somewhere a deficencie in somewhat. Oh could we see God in all his loveliness and beauty it would form and stamp our soul into his image and we should see nothing but him   There are Angels happy hopeful beautiful. Why should we not be so? I see no rewards or punishments anywhere, in what ever a Man does: that he is, and is so; if we could understand this we should understand all. Disobedience is its own punishment. The parent tells the Child not to do this or that not because it consults its own will but because it sees the hurtfulness and misery which it may cause. God inflicts no punishment. We are our own executioners   God gives us life and says here make it into what form you may but mind it is no frivolous play   You may surround yourself with the blue heavens the bright stars the pale moon the bright sun with the green earth beautiful flowers loving spirits beautiful Angels   And you may also turn all these into demons and hideous sights and make all things around thee a hell. Be an Artiste or a Devil.

Dec 14.

When I cast my eyes back it seems to me that I have made some progress that I have grown somewhat better than I was. Thoughts feelings & passions which were active in my bosom whose character were not to be well spoken of in truth have disappeared and given place I hope to a better state of mind. Altho my present state of mind is far from what I would have it to be, it is where I never anticipated it would be.

How am I now actualizing my spiritual life? this would be hard for me to say at this moment. Am I less willful? do I sacrifice more than I did? Am I more loveing? I am afraid at this moment that I am doing nothing more than I did. And therefore, did I take up this book to give an account of myself. Study takes up the best part of my time most generally   I say a lesson in the Latin & German every day and now intend to study the English Grammar again and then I read considerable and write letters to my friends. This with the time I have to spend in bussiness does not give me sufficient time to meditate   And here there is no opportunity for me to go into a retired silent place where I can be perfectly still. The last has the most internal effect on me and the best and most lasting. Two things I should and must do for my own souls sake; speak less and think less of my friends   This will give me a retired place and an opportunity for silence in the midst of all that is around me.[110]

I feel as if I am not doing anything for to ameliorate the social condition of those around me under my influence and partial control   Just now it seems there is a stand still in this direction. The Spirit promises to teach us in all directions. What would it have me to do more in this work? what should be my next step? My mind has been drawn partially off from this on account of the present poor state of bussiness which keeps us cramped in our funds. I have a fear of doing with less food than what I now do with for fear of injuring my health or else I should fast often. To day let me put in practice the two above mentioned duties silence and less thought upon my friends   And now Oh God if Thou helpest not I shall be worse than before. Heavenly Father as the flower depends upon the light and warmth of the sun for its growth and beauty much more do I depend upon Thee for life and progress. Oh Lord from the depths of my heart I would implore Thee to give me strength to aid me in all good intentions   Oh my heart overflows with its fullness of gratitude for what Thou hast done for me   And I know Thou willt not shorten thy hand or lessen Thy love. Therefore if I will come in an humble contrite and child like disposition Thou willt give me more of thy Grace and Truth. Lord let me see more of Thee. Open thou more of my vision   Give me a purer heart. Let me rest wholly upon thee   Make me feel this. Oh Lord I feel this is but the struggle of my soul to see Thee more completely and help Thou it in its attempts. Thy beauty

Thy loveliness oh God is beyond our finite vision far above our expression
and Lord all I can utter is help my weakness.[111]
Thanksgiving Day 5 oclock in the morning

This is my 23 d. Birth day.[112] And what have I been doing worthy of
my age? Alas I cannot point to anything   Oh God Thou knowest what my
heart is and what my circumstances have been and to Thee and to Thee only
do I look for guide encouragement and a Friend who knowst my secret
thoughts all my longings difficulties and trials. Oh Heavenly Parent willt
Thou fullfil all my wishes which are according to Thy Wisdom and Goodness. Oh awaken me to a higher Sense of existence; give me strength to
Love to live as one who was made in Thy own image. Oh Lord Thou
wouldst have honesty sincerity and uprightness in all our conduct and especially towards Thee: we know that we cannot hide anything from Thee
where ever we would go Thou art there before we. therefore Oh Lord forgive me the utterance and disposition of my blind and doubtless ungrateful
Heart. Tho I should feel grateful for every gift even the smallest that comes
from Thy hand yet oh Lord forgive me I cry   I do not feel grateful for the
greatest of all gifts the gift of life   How can I be grateful without seeing
or feeling that this life of mine is of some use to some object or is in itself
beautiful and has its own object in expressing itself? Alas Alas I see not;
my heart aches and I have no hope. There is nothing that can releive my
pain or answer to my wants. Oh Great God Thou art full of kindness and
loving-mercy. Willt Thou remove the hindrances in me to the inflowing of
Thy Spirit Love and Wisdom.

I have very great reason when I look back to be grateful to Thee for
what Thou hast done for me and while I am not thankful for life in itself
still I am silenced with emotion when I reflect where I was and where I now
am   Instead of being cramped by poverty obliged to walk the streets selling radishes and berries for which Oh Lord above all things I feel grateful,
I am now at least comfortable conditioned within the circles of persons who
I can call my friends who I never had the idea of being able to call so. Oh
Lord how much ought I to feel grateful for!

This being my birth day if I could I should like to give an account of
myself so as to walk the steps I may be led to take in the future but this at
the present moment is impossible. My mind is not putting forth any project
and what I am principelly doing is giving Culture to the Spirit which God
has given me.
Half past four on the 18 of December '43

                                                        25 Christmass.

I have written to Georgia an invitation to come here and if it is harmonious for her to be here for her to stay. I have just finished a letter to

Almira; it is now about 8 in the evening. This afternoon I whent to see Orson Murray of Vt.[113]

What so we see in the two most protestant countries of Christendom England and America but a strong vigorous reaction of protestant individualism to catholic unity. Men and Women affirming with great emphasis that Man is not an isolated being an individual by himself etc. etc.

31st December Sunday. Aft.

This almost past year I cannot cast back a glance upon without moving my heart. How different! how changed! Alas I may say what pain suffering and bitter anguish has passed through my bosom! This time last year I was at my dear friend OA Brownson residence filled with an unknown spirit driven from home by it and like one intoxicated not knowing who I was where or what why or wherefore I was so troubled and the influence of which tho regulated still is none the less power-ful (as my experience these two days back has proven to me)

From O A Bs I whent to Brook Farm remained there nine or less months and then whent to Fruitlands and staid there 3 or 4 week and was then induced to come home by the willingness of brother John to do anything in his power for any object I might have in view.[114]

Here I have been for now about 5 or 6 months and alas here I am now not so restless nor so chaotic as I was but ah not without an unbareable almost pain at heart and nervous excitability.

I have felt this month somewhat like a more peaceful and restful disposition here than I have this year or two back. I have said to myself the reading of books the hearing of great artistes in the City the seeing of friends and the study of some branches of Literature and Science do keep me active on all sides combined with the social reforms in the family and the interest I take in the religious aspect of the times hence I feel more settled than heretofore   A greater liberty has been given to my life. What I yet require is a room to myself wherein I can study write and be alone.

I have not the integrity of soul the nerve as yet to give an account of myself to myself still I have a growing disposition to do so and hope I shall before long: that is to say the vices sins and cloaked iniquities of my nature not the virtues and what ever these may be of good in me.

Tho I feel and hold Christ to be to me the highest conception I have of God still his naturalness his humanity impresses me more and more. His influence for good has been incomparable more upon Humanity than any other object in the Universe yet I have a growing disposition to reckon him in the same but the highest in the category of such men as Pythagoras Socrates Plato Zeno Epicurus.[115]

My restlessness proceds perhaps from the want of time for greater intellectual activity and in being without objects of sentiment to commune with. Man to be even able to live I will not say happy but even to be willing to accept life must be in such conditions wherein the three (so far as analysis has gone) element of his nature shall find such activity as is not to him painful or repulsive. Those elements are intelligence sentiment activity.

Since I wrote the above this afternoon I asked my brths John and George the question if there was anything in our relations with each other which hindered or other wise prevented them from actualizing their characters which they must feel is their duty and destiny. John said he desired greater order in our bussiness relations which could only be produced by an authority which would seem to us tyrannical. This on my part I disputed and said I should feel it my duty to submit to any authority which had for its object such as he stated and should not consider it as tyrannical because it was not personal but would have to object if it caused me to give up any principel. The conversation ended in this. He took the side of treating the men in our employ with rigor and as servants   And me the side of treating them with goodness and as far as possible as brethern. I spoke of myself as my disposition demanded more time for intellectual and Moral activity. George had nothing to say for himself.

I am now reading Goethe's *Dichtung und Wahrheit* which I have read in the English but am much more interested in it in the German. It is now nearly a year since I read his *Wahlverwandtschaften* and it has left an indelible impression upon my memory and every day I see clearer in the truth of its subtle principles. Men may say what they may about the tendency and influence of its principles still they are none the less true civil or well considered.

While at B. F. I read *Werter* in the German not having read it before then and just at that period there was much in it which I deeply sympathized with and now in reading the D. W. I can perceive the reason for it it being written in such a period or like it in which I was then passing through.[116]

Jan 3. A.M.

How can it be expected that Men should be beautifuller nobler better than what they are, surrounded as they are by unaesthectick uninspiring and vulgar objects which are constantly before their senses affecting them in the worst manner. Ugliness discord and ungracefulness are all about us instead of their affirmative side. The *subject* may be ever so pure noble and musical is here surrounded with opposite *objects* which he is by his nature necessitated to commune with; he will become comparatively impure ignoble and discordious.

P.M.

Difficulties afflictions are given to measure the degree of our happiness, tho too often they prove too much for us and wound us, we are so weak.

There is much in Greaves' *Affirmations* that is akin to Goethes *Elective Affinities.*[117]

Greaves my present impressions lead me to say told more and higher truth to his age than any other man of his time.

Jan

The measure of injustice that we do unto ourselves is the measure of injustice that is done unto us by others.

This thought was impressed upon my mind this morning in considerring some remarks made by the men we have in our employ.

By doing injustice to our own true Nature we place ourselves in such conditions in which we must bear suffering pain and injustice with the deprivation of our liberty so far as we have voluntarily done our true nature injustice. Every sin that we commit every virtue we omit we are weakened and deprived of that strength which it is our privelege to have and to enjoy. Every evil that Society inflicts upon me the germ of it is in me and as I free my-self from my vices will I free myself from the evils which Society is filled and punishes me with.

Be true to thyself and it follows as the night the day thou can'st not be false to anyone, *verite egale*   Be true to thyself and it follows as the night the day others cannot be false to thee.

Sunday. A M.

Society in protestendm seems to me to present quite a different aspect than what it does to many of my friends who believe in Association Communism etc. It exhibits the spontaneous elements of progressed humanity in an unorganized unsystematic form. Catholicism is humanity becoming in an organized order.

Protestant countries are showing forth if one may so speak to the external world the internal phenomena of the soul of the Church without order form or sacredness. All living protestants are now demanding what is already in an organized institution in the Catholic Church. The different Societies institutions and unions in the Catholic Church are the naturel developement of the needs of Men under the influence of the Christian dispensation and so long as Men remain under that dispensation they will respond to their pressing wants. Protestantism having destroyed these institutions etc. has destroyed the object of many and it may be said the most devout and religious portion of her Community; and Men are now seeking or the needs are now making demands for them in the shape of reorganization of Society, Fourirism, Communism, No-Property etc. Those who do this would deny such an interpretation they believing that it is a general a radical an universal reform of all Society that must take place whereas I cannot perceive this but only the necessary object for a portion of society which do not find their object in society as it is. This idea of universal reform has been in the minds of all reformers and founders of sects in Christendom from Fox down to Joes. Smith and the last gives a greater evidence of success than any of his worthy progenitors.[118] Every project of reform has had universality for its object and not one but what has prophecied the down fall of that old Babylon of the Apocalypse but there she still stands high imposing now more so than ever conscious of her character and claims abiding in full hope and faith the events of providence simply with all becoming modesty   I will enunciate my faith and that is I do not believe that any one Man can give the whole Science of Humanity.

As well might we expect an universal reform to spring from an idea of an association or community by one Man as from a painting or a symphony of an Artist.

We should never forget that all the judgments that we make whatsoever are individual judgments.[119]

Jan 20.

It seems that here and in other protestant countries the laity have turned ministers of Christs Spirit and the Clergy have passed into the laity. When Men find a demand made in the laity for a higher and more christian life in the people that is preached up to them in the pulpits it is no wonder that they have no disposition to unite themselves with such a body.

Unless the Priests are above the people in Christian Spirit in love and good works the people will soon disregard them.

The Church is not in sufficient advance of the people to attract the best Men the Men who seek to realize a better life into her bosom.   .

The Church does not hold up to Humanity the ideal of Christianity.

There are those who have more of Christs Spirit out of the visible church than those in her bosom, in fact as a general rule reform has passed from the Church into secular parties.

Instead of the Church being in head and front of advancement suffering martyrdom for Christ she is in a conservative relation with society.

The purest Gospel is taught out of the Church.

We do not say that the Church is not doing a work and that she has not done much for us that is the present church but She stops half way. She would have you to be without being Christians.

The Church is a great Almoner but what is she doing for to ameliorate and improve the circumstances of the poorer and more numerous classes?

She is more passive than active.

We speak of the Church in the sense she is exhibited by her bishops and Clergy etc. And we speak of her as we do only in this sense.[120]

Sund. Jan 28. '44

I saw a man with bowed down head in deep contemplation with himself and one passing by said behold God thinking himself.

I saw upon a pedestal in the Great Pantheon of Gods the Devil and Men passing by looked up to him and passed on.

We call that philosophy or Metaphysics which looks at truth from a subjective stand point—this leads to Idealism rather Egoism.

We call that Theology or Religion which contemplates truth as objective—this leads to Quietism self annihilation.

The first makes Men Gods, the last makes God Men.

The first apotheoses Man, the last leads to Pantheism.

Shakespere speaks of death with such fear and sense of its awfulness because he felt the reality of life in all its realness.

29

Man is the union of *body soul* and *spirit*. From the life of the body to that of the soul there is a passage a new birth, from that to the Spirit a still greater birth. Some Men are not clearly conscious of a soul   More are not conscious of a Spirit—*the Spirit*.

The Soul is the garment of the Spirit   The Body is the garment of the Soul.

If we are born body Soul and Spirit we most of us often fall as far as in the body looseing all knowledge of the other two. Few if any preserve any knowledge or consciousness of the Spirit; not many preserve the recollection or feel the conscious presence of Soul. Most Men live in the body, not in the Spirit in and through the Soul and body.

The battle between the Soul and Spirit is much greater than that between the body and Soul. It is the breaking of every bone and muscle in the body and the snapping asunder all the humane ties of the Soul.

He that is of the Spirit is of the Spirit.

The Spirit is *in us*. It is evidence of our fall this recognition. All that we are endeavoring to do is to regain what we have lost. From this day I date a clearer vision.

My being is full but must now stop.

Feb. 7th.

We ever should be in our trinity Spirit Soul and Body in unity.

The Circles the plates in the *Seherin von Prevost* of life was to me when I read the book and saw the desriptions which she drew unintelligible then about a year ago at B. F. but now they seem to me plain and intelligible and very important and profound. [121]

Looking back upon what I wrote in the first part of this book I find I can read what I then wrote tho I did not then know what I was writing.

Feb 15

It is some lapse of time since I have penned a thought in here.

Taking the three branches of History which seems to have had the greatest influence upon modern civilization Hebrew Greek & Roman we find that our present life is a mixture of all three. Constantly are protests made unconsciously against the exclusive Hebrew tendency of our Religion. The Roman Catholic Church unites it seems the forms & ceremonies of all the ancient Cultus especially the Buddhistic. Christianity seems to me more like the religion of Humanity than the product exclusively of Palestines soil.

The Shakers   I have or am now reading a book called the "pasttime of Shakerism." It gives me much light on the subject of the tendency of the human mind in all Ages when utterly denying all physical instincts from the point of their excesses and abuse to fall into the opposite extreme of spiritual licentiousness of intoxication. Such seems to be the fact with all modern spiritual sects.

19.

The Lord be merciful to me and forgive all my offences. As I am finite I sin. Increases my finiteness that I may embrace more of Thee oh Lord. Infuse in my Soul more and more of Thy love. Oh may my Souls capacities for thee be enlarged. Tho I am nothing yet will I be contented and satisfied if Thou willt fill my small vessel with thy Glory. If I would be greater it is that I might containe more of thy Love and Light   It is us oh Lord I know that place hindrences in our Souls to Thee. Lead me oh to remove them from thy Sight. Heavenly Father teach and counsel me as a child. May all presumption willfulness and worldly ambition be purged out of me with Thy pure love.

Oh Lord let me say that I am Thine.

Let my soul be as free from stain or any shadows as when it first came from Thy hands that there may be nothing but Thee in it. My sense of nothingness makes me feel the stronger That Thou art all and makes me feel the need of Thee and nothing else. Make me worthy of Thy Gifts. If Thou showerest down thy blessings upon us what will they be to us unless our Souls are prepared to receive them   Prepare my Soul for Thee and thy blessings oh Kind Good Parent.

29.

Georgiana came here a week ago last tuesday.

Can the soul be wedded to God and humanity at the same time? The Spiritualist says no.[122] If not then how can we be at all for if the past had been true to such an idea the present evidently could not have been. Shall Men ever be great enough not to act. Would it be greater not to act or no? Where should we have been where will the future be did we cease and had others ceased from activity? There is nothing lost in the Universe. Is this life humane life a good & blissful gift or a penalty? Some will say yes others no. But are the affirmatives in a condition to answer? They see no better perhaps, hence from their point of view it is the best.

If I shall exist after my Soul has seperated itself from this material body have I not existed before having been united with it? Is not this the reason of having lost the consciousness of a former life the taking of this fleshy body? It is a remarkable saying of Christs that He had taken and had power to lay down and to retake his body!! Should we not have the same power if we were purified by God as he was? Is not an union with God an eternal fact? If Christ had this power, power over death & life in this existence is it not possible for us? Should we not hope for the highest that has been done in Man? Perhaps we are and have always what we really have the faith in. Man in his darkness sees not himself. The condition of power is that of light and goodness.

As we pertake of God in his Spirit we perticipate in his love wisdom & power.

Oh Lord fill my soul with Thee. Not as it is can this be; therefore remove all darkness and stain from my soul.

To deny all other relations but the union with God is this our whole full decision of our Soul? Are our relations with humane beings and with material nature in themselves vicious degrading? Are these the leaden weights that are hung to our feet keeping us from our divine abode   It does seem to me the significance of the denial is this that the relations we have sustained in this respect were low and degrading in our present view of them but can we not have a possible divine relation with Nature & Man? Or should we give up these relations in order to be in conditions to receive higher relations which await those who give them up. Assuming Jesus Christ as the pattern the example of what we should be which Christians hold him to be of certain neccessity these relations should be cut off for in none of them did he enter. We must either place Christ in the rank of many Spiritual men and Reformers or deny with Him all these relations.

March. 8

My life is becoming more practical. I am now much occupied in my mind regarding my position and purpose in life so far as any seems to have been given to me. It seems that a bussiness life has very little hold upon me.

My nature will be half lived out if I submit myself to these relations. I am here now in body but not in spirit. The greater part of my true life is lost in my present position. Thoughts feelings and study which would oc- cupy my mind if I had my own course are so far as my time is occupied with them are so almost by stealth   I am neither living in the bussiness nor am I making much progress in my studies. In this case I do not benefit others nor do I see that I am much benefited. This should change. One of the two must cease as an object. The first has not been nor is it now or does it seem possible for it to be ever my aim in life. What then shall I do? And *how* shall the end in view be accomplished?

One great difficulty seems to be this: I cannot place any definite pur- pose before my mind and bend all my energies to its accomplishment   I am willing to be true submissive selfdenying self sacrificing for the Spirit of my nature but

10. At the above line I was called away.

10.

Since the above I have made up my decision of giving up my life my time to study for the field of the Church. I have written a letter to O A Brownson to ask his advice and counsel and much of my course will be influenced by his opinions.[123]

The devotion to study the difficulties the many anxieties waverings and almost renouncing of my plans in the future are now present to my mind but still I see no other way than to be faithful and go on.

It is certainly an individual importence the decision one makes which must effect his whole future life. It seems to me I am not accomplishing anything here in my present position life which adds much to the benefit of others or is of much advantage to my owns soul.

When I look around and see other young men what they are doing I feel encouraged to go on but when I look into myself I am ready to drop down in my weakness and give up all life all purpose all aim of being. Alas, Alas, faith-courage-trust-energy-hope is all that I can utter. Is it not so that any step of importence is always taken in faith in the invisible power which rules our destiny? Oh for that humbleness oh for that humility which knows no fear no doubt no mistrust. Action perseverance application these with a life in God will be more than promises. When I look around me and see so many of those who I am acquainted with, friends too now have given up what it is now my purpose to live labor and suffer for it almost turns my hope in to doubt & my courage into fear.

Which Church the Roman or Anglican? To which it is my duty to unite myself I am not fully settled upon. This I will have to leave to a future decision. Whether to prepare myself to enter in a College or to put myself under the direction of a well qualified clergyman who will direct my studies and make up for me in other ways what I am deficient in is not fully settled in my mind but the latter method seems to me the best way.

17 Sunday.

I have written a leter to Rev Mr Norris,[124] Carlisle, penn. with the purpose of knowing from him whether he would become a tutor to me. An answer to the one I wrote O.A.B. I have rec'd. He gives me hearty encourgement to go on in the purpose that is in me.

With the letter I wrote to Mr Norris Rev B F Height wrote one to introduce mine.

My plans seem to be much clearer and much more definite. Every day serves to increase my settled and fixed purpose of devoting myself to the interest of the Church.

I would be faithful truthful and sincere and the end the results of my undertaking leave to the wisdom of God. He has given me a being (for which I begin to be unfeignedly thankful)   The law of my duty is to be true to the energies faculties he has bestowed upon it. This is my duty. If I do my duty His Providence will watch for the results. I feel like giveing myself wholly up to His Care. Such peace calmness and deep settled strength and confidence I have never experienced as now seems to have been given me. There is no other cause of evil than *our* submission to it. Did we shut up our bosoms from all evil influences God would reign wholly and supreme in our breasts.

We want reverence in the place of self-confidence.

All Men are not equal in all their capacities therefore the need of listening and mutual submission.

For want of true reverence Nature Man and even God fail to instruct some persons.

Submission to the higher the highest is an honour to he who submits and he who submits is he who gains most.

He who submits voluntarily to the Good and the True needs no law but alas where is the one who does this in all things? Oh Lord teach me when to submit and all things will be then given to me.

Self submission to God is the highest act of Man. We honor ourselves not God in our submissiveness.

He that will not be provoked to anger by anger tho he can justify himself according to law is greater than he who overcomes anger by anger.

Integrity is more to be prized than any happiness gratification or desire. We should rather part with this bodily existence than the integrity of our Soul.

Freedom consist in submitting to the Spirit of God not in the denial of God and his laws.

He that would do his age and the future a certain permanent good must seek the laws of the progress of Humanity of the great purpose of the Race build upon and continue that which has been built in the Past by the good and wise on these laws; and tho Men should for a moment in history forget these when they come back to their senses they must take up where you have left and continue the *great designed work of the Race.*

Reading, Music, is only so far permanently refining and elevating as we make what we read and hear our own.

I feel the need of travelling to *establish* the breadth of thought & feeling which now exists in me.

I cannot imagine the domestic comforts the little offices of tender love which are now filled that I will loose by going from home to study.

Tho we purpose ever such a clear probable and most likely plan before us how unlooked and unimagined end may it all end in.

Some Men act more wisely than others but God is omniscient.

22.

I feel the presence of God where ever I am. I would kneel and praise God in all places. In His presence I walk and feel his breath encompass me. My Soul is bourn up on his presence and my Heart is filled with His influence. How thankful ought we to be! How humble and submissive! Let us lay our heads on the pillow of peace and die peacefully in the embrace of God.

The performance of duties is the means of opening the portals of heavenly blessing.

How cheerfully ought we to accept all the duties which are opened to us! How richfully we are blessed with life from good actions!

Alas is there no such thing as continuous peacefull progress? Must the Future be always built upon the ruins of the Past? Has not the Race a growth the same as the individual? Or is war necessary to precede all change? Must the Son discard the dwelling his Father has built for him or make use of it as stuff to a new Tempel? When shall the time come when nothing shall be uselessly done and the child shall be enriched by the fruits of the Parents and so be advanced by the labors of the past beyond the point from which his progenitors started? This would be building to some purpose. We are enriched by the past as the succeeding generation will be enriched by our labors but Alas how much is needlessly wasted?

Sin seems to me to be like a great mountain of darkness before us on which all true souls are laboring to excavate it. I feel like making my impress upon it.

I read yesterday something I had written just a year ago at B. F. The same purpose was then at work in me that now is at work but now it is more definite clearer and I have more strength and fixidness. It has grown with my growth and increased with my strength and now it seems as if the time had arrived when the step which is to decide the purpose is to be took. God direct me.

I was on wednesday to see Bishop Hughes of the R.C. Church for the purpose of getting information of the facilities if any which the R.C. Church presents to a person in my position. He stated to enter the priesthood it was first necessary that the person should have been least two years a member of the Church and then it depended upon the opinion of his priest whether he was fit and had the capacity to be a worthy Priest before he could be admitted to enter the order with the intention of becoming a Priest of the C Church. He said that their Church was one of discipline. I thanked him for the information that he gave and said it was just for such information that I sought him because he seemed to think I had inborn protestant notions of the Church.

So far this settles my present intention of uniting myself with R.C. Church. Tho I feel not in the least disinclined to be governed by the most rigid discipline of any Church yet I am not prepared to enter the R.C. Church at present. The R.C. Church is not national with us hence it does not meet our wants nor does it fully understand and sympathise with the experience and dispositions of our people. It is principally made up of adopted and foreign individuals.[125]

25.. *Mon.*

What are the objects of life which are presented to the young men of our time? The Church the State and Social schemes which are now presented to us. Those who have certain and promising intellectual gifts for poetry painting etc. are naturally from inherent impulse and conscious power led to the goal of their life destined purpose. Every true gift and true being tho not having for their aim the conscious purpose of benefitting the Race all lead and tend to help the advancement of Humanity. Tho we may not have been given all equal gifts nor of the same kind nevertheless we all have a worthy and real purpose in our being and the realisation of this reality in us is the highest and noblest work that we can here perform. Why should we murmur or feel mortified at the capacities God has given us that they are not greater? It is God's work not ours. Rather let us seek to make use of these capacities in the noblest way possible for us and if there is any shame or disgrace in us doing all that we can do who should have it? certainly not us and if not we who should the Creator be ashamed of?

Let us not be daunted by comparing ourselves with others nor be puffed up in so doing. God has given us an individual life which he has not given to any other. This individuality let us live. Why should we fear the judgments of Men　　Are these always the judgments of God? I fear not. Let us walk fearlessly before Men which we will do if we are pure before God and are sure of his confidence. Be true to God and we cannot fear.

Let us acknowledge our weaknesses our want of certain talents capacities gifts. Let us do all this. Let us take the lowest seat in the Temple. Let us be subjects not governors and submit rather than rule be despised rather than honored. This we will all do and more if we have the sure conviction in us that God is with us. But without God we are cowards false and proud. We must forsake all relations and be about our Father's work to do in us. This is proof of our mission that we give up all for God. That which we love we cling to, and if we love the pleasures of the body more than the delights of the soul, the communion with God, then shall we live in the body in this world and far from God. Let us give up to the Spirit and it will move us in the right direction. He that follows the Holy Spirit is never led astray. When the Holy Spirit leads us all our paths will be paths of pleasantness and all our ways be ways of peace.

I feel anxious and would be about doing something to further the purpose of my being but am kept in indecision waiting for an answer from Rev Mr Norris.

27

The Church holds up the ideal of glorified Humanity—Christ—as the object the goal of Man's Aspirations and the preaching of her divines and her ceremonies are the means to excite Men constantly to this highest ideal which the Race can possibly realize. She not only holds up before the vision of Men the perfect pattern of the God-Man but she also imparts virtue to their hearts that they may attain to the same holy state of being. This ideal of the Church is not the ideal of Man as he is now but as he was before Adam sinned hence it is not produced by Men but has come down from Heaven, "it was sent". It springs not out of the nature of Man (subjective) but it is God manifested in the flesh to us (objective). And it is only as we commune with this objective ideal we become inwardly formed into a new pattern after the form of Christ Jesus.

30

I have rec'd from Rev Mr Norris a reply to the letter I sent him. His letter was very frank kind & instructive. The frankness of it quite astonished me. He writes me to come and see him & make his house my home while there. He wished me to get a letter from Dr Seabury which he wrote in reply to some strictures made by a R. C. Catholic paper on his letter to A Sincere Enquirer. Mr Haight gave me a note of introduction to Dr Seabury   I called to see him two evenings ago and had a very pleasant conversation with him. His socialbelness and perfect openness of expression of his opinions I was quite delighted with. He frankly acknowledged that he thought that there had error been committed on both sides in the controversy of the Reformation between the Pope and the Anglican Church. He recommended me to examine those points which kept me from joining the Anglican or Roman Church before I should do anything further. As there were the charge of schism against the Anglican Church and Her neglect of discipline in Her communion. I told him the Church of R. may commit errors in practice; they had not committed any in principel and that it was easier to prune a luxuriant tree than to re-vivify a tree almost exhausted of life. I left him with an earnest invitation to call again with the letter of Mr Norris. Since then I have read Norris letter; it is aimed at Lutheranism almost exclusively   It attempts to show that the Catholic doctrine of the Sacraments is rejected by all the real protestant sects. He sent me a letter written in reply to the president of Dickenson College against Methodism. I think it is very probable   I shall write him an acknowledgment of the reception of his kindnesses and go to see him when Easter is over as he writes me to do.[126]

As Mr Norris is not prepared to accept the office of Tutor towards me I have thought of going to Concord under George Bradford to learn the Greek & Latin languages of him. I have written to my friend O.A.B. for his advice *where* it would be best for me to go and have submitted the above proposition to him. What his answer may be I am not sure of but I expect that he will not aggree with my proposition on account of the transcendental influence in Concord and that he will advise me to follow some other plan however of this I am not sure & on Mon or Tues I expect an answer from him. Geo B.[127] I have not asked if he would be willing therefore it still would not be a matter of certainty if even he should accord to the plan.

Introspection is not all that is needed for a true Culture. Our Culture must or should be as well objective as subjective. We must make ourselves accquainted with History & the facts of other Mens consciousness as well as our own. We must perceive before we can reflect. There is an outward world we have to become accquainted with as well as the spiritual inward world however the latter may be above the former. A good knowledge of History will prevent us from falling in to many Errors which ignorence would make us very liable to—which otherwise we would commit. Many lives are spent in vain worse than vain—injuriously—which a better knowledge of history would have saved and placed the individual on the eternal basis of truth and caused his life to be a great benefit to his Race instead of a Curse.

Almira has not written to me now in a month. It makes me smile for I cannot account for it. What does it mean? he cannot be sick in that case he would let me know in some way or other. I cannot have offended him— it is not in my nature—I never have offended any one to my knowledge[128] I do not see how possible I could. I mean no evil to anyone. And if I speak at any time so as to offend I am willing to repair and confess my fault if told. I don't want to do wrong, nor give occasion for cold or ill feeling in any ones bosom: No, Alas, one, but one tender emotion of love increased in the bosom of any poor human being by my influence is my greatest delight and joy. I have been absorbed in the plans that are before me and very probably what I have written to her has not shown that interest—love—as what I have previously written to her. If I knew that she desired to cut off all communication with me I would resign myself to it not I confess without a deep struggle and considerable effort but I could and would do it, still, this would not diminish my attachment nor cool my love towards him but stamp her image deeper upon my heart and engrave in my memory the many pleasant scenes and hours we have lived in love together in fairer lines.

To my own heart I cannot be false however fickle others may be. What ever others may say or do. The love and truth in my soul faithful and true will I be to it until my being shall cease to exist. If ever I am false it is unwittingly and he is my nearest and dearest friend who points it out to my detection.

If a low passion usurps the place of pure love if a blind prejudice usurps the place of catholic truth he who informs me of it tho my enemy (if enemies it is possible for me to have) I will receive him as Angel from heaven, as an instrument of God. My honour my consistency my character consists in this in faithfulness to God's love, Gods truth and nothing else. Let me be true to Him. How then can I be false to either Man or the World? Tis He who knows our secret thoughts we should fear (if fear we must) and obey.

31. Sund.

The question of Christs human personality is one of the most importent in its results. It is the one which divides the Christian Church from the innumerable sects and individuals who believing in Christ believe in Him only as a person in degree differing from them but not in Kind. Jesus, say they, was one of Adams offspring under the same temptations & passions that we are and was kept from sinning from the fullness of the love and wisdom of God that dwellt in Him. The difference between Him and we is this and this only that in Him dwellt grace & truth without measure but in us with measure. Therefore the difference is only in degree not in Kind. The other view that is held by orthodox christians that Christ is a second Adam the generative head of a pure perfect & holy Humanity as the first was of the present sinful & wicked Race   He does not belong to the same Race as the noble company of Heroes Prophets Sages & Martyrs of the Past

April. 8.

What will be the practical realisation of Christianity   Will it be association?

I had a conversation with Mr Ripley this afternoon. He said his religious views had been modified since I last saw him. I gave him the views I held and we conversed together for two hours. They seem to me earnest and enthusiastic to realize the life that they have but neglect the fountain from which they have received the life they have. Time will modify them much more. Association as the *object* of the Church to realize its life in matter seems to be necessary[129]

Concord. April 23. 1844.[130]

The prayer that I first uttered in this book with increased_____

25.

Last evening I was interrupted I had to break off above. My union with Spirit is my only peace and rest. Did I not *feel* Spirit sustained I should *fall*. Oh God take not Thy holy spirit from me. Keep near and support me. Daily I feel my self less & less weaker & weaker as I grow in Thee in strength in *Love*. My Soul would do nothing else but praise and magnify Thy name. In Thee we are a Host, without Thee less than the worm under our feet. Lord my God leave me not I entreat Thee. Oh Father Thou hast been Kind and kept me sustained me through until this hour. Thou wouldst have me to love Thee more. Thou wouldst dwell in our hearts. Thou wouldst abide with Men: remove then oh Lord all obstructions from my soul that Thou mayst fully occupy it. Thou art my delight & beside Thee there is no life love or light. Oh touch my heart with Thy celestial love. Lord I am Thine; do with me what Thou willst. Thou desirest our love should increase. Oh Lord increase it suddenly. Thy love dwelleth in my heart; without this presence I should be dead. Am I not Thine? Knowest Thou me not oh Lord? Hath not Thy Spirit taken up its abode in my heart? Can any thing give this delight that Thou givest? Do not Thy own children know Thee? I have been groping in darkness seeking where Thou wast not and found Thee not. But oh Lord my God Thou hast found me; leave me not. But abide evermore with me. Who has tasted of the Lord and not desired Him above all things? Who hath felt Thy sweetness and not smiled? Oh Lord my heart is more eager after Thee than the bird is for its mate in the Spring. Every thing fails to speak of Thee in Thy ineffable sweetness Thy celestial Love. Oh who can comprehend the Lord? Oh who can enjoy the Lord. Not the whole universe not the Heavens nor the Earth not Man Thy image no. None but the Lord himself none but He can feel His own Love   None but He can comprehend His own Wisdom & Power. Take up Thy dwelling in my heart that I may feel *Thy* love *in* me & Thy enjoyment shall give me pleasure & Thy wisdom shall give me light.

O my God Thou art loveing! And Thou my soul art happy. There is no work but Thy work; all other is worse than nothingness. If Thou art not the corner stone the building will fall and crush us in it while building. In the secret chambers of my heart do I take delight with Thee with Thy Love and the world sees it not. Thou art hid from all but Thy children. Oh who is the Lords let him keep peace with delight. I would speak of my labours but my love closes my lips with Her smiles and delights. I am charmed and cannot speak.[131]

26.

I have said two lessons in Greek & Latin to Mr Bradford   My spirit does not fail me. No doubts of my perseverance passes through my bosom. I am quiet and in peace. I hope I shall draw nearer & nearer to God daily. I feel that I am growing in His grace. To Him I look for support. Will he not impart wisdom as well as love? His wisdom is foolishness to the world but his children know their own. Did not Solomon ask for Wisdom and wast it not granted to him. The wisdom that giveth life is the only wisdom that I can recognise.

In giving there is double gain.

27. P.M.

This morning I have got out a Greek sentence for the first time—it gives me great pleasure!

Love feeds upon itself—self subsistent in a sense. There can be no single love. All love is dual.

A.M.

It is the life that flows through us that refines elevates & ennobles our being not that which we *use* of another.

He who is spirit born quickens the spirit birth in those who meet him.

He who is spirit lead has all things needful. He who gives up his naturel life will find his spiritual life.

We learn the Scriptures not by reading them but by the Holy Ghost in us.

We shall know more, love more, & do more, if we be more. It is Being which will give us knowing loveing & doing. With the natural water we cannot quench the spiritual thirst.

Spiritual gifts are irreconcilable with natural wealth.

The only permanent wealth are spiritual goods: spirit never dies but the body does.

The Spirit must give birth to Celestial love as the Soul gives birth to the Spirit.

Spirit is the body of celestial love as the soul is the body of the Spirit as the flesh is the body of the Soul. As the fallen soul is possessed by demons so must the divine soul be possessed by Angels.

It is easier to write history sacred spiritual history than it is to *be* sacred spiritual.

There is a greater degree of difference between the celestial and spiritual birth than there is between the spiritual & natural.

The body needs bread that it may live; the soul, spirit-truth; the spirit, *celestial love*.

There are much fewer who have celestial birth than there are those who have spiritual birth—their ratio is as 2:4::8 rather as $\overset{C}{2}:\overset{S}{8}::\overset{N}{32}$ greater still. The spirit craves for love as the soul craves for the spirit. Spirit enlightens; Love enlivens.

The Soul *is* in spirit but lives in *love*.

Love & Light are not one in substance but are oned in life. Love is the warmth of light   Winter corresponds to Light. Summer to Love.

Light is the medium of Love.

The enjoyment of Love is a much greater delight than that of Wisdom. Wisdom justifies but Love sanctifies.

There is a purpose in all things: and when it is the farthest hid from our sight, when we stand in midst of the thickest darkness, when we stand deaf & dumb before our own destiny, mute with a deep unutterable speech, then is our deliverance nigh, the dawn near and the scales ready to drop from our eyes. There is a physician for every invalid. There is a balm for every wound. Knock,—Seek,—Pray, and it shall be opened, ye shall find, and ye shall be given unto.

The subject which wants and the object wanted are not the same.

We must be willing to let the love spirit guide us if we would be guided by the love spirit.

Can we complain of our coldness & darkness when we shut the doors and windows of our souls to the Angels of love and light which our heavenly Parent is constantly sending from heaven to us fresh from his glorious presence? We must never forget that if we would give ourselves up to God that He is waiting, and ever ready, *to give Himself to us!* He is infinite in condescension as He is in glory in goodness.

Think of this that all the love and light we have is from God and that it is our willfulness and that only that is in the way of our receiving more & more unto perfect fullness.

We should think less of this world less of Men and more and more of the love the goodness and the mercy of God. And that by so doing we shall grow more & more in His image.

The countenance of Jesus is seen in the face of every true devout Christian. Did He not promise that He & His Father would come and take up Their abode in their hearts? He that thinks of this Earth and the things of this Earth becomes Earthly   He that thinks of the things of this World becomes worldly. He that thinks of Heaven and the things which belong to the Kingdom of God becomes Heavenly. Choose. Think of no evil towards Providence.

If we think of the Earth beneath our feet we shall be drawn down. If we think of those who are around us we shall be left standing where we are; if we think of the Saints & Angels in heaven and our Lord God above we shall be raised up above and be elevated to the company of the glorious Host before the bright effulgence of the infinite Love.

All the Good the True and Beautiful in Man in Science & in Art comes from the inspiration of God and the condition of more is the obeying that that has been given us.

Humility Reverence Meekness are the three primary conditions of Knowledge of Goodness of Love and Wisdom.

He that goes before he is called goest to destruction. He that goes when the spirit calls and fails to obey it is unsuccessful and he dies. He that is spirit called and obeys in all things whatever may be the outward appearance of his unsuccess he really succedes. If God *is* with us this *is* success; it matters not what Men say to the contrary. Men will be troubled so long as they have a mind of *their own;* but when their mind is Gods mind, one with His mind then and not till then wilt they find rest, peace, and joy. Man could as well live without the constant inspiration of God as he could without expiration of breath as a dead man could revivy itself to life again.

29.

Many persons affirm a truth but in the sense they view it it is a *falsehood* and often is more pernicious than a lie.

Men err on the side of self indulgence never on the side of self-denial

All the knowledge we may accumulate will be useless if we have not the love to make use of it.

When Love stimulates the Soul to acquire knowledge knowledge gives life: but knowledge accumulated without the love causal power is adding difficulties to the birth of the Love Spirit.

We must give up *our* purpose, for the love spirits purposes.

We must become agents for the love being and the spirit being.

We must submit always the personal to the universal.

Our permanent existence is in the non existence of ourselves—but in God.

Submission to the Love Spirit is the "one thing needful".

He that seeks *his own* life shall loose it. He that seeks to loose *his own* life shall find it.

Blessed is no-thing—for then we are in the spirit. Let us live permanently in the sweet delight of the celestial-unmade-love-Spirit.

Who is so meek so tender so delicate so soft as not to wound the Love spirit at times.

Except ye become as little children ye can no wise enter the Kingdom of heaven—entertain celestial love.

30

The value of principles governments & laws have been underrated because Men have not the life which first instituted principles governments & laws.

May day.

What the Lord will lead me to, for His presence is with me and directs my steps, what purpose of office of use however humble He may place me cannot be forseen. Oh Lord grant me humility patience peace and above all faith in thy ever-loving-Kindness. Oh give me calmness restfulness in every trial of mind or of body.

The Church is an armor through which no shafts however well directed or with howsoever so much strength flung can penetrate.

My heart feels so inerted with love this afternoon it knows no bounds— It will neither let me rest still, nor can it be expressed. It would do nothing but love God and embrace all loveful objects. It is humble and would wash the feet and be the servant of the lowest. Oh what love Jesus has given to Men! how unlike all other life that is upon Earth. How unwillful it is! how meek modest & retiring it is in its actions! How unlike the virtues of the ancient philosophers! Jesus! is pure love in essence! His love is given to the poorest and most Man despised mortal as well as to the Kings of the Earth and richest of Men. Oh Lord Thy love is exceedingly rich and makes the hearts of Men more tender than the flesh of Man can sustain. It melts the heart in an instant. A moments enjoyment of Thy love is infinite. Who can forget Thee. Thy love? Not he who has tasted of Thy sweetness—impossible! What other joy can be compared to the joy in the Lord. O Lord Thou art my highest joy and take not Thy spirit from me. Teach me how I shall ever submit to Thy love. Let me not grieve Thy Holy Spirit.

2.

This morning I feel like singing the whole time, "Oh I would die & be with God"   Which is only desiring to live in a diviner life which I feel within. "Oh I would die and be with God". "Far far from every mortal care".

3d

O Lord this morning would I praise thee with all my power of heart and tongue. How close my heart feels drawn to thy presence! My heart feels tender for thy love is ever softening it to thy praise.

4

This afternoon I am conscious of nothing but love but feeling tenderness. "Oh I would die and be with God." "Far far from every mortal care." To live for this world for the good of this world is a duty but how much more does the Soul desire to go to its home. It seems as tho my Soul would be drawn from the body and soar above to its resting place. My truest life seems most like a dream. We are blind now. We grope about in the spiritual world like one whose eyes are bandaged in the material world. Our Souls are like Harps which are touched by angels but they are mute interpreters of the Sounds, the music. The horse works, unconscious of the use he is put to by Man. The birds sing but know not it is heavens music they pour forth so sweetly. The flowers blossom and fade and are innocent of their beauty and fragrance. The heavens are so lovely but it is we who per-

ceive their loveliness. Thus are we put to higher uses than we are aware of.
Thus must we be passive unconscious and as innocent if we would live "a
life well spent." When man plays upon the musical instrument it answers
to his touches. When he calls to his noble animal it answers by its movements Is it so with Man? Does he respond to the touches of love, does he
answer to the calls of the spirit. We should blossom as the fragrant flower,
our Souls would descourse as eloquently as music and we should live in the
joy of Angels were we as innocent did we submit to the divine grace of God.

We can but speak of that which we hear, utter that which we feel, and
testify to that which we know. We have been laboring for the life of the
body when only the eternal life can satisfy the Souls desires. The body *does*
live by bread but the soul does *not*. The Soul lives from the bread of heaven,
the body from that of Earth. When the Eternal life speaks through us and
we obey its voice then are we the Sons of God joint heirs with our Lord
Jesus.

5.

This afternoon I took my Greek books and Shakspeares Sonnets and
whent to the woods called by the name here the Cliffs   I read a few Sonnets translated two Greek sentences and found their grammatical relation
and laid on the dry leaves and looked up in the blue sky. And wrote after
this a few sentences.

Mans greatest act is obedience. His Glory is in submission   He is
most Man when most divine. Mans spiritual eyes have been blinded by sin.
He is not born with his spiritual sight. Spiritual sight is an after birth. The
truths which should be his daily food he gropes about to find but seldom
gets them. Greater powers than we walk in our midst which we scarcely
feel never see.

The prophecy I was so eager to catch from others lips some 9 months
ago is now uttered by my own.

Lying on the bosom of my Mother looking up into the Heavens of my
Father while the birds singing in the Trees. The gentle winds filling all space
with the sweet fragrance of spring flowers. The water flowing so slowly
along mirrowing the whole firmament above   Oh I feel like being in my
native home; this is Eden.

My heart is like blue vault above flitting emotions like silver clouds
pass over its bosom leaving no trace upon its pure surface.

To the birds I listened and saw them hop from branch to branch from
tree to tree as if they were of the same element in which they moved   I
watched the skillfull spider weave his web and the busy ant build its cell
and felt how full of instruct is All and how divine is Man.

"Thou gentle stream, flow on,
How calm how noiselessly thou art,
Thus flows the stream of life
When Christ is in the Heart
He calms the ruffled waves,
And bids the winds "be still,"
And like Thy crystal breast,
The pure reflect His will."

                                                                    6

The only union that can satisfy the Soul is its union with God; this only can will or does.

How shall we secure a full union with God? By fasting prayer, and all kinds of self denial.[132]

Oh Lord willt Thou accept my Soul & let nothing else fill it but Thee.

I will supplicate Thee in and out of Season in all places not to depart from me but ever fill my Soul with Thy presence.

Let not my faith grow weak nor my life slacken. Of Thee my Soul has tasted and Thou knowest that nothing else but Thee can ever give it comfort. Thou art my only Comforter and Thou my only love. My Soul sighs after Thee and my heart aches for Thy return. Let my Soul rejoice O Lord in Thy company and my heart be delighted in feeling Thee.

Thou O Lord art the bride of my Soul and my elect. Comfort me   Comfort me O Lord and let not my heart be so disconsolate. O my Soul my Soul why art thou so disquieted and so cast down. What aileth thee? What can I give unto thee that will heal thy wound. Who has wounded my Soul and caused it to bleed. Lord my Physician and Consolator will heal its wounds with the oil of gladness.

No where can I find rest   I laid my head on the pillow to sleep and slept but when I awoke my troubles ceased not. Where else shall I look for quiet rest but to Thee. Oh Lord look down upon me in the deep trouble and anguish of my Soul. If the Lord cometh not to our aid alas alas we must despair. Is it Thy nearness oh Lord that moves my Soul thus? Are these Thy tender wounds then may my heart be touched in every pore.

Touched in every mortal part
Bleeding from every pore
Upon Thy altar I lay my Heart
Lord what can I do more.
Here Lord I give my Soul to Thee
Cleanse it from every stain

Then shall my sorrows have an end
An all my sins be slain.

6

To what ever sphere we submit to be it the Love, the spirit, or the nature sphere, we shall reap our true reward. (Compensation)   Where the carcass is there will the Eagles be gathered.

As you make your bed so you must lie.

We do not gather figs from thistles, nor grapes from thorns.

Knock and it shall be opened unto thee: seek and ye shall find.

I of my own will do nothing but the Father in me.

I of my own will can do nothing but with Jesus Christ I can do all things.

The office of the Priest is the most casual of all offices. He is the medium of the infinite to the finite. Touch not Gods anointed for thou shalt be struck with the hand of the All-mighty. It is the place that gives to the priesthood their sacredness not their individual character.

My complaints must be uttered tho ever so trivial.

If I had known that Henry Thoreau had taught the G. & L languages I should have selected him instead of Mr Bradford if I had known what I now know. Mr Thoreau has a better knowledge of languages, has more leisure, takes a delight in languages. Mr Bradford comes here when he has been tired out by his School, simply hears me recite, gives me scarcely any valuable information on the structure and the nature of the languages; and does not awaken any keen interest in my study; whereas from H.T. a few moments conversation gave me more instruction and delight than all that G P B[133] has ever said to me on the subject. G.P.B has so much other bussiness that takes up his mind that when he comes here I feel as if he felt his time was lost and that he is desirous to get away as soon as he can. He comes after 12 and has to take diner at one. Would he accept willingly that H T should take his place? I cannot say, I fear not, or he would have told me of Thoreau situated as he is. I must be patient and not too eager and this will all come right.

After having delivered myself of my complaint this morning G.P.B. came in and I had the pleasantest time with him since I have been here. Like most complaints we utter them after the birth or cure has taken place. Complaint is a much better sign than indifference: one evidences *life;* the other is no evidence except of death.

7

If democracy is a virtue the Church is the School in which it was born. What is the faith in the authority of the Catholic Church but the faith in universality of the inspiration of its members and hence its authority: the

very basis of Democracy. All Men are born free and—Vox populi Vox Dei
etc. etc. This is true when limited to the Church it being an inspired body.
But it is not true in the *highest* sense when applied to secular bodies or
masses of Men indiscriminately. It would be true in a political sense if all
citizens were members of Christs body being in full communion with God
filled with His Grace and being Christians in every deed but this is not so
and tho the Church of God cannot err because she excommunicates all he-
retics and so preserves the pure life and doctrine; this is not so with the State,
hence she is apt to commit mistakes as well as individuals.[134]

7

Life is more novel than any fiction, for fiction is but an *attempt* to *paint
life*. After I have gained that which my heart has longed for but which it
dared not hope for I say to myself in the future I will never despair; but,
how weak am I scarcely the next hour passes before I am as restless as before for some future object.

My heart pains me physically. The strong emotions which have passed
through my bosom have been too much for my heart. I seem again somewhat restless. I trust this will not last long.

If the Spirit leads us it has a design and we should meekly bear our
burthens until birth has been given to its purposes. It cannot be too often
repeated nor with too great an emphasis that all our involuntary spirit actions
are providential to the lower spheres of being. We must have faith and cast
our bread upon the waters. What hopeful and consoling lessons does the
Past teach us when we look upon it in the Spirit.

Our restlessness dubiousness and despair is because we rest not upon
the Spirit fully.

As Mans sensibility increases towards nature he receive the gift of in-
terpreting her secrets. Thus interprets the poet the flowers precious stones
trees etc. the mystic the animal Kingdom etc. He is receptive of their life
and all things in nature speak to him.

8.

When speaking of things above Man we should always speak in the
passive voice, when of things below in order in the active voice.

To the Lord I would devote all my soul and all the powers he has given
me. They are all His. He gave and for His purpose should they be employed.
Oh Heavenly Father teach me to feel that thy way is the way of peace and
that all thy paths are paths of pleasantness. O Lord teach me to let Thy will
be done in me.

How sad, how very sad I feel. Oh alas, I know not what it is. It is so
deep so very deep. There is nothing nothing that can touch the place. No

love sympathy no affection can do anything towards removing it. This is death   Oh worse than death. I am sad but it is not despair. It is worse. No friends none that I love or who love me could at this moment touch me. All is blank with in and all is far far away from without. Oh for why is this sadness? Why these many sighs unutterable sensations of the heart. What lesson are they to teach. What should have caused them. What do they mean? The singing of the birds makes me feel sadder   The heavens increase it and all that is beautiful and joyous add pang to pang. Oh what is the human heart that it can bear so much. My Soul is void of all consciousness of emotion thought or strength. I feel like one who has no Soul heart or any central life. It is as if nothing was moving but a hollow frame of flesh. Heart Head all is void and what speaks or moves is nothing but the shadow of that which was. My self my consciousness is lost and all seems to be but an empty chamber. All is inverted. It is if my spirit had fled and left nothing behind but memory. Tho my body is here my spirit is looking in another direction and is without the body. It is now the body that writes and I feel what the mere bodily life is without the Spirit. O return Spirit and revivify this frame   One human thrill now passes through my bosom. One human sigh I now just draw. Now all has ceased again. I hear all things around but it sounds within me like an empty chamber. There is no heart in all. A painful dart passes through my side. The pulses I feel beating in my head. And now I sigh again and my *heart* begins to heave. My spirit is away. It is in some other place and nothing remains by me but a blank existence.

Substance and quality—Cause and effect—Parent and child cannot be separated tho the quality the effect the child cannot produce the Substance the Cause the Parent. Therefore it is not the quality the effect the offspring of love or Goodness that we need but the Love substance, Cause, Parent. We want more than lovefullness Goodness we must have the Love and Good natures which shall generate these qualities.

9

Man is a very restless animal. Scarcely is one hope realized than a new and wider one springs into being. The birth of one only gives place to another still more heart rendering bosom aching pain suffering anguish for its realization. We call this life progress embodying the infinite alas such painful births will soon make an end of us all.

Life is one continual birth pain. One hope one dream after another is actualized and the same eagerness to reach forward to brighter and purer visions. Oh is there to be no end to this?

When shall we rest and find our *home?*
When shall this sorrow cease?

When shall this sadness have an end?
When shall we live in peace?

The hope of yesterday is realized to day and that of to day seems set as far
from us as the stars in heaven.

Love is united to sadness, Sorrow to Gladness, and joy is united to
Grief. Hopeing and despairing; pain and pleasure without measure & madness or death fills out the train.

One moment we are singing the next we are sighing
We weep and we sleep and we laugh at betimes Finding no consolation we
write a few lines.[135]

We note not the presence of those who we feel are ever with us.
The natural Man stands in relation to the inhabitants and glories of the spirit
world as the owl does to the natural world at mid-day. The ox may live in
the midst of all the beauties of nature without being the least influenced by
them. So is it with the natural Man even now wherever he exists as regards
the spirit world. "Heaven opens inwards"   "The Kingdom of heaven is
within you." The sublimest truths uttered by poets prophets Saints or Sages
are paraphrases of the utterances of Jesus. We cannot ever affirm with too
much force and emphasis the reality the substantiality the permanency of
Love and Light and all affirmations concerning and of them. The spirit
world is permanent real; the natural world transient and apparent.

10

Our bodily appetites spring not so much from the needs of the body as
from our prevailing dispositions; deny your dispositions and your appetites
will cease; feed not your appetites and your dispositions will disappear. But
before the external Man is willing to stop the food on which his depraved
appetites exist he first must be led to deny the internal disposition which in
the sight of the external Man is his ground of justification   The internal
is ever before, prior, to the external; tho exterior Man does not see this.[136]

If I truly believe that the life of Jesus has perpetuated in a body called
the Church and that this life is the true life & light of fallen and depraved
Man should it not be the primary and all important enquiry? Where is this
body that I may become a member of it so as to partake of this supernatural
influence and become the heir of heaven the Son of God? Am I not ne-
glecting the invitation of Jesus who is in our midst to the marriage supper
of the bride for the things of this world and the wisdom of Men. Is it not
with me as it was with the young man who asked Jesus in person what shall
I do to be saved that I am not willing to give myself wholly up to Gods
purposes to the Spirit to Love. Is it not the fear of Man of this world that
keeps me from being united to the body of our Lord? or is it skepticism? or

is it that the question *which is the Church* keeps me undecided? If the last question was clear to my mind there would not be any room for standing aloof as I now do; but, is this not the same question which the Jews put to Jesus art Thou the Christ or are we to waite for another? It is from my blindness that I cannot see and it is not one who lays claim to be the body but many and to submit that I may have the life given to me to see, & this submission to any one of the bodies or sects whatever they may be is the question which it is so difficult for me to solve. Which shall it be the Roman or Anglican the Presbyterian or the Baptist etc. etc. etc. It does seem as if I cannot do more than submit to the Spirit of God that is given to me where I am until I shall be led to see what I do not now see. I do not question that great blessings are bestowed to the Church and that to be out of its pail we loose much life which otherwise we should have in Her fellowship but among the conflicts of these times resulting from the errors of the past we must also submit to suffer the penalties for the Sins of our forefathers as a part of our destiny.[137]

True consistency consists in unconditional submission to the Spirit and Love life in the Soul. The only consistency is in being guided by Love and Wisdom where ever they lead, outward consistency too often purchased by inward inconsistency. True consistency will be gained as a result when we are perfectly unioned to Love & Spirit. Unity will produce nothing but unitary results: The nearer we approach God the more consistent we become.

11

This morning I rec'd a letter in answer to one I sent from Orah[138] one of the lovliest most love natured being that has met my heart. There is more *heart* in her bosom more heaven in her eyes than I have felt or seen from any other person. She is not lovely but love itself.

13.

I need to be alone in silence that I may feel and enjoy the Society in which my soul is and enjoys. The exterior Man thinks you are lonesome and alone if you are not in the midst of many bodily persons; whereas in such conditions the Soul finds the least Society and communion. Alone we are in Society, in society we are alone. What my heart feels my lips speak and if what my heart feels are not realities than my heart causes its own feeling a thing impossible for when we feel by any sense we always feel something which we touch or something that touches us therefore the feeling in my heart is much a verity as the perceptions of any sense.

We should speak what is given us to say not look to the audience which we are speaking to for what to say. Let us speak: we may be preaching to Spirits who are in prison waiting for their deliverance. He would be the best speaker who should drive every one out from the room in which he is speaking instead of exciting applause.

There are spirits bound in Men all around us suffering in bonds struggling for their freedom kept in the chains of *Self* will and to this abolition Society should we join and preach Anti Slavery. Tis the Slavery of Angels we would abolish. Freedom. Room for the Kingdom of heaven upon Earth. Our contest so far as it is a contest is for the Spirits in prison not for the freedom of Mens bodies. There are no greater Slave holders than our modern Abolitionists. Their own wills are in chains to self and they are in bondage to Sin and deprive the Angels of heaven of the freedom of their home their own Souls. The way to ameliorate Man is to drive out the wicked spirits in him not to prepare a feast for the feeding of these devils in him. You make a man worse by making his outward circumstances more easy for him, if you leave him to remain as he is inwardly. You lull the devils in him to sleep you do not exorcise them and this all that is needed. Nay you but give him the opportunity to entertain more of the same diabolical tribe.[139]

He that has exorcised the wicked spirits in himself is prepared to exorcise them in others.

Our souls are the entertaining rooms for Angels not for demons & devils.

"Madness to wit," faith to fanaticism, and insanity to genius are "closely allied." Men are not wicked but wicked Spirits have taken possession of them and have become masters of the house and what we have to do is to drive them out. We must entertain the heavenly visitants and if our house is filled with them the devils will not knock at our doors and disturb our peace. We must resist evil & invite the good. God is the Educator the Schoolmaster of the Universe and He will educate us all as we need and should be educated but His conditions are self submission willingness to obey His spirit and perfect reliance on Him. He will lead us into all truth and nothing that is hid but shall be revealed.

14

He who lives in the closest accord with nature in the complest harmony with all the laws of God is the most poetic natured Man; in other words the most godlike natured Man is the beautifullest & the best.[140]

15

This seems to be the fact and I stop my lesson to relate it. As my memory increases in learning my heart ceases to feel the constant inflowing of love and my intimate communion with the invisible is not as familiar nor so frequent. It is the heart alone from which all life issues and if that is given wholly to God shall it not issue forth the love and wisdom of God in the fullness of Him? It is really a very serious question with me whether I am not called upon to give up the course of study on which I am set. Will it not be found after having devoted so much life and time to the study of languages for the *sake* of *reading* what the Spirit has inspired other Souls to speak my own Soul has suffered in this intellectual acquisition, and what I have sought to find in others my own soul would have received immediately from the primitive source if I had obeyed its requisitions. Is not the course that I am taking the very opposite to that which they pursued whom I so much reverence and love? If this be so or no this is certain and sure that it is not eternal life that is given in the pursuit of knowledge. Will not the Spirit reveal all that is hid if we wholly submit to it and obey it in all things? I cannot get clear of the conviction that I now am quenching the flow of life from within and that I should give up my whole time to contemplation instead of this self active study of the intellect. My heart would have what my head is seeking for if I would but surrender my-self unconditionally to it. The delight and enjoyment within is so much greater than the happiness and pleasure without that constantly I am drawn from without to the conversation within. It is only at moments that I can study and those are when I am not inwardly engaged and this study does necessarily increase these moments. A good lesson is a sure sign of a nearly lost day. The conditions for study are as opposite to those for the Love spirit as heaven is above the Earth. One is child like submissiveness and the other is self willed activity. Is not the only condition of growing in Grace and the Knowledge of the truth in a total surrender of the soul to love. Will a knowledge of Greek & Latin increase celestial love or heavenly wisdom? Shall we not increase in these as the heart is unioned to God and the will is cooperative with the Divine will.

Is this study an appointed means of God of receiving his grace and the knowledge of the truth? Does Jesus promise any where that the Holy Ghost shall be given or the Comforter through the means of wordly knowledge? Will not Jesus who now sits on the right hand of the Almighty father who did promise that whatsoever we should ask in His name should be given unto us will he not give us the Holy Spirit the Comforter as was given of old if we really ask in His name? Shall we not be prepared to meet all occasions if we put our whole trust in God. Should we be engaged in any work which does not draw us closer to God in every motion. I laid this book down to commence my study again but have to return to it. The question is of some serious consideration concerning these studies. What are Greek & latin and a course of theological studies to me if in me is already what these can give me? Was not God with them and they spoke as God gave them utterance and why not we? Let us be oned to the love and power which they were united to and we shall have our measure of the same wisdom and love.

Does all knowledge that is true knowledge come from above or does it not if it does what are the conditions for its reception. Is God God or is He not? Alas that I even put these questions after having received such testimonies as have been given to me. Men ever quote that which is better than they are; cease quotations and be silent until you are equal to utter that which will bear being quoted even as you would have quoted. Quote from God as all genetic Men do, not from second hand. You must become a fore man in Gods working shop. Give reverent Ears to the voice that speakes from above and the vain bable below will cease to annoy you; God has given you Eyes See yourself and be not satisfied with other Man's seeing for you. Be consistant with heaven however inconsistant you may appear on Earth. Is not the maker of laws greater than the expounder of them. Is not humanity greater than the historian.

It was really unlooked for by me that this question should have come up so soon and with such a hold as it has upon me. Why do I wish to Greek and Latin; is not the same Holy Ghost given to all which carries with it apostolic authority and canonical sanctions? The fathers of the Church the Greek Poets the philosophers all did they not see with the same eyes hear with the same ears in all the same as we? Is not the heaven the same　　Do not the Stars shine as then? Is not God Man nature the Same? Are we not to be Men and stand as they did on their own feet. Is not the Holy Spirit to be spoken through us or are we too but faint echos of the sepulchered past? We say let the dead bury the dead.

17.

He that has intuitive sight needs no long drawn prosaical demonstration of the realness of the truth he perceives nor does he demand that it should be clothed under Symbols Parables or material forms. These are the toys of infant Men serving for a time to amuse but blasting the perennial life if too long played with.

What we need and demand is not that we should read what Poets prophets and Sages See hear and receive but that we shall have poetic sight prophetic hearing and the Sages wisdom. Let *us* See what caused the poem of the Poet and not be satisfied with the picture of it. Can we not be unioned with the poet nature if we supply the subjective conditions? If we were all poets poetry would cease to be written. The ever all conscious present to all we intuitively recognize and of this we know of in silent. All we can do for another is to recommend him to the unknown for real knowledge from which all known springs from which we have received. It is absolute theatry to profess to give any thing from ourselves: we have no power nor right to give what we are only agents for: This is the very ground of Satans sin usurping the authority and glory of God. It is only as we are passive agents for the Love Spirit the Light Spirit & the Life Spirit do they work upon others for their purposes for their 1, 1, 1, purposes, we of ourselves can do only worse than nothing. It cannot be too often repeated in the present state of the public mind on Education that all that is is from God and if we wish fresh thoughts we must go to the Source of the Spring not drink from some muddy lifeless channel. The nearer we are to God the more original our relations are with God the nearer we shall be to Man and Nature and the more genetic will be our nature and by consequence all that flows from this genius nature. Be willess and you will be pursued and overtaken; be willful and you will never reach the golden apples but still and they will drop in your mouth. We must be taught by that which Pythagoras, Socrates Jesus and Shakspere was taught and we shall be as they were and by consequence teach as they taught. This is the relation that Jesus came to establish between the Soul and God; he was the Medium the Uniter of this relation. The conditions for progress are the perpetual giveing up of the lower for the higher and what these are the Soul of necessity in Grace must be its own judge, "it must do with its own as it will".

A great Man cannot be of necessity a very learned Man in the Sense of the world, they are all taught of God, and in this consists their greatness. They are what the world calls inspired Men. He who is by birth right conditioned for the immediate reception of God is called a genius. Genius of consequence becomes more and more genetic as it depends upon the genius nature. He that does not rest on God becomes weaker & weaker however strong he may seem this appearance may be kept up for some time but it will be pierced through if not in his own age the next will not be blinded by the apparent, and it will uncover the Sham and show its *shame*fulness.

Let us us never loose sight of the permanent in what ever we do and our acts will partake of its character. Whatsoever we do which is not of the permanent nature is waste of time, worse than nothing, and never will leave an abiding impression. The Eternal can only produce Eternal results-effects: Love the same Light the Same. By whomsoever we are begotten his works will we display. Socrates would be the first to acknowledge the divine superiority, the incomparable divinity of Jesus, if he were now here. It is most unsocratic to deny this. As Men become real they leave off the apparent, they play no more with toys, nor do the Symbols engage them as they have done. Jesus, Socrates, Pythagoras, were so real in the faith of truth they did not doubt of its perpetuity, they even did not write carve Statues or paint pictures to perpetuate but trusted to God and the hearts of Men and as Men become genetic the more will this be the case Shakspere took no care after his productions and the penny scribbler is more careful than Paul was with his Epistles or the Apostles with their Gospels. As the living faith ceases Men depend more and more upon the record.[141]

19 Sunday.

I have been very willfull indeed these two days past. The spirit has chastised me by its receding from me for a distance and a while. I begin to feel youthful again. The *under* standing's office is to submit to the superior standing   When ever it attempts to officiate in the place of the superior standing it makes but poor and botch work of all its attempts. The union of the Spirit with me is transientially taken place but not permanently established and I am too willfull to let it permanently be with me. I can as yet only supply the transient conditions. No one can imagine what the permanent conditions are who has not been permanently united with Spirit. Alas, Alas, what am I yet to suffer from the persistency of opposition from the pschical & physical spheres of being to the divine the moral. God desires to educate me and I have not the will to let him, o how wretched I am. The sooner I submit to it the sooner it will be over. While this is going on there is nothing that I can do but be perfectly submissive to its own direction and motions. My study will have to be laid one side for how long a time I cannot say I hope not forever; however if this should be the fact I must submit and the result I am verily aware of will be productive of generative results such as nothing else could have been to me.

Mond 20.

These leaves I happened to skip[142]   It is a plain fact of my present experience that the conditions for the psychical spirits growth are not the same as those for the love Spirit. Of this there is no question. And this is equally true that the conditions for the physical nature are not the same as for psychical sphere. If we give wholly up to the Love nature shall we be supplied with the psychical and physical food? Are not we to supply the triune conditions of our triune being   1st the primary love   2nd the secondary light   3rd the extreme—what we call life? May we not as well expect wisdom from the food of which the stomach is supplied as to expect Love from wisdom   And is not the contrary as equally as true? namely as well expect wisdom from love as material food from wisdom?

How true is it that if we are wholly united to the Love nature it will place us in the true receptive conditions for the Light and Life Spirit? Should our time be wholly devoted to supplying the conditions for the union of the Love nature with our Souls and depend upon it for the other results or should we divide our time as we feel there is need between the 3 natures.

21.

A proper subjection of each of the triune natures would place us in direct communion with the triune spheres of being. There seems to be no doubt but that the mass of Men are in greater subjection to the physical nature than to the pschical and to that than the divine love creative nature. This is the redemption of Man to place in such conditions as to unite him in full communion with the Love and Light nature. His fall consists of his having fallen from this communion into the lower nature the physical. He lost his communion with the Father as it was in the beginning through the willfulness of his will and the Son of God *came* to restore us to the bosom of the All love embracing father. That we may give "thanks, with joy, to God the Father who has made us worthy to be partakers of the lot of the saints of light." Let us commune with the Angels of love and light in the courts of our hearts, Gods temple, not made with hands, but through the power and love of Gods grace.[143]

How good is God when all that we have is from him as a free gift! How much rather would we have it a free gift than otherwise! We must become harmonized triune beings. Do-Me-Sol. Each note must have its own proper degree of tone to be in unison and produce in cooperation a perfect harmonic being as its result. Do-Gift-Me-to Me-Sol-Son of God-   The gift of God makes me his Son.

22

Death but shuts out one of the mediums of mutual communion, but there are other mediums through which we commune which are none the less real and much more intimate interior than that of the body. Our interior vision has not been so clearly opened that we can recognize so distinctly those we feel and meet in the interior spiritual world as we do through our bodily senses those like us in body; but that this is attainable the records of many devout and holy individuals plainly teach us in Scripture and in Church not to deny the history of many remarkable in fact of most every remarkable individual of profane history but much more of sacred history and even our best moments for Jesus came to open heaven to us which had been shut by the sins of humanity. This meeting through the medium of the body is very transient and most superficial and becomes more and more unsatisfactory as the other spheres of our being are opened inwards. When the three spheres are opened in harmony within us the love sphere the Light sphere and the life sphere, we can meet those who are in the lower physical or in the psychical or in the love sphere but we ask for the most interior for the enjoyment of it as for the other spheres happiness.

23.

We are best educated when we pursue the paths on which we are led, to strive for an object in which we feel no pleasure, to please others, is degrading ourselves and worse than idleness. Those we copy copied no one but obeyed their own elementary feelings; should we do so we should be as they were true to themselves and by so being being all that they were the very most a being can be.

[May 19]

This afternoon brings me to the close of this book. How different are the emotions with which I close it from those with which I opened it at B. F. now little more, (a month) than a year ago. How fruitful has this year been to me!! how strange! mysterious! And beautiful. And now my Soul foreshadows more the next than ever it presaged before. My life is beyond my grasp and bears me on willessly to its destined haven. Like a rich fountain it overflows on every side and from within flows increasingly the noiseless tide. The many changes and unlooked for results and circumstances within and without of the coming year I would no more venture to anticipate than to count the Stars. It is to me now as if I had just been born and I live in the sabbath of creation. Every thing that I see I am called to give a name, has a new meaning to me and should this life grow as the last year has grown what—Geo & Burrill Curtis came in & I have just returned from a walk in the woods with them—May the buds within blossom and may the fruit ripen is my prayer to God.

It is a singular fact that tho being conscious of a more interior and potent power to work within I am more quiet and willess than I was at first when it affected me. I feel like a child full of joy and pliability and all ambition seems to have left of any character. I see where I was heretofore and the degree of externality that was mixed with the purposes which I cooperated with and feel now free from tho it does seem to me that all wordly prospect that ever was before me is gone and if I was weak very weak in the sight of the world; and so I really am and I feel no more potence than a babe yet still a willess power of love which will conquer through me which oh gracious Lord I never dreamt of.

It is ever that Gods ways are not as our ways and if Man had his way it would but lead him farther & farther in the way of destruction than that of peace and true glory. The craftiness the deception of the Evil one is ever deeper than that of Mans penetration and the only security that Man has is in giving up his soul to Gods watchful care. Here I now am; where this birth will place I know not. My whole experience of these 2 years has been strange to me and this seems to place me in another sphere of life. I ask no more where it will lead me but submit to be led. Sunday evening 19 of may 1844[144]

Unendlich ist das Werk, das zu vollführen
Die Seele dringt. Iphigenie Goethe.

Allein, O Jüngling, danke du den Gottern
Dass sie so fruh durch dich so viel gethan.
                    Ibid.
Zu einer schweren Tat beruft ein Gott
Den edelen Mann, der viel verbrach, und legt
Ihm auf was uns unmöglich scheint zu enden.[145]

Red oder schweig nicht immer anst du vissen,
Was mir im Herzen ist und immer bleibt.
Um Guts zu tun brauchts keiner Uberlegung.
Der Zweifel ist's der Gutes böse macht.

Der Begreiffende steht immer höher als das Begriffens; Ne
          aber
im Glauben ist es um-gekehrt, der Glauben steht immetiefer
als das Geglaubte. Kein Wesen in der Schöpfung
Kann sich ans einem Kleineren in ein
Grösseres entwickeln, ohne das ein Prinzip der
          Entwickelung
in dasselbe gesezt werd.
Eckermann.[146]

Now it was given me to understand, that there is a Threefold coming of Christ.-His first coming was in the flesh. After which, before he left the world he engaged that He would come again *in spirit* to his own that were in it. *This has been accomplished.* This was his *Second Coming.* Upon which we have lived, and spent upon this stock of Life ever since his departure. I mean such, who for this worthy gift, *have, with great seeking,* obtained it. This the Apostles had more richly and abundantly, as to the manifold working by powers and gifts, than any since. But yet they were still looking out for his next coming;—for, by his Spirit he was to make meet and ready; that the inward Spirit, with his *Mind,* Will and Senses, should be all internally transformed; (as the New Testament runs much upon it) to *be found sinless;* spotless, and blameless, against the coming of the Lord

And what is to be done at his third coming, *but to change our vile bodies, and to fashion them Like Unto His Own Glorious Body* by that power which shall open the Element, (*the Eternal Nature*) which the Celestial Body shall evermore consist of. Christ's third coming will be to this purpose, *To Redeem Bodies* out from all those evil events that Sin brought in, so that every spirit may come to have *its own Native Body,* and the spirit may no longer draw one way and the Flesh another. Divine. Rev & Proph. by Mrs Jane Lead Pub in London first in 1700. 1830[147]

The character of Luther like that of most true Teutons was compounded of hearty joviality and deep sadness. Maurice.

"This sentence appears to me must have been penned by a Teuton or a son of one. If Maurice is an Englishman he never penned it but borrowed it"[148]

Zoroaster believed That the time would come when Man would not eat or need any more food nor would he then cast a shadow.

An utterance of a divine instinct which lies in the souls of all reborn Men—The aspiration—the prophecy of to-day as it was in Zoroasters time.[149]

Philosophy seeks, Theology finds, and Religion possesses—the Truth. Johann Picus.[150]

Goethe says in his old age that the love for Lilli continued still with him and colored his poetry and life.

How I wish I could love Men! for amid all life's quests   There seems but worthy one; to do Men good. It matters not how long we live but how. For us the parts of one Mans pain while here   We live in every age; we think and feel   And feed upon the coming and the gone   As much as on the now time. Man is one: And he hath one great heart. Festus[151]

Let us think less of Men and more of God.

Buddha Commandments

1st Do not kill: 2nd Do not steal: 3d Do not commit adultery: 4th Do not lie. 5th Do not slander: 6th Do not call ill names: 7th Do not speak words which are to no purpose but harm: 8th Do not covet others property: 9th Do not envy: 10th Do not err in the true faith, or think it to be false.[152]

INTRODUCTION TO VOLUME 2

May 30-July 12, 1844, was one of special intensity for Isaac. During the last week of May he had used his vacation time from George Bradford's language school to visit Boston. There he planned to see some old friends like Mormon evangelist Parley Parker Pratt and Brownson while staying at Leaches's Graham boarding house. He took in some cultural attractions, viewing Crawford's statue, Orpheus, and Alston's painting, Belshazzar's Feast (see Hecker to Family, May 23, 1844, and May 27, 1844; Hecker to Catherine Hecker, May 31, 1844).

Yet despite those delights, it was a restless time for him. His efforts to see Brownson and Pratt were in vain, since they were out of town. That disappointment gave rise to a feeling of alienation in the city and sent him "home" early to Concord, more intent than ever to attend to his own inspirations rather than to the externals that had disappointed him in Boston. As any youth, he was ready to take a bit of inevitable bad luck as a providential sign that he should attend to his own inner life and not look to others for stimulation. He was also ready to resign himself to the fact that disciplined study was not for him.

Thus motivated, he filled an entire notebook in a six-week period. The intensity that he brought to the diary accompanied a crucial development that culminated in his decision to become a Catholic. The opening entries include some of his better musings on poetry, art, and the spiritual nature of genius. Emboldened in his introspective mode, he writes to Brownson on June 4, including a previously written letter from May 24. The two letters strongly present his reasons for not being able to study. Eloquently he argues for the primacy of contemplation over study and assures his intellectual mentor that the inner union with the Spirit that he so effortlessly experiences is a "source of so much more life in every direction that all

191

other sources seem to me lifeless." That life of contemplation is a life of "perfect submission to God" in which all willfulness, pride, and ambition are yielded up.

Immediately after sending those letters he receives a note from the one person among his Transcendentalist friends most like him in his asceticism and intensity, Charles Lane. After the fold-up of Fruitlands, Lane had taken up residence at the Shaker United Society in nearby Harvard, Massachusetts. From there he wrote to Hecker urging him to come for a protracted visit and assuring him of the rightness of his inclination to abandon study for a life of inspiration. Lane is the protagonist who represents the no-church, radical, "mystical" school of reform. As he asked Hecker in his letter: "How indeed can the living, youthful Spirit think of adorning itself in the dead antique garments of a bygone world?" The social structure, as well as the individual's consciousness, had to be reformed, starting from the most basic awareness of the Spirit's work within. That Spirit for Lane was the spirit of newness that was removing the lifeless social structures, religious institutions, habits, and beliefs and replacing them with fresh ones. Lane saw no hope of revivifying the old. His approach was to come out from among the dead, and so he did, leaving a career as a London accountant and joining the utopian efforts of Alcott and then the Shakers.

The other protagonist in the drama of Hecker's conversion was Brownson, who was the foil to Lane. Brownson's trajectory was in the opposite direction. He had come from his own utopian period to a time when he railed against "Come-Outerism." He saw a flaw in the radical schemes of Lane or even of the less radical Associationists: They separated themselves from the very structure through which life was communicated to individuals: the church of Christ. More mindful than everyone of the need for the grace of Christ to redeem the individual and the society, he had come to see that he could not "attain to purity and sanctity of life." He needed "the councils, the aids, the chastisements and the consolations of the Church."

We see played out in this volume of the diary the interplay of these two opposing viewpoints and their effect on Hecker. The entries of May 31-June 6 pulsate with the vibrations of the age of the Newness. But on June 7, he receives a letter from Brownson which chastises him with a fatherly tenderness and firmness and warns him to take care "not to mistake the mental habit into which you have fallen for the guidance of the All-Wise" (Brownson to Hecker, June 6, 1844). He must instead learn to give up the spiritual luxuries of idle imaginations and learn to fix his mind with discipline on whatever subject he pleases. That warning hit home, but not with as much force as did Brownson's exhortation to join the church and, most importantly, his revelation that he himself had decided to become a Catholic. That revelation evoked an immediate response in Hecker which sent him—no longer creeping but now running—to the Church of Rome. The day after receiving the letter he traveled back to Boston, the place he had been so eager to leave a few days previous, and visited both Bishop Fenwick and his coadjutor, Bishop Fitzpatrick, on Monday, June 9. He left Concord for good on June 16, withdrawing from Bradford's school. On June 18 he arrived at the Jesuit College of the Holy Cross, which Fitzpatrick had begun in Worcester. On June 21 he left Worcester and returned to New York by way of Boston and began meeting with the coadjutor bishop of New York, John McCloskey, receiving instruction for reception into the church.

He had long been struggling with the church question and, as we have seen, voiced serious doubts about whether the Catholic church would meet his needs virtually right up until June 7. Most often those doubts were expressed in cryptic terms such as "the church does not meet my inward wants." Usually, however, he does not cite specific theological disputes with Catholicism. Rather, he complains of the foreign character of the church, of its incongruity with American life, or of its failure to understand the animating forces of contemporary society. Brownson's declaration of his intent to join the church quickly cleared up Hecker's problems because they were essentially misgivings about the social character of the church and about his own doubts about being able to fit into a "foreign" group. As he says in the entry of the 11th: "The Roman Catholic Church is the most despised, the poorest and according to the world, the least respectable on account of the order of foreigners which it is chiefly composed of in this country." His awareness of his own foreign roots had largely disappeared, even though his parents were born in Germany. It was, no doubt, the hoards of Irishmen that were flooding Boston and New York that Hecker had in mind. Brownson epitomized Yankee intellectualdom for Hecker, and seeing so famous and established a figure embrace the Church of Rome emboldened Hecker to do what many of his intuitions and reasonings had been leading him toward.

His conversion brought with it a resounding sense of harmony. Thus his entry of the 13th is bathed in the inner light and rests in the peace of conviction. His declaration that "no exterior relations, events, or objects can disturb this unreachable quietness nor no event can break this deep repose I am in" was indicative of the degree to which conversion centered and integrated his life. After it the larger questions of his purpose in life and the meaning of existence are answered. As he writes on June 14: "All is unity with me—Love." His conversion becomes an essential part of his personality, so much so that events later in life cannot shake his faith in the church. It is this tone of serene fulfillment that inspires the closing section of volume 2. There Hecker's musing on the inner life takes on a new confidence and balance. The perplexity of the earlier volume has given way to a concern for the truth of his new-found faith and a celebration of its mystical richness.

VOLUME 2

Concord. Mass. May. 30th 1844. Thursday.

Yesterday evening I returned after 3 days visit to Boston B.F. etc. I whent with somewhat of an intention to see whether in mixing with the world I should not be somewhat influenced with their life and be brought into new relations with my study etc. but it was to no purpose that I whent, on wednesday afternoon I could no more keep myself there than one could sink himself in the waters of the dead Sea. And so I had to come home.

I feel that I move in an element as different from those around me as the bird does from the fish and to meet them is alltogether out of the question in fact I feel no desire to do so, nor any need of it. There was no inducement that I could imagine strong enough to keep me from returning. Ole Bull[153] was to play the next evening who I wished to hear again very much, and a friend Parley Pratt[154] who was to be in town the next day or two who I had not seen for a great length of time who I did wish to see and many other objects to keep me there for a day or two longer but they were all without the least effect.

I feel a strong inclination to doze and slumber more and more and these slumbers the dim shadows that appear in my wakeful state are clearer and my conversation is more real and pleasant to me.

I feel a double consciousness in this state and I think now is not the real, I will recollect it all what I saw, and what I said, but, it flees and is lost when I awake.

While I was in the City I could scarce refrain from sleeping at certain periods it mattered not where I was. I say sleeping, but sleep it is not for in these states I am more awake than at any other time.

Humbly and freely I confess with a deep sense of humility that all my labour is useless and my ability to benefit or accomplish any thing in the view of the world christian or wordly is daily becoming to me fainter and fainter. The Spirit which guides and controls me I have no disposition to rebel against but would meekly submit to its supreme and perfect guidance and do feel that in this my life light and love is the greatest however small and insignificant it may seem to the world and in reality it may be. It is all that I can be and attempt to be more would end in making me less. It would seem that I am doing very little indeed here but this is no criterion for what I feel conscious of what I feel is being done for me and through me and if this be a delusion how to awaken my self from it is to me unknown. O I would submit to be guided by a little child, be willing to obey a stranger in the street, to do anything if the Spirit permitted me to do it, but unless so, there seems nothing so impossible for me to do as to disobey it. I have no fear but that a holy pure trust in God will do more than any other, than all other efforts, have the power of doing.

31. A.M.

Restlessness may be attributed to me with what degree of justice I cannot judge but it seems quite evident to me that my state of mind now is such that study seems to be out of the question. Candidly I confess that what to do I know not, but that to remain here for a time until some thing seems plainer to me than what now does. To bend all my energies to some ultimate objective purpose as many young men do. I have not the ambition, or impulse to do so. To return home and engage in bussiness life, seems to be more impractible than the former. I see not but that the only thing I can now do, is, to remain here where I am, as quietly as possible, and take this event as one of the many lessons which life has in store to educate us for unseen purposes.

Was useless for me to ask advise, as it seems to me to ask myself on those subjects which I feel need of advise upon. Who can give me other advise than their own lives, their own experience, and those I would ask their opinions I already anticipate what they are and therefore have no interest in asking that from them.

If I ask of the bussiness man, his advise will be of the character that has led him to his pursuits, if I ask of the Politician, the Metaphysician, the Literary Man, the Poet, the Moralist, the Theologian, the Divine, they will all give such answers as spring from the nature which has led them all to their several pursuits.

The question what am I to do? what is my work? I have no answer as yet except it is not to ask the question and be satisfied and live as I do for a time.[155]

It does seem astonishing how little the greatest have accomplished permanently in this world.

There is nothing that I can do that satisfies or will satisfy the deep internal permanent existence I am conscious of within; and whether there ever will be or no⟨t⟩ I am at loss to say. So long as this remains and does not find its outward freedom, so long must life seem to me dubious and painful to a greater or less degree.

The Man who is engaged in the material objective life, the Man of Science, of Art, in all their great and numerous branches which have to do with the objective material world seems to gain slowly and perseveringly by a steady march the goal which is ever before him. He learns what has been done and known experiments anew himself, multiplies the past with his own original observations and adds to the store of the Sciences. But with the objective spiritual world of Truth and Goodness this process is not so tangible sure and progressive and the labour is of quite a different sort as the difficluties and rewards are of quite a different character. Mans spritual senses are not so well trained and refined as his material senses are, hence the former road is so much more difficult, than the latter, and his labours speaking from the worldly side much less appreciated in this direction, in fact they are to a very great extent derided and spoken of as vain foolish and mere delusive fancies of his own fertile brain.

It seems to me the body is a very costly machine at the cheapest rate to keep a going in a healthy condition, and as for myself its productiveness seems not to me to pay the cost of the expenditure for its sustenance, and so far it is a loosing concern. But the tree requires some years before it bears its fruits and so I trust it may be with me. Patience and calm trust are godly fruits of life.

[June] April. the 2nd Sunday P.M.

It sometimes seems to me that I shall settle down in some retired spot and there live a quiet life and then again this seems almost impossible when I reflect that I shall not find my wants supplied by such a life.

This afternoon in the woods with a lead pencil I dotted down a few thoughts that occurred to me. I love to put my naked feet upon the bosom of the Earth and feel the gentle breezes play about my body.

The Earth heaves and sighs from its very heart with sympathy for Mans woes and sorrows, and Men rest upon her bosom as upon the bosom of a kind mother and she drinks up his bitter tears in compassion and extracts the painful poison from his heart and pours in his heart instead the waters of joy & gladness.

We are Sisters to Nature: She is a child of God as we are and She has partaken of the same penalty of Sin that we have.

Nature is redeemed by the same Redeemer that we are, and by no other.

Man is the medium of the Redemption of Nature as the God-Man was the medium of the Redemption of Man.

Do we feel the same in the presence of Nature as we do in the presence of an immortal Spirit? Should we not?

Does nature shame us from doing evil and prevent us from committing sin in her presence the same as a virtuous human Spirit would?

As the countenance of a man shines back the beauty of God when Man loves God so does nature reflect our love when we love Her.

Has absolute nature self-consciousness?

The Soul acquires knowledge of nature through the medium of the body as it becomes acquainted with God through the medium of the Spirit.

What are the physical conditions necessary to a perfect communion with the Soul of Nature?

June 5.th

Yesterday I sent off to OAB. two letters one was written two weeks ago but which I did not send on account of its subjectivity the other was written yesterday. In these I spoke of my difficulty and my purpose in coming here and the result of my efforts.[156]

Reading an old Review yesterday I met with a short and amusing Autobiography of Alexander Dumes in which he says he studied for two years different branches of sciences and languages when he first came to Paris being then near 21 without knowing why or wherefore and without having any purpose; but after two years had elapsed he whent to the Theatre and saw Hamlet played which awoke in him all the energies of his faculties and opened to him his destiny.[157]

Yesterday I said a lesson in Greek and Latin to G.P.B.;[158] it was better than I had expected.

George Curtis gave me to read a desription of his character by Anne Parsons[159] a clair voyant in whose hands was placed a letter of his to J.S.D.[160] She speaks of him as a person of decided character, a good friend. She speaks of him as one having considerable fun and imagines him wrapt up in a cloak and can't say whether it is an inward or outward cloak. There seems says she a great deal holy tender & deep in this person. His mirth is not common it comes from a high source. He has some creative powers. Not strikingly energetic, but no want of it in his love of contemplation. He is pure. Conscientious without any thought of being so. Poetry is his vocation. His poetry will influence mankind most. To write may be his mission. Does not ⟨possess⟩ his own powers yet. He will make some sort of furrow in the worlds surface. W.H.C. would make a broader deeper straighter furrow. Would not do so much to advance the cause of humanity, his influence would be confined to a narrow circle etc. etc.

It makes me smile when I fancy how dumfounded we must look to those who see our destiny so ligibly written out while to us it is so dubious. Not that the above is of this character any farther than a little more than an ordinary sensibility to the peculiarities of our character.

This is our destiny to do the best and greatest that is now to be done. He is accomplishing his future celebrity who was doing, matters not in however great his obscurity, the greater the better, whats noblest for him to do at this very moment.

I like Swedenborgs definition of perception "Perception is nothing else but the speech or thought of the angels who are attendant on Man." "a sort of internal speech."[161]

When our hearing is sufficiently delicate we hear this speech. When our sight is sufficiently illumined we see the angels. And our sense of feeling when delicately sensitive we feel the influence of their presence. Wordsworth says:

> "for from the starry sphere come secrets,
> whispered nightly to his ear;
> and the pure spirit of celestial light
> Shines through his Soul—
> "that he may see and tell of things
> invisible to mortal sight."[162]

Dryden says

> "Reaching above our nature does no good:
> We must sink back to our own flesh & blood."

These lines from Wordsorth struck me as I read them passingly.

> "How oft high service is performed within,
> When all the external Man is rude in show;"

Speaking of the poet the same writer observes. For all good poetry is the spontaneous overflow of powerfull feelings; and tho this be true, Poems to which any value can be attached were never produced on any variety of subjects but by a man who, being possessed of more than usual organic sensibility, has also thought long and deeply. For our continued influxes of feelings are modified by our tho'ts, which are indeed the representatives of all our past feeling; and, as by contemplating the relation of these general representatives to each other, we discover what is really important to Men, so, by repetition and continuance of this act, our feelings will be connected with important subjects, till at length, if we be possessed originally by much sensibility, such habits of mind will be produced, that, by obeying blindly and mechanically the impulses of those habits, we shall describe objects, and utter sentiments, of such a nature, and in such connection with each other, that the understanding of the being to whom we address ourselves, if he be in a healthful association, must necessarily be in some degree enlightened, and his affections ameliorated.

Schiller seems to me to be a sentimentalist.[163] Jean Paul was one in whom there was a genuine healthy flow of delicate tender love. The first in this respect seems to be of a hotbed growth; the latter of sweet healthy nature.

The only pure incitements are Religion, Music, Poetry, Painting, Sculptor and last and not the least of the latter is Nature in all her beautiful variety. These are the influences that are to redeem regenerate Man and the first of all is Religion. Without that Man art & nature decline, degenerate; The Church the Arts and Nature are the triune mediums of approaching the unapproachabe love beauty and grace.

The Catholic Church has always cherished and with a mothers care fostered the latter & infused purity and elevated them with Her divine spirit.

Man being the creative medium of the Arts as the Soul of Man was purified and refined by the gracious influences of the Church the arts necessarily received their share of this refinement and elevation.

My thoughts constantly carry me from my study. To sacrifice my thoughts seems an impossibility. What to do, than to do what I can, who can tell?

Man is the creature of circumstances spiritual, psychical, and physical.

The germ the seed of the strawberry will never produce an oak in any circumstances. Nor will an ill born person in the same circumstances as well born person ever equal the well born person in any of his actions.

"Education can never wholly repair the defects of birth."

I feel before my attention can be changed to intellectual study I needs must have a genetical change. It is not the channel through which my life flows, but it is in the quality of the life that flows.

If I understand the associanists they say good physical circumstances are necessary to the spiritual regeneration of Men   And it seems to me spiritual regeneration is primary and must take place prior to physical amelioration.

Universal love the Arts and sciences and the beautifying of the Earth are the effects of spiritual regeneration and not necessary to the working of its original power but are reflections of it.

Men they say are not prepared to adopt all the grand discoveries of Fourier, why? because they have not been educated for it etc. etc. Query how will you educate them for it by physical or psychical socialism if that is all you have they both will be impotent to move Man to a higher and more noble destiny.

When you make *catholic* provisions for the spiritual nature of Man then and not till then will the religious public be convinced of the sincerity of your protestations however serious you may be in proclaiming them now.

If you have no better to offer than those that are and you do not deny the need of such institutions why do you not recognize those that be? Have you better, then why not offer them to humanity? You should have offered these first if you consider them primary and essential to successful efforts in the cause of Mans progressive well-being.

One of the greatest liabilities of Men is to attribute certain effects to wrong causes.

We must be one with the cause before we can certainly trace distinctly its effects. How shall we prepare for a practical life—is it not by beginning to practice?

It is not by secluding from the world that we are strengthened in practical virtue. It is a sin to divert our attention to reading when God would fill our hearts with the fullness of the Holy Ghost.

What tho death awakes us to a more angelic life? Shall we not fill these now empty hours of senseless time with that foretaste of heaven in mutual love. Heaven itself will not receive us until our Hearts have shapened been by pure love here after the pattern of those whose very form is love and beauty. How sweet are the wounds that are made with the arrows of love. It wounds us that it may love us the more.[164]

P.M.

Tho my meals are made of unleavened bread and figs, & my drink water and I eat no more than supports my body, yet do I feel sinfully indulgent.

I like this of Novalis which came under my observation to day. "Alle Thatigkeit heill-auf, wein das wissen eintritt. Der zustand des vissens ist Eudumoni, salige Rube des Beshunug, himmilischer Quietismus." All activity stops when knowledge steps in. The condition of knowledge is Eudamonic, (Genius, fortune) holy peace of perception, heavenly Quietism.[165]

The thought at bottom is not unlike the definition of perception of Swedenborg a leaf or two before this

6

I have made up mind to accept the life of spontaneity which now prevents me studying. My not studying shall not trouble me any longer and upon the consciousness of the superiority of this life tho it does not promise prospectively the acquisition of certain desirable advantages. What I am I am by it and my trust shall not abate. Lane in a letter to me yesterday says "the thought came in my head that "Studying" was the name to cover to the exoteric eye that deeper work which was to go on in the retirement, peace, and leizure thus best obtained. In the fact it appears I was correct, though such was not your conscious design." "What you express he says Concerning the effect of study my own soul confirms."

"It seems to me frequently that a soul born with genius equal to Shakspere's could not go through any process more calculated to suppress it than that of reading and studying Shakspheres works."[166]

There is much discernment traceable in these remarks of Mr. Lane's. As for the last it is saying in other words that if you would advance, make progress, you must commune with yourself to something more advanced higher than yourself which the product of a Soul equal in genius to your own is not. I have a notion to write a letter to Rev Mr Height[167] but think it is better for me not to do so. Then come to think of it it would be better for he being professor of pulpit eloquence and it being his duty to over look the compositions of the young men at the College etc. his experience must be wide and probably (I smile) he can give advice which would be profitable at this period. I will attempt it I beleive. My desire to write to certain persons who I have written to is all most ceased for my sphere has been so much changed while they have remained stationary.

The fact is evident in others, proven by observation, that the education of Men is always mysterious to them when they are in the midst of their instructions.

Goethe's many sidedness was the result of this numerous partialities of his youth.

My whole heart these two days past like one fresh wound.

What would the Spirit have me to do? to say? it seems to give me no rest, would it have me to be still quiet and peaceful?

What is the work that the spirit is doing now within me?

Should the elementary feelings, the internal eternal affinities be the basis of all our thoughts feelings and actions, the rule of all our conduct? The Spirit draws me ever inward and will not permit me to read think or do anything else but attend to it. It is like a young bride it would have me ever in its presence speaking of its charms.

In giving fixed names to our being we are led to deceive ourselves. Think of this, of your name, what you comprehended under it some few years back and what you now comprehend under the same cognomen.

My heart is drenched in tears. The heart often weeps when the eyes are dry. Our vision does not penetrate so far within as the origin of our feelings. Did it we should see angels the host and the Kingdom of God. The holy city is within. My heart holds conversation which my ears do not hear, and it escapes but the effect of it remains impressed upon me. Oh my heart what aileth thee? and with whom doest thou commune? and wherefore doest thou weep so bitterly? I would clasp thee in my embrace and drink up thy bitter sweet tears and gladden thee with my love.

Reasoning and demonstration are not the highest forms of knowledge. Neither of them is the purest style. The higher the wisdom the simpler the words and the style. The child talks almost all in monosyllables. No poet has yet been able to describe the simple truth tho they are charged with exaggeration.

Every full inspired life utters itself in proverbs sayings & maxims. Budha left many thousand precepts which his preachers have to study.

It is easier to speak wisdom when we are wise than it is to speak foolishness in our folly. In wisdom there is no folly but in folly there is always some wisdom.

Poets do not create but perceive; the unpoetic is but half true always, some times a greater allowance must be made for the proser. The truth of prose is in its poetry and no farther.

As music is the harmony of sounds, and, when in the whole there is no harmony tho there may be discordant notes which make harmony by the variety of combinations it cannot be called music.

Music is the poetry of sounds. Some writers are ever poetic but never poets. None are poets but those who habitually live in Paradise, Eden. Moments most all Men get a glimpse of heaven. He is a true philosopher who rests upon the permanent grounds of being and reflects on the eternal affinities of the Universe.

The more we draw from the well of life the deeper & richer becomes the source from which we drink.

When angels would have music they touch the chords of poets hearts.

Oratory and sculptor are analogous. This truth will bear historical proof.

So is Poetry and Painting. And So is Religion & Architecture.

If we are oned with the great artistes we shall create the objective forms of art unstudiously instinctively

Genius is ever spontaneous, feminine, willess, conceptive, creative, productive and Loveful. Art will reproduce itself so soon as Men are unioned with the great artiste. Art is the product of the great artiste acting through perfect mediums, the Souls of Men when beautifully formed. Poetry reveals the occult union and mystery of words, it places them in their original connections.

It has ever been a part of my character not to read any book for the sake of having it to say that I have read it or to cram my memory with one passage to repeat for display or others pleasure. What ever I have done or do is because I feel a deep interest in what I have done or am doing. This it is now that governs me and is the cause of my cessation from study.

This morning I commenced a letter to the Rev B.F.H. but after having written about two thirds that I wished to write the thought came to my mind that by judging of the past of my life passages of different states of experience had been passed and then more threatening than this now seems and I should be as well off in 3 months from now without sending this letter to him as I should be if I had. This reflection governed me and there the sheet lies half finished and unless a new impulse is given me in that direction there it will lie without further disturbance.

My present position was the choice of two which was before my mind and the other one I feel as little inclined now to accept as any other ungenial occupation which is to put myself under the tuition of some clerical person with the object of educating me to the same sacred office.

However this allways was my affirmation   I would study to acquire what seemed necessary to this object if possibly I could and if in the end I should feel inclined and discovered that I had the ability of being useful in this function, tho I could not promise that I would, I should be governed by the highest sense of duty in the choice.

The simple fact is I do not feel drawn to any particular course of life in my present state of mind, and it does seem necessary that one should know in forehand his future occupation in order that he may direct his attention (he direct his attention?) to such studies as shall be immediately connected with this pursuit. My life is always sincere and at bottom earnest but how to employ this is the difficulty. It is out of the question for me to take up any thing in which I feel an indifferent interest in or which any way hinders me from obeying my deepest convictions. Honestly I confess I have no idea of having more than ordinary ability in any one direction and so beleiving what can I expect but ordinary *success* in the spiritual meaning of that word I mean.

If I should put the pen of critisism upon myself I should leave but little worthy to spoken of and with all the honesty of friendship so much spoken of there is not a friend I have who has the frankness to use no unkinder word to tell me this.

Before my coming here this very question I put to O.A.B. who I did expect would have spoken otherwise than what he did and frankly his answer I waited for with no little uneasiness but what did he say? He gave me words of much encouragement and now thinking of this I will recur to his letter and read it again. I then wrote to him with a faint idea of studying for the ministry and he said in his letter to me, "I say frankly I should rejoice to see you devoting yourself to the ministry. I beleive it your vocation. I have beleived so ever since I have known you, and on this point my mind is made up and I have no hesitancy in sayng devote yourself heart and soul to the ministry". This was to me encouragement coming from one whose judgment whose zeal and wide experience and knowledge of me gave me much confidence in; and others who I had reason to put confidence in gave me the same advice but still I am again afloat and am nothing.[168]

Oh Heavenly Father give me a due sense of my real inferiority and a deep humility which shall never leave me and if to accomplish the ends of thy providence it is necessary for me to be blind as to what the future is to be to me or that my labour is to be the humblest upon Earth grant oh Lord that I shall never forget Thee or Thy love.

7.

I did intend to spend this day in perfect silence and free from reading writing or studying but having received a letter from OAB of such interest makes me wave my resolution. He says he is preparing to enter the Roman Catholic Church, and that he has made up his mind to do so. He speakes strong against my present tendency and asks me if I beleive in the Gospel? Do you really beleive the Holy Catholic Church? If you must put yourself under Her direction etc. etc. And says either I must join the Church or be a Mystic etc. How to answer this I can scarcely say.

OAB is a strong man and has had a great influence upon my character. The Church I have no objections to, & have said repeatedly that the best thing that I could do would be to unite myself to it. To be consistent with my faith to be true to my convictions to the extent that I have always been would lead me to unite myself to the Church and that to the R.C. Church. I have sought in all the numerous protestant sects for that which should sat-isfy all my wants and my seeking was all in vain and having examined the Catholic faith and finding it to answer to all my wants what but willfulness on my part can keep me from joining the Church Catholic? What have I against the Catholic Church? This moment I cannot say that I have anything essentially against her and She meets all my wants on every side. Oh this is the deepest event of my past life. I would have united myself to any one of the protestant sects if I had found them to be what would have answered the demands of nature and why should I now hesitate when I find the Cath-olic Church will? Is not this the self will which revolts against the invol-untary will of the Soul? I feel there would be no doubt that if I should unite myself with the Church that I should pursue my studies with vigour.

I feel like throwing all up. Some cannot rest. How much better it would have been could I have remained in quietness in my daily pursuits and not have been lead as to where I now find myself. I certainly should recommend any person in my position & disposition as OAB has reccomended me and his reccomendation was partially anticipated.

The practical working of it cannot be otherwise than this: should I ever make up my mind to join the R.C.C. my indisposition to study would not be removed   He thinks it would by the Church discipline etc. etc.   If so that would be some time before that could take place. The fundamental question is am I willing to submit my will to the guidence and direction of the Church if it is the body of Christ, if it is the channel of the Holy Ghost, if it is the inspired body illumined with Christs spirit, in a word, if it is the Catholic Church. If I would serve God and Humanity, if I would secure the favor of God and heaven hereafter, why should I not submit to it?

Tuesday 11.

This morning I returned from Boston having gone there on Saturday to see Bishop Fenwick of the R.C. Church. I saw the Bishop and his coadjutor Fitzpatrick. The latter I spent some time with yesterday afternoon and enquired particularly as to the preliminary steps in entering the RC Church. My mind is made up to join the C. Church, and this soon. Next week I intend to close my account here and go to the Catholic College on a visit that situated at Worcester.

Fitzpatrick, called Father John, offers to give me a letter to the head of the College a man he says who I will be much pleased with. There I intend to stay as long as it seems pleasant to me and then go on to N.Y. and there unite myself to the Church. I sigh and feel this is a step the most important in my life.

My highest convictions my deepest wants lead me there and should I not obey them? This permits no room to harbor a doubt in. My friends will look upon it with astonishment and probably use the common epithets—delusion fanaticism and blindness—but so I wish it to appear to minds. As they are otherwise to me this would not be satisfactory. Men call that superstition that they have not the feeling to appreciate and that fanatacism that they have not the spiritual perception to perceive.

The protestant would admire extol and flatter him who will speak and write high sounding and heroic words. Who will assert that he will follow truth wherever she leads at all sacrifices & hazards etc. and no sooner does he so than it slanders persecutes the Man for being what he proffessed to be. Verily it has seperated faith from works.

It is a heavy task, it is a great undertaking, it is a serious sacred sincere solemn step, it is the most vital and eternal act, and as such do I feel it in all its importance weight and power   Oh God Thou who hast lead me through Thy heavenly messengers through Thy divine grace to take this new unseen and religious act of duty. Support me in the days and moments of trial; support me oh Lord in my confessions. Give me power & purity to speak freely the whole truth without any equivocation or attempt at justification. Oh Lord help thy servant and support him when he is weak and feeble and would fall.

One thing that gives me much peace and joy that all wordly inducements and self gratifications, all temptations whatever are in favor of the
Anglican Church and in opposition to the R. Catholic Church & that on this
account my conscience feels free from any unworthy motive in my joining
the Church.

The Roman Catholic Church is the most despised the poorest and according to the world the least respectable on account of the order of foreigners which it is chiefly composed of in this country. It is no sacrifice no
task of any or the least difficulty in this respect to me but the new relations
in which it will place me and the new customs which will be required of me
are new to me and hence I shall feel all their weight at once.

13

I feel very cheerful & at ease in perfect peace since I have consented
to join the Catholic Church   Never have I felt the quietness the immov-
ableness and the permanent rest that I now feel. It is inexpressible. I feel
that essential and interior permanence which nothing exterior can disturb
and that no act that it calls upon me to perform will in the least cause me to
be moved by it. It is with perfect ease and gracefulness that I never dreamed
of that I will unite with the Church. It will not change but fix my life. No
exterior relations events or objects can disturb this unreachable quietness
nor no event can break this deep repose I am in. I feel centered deeper than
any kind of action can penetrate feel or reach. [169]

The exoteric eye is double; the Esoteric eye is single.

The external world is divisional, the internal world is unity.

The Esoteric includes the Exoteric, but the Exoteric excludes the Esoteric.

The Man can move all faculties organs limbs but they cannot move the
Man.

The Creator moves the creature and the creature moves the created.

We know God through looking with the single eye towards him.

14.

A transcendentalist is one who has a keen sight but little warmth of
heart: Fine conceits but destitute of the rich glow of Love. He is in rapport
with the Spiritual world unconscious of the celestial one. He is all nerve and
no blood colour less. He talks of self reliance but fears to trust himself to
Love. He never abandons himself to Love but always is on the look out for
some new facts   His nerves are always tightly stretched like the string of
a bow, his life is all effort. In a short period they loose their tone. Behold
him sitting on a chair! He is not sitting but braced upon its angles as if his
bones were of iron and his nerves of steel. Every nerve is drawn his hands

are clinched like an miser it is his lips and head that speaks not his tongue and heart.

He prefers talking about Love to that of possessing it, as he prefers Socrates to Jesus.

Nature is his Church and he his own God.

He is a dissectin critic heartless cold and what would excite the love and sympathy in another would but excite his curiosity and interest. He would have written a critical essay on the power of the Soul at the foot of the Cross.

To morrow I go with R W Emerson to Harvard to see Lane and Alcott to stay until Sunday   We shall not meet each other for on no other grounds can I meet him than those of Love   We may talk intellectually to-gether and remark and reply and remark again[170]

How vain are all speculations regarding the future has been repeatedly shown me in my past experience and on the eve of my departure from here   I shall not attempt to speculate any farther upon it.

After this event of my union with the Church when all is calmed & at rest where I will then be it is not possible for me now to say.

The events of life no one can foreknow or predict.

That the shaping of events are not wholly in our hands my present un-anticipated movement is clearly demonstrated to me   When we are in the midst of destiny our acts have no time & space fore or after.

I do not know of any act that I now could do that will have more influence to shapen my destiny than my union with the Catholic Church.

The more important actions we do, do, sincerely, seriously, the better are we acting our part in this present life of ours.

It is very certain to me that my life is now as it never was. It seems that I think feel and act from my heart. It reads talks hears smells sees and all.

All is unity with me—Love. Instead of exciting thought ideas etc. as all things did heretofore they now excite Love cheerful emotion and gladness of heart.

To the spirit within I address myself. So long as I struggled against thee I had pain sorrow anguish doubt weeping and distress of Soul. Again and again have I submitted to thee tho ever reluctantly yet was it always in the End for my good. O! how full of Love and Good art Thou to suffer in us for us that we may be benefetted and made happy. It is from thy own pure Love for us for Thy happiness cannot be increased or diminished that thou takest upon thee all the suffering of thy Children.

Lord if I would could or should give myself wholly up to Thee nothing but pure joy complete happiness and exquisite pleasure would fill all my Spirit Soul and Body.

The Lord desires our whole happiness; it is we who hinder him from causing it to be so with our struggle against his Love working Spirit.

Lord keep me ever in the permanent Love Spirit substance and let me not descend otherwise than in the Love Spirit in understanding & sense. Keep me from all disputation and arguing.

Keep me from all reasoning and demonstration.

Keep me from all self effort and self confidence.

Keep me in unity in Love

Keep me in the centre in the eternal purpose   And let my words be few and those not mine but thine the Love Spirit   Let not my mouth speak when Thou wouldst have me to be silent. Let me not answer all that asked for often silence would answer more effectually.

Let me not speak unless thou prompts me to it and shame and confusion will not follow me.

Who is the Lord; is He not our nearest Friend   Is there any one nearer to us than our Lord when we are Good. Is there any one farther from us when we are wicked. The simple presence of the Lord is blessedness. Our marriage with the Lord should be so complete that nothing should be able to attract our attention from him.

We shall speak best to Men when we do not think who we are talking to. Speak always as if in the presence of God where you must be if you would speak to benefit your neighbour. If we are pure before God the eyes of Men will never make us ashamed.

We must be blind to all things and have our Single eye turned towards God when ever we would act in any manner upon Earth when we would heavenise it.

On the Hypocrite

"No Mans condition is so base as his,
None more accurs'd than he, for Man esteems
Him hateful, 'cause he is not what he is;
God hates him, 'cause he is not what he seems.
   What grief is absent, or what mischief can
   Be added to the hate of *God,* and *Man?*"

On Affliction

"When thou afflicts me, Lord, if I repine,
I shew myself to be my own, not thine.
                    B Fran. Quarles—1687"[171]

"If such be Gods; if such our helpers be,
O, what are Men! How more than Beasts are we etc."

His presence made the rudest peasant melt.

Marlowe[172] *Vishnoo Sarma*

"Fate succeedeth not without human exertion"
"Hospitality is commanded to be exercised, even towards an enemy,
when he cometh to thine house.- The tree doth not withdraw its shade from
the wood cutter."
"A wise Man is worthy to be advised; but an ignorant is never."
"A draught of milk to Serpent, doth nothing but increase his poison."
"It is a kind of slander to trust rumor"

Ben Jonson[173]

Seek! Shall I seek! the Gods above
should give,
they have enough and we do poorly live.

Cowley[174]

New York June 23 Monday
Friday last I arrived here. Since I left Concord I visited the Catholic
College at Worcester and have visited the N.A. Phalanx at Jersey.[175]
I scarce have a word to say here.
I still feel that my consciousness is interior to all life. Interior to organs
faculties or material mediums.
My intention is to go to see the Priest that Bishop Fitzpatrick gave me
a letter of introduction to. Not one word has passed between my friends and
me respecting my being united to the Catholic Church.
I see no practical way for me to pursue in my present state of mind. I
need none. This a demand of the understanding not of the superior standing
in which we should always live, be.
The wordly Man & the intellectual Man thinks all that time is misspent,
absolutely lost, that is given to the spirit while the Spirit begotten Man feels
he includes the other two when he is wedded and enjoys the communion of
the Spirit.
The Spirit Man generates knowledge; the time Man acquires it—acquires what the Generative Genius generates, creates. What one has the
other seeks to possess.
We never should permit ourselves to be moved from the interiormost
the centre on any conditions whatever external to it, and this we should not
do on any pretext whatsoever. Let the body perish and all be destroyed but
cling to the Spirit, to God.
One victory over the world, over the body, is two gained for heaven.
It is to the interior life and that only we must look for support approbation

or whatsoever we need. If we loose for one moment our hold on this we fall in the dark unfathomable hades of Sin.

If we trust to it it will give us all that we need for body mind or Soul. The Ravens will bring us bread and Angels will minister unto us in the deserts of Life.

Lord our Souls ever praise thee for thy loving kindness. How sweet are the blessings of thy Spirit.

We must be so oned with Spirit that we can be still in Spirit where ever we are and be above the sense of hunger thirst cold nakedness reproach unkindness heat rain or any outward power, cause, whatsoever.

Our being must be in Spirit and then our ex-istence will be Spiritu-al. The only thing we have to do to secure heaven hereafter and to succede in this world is to place unconditional trust in God.

Let us surrender ourselves completely & perpetually to him and He will take all care and provide for us.

He keeps saying to us in heaven Let me take all the trouble. Come unto Me all ye that are weary and heavy ladened, and I will give You rest   My yoke is easy and my burthen is light but we keep heaving out a stern of our Self will, which will not hold water and at the last day we shall find that our labour has been evil and our trouble was all in vain.

Trust, faith, submission to God is the one only condition of right ex-istance.

25.

This morning I whent to see Bishop McClosky.[176] I found him to be a man of fine character mild disposition and of a broader education than any of the Catholics that I have had the pleasure of meeting with. He was accquainted with Brownsons writings & Emersons & personally acquainted with Wm Channing who he had met at Rome.

He loaned me some books on matters pertaining to the Church. He is to begone a fortnight from N.Y. and I am to wait until he comes back before I take any further steps towards being unioned with the Church.

Man is a mystic fact.

The interiormost is ever mystical and we should ever be in the centere of the circle of the mysticlife. We must unfold the mystical in all our expressions, actions thoughts & motions. It is the mystic life only that can fully interest Man.

This is deeper than all conditions behind all organs faculties & functions. We must hear those who speak to us in the interior world and hear the mystic Man speak through us.

The mystic Man is ever youthful fresh & new

The mystic sphere is the kingdom of heaven within.[177]

I cannot study sit down and read for a length of time; the new man will not permit me; ever he calls me from it to meditate and enjoy his presence.

He says I am all; ask of me and I will give you more than has been written than you can find or dig out by study.

Be my spokesman this is your office   Submit to me this is your glory. I have taken up my abode in you on condition that you will be obedient faithful and submissive.

You have no bussiness to ask of me what I am a going to set you about. I am and you know it and this is enough for you to know.

This is my condition of remaining with you that you entertain me and me alone and no other on any pretext what soever.

I am all and this suffices.

You have nothing to say do or to be troubled about; only do as I bid you to do; follow what I tell you and be still. If you neglect me in any way forget me for any other object now after you have enjoyed my confidence love and blessing I will not abide with you any longer.

I want all your time and to speak all that is to be said   you have no right to speak a word not a word of your own. You are not your own   You have given yourself up to me and I am all; I will not leave you unless you leave me first and then I shall ever be the nearest to you but you will not know it.

I am your Friend the one who loves you and I have discovered myself to you and will do so more but the condition of so doing requires ever more faith tenderness and submissiveness. Nothing is so real so near so full of enjoyment as I am to you and you cannot leave me without giving up the greater for the less.

I talk to you at all times and am with you at all seasons and my delight is to be in your presence to love you and take delight in the love I bestow upon you   I direct your pen speech thoughts and affections tho you know it sensible but you shall know it clearer who I am and all respecting me if you but comply with my requirements.

You need not fear you cannot make any mistakes if you submit to be directed by me.

26

Is it not better to teach those who depend upon charity for their subsistence to live so as to be independent of alms than to be charitable? There is no doubt there are those who are essentially dependant upon the charity of their fellow Men for their physical existance but a large majority of those who now depend upon charity are not of this class.

27.

Discipline what is it? and what is its value? These questions have presented themselves to my mind this afternoon. Whether a complete reliance upon and faith fullness to the spontaneous nature would not give us more than education and discipline in the common meaning of these words is to me a question upon which I ponder.

June 31.

Under the influences of nature & Man humanity has degenerated   Under the influence of the Church She has been regenerated. This truth admits of historical as well as individual proof. Religion is an influence that comes down from heaven to Man not a development nor a growth of Mans nature. Mans growth is the consequence of it.

Where is Egypt with her Zoroasters and her Pythagoras? Where is India with her Brahmas? Where is Greece with her Socrates Platos? Where is Rome with her Catos & Zeno? Where is Israel with her Moses & Prophets? Where are they all? All are included in Christ the God-Man who has established a Kingdom which is immutable and cannot fail.

July 5th.

It is the duty of every Man to do that which expresses the divine life which stirs within him and not to do anything which is inconformable to it. So far as Man falls short of this so far he falls short of his duty of his perfection and divine beauty.

We must be true to the divine life within and I think we may say with very great certainty that this is the only way of obtaining happiness in this world and eternal felicity in the world to come. It is to this that God calls us, but we, no not truly we, but the Man of Sin ever flatters us as Eve was at first that if we follow him we shall not die but become as Gods and we to day have the same temptas to overcome as Eve had. O how much greater God would have us to be than what we are but we will not. We must cast out the Man of Sin and submit to the Paradisaical Man. This we are enabled to do blessed be heaven by the grace of God through Jesus Christ.

What are the temptations which hold Men back from following God and living a divine life? In one word—the World. Pride, Love of Praise, Riches, Self indulgence, and all that refers and looks to time instead of heaven-Eternity-God.

We should encourage all that gives us an impulse heavenward and deny all that tends to draw us down more in the body-sense & time. Man alas is weak powerless and unable to perform any good deed to raise himself to God to serve heaven without the free gift the blessed grace of God the Holy Spirit.

We all fail to act up to the divine grace which is given us. Oh Lord forgive me my manifold transgressions and empower me to be more and more obedient to Thy holy Spirit. It is the desire of the inward Man to follow thy Spirit but the appetites of my members ever war and often subdue and overcome the inward Man. Strengthen oh Lord the inward Man and enable him to govern my whole three sphered nature.

Send down oh Lord into my heart thy celestial love and quicken all my heavenly powers. It is very true that no Man can serve two masters. Between these two there is no compromise no mediation—God & Mammon   Lord make me fully sensible of this and strengthen my resolution to follow thee. I do look to the Church of Christ for help. Oh may I find in the Church that which the Apostles found in Jesus.

July 6.

The immediate effect of Christianity upon humanity has been to increase Mans sensibility of the objects of the Spiritual world. Poetry Music the fine Arts are ennobling and spiritualizing only so far as the nature of Man has been divined by the influence of the divinity. Previous to the Coming of Christ the Arts had rather on the whole the tendency to encourage vice licentiousness and Sin than to elevate and refine Mans nature.

The influence of Christianity has been to restore Man to his primitive gracefulness excellence beauty hence the expression of Mans—Art, or rather the expression of the divinity in Man has been diviner purer and more beautiful in its character.

The mission of Christ even to infuse into the heart of humanity a divine life the character of which was never before so fully experienced. This is very evident from the fact of His immediate influence upon the Apostles and the effect of the Church upon the history of the Race.

Jesus has given to the Race a new birth which has expressed itself in a more refined beautiful graceful musical and poetical forms than was in the nature of the previous humanity to do.

In affirming Jesus to be the basis and life of modern civilization nothing is detracted from the great & good which preceded him nor that they have left traces of their genius upon modern Society.

When we speak of Jesus as God we affirm him to be God the source of all inspiration from which all ancient & modern have derived their life genius goodness & divine beauty.

Jesus quickened the spiritual powers of the Soul which were deadened by the fall and Man again saw heaven and angels descending & ascending to & from the throne of ineffable Love.

All the promises of Jesus refer to gifts of spiritual powers over inanimate matter the animal creation and the Man of Sin.

Jesus came to give a spiritual life which would generate all knowledge and physical well-being.

Jesus came not to teach a system of philosophy how ever useful this may be to direct Men how by the least possible outlay of physical strength he can procure food for his physical subsistance however necessary this may be but he came to give a Man a new nature which shall more than do all this which will not only secure his well being here but his eternal felicity hereafter.

As we rise above our time nature and are united with our eternal nature we feel more and more our indebtedness to Christ. It was to this he called us in all his words and now calls us in the Spirit.

P.M.

We do not say that the merchant the Trader & the Mechanic & Laborer may not and that some do not live a divine life but it is the divine life & that only that we should live & all inconformable conditions must be made to conform to it or be given up. We cannot say for another what conditions are absolutely necessary for the manifestation of the divine life within him but this that it is the imperative duty of every Man to create and seek such condition as are really necessary to the existence of the divine life at all sacrifices be what they may.

We must place absolute faith in God implicit confidence in his providence and in doing this we have done the greatest act of our being. This is the consummation of all acts. The act of all Actions.

Our worldly activity proceeds from the wordliness of our hearts and the last must be over come before the first will cease.

So long as low appetites are cherished and selfish passions are harbored and vanity allowed a seat in our bosom so long will Men be slaves to their stomachs, backs, bussiness. Every quickening of our sensibility towards Love Heaven & Equity will lead us to change our circumstances conformable to our new inward life.

It is for *us* to be true to God however unlike the world we may seem. It is here in silence in private alone that deeds can be done which shall outstrip the Alexanders and Napoleons in their eternal effects.

July 7. th

All that we contend for is that Man should obey the will of God and cooperate in the work of God with his will and not against it. Interior submission to the Love Spirit is the answer to all questions concerning Mans welfare here and hereafter. Whatever a man is lead to do in obedience to it is well done and Godlike tho it leads him to offer up his only dear Son.

We do say this with great emphasis that nothing under heaven should prevent a man from following God.

Unless Man can give up all and follow Christ he is none of his.

Every true Man is a genius.

All genius is Religious.

The objective forms of genius are the expressions of the beautiful the good and the true in one word—God.

He is a genius in whom the beautiful the good & the true permanently inhabits. In whom it has become an abiding permanent substance.

The genius in every work of art is religious whatever the subject may be.

The artistes performs the highest act of religious worship in painting the Madona The composer in symphony or in oratorio   The Poet in his Paradise Lost or whatever may express the highest within him. And so does he who sows the smallest seed or plants a blade of grass.

We repeat that every Man is called to give expression to the highest, best, divine in him and to this and this only is he called.

We add also that the Catholic Church is the medium of this divine life and she has nurtured and encouraged Men of genius in her bosom as a fond mother.

We do not mean to say that the Church has made Men of ordinary stamp into geniuses but that she has given to the inborn capacity of genius the highest inspiration and so been the means of their being more than they would have been without her, even so with the most ordinary Men.[178]

We affirm that the influence of protestantism upon the bussiness world has been to make it much more unchristian than it was under the influence of Catholicism in the middle ages[179]

July 9.

It seems to be a common experience that in our present conditions of life that we are compelled to sacrifice daily the ideal in a certain measure to the material the Eternal for the temporary the unconditioned for the conditioned.

If I could give a true narrative of the inner & interior life which I have passed through these two years back or more it would be a picture not uninteresting I imagine to a few.

It would be a story of the birth and youth of the Ideal.

Previous to these following two years it was within my own bosom and had not exhibited itself in external actions but since then it has.

My visit to OABs for a month then my residence at Brook Farm for 8 or 9 months after that my being at Fruitlands for 3 weeks or more my return to N. Y. and with what objects then my going off again and residence of 3

months at Concord and the objects that were then in my mind and now my
return to N. Y. and the cause of my return these if I could em body with
the incidents which have been connected with them would be material for
one who could work them up for a Wanderjahre.

The first Period should be named Youth giving the Ideal and the Actual
in Youth.

The second should be the struggle between the Ideal and the
actual   The third should be the mastery and the supremacy of the ideal
over the actual material.

The fourth period should give the absolute union of the Ideal and the
eternal absolute in their individual existence.

The fifth should give the eventual oneness of the Ideal absolute with
Humanity and Nature.

July 10

Under these five heads I have in mind materials sufficient to make
quite a Volume but need the close application to connect them tho I do not
say they would be readable when done.

It would be the esoteric and exoteric history of my own life of 10 years.

I have thought of undertaking to write under these 5 heads each day
whatever finds at the time place their and since yesterday much has come
to me that almost forces me to do so. I should give letters and leaves from
a day book of the period in which I should carry the person of the narrative
which had been written about that time and letters received by him.

This attempt would be useful to me as a task if nothing more should
come from it. Or it might serve to some future purpose. I now think if I had
the leisure and a quiet place that I should set my whole heart Soul and mind
to work at it.

The first period would be the unconscious period; the second the beholding of the ideal; the third the identity of the ideal and the Real I mean
the Union of the Ideal & the Real. I should have before my minds eye to a
certain extent the novels or narratives of Goethe and Jean Paul.

I feel periods that I have passed through with intense and unearthly
excitement which heretofore I had not the nerve to describe   I should be
able to do it now with sufficient life to draw still the deepest from me.

This I will think more of and see how my mind will settle upon the
matter. I think I should wish but to identify myself but partially with one
character and as it were not to give myself up to my conditions. For in fact
so do I feel. It is not because I take the part of certain principles or institutions when I meet certain persons that I rank myself wholly under their
banner for the next moment if I should meet a nother party who I felt did
not justice to the side I had attempted to place in its proper harmony with

all other great principles I should certainly take the opposite side. I feel if it were possible and I sincerely confess with my whole heart in all its candor it is not possible I should like to keep myself in the relation of a soul of a Biographer and auto biographer. I have never attempted anything and this must be my first attempt God willing helping and acting.

What should I first open the first chapter with—this—Let Men say what they will God above us the human Soul and all surrounding nature are great realities eternal solemn joyous facts of human experiences

Something in this vein I would give in a short pseudo preface in a style a la Jean Paul with a thrilling vein of deep heart stirring earnest ness Car-lyleian. I make mention of these men because they figure to me my own life.[180]

I could not commence and go on with the narrative consecutively but would have to think much collect much and construct much before I would be able to give form and shape and certain air of reality to the story.

I laugh at this and say will this but show my folly? Let me see and with the help of God wait and see what 24 hours or more may effect my resolution. This I can say if I have the ability and my resolution increases as it has since I first tho't of it somethings may happen which have not been. I will think dream and sleep and pray upon it.

11.

To day I arranged the letters I sent home from my first going away until my last stay at Concord. I think I shall attempt to do something towards the thought which occurred to me on the 9th.

It should be done by selecting the best the most interesting parts of my life and experience of some years.

12.

We make no question that God gave to all nations previous to the birth of Jesus Christ his *beloved* and only *Son* dispensation of light and love in their great Men and lead them from time to time to the stage of civilization to which they had arrived. The Christian affirms and is the first to affirm that God is the Parent the Father of Humanity of every human being and it would be in direct contradiction to his own faith to deny this. But when Jesus Christ came he came to introduce a life in to humanity whose light and love should so surpass all that had been before him as to make it appear as darkness compared with light. This life makes no war with the good and true that existed in Men before him nor does it deny all that had existed but embraces includes and fullfills it all and gives to Man more than Men dared dream of previous to his coming. That Christianity is of this high character not only did its author show by his life example and death but it has shown itself to be so subsequently wherever it has come in contact with any of the old forms of religious faith and doctrine. It has shown a power that is superior and which over comes all that arrays itself against it.

We do not say that Zoroaster Pythagoras Plato Socrates Zeno Cato etc. etc. were not good great and religious men and were above their age in which they lived inspired by a life superior to their time and even above the life of a great part of Christendom so called but this we say: that Christ gave to the world a life infinitely above that which they lived and had they lived in His or our day that they would have been far superior to what they were as the inspiration of Christianity is above that which they lived under.

13.

To day I have been with some friends to Fort Lee but have been far from them in thought and feeling.

At present I am out of all outward engagements bussiness study all subjects of interest all objects of an earthly existance are not a part of my thoughts. This cannot long continue so nor should it. Something must be done either one way or the other before long. I don't expect that I have any talent or genius in any direction in particular and that my mind is of a general and ordinary capacity without any remarkable aptitude for any thing particular. I should do some thing yet what to do is what I cannot say. Nothing engages my interest and I do not feel inclined at present to take hold of anything. I feel that if I should attempt to study the languages again I should be drawn from them as I was in a much less shorter period than I was then. To believ any thing in a particular sense providential will happen to me I do not and should not.

It is a clear and bounding duty that every one should in some way or other recompense the world for that which he consumes from its store. Now for me to do this consistently with the present state of mind that I have I see not how I can do it. To be sure I have contracted my wants so far as respects eating as it seems to me possible; somewhat in dress but not so far as I should and can do in this latter source of much expense. Otherwise as for pleasures and many other sources of expenditure I trust I am not immoderate. But still it leaves me here. I do not and do not see how I can give my attention sufficiently to our bussiness for to satisfy my self or brothers. To so condition myself as to force myself to engage my attention in bussiness the greater part of my time as for instance by marriage I have no desire to do so and therefore cannot. The life I now live is more to me than anything living and I feel prepared to sacrifice all for the sake of its continuance and to my obedience to it. I see no place of usefullness for me with my life as I am and would rather give up this earthly existance than to part with it. My present position in this part of the world as it is is one which I do not see any prepared congenial conditions for nor am I in condition to remain long as I am. If I were in Europe I should find in the Catholic Church institutions were in I could enter for a time until his period of my life would either fix itself permanently or give place to another by which I could see my way clearer. But here I am and not in Europe   If I cast my eyes all around my way seems difficult and I am at loss what my fate may be. Some thoughts have arisen in my mind and I will state them which may come at some future time in the range of the possible.

If I am joined to the Catholic Church may I not if there is such an institution in Europe go there and live for a time? Ah is this possible?!

If we owned a spot of ground I would be willing to go on it and engage as much of my time as possible in cultivating and improving it.

Last I do not know what may be the advice and influence of the Catholic Church upon my mind and do have a slight hope that I may find the exact remedy that I need in my union with Her.

I feel the assurance that if I follow the Spirit of God and place all my confidence in it that it will do for me what I dare not hope for myself.[181]

14.

We should not wish to forerun our, no God's, time. We should be patient and satisfied with what the day brings forth. If we have one step before us to take we should not ask what will or may the next one be. The condition of knowing the next is in taking the one that precedes it. This is one fact which we should be assured of in our inmost soul that is God is our Father and watches over us all. We are in the hands of him if we place ourselves there who is infinite in Love and Wisdom. All that I ask and wish is conditions adapted to the expression of the life given me. It is true we all must be able to create those conditions necessary to the life which stirs within us. This seems to be the law of our own individual existance and of necessity so. We must have the heroism the fortitude to create or procure such circumstances as will best express our own individuality and this we are called upon to do both by God who created us as we are and that which makes us differ from all those around us. It is for this we are created that we may give a new and individual expression of the absolute in our own peculiar character   As soon as the new is but the expression of the old God ceases to live. It is ever that the mystery is revealed in every new birth. So must it be to Eternity. The Eternal Absolute is ever creating new forms of expressing itself. It is it that calls upon us to be ourselves, to be Godlike, to be that which is godgiven to us whatever that may be, to be anything else is to be nothing, is to deny God is, and lives, and our own individual existance. This is true and we are called upon to be true to this truth, for all other things are subordinate to it—*sacrifice.*

It has ever been and we suppose it ever will be the condition of those who are most true to this god given life destiny that persecution poverty and sometimes martyr-dom is their lot. Their whole life is one of living death of perpetual martyrdom and their suffering here is the condition of enjoying heaven-within-hereafter. These are the true Prophets-Seers and Poets-Messengers of God to Man, the saviours of the Race, and the world is never in want of Pilates to crucify them. Christ is crucified daily on the cross of selfishness indulgence and all kinds of vice. He that indulges in his soul heart or senses anything contrary to the spirit of Christ is partaker of the guilt of the crucifixion of the Redeemer the Saviour of Man.

We say if we were of the generation when Christ was upon Earth, if we had lived in his time, we should not have done as they did, behold Christ lives to day as truly as he lived 19 hundred years ago and we daily persecute deny him and pierce his dear body with spears sharper than those of wood or iron and when he asks from us in his lovely and sweet voice for water to quench his thirst we give him to drink that which is bitterer than wormwood and gall.

The Jews did all this after a sensible and material manner but we alas do worse; we do it in our hearts in an invisible and spiritual way.

We say Jesus was the Christ not that he yielded himself to the Christ Spirit as Pythagoras Socrates Plato Zeno etc. as many nowadays do contend. Jesus was the Christ, the Word made flesh, sent from heaven, not one of the human species, born of the Immaculate Virgin, conceived by the Holy Ghost.

The Catholic Church has preserved unity without encroachment on individual liberty and has preserved individual liberty without the loss of perfect unity. Unity without individual liberty is impossible as individual liberty is without unity. When the tendency is to consolidation the effect of this is immobility slavery death; when to seperation we have obstruction lawlessness and wild fanaticism. It is only in catholicism Unity and Individuality in divine unity that progress liberty and life is secured and perpetuated.

15.

Poetry is a clearer and purer intuition of the absolute under the form of the beautiful. Philosophy of the True, Theology of the Good.

Religion is the mystic union of the Good True and Beautiful under the form of the HOLY.

The intuition of the holy is the highest action of the faculty of reason.

Sensible perception or intuition

| Philosophic | D— | " | D— |
| Imaginative | D— | " | D— |

Religious   D—   " D—

The Church embraces in its cultus the absolute Holy in all its forms of expression as consequences not as causes. It is the generator; It is not re-generated by them. We hold that Poetry Philosophy the Arts and Sciences are the immediate consequences of the inspiration given to Men by Jesus Christ through medium of the Catholic Church. That prior to the introduction of Christianity the nations the farthest advanced in these higher branches of knowledge were uncivilized barbaric.

P.M.

This morning I saw Bishop McCloskey. In 8 or 10 days I expect to recieve conditional baptism from the Catholic Church.

He said that my life would lead me to a contemplative life and that in this country the Church was so situated as it required them all to be active etc. I did not speak farther on this subject with him. He asked me if I felt like devoting myself to the order of the Priesthood and undergo their denial discipline be missionary etc. etc. I answered that all I could say was that I wished to live the life given to me and felt like sacrificing all to it, but would not say that the priesthood would be the proper place for me.

I feel that if I could for a certain length of time under the discipline of the Church have conditions for living a life of contemplation it would be what spirit now demands of me. Whether by following some other way I shall not be compelled back to this step I am not perfectly sure. If there are brotherhoods in Europe which are instituted genial to the state of mind that I am in which the Bishop intimated that there were if I could go there for a length of time why should I not go? why not? I will see farther about this subject the next time I speak with the Bishop. There is a College at Fordham a few miles from the City which tomorrow there is to be a commencement which the B invited me to go and see. Perhaps I shall find this place to be suitable and it is possible I may be led to examine and try it. The Lord knows all; into his hands I resign myself. He will do for us if we trust in Him more than we dare hope for in our dreams. His ways are not as our ways; what ever he does is greatest best and right for us, let that be what it may. Jesus conquered upon the Cross not upon a Throne. His crown was made of Thorns not of gems and gold. Be ye followers of me said He.

17.

Instead of the denial of the supremacy of the physical nature and the subordination of it and the pschical nature to the spiritual nature which was the chief characteristic of the Middle Ages we have in our day the gospel preached of gaining heaven by sensuous gratification and the supremacy of matter.

Fast days have been turned into feast days and days of prayer into those of secular bussiness and trade. There was a time when Men sought for all kinds of hardships trials and possible endurances that they might love their Master more and be more like Him but now this is said to be useless self torture and the fanaticism of spiritualism. The world believing Man can only gain heaven by means of material wealth, he calls that righteous, and that only, which aids it in its outward material accummulation which sinks the Soul deeper & deeper in sin sense and shame.[182]

Man must deny all that is below his paradisaical nature which has usurped the place of his true elementary being the image of God. This we do not call in strict language the denial of our true God created immortal self but the denial of that which is not myself which has taken usurped the place of our true eternal heavenly Adamic being. It is the restoration of that defaced image of God to its primitive divine beauty grace and sweetness. We must feel and possess the love and light from above before we have the disposition and power to deny the body and the wisdom of this world.

If we have the Christ Spirit we will fulfill the Christ commandments.

Thus was it with Man prior to his spiritual death, his fall, he lived in, and enjoyed God and was in communion and society with Angels not knowing Good and Evil. His life was spontaneous his wisdom intuitive unconscious even as light would be if there were no darkness, we should see and be recipients of all its blessings without being conscious or knowing its existance. But darkness came—Sin—and Man knew Alas and in-knowing lost all he *possessed* before.

Jesus came to restore Man to that Eternal Day from which Adam fell.

18.

We hold and identify the life displayed in the morals and Aestheticks of the Greeks to be in its highest manifestation the same as that which was displayed in the Jewish Nation and which was made flesh in Jesus for which a body was prepared through the instrumentality of the Holy Ghost and the Virgin Mary. We would not deny the Absolute under any form of its manifestation; we should hold ourselves culpable if we did, but let it be understood that while we would not do this no more than to deny our blessed Lord and divine Saviour we do hold that the Catholic Church is the divine appointed medium by which Man is given a new birth and saved from Sin given a new birth reunited to God made partaker of the glory and blessedness of the Angels of Love and Light and an inhabitant of Heaven and brother of Jesus. Jesus is the incarnation of the Absolute God; all prior manifestation of God was qualitative and relative.

Is there not a mode of certainty of reason we may call absolute, a priori, synthetic intuition of the One, the Eternal Centre: Unity, Unconditioned Being?

All reasoning is subject to dispute and we do not see how this possibly can be avoided.

The a priori method of demonstrating this Catholic Church as being the Church of necessity is one. And then the posteriori method is the other she having proved herself to be so. The first goes back to original Sin; its proof then the absolute necessity of a Redeemer and the necessity of his being a God-Man then the institution of his Church as the medium of his influence and of consequence its perpetuity universality and infallibility and power.

The other method would be historical evidence miracles etc. etc. We confess we do not perceive how that Man can be brought to see the truth as it is in Jesus without the operation of the grace of God a priori in his heart; and the condition for this is still within the power of unregenerated Men. Before the sinner knows that he is a sinner in the orthodox sense he must be the recipient of Gods free grace.

18

Every Sinner of necessity must have the ability to supply the conditions of receiving Gods Grace otherwise we do not see how he can be redeemed freely from Sin without the destruction of his freedom. We do not say he has or possesses grace unto salvation, but has the power to create the conditions that grace may enter and abide in his heart unto his salvation.

Thus the sinner who hears the Gospel preached partially perceives the truth of it and feels its power and has the power to submit himself to the conditions it requires of him that he may possess the power and grace of God unto his eternal salvation or he may if he so pleases, continue in the way of darkness Sin and Death.

Grace is the free gift of God. God being Universal Love will consequently give his grace to all those who will submit to the love conditions of his universal Love.[183]

The highest object of Mans earth existance is to be the same as Jesus to submit to Christ to yield to heaven. To labour for the Redemption of Man the establishing of Gods kingdom upon Earth.

Yield yourself to the Absolute All embracing Love and let it act in, through, and with you in its own infinite loveful manner. Co-operate with it in all its loveful purposes and this is your work and none other. He that seeks for a work will never find it but he that submits himself to the Creator will always be at work. We have not because we will not, we will have so soon as we will not to will have.

If we possess the Spirit, rather if the Spirit possesses us it will lead us to our undoubtful work.

If we are inspired we must do, actualize it which is acting us.

We must be before we can do.

We must always be—doing.

Submit to be and of consequence we shall do, must do.

The Seed must grow if it is placed in growing conditions; the plant must blossom if the seed grows. And the blossoms must produce fruit if the plant grows, and the fruit must produce new seeds if the fruit is permitted to ripen.

Oh God give me grace to yield all myself to Thee. This is all that I wish desire and long for. Oh give me Thee.

20

Yesterday I spent with a party at Fort Lee in the woods. I was one hour in silence alone in a pleasant spot which over looked the river on the high palisades rocks. I seemed to be in communion in all the deep avenues of the Soul with the infinite invisible all around us. To me this is society, inspiration, life, being. O nature couldst thou but utter thy unutterable Soul how much nearer and dearer wouldst thou be to the heart of Man and Man to thee. But we do hear thee in the deep still voices of the heart. It is thee who fills our heart of hearts with deep unutterable universal life. Thou art a Being as we are not a mere expression of the Infinite. God has given unto thee a joy and sweet existance of thy own. Our hearts feel and tell us so.

We affirm from knowledge perception experience that there is a function of the human Soul through which knowledge is gained which is higher than that of human philosophy by analysis induction or any other human method. Call it inspiration intuition or faith it is and that it is is all. It admits of no controversy; it is absolute affirmation but not dogmatic in the odious sense of that word. It is the perception of the Eternal Spirit or Laws which are the one unitary foundation of the Infinite in Man & Nature. It is the perception of the unconditioned on which the all conditioned is based. It is seeing the unseen the ideal in the seen and actual.

We should rather let this body of ours return to the dust from which it was formed than to let the Spirit suffer and die within us.

We must be able to set still and subsist without meat or drink and let the angel take its flight up towards heaven and leave *the outward shell of the chrysalis behind*.

21.

We should suffer ourselves to be raised up unto the highest heavenly atmosphere of divine life wherein all demonstration argument and dispute ceases and all external enthusiasm proselytism and physical might is not sought after or thought of.

Into the high region of pure affirmation which springs from simple divine intuition of the eternal affinities of beings things and actions.

All controversy is the mixture of light and darkness; let the light alone be affirmed and the darkness will cease its parasitical existance.

Let us always speak the deepest and most universal affinities which we experience.

We shall exorcise the spirits of darkness selfishness ambition and pride if we submit to universal disinterested Love.

Are we so related to evil Sin & darkness that we cannot exorcise them without fear of losing our own existance? Separate, separate, the light from darkness and let not your being be a blank chaos.

Heaven help me. The Lord knows what I need; I do not, only that I need. Grant o heaven.

All things pass by me and are doing Gods work in doing their own, and I alone set still looking on with still seeing gaze. It is as if I were an inhabitant of a different sphere breathing another atmosphere. Separate from all around, inside of all. Doing nothing; yet it seems they add not to natures store but of all most deluded in thinking that they really do. The future will rank them most real who seem to be most visionary now and those who scoffed them possessed with darkness not knowing what they did. No one can gain heaven here peacably.

Not to have loved is a greater crime than having in love committed sin.

22

The absolute beautiful true & Good displays itself in the works of a Sculptor, Painter, Architect, Composer, and the life of a Saint as it does in that of a Poet, Hero, and Statesman. We do not deny the Great Manufacturer, the Merchant, or Mechanic Genius of the self-same stuff as that of Homer, Phidias, Michael Angelo, Raphael, St. Bernard, Shakspere, Dante, Napoleon etc. Wealth of any kind really accumulated is evidence of genius.

The Good the True and the Beautiful are worshipped in mystic unity under the form of the HOLY in the Catholic Religion, in the apriori synthetic intuition of faith which is a more elevated and purer mode of activity of the faculty of Reason.

This is a subjective understanding, conception, of the object of Catholic Religion. The objective form would be the showing of the objective Holy incarnated in the flesh made visible, subjective, in the form of Man.

The moralist says be good; the philosopher, be just, be true; the poet, be beautiful; the Religious man, be Holy. Religion comprehends all virtues in the word Holy if not as an aggregate but as the Cause and they as consequences. What virtue, what beauty—grace—is not sweetly seen in the Maddonas face.

23.

Christ to have benefited the human Race must have been an object of the Race higher than it not one of it, for the human Race is the human Race and nothing more nor less and cannot be its own object at any time and if so, if it could be the subject and object at the same time, there would be not be anything in the subject that there is not in the object or in the object that there is not in the subject, hence nothing could be gained if this could possibly be, which it cannot be   Ergo if Christ has benefited the Race he is not one of the human species but as the Scriptures say the only begotten Son of God made flesh. Here lies the great difficulty in distinguishing Christ from the great providential Men who have existed in the history of the Race. By what right do we place him above and not as one of the human species? By the same mode of reasoning may not all great Men claim in *degree* the same office? Is it by the prophecies which were prophecied before his coming? Is it by his power and miracles? Is it by the effect he has had upon the progress of humanity? In all of these perticulars other nations show in a degree a paralel, especially the Hindoo nation. But the great that have been since his time admit his divinity and infinite superiority but do they not prove themselves more like him in doing so? We do not question that Christ has done all for humanity, A fact that the most orthodox may affirm. But are we to beleive in his special divinity or in the doctrine that the infinite God incarnates himself in his own time & seasons in the human form to Save the Race?

24

No, we are not to beleive the last proposition for they, the geniuses of the Race, were so by the inspiration derived from God which inspiration was made manfest in the flesh in Jesus Christ. In him it took the human form. Jesus was the eternal underived substance one with the Father, the Same. In him the unknown God, the invisible Spirit, was made manifest unto all Men for he was the Light and Life of Men and the Truth.

In all our reasoning we must understand that the criterion of truth is not the individual judgment of our personal Reason but the universal voice of the Catholic Church. Not that the individual Reason is to be trusted in some Cases nor that it has not light, for the Voice of the Church is based upon the light of Reason, but it is this: the individual reason is not competent to comprehend the universal truth, hence no individual judgment is the criteria of absolute universal truth.

Oh heaven what is Man that he should be the tool of such low passions.

This seems to be the greatness of life to concentrate on whole nobleness in one great deed and leave this world.

The time is near when I shall receive conditional baptism in the C. Church. This is the first step of placing myself in new conditions under other influences from what I have been in.

This will cause new feelings thoughts & actions to arise within me. What character this will give to my future life is impossible to foresee. It is such acts as seem to us unfathomable in which we act because impelled by the infinite unknown called God Fate Fortune Chance what ever it may be named that are the all of life and are unoblivious eternal. Such should be our every-day-life. We should ever do that we dare not do if we would conquer the impossible. No conditions can conquer the Soul, in it is the stuff on which they depend—the Unconditioned.

The Hero is greater than the Poet who sings the song of his noble exploits.

Occasions do not make Heros but Heros create occasions. Godlike from the Chaos around him he forms a world which shall represent him.[184]

God himself gave birth to a being which imaged him, is it ignoble in Man to do likewise? It was earth dust mud from which the form of Man was shapen   Gods fingers were not soiled. The same words are used to write the revelations of heaven as those to write our worst crimes.

The every day revelations of a Mans heart is proof that our common life would be great noble heroic if we would be true.

We know not which is the greater sin: to suffer the inspiration to die out of us in ordinary life or to blindly go forward and do some deed as at least shall seem to satisfy the God within. Expiation, Sacrifice, it will have, and if it needs be, give it thee.

The greatest truth ever expressed in the condition of finding life is in loosing, in yielding it up. To yield up our mortal life is giving death for immortality.

Man is more willing to play a loosing than a winning game from his cowardly fear. Unless we die we cannot live. Life is in Death and not otherwise. The old bark must give place to the new or the Tree must shortly cease to be. We are no two moments the same. The present is an indivisible point, too swift to be seen by mortal sight.

To be true to God—genius—is not necessarily to be externally different from other Men for they often seem to be what they are not. Genius exists in your submission to it and when your submission seems most uncalled for then must you yield implicitly.

If Men were as true to God as they are to Satan there would be then as few devils then as there are now Saints.

INTRODUCTION TO VOLUME 3

The third volume of the diary was written between July 25 and August 28, 1844. During that month Isaac is living at home with his family and dividing his time between working at the family business in the mornings and spending the afternoons reading, writing, praying, and musing as he felt led. In the joy of his new-found convictions he writes letters to his old Brook Farm friends—George and Burrill Curtis, William Henry Channing, Charles A. Dana, and Debora Gannett—telling them of his conversion. Each responds sympathetically, though each makes clear his differences with Isaac's opinions. Yet it is a time when his mind naturally thinks of them, those who struggled with him searching for more light, because he is sure that what he has found will benefit them.

The most significant events of this period are his entrance into the church through the reception of the sacraments of Baptism, Penance, and Holy Communion. Yet oddly enough, there is very little mention of those events in the diary. At one point, when writing to Brownson, he even complains that the gift of contemplation and interior prayer that he experienced in the past has dried up and he wonders whether God is testing him.

Despite that touch of unexpected aridity, his interior life takes on more focus and breadth during the writing of the third book. The entries are longer and more pithy. Though he still is given to aphorisms, there are more attempts to develop his points. And clearly his command of the mechanics of the language continues to improve. The commitment to interiority that has been present from page one of the diary is still strong, but now the confusion about the nature of his inspirations and the meaning of life is subdued by a growing confidence and maturity.

Yet the perplexity is still present, albeit with a different focus. With the larger church question settled, he is free to focus on the question of his *own vocation—by no means a new concern in the diary, but now undertaken with a desire to acquire manifestly Catholic forms of piety and ways of life. The idea that grasps his imagination most strongly is that of making a pilgrimage. Like the faithful of the Middle Ages he wishes to journey on foot throughout Europe to Rome, blending penance and heroism in one quixotic adventure. And who shall accompany him on this journey? None other than the great Transcendental pilgrim himself, Henry David Thoreau. He had gotten to know Thoreau well when he boarded in his Concord home from April to June, and knew Henry's love of long walks. Indeed the idea for the pilgrimage captivates his imagination for the month and almost comes to fruition. Thoreau seriously considers going but then declines, choosing instead to make his own pilgrimage to Walden Pond.*

Disappointed but not crushed, Hecker closes his diary wondering what one such as himself who has no talents should do in life, but resting in the riches of his inner consolations and in the solace of his new faith.

VOLUME 3

New York, July 25–1844.

Being truly thyself thou art more than in seeming to be greater than what thou art. All sham is shame ful. Yesterday I saw the Bishop—next Monday he is to appoint the hour on which I shall receive the sacrament of baptism.[185]

Sweet Stars and thou Melancholy Moon and the Deep Mysterious Sea ye are true symbols of my own inner life.

I cannot look upon the rushing impetuous stream in a moonlight night without a madness seizing me.

Could I but give up all my time to contemplation, study, reading, and reflection!

This morning I read Fredricka's *Solitary*. So far as the inner life facts are concerned they are parallel with my own. The expressions are often the same and even the external relations.

Let us speak to each other as we are for all else is truly ''Babel''.

If you cannot hear the true word speak through your brother be still and desire nothing else. You are the truest friend to him whom you dare say the same as you dare to the silent Stars.

If you cannot speak the absolute truth to the one whom you call your friend better to be silent then to equivocate.

The object of friendship is forgotten, it ceases to exist, when you are conscious of his separate existence.

To your friend you *reveal* yourself, to all others you converse, speak. It is not the agreement of opinions that makes friendship a deep oneness an inner affinity.

He is a friend to whom you can speak unhesitatingly almost unconsciously.

Friendship is as involuntary as your own existence, being, and so must friends feel towards each other.

26.

We do not know that an author is the best interpreter of the tendency and purport of his own productions? It is quite a common fact of two men giving original birth to the same idea and sometimes the same expressions.

There is a life which is too tender to be thought much more to be expressed. The Catholic Church discipline says open not your interior life to any but your confessor.

Christianity has the highest appreciation of the nature of Man, it believes that he has the faculty of committing such Sin that none but God himself can wipe it away.

Holiness, Piety, Love, are elementary. Eusevia—Piety—is joyfull worship.

There is a divine certainty a philosophic certainty and a historical certainty. The first belongs to the heart the second to the intellect; the third to the senses. Catholicism appeals to all of these methods of conviction. The first certainty of consequence includes the two latter but the lower do not include the higher.

Love includes Light and Life. God is in, and includes all, but all does not include God.

Genius in Greek is Eu-damonie that is a Good Angel, a heavenly demon. Not so eu—means good; Damon means genius. Cupid is represented with his mortal eyes blindfolded because love is Spiritual, transcendental, unseen.

Nothing is so sure as his arrow, nothing so certain as the certainty of Love. To know that we love is to know more than knowledge can embrace.

We may know that we love but to know what that love is we cannot. Paul says "May the love of God which passeth all understanding" etc.

Our likings will be lawful when we are transformed into our primeval innocence.

27.

To the barbarian we are prophets, clair-voyants. So are the authors of the New Testament to us.

Christ came to introduce that pure excitement which should become permanent in humanity and place us en rapport with the unseen to us as we naturally are. The Church is the means by which we are put in rapport with Christ, God, the Holy Ghost.

It is by her mysteries we are magnetized with Love Light & Life. We are raised to a supernatural vision permanently by being in union with the Church through which flows this invisible influence by which this elevation illumination is given.

28.

Man thinks he knows more of himself than woman does, and so does woman think of herself, but it is the contrary in each case.

I have commenced acting. My union with the Catholic Church is my first real true act and it is no doubt the forerunner of many more—of an active life.

Heretofore I did not see or feel within me the grounds upon which I could act with permanence and security   I now do and from this basis my future life will be built. Whatever my actions may be I care not; it is this deep eternal certainty within I did wish to feel and I am now conscious of that the lack of it was the reason for my inactivity. With this guide I ask no other nor do I feel the need of the support of friends or kindred or the world. Alone it is all sufficient for me tho it contradicts the advice of my friends & all my former life. Its certainty seems to me absolute, if any error arises it will be in my disobedience. We would not strain to act for we live in being.

This is to me the Star which if I follow will lead me to my life-destiny-purpose. This may be a mistake, if so it is to me a glorious one, would to heaven I had the opportunity of commencing them in an earlier period of my being, we thank God for it now.

This interior consciousness of our true being's existence is all the recognition we ask in any shape; it is enough. We are contented in full being, not asking what are we or what we are.

Our union with the C. Church does not necessarily indicate the colour and tenor of all our future acts, we see it but one of a series of acts, and these may in many respects be quite different in their appearance.

Our life is such as not to be expressed by one simple mode of activity.

We feel free from the external world, ready to act through every form, at any place, and prepared to cease acting. Our consciousness of existence is not fastened to the material world, it is but put in rapport with it when we will.

We have no contempt for the body but are very grateful for having been given one, by which we are enabled to enjoy all the beauty of the material world and through which we can act upon it, and impress upon it the ideal spiritual forms perceived in another world.

30.

If Jesus was the God Man and the Catholic Church is the medium of introducing his life into the heart of humanity it follows necessarily that those ages in which this power had most sway they must have displayed compared with others of less of this virtue a purer and higher life.

The inward voice becomes more and more audible, it says ''I am''— ''obey''. The new clothes itself in new dress.

What proof does a man give, if he does only what has been done, that he *is*. Can a man repeat the past with genius? If I should do now that which my ''demon'' would lead me to do I should go to Europe, work my passage there, and Aller a pied.

One true act opens the passage for ten more.

Man is left to his own destiny; religion but sanctifies it.

The only Catholicon for Man is in being true to God, humanity, himself.

We cannot repeat the past, it is impossible, but we can continue and perfect it.

If we have not the power to institute any thing greater, and we have not, we are bound by duty, humanity, God, to perpetuate and fullfil the present in order to realize the future.

·The life of humanity is one continuous flowing stream in which there are no stoppages and broad chasms, if one link is broken there is no repairing of it.

Sin is the submitting Reason Conscience to flesh sense appetite. It is suicide.

Friday, to-morrow, next day morning at 9 o'clock A.M. I am to receive the sacrament of baptism at the Cathedral. The next day morning I am to attend the sacrament of penance.

We have in good earnest this afternoon commenced a Novena for the purpose of making a pilgrimage to Rome. To work, beg, and travell on foot so far as land goes to Rome.

The idea has seized me and I should not hesitate to start to morrow on the journey. I mean to write to Henry Thoreau on the subject. We know of no pleasanter better way both for soul and body than to make such a pilgrimage in the old middle age fashion. Suffer hunger storm cold heat thirst all that can affect the body of flesh. If we receive hard usage rough knocks etc. much the better will it be for us. Why thump ones flesh here; let it be done by others while in the mean time your soul is looking on higher objects: We like the idea it is a much better one than a monastery or any kind

of seclusion. What if my friends should oppose it there is only another difficulty added to many more the impossible is unknown. We say go. We feel
we have the stuff to do it in us. We say we should love to work and beg our
way to Rome if it costs us ten or fifteen years of our life.

It is the best thing we can now do. We have a good constitution can
live on bread and water why can't we take a walk over the fairest portions
of this Earth planet and make it ours by seeing it. It would be so for more
than that the owners cannot do. We say again go.

We would say if H.T. consent to go therefore it was we were sent to
Concord. Who knows. Horatio etc. ''God works by mysterious ways''. We
will write to Henry Thoreau. Nothing is impossible.

We cannot write to him now the idea is too strong for us. We take no
supper tonight as a preface to a large edition of the same in future.

We have talent to do this we know, and do it we can, and do it we
may.

31

Somehow or other we have passed from I to we. We know not how.

This afternoon we sent a letter to Henry Thoreau respecting a journey
to Europe.[186]

August 1st Friday. 1.P.M.

This morning we were baptized by Bishop McCloskey. Tomorrow we
attend the tribunal of Confession.[187] We know not why it is we feel the
internal necessity of making use of the plural pronoun instead of the singular.[188] It has come to a bad pass when we cannot perform miracles nor
work in good earnest with our hands. Why is this, is it because we stop and
have not the valour to procede? We cannot stop long on the mystic bridge
between Earth and Heaven if we once have started on our journey. There
is no half-way-house, it is either onward or backward.

The true being of Man is mystical   We say we know not what Man
is. The stones with which the streets are paved, which we walk upon we
feel a mystic union with. Matter seems not to be a hindrance to spiritual
perception, rather it is the form in which the spiritual is cognizable.

We do not feel the want of conversation with others. Our own company
is all to us. To ask and to give are the proper modes of being. It is a profound
fact that when we meet friends we ask them ''what news''   A man must
be dead if God does not reveal to him of the new heavens and earth.

Vision, seeing is a higher order of somambulism in which consciousness is retained.[189] Life is a double consciousness in which we dream we
are dreaming. We live in a world within, the body lives and moves in a
world without. Life is said to be a dream when we are awake permanently

in the sphere of the dream world. Beautiful are real, pure, dreams, they are visions, glances of heaven. The me must be centered in the interior sphere the mystic world. It is possible to supply the conditions for the every-day-life to be as pure and clear in its perceptions as we are at times in the condition of bodily sleep.

The body should be as passive to the Soul as it is to the Spirit. Dreams are realized hopes and these may be actualized. Our ordinary life in many cases is more than a dream to the hottentot.

Dreams are the history of the future. No union of parts of the same thing can make a unit of the same substance. Unity is original, uncreative, imperishable.

Resolutions and perceptions of purity have been revealed to our soul of greater strength depth and clearness than ever have been before this day.

The will is in the Spirit, Spirit is not imprisoned in matter. Matter is not impassible to Spirit. As we become spirit matter vanishes. The senses see nothing but the sens-ible. Sin imprisons Man in the flesh. Purity liberates him. Jesus could lay down and take up His temporary life at will. We know not what Jesus was but we know what he has done for us. The will is interior to body & Soul. Sin is an act of the will, hence its sinfullness.

True temperance is better than times of fasting; fasting is better than no season of self denial. Theopathy is the most mystical of all sciences.

We cannot remain long enough one Man to do or finish a thought; it is true

> "Oh what a thing is Man
> He is some twenty Men;
> Each several hour."

Baptism is the declaration of our intention of becoming naturalized citizens of the holy city of God—Jerusalem.

Christianity is the reunion of the inernal and external. Religion means Re-union. To know is to distinguish. The tree of knowledge is the forbidden tree. Christ is the Mediator the Physician who will heal the seperation.

We do not see any reason why fairies are not as probable as giants.

The end of true reasoning is pure intuition. The intellect asks, the moral nature possesses, the physical nature wants. The intellectual and physical natures are never satisfied by what they ask; they must submit to the moral all supplying nature as the only remedy.

We have been divorced from God. Re-ligion is to re-bind us to Him.

The Artiste is rich enough to give or otherwise dispose of his works; if we have that which supports the artiste we have more than his works. If

we have that, we have an all tempel were ever we are, full of beautiful statues fine paintings and the dreams of poetry.

Let us always affirm what we see and never construe it into denial of
something we dont know. Many errors if not all would be avoided if we but
affirmed what we see and the condition in which we saw what we have seen.
If we have seen an Angel if called for, affirm it; if we have not, it would
be very foolish in us to say therefore there are none in the face of the testimony of so many who have seen them.

There are some that have their natural sight very dim so that they cannot see distinctly. Now it would be very absurd in them to deny every thing
that lies beyond their horizon. There are about as many probably less who
have their spiritual eyes open as there are those whose material eyes are
blinded. We grope about and feel our way in the spiritual world as the blind
man does in the material world. He is governed by his feelings in the unseen
& so are we, neither of us sees.

The moral nature must submit itself to love and it will direct the intellect to Light and the physical nature to purity. Yield your whole nature
to purity. Yield your whole nature in its trinity to Love, Light, and Life.

Piety,	Philosophy,	&	History.
Feeling,	Seeing,	&	Doing.
Heart,	Head,	&	Hand.
Interior,	Medium,	&	Exterior
Centre,	Radia,	&	Circumference
Inner,	Middle,	&	Outer
Substance,	Form,	&	Expression
Will,	Thought	&	Act etc. etc. etc.
Angel,	Man,		Animal
Heaven,	Air,		Earth
God,	Man,		Nature etc.

Mathematicks is the physical expression of divine truth. Mathematicks
is one of the most mystical of all Sciences.

Pure Mathematicks Love and Truth are of the same stuff of the same
land. The word is used for astrology in Latin. The basis of Mathematics is
pure axiom intuition. The axioms are based upon invisible uncognizable
ideas.[190]

2

—Penance. Joy! Unbounded love! O! Sweet Jesus Thy love is infinite!
Blessed faith! Sweet love! We possess an internal glory. A glowing flame
of love. Let our whole life be one act of penance. O dear Jesus the Life-
Giver. The blessed giver of sweet joy. Oh what a sweet thing it is to be in
the way of loveful grace! Darkness is turned into the light of diamond. Jesus

keep me near thee. O how great a condescension   Jesus is our friend. O!
who has the conception of Jesus being his *FRIEND*. Feel him to be your
friend. O ancient faith how dear how good is God in giving us sinners thee.
Blessed is the grace of God that leadeth sinners to thee! O how thou hast
comforted the Soul. It would turn from thee but thou strengthened it. The
cup was bitter but infinitely more sweet is the joy thou givest it. Our soul
is clothed in brightness. Its youth is restored. No clouds obscure its lustre.
O Blessed ever blessed unfathomable divine faith. O blessed faith of Apostles Martyrs Confessors and Saints! O holy Mother of Jesus thou art my
Mother. Thy tender love I feel in my heart. O holy Mother thou has beheld
me! Bless me Virgin Mother of Jesus.

The ridicule of the times is the birth symptom of coming events.

5. Monday.

The heart seems to be very active to day but the intellect seems very
dubious. It may be that I read too much. We seem completely enveloped in
a mystical life. Our attention seems to be involuntarily fixed. We love, oh
infinitely. But it is vague indefinite. We cannot be still nor do we know
what to do.

We have thought over our pilgrimage to Europe etc. and are still firmly
inclined to undertake the journey if H.T. consents. To-morrow we intend
to speak to B. McCloskey respecting it. We seem to have become extremely
passive, some would call it a weakness, but we feel it is not so. We desire
to do some thing that is definite, yet we are unable to say what it is we
should do, for we know not what it is we can do. We would cry out in tears
of our heart, Lord I am here, what wouldst Thou have me to do? Oh Lord
what wouldst Thou have me to do? We are nothing   Thou art all. Can we
not rest in peacefulness if thou commandest us not to stir. Willt thou not
call in thy own time and season? Surely we should be satisfied, if the lord
is, in being as we now are. If he would have us to do, he would call us to
the work. Oh that my heart was more tender that we might feel more sen-
sitively the inspiration of the holy spirit. Oh that we hearkened more to the
voice of our God. When we compare ourselves to others we are nothing and
we never shall feel otherwise. We feel what we are is the love and truth that
abides in us. We wish to yield all to love and truth under all forms in every
shape & conditions. Oh blessed and infinite God give unto us the light to
see ourselves as thou in thine infinite Love and Wisdom seest us. Make me
O God as thou wouldst have me to be. Teach me O Lord how I shall know
thy will. Shed down O Father Thy blessing upon me. I am deeply sensible
O heavenly Parent that I am unworthy of thy love and need thee therefore
infinitely more on this account. Oh Compassionate God bestow but the

smile of thy countenance upon me and I shall revive. May the Lord not forget his unworthy humble servant.

6.

We would rather live in a tub Diogenes-like than to sacrifice our inward freedom. We seem to be here in an almost constant constraint on account of the bussiness that surrounds us. We hope with great earnestness that H.T will accept the invitation to go on the pilgrimage we have spoken of. It seems to be the act for me and we know of nothing better that we can do. We wish to abandon ourself to providence. Our whole life should be but one perpetual abandonment act. We do this not willfully but obediently to the inspirations given us we beleive by Gods holy spirit. We do not expect to be understood why we should do this, nor do we feel the need of this so long as we have this grace within us. We see not what external riches can give us that we need, desire, or wish for, why should we labour for them then, we cannot, for the will for them we have not. God is all-bountiful; we feel this, and what little we need he will provide for us all sufficiently. We have no desire to study; we fill up our vacant moments with reading.[191] We know not what we are but we feel willing to yield up our whole selves to the spirit of God. We ask not for any thing external for which the world are seeking; Lord in what consists our sin?

We have tried in vain to write to a friend of ours but could not with all our effort succede.

Our life is involuntary, should this be so, so completely? We feel strong in grace but nothing in ourselves. Our life is objective-subjective. We pass from the I in the We where in the I is dissolved and the We is all. The I is not the We; it disappears in the We as shadows before the brilliant light of the Sun of Suns. The I is the negation of the We. The We in its fullness and completeness is universal consciousness but not conscious without the I. Consciousness is the reflection of the light of the Universal We striking the individual I. This is so sudden electrick that we should not be able to seize it unless memory retained it and the constant repetition of it makes identity. The I is historical, the We is mystical ineffable infinite. Until the I becomes the We it knows not itself but then it knows all. The I is absolutely negative unprogressive essentially nothing. We know by ignorance. God knows not, He IS. Genius is uneducable. Union with God supersedes all knowledge. Knowledge is evidence of the Fall.

Our life seems like some sommers day. At one moment the heavens are beautiful, the Sun shines bright through the silvery clouds, and all above is pure, joy ful, and heart quickening to look up at. Alas! in a few moments all is changed, black clouds are gathering, the Sun is hid, all variety is changed from dark to darker only, the lightning flashes, and the heavy rain drops like large tears, all is dark, the thunder claps, and all is changed into a dreary, sad, countenance.

All that is worthy of thought, action, speech, is the Universal Law; but for the true utterance of this in any mode worthy of it is wanted Genius. There are but few of the Race who have been worthy interpreters of it. A Rafaelle a Shakspere a Dante a Mozart Beethoven a Canova a Bernhard a Salles and a few others of the modern world have given us some glimpse of it.[192]

7.

One day passes after another and we seem to remain where we were. What new or fresh event do we add to the history of the Race? Alas none. What act do we that has not been repeated oer and oer again? Alas none. Do we increase the field of the possible? Do we increase the Known? Do we conquer the illimitable, all unconquered, and unconquerable except by the infinite in Man? Why ask these questions? We know we do not. Mans destiny is set to face the impossible the unknown and to conquer it. There is nothing sure than that we are born to war, struggle, suffer. The thread of life is only unwound by rough trials and sharp unearthly struggles with foes visible and invisible. We must push forward and make some advance upon that which we have if life should be to us little better than a malediction.

We are born to be more than Men or else Men now are no type of what Man should be. There lies within us the impossible which asks for being, and it will only answer to the outward impossible around us. Like only responds to like. Abandon thyself to the outward impossible if thou hast not had the revelation within thee and it will spring into being all armored for the contest. Mans power is greater than all his conceptions. The power that acts in the Actor is always greater than the Actor. Thou canst be more than all thy sublimest dreams. That which dreams lies within thee if called into being will realize itself in actual life. Let us wake up our everyday life to that of dreams and our existence will realize them, express them.

The conditions for Mans spiritual well being in the present state of his nature are in an inverse ratio to his material well being.

The harmony, the divine order of Mans whole being is the end for which we should labour, its present disarrangement is in the subordination of the spiritual and intellectual natures, to the physical nature, and this must be reversed to cause harmony, & order again.

The first act of disobedience to the divine order, disabled Man of his power to restore himself, and made him dependant on the special grace of his God Creator.

The reception of Grace is the first condition necessary, prior to all real & effectual reformation. All attempts at reformation with the nature of Man as it is will reproduce the evils of that nature, which are largely more than its virtues. The larger the association of Men the worse will it be, the evil elements increase almost geometrically. There can be no association, no government beneficial to Man which is not built upon the principals and in subordination to the Church of God.

The Church of God is the source and centre of all permanence, progress, peace.

9.

Man is a perceptive-receptive-active-being. These powers answer to the visible the invisible and the actual world. Also to perception inspiration and action. Thinking feeling & doing, etc. etc.

We have just finished Dante's description of Hell. We cannot justify the horrid hideous and deformed pictures he describes by the rules of taste as we understand them. We feel they do shocking violence to our taste at least. On the whole we cannot but say and this may be sufficient to justify the poem that its general influence does lead to morality   yet to use such means to such an end seems that there is but slight shade of difference between them. What should be required of a work of art?

First it must not shock the moral sensibility.

2nd it should not offend aesthetick taste.

3d it should not degrade the human form.

4th its pictures should be in keeping,

" devils be devils and not Men, this is degrading the

" human spirit otherwise.

5 the effect of the work should be to elevate

" the Soul either by its positive or negative influence.

6 we require of a work of art as we do of a man it should be something and that worthy too to be.

We read the lives of the Martyrs not for the purpose of reading the cruelties tortures and sufferings that were practised upon them but for the holy heroism angelic beauty and patient firmness they exhibited.

When physical deformity teaches us disgust we see no good that it teaches in religion morals aestheticks or any branch of human cognizance.[193]

Men beleive in studying and following the classics in their models of taste etc. but in matters of far more interest religion & morals they assume they have all and need no models or instructors. They religiously follow one and athestically deny the other.

What the Greeks and Romans are to them in aestheticks are the Apostles and Fathers of the Church to us in Religion & Morals. Consider this, they are of a quite different character. The latter does not necessarily exclude the former by any means, the foremost in recognizing their greatness and sublimity have been of the latter class of Men. Some of them we fear to their detriment and injury to the justice of the cause they held permanently to.

10.

The mysteries of the Church are the channels of the mystic life.[194]

Oh life is leiden.[195] "Tis not happiness tis deeds—those far distant stars of the night—this is our goal".

The Catholic Church sanctifies all true life whatever expression it may take the anchorite the statesman the artiste and the labourer all if true to God are equally Her children.

When we take into contemplation the omniscience of God we must conclude that God foreknew that some would choose salvation and others not, but this does not necessarily prove that they were so predestinated to choose.

It is a tender and delicate point for one to decide how far he should trust in providence and how much is dependent upon his own exertions. We must have a worthy end in view or else we cannot wisely expect the aid of providence in our favor.

We feel deeply and strongly that the circle of family happiness is not sufficient for our nature but what to do that we can profitably do outside of this we have not the ability to say.

Our real wishes are presentiments of our capabilities is a very true proverb no doubt, but are we not most unconscious of these? We seem to think we are all unconsciously educated for unknown ends & purposes.

Is he not greater who cheerfully of his own free choice chooses rather to suffer with the children of God than enjoy the Kings Palace than he who submits to the same end without having the like temptations.

I look upon my self as belonging to that class of decided unfortunate beings who have no particular talent for any particular persuit.

The word talent and genius has for me no application whatever. I stand on the confines of both worlds not feeling the necessity nor having the true valor to decide for either sphere.

Oh heaven why was this deep ever burning life given me, was it that I might be slowly and painfully consumed by it? All greatness is in the Actor not in the act. He whom God has blessed with an end in life he can laboriously labour to accomplish that end, but alas for that poor mortal whose existence answers only to fill space in this world. How excruciating is it when he is conscious of this! Oh Prometheus!

Simply to be what God would have us to be is to be greater than to have the applause of the whole world otherwise. All such statements as these are necessarily one sided. Because, in the world there are always good & virtues Men whose approbation is that of Gods.

There is an instinct in Man which draws him to danger as in the battlefield stake etc. as there is in flies that draws them to the flame of light. It is the desire of the spirit within for Release.

11.

Since I have left Concord ⟨the gift of tears, of contemplation and interior prayer⟩ have all been taken from me. How hard has it been for me to go through with all these solemn mysteries & ceremonies without experiencing that great delight which I have felt. Why is this? Is it for to try my faith? Oh Lord how long shall I be tried in this season of desolation. Are these never to return oh Lord and why? Have I acted unworthily? Oh what shall I do to receive these blessings again? If I remain at home with the help of Gods grace I will live upon bread & water alone for nine days as a penance and Novena for the restoration of his blessings.

The highest state of perfection is to be content to be nothing. Lord give me strength not to ask of Thee any thing that is pleasant to me. I revoke for what I have asked above and will try to do all without the hope of recompense. Lord if Thou triest my Soul let it not go until it has paid the uttermost farthing. Give me oh dear Lord but the grace not to despair nor sink under the weight that thou in love putteth upon me.

We see ourself to day more than we have ever before.

As we learn some animals to spring up in the air for the food we hold up for them to catch and hold it ever higher that they may learn to spring farther so does God entice us with the heavenly food Love that we may ever rise to a higher state of perfection.

14. Wed—

We are drawn from all sides of our being and that keeps me where I am.

"Oh what a thing is Man! how far from power
    From settled peace, and rest!
He is some twenty several men, at least,
    Each several hour."

"Oh, what a sight were Man, if his attires
Did alter with his mind;
and like a Dolphin's skin, his clothes combined
With his desires."

I have not as yet rec'd any answer from H.T.[196] I cannot imagine whether he is inclined to go or no.

Ora has not written to me for some time. Almira has lost all, or at least so it seems, all affinity with my life. We do not feel any loss. Last evening in my dreams I seemed to have repeatedly the sense of being separated from all sense. We feel at present no sensible relations with any one.

I think that I should not hesitate to go to Europe if H.T. consents. Bishop McC.[197] who I spoke to concerning the pilgrimage tho't that it might be very useful to me and seemed inclined in favor of it. He said tho it would be surely necessary for me to have some money on which I could depend that in some circumstances I could not get along without it. My brothers tell me that it is impossible for them to spare anything out from the bussiness. This would not hinder me from going. We should go as far as we could go. Across the Sea we certainly could get. We do not value *this* life of ours at a dear rate. We trust that H.T. will go. Oh what else can I do at present, the study of the languages I cannot now pursue for they have but little interest for me. And then I should not be here at peace even in that if I did not lay down some end in view to suit my friends. I have no plan of life. If God or Fate has not in given me a head planned something we cannot project it. We sail upon the Sea of life but heaven knows to what haven, I not. Perhaps to cross the Sea would be emblematic of my present state. Good! We think it is. Our resolution has raised 20 degrees! We will cross the Sea and not be tossed upon its billows longer.

When we meet a man in the street he excites in us the sentiment of reverence for the human species. A woman inspires us with love above all limitations.

Honors crush those who win them. "I am richer," says Jean Paul "in a receiving than in a creative imagination." He was then 18. Was not this more on account of his youth than his real nature? Is this not the case with all youth however rich comparatively? We think so.[198]

"Mans duty says JP.G.[199] is to work only in harmony with the inconceivable. "Choose for your choice is but brief but endless"

This morning I attended the Cathedral and saw six young men admitted to holy orders.

We feel always a mystic influence acting upon us at the ceremonies in the Church. Not unlike the first symtpoms of magnetic sleep.

The Saint the Artiste in Sculpture Painting & Music the truly great Statesman the Architect all do seek to realize the self same unfathomable absolute life in their works. So is it with the Martyr Hero etc.——It is all the preternatural perception of the beautiful good and true that they labour to realize in actual life.

"They sin who say that Love can die."

Christianity gives inspiration to Mans being; this may show itself in moral industry—Saints—in intellectual industry—Artiste etc.—and in material industry in Labour for the good of humanity.

We seem sometimes to think there ever is a greater end in all our own purposes than we with finite reason can fathom or foresee. The Man who is true to God tho to all other eyes he may seem false does more than if his actions proclaimed him greater than a Caesar. How sad is he! Who is devoid of moral intellectual or physical industry. Who dare to himself be true in word deed & thought is a Hero. Oh what is there in Man that should make him fear himself. Who fears not himself fears none other mortal like. The first foe that Man encounters is himself if he is faced all others vanish like dreams at the approach of morn. is it not thyself who dreams of terror fear and the like, dare these phantoms in their den and scorn them with thy looks. Make all thy powers yield to thee and minister to thy purpose. Master thyself. Make the rebels serve heavens high purposes. Not even give them the common freedom of the choice of death.

Thinking depends more upon the will than feeling. Hence women are more impulsive than men.

Women believe, men perceive.

Woman is mystical, man historical.

Women are realists, men are idealists, etc.

The woman in man gives to man his life, and the man in woman gives to her her strength. Woman is the beauty of man. Man is the strength of woman. We see the wife in the husband and the husband in the wife. They love each other for that which each in themselves have not. If like in all cases loves like why do not men love men as they love women. In heaven there are no sexes; woman again is oned with man. Oh God awake our slumbering powers, restore us to our day.[200]

We feel within each day each hour our original self awakened to higher being. Take this dim veil from before our eyes that we may see and feel as we are seen and felt by unseen agents of thine.

More lies hid in the virtue of Christs power than Man dreams of in the highest flights of fancie.

As in Adam all died etc. There lies a world within us hid nearer to us than our own bodies but alas farther distanced from us by sin than the farthest off star.

The Kingdom of Heaven lies within you. The measure of our influence over others is in proportion to our submission and purity towards God. The boundaries of Mans powers are only limited by his own sin. If ye believe in me greater things than I do shall ye do. God is on our side our greatness is his glory.

If education cannot repair the defects of birth what but the original creative power can?

A man who has power to do some thing worthy to be done & is doing
it or he who feels within himself the conscious power for doing & is preparing himself within himself the conscious power for doing & is preparing
himself to do these in hope and joy may be delightfully content with gratitude to Almighty—God. But he poor useless mortal who, alas, neither feels
the latent spark of Prometheus birth nor is doing his work, he oh ye pitiful
gods! compassion on him this luckless object nonentity. How few there are
who look with the inner eye alone!

To be sincere is a duty. To what? to all that your mind is inspired with?
No. To what then, which reject, and which cherish, who shall judge? Yourself! that were strange; it is you that should be judged. My thoughts and
emotions are me, these are the offspring of myself, and I can but look upon
them with a parents eyes. He that attempts to judge himself has no limits to
his censure or praise he is either friend or foe unto himself. We read the
lives of the Saints on this point, and what light do they shed upon it? If we
are to judge from our own result they leave us just where we stood before
we read. They all seemed governed by their own best judgment in obedience
to their spiritual advisers and this is the best Catholicism we can have I suppose.

When I feel the need of warm *human* sympathy I take up a Vol. of der
einziger Jean Paul and read a few Chapters which answers my deep human
longings. We see in Jean Paul the same vein of sweetness and angelic purity
that we find in the writing of Saint Francis of Sales. Oh how many Saints
has protestantism robbed the Church of, who under her cold freezing influence have struggled for heaven like angels in darkness for heavens dear
light.

The objections of the irreligious to religion are the joys of the truly
religious.

''Penance dreams her life away''

Do not our real dreams foreshadow future events?

Truth in a bigots mind finds no friendship but a prison darker than
hades. There are things so secret within us that we cannot bring them to our
lips much less to our pen to fix on paper.

How insensible are we of the gratitude & thanks that are due to Jesus
for all that we now enjoy!

We are as liable to put in heathen authors who we read what they never
thought or dreamt of as we are to fall short of many christian writers who
tower far as the Stars above us.

The perception of the beautiful in nature external form in many but not
in all respects unquestionably the Ancients are *still* our masters, but all that

respects religion, morals, certain we are they never had but dim glimpses of the light we now possess. The Sciences we cannot say, this is, and we do not know with how much justice disputed. A full and accurate knowledge of their proficiency in them probably we never shall obtain.

Greece Rome & Judea have been incorporated to a very great degree in modern civilization and thru much of that great and mystic land EGYPT. Egypt to us is replete with intense interest. Source of immense unknown influence on the destiny of the Race.[201]

15.

To day is the holy day of the Assumption of the dear blessed Mary mother of our Lord and Saviour Jesus. Oh may I be found worthy of her regard and love.[202]

Nature seems more and more to us to be in all her varied humours but symbolic of Mans own life.

How rich and gifted is Mans nature! How much he has capacity to enjoy! Had he to pay for the favors which in one brief hour he receives all life from the cradle to the grave would not be sufficient to pay the debt. Great God teach me gratitude to thee; let every breath breathe praise and every sound sing thanks to thee the All giver of Love Light & Life.

Oh Man is own worst enemy, he spurns his own salvation rejects his Saviour his glory joy peace happiness & All Lord teach him to see his own blindness that he may exercise true pity on his own poor Soul that it may soften and shapened be in Christ.

He that has not learned the bitterness of the drops of woe has not learned to live. One hour of deep agony teaches Man more love and wisdom than a whole lengthened life of happiness.

Some Men do live as if they had a right to live and to all things beside; blind mortal! thou hast forfeited life once and only livest now by permission of Gods infinite loving grace. For thy Sin against him he has given thee his only Son and grace to boot. In many faces I see passing through the crowded streets a veiled beauty an Angel quickening me with purer life as I pass by them in anxious haste. Do we not see the hidden worth, glory, and beauty of Men as our own becomes revealed to us? Would the Son of God have needed to ransom Man if he was not of incomparable value? A Church without mysteries is a misnomer. Abstract the mysteries from the Church you abstract her soul. And this is what Protestantism has attempted to do and for itself has done.

The greatest difficulty is so to frame your speech as shall not do injustice to any party and shall express the whole truth.

The mere assertions of great Men too often pass current without examination, they are not great in all particulars, hence if many of their opinions were scutinized more would be found spurious than the multitude imagine. After Men have acquired a reputation they are apt to speak heedlessly and without sufficient data for their assertions.

Carlyles Past and Present is a book that has not as yet to our knowledge been sufficiently examined. The man has too much fame to have justice done him. He seems to us an observer and has a keen penetration in particulars but lacks depth of profound general philosophical principles. He sees deeply but his reasoning is superficial. He is a painter not a philosopher. He is deficient in consecutiveness. His paintings are only sketches a la Ret⟨z⟩. He has been, and is, much more praised than studied. He has the prophetic gift but in all his own deductions he fails most sadly. It is not an anomaly that a prophet does not understand his own prophecy and fails in his attempts to interpret it. Mr Carlyle is a prophet but not an interpreter. His genius is in foresight not in insight. His interpretations are all special.[203]

18.

Yesterday I rec'd an answer to my letter from H. Thoreau. He declines going. He says he retires from all external activity in disgust and that his life is more Brahminical, Artesian well, Inner Temple like. Such a tour has been one of his own dreams he says etc. etc. The day before the 17 I sent him another letter before I rec'd an answer to my first and I think it is yet possible that he may make up his mind to go. However it is most likely he will not, and then I am set upon my wits again what to do. It seems almost impossible that this should fall through for what else to conceive of I am at a loss. Should I undertake to study the Greek and Latin again to what end should I do it, none other than that of self education. Probably if I cannot see any other way I attempt to do this. Thoreau may yet decide to go. I am half inclined to stay here in Darien next week and in the mean time think over all the matter.[204] Here in the silent woods and in the perfect sweetness of being in these conditions so favorable to interior life the oracle within may whisper that which I am now waiting for. Life when hampered in on one side like the tide will put itself forth in some other direction. We should have no fear or despondency having the life all the rest is infallibly certain. Having this not however sublime our projects may be they will prove to us the reverse on putting them to trial. We have no doubt that this life within will find better expression the more it is denied and for a time thwarted. Let it lay in fallow; it will enrich itself by so doing. We are too often so it seems to me too intent upon living and not enough in being. Sometimes we are inclined to think what ever a man does in any sphere of being should be for the same reason that the tree grows, plants flower, and the birds sing. We must answer a higher end than our own in all our actions if we would ennoble ourselves and the being of others. In our being agents of God we become more than ourselves. Our being is impressive of that which we commune with; let us not be friends to that which is lower than ourself but rather teachers.

Oh what a serenity and quiet calmness nature bears and infuses into all that is in harmony with her. It is a pschical after birth the sensible consciousness of nature, as the self consciousness of the "Me" is. And so is the feeling of the being of God an after birth in the phenomena of the Soul. The invisible Parent, the visible Parent, the Child. Principle, Agent, Deed. Man, Woman, Child. The germ, the tree, the fruit. Light, Love, Life. Substance form, being. Air, water, Earth, etc. etc. Inspiration, Action, Deed, etc. etc. etc. "All that is not God is nothing"

> Blessed are they, whom grace
> doth so illumine, that appetite in them
> exhaleth no inordinate desire,
> still hungering as the rule of temperance wills.
> *Dante Canto 24 Purg.*[205]

The women of old Rome were satisfied with water for their beverage, Daniel fed on pulse, and wisdom gain'd. The primal age was beautiful as gold and hunger then made acorns tasteful; thirst, each runlet Run nectar. Honey and locusts were the food, whereon a Baptist in the wilderness fed, and that eminence of glory reach'd that greatness which the Evangelist records. Dante Purgtor. Canto XXII

He cannot err whose nearest friend is God. There is in each Man that which none but the infinite eye can see and only His advice and counsel is able to direct.

19.

In whatever I may turn my attention to the end it must have in view must be invisible, God. We cannot engage in any thing which has a visible temporal object in view. We would reverse the order of the world; we would spend 3 hours of our time to spiritual life 2 to intellectual life & one to the physical life instead of 3 hours to the physical etc. etc. as the world.

We are prepared to give up those Sensible objects & enjoyments gained by devotion to the world such as fine costly luxorous of the table and gorgeous dresses and magnificent houses & furniture for the splendor and delight of the invisible inconceivable object in heaven not made with hands. We wish to live for the invisible as the primary duty of our being. This is to us that bread and drink whereof if a man does partake he shall never hunger & thirst. Oh good Lord give unto me this eternal food and take me from this dependance on this temporary nourishment.

It is only by self-denial we gain heaven having lost it by self will. Every time we overcome a selfish desire with the love of God we mount one step higher on the ladder which reaches to heaven. Lord give me strength that I may at least take one step advance daily and let me not fall any farther by self indulgence. When some think me good I am so ashamed that I would hide myself forever from the presence of Men.

20.

Scarce do I know what to say of myself if I accuse myself according to the conscious the light given me it would lead me to leave all around me. My conscience thus accuses me. And in partaking of the worldly things and going in the company around me my interior self has no pleasure in and the labour & time afterwards I feel is misspent. How to live a life which shall be conformable to the life within and not to separate from all those around me and the circumstances in which I am in I cannot conceive. I am now like one who tastes a little of this & then a little of that dish and his time is wasted and his mind is distracted from that pure enjoyment which is a fore-taste of the bliss of the Angels. We feel our primitive instincts the unvitiated tastes are becoming daily more sensible and our heart more susceptible of inspirations from above the invisible. The ideal world the world of pure ideas the soul world the interior the kingdom of heaven within we feel nearer to us as if we were more a friend of fellow citizen of it.

Oh Lord my heart would break forth in praise of the riches of the Life given within. Its richness is incomparable with the external riches we perceive around us.

It seems in this we enjoy all know all and possess all. If we have thee oh Lord if thou hast taken up thy dwelling within us we enjoy heaven within and Paradise without. Let our hearts be thy Holy City and do thou enter the chambers of thy inner temple. Lord we have a temple within where thy presence ever is, where holy service in silent may be perpetually offered to thee, under all circumstances.

21.

When we incur the displeasure of Men of this world we quite often receive the approbation of God and the smile of Angels.

Shall we not as we are disencumbered from sin be freed from all its penalties? And are not Death nakedness and labour consequences of sin? The object of Education should be to place every individual mind in vital union with the One Universal Educator. Instinctive union with the holy pure good right beautiful is what is needed. The only pleasure for Man is his union with a priori principles.

Being not representation of being has the faculty to generate being.

Universal progress is accomplished by individual endeavors. Many-sidedness if the union of repeated one-sidedness. There can be no opposition to God if he is truly seen as he is. Genius is always mystical.[206] The destiny of the Race is universal genius.

22nd

Our own life has its seasons as nature has, we should call our own at the present time April, the opening, the spring.

23.

Life is an enigma, rather being is a mystery. We shall never rest peacefully until our being is eternalized. The time and space Man is always in anxiety and trouble. Never look to what you shall do to outward showy deeds. Be true to the holy inspirations given within the inmost circle of the Soul and let nothing more external affect your conduct.

When you are in want of counsel or advice ask of God we know no other remedy. Man by Man cannot be counseled as he ought. True and wise counsel can only be sought for in the omniscience of God.

Feel a great deal think much and read a little is much better than to do the reverse of this. All our true nourishment comes from the invisible world; the root of the visible lies buried in the invisible. If our life is not hid in God it is of no value.

Man ceases to be a revelation of God as soon as his soul looses its union with spirit. In the spirit alone Man lives & moves & has his existence otherwise he is dead. We have had seasons of rejoicing and have said we will in future always trust in God; alas! what a wretched being is he, Man, forgetful of the past, and of the infinite bounties of his present condition, he craves for more not knowing that gratitude is the price of Gods gifts. A heart ungrateful is never blessed. I have had a second answer from H.T.[207] and he still declines going. All is well. We could go but are not very anxious to go. It is a thing we feel the faith in us to do therefore to do it would not be of such great advantage. We know not but that we have received the greater advantage in the pure resolution of will to go than we would have in the event of going. There is a sphere within which costs more strength to act tho not visible to external show than all our world applauded deeds.

Mans eye should be fixed on God not on this apparent unreal world.

The respect and veneration we bear ourselves is the measure that others bear towards us and this is in proportion to our purity sweetness & heavenly virtue. Oh how slow a process is the growth of virtue.

Who can deny there are Angels when we see some around us who bid fair promise of becoming members of the Angelic choir. Many that we see as we pass them by seem to us like veiled Angels. Oh could we see Man as heaven beholds him. We believe in the greatness of Man because He who spake as never Man spake said if we beleived in him greater things than I do shall ye do and he knew all that is in Man. Oh what must Earth become when Man shall be freed from sin by Christ.[208]

If we had divine resignation we should possess more than we have the desire to ask for. We are willing to suffer the judgments of Men but let God be our judge.

Man retires from the exterior world as he finds objects of communion in the interior world. The Kingdom of heaven is within us, said one who knew. Think of this. We know not but the idolatry of the Egyptians is more tolerable than the unbelief of modern times. Without faith of some kind Man is dead. Pure faith is the highest act of Reason. Thus would we classify the functions of the faculty of Reason.

1st Simple external posteriori perception
2nd Pure a priori or transcendental perception of ideas or principals.
3d absolute revelation of faith.
The first is individual;
the 2nd is universal;
the last is absolute.

The more a man descends into the animal sphere of life the more he has to labour for the support of his existence   It is only the animal life that makes Men slaves to physical labour. Cease to be animals and slavery poverty will cease.

If the animal passions are indulged of consequence you must pay the cost.

If you get a large family of children around you and please your animal appetites with all kinds of luxury and indulge your pride in all the foolish fashion of show do not wonder that it costs all your time to uphold such an expensive life; this is necessary of consequence unless you cheat someone else out of his hard earned value of his labour. We cannot perceive how a christian under the present arrangements can become wealthy without violating repeatedly the precepts of his religion.

The heart of Man is the Sun of his life, the intellect is the moon, and his thoughts are stars, his hopes bright silvery clouds. The heart is heat the intellect is light the will is power.

Where shall we find God? within. How shall we hear the voices of angels? listen with the inward ear. When are we with God? when we are no more ourselves. When do we hear the music of heaven? when we are interiorly silent. What is the effect of sin? confusion. Where does God dwell? in silence. Who loves God? he who knows nothing & loves nothing of himself. What is prayer? the breath of silence. What is love? the motion of the pure will. What is light? the shadow of love. What is force? the power of love. Where does God dwell? where there is peace. Who is most like God? he who knows he is the least like him. What is the innermost of all? stillness. Who is the purest? he who is the most beyond temptation. What is the personality of Man? the absolute negation of God. What is God? the absolute affirmation in Man. What is? is by what is not. What is it to know? it is to be ignorant. What is it to love? it is to have the want of it. What should we desire? not to desire. What is the most positive answer? silence   What is the truest? that which cannot be proven.

25.

In silence suffering without murmuring. An eternal thirst enduring without being quenched. Infinite longings without being met. Heart ever burning never refreshed. Void within and mystery all around you. Ever escaping that which we would reach. Tortured incessantly without relief. Alone bereft of God Angels Men—all. Hopes gone, fears vanished, and love dead within. These and more than these must Man suffer

26.

Every new relation awakens fresh life into being. All that we perceive however unconscious we may be of the fact changes our character. All the scenery which surrounds us works imperceptibly on our nature and makes it what it was not. Look up at the heavens, look at the silent far off stars, behold the beautiful around you on every side, tho you know it not it works more upon your character than you are aware of. Refrain from frivolous company, listen not to idle words nor look upon evil however light may be its shade, the memory of them is immortal indelible. Be watchful of your eyes if you would have sweet and pleasant hours of meditation for they engraven all they see on the tablets of memory. Man is in a retrospective sense responsible for his sinful dreams. Because we are insensible of our sins this does not free us from their guilt and punishment. We should always act and speak as if we were in the company of angels. Because we are. Fear to think anything that you would be ashamed to speak before Men for the Angels see all your thoughts and know the secrets of your hearts. How much more care ought we to have for them!

Since for the present I see no prospect of my going to Europe I feel an inclination springing up within me to recommence my study of the languages: If I should well order and husband my time and devote myself singly to such things that are to me of of the greatest interest and highest import I would find perhaps time sufficient for all of these. Singleness, perseverance, and firmness, of purpose, these are the virtues required for success. Man works ever to some unknown end. There is more gained in conquering our desires, tho they may be even permissible, than there is in satisfying them.

28.

We know not what we are. Where are we and how shall we find ourself? Christianity sanctifies our destiny but does not change it, as it sanctifies Art, elevates Literature, and diffuses the benefits of Science to the mass of mankind, and ennobles our actions. Have not we been too much engaged in reading, and paid too little attention to the center, that has caused us to loose ourself as it were? Our position here distracts our attention and we loose the delight and intimate knowledge and sweet consciousness of our interior life. How can this be remedied? We are constantly called off to those objects which we feel no relish in and if we retreat for a short time they rest like a load on us so that we cannot call ourself free any moment. We see the case as it stands and feel we are loosing our interior life from the false position in which we are placed. The humane ties and the material conditions in which we are, should be unquestionably sacrificed for the divine interior relation to the one, the Love Spirit, which we alas! HAVE so sensibly felt. Can a man live in the world & follow Christ? I know not, but as for me I find it impossible. We feel the necessity more and more for us to leave the society and the distracting cares of a city bussiness for a silent and peaceful retreat to the end that we may restore the life which we fear we are loosing. Our material interests should be subject to our humane ties our humane ties to our spiritual relations and who is he who brings these all in divine harmony?

How shall we make the sacrifice which shall accomplish the sole end we have & should have in view? Twice have we left home for this purpose and each time have unavoidably so it seems to me at least, did then returned home. Once more we trust will be a permanent and immovable trial. Man is a triune being and of innumerable relations, and the science of his true Being is incomprehensible because he is infinitely progressive in his nature.

By patiently waiting we prevail, but there are conditions which to wait under is no virtue. The state of the mind often perplexes the wisest The counsels of others are as various as there are counsellors. Man is separated from Man as one fixed star is from another. Each has that which none other but God himself knows. Seek the a priori Counsellor for the a priori mystic life. Depend on the one on which the all depends and not on the dependent. Union with the independent unconditioned will free you from all dependence & conditions. As your friendship is so will be your life.

INTRODUCTION TO VOLUME 4

The fourth volume of the diary stretches between September 9, 1844, and January 3, 1845. It is full of short entries that are made in a scrupulous manner except for one week between October 27 and November 5. The form of the book is an indication of the new use to which Isaac puts his diary. This book, he declares at the outset, will be a record of "the many smaller venial sins which beset my path." A preoccupation with his own sinfulness and a careful attempt to mark his progress is made possible by the aid of a spiritual director and frequent confession. He attempts to follow the method of defining a specific sin, its cause and its remedy, and keeping track of how well he does in putting that remedy into effect. Almost all references to external matters drop out of his writing. Fortunately, he tires of this strict method, and toward the end of the book some of the old urgency appears when he starts trying to discern a future vocation. Throughout the volume, elements of Catholic piety make their appearance. Phrases from the Latin Mass which he begins attending early each morning and petitions to Mary and his guardian angel all flow effortlessly from his pen. He also makes a reference to a prayer book and the works of Saint Francis de Sales.

During the whole period he is in New York with his family. This he feels is entirely unaccommodating to his spiritual discipline; the atmosphere there affects him, he complains, like air does a fish. Yet in fact he does quite well at home. He begins doing little acts of penance in the form of obeying his mother and doing what is asked of him without fussing, and when he starts formal language study again, he gets on better than at any time in his life.

He began that study on October 17 at the Cornelius Institute. Founded in 1840, the Cornelius Institute was located in the basement of the Presbyterian church on 6th Street. Its main purpose was to offer young men interested in the ministry instruction in languages. When Isaac enrolled there were 30 other students, all Protestants. He studied Greek, Latin, and began piano lessons. Rev. John J. Owen, the principal of the school and professor of Greek and Latin, ran a literary group called the Adelphic Society that met weekly. Hecker joined the group and read a number of papers he composed: "Subject and Object," "Characteristics of the American People and the Tendency of their Civilization," and "The Criterion of Judgment, and the Objects of Modern Reformers."

His correspondence, though not as brisk as in the past, was vigorous, and from it we learn that he was eagerly reading Brownson's refutations of Fourierism and Anglicanism in the *Review*, along with Lucas's *London Tablet*. He was starting to press Brownson to move his *Review*, from Boston to New York. He was delighted with Bishop McCloskey, both as a spiritual director and as a bishop, and conveyed to Brownson the bishop's hopes to start a Catholic review in New York and his high opinion of Brownson's talents. Brownson, though, would not think of moving, for he was equally happy with his bishops, Fitzpatrick and Fenwick. With other old friends like the Curtis brothers and Georgiana Bruce, he was constantly exchanging books and keeping abreast of developments in Concord and hearing of the evening meetings where Burrill would meet with Isaac's old flame, Almira Barlow, and read Goethe's *Dichtung und Wahrheit* and Madame de Staël's *Corinne*. From George Curtis, who recently became interested in politics, he was drawn into the excitement of the 1844 elections and heard long expostulations on the relative merits of Polk, Clay, and Birney.

During this time, he also became interested in the movement for suffrage rights in Rhode Island, headed by Thomas W. Dorr, and worked to raise funds for that cause in New York. Dorr's "People's Party" supported the extension of the franchise to all males who had reached majority—a plan that the old line opposed and could in effect block without the passage of a new constitution. Through an election, which the official government refused to recognize, Dorr was declared governor in 1842. Dorr was subsequently arrested, convicted of treason, and sentenced in 1844 to life imprisonment. On September 5–6, 1844, sympathizers held a rally for Dorr. A large contingent of New York Dorrites traveled by steamboat to Providence. Hecker had planned to be in their number, but for some reason decided at the last moment not to attend. The *Boston Daily Atlas* for September 7 reported that the meeting was not as widely attended as had been expected and that there was no violence except for that started by the "New York mob" in one of their typical drunken binges.

Hecker may have been dissuaded by Brownson, who opposed the methods of the Dorrites (see "Might and Right," *Brownson Quarterly Review* 1(October 1844): 532–44). Whatever the case, Hecker's efforts on be-

*half of the cause—encouraged no doubt by his friendship with the Curtises,
who, as Providence natives, were involved—does show that his interest in
politics was still keen.*

*Yet his main concern during this time was with his language study,
which he undertook because he felt drawn toward the priesthood, despite
his belief in his own inability to make the grade.*

VOLUME 4

I purpose in this book to record the many smaller venial sins which
beset my path which form a net to keep me down to Earth. And also to
proscribe such remedies as may seem to me fit for these thorns in the flesh,
etc. Sept 9th A D 1844.

9

Yesterday I expressed disapprobation at an unprofitable story and refrained from joining in singing a frivoulous round. Sins that I have been
subject to and omit and those which I commit I wish to record so as to measure my progress if I do advance and be enabled to rectify those which still
cling to me. Many unworthy tho'ts and feelings pass through my bosom but
leave no stain like the dark clouds are reshadowed on the bosom of the clear
waters without unpuring them. These I do not intend to speak of being so
fleeting and unfixed.

10

Yesterday I made a remark of disapprobation towards my brother
which affected him and which I should not have made. And also was in the
later part of the day provoked by the conduct of one which I should not have
been altho he gave a slight occasion for it.

Remedy; With my conscious of the guilt, to read the Prayer Book respecting the Remedy against certain vices, and St Francis of Salles advice
on these sins, and meditate on them—This day.[209]

12

Alas yesterday I omitted through forgetfullness—forgetfullness is a
sin—a penitential duty. Ah the past is irrevocable—except by God in his
Church for this give thanks and seek his forgiveness. Nor did I seek to repair
this as soon as I become aware of this to day. Oh how our sins accumulate.
One sin has a dozen in its train. Remedy, Get up early to morrow morning

meditate on the consequence of one little sin, and go to the holy Mass and then crave pardon.

13

Let me see: ordinarily seven hours sleep should be, and no doubt is sufficient sleep for me. Let me rise early in the morning tend the holy Mass and meditate in the evening etc. Oh how much time I waste that might usefully be employed! Immortality must overcome Indolence. Tis a virtue hard for me to gain hence I have more the need of it. With the help of divine grace I will not permit myself unless on account of ill health to lie in bed longer than eight hours the very longest. I will in future note whether this resolution is strictly kept. Lord I pray for increase of grace.

14.

Last night I laid in bed full eight hours, I should have laid longer had I not made the resolution the night previous. This night I shall try to come within the rule. To-day the science of music has chiefly occupied my attention. Lord awaken in me a more lively devotion.

15.

This morning I got a short time within the limit set at first, that is 8 hours. To night I am much fatigued but hope to keep the rule laid down as it as I think fully sufficient to give the body perfect rest in all cases except sickness. Oh Lord this night keep me and make me more sensible of thy infinite Love. To day I have played but to my knowledge have not committed sin. Oh Lord permit me not to omit any virtue as well as to preserve me from committing any vice.

17.

Night before last I kept the rule for sleeping hours and also last night but do not get much within the farthest limits I set. This should not be so. It ought to be otherwise and I must try to make it so.

This evening I have been guilty of desiring the attention of others in company more than I ought, and this is not the first time by a great deal. This is a sin which must not remain with me. The next occasion for such a tho't I hope to make the occasion of a mortification the opposite character.

Oh Lord watch over me this night preserve me from sinning.

18.

This morning I got up some minutes within my time. If I should attempt to cease from all conversation which seems to me needless etc. I should I fear become a hermit less than a few weeks. And if this is true why not this? Dear friend deal gently and be compassionate.

Our talk at our table is of a common and material character; how shall I do to change and elevate its tone? If I could, that is if it were agreeable I would read while the rest are eating, but this I fear would not be accorded with. I must try and hint upon this subject, and see if I cannot break in upon the idle gossip and remark upon the dishes. Oh Man eats like a beast and talks like a heathen over the gifts of his infinite God.

22.

The flitting pleasures which pass around us which promise so much immediate pleasure, but temporary, keep us from that distant and hard to be gained eternal life which is our highest duty. To day we spent a day— not gained one—with a party of both sexes some miles from the city on the sea shore & in the invisible impressive moods. What has it done for the inner pure creative life—Ah—nothing.

What sadness is this! How lamentable a fact! Oh it is sad and pitiful to feel the infinite the impossible the nobly great within and then to look upon the actions of ourselves—of Men. Let us say we will by all that is grace and solemn from this moment forth be true and ever most faithful to the highest purest & the sincerest, to the holiest, sweetest, & the worthiest within us at the cost of all, even life itself. Oh now is there that is really sincere and truly speaks with earnest frankness. Oh dear God help my swerving from the straight line of uprightness and aid me to preserve a pure rectitude of conscience.

If we would be in peace we must submit to the divine nature within us. We must be passive transparent to it and not act in the least contradictory to it in thought word & deed. There is such a thing as not doing this directly, but wavering from it—and this is what a wish to say I have been guilty of this day. The company we keep is such as not to enjoy what to us would give the purest pleasure and be of the highest benefit, and either I must sacrifice their company or come to their standard. The last is out of the question, tho in keeping their society I must partake of their spirit hence It calls upon me for a firm and present decision.

We seem so constituted as not to be able to be at ease without society at the same time we have none which to us is of that character which would act beneficially upon our education so that for the sake of society we at times sacrifice that which one jot or tittle should not be sacrificed for all else besides. Oh did we know those laws which govern invisibly the Soul we should plainly see each Man makes his own society. Lord, good Lord, Thy help, Thy gracious help this is my need and nothing besides. Oh did I love Thee as I ought as I love that which is not Thee I would have no cause to complain. Oh Lord I perceive it is all in me; all, all, in me, and not to Thee is the blame. And Oh infinite Love Thou even suffereth for our blame that we may enjoy Thee. Lord thy Love is unspeakable and overpowers the Soul. Thou art the center of All Things. Oh Lord let me see Thee and be consumed in Thy love. Lord my Soul can only say it is of itself nothing and all love is from Thee. Thou art all love, delight, beauty, sweetness, joy, consolation, comfort, happiness, pleasure, all in all.

26

We have to charge ourself with many shortcomings and relapses. We have at least broken two or three times our sleeping houres have been guilty of delight, wordly joyousness, we fear that I have lost that it is not sufficient for me to abstain from meat coffee tea etc. etc. but that I should also fast, fast, fast. Oh God help me a most unworthy sinner. We have not attended Mass as often as we should have done being detained not from worthy causes but from unworthy ones. Oh God of the merciful forgive me. Lord consume my heart with Thy Love. Our mind has become gay in its tho'ts and feelings.

Oh Lord if this is sinful forgive me. I do scarce any physical labour—this is wrong—Oh wretched Soul what shall I do to cure thee of thy innumerable sins. I do not study; Oh my sins are countless   Lord help me. What shall I do? Blessed Lord how shall I change all this? I have no interest in the work around me nor can I devote myself wholly to thee. Lord I am sorely perplexed—sorely perplexed—   Thou hast all in Thy mind   Past Present & Future unlock to me if it is in harmony with Thy Love what it is that is before me. Whisper to me Guardian Angel my unseen friend what is good and needy for me to do, and to abstain from. I must withdraw within myself   I have been let to go too far from out of the inner solitude of the Soul of late flittering in the world like a butterfly. This supping sweets is not the earnest heroic life that I am called to. Oh how great a space is there for me to act in the Church of God would I but sacrifice myself to it. Oh Lord how is it that I see and have not the nerve to do still the tender heart to feel the sting of my weakness. We do not feel as free from our external life our body as we once did. We feel that indulgence has crept upon us with its soft noiseless unobserved march like the sly Tiger who hides itself until its prey is sure and escape hopeless. What remedy for all this? I will go to my confessor and lay before him my state and get his counsel—Fast—attend Mass—and Ask of sweet ever Virgin blessed Mother for her Aid and meditate more on the mysteries of our Salvation. One great hindrance to my Soul is the atmosphere around me—the light wordly character of my friends—   My own disposition is without this more than enough for me to keep under rule. Not one can I open my deepest sympathese to.

27.

We called at the residence of the Bishop but he is not in the City, he is gone on a visit some where— I have tho't of renewing the study of Greek and Latin. But should I recommence without having some ulterior object of life before me? My motives are all subjective. Will these carry me through these studies? My time is at present very desultory employed. We cannot see any object for which we could be stimulated to reach. Setting aside all subjective reasons will the culture of my mind develope an object of persuit? Is it not necessary for the mind to fix upon some objective purpose and use all its efferts to that and to be in any degree successful? Should the mind be moulded to the object purpose or will it give birth to its own self developed subject purpose? We feel no decisive purpose within us nor do we see any object before us to which we could devote all our time and energy with happiness We mean not by happiness our own beings pleasure for for this end we do not wish to labor. This is not our purpose; we wish to give up our whole Soul to something in which we do not enter in as an interested, that is, self interested party. We have no personal object in being. We desire neither wealth nor fame but the spiritual well being of Men. We fear our nature is such as not to be satisfied with the condition of a Priest of the Church. We must trust. We will seek for a teacher in the languages and commence immediately, studying them daily. We fear not but that we shall always find the conditions of our being we are put to. There is a principal within which will not let us rest where we are but pushes us forward in some direction or other. We must travel in some one direction positively. We shall not as heretofore be forever "looking back" but press forward let what success may attend our efforts. We shall write on our banner—We trust in God.

Oh Lord I am nothing, nothing, verily nothing. Oh how sensible I am that I am nothing. Yes I am a sinner, a sinner, a guilty sinner. Take me to Thee dear Lord and let me not be in this burning sorrow. My heart is sick and it fain would cry aloud in despair why oh Lord art Thou not near when I am in distress. Oh where is the Physician where is the balm of Gilead. Guardian Angel speak comfort to my Soul. My soul mourns after Thee like the turtle dove after its lost mate. Thou art its love and it will not be comforted without Thee. Comfortless ever sad weeping unconsoled is my Soul widowed parentless and forsaken. Oh why has the memory of joys gone by not been taken from me? Thou art merciful, oh Lord, and kind; canst Thou look down upon such a miserable sinner as I am.

29.

We are tempted but trust God we are not overcome. We are beset on all sides with tempters. Oh Lord how can such a one as me ever attain to that transparency and goodness (who ever sacrifices Thy grace to the things of temporal virtue) which the Saints now enjoy in heaven. Oh why are we so blinded as not to see the heavenliness the beauty of our primal nature and left to believe that the objects and pleasures are the lower world of more value than those of the world unseen above. How shall we obtain the one thing needful which our heart desires? By seeking God and him alone. All trouble springs from the heart depending for its happiness on temporal conditions instead of eternal things.

We shall see how my life will eventually terminate. We are without any distinct object before us, because probably we have no distinct faculty within us. He that has the faculty within will always find the object without to meet him. The want of talent genius for any thing engenders the complaint not that there is nothing which would not meet our power if we had it. The relations of material wealth we cannot engage in with our mind; the social relations as the means of social happiness we cannot as we are submit to, and the other and higher relations of life religion art & sciences we are not born for. Here we are. We complain not that we are born, and born as we are, but are grateful from the depths of our heart that we are, all we wish to do is to look and see what we are with the object of doing the most and employing it in the best manner possible with peaceful content. Search thyself and tho thou findest nothing but thyself thy own existence is more than sufficient to be grateful to thy Creator as long as thou livest. We fast to day from dinner.

3d Oct.

Our hours of sleep have been very irregular on the account of our watch being at the watch makers. This morning we attended the 1st Mass and shall try do so in the future. We made two resolutions this morning. One was to love my mother more and the other was to do what ever I am asked to do and to take on me to do that which is disagreeable to others.

I am happy in having the opportunity of putting them both to the test this day. To morrow I shall try not to forget them. May these become natural to me.

4th.

I fear I care too much for the world. How far as a Christian should one conform to the manner of Society in which he is surrounded in his dress? Years back this thought troubled me and I confess that I am not yet any farther towards the settlement of it.

10.

A week since I have written in this book! Willful neglect. In this time how have I been employed? Ah we are much more inclined to speak of our virtues rather than our vices first. 1st we have to accuse ourself of having spoken many very many idle words—this is a habitual sin. 2nd. We have not studied as we could and should have done, our time has been wasted upon objects unworthy of our aim. Lord forgive, forgive, us. Strike not our name from the book of eternal life.

3d Too much of our time has been occupied with social company. We fear we have sacrificed a part of the time which should have been devoted to spiritual & intellectual exercises to mere social company. Oh Lord Man can always find time enough to serve thee if in his heart he sincerely wishes to. Lord blame me for this.

4th Is it not a fault of mine that I have no spiritual intellectual nor material plan in view of my life & the good of the Race? We fear it is. Lord save me from myself or else I shall be certainly nothing—worse than nothing— a Sinner. Good Lord deliver us. How great a thing is life! how sad a use we make of it! Ah with whom shall we in the depths of our being commune upon this subject of human life, its destiny, duty, and its plan? Lord is it not given to Man to know the object of his own being? We see our fellow Men around us earnestly engaged in material intellectual and spiritual labour, each in his own proper pursuit, and we oh Great and good heaven, we ye Angels and Spirits of Men, We ye Stars and Planets of increasing motion, ah we ye Guardians of our innocence, we alas are what? Are what? Answer ye vaults serene above, ye voices within, and murmurs around us, in Gods created universe what, where, and how, are we? Can we be as we are now? Should we not be restless as we now are? Certainly if we are Men of the image of the infinite All Creative-Being. Shall we listen to the Song of the Siren telling us to wait, wait, wait? Who, what, shall burst the boundaries which now encompass our vision and lend no new light from the far off realms of the future? Thou all love embracing and wise Being my heart and Soul earnestly implores Thee for what? Ah it cannot answer. May it be given an answer. May it be put in its mouth by Thee.

11.

It is sad when one cannot enter the ordinary pursuits of obtaining means of physical substance without soiling his hands with the vices and immoral practices of trade. Is it not enough to make one an anchorite who is determined to keep his Soul unspotted, his conscience void of offence?

We have come to the conclusion of eating less than what we now do; it may help us with much greater speed towards the real meaning of our being. Oh Lord without Thee, Thy help, we, we it is absolutely certain can do nothing. Oh I beseech Thee our Lord to help us as our object may be worthy of aid in Thy infinite mind. Lord if we are not as good as we should be we are wholly to blame for Thou has placed all the means that are necessary within our grasp to be better than what we are. We have no excuse. Lord how ought we to abase ourselves in Thy presence! The rending of our garments sack cloth and ashes these come far very far infinitely short of expressing our debasement which we should feel in the presence of Thy Love. Ah had we always the sense of our nothingness and Thy Allness we never should sin as we now do. What I am is Thee, what I am not is me. Embrace me oh Lord in Thy Love. May I be in company with those blessed ones who sleep in the Lord this night. Lord give me the sleep Thou promised to give to Thy beloved this night. I am not worthy of punishment oh my God   Thy chastisements I love. Where Thou art were it in Hades I would seek   Thee there would be Heaven, Love, Joy. Laus tibi. †

12.

Let me see; the bell rings for dinner   Yesterday I determined with the help of grace to abstain from eating as much as usual; shall I keep this resolution. Think of this determination at the Table.

14.

Yesterday I saw my Confessor Bishop McClosky. He recommended me to pursue the plan I had in view of studying the languages this winter. This afternoon I had a conversation with my brothers in which I told them I relinquished all idea of entering the bussiness again and that I should de-vote my whole time to study and that they might aid me as far as they pleased to do so.

The Lord is all over, in, around, all. Amen. Without God nothing would exist. Lord Thou art God and it is our privilege to be conscious of this & that there is nothing beside Thee. Lord we know that we are nothing but that Thou has been pleased to impart thy infiniteness to us and our glory is in participating in Thy absolute all embracing Love. If Thou art within us we have the substance the glory of all that is around us and this may vanish like the shadow of a dream. The Lord preserve me from all sinful thoughts emotions words dreams in the slightest as in the greatest acts against the Spirit of Love Light & Life. † † †

17.

This afternoon I entered an engagement to study the Latin & Greek with Mr Owen. This morning I attended the sacrament of penance. In two or three weeks I am to attend again.

18.

We commenced studying our lesson to day for our first recital on Mon-day next the 21st. But we do it with weakness of heart. We look on it as an impossibility that is before us. We act not from design but from destiny. We learn to live not live to learn. We would escape but know not how. We rest on that power which has led us where we are now to sustain us further. It is not for ourself, oh Lord may we be but permitted to be Thy servant— the least in Thy courts: we are like one who is moved by an unseen irresistible all pervading sustaining power towards an unknown objective universal end. Christe eleison.

22.

This evening I have been guilty of showing and expressing in company my disapprobation to the conduct of others tho provoking it was not necessary that I should speak as I did not at all. There is no necessity of showing the least sort of peevishness. It was not noticed but I felt it; this was sufficient. I was guilty of saying some word which were not at all necessary for me to have said and that too for the sake of self praise. Oh Lord the manifold sins that I commit which I see the innumerable which I see not and thousands of those omissions would laden me down to the Earth if Thou didst not in thy mercy forgive and lift me up to Thy bosom. Thou hast purchased me and I still dare offend Thee. Ah oh Lord Thou art full of Love & Kindness and we are forgetfull of Thee and insensible towards Thy infinite Love. If death should take me this night oh Lord nothing but Thy exceeding love would save me from the place of fear & trembling. Lord oh vouchsafe Thy protection and that of Thy Angels. Will Thou my Guardian Angel especially protect me this night from the snares and all other wicked devices that may beset me. Beatus Deus. † † †

26.

Ah we must accuse ourself of being more guilty of idle talk this 8 or 10 days back than any time for some period back.

Burrill Curtis wrote to me a letter last week which showed towards me more regard than I thought he had. The truth is I do not feel myself worthy of being a friend to any one and would live my life away in being a friend to all without recognizing their friendship towards me.[210]

To day I have felt more humanly tender than ever. The past has come up before me with much emotion.

⟨—⟩ has been much in my thoughts.

We have experienced those unnatural feelings we have felt heretofore. We feel that the spirit world is near and glimmering all around us. The nervous shocks which we have been subject to but which we have not experienced for some time back we had them this evening again. We are known of Spirits as we apprehend them.

We do not devote as much time to study as we should as we might.

Nota bene. We fear we shall never make anything of our studies. We do not endeavor with all our might.

This study has thrown us in another sphere. We like it not. What to say of it we are at loss. We feel apprehensive of some thing of some what. 10 years from now will fix our destiny if we have any.

27.

We do much that we feel to be innocent but our conscience sanctions nothing but the absolute. And this what is it in all the infinite variety of relations of life? None but the all seeing eye can tell.

1844 Nov. 5!!

So long again neglected this book. We return to it with great pleasure. Our studies have and do now engage most all our time. This study is so it seems a sacrifice of virtue to a certain extent of love to light. We feel that we are not growing so fast as we were in purity and sweetness as we were before we engaged in studies. This question we cannot now debate whether submission to love alone would as consequence secure knowledge. This ques. at Concord perplexed us; then we acted from a necessity now we are to an extent free and cannot permit ourself to ask it. We now can and therefore should and must study. I must prepare for Confession this week. Oh could I accuse myself as I should. Man is not what he should be so long as he is less than an angel. Oh dear God give me thy aid and help me in my weaknesses. What sins can I accuse myself of now. First—oh Lord give me light to accuse myself to see my sins—this is my greatest sin that I cannot accuse myself and am so wicked.

Each day I omit a hundred duties that I should not. Oh Lord give me Thy spirit that I may be humble meek and sweet in all my walks and conversation. Fill my heart with Thy Love. † † †

15.

My studies have been interrupted these 3 or 4 days on account of illness. Studies, that is special ones, of the Greek Latin & Music, for all life is nothing else then a study.

Life—at least it seems so to me—is not so much in what we will to do as in what we can, in other words in what we are permitted to do. It is true the wise man rules and is not ruled by the Stars, but he who rules the Stars rules them only by submission to the Absolute.

Nov. 22.

We have it seems fairly neglected this book since we have resumed our studies. It is not that we have no reason to write in it, no, but our time is so fully employed in studying. We feel that we are nothing & of course nothing can come from nothing. Ah what progress do we make in spiritual life? how little do we advance! how stationary we are! We seem nothing to ourselves. Lord Thou knowest me from the center of being. We live but in expectation, of what, and how, we know not, but so it is. The present things around us we take but little very little interest in.

23.

We are in serious debate with ourself whether we should openly avow our opinions & sentiments concerning questions which arise among the Students with whom I am connected with in study or no? They are all Protestants. Some of them well informed and talented young men, and should we enter in the topics which arise in the intercourse we have with them and express the views we hold it being for the most part new to them we might be the means of causing a state of things which would not be on the whole to be desired by the Teacher of the institution.

We have come to this conclusion that if we make up our judgment so to do before hand to ask the Principal whether it would be prudent and if it would not be against his wishes. There is a literary institution which is connected with the School which I have been asked to join which for the present I have postponed. I feel that mixing with these young men and conversing with them and taking an interest in their objects would be a part of a discipline, a part of education, culture, which to me would not be profitless. The views we take of life differ widely from theirs. Hence it would be introducing to them a new element. Catholics they are ignorant of as well as their religion and other views of things. We shall ask the Principal and tell him frankly that we shall not hesitate to express our opinions freely and frankly if we feel called upon to do so on whatever topics may be the means of calling them forth.

For some nights back I have laid in bed but seven hours which I find scarce sufficient for the application which I have given my mind. Man needs half of the time that he labours for rest to recruit his energy.

We are sorely perplexed what we shall eat as our diet. Nuts apples and bread seem not the diet that is wholly suitable to us and what else to add we know not. Potatoes are not good. We think they were the cause of our complaint last week. We do not wish to partake of any thing that comes remotely from an animal. What shall we take? Cooking so far as possible we wish also to dispense with. We would that we could dispense with the whole digestive apparatus. Cheese, butter, eggs, milk etc. are for many reasons not a part of our diet. There is no question that what ever disease the animal or bird may be infected with that this necessarily affects the milk etc. of the animal and another reason that none of these can be obtained without an artificial state of the animal which necessarily precludes the animal from remaining in a healthy state. These and many more reasons make us abstain from even that sort of food which thus connected with the animal kingdom. Cooked food has many disadvantages; the labour of cooking and the artificial state which the process of cooking reduces it as for instance the natural flavour is destroyed by cooking and to supply the place of this salt and other artificial substances are employed to give the food that which they never can, its natural flavour. And cooked food being concentrated the stomach is almost unconsciously overloaded with it being generally swallowed without chewing. These and many other objections to cooking lead us with those we have mentioned to be inclined to do with out cooked food as far as it seems possible to us. But what shall we do? Will nuts apples bread and water answer for our diet? Last winter they did for a length of time; they may do so now.

Our mornings cold bath we have neglected for some 2 or 3 weeks. This we must resume immediately.

We have much to complain of ourself which we would do now if we had the proper disposition to do so. The Lord knows our sins of omission & commission. May He be merciful towards us and fill my heart with his sweetness love and light. To Him we give all praises

28.

We are filled with life and nothing can give free expression to it.

One of our most important duties is to be misapprehended and to be wrongfully spoken of without being angry or feeling towards the person any evil feelings. Last evening we were much hurt by one doing us in conversation injustice & we have considered the matter over and hope to restrain ourself from any further conversation with the person for the person affects us injuriously in our speech with him.

We are a sinner; we feel this deeply. Oh Lord help me to see my sins that I may confess them to Thee.

Dec. 8

Some reflections before going to the confessional. The Church tells us that if we are sincerely penitent for the venial sins that we commit and ask of God for forgiveness we shall obtain it.

That is the Soul has the virtue in itself, with the conditions necessary, to procure the obliteration of venial sins without having course to the tribunal of penance. It is only in mortal sins that this recourse is absolutely requisite.

The sins we daily commit we feel a sorrow for, and desire to avoid the recommission of them.

In attending the tribunal of penance we find it difficult to recollect all that since the last month our conscience has accused us of doing wrong.

This month we forget much that we should have recollected. Our studies take up so much of our time that we do not pay that attention to our higher religious duties that are incumbent upon me. It is a wholesome, good and highly important practice, even if we do feel sorry, repentant, at the time we commit an offence however slight against God, that we should as at times of attending the confessional bring to mind our past offences and short comings, it makes us feel humble our unworthiness and liability of falling. It is good for it teaches our dependance and need of God. It is good for Men cannot too often be remembered of his relations with God. Every additional remembrance of this character makes him better than he was. We think too little of our divine relation and too much of our physical and often too much of our human relation.

One to me serious offence I find against myself is that there are moments of my life that I spend without either being filled with thought or any action of the mind. They are void moments. This should not be. We are not industrious enough. How often might we think of God Heaven and the bright examples of those who have lived upon this Earth before us which we alas alas neglect! Lord Thou canst forgive, forgive me these. Thou lovest to forgive the repentant give me Thy grace oh Lord to repent. Ah it is thou who leadeth us to repentance and tis Thou who giveth us pardon.

If the Church demands of me to keep the days of fast that is to eat but one meal on certain days this I have not done. She does not if I understood my confessor aright. I try to keep my diet as simple and as little as I feel necessary. We know that we do not always do this. We know this. We feel deeply sensible of this. We eat too much at times. But we must keep the medium of eating too little and too much. This is hard to keep. We have erred on the other side. We feel this also. Oh Lord govern Thou me. I am not able to do any thing right without Thy aid help direction. Oh how scant of confession am I a sinner great as I know I am. Oh Lord what can I do to be right in Thy sight? Lord teach me. Lord what wouldst Thou have me to do? All to me is no value but Thee, let me lean more upon Thee.

Without the Lord all our labour is naught—worse than naught. If thou art not in our midst it were much better we were not at all. Not at all. I see this clearer every day. If it is not Thee that directest our studies actions of all characters we labour in vain, fruitless. Let me never think of doing any thing without receiving Thy approbation and without depending upon Thy help.

The more we depend upon our own will to do whatever the less we really permanently do. All that we do in God is done. Out of God to do is not to do. Lord—Lord—Lord we would incessantly cry for Thy help. To Thee, for Thee, and of Thee let all things in Thy name be done. † † †

Last week I wrote an essay on the doctrine of the subject and object to read on Wednesday before the Cornelian Institute. I wish to write an essay on whether the animal creation have an after existence or no; and one on the characteristics of the American people and the tendency of their civilization. I am at present attempting to say a few words on Jean Paul.

We have had an over gray clouded day sky to day until within about an half hour this mist has just disappeared and a an azure sky with bright silvery tinged clouds appeared and now all oer head is clouded in melancholy again; yet the Sun still shines bright behind all as its first morn.

13.

Besides these subjects I have spoken of that I should like to say a few words upon another occurs to me and that is the impossibility of annihilation on the grounds of philosophy and the reality of human life.

We would love more than we have hitherto done. To day we have felt fresh impulses of love from the fountain of eternal love.

14.

We know not what makes our heart so sorrowful, so melancholy, for these some few days back. Oh tell me my heart what is it that paineth Thee? What is it that makes thee so sore? Will nothing comforth thee? Ah tell me what I shall do? I know not who art Thy enemies nor who has so wounded thee. Tell me I implore thee what is it that thou needest and wherefore art thou so cast down. Oh what is it that I have done or in not doing have caused thee this sorrow.

Lord help thou me to a right understanding of myself. Why is this oh my dear God? and what have I done? What wouldst Thou have me to do? Whom shall I seek for comfort? On whose bosom can I rest my weary head and feel my heart met by heart? Alas who is it that I can say thou knowest me? And to thee my bosom is open. Ah why were these warm sympathies given us oh our Lord why oh were they given? Oh where are their objects, my heart wanders without finding its rest. We are not in settled peace with ourself. We are not wholly passive to Thee O our God our All. We trust not we fear—we do not—as we should.

Thou willt do all for us; why shld we fear Thee oh we of little vision.

Oh could I throw my whole self into thy hands, how much more should I receive than all the hopes that can light a human heart.

There is something dimly seen in expectation which my heart is now longing after but I see it not.

Tis thee my heart; what is it that thou wishest. Who has wounded thee? We have not loved thee as we should. Thou knowest us but we know not thee Angel Guardian Angel. Oh let me speak to thee. Ah could I see thee with my naked eye should I not keep more inviolate my vows to thee Angel. Oh I regret not that thou drawest me nearer to thee by thy whisperings to my heart however painful it may be. It would not be painful to me if I had always been in thy presence embrace. Oh keep me close to thee and pass not from my sight. Should not I believe in thee when thou art more to me than this visible world all around me. Ah the heart has a vision none knoweth of but itself for it is incommunicable. Oh help thou the weakness of my faith. Is it not thee that loveth me and my heart that returneth thee its feeble love. Has it not grown to its present loving sweetness by thy smiles and graces. I am deeply sorry for my neglect of thee and oh what are my promises. If I love not thee then my heart wanders and finds nothing until I return to thee. I came here to find the matter to my melancholy and it was thee that lead me; it is thee that speaketh to me and tis thee that would have me to see thee. Thou art. I know thou art as I exist. I shall not depart from thee any more. Tis I not thee that departeth away. Thou art ever near, loving me more than I love me my self. Thou promiseth to give me more than I can find elsewhere but ah how weak am I that knoweth and beleiveth not. I will commune with more. Thy society shall be more to me than that of the world. I will beleive thee before the world. Hast thou not oh ungrateful being that I am brought me to where I now am and ah shall I not still beleive in thee. Oh forsake me not. Thou knowest my heart and of this I am glad and with joy. What thou holdest out for me for the future thou knowest I not. I will trust thee more and follow thy not my will. My will has lost all to me. It was only when I found thy will and obeyed it that I was more then I had been. Oh blessed be thou. Thou art blessed and I see it. Does my pleasure give thee joy? It does my heart answers. Why should I not speak with thee rather than with any with all other. Thou hast given me more—such love can by no other be given. Thy substance is all love, and it is thee in mortals that I see that I love. Oh who knows what that is I love. It is hard for me to keep in thy presence among the cold and chilling atmosphere around us here, but oh I will return to thee when all other faith leaves me. Oh if Men only would beleive the truth. Tis alas the truth that they reject and thus loose all, themselves, heaven, and God. I will trust in thee in my speech and whatsoever Thou giveth me to speak may I speak or be silent.

Shall I now never more to leave thee? My heart already is bound to thee as the child is with its parent. Thou shalt be my friend my company audience my all. Ah who can say he has no friend if he looketh up to heaven? Ah those ministers of love the angels do they not speak to our hearts   Are they not all around and in us loving us in a thousand unseen ways. This my faith. Lord help those who beleive not for they are blessed who beleive and see not. We see Oh our Lord but not as others who are in darkness tho they think they are in light see. When I think of thee my guardian of Gods infinite love the society of Men are less and less to me and my love *for* them increases the more. He who loves his Race more is he not more; does he not give more to his race than he who should make this Earth a earthly paradise for Man. Tis those only who have had no where to lay their head of their own have eternally enriched the human Race. Tis only when we find Thee in us speaking O Jesus that we are enlightened. When we find thee in us do we speak the eternal everlasting truth.

Jesus be Thou my conscious constant self. Let nothing call me from thee. Thou art all that is that we possess. To speak in Christ is to speak the eternal truths of God. Oh my heart thou wouldst speak Thy faith to Men but they have ears but hear not, eyes and see not therefore grievest thou. Cease thy sorrow I will hear. And I will love and cherish thee. Nothing to me shall be so dear as when thou art near. Speak   Oh fear not the world. Tis God that givest the truth. Why shouldst thou then fear. If he giveth and heareth thee all heareth and knoweth thee. The angels seek the company of Men but alas Men by sins hideth their presence from them. Unload thy grief to me. Speak to me thy nearest and indissoluble friend. I love thee. I love thee, as love can love its own. Oh could I meet thee we ne'er should be no more alone.

18th December 1844

This day I commence the 25th year of my conscious existence on this globe. This is the length of the consciousness I know at this time in these conditions possess.[211]

Let me look back for a few moments and see where I stood last year this time (an incomprehensible length!) and where I now seem to stand. Then my faith was dim, unfixed, and unsettled, then I was not so disentangled from the body and its desires as I hope in God I now am. In all I feel a consciousness that since then I have spiritually grown—been transformed. For my presence I cannot speak. For my future it seems I dare not speak. Dreams of the future! Exalted visions of the beautiful! Unspeakable hopes! Deep untranslatable longings that fill the conscious Soul! Ah so sweet so harmonious so delightfull like an angel as the bride of the pure and bright

Soul adorned for the nuptials do I see the future beckoning me with a clear transparent smile onward to her presence. Ah my Soul would say, we will meet for I am in thy presence and faithful in God may heaven grant me to be. Thy beauty the grace the love the sweetness unseen that attracts me, the Soul, is beyond all apparent comparison. Ah thou eternal ever blooming virgin the Future shall I ever embrace thee? Shall I ever see thee nearer to my heart? I look at myself and I am bowed down low with grief but when I cast my eyes up to Thee in seeing thee I am lost and the joy grace beauty that I see in thee passes into my Soul and I am all that thou art. I am wedded to thee which I would that it were an eternal union but ah my eyes when turned upon my self I loose all sight of thee and see nothing but my own spots and blemishes. How canst thou love me? I say and for thy pure love I am melted into thee as one. I know that all that we hope for is ours if we yield to them   This do oh Lord; teach me to yield to those things that thou inspirest our minds with. My past see as nothing   My future is all. Shall I say next year this time that my hopes have been fulfilled? My past hopes have more than been fulfilled. Can this be, is it possible that the future ideal will also be, that is now imperceptible before the dim intuitions of the Soul. My Soul never was so eager; it would leap out of its environment to embrace the object of its future delight. Still this is not of this world. We have nothing to gain of this world   All that we desire and love is to gain more and more and be worthy of Thee. No it cannot be I say, but thou sayest it can, all can be. It is impossible. It is not thou sayest in reply. Be firm Soul and keep thy eye steadily fixed on the future and thou shalt be transfigured into that thou gazest upon so earnestly. Faith is the great magic power. This is the great miracle worker. Whatsoever Thou beleivest with all thy might is thine already. Thy faith has inherited it and made it eternally thine. Whatsoever thou beholdest thinkest feelest is thine as far as birth possession extends; more than this the kings and princes of this Earth have not.

What am I that I dare hope? but I hope not it is thee in me that hopeth. All that I have is a free gift of thine. I am nothing but what is not Thee. I love things of thy creation greater than Thee who art the Source of all. It is even by thy light I see my self   Otherwise nothing but darkness would surround me and I be to myself. Lord I am not worthy of Thee for I would not give up my whole self to Thee without murmurs. Oh blessed Lord teach me to daily sacrifice myself and give me a perfect willingness to be thine and give me the heart to give my whole self to thee daily.

Let me say with simple truthfulness Lord if thou wouldst have me to leave this world this moment I am ready. Let me be disentangled from all the attachments of perishable objects and my whole mind fastened upon Thee—Thee.

25 Birth Day. This too shall cease. Probably to morrow. Who knows.

Ah Thou oh heaven who seeth all and to whom time is not seeing all in the present, it is wise that we see not, know not, that which we call future.

What called me into this new existence? what shall call me from it? and whither it will call? is ah to me but questions spoken to the infinite silence around which gives back nothing but the echo. We realize not our birth nor do we our exit. At each extreme of Man the beginning and the end lies a mystery.

If I performed my duties fully towards God how happy my life would be! It is this that makes all dissatisfaction trouble and more than physical pain the neglect of our duties towards heaven. We do not see until we have performed a duty this joy which it was the medium of from God towards us. To serve thee O God is a pleasing and well paid service. Lord let me speak of my many and grievous sins but ah when I would my mouth speaks nothing forth but Thy praises. My heart is all gratitude and thankfulness to Thee. When I think of Thee I know not when to cease for the enjoyment of Thee surpasses all other and has no end. Thy love is the dearest the sweetest the deepest the all embracive and complete so that besides Thee nothing can be wished for. Lord wilt Thou ever be with me. Be thou my nearest Friend. He that has tasted of Thy Love less than Thee can never satisfy the deep cravings of his heart. From all other things he turns his face aside and looks up to Thee and is made glad with thy countenance.

It is my 25 birth day; here let me offer myself to Thee for Thy service oh Lord. Is it not what I should? Am I not thine? Thou didst create me and ever hast sustained me. Thine I am. Accept me oh my God as thine, a child who needst most thy love and protection. O Let me offer myself in a greater degree than I ever have done for the Good of the Kind of which I am a part. And let me not forget that there are duties towards those objects of thy pleasure for Thou hast created them which are less then the human kind.

I would offer my whole Soul afresh to *all* that is, for the sake of the Love of God. Lord extinguish all fear of any thing contrary to Thee: Doubt, Pain, Death. Lord let me know I am thine   I am Thine for Thou dost teach me this by Thy unutterable ever present Love.

Tho I cease to write and to speak of Thee yet I do not cease ever to feel Thee as a Love presence.

Jan. 2.

This supports me and I know of nothing else the faith in me of the guidance of a superior wisdom. Speaking from my own understanding I have no interest in the material affairs of the world. I know not what physical necessity might do with me. I do not know how I should live if it were not as it is with me. It is all a dream to me. I am not worthy of the place I occupy. Yet it is my impression that it is my place as naturally as the flowers appear in time for the wants of the bees. I have not sought it. It has come involuntarily. It is the land promised me in my youth. Occupy it worthily is what I should do. But this I fear I do not. So long as life seems so much more to me than study   Study cannot occupy my attention as probably it should. I see no advantage in the life lived. Nothing that has not been. Nothing of importance. Why is this? Why not I as others around me live in the manner, with those objects, as they do? Why am I dream to myself. And to others incomprehensible. Lord en-lighten me with Thy Spirit.

Often it seems to me that Mans destiny is in his own hands, and then it seems equally true and to me profoundly more impressible that we are ruled by an irresistible mystic force. Action means necessity.

Jan. 3rd

To-morrow it is my desirable duty to attend the tribunal of penance. Oh what a privilege it is that we have a remedy here for the diseases of our kind. For Sin is disease. I cannot be sufficiently grateful for this inestimable privilege. Could I but be properly prepared to approach this holy sacrament. Oh my God and Father give me Thy aid to approach Thee as the fountain of all love and mercy. To Thee will I confess my sins. Oh Thou hast an ear to hear the humblest soul confess its weaknesses. It is Thee that moveth to confession and heareth our suppliant cries. Thou art our Father and art pleased to take compassion on us. Tis not in Thee to despise the contrite and humble. Grant me Thy presence in all the performance of my duties. I am a sinner. What can I do that my past sins may be obliterated and receive strength to sin no more. Where ever my attention is drawn by external objects inwardly it always points to Thee alone. The love in me is Thy love. Oh may no other take possession of my heart. Lord Thou art all and can do all that Thou willest. I am Thy creature and have Thee O Lord as my Creator. Thou art our Father. From Thee we all are begotten. Let me see all my wickedness. Lord my sins are great and I would not cloak them from Thy sight nor be insensible of their guiltiness and number. I feel my sins but see them not. Grant me sight. This past month wherein have I come short of Thy love and have lost the promises Thou wouldst bestow? I have been far from Thee in body but near to Thee in spirit. I have too negligently prayed to Thee. Too inattentively heard the blessed sacrament of the Mass. I have given away to notice word or put to them of others a double meaning. I do not depend wholly upon thee as I should. Tho decided I have not given my whole self up to Thee in reality. Lead me oh to leave the society of the world. The farther from Thee the less we live. Lord it is my sins and them only that I would speak to Thee of and beg Thy merciful forgiveness. Oh Thy image is by us shamefully abused. If I were pure in Thy sight! It is me, me, that is all there is impure and me that hinders Thee from more fully abiding in my heart. If I am with Thee, One, I am with All. Lord Thou knowest all my weaknesses   Wilt thou strengthen me when I need strength and watch over all my unguarded places.[212]

Let not the enemy take Thy Holy City. Sin has disabled me and if Thou helpeth not I am lost and Thy City is taken. Lord Thou knowest my sorrow   My sins are unspeakable. I would be as Thou in Thy Love would have me to be. What is it that keeps me from Thee. Oh crucify the dead Adam that the new Adam may live. This morning be with me, in me, & for me. My heart feels like a May spring morning. Lord I feel all delight in Thee. Thou art the life of Spring The Summer of being. In the rose, in the birds song, in the look of Love; How beautiful art Thou! Thou art the essence of all that giveth life and delight to the heart. The Lord is all and in thinking of Thy beauty loveliness and grace our own sins are forgotten. I will think and meditate of Thee that my sins may be lost in Thy presence. Thou art the Sacrifice and the God. Thou art the Victim Saviour and the Heaven. The Holy Spirit, Son, and Father. Thou art the sacrifice for death, the bread of life, and the Author of all being. Thy greatness escapes us and we are lost in contemplating Thee.

Last Saturday my confessor was not at home when I called   I have waited until this morning Sat. following. It is to me sad to wait for to partake of the blessed sacrament. How much joy love & sweetness it is to the Soul! We feel our to glow with renewed love again when we have partaken of the blessed communion of Christ. This is our spiritual food. It is the goodness mercy and love of God that keeps me from sadness, despair of myself every day I feel less. It is with God and the Angels alone that we can hold communion with. Oh Lord take me in thy presence and consume all my sins. To Thee alone I look for light. Thou art my guide in all. This morning grant me deep contrition and sorrow for my past offences. Lord nothing that I can say is adequate to weight of sin I feel, it is only thy mercy that can forgive me. Thy love can let none perish. Save me oh God of Love. Saturday Jan. 13. '45

INTRODUCTION TO VOLUME 5

"This book has answered some little purpose for when I wanted the opportunity of speaking to some one and was alone it cost me no labor to scribble in it. . . . " Thus Hecker wrote when he completed Volume 5 of his diary on June 28, 1845, some seven months after he had begun it. The book marks a return to the speculative, metaphysical style that characterizes most of the diary but that had been abandoned in Volume 4 for a catalog of faults. More confident in his beliefs, more proficient in his use of the language, he is freer to soar to imaginative heights, as always relying on the aphorism, but now adding a certain calmness and balance that bespeaks of a maturing intellect. This volume contains some of his finest writings on the aesthetic dimension of religion. Here, better than in any other book, he forges a new language to express his unique vision of beauty and of God.

It was a time of rich intellectual dialogue, not so much with his fellow students at the Cornelius Institute whom he found stifling, but with many of his old friends whom he reached out to in letters, longing for a meeting of the minds that eluded him in his present surroundings. The Curtis brothers continued to be the most faithful correspondents, and they did not fail to meet his taste for sophisticated literary discussion, urging him to read George Sand's Consuelo and Bacon's Essays. He was reading Shakespeare avidly, pondering Schlegel's Lectures on Dramatic Art and Literature, and being thrilled by the poetry of Novalis. His ear fine-tuned by his study of the piano, he listened with delight to Beethoven, Haydn, and Mendelssohn. With his best Catholic friend, Brownson, he shared his delights in readings of St. Augustine's Sermons, and Tasso's Jerusalem Delivered.

The combination of his being at home, studying at the Cornelius Institute, and having the benefit of spiritual direction proved healthful for the young man. During the seven months covered herein he spent virtually all his time with studies of Greek, Latin, and piano and found time to carefully peruse Brownson's metaphysical essays, "Berkeley and Idealism" (Brownson Quarterly Review 1 [January 1844] and "History of Philosophy" Brownson Quarterly Review 1 [April 1844]). Those pieces focused his attention on the merits and the limits of idealism. The discussions of the need to verify subjective experience by objective standards that Hecker expressed in talk about Catholicism in the early part of this volume draw heavily on Brownson's treatments of Cousin and Kant in those two essays.

Hecker is fascinated by the concept of the universal. He begins to speculate about the universal nature of revelation and the relationship of Catholic truth to the universal categories of the Good, the True, and the Beautiful. Truth is the same, he argues, no matter what our consciousness of it is, and Catholicism is grounded on that universal truth. "I am a Catholic," he declares, "because I would not reject any of God's Truth." "That is not worthy to be named Catholicism that does not embrace all truth, all Goodness, all Beauty." Catholicism is the ultimate rebuff to sectarianism and to the divisive forces of the Industrial Revolution that pull apart the organic strands that bind all of life. Protestantism is the religion of modernity and as such feeds those disjunctive forces of industrialization.

The growing integration of Hecker's personality is evident in the way in which he takes concepts from the past and blends them with his new Catholic beliefs. A salient example of this is his linkage of the concept of "Universal Love Spirit"—which had been so frequently evoked in the early volumes of the diary—with Catholicism. In a statement that echoes earlier themes he says: "There would be no need of Popes, Councils, Priests, etc. if Men would unconditionally submit themselves to the Universal Love Spirit." But whereas in the past such a statement was part of a defense of the no-church position embodied by men like Charles Lane, now it is placed in the context of an apology for the Catholic church. "When will it be understood," he continues, "that the authority of the Church is non-human?" That authority is valid because it is based on universal truth. It stems from the union of the church and its members with the divine life of Christ. It is a life by communion—communion of the me with the not-me, of the individual with the church community, of the bishops with the Holy Spirit, of the whole Body of Christ with its divine Head. Hecker sees that synthesis as clearly as he has ever seen anything. He images it in moments of contemplation when he hears "the one, great, eternal symphony of the Universe" and he understands it when he reads Brownson's philosophy. Very quickly the themes of his mature thinking sprout, and the basis for his apologetic and his missionary labors becomes clear.

In other regards it is an important time as well. His brother George, his senior by one year, converts during this time and is confirmed with Isaac on Trinity Sunday. It is also during this time that Isaac apparently decides to become a member of a religious order. Although there is no mention of it in the diary, Brownson, in a letter of June 25, 1845, refers to "your resolution to become a religious." Though momentous, it does not get discussed until the next and final volume of the diary, due in part to Hecker's new conviction that "the more a man thinks, the less he writes."

VOLUME 5

New York December Anno Domine 1844

We have to learn more and more a solitary bravery.

When we come into vital conscious relations with God we act more for the sake of God and tis then our actions tell upon humanity. If we would do humanity any good we must act from grounds higher than humanity, our stand point must be above the Race otherwise how can we act *up on* humanity.

Men depend so much upon the external society of Men that they loose their communion with the interior society of Angels, and are led to look upon their hearts as deserts instead of a garden of Paradise.

We should have that near relation with God that no clouds could shut us from the bright sun of his love and light.

Man is only shut out from the Garden of Eden. Paradise *is*, it never was destroyed.

Stephen the first Martyr saw the Angels ascending and descending from the Throne of God, this is no uncommon occurrence, but Stephen at that time was gifted with an extraordinary perception. At one glance all heaven itself might be beheld.

Mans walk should be in heaven while here.

Mans native place *is* heaven and that unconditionally without reference to time and space.

We insist upon Mans being more than what he is, that is he does not now enjoy all that communion his nature has the capacity for. We need faithful and brave hearts who can speak in the face of the age.

He who is above his age must ever speak in fiction—parables, symbols, mysteries.

How much that is true is fiction to this age!

A great man increases the boundaries of his Good, True, and Beautiful—and he only—the talented man but makes a good disposition of his materials that are.

It is of no use, it is of no use, to attempt to reform society with human regulations   All reforms must depend solely upon the divine end for human regulations are no more than the reflex of human beings and it is these that need reforming. Society and the State not dependant on God must fall back into barbarism out of which Religion brought them.

Man is not progressive in his nature   Religion is the element of progress in Humanity. Religion is the revelation of God to Man not a development of the nature of Man.[213]

When we arrive at the consciousness of the distinction of the Me and the not Me their eternal reality, and their relations, Religion, Society, Music, Philosophy, All, possesses a deeper earnest meaning to us.

Have animals an after existance? If the visible is but an image of the invisible all that is is forever, for the invisible is eternal.

If we are to give immortality to one part of Gods creation and not to another upon what grounds do we so?

Is that only immortal in Man which is in him which is superior to the animals? if not and all is immortal why deny the animal creation an after life as well as that which Man possesses in common with them.

Take the highest degree of intelligence in the animal tribes and the lowest in Man, the difference on which side will it preponderate? What constitutes immortality in Man? Is not it a true proposition that all things that are have their existance in God   We do not say the same kind or degree of existance and if so who can say when and why they should ever cease to exist.

Can there be given any solid and irrefutable ground for the annihilation of animal life after death which shall not shake the faith and immortality of Men? As non existence is an impossible conception in any respect whatever how shall we predicate the external extinction of animal life?

If animal life after its brief period of exhibition flows back to its original source the Creator and thus reabsorbed where does this reabsorption stop in the scale of being and where does it commence?

All things exist in the Divine Mind and it is as impossible to conceive of the reabsorption of any act of our being that we have once performed into its original substance as it is the reabsorption of any actions of God.

Death is the precise opposite to what we are now, and it is impossible for Man to conceive that which is not, as he now is, death is an impossible thought. As we know not where we are nor what our state is when asleep while we are what we call awake so neither do we know the reverse. The condition of one excludes the other necessarily. Mind this: if the animals are given an after life whatever we may say in the affirmative or otherwise alters not their state.

Who can look upon the animal creation in all their divine beauty and deny them a future existence. See their graceful motions! their beautiful forms! and the many pure instincts they exhibit! Did they not share in common with the curse that was pronounced upon Man? do they not groan for their deliverance with Man? And are they not promised a participation in the restoration, the Millenium?

18

Why should such perfect objects of the exhibition of the divine power be annihilated? Can God desire it? Is it not the wish of Man? And if they could speak would they not plead with all their gifts for future life? If then it abounds to the glory of God and the happiness of Men and the gratification of the animal creatures of God that they should possess an after life who would even now deny them this?

The question is should we or should we not believe that animals have a future life? and to us it seems that we should as it is in harmony with the idea we have of the infinite Parent and not contrary to any thing we know.

They stand between Nature and Man as the Angels between God & us. They were created immediately before Man.

He who loves not God supremely is not prepared to suffer for the good of his fellow Men.

Only when the Universal Love Spirit is supreme in the Soul does Man act for the Universal End.

The Universal Man must be first born in the individual person before he can see that he is not to live for himself but for the Universal Man.

He who adds a fresh impulse of divine love to the Race does more for Men than he who should add the riches of princes to Men.

Until the reformer yields himself up to the great Artiste to be formed he cannot re-form others.

Faith is one of the highest gifts of God to Man. It is the sublimest faculty of the Soul.

It is my custom to trace all the civilization of modern Society to the appearance of that mysterious man Jesus. What should we know of the Greeks who unquestionably have been and are the means of refining in many respects the tastes of Men and the Latins & other nations of antiquity of Christianity had not by its spiritual influence given us a perception of the good true and beautiful hid in their universal history.

It never can be too often uttered that Catholicism means the Universal Good and True and Beautiful. That is not worthy to be named Catholicism which does not embrace all truth, all Goodness, all Beauty. Our allegiance is alone due to God and to Catholicism because it is the universal revelation of God. The measure of Catholicism is the measure of Gods love to Man. I am a Catholic because I would not reject any of Gods Truth. If faith in God is sectarian then a Catholic is a sectarian not otherwise.

It must not be taken for granted that all that proffessed Catholics have said is Catholic.

Catholic truth must be conceived as it is for it must be considered all expression of it is necessarily special. It is only he who can hear the one great eternal symphony of the Universe that has an idea of Catholic Truth and hears a fit expression of it. Catholic Truth *is;* it depends not upon Scriptures, neither Councils, Bulls, nor Sermons.

If there had been no opposition to its introduction none of these would have been needed.

These are accidental facts growing out of Her history. He who has arisen to a clear and broad perception of the beautiful, True, and good, is Catholic—hence the reason of so many artists becoming Catholic—many more who are Catholic but know it not.

Christ was the incarnation of God the full Catholic revelation of the Infinite.

It is this that makes the Church Catholic: that it is one with God the Universal Love Light and Life.

It is a very false notion Men harbor that union with the Catholic Church diminishes their true liberty; If union with God results in slavery then are they right not otherwise.

What are the Popes Councils and Priests? when acting authoritatively in harmony with the Church but the Agents of Christianity. We deny it with emphasis that the principles of love of truth can ever err, and it is to these and these only that Mens Souls pay obedience.

The Popes, Councils, Priests, bow to that which the simplest and least member of the Church bows and all his authority is in *it* not in him.

There would be no need of Popes Councils Priests etc. if Men would unconditionally submit themselves to the Universal Love Spirit.

When will it be understood that the authority of the Church is non-human?[214]

The authority of the Church is as much binding on the Popes etc. as it is upon the least member of the Church.

The authority of the Church is no more the reflex of the will of the Pope the members of a Council or the Priests than it is that of the humblest member of Christs body. The heads of the Church yield to the same authority as the members do and no other. We pronounce all which is not in obedience to the eternal principles of Love & Right as uncatholic being Catholic.

Christ has promised that his Church should never fall into error; he has left no room for Protestantism. Protestantism is no more nor less than a denial of Christs promises.

Every protest against the Church is unconditionally false and to be condemned otherwise the promises of Jesus are to none effect.

There is no half way house between Catholicism and infidelity.

When we join the C. Church we do not join the Pope etc. but yield to the same principles he has yielded.

The Catholic Church yields to Christ its head, its life; the members have no authority over each other in what ever station they may be placed.

Is all that the Popes Councils & Priests have done in matters of faith truly Catholic? yes if recieved by the Church of Christ.

Whatever—is an expression of the universal Church must of necessity be true and incontrovertible as the very words of Jesus Christ if we believe in him.

If Men truly renounced the world—that is truly performed their baptismal promises—there would be no room for the Sacraments, for the Church etc. but this is impossible, therefore the need & the necessity of the Church.

We are infants in Christ and need a Mother. I ⟨——⟩ as much as ⟨——⟩ have had a natural Mother.

Regeneration is a progressive work—tho an act of an instant. We must be conceived by Spirit, born again, in the manner we were born after the flesh.

Unless a Man is born again he cannot see the Kingdom of God.

The Spirit of God in us is ever giving birth to the new Man, the eternal youth, Adam.[215]

Each one of us will find that Adam means us when we know ourselves better than we now do. He that is made a live in Christ knows that he sinned in Adam.

The light in Stars, the music in the Song of birds, the beauty in the flowers, we must not imagine is gone because it disappears from our limited vision. We imagine there is more power in Man than he wots of and more around him too.

That Soul can only embrace all truth which is free from all human systems.

Is it not God that we desire to embrace? Why fear we then to embrace all that comes from him?—he himself where ever, whenever, we see him.

It is He, enough, why enquire we farther.

We complain not of the love of the humanitarian, of the lover of nature, we would not wish either of them to give up one jot or tittle of their love but to cast their eyes up and see there are things to love—perhaps supremely too—besides these dear friends.

He who loves purely it matters not in what direction his love takes is to be commended for his love as such but not on this account for all that he does. It is possible for an infidel to paint a good Landscape etc.

The only worthy object for Men to labor for is to increase the vision of Men towards loveful objects.

He who increases Mans love diminishes his wants at the same time he increases his possessions.

He who loves all possesses all, is a lord. He who possesses all loves nothing has nothing, is a beggar,—worse,—less than an element.

How rich is life with love, in it we travell to all the objects of our love in Spirit—to all that we have seen and can imagine—to friends, summer scenes on earth, above the mild sky by day, and a still beautifully night, and more dear still the escape of deep involuntary sighs, an accidental look, a half timid glance from another eye, an electric touch of the hand of love which like liquid fire finds its way to the heart,—a reverie—floating shadows of beauteous forms, ah love unlocks all the possibilities of Men and makes our common life a sleep. Ah he only is awake whose life is nothing else but love. Ah to him life means all reality—time is lost in being

Protestantism is the spirit of individualism antagonism selfishness competition definitiveness and we hope for no good towards the Race from all the measures that are before the Public so long as the protestant spirit in the end prevails over the results of all their efforts.

All the advantages of science of important discoveries so long as the competitive spirit reigns in society tend to accelerate the speed of society towards wretchedness crime and increased selfishness.

The Catholic and The Protestant civilizations are antagonistic and wherever they come in contact they must generate war. It is only to the progress of catholic influence upon the Race that we look for any real good to Men. We feel quite satisfied that Catholicism is destined again to be the only faith of Christendom. Its progress is progressive silent and permanent on the other hand Protestantism is unprogressive and must eventually become extinct.[216]

It is a singular fact that protestants imagine that they only are the advocates and friends of progress. Does not the doctrine of private judgment if Men are selfish tend necessarily to selfishness? If Men were pure and universal which they are not we would have no objections to this doctrine   The sooner it is known the better that Catholicism and Protestantism can never agree in the same community. Both are productive of entirely different states of society.

Emerson says Jesus would absorb the whole Race. He does not see that through Jesus we first become Men. What are the Race outside of the influence of Jesus of Christendom? We wish E.- & his school once possessed the true view of Christian philosophy.

If the Soul is progressive in & of itself why is it that those people on which the influence of Christ has not been spent remain in a state of immobility? This is the error of E. and those like him that they do not perceive there is no truth whatever old or new that is not embraced in the Christianity of Catholicism.

C. Christianity does not deny the past but fullfills and increases it. Transcendentalism can only spring up in a protestant country where the people are ignorant of the Catholic faith.

We do not wonder that Men of culture and breadth of mind should reject christianity if that is christianity that goes by the name of protestantism. We in our earlier years repudiated this because it did not satisfy all the true and essential wants of the Soul.

As soon as we saw Christianity in its Catholic fullness we did not hesitate for our motives ever were to accept all that tended to increase our love and give us higher views of truth. We say many Men reject protestantism through the grace of God. This grace is given them in their infancy by means of baptism and when they have grown to the age of maturity they reject the so called Christianity around them because it is not up to grace in them.

If Christianity is the divine religion no Man can make any pretensions to seriousness, to sincerity, and, if he is acquainted with it and reject it. If any one does, and lays still claim to these virtues, we demand of him a religion superior to that of Christianity or else why reject this? When we find one ignorant of Christ exhibiting a power greater and preaching a religion higher than Jesus did then and not till then shall we be disposed to give any faith at all in the speculations of the transcendental philosophy.

Transcendentalism is a sect of protestant Christianity; out of this category they cannot get.

All that tends toward a higher stage of perceptivity moves the individual nearer Catholicism.

The difficulty is not in the truth of Catholicism but in the destitution of spiritual perception in Men. They account all that superstitious which with their intelligence they cannot grasp.

What is there noble in philosophy, beautiful in art, pure in ethics, divine in religion, that Catholic Christianity does not embrace but gives a higher and deeper significance to?

We cannot with indifference be present and here such names as Zoroaster, Pythagoras, Socrates, Plato, Zeno be called pro-fane if by that is meant irreligious. It is not true. They are more to be reverenced than we; had we been born then no question we would have shown much less religion than they.

This is new years morn. Every morning—moment—of love is such. Every moment of love is the commencement of a new childhood. Every morning is the beginning of the creation. The Sun rises, the birds sing, the flowers bud, and all is as it was at the first day. Love is the mystery in mysteries. To say a man can love is to say that all things are possible. Always remain true to the interior life whatever apparent inconsistencies it may subject you to.[217]

Is it well to receive the homage of Men. If we act, if we do the thing, why not burn up our M.S.S.[218]   why publish it. is it not done and that for all eternity. The fear of being unknown is proof of the unworthiness of being known. If we are known of God, in the courts of heaven, why affect the manners of Men. The less we seek to be known the more we shall be known. He that publishes himself is never read.

Doubt never disproves a fact, no more than the extinguishing of light annhilates objects. That which has been once seen so far as human perception is the foundation of our knowledge is and ever will remain an eternal fact whatever may be the changes of the human mind in its history. Revelation stands opposite to Doubt; the one is a clearer perception of the truth, the other a dimmer perception of the truth. Neither disturb or destroy the objects of divine truth. To doubt is to be doubtful of something, of some immutable fact; this exhibits the state of human perceptivity not the unrealness of divine truth. Doubtless there are truths beyond the reach of the most enlightened perceptions of genius, and others again that are perceived by gifted minds that the ordinary perceptions of the mass seldom if ever reach.

Truth is the same whatever may be our intelligence of it.

Proove to me that a thing was once seen, or give me reasonable evidence that another that has seen and made the affirmation is to be relied upon, the fact is as well established as tho all Men had been witnesses of the fact. The sight of Stephen the first martyr at his death, that of the Apostles, when with Jesus on a certain mountain, was a miraculous degree of the perceptive power, the things they saw were before there perception of them, were then, and are now to day, this moment and were we gifted with sight as they we should also see them.

"Were not the times so unsociable,
The Past and Present and the Future would be one;
Spring would unite itself to Autumn,
and summer and winter,
Play ball earnest youth would be wedded to old age:
Then my sweet Spouse would dry up the source of Pain,
All sensible wishes would to the heart be granted".
                                        Novalis Vol 1, 256[219]

Too frequent we are apt to accept skepticism and doubt for argument and proof. It is what a man sees that is; the absence of sight prooves nothing but personal blindness. An intelligible faith is sight. Even a superstitious faith has ever an important truth included in it which a higher revelation brings to light.

The Heathens beleived in a God, the same God as we, the difference was, to them he was the unknown, to us, our Father who art in heaven. Superstition is ever to be preferred to doubt as reality is to nonentity. Christianity is the fullfillment of all faiths that ever were. It is the universal everlasting revelation of God.

There is no direct proof for the immortality of the Soul. It is the proof direct itself. What proof direct can one give to another that he sees. If I see a star what proof can be given to another that I actually do see it? If I point his vision in the same direction and he observes it also this adds no evidence to the fact that I see, but only that he sees too. Consciousness is incommunicable. We know that the Soul is immortal by the same law that we know our personal identity, that we are, the world is; and all other such truths. To prove a thing we must have some other thing besides the thing itself; it cannot be a witness for itself, for it is it itself that is called in question, how shall then I prove that I am, the world is, or God is good?

I cannot get out of myself; There is no other world besides this for this includes all that is; And out of God there is no goodness. They are incapable of proof. They are. I would not doubt them if they were not. To doubt of that which does not exist is no doubt at all. We cannot think of a thing which is not. Thought is the *result* of the perception of objects. The sense of immortality is more or less intense in different people. The loss of it does not annhilate the Soul. But he that doubts the immortality of the Soul has not lost it, for were it wholly lost there would be no room for him to doubt it. No sense is ever perfectly lost; it differs in a greater or less degree of activity. What *is* ever must be. In the universe of things there can be no total loss. What now is ever will be because it is now. I am therefore I am immortal; This is the purest affirmation of Truth. Man exists in the mind of God as the actions of Men in theirs. If Men are immortal their deeds are; the logic can be carried higher up. The affirmation I am includes all, God, myself, Nature. For I know myself only so far forth as I am distinguished from these. What is not them is me. What is not me are they. Tho I can choose between actions, I am forced to act by an irresistible force of my nature, being finite, not so with the infinite, action with him does not mean necessity, hence are we, and all that is, creatures of Gods own free pleasure.

What a glorious thing it is to be! The very fact of our existance is enough to call forth from our hearts eternal gratitude & praise. Our existance is the pleasure of God. We finite beings live to give pleasure to God! We are his acts of joy. It is said it is his delight to be with the children of Men. God has called us forth from nonexistence into eternal life. All his acts partake of his attributes: Eternity, Love and Wisdom. These are imaged forth in the Souls of Men. To say that Man is mortal is in sense to say he is not. If Men were mortal they would be ignorant of it. Do Men know what they are not. We are all that we know and more having the possibility of indefinite progress in us. Man is every thing and more—he is Man. He is all that faith can reach, thought penetrate, and feeling comprehend.

Jan 14.

There is but one universal movement in the world of things in history and that is the Regeneration of Man. This is all that gives new life to the world. It is this that upholds the world, it is this that keeps all from falling back into the chaos of total darkness. All labours that help or have not for their end for this one great cause the reunion of the Soul with God are destined to diminish in importance until they pass into utter oblivion. Only as we are united with God are we, and the things that we do immortal. Aside from Jesus Men degenerate

It is only poetry whatever shape it may take that is worth currency among friends. Less than this is of no value; it is all mortal.

A man writes an essay labels it the Poet the thing that is just that which cannot be told.

None but the Gods knoweth the poet.

Painting is embodied poetry—music.

Forms have magic power.

Ordinary persons feel harmony, Music, the composer (a poor name for the Tone Dichter) *hears* it.

There is no difference except expression between the Poet Painter and the Genius of Music. They give all utterance to the same interior fact.

Every soul that feels hears & sees must experience the inadequacy of our common Talk to express his life. The expression always ceases where it should commence. Like some books we read we would have the authors to have commenced with their conclusions as their premises.

The all reality can never be crowded with expression; it escapes it on all sides.

Oh we see that music in some faces that ravishes our heart with delight. It is quite a mistaken notion that enjoyment is diminished by temperance, Chastity, Purity.

We must kill the man who is blind or else the Devil will have him whole. He should pray Lord save me from myself. Kill me before it is too late. Stop me on Thy way.

In Emersons essays there is the sameness of the state of mind but he speaks at the same time on foreign subjects.

The fabulous the mythical Spirit is to be sought, is to be possessed.

As in cases of clairvoyances the language the style and influence is more elevated so is it that we are to be permanently gainers not by transient influences but by the constant influence of God.

The more we depend and look for support from the transient causes the farther we shall remove ourself from the permanent all sustaining Cause.

The genius of religion is divine inspiration.

The influence of the Church is divine excitement.

The only healthful excitement is the Love Spirit.

All absolute difference is insanity.

Memory is not a faculty but a state. There are *no* faculties.

He who seeks knowledge otherwise than through and with the divine Spirit gains nothing but folly.

Men look elsewhere as if God were not Wise—for wisdom.

All true wisdom is hid in God and as we partake of his Spirit all that is hid will be revealed to us.

Knowledge—true wisdom—is not acquired but comes from the inspiration of God.

Knowledge is acquired; wisdom is given. Wisdom is genius; knowledge is talent.

A prayerful spirit is the condition in wisdom. Genius is faith. The Genius is always a Hero. Genius is permanent clairvoyance.

We become daily more and more intelligent of our ignorance.

Our "knowledge" is fast disappearing. Christ is the Redeemer from all our inherited "knowledge".

We know less now than we ever did. We hope we shall ever keep knowing less & less whilst we are doing more & more. God knows all, this was our fall in our attempting to know. Nothing but God knows. God is absolute intelligence, love, and power.

Self-knowledge is the parent of all crime. I thank God that I know nothing but evil and this is becoming less and less. I would that I knew nothing. I am ignorant insomuch as God does not know all, that is my own knowing is the cause of all my want of knowledge. Self knowledge is the cause of all ignorance.

Before Adam knew there was no ignorance. The object of education should be and is to unlearn what we know. When the Soul is perfectly free and unobstructed God will dwell in it with all his glory. He is the wisest who knows nothing. It is only self that knows. Remove self and all knowledge ceases. Let the primal Adam take place of the fallen I and wisdom will be the birthright of Man.

I wish Men could see that in each is the Adamic Man glorious as when first created waiting for us to be crucified on the Cross that he may appear in all his primal beauty grace and wisdom.

We must all bear the same Cross that Jesus did if we expect the resurrection to life. In truth Jesus said before Abraham was I am. *I am* was before all Men things past present or to come.

The permanent grounds of the eternal present must be sought after in every Soul and when discovered it must be clung to with a deathless attachment.

The Wisdom of God is the revelation within. The wisdom within disavows that without. The wicked are in the midst of the Garden of Eden but know it not. Sin is the only barrier between *us* and All.

We look upon the past as dark, why is this? what is our standard of light? There are ages we call as a stigma dark ages, wherefore is this? We call their faith fanatacism, their devotion idolatory, their piety superstitions. What shall be said of us in after ages?

What shall be named our eagerness for wealth, our indifference in religion, and attachment to the perishable things of life. Can there be greater fanatacism than this! greater idolatory and superstition!

We say that there is good in what we do, that their is a poetry in machinery, a chivalry in commerce, a some thing not to be denied in exterior beauty. We are not inclined to deny this. Let this be so. But consider this the ages that shall follow us will not be engaged in the same objects that we are, hence they will not be in the position to see in our pursuits that which we do, and if we could hear there comments upon our labors, if they were actuated by the same prejudices we are against the past what righteous indignation would arise in our bosoms when we should hear them speak on this subject.

What is the standard of our judgments? We should ask ourselves why is it that I approve this and disapprove that. Back of all our judgments lies a certain rule or canon by which we speak of things. In every judgment there is consciously or unconciously a standard by which it is formed. We cannot make universal judgments unless our standard is universal. We cannot possess a universal standard without our submission to the Universal Law. Now what is the universal Standard or Law? And how shall we know this who are in want of it? Each individual Soul possesses more or less a part of the universal Standard of Criticism on all subjects. No one possesses the complete standard of criticism on one single branch of human Knowledge much less the universal Law. The Soul of the greatest Genius of the Race is still individual and fails to express in only a lesser degree the whole unconditional truth. Even the object seen is not all seen at the same time. We come short of not seeing the depth and height of the truth as well as the breadth of the truth. All the Race and nature fail to reflect back the whole Sun of truth. The infinite is and he only to comprehend the whole truth. But he is the Truth. It is only God who knows himself. The finite looses its character as it becomes infinite. The finite without God would be Infinite. For what is not God is Nothing.

It is a strange fact this faith in a Sacrifice. Nothing but blood will satisfy. I know not how it is this thing seems different to me now from what it has. I never could contemplate this faith of the past in a favorable light until now. If I were a Hebrew Greek or Roman I could have sanctioned their sacrifices   Shall I not say even the sacrifice of virgins by the ancients. It is true that true love is most cruel. See what Abraham in will at least did do. Jean Paul in Titan the 1st Vol he makes the father of Albano wound his son in their first meeting. & Goethe in Wilhem Meister when Wilhelm speaks of his first I believe love to Aurelia she wounds him by drawing a knife across the back of his hand. These and many such facts I have not been able to give a right account of until now. They are strange but nothing truer. Revenge & Love do act alike. We would kill that we most love— shed its blood. This is the virtue of a Sacrifice that it be that which is pure and of our deepest affection.

Shakspere seems very near to me now. I feel as if he were a contemporary author of our time. I feel his beating heart. He has lost his objectiveness   And it is if I were in communion with his heart. How warm how large and over flowing heart of life he possessed. Greatness has no individuality. Dante, Shakspere, Tasso, were instincted with Love and heavenly childhood! What a life did Shakspere live! What passed through a heart like his! He seemed to possess the free scope of Spirit. How much to him was known in solitude. Oh that great heart if it were opened to us now with all its richness.[220]

No one who would realize the christian ideal of life in any sphere but requires the heroism of a Martyr.

We are not to be slaves or mere passive agents of the past. No, Martyrs Patriots Heroes Saints the present demands which shall be to the present what the great were to the past. The illimitable boundaries of Science of Love stand before the gaze of youth this moment whose delight is in being known of Men as when Adam first opened his eyes in Eden.

Devotion Self denial Disinterestedness these are the keys which will unlock the rich stores of the Future.

Think nothing is gained; what is the future is infinite. No science is perfect. Science if it means perfection there is no science. Ask not for time place or condition for action when the whole unexplored future lies hid before your vision. Be sure that it is not gained by those who do not pay its immortal price. If you would gain the great you must give up the mean. The price of genius is self sacrifice—and ever present death—. If ye fear the scorn and derision of the world expect not to be named with its heros, those in future ages whose lives have been generously spent in the cause of God, Love, Right. He that would live let him once and for all not think of life but loose it in and devote it to God. Be so great as to give thy life to something that is nobler than thou if thou wouldst be ennobled, immortalized. He who can loose his life in some thing that is greater than himself to him greatness is not his master but his slave. He who sees nothing greater than himself has ceased to live. Be employed by a greater Artist than thyself; labor not for one so mean as thou. Say to thyself I will be not thine but someones greater than thou. If thou wouldst move the Race to greater good and higher virtue loose thyself in the universal and fear not by this thy own extinction, thou shallst gain distinction by this.

Get above seeking distinction if thou wouldst possess it. The Gods are famous, Men seek to be. Know this thy highest sublimest conceptions are a part of thyself and possibility. If thou wouldst have greatness be great to thyself. Do thine own impossibility: Do what thou fearest. Canst thou not actualize a greatness in solitary bravery the world will not call thee great. The world only calls those great who are greater than the world. In the long run the wash wears off and the false metal is unhid. Thus the voice of ages proves the genuineness of genius. If thou hast not in thyself accquired imperishable fame however the public may now flatter thee the ages will discover thy deceit. Sooner or later thy heart will lie bare to the gaze of the future. True genius is imperishable, a mystical perennial fountain of inspiration for all ages. The martyrdom of the 19teenth Century is the heroism to live and labor in the Cause of truth of Christianity. The martyr the Hero of the 19 century must be great enough to turn the heroism of the past in to mediocrity. This is the sublimity of heroism to live truthfully. Death for the Cause of truth is but one moments act; heroism of such stripe our whole life should be made of.

What is it to educate is a question that cannot be answered until another one is answered which lies deeper than this on which education depends. That question is what is the destiny of Man? If we know the destiny of Man the character of true education will be such as to facilitate him in the realization of his destiny.

We need a full complete logical statement of the theory of the Catholic Church in the language of the day. The influence of the Catholic Church was preeminently favorable to the free development of the highest elements of Mans nature.

The 19teenth century is the least remarkable except it be, no without exception, of any age since Christianity.

The Catholic religion is a mystical religion and its members live a supernatural life. Catholicism is Christianity and all must be denied that is not Catholic, it is the standard of truth and is not to be pared down to the credulity & understandings of Men—The Church has said it therefore it is true—Enough. This is the highest testimony of truth.

Feb 26

Man possesses to a fearful extent the power of directing the course of his own destiny. Oh Man what an awful responsibility rests upon thy conduct. Thy choice of ways is one of eternal consequences.

The demonstration of authority is the only method of demonstrating the object of "faith" to one who is in doubt or disbelieves them. The fact is this they are only apprehended by faith—and it is this (faith) that he is in need of in order that he may perceive the truth of any demonstration except that of authority.

Jesus tells me the Kingdom of Heaven is within me that the Angels in heaven rejoice more over the conversion of one sinner than 99 that need no repentance and many other supernatural truths that I am not in the condition to verify by my own personal experience. Now knowing his character by the many divine acts of his which in some measure I can apprehend and appreciate by my own experience these naturally give me confidence in his veracity and I believe those things which he affirms tho they are not apprehended by me. This is the method of teaching by authority or testimony and this seems to me the only method that we can be taught those truths which *now* transcend our feeble capacity. Faith is one of the most precious gifts of God and for which there are no substitutes. Philosophy, deduction, induction, no method of demonstration whatever, can supply the place of it for a moment.

It is all idle the study of metaphysics, philosophy, science, literature in a word all culture is as nothing in comparison to it. It is the fountain of true life, love and divine wisdom. It is faith that vivifies all things. It is the power of faith that apprehends all things. Give me faith; give me this and all other knowledge shall be my servant. Faith is the wisdom of God. Faith is the highest intelligence; it is the blessed gift of God through which we apprehend the hidden things of God by & in & through his own brightness. Faith is a distinct and supernatural gift of God for which we should earnestly desire it from our God. Faith is the gift of divine illumination. He who has the gift of faith cannot but love and worship God because in faith he sees God as he is the ineffable love and light which quickens the hearts of the saints. Faith gives love, light, humility, meekness, charity, patience, firmness, perseverance, zeal; faith is the parent of all other virtues. Through it we are united to God the ineffable fountain of all love. It is the channel of all blessings. Man is all powerful to the extent of his faith. Jesus is the giver of faith. Unbelief is the result of sin and the mother of death. He who can ask for faith with a sincere heart is already half convinced of that he would beleive. There is no better state for the soul to be in than the earnest desire of faith. Faith overcomes the world and raises up to God. Through it we are half in heaven while here. By it we converse with Angels & hold communion with Saints tho we move on Earth midst Men. To the eye of faith all is present past—present & future. Faith penetrates beyond all proof and seizes hold of the ineffable the eternal is. It is the highest action of the superior faculties of the Soul. When the soul is in faith it speaks with God involuntarily and enjoys his ever loving & mysterious presence. It discourses by communion of affection—love—light——When we make a pure act of faith Angels visit us and darkness disappears. Tis only doubt that even now shuts us out from heaven. All are as they were in the beginning; excepting Man who is fallen. And if raised up again by faith in Jesus heaven will reappear to him.

Tis sin not conscience that makes cowards of us all. Tis sin that gives consciousness—self knowledge. Cowardice is the absence of virtue. Virtue eliminates the fact of conscience.

Catholicism includes the positive in all faiths ancient or modern, of profane or christian sects.

A pure logical system of Christian theology which shall include all theologies of the profane world in the language of this age is a work that is called for and much needed.

Government is the power which governs. The power which governs in civilized nations is characterized by the definite forms through which it exercises its governing power. Thus we have Monarchy Aristocracy Democracy. Tho in modern times we have no pure example of any of these forms. Now the end of all government is the same, that is considered abstractly, which is securing the nations destiny in the speediest time possible. The end of government is the good of the governed—the whole. The form of one kind of government may suit the character of a certain people and their situation more than another.

The andante movement in Haydns symphony in b seems to me like the apprehension of the spiritual world by the heart; Beethovens Geister Waltz the same apprehension but clear and spiritual as by the intellect. The Lobegesang of Mendelssohn seemed to me to feel like the production of a foreign and ungenial mind.[221]

There are three classes of opponents which the Catholic Church has to defend herself against. These may be divided under three heads
1st Those who deny the divinity of Christ: Unitarians Deists etc.

2nd Those who deny the primacy of the Roman See: the Anglicans the Greek Church etc.

3d Those who deny the infallibility of the Church: the whole swarm of protestant Sects.

It is the fate of heresies to become extinct.

It is an experience all have to testify to at some period of their lives that the deepest desire in the heart is the desire for God and that this is the germ of all other desires. All attempts to satisfy this central affinity by fixing it on an exterior object proves in the end unsatisfactory & useless. Love of God lies deeper than all other love however close these may be. All other love is predicated on this. He only can die for a friend who loves God more than his friend. Friendship is a deep faith in God. He that loves God has Gods love which embraces all and is *in* all. Man at first places his trust in one and another object in a friend—wife—children—and only at length when all has failed him does he find that God only can satisfy this immortal want. Blessed are they who find this treasure before it is too late. Blessed are they who devote themselves from their Youth to the love of God alone.

In God we must find a wife, friend, in a word, all.

No one truth impresses itself upon my mind with more force than that the only permanent relation that we here can establish and enjoy are only those we have with God.

April 2nd 1845

Since I have thought of the question whether the rise of protestantism promoted civil liberty I have been somewhat surprised at the result. All the principles of civil liberty and the great bulwarks of the rights of Man have their origin in catholic times & among catholic Men. For instance The doctrine of representation—the magna charta—Trial by jury—the Common Law—the Italian Republics—Switzerland etc. etc. Protestantism has not introduced any new principle in the civil rights of Man.

The memory only is a faithful record and perfect index of the mind— how much passes through the mind that never has or can be written however familiar Men may write.

We must come to it and why hesitate in stating the fact that our relations with God are to be first established and these are peculiar, unlike all others. After all God is nearer to us than Man or Nature. Say as one pleases, no other relations do satisfy the wants of the Soul but those of religion and all other attemps will as they have ever prove fruitless.

How opposite is the calling for the Capitalists for aid by the Sonnerites to the driving of the Money Changers out from the Temple by the Son of God. They pretend to be Christians too. When Socialism moves one to shed his blood for its advancement we will have some hopes for it; not till then.

Probably the three greatest Poems of Civilization of the Christian ages are Dantes Divine Comedy Miltons Paradise Lost—and Goethes Faust. From the first to the last there is a great decadence. The Satanic Titanic element which is the chief burthen of the two latter songs is to be found in the first but only as a small brook beside a flowing majestic river. There is more heathenism on one page of either of the latter than can be found in all the divina comedia. Dante seems rapt'd up into a beatific vision so that he can scarce utter audibly while Milton is a sublime rhetorician gifted with moments of a poetic vision Goethe tho a great Poet and tho he makes use of non natural machinery in his Faust he never falls in a rapture and transports us beyond the human. There is a strength and humility a sweetness and intensity a delicacy & terrific terror in the Commedia that is no where found in the two latter. The first is all Christian in its imagery; the two latter are heathen. If these Poems are an expression of the life of their epoch the 14 century far surpassed the 17 as that the 19 century as a gothic temple a modern meeting house.

The great question of life is how to live in time for eternity.

This is a great thing to bring back the mind to its original uprightness.

The highest heroism is to deny sin—to be a true religious Man.

It is much easier to suffer and endure physical pain from another than it is to deny oneself.

All art from a proper point of view is religious.

Art is the expression of life and if the life is not beautiful the expression of it will be the same. God being the beautiful Good & true He giving himself to Man under the veils of the sacraments hence the state of religion of any age will be the measure of its Art.

No great Artist ever was a—heretic. C'est impossible. No great artist ever was an infidel even among heathen. If poetry means some thing it means the perception of the beauty of objects and this perception is dependant on a like life.

Art is the expression of religion. The creed is in every Gothic Temple—so time is this art. The greatest architect at present of England was led to be a Catholic from the study of Gothic architecture. Raffaelo did not *lend* his genius to religion but religion gave life to his genius.

Religion is pure excitement or inspiration Men can do some thing without religion but it is very feeble. Religion is the Cause not the result of art.

We say Raffaello was pious or else he never could have depicted piety.

"He painteth best who loveth the best"—and what he loves best.

Religion is not a tender sense of a dependance on a superior power; it is a participation of the divine nature in a supernatural degree.

Religion is a supernatural participation of the divine nature which restores Man to all his original sensibility beauty & grace.

It is he who best expresses the life of Christianity that will be the greatest with the future whatever may be the character of that future such as Dante—Michael Angelo—Raffaelo.

Religion is the reunion of the divine and human nature which were seperated in consequence of the original sin. In the sense we use the word religion now there would have been no meaning for it if the fact of original sin had taken place.

The present object of our existance is to regain what has been lost and this is accomplished only by religion. Religion is the gift of God himself to Man which the faithful receive under the sacramental veils of the Church in a mystical manner and by which the reunion of the divine & human nature is again effected.

It is a greater gift of grace to remain faithful under spiritual dryness than is the gift of ecstasy, vision, & tears.

It is better far to receive the discipline of God than he to be a stranger from us.

I have never felt the inutility or weakness of reason in giving any real and permanent grounds of truth or faith as at the present moment. Reason is finite, erring, rash and feeble. All its attempts at comprehending the incomprehensible are futile. Reason serves only to show its own weakness. However illogical this may seem it is so. Grace is all in all. Reason is usefull to divert the mind for a while. We must ever follow the guidance of the grace of faith if we would keep from the paths of error and doubt. God is the author and establisher of our faith—The Alpha & Omega.

There are but two things that we need to have be fore us constantly if we would preserve our souls pure from the stain of sin—Eternity and the suffering of our Saviour.

Eternity and the Passion of our Lord beholding there all our labors all our sorrows all our disapointments—all our misfortunes and wants—are easy, light, and are cheerfully borne.

Blessed Jesus hold these ever before my eyes that I may not walk out of the path of life nor complain of anything here below. There are many arguments that are used by christians for the Christian Church that are not substantially in and of themselves valid. For instance—The one of miracles. Why? The Hindoos and all other religions display a list of miracles equally as bright. Shall we say, only the Christians ones are true and that all the rest are untrue? Sanctity is also one that when we read the self denial and interior life of some of the Priesthood of the hindoos we are at least disposed to consider awhile on this matter. Another The argument of numbers This is a lame one for is christianity any the truer now than it was when it numbered less thousands than now it does millions? And even now taking the whole race into calculation Paganism is the true faith if the numerical strength is the proof of the truth. We say the truest religion will give birth to the holiest lives, the most heroic deeds, and the beautifullest specimens of art as a necessary consequence of its divine character. Not only this   As civilization and all the discoveries of what ever character they may be are the result of enlightenment that the purest religion will be the means of producing the highest civilization.

We have much to learn before we know all that union with God means, all that loneliness demands, all that Man is. Alas how few live solely for God—Mary—John the Baptist—these from their birth were consecrated to his work alone.

To learn the vanity of the world and the nothing ness of Men is a long and hard lesson but this must be perfectly learnt before the Soul can be united to God.

I am now reading Schlegels Lectures on Dramatic art & Literature. I have read the Vol to The English Stage and a part of this. Throughout he impresses me as the profoundest professed critic that I have as yet read. Now and then a remark escapes him that admits of no fathoming—it is a study—it is genius. Heyne, Heyne, that Heyne, the rascal had given me by his diabolism a sort of contempt for Schlegel as a stiff ruffell shirted french pedant. He is a rascal for cheating me in this manner. After all I have never known an instance where either wit ridicule or sarcasm did not have to obtain its own end by lies and hence in vain.[222]

Poetry is the truest description of things as they *really are*. Poetry is the most natural speech of Man—the primal Man in his primitive state. Things as they really absolutely are are either beautiful or deformed—Good or bad—True or False. The absolute in all things—the good and the true—if seen and which the true poet does see is ever beautiful. If the poet could imagine things more beautiful than they are or were he would the originator of all in his power and richness of his nature.

The Poet is more eternal and less historical. Poetry is more mystical than superficial. It is higher than the reasoning faculty. It pursues the apriori instead of the posteriori method. That is it arrives at its truths by intuition not so much by the understanding faculty. Hence Pope was more a philosopher than a Poet.[223] The Poet is more of a prophet and Seer than a historian or philosopher. Tho he includes both of these. He is an epitome of all in their essence. A great poem, painting or peice of music is an incarnated deed of nobleness of beauty of goodness whose elevating influence will last as long as time. The Poet sees the Soul, essence, the spirit of things. His inspiration is a part of that which Adam was first endowed with; he calls things by names that which they are. He lives in the midst of profound realities in which the meanest thing is significant to him of the profoundest meaning. Had we profounder vision we should see the whole mystery of the Godhead hid in a grain of sand a universe in a drop of dew.[224]

"There is no great and there is no small,
To the Soul that maketh all.
Where it cometh all things are,
And it cometh every where."[225]

Odours, sounds, colours, all speak to him secrets which the common ear never hears—hence his madness—divine madness.[226]

It is folly to imagine that Men can imagine that which is not for in the omnipresent present are all things that were and are to be. We are in the midst of all for in God we live and move and have our being and what is outside of Him is nothing. Is it because others see more than we do therefore it is imagined? Are our optics the measure of every other Mans vision?

We all live in an infinite reality which it is impossible to grasp & express. That which is to be noted is not that more is said than is but so much less. Nothing less than God himself has the ability to express the universe of reality in Eternity. What meaneth these voices of birds these beautiful flowers the winds and the Stars? All things that are have a meaning and that too profound. Could we trace back the slightest thought or emotion of the head or heart it would lead us to heaven to God. God is the pure truth of all things.

We come in contact with the infinite in the humblest flower that blooms as by the touch of the garment of the servant of the High God. The visible is the veil of the invisible and we are hemmed in by shadows. Man is more than Men imagine. The son of God valued his salvation more than his own bitter sufferings and his cruel death. If we but place our hand upon a stone we are in communication with the infinite of all things.

Nothing is or exists independent of him who made it and had we not fallen we could even have named them all as Adam did. Could Men gain their primitive instincts in their primal purity they all would be poets. We see now but darkly; did we see the immense reality that is all around and above us we should be crushed being as we are. Sin has corrupted Mans heart shortened his vision and debilitated his power. He sees but the hull and crust of things. This beautiful world which we tred upon and is above us he would to adapt it to his own superficiality reduce it to hydrogen & oxygen & even God to a Gas. Indeed shall we limit our vision to those who would reduce music to certain vibrations of the air poetry to rythm Man to a machine to digest animal & vegetable matter into tissues and the metamorphosing these tissues in digesting—Religion a delusion the universe into hydrogen & oxygen and god himself into a gas?

Men who think more of a steam engine than of the Divine Comedy, of a ship than Raffaello's Maddona, of a successful politician than a Saint?

Here ends the sheets of another book. Seven months since I commenced. It may be said that the more a man thinks the less he writes. Because he then sees so little worth writing. He that thinks seldom will fancy all tho'ts to be of rare value and he that thinks much knows that very few are of any and even those are not new. The last book we wrote we sent to a friend, this all that has any worth to me I could put upon two sheets. I look back for a few years when I was ignorant whether to commence a sentance with a capital or no, and many other such little things and see where by perseverance and study I am tho nothing. I laugh at my simplicity and earnestness. Is earnestness only allied to youth and simplicity?

However this book has answered some little purpose for when I wanted the opportunity of speaking to some one and was alone it cost me no labor to scribble in it a book. It would give me great pleasure if I had a friend who would exchange such reliques of himself to me.

June 28. 1845.
Isaac †

INTRODUCTION TO VOLUME 6

The final two volumes of the early diary overlap chronologically. The diary which I have labeled Volume 5 was begun in December 1844 and finished on June 28, 1845. The volume that I have designated Volume 6 begins on January 20, 1845, and ends on July 28, 1845. Whereas the entries in Volume 5 are long and often undated, those of the final volume are shorter and more carefully inscribed with dates. That carefulness is a clue to the tone of much of Volume 6. It is in many ways the shadow side of Volume 5. Whereas in that book Hecker looked out at the world with a verve and intellectual acquisitiveness, in Volume 6 his gaze is fixed within. In Volume 5 he expressed a balance and maturity that enabled him to turn his attention on the role of Catholicism in the world. But in the sixth book he is often helpless to lift himself out of the pit of scrupulosity. That they were penned in part during the same period illustrates the complexity of the young man's life at this time. The tortured style of the troubled Romantic was not entirely effaced by his conversion; rather it was given new forms, more Catholic forms that centered on his experience of the confessional and his interaction with his spiritual director rather than on the musings of an Alcott or Lane. The effects of the instruction on preparing for Penance that he received from *The Pius Guide* he took very seriously: *"Examine your conscience diligently. Excite true and sincere sorrow."* Whereas in his first book he mimicked Jean Paul, here he imitated the bathos of the Guide's *"Prayer of thanksgiving, to be said by the Penitent when preparing for Confession: What am I, O Lord! that thou are mindful of me? I have lived in sin, and have daily repeated many iniquities, faults and imperfections— still thy goodness spares the life thou hast given me."* Or he could turn to the excesses of *"A most devout Act of Contrition"* as presented in *The Key of Heaven* and say, with the author, *"I would willingly bewail the enormity of my sins with tears of blood"* (p. 109).

Yet although the perplexed, melodramatic tone dominates, there are some bright spots at the start of the book. In the opening pages Isaac talks of a return to the inner life of contemplation. *"All seems mystical,"* he proclaims in some of his best writing on the beauties of the contemplative state. There in those moments he attains a fresh language, however inchoate, that gives vital expression to his unique Catholic American experience. In it the themes of perfection, of Dionysian reliance on the inner Bard, of hope and thrill in the presence of newness within and without the soul are blended—however briefly. A modern sense of helplessness in the face of being, of surprise over one's consciousness of being emerges before falling under talk of sin and scruples.

The concern over his sinfulness becomes the backdrop against which the vocational question is worked out. We know from previous books that Hecker's concern for religious life was motivated by a larger concern for social reform and encouraged by the communities of perfection that he experienced before his conversion. But in this book the motivation that is most clear is that of wanting to find a new environment that will help him save his soul. He longs for a discipline that will, as he tells Brownson who visited him at his home in New York, *"kill me dead."* Once he accepted the idea that he needed the grace of Christ as mediated by the church to save him, he became adamant in his desire for more effective discipline that would bring him closer to God. His experience of spiritual direction with McCloskey was so good as to convince him that he needed more. *"Oh that I cannot get rid of myself,"* he laments. Both McCloskey and Hughes, who sat in for his coadjutor when he was away, encouraged him to seek the priesthood. He was sure that he did not want the secular clergy, although Hughes was happy to try to encourage him to wait for the opening of the seminary at Fordham or go to St. Sulpice. Yet his conviction to try the religious life only deepened. He was unsure of which group to affiliate himself with, having considered the Dominicans, Sulpicians, Jesuits, and Redemptorists. The diary ends only with a decision to definitely go abroad.

VOLUME 6

Jan. 20—A.D. 1845

Tues. The Lord is over good to me.

Last Wednesday I felt uneasy about the system of renting pews at the Cathedral and other Catholic Churches and thought of abstaining from occupying them. But before which I called on Bishop McCloskey and spoke to him of the matter. The conversation I had with him led me to be more at ease but still none the less opposed to the whole system of hiring out the Temple of God for gold and silver.

He presented the side of the necessity and prudent view of the case whilst I felt that providential and unconditional faith on God would be the true the only course for the Church to persue. However as the thing itself is but temporary not permanent but rather repugnant to the spirit of the C. Church and which will it is to be hoped eventually be abolished the conclusion forced itself upon me for to rest awhile.

As a protestant I never sat in the pews from principal: how much less could one tolerate it as a Catholic. I wrote a letter to O.A.B. in which I gave vent to my feelings on the subject. And spoke that there was temporally speaking much for to be done and undone in the Church as it now is. May the Lord give me his grace to lead guide and direct me in all his ways.[227]

I cannot speak of myself as I would. I feel interior sympathies which control my speech. I would make these sympathies definite but nothing that I can do defines them. Nothing but He who is All, above All, and in All, can meet and satisfy them.

I feel every day more my lessness, and the greatness of God of Love. The inner life is becoming ever more real. It seems that the more we are enlightened and enlovened our memories are restored and that we become self-conscious. Do we know what self consciousness is? We are not fully aware of its full meaning. Ah who is it that has seen the angel primal Man of himself in all its prior beauty, innocence and grace. I find myself making gradual and respectable progress in my studies. To what end? or wherefore? The Spirit that guides me knows. I am blessed with innocence on this matter.

22

The idea I had some time ago of attempting to put my life in a biographical form seems now to come again to me with some strength. I know that I have not the means of doing this at all as it should be, besides it means very great enthusiasm to do it well. The past does not sufficiently interest me of my life to give me the enthusiasm to do even as well as I can do it. Since the last time I thought of it some 8 or 9 months ago or less the plan I then had does not seem to me as well as the one now at this moment has struck me. That is this. I think it would actually be more fictitious or seem so at least by making it more real. First to give the actual state of my mind & to introduce the different characters and events that I met with in my progress. My former view was somewhat different. I attempted then to commence and did write a few sheets. Shall not I attempt it again?

I should have to state the peculiar state of my mind before I left home and the incidents prior to my departure, then the events that happened to me interiorly and exteriorly subsequently. My heart is moved with the thought. Oh that I had the faculty to do this! It would be for my own gratification. I wish not for any other purpose than for sincere reflection & beneficial emotions it may excite in my bosom. How to do this? How to begin? A plan I should first propose to my mind. Make first a skeleton of the whole and then improve and fill it up at different times.

Since I wrote the above a few hours ago I have attempted to write and have written six sheets full.[228] The next time I write I wish to give a description of the family of the subject of the story. His position with those whom he is related. Introduce a conversation. New views of life, of friendship, of relations, of sleep.

I will at least do something for myself in this. This new position which I have placed myself has given birth to many new thoughts I dreamed not of before. Every new relation is the mother of a whole brood of new thoughts. Experience is the parent of all history. Poverty is the parent of Experience.

Another day has passed. Ah and wither has it gone? And to what end is it that it has been spent? Have I been moved a day closer to God by it? Ah in whose hands the destinies of Men are and who keepeth record of our lives whitherto and what is this life of ours? I know nothing but this: that I am ignorant. Daily instead of gaining I loose knowledge. Would to heaven that all my knowledge were taken away from me.

I feel as if I should like to say something on friendship because I am conscious that what I have heard said does not meet all that I feel on this subject.

I know not what by labor I may not acquire, therefore as much has been given me which before I did not expect, I am encouraged to go on from the experience of the past and the hopes awakened in me in the present.

It is my desire if I can through the grace of God to live through lent on one meal a day. Oh that I were more abstinent more self-denying. Oh Jesus never let me slacken my fervor in spiritual progress. Jesus, Jesus, Jesus.[229]

This week and the week past I have felt more the necessity of my giving up more and of greater self denial if I would continue to increase in the love of Jesus. Oh that I would give myself wholly up to Jesus how much more should Jesus be to me. I see in Jesus more than all the wisdom of the world and power omnipotent.

If I would practise greater self denial I must begin by a greater practice of devotion. The more spirit we are the less matter we need for our support. Oh Lord make me as one of thy holy Angels that thy Spirit is all its meat and drink. Lord lead me to look more to thee less to Men still less to Earth. Learn me to feel Thee and to think Thee interiorly rather than to speak fine words concerning Thee. Lord take me up to Thee. Lead me oh Lord—but I am an unworthy servant not worthy of any of thy gifts. I thank Thee O God for what Thou hast given and take not these away for my ingratitude. Lord what can I say sufficiently to tell my unworthiness. No language can speak it. Thou knowest Lord how wicked I am. This moment Thou seest how I fear Thee. How little trust I put in Thee. Oh Lord it is a wonder that Thou sufferest me to live. Mercy mercy mercy oh Lord God on thy unworthy not to be named Thy Child. † † †

Jan 30.

In my present state of mind I am at loss what to say of my self whether it is what I know not of or no. Responsibleness, Conscience, Duty, Right, Justice, Love, Feeling, Consciousness; these and many more like words seem to have lost their accustomed meaning to me. Pain is not pain. Nothing seems to me as it is if it is not what is seems to me. There is a silence within which not even the deepest disturbs. I fear if I could fear of my present state. My spirit feels free from all time & space conditions. Tho I am in the body yet I am not here. My Childhood seems to return. It is as tho I had drank of the waters of Lethe and the nectar of Gods which restores us to youth.

When shall I end in denial. What shall I do. Where there is no standard there is a loss of all end object & rule. I fear myself. I know not why or of what. Things seem strange to me now. If I did do willfully wrong I should fear I had lost all conscience. Lord thou knowest I am a great sinner. Unmindful of thy gifts. Oh that I had grace to be grateful. I am all and worse than all that is sinful. Lord sinners repent and follow thee but I alas sin constantly. Lord that I could speak from the very center of my soul of the deep compunction I would feel. Lord I think my life is most wicked. Nothing but thy judgments can make me good. Oh that I had eyes that I might see. Lord if thy severity must save me oh spare it not upon me. I would rather be saved as if it were by fire than to loose my soul with all the world. Lord I desire not ease pleasure; give me thy own punishment. In to Thy hands oh Lord I commend my spirit. Oh may I be a brave & valiant soldier in thy cause. Oh Jesus take pity on me. Thou knowest our human frailties! Forgive and bless me oh Jesus. The enemy lies always in watch of us. Jesus. Jesus. Jesus. † † †

Lord forgive me the many sins I feel weighing heavily on my sinful weak heart. Thy mercy is our only security hope and dependence. Oh Thy mercy oh God Thy mercy. Lord awaken me to a sense of my sinfulness and the sinfulness of Sin. Ah deep have my sins penetrated into my soul. From the depths of my soul oh Lord the God of forgiveness forgive & have mercy

upon me miserable sinner that I am. Ah Ah how shall I express the sinfulness of my heart. Only Thou O God canst know its wickedness. Oh that I
could see all my sins. I will interrogate my soul. Wherein hast Thou sinned
against Thy God and giver of Life oh my Soul? Wherein hast Thou neglected thy duties towards thy blessed Saviour Redeemer and Love? He was
reviled suffered crucified for thy salvation and how hast thou treated Him
wicked, ungrateful, hard, impenetrable, unrepenting rebellious, proud,
empty heart! Ah what should not be thy punishment? If thou receivedst thy
full due thy soul could not bear it. Ah Jesus blessed Jesus Thou innocent
Lamb was for us condemned that we might live. Oh wretch that I am what
shall save me from committing sin against Thee.

I have not been grateful to thee oh God for the many benefits thou hast
bestowed on me.

Ah oh Lord grant me this that I may see my sins that I may feel compunction for them and all the foul stains be blotted from my Soul. It is not
one particular Sin, oh no my whole Soul is sick with Sin. I think not enough
of thee dear Jesus! Oh Mary Mother of God do thou come to my help and
aid me in my distress. Give me compunction of heart, detestation of sin,
Love of God.

Keep me oh Lord this night from all evil. Send thou thy messengers
to guide me　　Give me a willing Ear. Oh my guardian Angel be always
near and keep me from sinning. † † †

Tomorrow I go to the Confession. Ah that I were deeply sensible of
all my sins of commission and omission. The Lord be my help. I am in want
of greater love for those around me. Too negligently I perform my spiritual
duties. Too little of my time is devoted to spiritual exercises. I feel all over
sick with sin. Ah that I were free from the disease of sin. Thou oh Jesus art
our Physician. Thou has given to us a divine Remedy for which no gratitude
can pay Thee. Lord accept my weakness.[230]

Feb. 16.

This week I have spent mostly in company with OAB who has been
here.

A dim unconsciousness seems to hang about me like a cloud this day
or so. I know not what to make of it. In fact as I now am and have been for
some time back is to me inexplicable.

I am to that degree willess that it makes me feel that all around me
is different from what it was. All seems mystical. Nothing is definite. I
have no settled views or clear thoughts of my own. I speak and write as
it were without consciousness. I know not what I say, or what guides the
pen. I am bereft of all that makes me feel personal. I am like one who
acts acts but from what or how I know not. This is to me inexplicable.

I am drawn to contemplation. If I should give up all of my attention would be attracted towards spiritual objects. My study would be neglected. They are even now. Ah this should not be. I have as much as I can do to keep my thoughts on study   Still I do not feel that I do my duty. That I feel and devote sufficient of my time to thoughts of spiritual, religious objects. My life seems barren to me of good works. I cannot point to any thing that I have done that is a moments pleasure to me. Thou knowest oh Lord my unhappy condition   Shed down Thy mercy upon me. Oh my guardian Angel be with me and direct me. Leave me not to myself. Be Thou ever present with me. If I am left alone I am most miserable. Without thee I am blind. Whisper to my Soul divine advice. Keep me from all dangers of thought of words and actions. Keep me from the influences of the evil ones. Be thou my protector. Let not my ingratitude send thee far from me. Teach me to act so as to please thee. Ah say that thou takest pleasure in me. Oh say that thou willt not forsake me. That I am thine. Spirit of love! Spirit of Grace! Spirit of beauty! Be thou my only object. Angel of God. Channel of love. Medium of Light. Let me behold thee. Stir up my heart to good. Give me humility. Greater love of God. More wisdom. Devotion. Love towards Men. Self sacrifice. Greater faith. Knowledge of thee, heaven, and the hidden things of God. I pray thee I pray thee be to me what I need not what I ask.

I feel much like giving up all my studies to contemplation. Ah what is all human learning! Ah nothing! Worse often than nothing to the soul. Thy grace oh God is all in all. We neglect thy grace for human learning. Ah Ah that I were wholly submissive to the motion of Gods love. I know not, I know not, what I shall say, or what I shall do. Oh Lord do Thou with me what Thou willst. Lord willt Thou wholly take me to thyself. Ah that I did but give up my whole self to thee. Lord embrace me and say that I am thine—all—all Thine! Here is my difficulty oh Lord and do Thou direct me   I am always in doubt when I do not think of Thee alone that I am sinning and my time is misspent. Yet how can I think of thee at all times when my studies call my attention from Thee. These oh Lord I offer to thee with deep humility. May all that I do be done alone to Thy great glory. My heart would be drinking always from Thy living fountain of love. But how shall I best serve thee oh my God and Saviour? Ah let all be devoted to thee, to thee alone. Let me not be distracted from Thee. Oh Jesus who gavest up thy blessed self for us unworthy sinners, who countedst thyself nothing that we might be saved, to whom all things were as nothing in comparison to our wretched but immortal Souls, Ah Jesus blessed Saviour give me a taste of Thy divine humility and detestation of this world and all its empty and vain things. Oh Lord purify me from all self, pride, ambition, and love of the world. Let me look to Thee thine Angels & saints above. Lord I cannot depict all my sins if I should speak forever of all my offences. Lord I cannot ask Thee to wash out my iniquities for they show to me my sinfulness and teach me the virtue of humility. Ah let this ever be my motto: All for thee, to thee, and with thee.

Subjects that I would ask my spiritual Director to morrow morning when I go to see him his advice, counsel etc. I wish to throw myself more into his hands, to receive his direction in my present state of mind and conduct than what I now do from him. I do much that I am in doubt of the propriety of doing. I feel deeply the want of one to whom I can open my mind with greater freedom than what I have done. I can find no fault with my director for I believe he has met me with all the frankness in our social intercourse that I have shown towards him. My present state of mind is developing certain tendencies that need the counsel of the one older and more experienced than myself such a person as my spiritual director is. I will with the help of grace open the doors of my heart wider than I have hitherto done to him. I feel that it will not do a mere hasty expression of a few words of encouragement or impersonal remarks. If I am to return to the state of which I was at Concord which my present state seems to lean that way I would have this to be with the advice of some one in whom I may place confidence. I cannot say that this will happen but only that it may as I am now going. All my attention and faculties & powers are being absorbed more in contemplation and my interest and attention in studies necessarily decrease. I fear that even my desire to give myself wholly and alone to God is not pure. How can an imperfect creature make a perfect act. Ah! How much is lost by the many distractions of my mind from the One the needful thing. All that time is lost that is not solely devoted to Thee oh Lord. What matters it where we are or what we are doing if we are laboring in & with the Lord. He is everywhere the Same. In him we forget all other ties & things. In him alone we live & move & have our being, all else is nothing. I know not is it lawful even to desire to be good? Lord help me with Thy grace to make a pure act of faith. Oh that I were so humble and so pure as not to desire nothing but God but wills me to desire,—that no self, pride, vanity, did not mix with all my acts. Oh that the Lord would teach what sin I harbor that keeps me from approaching nearer to him. I would say with a pure and sincere heart Lord all that I have is thine; do with me as Thou willt. All I give up & devote to thy holy service. Nothing I ask for myself. Pleasure, gratification and all that leads to the delight of self I would banish and labour alone for thy delight and glory. Lord accept me as thy child, servant, slave. What is there that Thou wouldst have me to give up—sacrifice—that is now in my possession?

What further denial wouldst thou have me oh vain and sensual creature have me to practice? There is nothing that I can do that is good   Thy grace does all, all that I can do is wholly to give myself to Thee. Accept me oh Father. Oh that I could make such a gift that thou couldst not reject. A gift with the whole heart not with the lips alone. Lord give me the grace of self abandonment to Thee. Let every breath be a prayer to Thee. When shall I be wholly freed from self and Thou be all in all in me? Shall I ever attain this? Oh no not here. Tis self alone that vitiates and destroys all the good I would do. Lord I depend all, all, on thy grace and mercy. Whatsoever Thou doest is right. May I enjoy the contentment to be nothing. Enlighten me that I may shun the evil & walk in the midst of Thy path. Give me Faith, Hope & Charity Father of blessings.

Oh that we could make a clear and perfect offering of our whole self to God. God only works effectually and until we are his servants all our labor is naught. It is only as he wills in us to be to do & to suffer that we make any advance towards our perfect state. We must learn to cease to will & let God will for us. It is not by the knowledge of science or any discovery that our wills are made conformable to the divine will but by the denial of self will and perfect union with God. Union with God is an interior act of the Soul not the result of any external arrangements. Everything must be judged in this world in the light it stands in regard to our fit preparation for the next. Whatever condition fits Man best for future bliss is the best condition for his present being. Be that poverty self sacrifice, martyrdom, or sickness whatever it may be. Man is not to gain heaven by ease and self gratification with folded arms   No it is in being stretched on the cross of self denial

March. 3d.

I am in much doubt concerning the relations we should hold to each other in this life. I have a relation respecting that I know not how I should act respecting. It is true that we should hold no relation with anyone that hinders us from approaching nearer to God. That is not beneficial to us or to the one we are in friendship with. Every relation should be the source of good to us or to others. For this is the office of friendship between Men. But here lies the difficulty with me in judging whether certain relations are or not useful in the true & highest sense to me. Heretofore I have acted as my nature seemed most inclined to dictate trusting that it would not lead me into wrong but now I am somewhat in doubt and scrupulous about it. If I feel that I would make all the progress towards God Heaven Purity, that I can possibly make then it is my imperative duty to cast off all attachments that I may think hinder me from securing the true end of my being. Ah here is the question. It is hard and difficult to cut off any attachment that we feel for a friend even tho we may suppose that it is in the way of our advancement. Friendships may in a certain stage be helps to ones progress but may prove to be at length great weights if held on too long. They may occupy too much of our attention and attract our minds towards other objects than that which we would have them dwell upon. Shall I or shall I not labor to give up all attachments to those I feel and have a degree of friendship for? The purest and the best have held and enjoyed the pleasure of deep friendships. I do not feel that they would be the slightest cause of hindering me from treading the path of my duty. It is a question I cannot settle & must leave rest for some more thought & reflection.[231]

March. 12.

I am not so easy and peaceful at heart as I have been. This I am sorry to say. I believe it arises out of my too great desire to make progress. Also from some doubt that still lurks in my mind concerning the end to which all this is to result in. I do not live enough in the eternal life to forget the accidents of time. Oh am I not getting more wordly? Do I not let the motives of ambition enter my mind? I fear that I do. Or else why should I care for the future if I did all my duty in the present. Ah that I knew what I could do this moment that would prove my love of Christ and be accepted of him. Not to doubt his goodness is truly my duty but ah I fear that I am a miserable wretch in whom there is no good. And oh that I shall not see his face hereafter. Ah no expression can utter the unworthiness that I feel. I am unworthy profitless and a stumbling block in the way. Ah when I attempt to do any good act evil is always present to me and takes away all that is virtuous which makes me feel worse and see my hideousness more than ever. The Lord has given me to see myself and oh what a cloud of darkness of deformity & sinfulness I am. Ah oh Lord unless I knew that thou dost all that is right and good I should despair. Thou hast kept me from my own sight until thy own season and now thou hast given me to see the inherent deformity of my Soul. Ah it is dark, disobedient, & ugly. It cannot do one good act. Whatever I do is tinctured with its vices & impropriety. The more I see what I would be I see what I am and am not and that there is not health, beauty, love in me. Oh what can I do to get rid of myself. I will ask my confessor how it is, if it is so with others that they feel no sense of things. No joy, no reality, no emotion, no impulse, no positive something within or around me. No love, no delight, nothing, nothing, nothing. Is it me? is it my fault? Oh Lord teach me the way. No sense of anything Ah what does this mean. Now what to say I know not. Oh that I could weep or could feel that I loved. Could be sensible of any thing. All that the head can think, all that the heart can feel, or the hands execute,—seem—yes seem—they are not real. I must go to my studies but ah it is all mystery to me. All my dependance is on God. Like one who is on an illimitable sea without compass or rudder. God on Thee and Thee alone in thee I put my whole trust. I feel no other relations and to Thee I cling with all my strength.

March 15.

Should I picture myself as I am sure that I am   Ah what a wicked forgetful ungrateful creature would it show me to be! I cannot say nothing but mercy mercy mercy oh God. Why am I not better, more devoted to God, more industrious in things concerning my souls affairs? Alas I am a sinner full of sin. Full of the world, pride, ambition, self, and all kinds of wickednesses and if left to myself would fall into all sorts of vices. Oh it is thy grace alone that sustains me. Ah why do I begrudge the time I devote to Thee only and not that which is worse than lost. If I shall have to give an account of all my misspent time what a weight of sin will be mine. Oh Lord Thy grace shows me in all my ugliness to myself. Ah—Ah—I have no complaint that I can find nothing to confess All, all, sins are mine and more my own. Ah wicked man no grace can cure thee from all thy innumerable sins for thou sinned every moment of thy poor dependant life. Oh self deceiving self gratifying self indulgent man what torments must thee endure before thou art wholly subdued. *Verbum sat* of thee wicked perverse and destroying self.

This fortnight past I have repeated the litany of the blessed Mary Mother of God for the sake of the conversion of my friends. I have ceased & intend to repeat this habit again so that I may do it with more earnestness. But I pray for others when I am not able to pray enough for myself.

Oh Lord help me—me—me. Not for my sake but for my Souls sake—may it not be cast unto the place of darkness & death. Mother of God befriend me. St Augustine aid me in my studies. St Francis oh give me help to love and practice the poverty & humility thou didst. St Teresa teach me the spirit of obedience & meekness. Oh Lord save me not for myself but for the glory of God alone.

Here I am in the midst of a body of protestants so situated that it would be all out of place if I should really give full utterance on the subjects which interest myself and which are brought up by the others. I now mean the institute in which I am studying. It is a part of my duty to write an essay to be read on Wednesday at the institute and this I have repeatedly attempted to write but cannot for the reason if I write to suit my views of matters as a Catholic they would be out of place and if I do not I cannot say any thing that gives me any pleasure. I have attempted to write on different subjects—what is the criteria of judgment—on the objects of modern reformers—on friendship—and I must stop before I can get to the end of the story.[232]

The Holy week is just passed.[233] I have attended all the appointed ceremonies and festivities of the holy blessed Church of God. This has not been without some fruit I trust in myself. Never have I felt the passion of our divine Saviour the God-Man as I felt it at this holy season. But what can I say more and with more certainty than that I am a great sinner. A weak unfruitful and cowardly christian. Doing nothing. Oh Lord if I cry to thee for mercy what answer can I expect when I go and sin again against Thee Thy Love & Law. This is my theme and my only theme: my sins and my ingratitude. Oh what defilement ugliness and deformity of heart hard obdurate wicked doubting and unbelieving fickle wayward double heart that I have. Oh Lord I cry from the depths of depths to Thee in heaven; what shall I do that I may be freed from this weight of sin. I am beset on all sides with innumerable enemies—Pride, Ambition, Vanity, all that can tempt a temptable and wicked heart like mine. Ah where can I hide my head that sin will not enter. Thou art oh sin every where and we can hide nothing from except we hide our whole hearts in the bosom of our blessed Saviour. Blessed saviour how can such a wretch as me call upon thee. But ah thou art all Love and Mercy. When I begrudge almost a few moments to be spent in Thy presence how can I expect Thou willt be pleased with my petitions. Ah I am all over sick. I know not whither to flee. There is no truth in me. No good. Wretched man that I am who will deliver me from this bond of sin? I see nothing in me but sin not a spark of good. No response of love; all is cold, barren, void, dry, & dead. My prayers & devotions & alms rise up against me. Every thing is an instrument of evil to me. I cannot fly from it oh God. I am a barren & sapless branch. Nothing. Nothing.

Tomorrow is the day for me to see my confessor and approach the confessional. I have endeavored to recollect this month the numerous sins that I have committed and duties I have omitted. But ah what shall I say but that I feel that I am on all hands beset with innumerable temptations.

April 2nd—

I must get more back to myself than of late I have been. Give more of my time to definite objects. Give more to silence, recollection, and calm thought. This it is that gives more depth & breadth to our spirit. The external is ever ephemeral and illusive. A hindered and distracted attention is soon wearied and is fruitless in results. The mind like a tree must be confined to a few branches if it would bear large and flavored fruit.

The last time that I saw my Spiritual Director in conversation he spoke to me respecting the sacred ministry, of my devoting myself to such an office. This is a subject which I feel an unspeakable difficulty on. I told him I desired to place myself wholly unto his hands and whatsoever he directed me to do I should do and the more he gave me direction the happier I should feel. Of myself I do not wish to be any more than nothing. I give myself up and am willing that anything that is best for me to do should be done with me. I know not what God has given me this life for otherwise than to submit to his will & follow his direction. So far the Lord seems to be with me and I hope he will not forsake me in the future. All that we can do in this life is but very little and this of less importance than it seems. God in thy hands I put myself. All that Thou wouldst have me to do teach me.

Some tell me I have a tender conscience approaching to scrupulousness. I know not that this is so. This I know full well that if I did all that I could easily do much more would be done by me than what I now do. Certainly I am not scrupulous when I compare my actions with those of good Men & saints. See what self denial—what abstinence from worldly nay even from not harmful pleasures they denied themselves. I lay this down as a principle that we deserve nothing and therefore all that we have is given us from Gods mercy and for which we ought to be profoundly grateful at all times.

The attention that my studies force me to place upon them keeps me too much from meditation & other spiritual duties. When I think of what I have enjoyed and the state in which I now am I see that tho I am safer now than I was then still I am bereft of much that was mine. If I could devote my time as then to no other than spiritual exercises it might be that what has been lost could be regained. I know not all that I say says not the one thing I would express. I am drawn by two tendencies: by doubts and hopes. I feel not like remaining still as I am. Perplexity meets me on all sides. To remain still is almost an impossibility to me and to whom shall I unburthen my soul? My spiritual Director I would not occupy too much of his time. In going to the College at Rose Hill on the first part of this week Bshp McCloskey promised to introduce me to some of the converts at the institution professors, which he did, but they seemed not to be those with whom I could have that intercourse that to me is desirable. Next Saturday morning I will go and see my Director again. I feel unsettled, uneasy and know not what to do.[234]

Sat 19. April.

When I seem to labor on one side on the other I loose what I gain on this. I try to watch over my eyes that they may not be drawn from the interior and then other sins take hold of me.

The Bishop advised me to read the lives of St Ignatius & Xavier & think of the office of the Priesthood and make it a subject of thought before I decided for either. I have just read Butlers life of St Ignatius. I have read that of Xavier.[235]

I rece'd a note from a person known by me some years ago a Catholic

that a Priest a German desired to see me. I went on Monday last to see the
Priest and saw him this afternoon. He is one of a number of Missionary
Priests of the order of St Aloysius. He wishes me to make a spiritual Retreat
for the object of discovering the order in which I am or may be best adapted
for in the Church. He is very desirous that I should do this immediately and
at their place. Their order is one quite strict in its discipline and seems to
me of a very good character. He seemed to think that the discipline and
standard of religion is not so high among the english & irish Catholics. This
is I believe true. He is a very zealous person and too much so it seems to
me.[236]

It is a subject of much deep concern to me in making a choice of the
order under which I shall place myself. I know not unless the grace of God
is given to me in a greater measure what I shall do about it. It is a new step.
Unquestionably an important one. I desired my confessor to say to me what
was best for me but he thought I had best think over the subject. It seems
greater to me now than it may really be. God gives grace according to the
destiny to be realized. There is the order of the Priesthood—the order of the
Jesuits—and other orders in this country not tho numerous to which I might
be united. Oh Lord choose Thou and with the help of Thy grace I will follow
Thy voice.

April 24—

No I cannot put myself under other hands. I must leave the German
Priest. I shall see my Confessor to morrow morning and converse with him
on this matter more. The Lord—the Lord—the Lord—ah it is need that we
call upon thee for help & consolation. I am nothing and ah what wouldst
thou have me to do. There is nothing in this world that is of any interest to
me. Oh Lord help Thou me in my dimness—make plain my path—open my
eyes that I may see—give me grace that I may walk in thy way—Lord what
shall I do? Thou art Almighty and all knowing   Give me oh Lord grace
& wisdom. Lord I commit myself to Thee; reject oh not such a great sinner
as I am. What can I do oh Lord could I but come to Thee. Lord help me in
my troubles and let me not remain in darkness. Ah what am I thus to be so.
Who will give me aid? Lord none but Thee. Come oh Jesus open Thou my
eyes. Ah who will intercede for me? Oh Guardian Angel speak. I will have
faith in God in all things † † †

25

These are the things that give me trouble. Tho the world has no particular hold upon me,—to say that I give it up once and for all. My perfect
want of faith in myself in being any way useful.

I saw my Confessor yesterday. As I thought I will not have any relations with the German Priest. If I make a general confession the Bishop recommended me to make it at the College where there can be no bias on the minds of the persons as there would naturally be at the place of the G. Priest who belongs to an order and for which he is exceedingly zealous.

I will try to keep my mind composed and easy about this matter hoping that the grace of God will in due time enlighten me on this matter. If I look back all has been opened to me in due season and at present why should I be anxious. God give me thy grace to help me on in the way that Thou wouldst have me to go. Give me hope—grace—love—Jesus come to my soul and give it the true courage of thine own. Be thou with me oh Jesus and the world friends and all will be no hindrance to me. That which seemeth to me will be light and easy and my heart will be with thy joy filled in all distresses. Jesus thou art almighty and full of Love. Give me from thy abundance and I shall be strong. It is a pleasure to suffer for Jesus more sweet than the joys of the world. Agnus Dei tollis peccata mundi dona pacem.[237] † † †

Spoken hastily twice.

Neglected repeatedly to give thanks at my meals.

It seems an essential disposition of my nature to study art as well as the source of art the spirit the consciousness of Man. The interior as well as the exterior   And the exterior as well as the interior. In deciding on the life the order in which I feel best adapted to this fact will have some weight. To lead wholly an interior spiritual life this it seems to me my nature tho much drawn in that direction could not permanently remain in such a state without some disinclination.

April 26

In making choice of an order it is the spirit of God to which I should listen and not my own will. To hear the will of God I must put myself in proper condition. And this is to be accomplished by prayer—silence—and interior recollection—and self abnegation.

When I look back at the repeated and unsuccessful attempts that I made to bury myself and attention in bussiness I cannot for a moment doubt that I am called or destined for a different sphere of life. It is law of divine Providence tho up to this faith in my personal affairs I have not acted that he gives his grace to fulfill the duties of the station to whomsoever he calls to the office. Subjectively attractions are in proportion to destinies.

By July next I am to know in what order I feel inclined or am led to embrace. True the assent is not irrevocable. Yet as such I should consider it if I would not loose any time in preparing for its duties. Lord I am nothing. Give me Thy grace to enlighten me in my present darkness. Give me Thy grace of perseverence to embrace and continue in whatsoever Thou mayst call me. Lead me oh Lord in the way I should go. Let not my thoughts be distracted from this one thing in view. May all my attention be directed to this one point until Thou shalt enlighten me as to Thy purpose in my being. Oh Lord I renew my promises made in baptism. I renounce the world the sense & the Devil and give myself wholly to Thee. Do with me oh Lord as seemeth good in Thy sight. I desire to overcome all self and be nothing else but thine alone. Help me oh Lord to overcome my self will. Whatsoever is in my way remove it oh Lord that I may see. Grant this oh Lord for the sake of Jesus and thy saints. misarere nobis—† † †

27—

This evening I listened to unprofitable conversation which I should have gone from or have changed it if possible.

27

My chief passion I believe to be a desire to be thought more of than what I really am. This frequently leads me to say things I fear too often for an effect. That is in what I do say this passion enters in as a part of the motive which it should not. Ah Lord give me grace to confess and overcome all my sins. Tis this I ask oh Lord and this Thou has promised to grant to all that sincerely repent. From the bottom of my heart oh Lord with all my will I repent of this and all other sins and ask of thee power to overcome them all. Let me be clean & upright in Thy sight oh Lord. 29.

May 1.

When the gifted the talented emperors, kings, queens and princes renounce the whole world to follow thee oh God why should not I who am poor in mind and in all things give to Thee the little I have when others have given thee so much more. Lord help me to say I am all thine from henceforth—forever. Amen.

2nd.

This I should learn the first lesson of all to be perfectly willing to be nothing. So long as I feel or harbor any self will so long shall I feel and harbor trouble in my bosom. Oh Lord Thou knowest this is no easy thing for me to learn. If Thou givest me not Thy grace I shall never learn this all important lesson. How shall I get rid of this which gives me such anxiety, desire trouble and all manner of sorrows regret & unsteadiness? Lord it is of Thee I ask and willt Thou not answer to me? Ah to whom else shall I go? Thou knowest all my wants and weaknesses and thou givest to those who ask of Thee liberally   Here I am oh Lord Thy servant imploring Thee for thy grace not for myself but that I may overcome myself. Grant me this oh Lord in the name of Jesus Christ the only mediator between God and Man. Lord our God have mercy on me and keep me in the hollow of Thy hand. Give me victory over self will. Enlighten my Reason. And give me the graces of humility submissiveness Love & Charity. Lord I ask these of Thee because Thou hast said ask and ye shall receive knock and it shall be opened. I ask oh Lord I knock oh Lord and here am I oh Lord thy servant and waiteth upon Thee. Send me not away empty; let me not go from thee cold and blind oh Lord. Give me faith not to despair and courage to persevere. I ask all these things for it is Thy delight to be with children of Men—Hail Mary—Blessed Jesus † † †[238]

Oh God Thy grace bestow upon me miserable sinner.

I must learn self denial now that I may not when I come to enter the order which Gods grace may call me that I shall not feel the way too hard and the discipline severe. Tho we give up many things these in the end become a habit and to progress in grace we must learn to give up still more. There is always plenty that we take that we may give up with great benefit to ourselves. If I detach myself from the things that are around me now with how much more cheerfulness will I follow the voice of God whithersoever it may call me.

Oh Lord I desire to give my will wholly to Thee. Receive oh Lord this my gift and direct it as Thou willt. All my desire is to give up my will. Pray for me oh Holy Mary. Help me in this moment of my life my Guardian Angel. Lord speak to me that I may no longer be troubled with my own will. Free me oh Lord from this great and original evil. This is all my trouble and all that hinders me from approaching thee nearer. Ye liberated saints who have suffered as I now do intercede for me that I also may be freed from this source of all evils. Lord teach me now and at all times that whatsoever Thou biddest me to do or whatsoever I may be bid to do and Thy authority that this is the best for me to do whatever it may be and that I may do it with meekness humility & sweetness.

The doubts that are in my mind are these whether I should choose the vocation of the Priesthood or that of some order which is of severer discipline. But the Church needs mostly Priests. And in the vocation of Priest the discipline could be drawn as tight and severe as it is possible. Then it is possible for to choose a higher or a more self denying place if the vocation of priestly orders should be found not sufficiently so. But then it must be considered there are stations in the duties of the priesthood that call for great self denial, humbleness, and self forgetfullness. But here arises the disadvantages: my want of talent and culture for this order. I will lay this all before my spiritual director. Sunday evening—

Thus—I said that I did something which I did not tho it was my intention. Again I gave way to my curiosity to a greater degree than modesty should have.

June 1.

It is some weeks since I have written in this book. Study has prevented me from giving my time to this and other duties. Tho I consider study a duty still not one that will supply the place of these.

On Trinity Sunday I was confirmed with my brother George.

I selected St Thomas of Aquinas.[239]

At present I am much tormented and tempted with wicked and loose dreams. Every now and then they give me a great deal of pain and trouble.

There is no good at all in me. All that I see is sin. I see no escape. Patience and contest is all that I can do.

2

Lord I am inexpressibly grateful for all thy goodness towards me a miserable and sinful sinner. I am weak, wicked, and full of wrong. When I think of all thy kindnesses I should be willing to go as dry as I am now and as barren to all Eternity for what Thou hast done for me. Lord give me strength not to complain nor to ask for Thee. Let me live as tho nothing was for me.

3d

This morning I go to the confession   My confessor leaves the City for two months. The duty of the Confession keeps a constant guard over myself in order I may make a free and full confession when I approach the tribunal. Frequently it happens that I can only accuse myself in a general manner. This I feel is not all that I should do but am at loss what more to do.

12.

It seems every new effort that the Soul makes after a higher state of purity the greater are the efforts of the enemy of Souls to keep it from attaining the end of its aspirations. I feel this sensibly, always after partaking of the Eucharist. This week I have been so tempted that I feel inclined to say that I never knew what temptation was before this.

15.

Yesterday I saw Bishop Hughes respecting my embracing one of the orders of the Church, the Priesthood most probably. He said by September the Seminary will be sufficiently finished to take persons with the intention of embracing the Priesthood and he advised me to remain at present here until then. This is what my confessor the Bishops coadjutor had already advised me. The B. was about going somewhere and I had not the opportunity of speaking to him as I had desired. My want of humility talent and culture seem insuperable barriers to my usefullness in the Priesthood. They would keep me from it if something did not with a greater and irresistible force push me forward. I submit, I go, the end God knows. He knows all and I follow the will I hope of him not my own. If I follow His will the true end of my birth and existance undoubtedly will be accomplished. This is all that I know that I am I and here and that I strive to submit & follow His will.

Death is a serious event. Are we prepared to meet it? Who is there among us all that can answer yes. Ah we fear no not even one. Let us then take this fact to heart as immortal souls, as Men. Here is something that is real and seriously so that we have not met, and will have to meet. Is it possible that we knowing this, knowing it too to be the inevitable lot of us all, that we can rest peaceable for one moment of our lives unprepared to meet this impending event. No this is not possible. We cannot rest without presumption or insensibility on our part. Where would the world be found? where we, if at this moment we should hear the summons from on high "to judgment"? Can it be that we are immortal? Can it be that we are Men? and give such little heed to our future life and our present state? As immortal souls what can be of higher interest to us than the life after this? As Men how shall we seem to ourselves when death shall grasp hold of us? On the former we cannot reflect with pleasure nor can the latter give us anything but fear sinful and vulnerable as we are on every side. There is no cloak with which we can obscure ourselves from the eyes of God when we receive the mortal wound. Nor as we are can we die with the innocency and smile of Childhood. There is no escape for us either from without or within but by faith and goodness. And with these, alas! Who is so well armed as not to be wounded? What a picture is this of an immortal soul! of Man! Who could imagine this of him seeing him in his daily pursuits? Of such great destiny and in so great danger busy about such little things. Higher in nature lower in action, than a brute. Feasting and making merry at the very moment perhaps his brother his nearest friend is summoned into eternity and the sword is descending to cut off the thread of his own life. Oh what a thing is Man! A profusion of the costliest gems mixed with the basest metals. Death is a blight a scar on this beautiful creation. We all feel it to be so. It does violence to nature, and interrupts its peaceful onflowing. It is tragic. It is a result not contemplated. A discordant note in the harmony of nature which changes the whole character & feature of things. The purer instincts of our own nature tell us it was not so in the beginning. Now alas its seeds are impregnated into the merest atom, and the great universe itself must crumble. All nature groans with the self same curse. It inevitable is. It will meet us and we must meet it. We have a remedy against its poison, and we may swallow it up in victory. It may be made the beautifulest event in life and the sweetest note in the symphony of Mans existance. And it is to this end as we can not escape it, which may for all be the greater, that we are called to live & labor for. What love what gratitude should we not bear towards that Physician who brings to Man weak and impotent a remedy by which he is enabled to burst the tomb tho it be covered stones too heavy for human strength to roll away, to disarm death of its sting, and make the bitter sweet, and turn the curse into a blessing. He asks us for nothing but that he may cure us. His pity and compassion for us is infinite. Oh could we but see ourselves as he sees us even our stony hearts would melt with pity.

What is more touching and affecting than to see an immortal Soul spurn its own salvation?

June. 21.

I strive to follow my spiritual director or else I should be fearful of my state.[240] All my difficulties sins & temptations I make him acquainted with. It is said by many of the most renowned spiritual writers it never has been known at any time that a Soul has been lost that has obeyed its director. I fear that I do not sacrifice more and more daily and without which there can be no progress towards God. I am not at all desirous to consider where I am but what is still before me. Oh that I gave more of my time to silence and divine abstraction. That I would not consider this time so devoted as lost. That I could free myself from all vanity pride and self-esteem. Oh Holy Mary Mother of God who was untouched by sin tho tempted as we all are do thou pray for me that I may be given such grace as was given to thee. I am sinful and would speak to all of my sins even in this I fear that my vanity would feed itself on. Even my desire for goodness is not free from selfishness. Oh where shall I fly in order to get free from sin? Oh that I could break through these unreal difficulties that beset me. That I could form new resolutions and keep them. If I am rewarded for my prayers then I think how much greater it is to live by faith. And if I am not rewarded then I think it is because I am so evil. Well well I see no way for me to get free from these trials. They must be born. It is the lot of us all. If we should be freed from uncertainty then we would fall into presumption immediately. "O what a thing is Man! How far from settled peace and rest". † † †

Oh Lord free my Soul from the burthen & travail which now rests upon it in its desire for the peace and salvation of those who are dear to it. Bring them to the light and give them Thy grace that they may be strong and embrace the eternal truth. Lead them oh Lord in thy way. Fill their hearts with the desire of Thee. Let them not rest untill they shall have found and united themselves to Thee. Lord if thou lookest with delight on the soul that seeketh the salvation of another do thou answer its call as thou hast promised thou wilt do. How can I rest and be at peace if these shall be lost and find Thee not. Oh all ye powers intercede to the Lord for their salvation. Ye ministering spirits inspire their hearts with holy thoughts and firm resolutions. Oh all ye saints martyrs prophets and virgins pray for them. May all that they see quicken their hearts towards thee oh God. May the prayers of the faithful here oh Lord be effectual. Lord take from me and give to them. Lord let me suffer and they rejoice. What may I oh Lord do for them. Thou who art all give answer to my weak desire. Relieve and Release me oh Lord. My Soul is troubled and all the day is wrestling before Thee for them. Thou knowest oh Lord this is my desire but how far short do I come from it. Oh that my asking was effectual and could not be repulsed. I will hope and never despair.

Pray for my soul and be always with me my blessed and good Guardian Angel. † † †

22

When shall I oh Lord fully learn this all important truth, that in following my own will, in any, in the least respect, I am detached from Thee, and instead of gaining ground as I may seem, that in reality I am loosing rapidly. Oh that this truth was never out of my mind. That I were perfectly obedient to thee however little and mean I might appear in the eyes of the world. Must we not become fools for Thy sake. Let me never forget Thee and remember Thee in all that I do.

When shall I become nothing for Thy sake hasten the day oh Lord. Give me a heart to follow Thee. Let me look on all other things as worse than nothing as accursed. Oh Lord grant this my petition. Teach me Thy way. † † †

28.

I cannot get beyond the fact that all our anxiety trouble and uneasiness arises from our own willfullness, and that if we would wholly submit to God, we should live and enjoy such peace love and quietness that is His. Our estrangement from Him is all that is wrong and our reunion with Him is the remedy which will make all wrong right. It is not, it is not, that society or nature of Man that disturbs and disquiets us; we have the disturbance and restlessness in us. Oh how deep are the words "Consider the lilies of the valley they neither toil nor do they spin" It is true, too true, that our want of faith and confidence in God is the source and ground of all our fear, doubt, & trouble. Perfect love, purity, & faith, cannot be disturbed or riled. Oh what a life is Mans. How far from settled peace and rest. Could we only give our whole Soul to God. We are ever striving from him. If he did not cling to us with deeper attachment than we to him we should be for ever seperated. Oh my Soul why art Thou so wilfull. Surely this is thy nature not my act. Wherefore is this, and why doest thou spurn thy own salvation? What makes thee so disquiet. And who can advise thee? Where is the Counsellor of thee? Alas no wind speakes to thee. The heavens are still and the Earth makes no noise. No Angel or Dove descends to whisper peace. The Soul is alone in its grief. It must feel all trials and sufferings. Hope is not even left to it that it may suffer all. And what is sympathy where it cannot reach. Well, well, here I am and this is all. Without sense is any thing but sin. All, all, actions, seem superficial. Nothing springs from the center or reaches there. If that would act. It is a wish, a wish, a wish. It is, and why say it is not; it is. It is too, the deepest fact of all acts. The jeers of Men, the prison, or the rack, cannot touch it. Love cannot warm it, Hope cannot inspire it. And thought cannot reach it. There is no balm in Gilead and no Physician. No Prophet has prophesied it. No Seer has seen it. It is deeper than life and beyond which there is nothing. It is beyond prayer except it be prayer itself. A still desire. A sleep deep in God.

Study I have tried to day but I cannot. Is it not the bussiness of Man to save his own Soul and this before all things? Does the study of greek and latin help a soul towards its salvation? Is it not quite a different thing from Grace? Sometimes I feel strongly inclined to set aside all study all reading as superficial and not so important as contemplation and silence. It is said look to some who have studied and at the same time made the most rapid approaches to God. Good, well, so be it. John ate locusts and honey and Paul shaved his head. Daniel ate pulse etc. What does this prove? It proves that they did so and so and this is all. No one man all in all is an example for another. When we most need advice the friend is sure to be wanting. There is no book that ever was written that answers all in all to our wants. Almost we may say a book is not profitable to us until we have no need of it. If we follow it it may do us more evil than good. And to read it with judgment we should be equal with it. We must learn to depend more and more upon that which those depend on who wrote not upon what was written by them. Shall we depend upon the Bible when we have Jesus Christ himself? We speak this not presumptuously but with truthfulness and humility. Were the book as the Bible unquestionably does point out the way, and is taken as a guide to the way, and not as the way the truth and the life, in such a case, it is invaluable, but experience has proven that too often that the letter has crushed the very spirit it was written for to cherish. But this is not the subject of my present reflection. In matters where there is no infallible judge to guide us and distract us we have no higher ground for our action than our conscience and reason to follow. It is a question that can only be solved by each individual soul in and for itself what will & what will not aid it in its union and approach to God. The Bible the Lives of the Saints and the Ascetic and Spiritual writers are in this matter no infallible rule—nor do they pretend to be. The thing itself is impossible. For how could such rules be laid down for each individual soul which is different from all others and should be as well adapted to it in its peculiarities as it is to those of very unlike characteristics? New diseases require new remedies. New times new measures. New masters make new laws. Hence it is each individual so far as he is truthfull to the character bestowed upon him by his Creator must tread upon untrodden ground and sail in a different course. To make that similar which in the wisdom of God is dissimilar as the characteristics of Men are would be sacrilegious not religious. Hence the true Church is Catholic. It meets all the wants of each individual of the Race. Hence God in his fullness is its Author. Hence the different sacraments and orders in the Church, the first which fill the wants, the second which cherish their perfect expression. But the difficulty in this matter lies here with me for it is matter more personal I imagine than general—what is the path that Gods providence has destined in obedience for you to pursue. We may in our willfullness or even in our weakness follow that which He has not designed us for. As for example we heard a religious the other day say that he had served some 30 or more years in another order until within late when he saw that his proper position was where he now stood. Now the intincts which lead us in opposition to some things which may be good in themselves for others, and the attractions we feel towards other objects which also are proper and good, these dispositions when they are not very strongly marked, and are clearly to be perceived, present a difficulty which with all our prayers and efforts is hard to solve and overcome. There is no voice that will as it did Paul direct us on our journey to whom we shall go in order that our blindness may be taken from us. There is a voice not less certain to be sure but tho this be so, are we to look for such an action of it in every case? It has not pleased itself to manifest itself always in this manner and hence it is not always thus to be expected. Where shall we find our Ananias? This is the question. If we asked as Paul did in the same sincerity and willingness Lord what will thou have me to do? the answer to us might be as plain. Grace is our only hope.—28

Sunday. 29.

O.A.B. is here.[241] He arrived this morning. Tho he is a friend to me, and the most critical periods of my experiences have been known to him, and he has advised and frequently given me his sympathy yet he never moves my heart. He has been of inestimable value to me in my intellectual developement. He is too a man of heart. But he is so strong and intellectually active that all his energy is consumed in thought. He is an intellectual athlete. He thinks for a dozen men. He does not take time to realize in heart for himself. No man thinks & reads more than he. But he is greater as a writer than as a person. There are those who never wrote a line but whose influence is deeper and more extensive than those who have written heavy tomes. It is too late for him to give his time to contemplation and interior recollection. He is a controversalist a Dr. The last he will be before long. Some have wondered why we could have such a friendship for O.A.B. They imagine him to be so harsh and dictatorial. We have not felt this. His presence does not change us. Nor do we find ourself where we were not after having met him. He has not the temperment of genius but more of a rhetorician and declaimer. He arrives at his truths by a regular and consecutive system of logic. His mind is of a historical more than of a poetical mould. He never startles us with profound truths rushing from his brain like Minerva from the head of Jupiter already armed. We see both the genesis exodus and revelation of his thoughts. He never will be charged of holding two doctrines one esoteric and the other exoteric. As a man we never have known one so conscientious and self sacrificing. This is natural to him. His love of right is supreme and his greatest thing he detests is bad logic. This makes him peevish and often riles his temper. He defeats but will never convince an opponent. This is bad. No one loves to break a lance with him because he cuts such ungentlyman gashes. He is strong and he knows it. He has more of the Indian Chief than a chivalrous Knight in his composition. He has both. Tho nothing of the modern scholar so called. He is wholly wanting in genuine pathos. He whines when he would be pathetic. His art is logic but he never aims at art. He is a most genuine and true man to his nature. None so much so. By no means E.[242] who ever prates about this thing. If he attempts embellishment you see it's borrowed. It is not in his nature. There is a pure and genuine vein of poetry running through his nature but not sufficient to tincture the whole flow of his life. He is a man of the 13 & 14 centuries not of the 19teenth. He is an anomaly among scholars, writers, and divines. He is not thorough on any one subject tho at home on all. What a collegiate education would have done for him we are baffled to conjecture. He is genuine; we love him for this. This is the crown of all virtues. But we must stop we only intended to mention he was here.

Monday. even 30.

Here I would make a vow. But it must be considered. I would uproot by all possible means all my love of praise and ambition. Destroy everything that would feed it. Do all that would crucify it. How to do this? What measures to pursue. To live wholly for God for Eternity.

July. 2.

The scripture says the pure in heart shall see God. If we then approach God as we are cleansed from sin, and if we are illumined with the light of God as we approach Him is it not unquestionably true that the sole duty of Man is to purify his heart? And if learning does not tend to purify the heart should it be encouraged or even sought after? Did not Jesus say first seek the Kingdom of God & his justice and all things shall be added thereunto? Learning and Grace are two distinct things. We can gain heaven with the last without the first but not with the first without the last. Christ will not ask us if we can decline amo, or if we have sound views of the middle voice of the preterite tense of the Greek verb. His question to us will be have you fullfilled the commandments which I gave unto you? Perfect submission to the Spirit of Christ will necessarily lead to perfect obedience and harmony with the Church of Christ. Hence we say that the Church in uniting us with Christ frees us from all documents, books & records. These are helps, aids, guides, but are not the Spirit upon which we are to depend and follow tho without doubt that the one being a record of the other they harmonize. When we have the substance we need not to rely upon the account of it. But however this is not the question we started with and now neglect our studies to settle. We feel as we did when we were at Concord that study was an interruption to our more rapid approach to God. That it called off our attention from him. That it dissipated our life. It is a sin to give up a higher for a lower. There are certain deep affinities we cannot control nor pray against. These are what is deepest in us. This may not justify them. Luther said "Here I am and I cannot do otherwise so help me God". And this too in objecting against the Church of Christ. Martyrs have been for error. That is Error has had its martyrs or those who have died for her. O what a thing is Man! is what on more than one occasion has been my ejaculation. Then too we read of many of the Saints such as St Francis St Thomas of Aquino who formed or were led by certain resolutions to leave all their former positions in life and prospects like even St Ignatius and devote themselves to something of quite a different character. I know not how it is with me. One may say give up this thought of yourself and go to study. Good advice. It would be better if those who would give it gave the power at the same time to follow it. It is something that acts so powerfully on my heart as to draw my attention from my study towards it and without a greater power or increased strengthening of my will; resistance is of no avail. We are told to deny ourself. Good, but this is not ourself that moves us. If we are deluded we must be made to see ourself for we cannot.

July 4.

The doctrine of infallibility of the Catholic Church is the only ground upon which there can possibly be any settledness and security in our faith. If the Church may err, if the Councils may err as undoubtedly individuals do then have we no surety of our faith and consequently of our salvation. We are left orphans and without a guide. The Question is not whether we differ from or what are our opinions on matters of faith and morals but what are the decisions of the Church and we must give up if we differ and submit. This is all. The Church is the pillar & ground of truth. Not the Bible as interpreted by private judgment. If the Church has not this infallibility then where else shall we find it? The Church has it and for its evidence it produces the promises of its Founder its own uniform doctrines and its continuous faith.

9

I have studied little but written much these few days past. There is a war within me between what I feel, or between my life, and study. Between the interior life and the exterior. When I shall be freed from my own control I shall make more progress in either one of the two. I long for that day. I too may use it when it comes. But he that does not trust knows not what life is. *He that looses his life shall gain it. These words are all.* He has all time, eternity, to work in. Time makes all our sadness.

I think of going to New England in the vacation. Probably next week when O A B returns from Balt.[243] True I have little to call me there. Why should I go? Why? I fear that I am not led from the higher sources to go. It may be dangerous. It may not. I will leave it until then for decision. One inch of self will moves us an ell from God. O that I were still when He would have me to be still. Ready to go when He would have me go. To suffer to joy in everything as He would have me to be. O that I could loose myself in God. O what a gain this would be. O Lord take me to thee that I may be lost in gaining Thee.

I think that I shall go East. But the word almost dies in the pen. I fear that I do not go to gain. To share I have nothing.

July 17.

Yesterday was the commencement. My connection with the Cornelius Institute is ended. The young men I have met with there I have no great interest in. Perhaps I should make one exception—E. Wall. They are as a body not in that deep earnestness which is a characteristic of a mind of any value. The world will never be moved nor Sin put to rout by such. There is such a mass of ignorance prejudice and such a want of humility in the protestant community that I am glad to get free from its disagreeable presence.

It is like ploughing among stones & rocks. My going first to C. Institute has been a useful experience to me, and chastened my hopes. I have been by means of it much deeper in the workings of protestantism. Its want of deep spirituality, its superficiality, and its inevitable tendency to no religion.

O A B I expect this afternoon. I had resolved to go on East with him but my brothers desire me not to go on account of the expense. I think I shall remain here. It would not be one half as expensive as they imagine. However if nothing turns up I shall remain here. I did have some thoughts of making a pedestrian tour on to Boston but this does not seem to me very inviting. It would be to me a pleasant if I could get some one to make a pedestrian tour to Catskill Mountains and then from there on to Boston. This I could do for a few shillings. But I know of no one who would be willing to do this.

19

Now that I am freed from the regular routine of studies my attention is drawn towards general and more important ends and aims of being. I consider myself and the motives and ends for which I act. All that I do, and all that I leave undone, is full of vanity, impurity,—& self will. It is me which does, and it is me that restrains from doing. How to free the soul from Sin, and disenthrone all earthly affection in it, is a hard, a difficult, and almost impossible work.

20.

Our union and conversation with God, our love & obedience towards Him, is unquestionably sadly neglected. It is only as we have his love in our hearts that we can do any good whatever. We ought in silence turn our energy towards him instead of wasting it upon the things of this world. How little do we think of God; how much upon the things of sense & creatures of death. O that we could collect all our senses and turn them up towards Him. Alas alas alas we did from our interior attraction towards him wish that all our senses were shut that we might be wholly occupied with Him but now where are all we. Have we lost our interior life. We then had power over ourselves but now we know not what this is. We cannot reach even where we there then. What means this. How is it possible that we should have such a knowledge of God as then when we give the better part nay most all of our energy to study and other occupations. And then too here are so many inducements to talk and speak that which is not profitable. All these things work against me. I feel a loss and want which makes me not peaceable and not restfull.

July. 23

Old and forgotten sins of the past are revived and come up fresh to memory, and actions that I thought were not sinful seem now to me full of sin. Alas I see myself as I never saw. Alas I am a man of sin without bottom. What a work a man has to do. What courage, truthfulness, & humility, does he not require. Without Thy Grace O Lord I can do nothing. I sink, fall, die unless thou sustain, encourage me, & lift me up. Thou knowest my weakness and what a coward I am. Help! Help! Help!

July. 27

I have decided that I will leave this country in order that I may prepare rather be prepared for whatever labor the grace of God may lead me to. Bishop Hughes recommends me to go to St Sulspice. This would be in order to prepare me for the secular clergy. So far as I can judge of myself I never wish to be one of the secular clergy. At least one of the regular clergy. But of this I cannot speak now. The Redemptorists have been much in my thoughts. Then too this afternoon I have considered of the college at Rome where the education is free, that at St Sulspice would be quite expensive I beleive.

28.

What tho I should know all about the expenses & character of the college of St Sulspice, and that of Rome, these are still for the secular clergy, and one of the secular clergy I do not wish to be. That is so far as I feel and know now about myself. To be sure the Bishop said that in my one year of novitiate at St Sulspice I could see the different religious orders and then if I chosed I could join the one that would seem that I am best capacited for. But then why should I put my choice off when I feel to a certain extent prepared to make this choice now? Here I am at stand I confess. Even if at St Sulspice there is thorough & exact discipline still the end is that to which I do not feel is the one for me. To take the step that I am called to do and not to go too far so as not to fall back is difficult for me. Oh Lord direct me and all my ways and actions. Oh Lord, what wouldst Thou have me to do? At Rome there are many objects of attraction that draw me there. At St Sulspice there are many objects that would attract me there.[244]

NOTES

1. Two sets of fragments have come down to us with the diary that from their dating, style, and contents clearly were diary entries made before Hecker started writing in bound books. The fragment I have designated Fragment A-D is undated, but by the reference to Brownson and his idea of Communion it is likely that it was no earlier than the summer of 1842, at which time Brownson was writing on Pierre Leroux's notion of "Life by Communion" in *The Boston Review* and, in July, penning his famous open letter "On the Mediatorial Life of Christ" to William Ellery Channing. However, it appears from the paper used and from the fact that Fragment A-D has come down to us always grouped with the January 10, 1843 Fragment E-H, that A-D Fragment I was written right around the same time. I have placed it before the other fragments because that is the order of the original sources as they have been handed down and there is nothing to suggest a much later or earlier date.

2. The son of German-born parents, Hecker learned to speak and read German as a boy. This enabled him to read the works of Richter in the original. He read all in German but *The Autobiography,* which was published in Boston in 1843 in an English translation, which explains some of the German quotes in the early stages of volume 1.

Johann Paul Friedrich Richter (1763–1825) took the *nom de plume* Jean Paul after Jean-Jacques Rousseau who in many ways was on the vanguard of the Romantic revolution that writers like Richter created. In his first novel, *The Invisible Lodge,* he developed the notion of *höhen Menschen,* the lofty superhumans elevated far from the trivial activities of the masses, suited more to a transcendental existence and ready to suffer death rather than to compromise with the imperfections of this world. That theme followed through in his second novel, *Hesperus,* and reached its finest form in his masterwork, *Titan.* In *Titan* the book's hero Albano is a titan, one of the *höhen Menschen,* whose interactions with Schoppe and the other characters draw out his quest for an harmonious existence, in love with pure love.

Doubtless Hecker finds these characters attractive. They become vehicles for his own aspirations. Through them he follows his own hopes and sorrows, and his sufferings. In a quite literal sense he is right when he says that he has "not yet attained a power to speak it''—neither the power of understanding or of expressing it in written form.

Regardless of what language he was reading, the fact that he was reading so much of Richter is of crucial importance in understanding the first volume of his diary. The five massive works of Richter that he names comprise over 3,000 closely-printed pages. That anyone could endure reading so much of Richter in such a short period may be hard for the contemporary observer to understand. In first encountering Richter one finds the words of Thomas Carlyle appropriate: ''The style, the structure of the book appear alike incomprehensible. The narrative is every now and then suspended to make way for some 'extra-leaf', some wild digression upon any subject but the one on hand; the language groans with indescribable metaphors and allusions . . . flowing onward, not like a river, but like an undulation; circling in complex eddies, chafing and gurgling now this way, now that, till the proper current sinks out of sight amid the boundless uproar. We close the work with a mingled feeling of astonishment, oppression, and perplexity and Richter stands before us in brilliant cloudy vagueness, a giant mass of intellect, but without form, beauty or intelligible purpose . . . the very high priest of bad taste. . . . ''

Yet upon a second reading Carlyle found something else: ''His works are hard to understand but they always have a meaning, and often a true and deep one. In our closer, more comprehensive glance, their truth steps forth with new distinctness; their error dissipates and recedes, passes into venality, often even into beauty and at last the thick haze . . . melts away'' (''Jean Paul Richter'' in Thomas Carlyle, ed., *German Romance,* in Emile Tennyson, ed., *Nineteenth-Century Literary Criticism,* vol. 7 [Detroit: Gale, 1984] pp. 227–29).

That long quote sets the scene not only for an understanding of Richter but also of the diary, since the young Hecker attempted quite clearly to mimic the style of his German literary hero. Without ever having had the benefit of a formal education, ignorant of English grammar and spelling, he launches his diary after having read the massive accounts of the conflict between the real and the ideal, the search for harmonious existence, the dualism of soul and body and of this world and the more perfect one above, that make up Richter's novels. He imbibes also the technique of blending dreamlike passages into the narrative and the attempts to create a sense of wonder, confusion, and helplessness over the course of one's life, and at the very act of consciousness that made Richter one of the century's great precursors of the modern psychological novel. The entire formlessness, overcrowdedness, and complexity of the novels cannot in fact be fitted into the diary by a man of twenty-two with little education and only moderate literary talents. Yet he tries. At times the attempt succeeds; often it does not, but always in volume 1 it is an effort *à la Jean Paul.*

3. ''You are searching for something of a higher power that is beyond life—the eternal, the First Cause, God.''

4. On images of the feminine in the 1840s, see note 37.

5. The reference is to Goethe's *Die Leben des jungen Werthers* (*The Sorrows of the Young Werther*) first published in 1774. Later Hecker will at times speak more quixotically about suicide, mimicking the heroism of a titan who would rather depart

this life than compromise with it. But the more "manly" attitude demonstrated here is more typical of Hecker who was writing to his worried mother not to fret about him: "Take noting that I have said discouragingly. Turn fears into hopes and doubts into faith, and we shall live better if not happier" (December 24, 1842).

6. Brownson had become interested in the ideas of Pierre Leroux in 1842. Leroux's work *De L'Humanité. Son Principe et de Son Avenir. Où se trouve exposée La Vraie Definition de la Religion et où L'on explique Le Sens. La Suite, et L'enchainement du Mosaisme et du Christianisme* (Paris: Perrotin, 1840). The book begins with a quote from the First Letter of Paul to the Corinthians: "We are each members of one body and we are all members one of the other." He argues that "La vie est une communion: communion avec Dieu, communion avec nos semblables, communion avec l'univers." But humans are not able to commune directly with God nor with creatures other than man. It is, however, precisely by communion with humanity that humans are able to commune legitimately and normally with God and the universe (p. 191). See note 24.

7. This is in all likelihood the January 7, 1843 letter of John Hecker to Brownson in which John thanks the doctor for his kind and patient dealing with his younger brother. He explains that Isaac has of late become prone to "nervous spells" during which he becomes peevish and melancholy. He is always better when about to undertake a journey or when expecting some special event. After it occurs he becomes discouraged. "Anything like physical labor mentioned to him had a very disagreeable effect." John thought that it was caused by "too much exercise of mind," and wanted to hear what Brownson thought before allowing Isaac to go off and study further at Brook Farm. John paints a picture of a younger sibling who was "spoiled" and never did his share of the work. John was bolstered in his opinion by an unnamed New York physician who thought that if he could get his mind on some "physical employment" he would improve. That opinion of himself Isaac was keenly aware of, and would often find himself torn between desires to study and a guilt that he should be doing something more practical.

8. Hecker's mention of the phrase "born-again" is interesting because it calls attention to the change of disposition that occurred in the second half of 1842. During that time, Isaac became increasingly interested in matters of the soul. He desired to spend more time in study and far less in working at the business. As we have already seen, and shall see far more in the future, the turn within had a good deal to do with his own sense of identity and vocation. But it also had an expressly Christocentric element, which his mother, faithful Methodist that she was, recognized right away. As John told Brownson in his January 7, 1843 letter: "Mother thinks he is under a severe religious change or under peculiar convictions which she thinks all persons must have before they are Christians. . . . The only thing she thinks he is looking for or wants is a giving up of his whole mind to Christ. . . . " Why in fact Hecker wanted more than to simply live out a commitment to Christ as a good Methodist I have dealt with at length in *An American Experience of God*. I should only wish here to point out that he was focusing on the question: What must a man do to be saved? while he was at Brook Farm. As he says in a January 19, 1843 letter to his mother, "that question has for me at this time, and for some time has had,

the highest interest.'' Essentially the Methodist answer to the question was unappealing, not only in its theological import, but in the cultural package in which it came. As his brothers were moving up in society economically, he wished to do so intellectually and culturally. Methodism was not the religion of the New England Brahmins or even of the New York captains of industry. Even in its more refined urban form, it had the rough edges of a frontier, missionary faith. Those rough edges were wholly unappealing to the young Hecker, as they were, incidentally, to his other brothers. Catholicism certainly had as many and more rough edges, but interest in it, at least as an ideal, was far more fashionable among the Transcendentalists than was Protestant revivalistic faith.

9. The fragmentary nature of this section is evident from the first line. It was written from Brook Farm, where Hecker had gone to live on January 4, 1843. The dates 4 and 5 which appear later in the fragment with no month or year must be between February and April, since he is already at the Community when he begins Fragment I-L, as we learn from his comments on the opinions others at the place might have of him. The first dated entry in the first bound volume of the diary is April 15. This suggests that there were probably entries made to the diary written on loose-leaves between February and April that are not extant.

10. This reaction to the people at Brook Farm betrays Hecker's own fears and misgivings as much as it does the actual response of the members of the community. There is abundant evidence to show that he was well liked by many at the West Roxbury community. Later he himself came to realize this and by the time of his leaving Brook Farm is aware of the affection of many of its members.

11. The inability to work at his family's business is, in and of itself, explainable in the context of his desire to be doing something else with his life. What is more perplexing is that a pattern emerges in his life of not being able to attend to the subject at hand. He cannot work at the bakery because he wants to go off and study. When he goes, however, he cannot study because he wants to attend to the inner spirit motivating him. Even after his conversion this pattern is present. When he enters the Redemptorists and goes to the novitiate at St. Trond, he cannot study. When in the 1870s he begins to become ill, he cannot, after his return from Europe, attend to the business of being the Superior of the Paulists. At that point the reason, though, is obvious and much easier to understand. He has a disease which today would in all probability be diagnosed as chronic leukemia that saps his strength. Was there any psychological link between the chronic problem of his old age and the intermittent problem of his youth? As tempting as it is to think so, it is not likely. The malady of his youth was most likely a combination of the simple laziness that John Hecker saw in his brother and a genuine gift of contemplation that made attending to the inner symphony far more appealing than it would be to most.

12. This prayer was written on the opening leaves of the first volume of the diary. It is followed by the dated ''Brook Farm'' entry, as it appears here.

13. This entry gives us some hint of what comes out rather strongly in his letters from this time: going to Brook Farm was part of an effort to become an educated, refined person that was motivated by a desire for upward mobility that

differed from that of gaining prosperity through business, a method to which John Hecker was totally committed. Cf. note 28, below.

14. As Thomas Wangler and Ann Taves have recently pointed out in different ways, the architecture and decoration of the American Catholic churches of the 1840s was designed to bring the worshipers into a sacred place that in its visual symbolism represented the kingdom of heaven. That movement within the sacred space brought the worshiper in touch with an array of saints as well as with the persons of the Trinity, each depicted in emotive styles that were intended to function both as gateways through which the faithful could pass in contemplative rapture and as didactic statements to instruct in the doctrines and laws of the church. See Anne Taves, *Household of Faith* (Notre Dame: University of Notre Dame Press, 1986) and Thomas Wangler, "Catholic Religious Life in Boston," in Sullivan and O'Toole, eds., *Catholic Boston* (Boston: Northeastern University Press, 1986).

Obviously the effect on Hecker was profound, as it was, interestingly enough, on another convert of the 1840s, Augustine Hewit. Hewit, who was to become one of the co-founders of the Paulists with Hecker in 1858, was the son of a Bridgeport, Connecticut, Congregationalist minister and a graduate of the Hartford Seminary. A trip to New York's St. Patrick's Church left him in reveling in the sense of God's holiness that he had experienced. See Hewit diary, PFA, pp. 3–5.

15. Although Almira Barlow was the heartthrob of many Brook Farmers like John S. Dwight, who sought her affection in vain for years, she took a shine to the little New York baker, some twelve years her junior. Her efforts to entice Isaac were noticed by the leaders of the community, who shortly after moved Almira and her family to new quarters away from the Hive building where Hecker lived. As this and later diary entries show, Isaac had a genuine affection for Mrs. Barlow but kept her somewhat at a distance. In an entry for May 16 he explains that his present state of internal transition would make it impossible for him to make any lifelong commitments to a person, even though he was attracted to her. After they had left Brook Farm, he returning to New York and she to Concord, they exchanged letters, which Almira complained were too cold. Soon she gave up the chase. See Holden, *Yankee Paul*, pp. 50–51.

Isaac's status as a member of an up-and-coming family business was not lost on his new friends, and one wonders whether the thought of a young, well-off provider for her three sons did not motivate the Brookline beauty's interest in Hecker.

16. The entry for Tuesday afternoon, April 18, clearly shows the deep interest Hecker had in the questions being raised by the Oxford movement. He and his brothers were reading the *Tracts for Our Times* and being greatly affected by them. It was through their influence that John decided to become an Anglican and George and Isaac were moved to Catholicism. In a March 1, 1843 letter to his brothers, Isaac had told of his conviction that the ideas of the Oxford divines and those of Brownson shared a "oneness and unity of doctrine. Furthermore the views of the Protestant bishops of Prussia and the Bishop of Geneva also coincided with what he saw to be a providential move "to bring all the scattered sects into one Church, one Body."

The controversy over the Oxford movement that rocked the General Theological Seminary of the Protestant Episcopal church in New York was very familiar to the Heckers. The trial of Arthur Carey commenced in June of 1843 and led to bitter controversy over his ordination that dominated life at the seminary during the next school year.

Stimulated by that controversy, Isaac decided to delve deeper into Catholic doctrine and did so by reading a newly published Boston edition of the catechism of the Council of Trent and Johann Adam Moehler's *Symbolism,* which he borrowed from the library of Theodore Parker.

17. An allusion to Matthew, chapter 24.

18. This sounds like Spinoza whose *Opera Postuma* (Amsterdam, 1667) was owned by Alcott. We know from a September 1, 1843 diary entry that Hecker by that time for certain knew Spinoza.

19. Dreams played a key role in Hecker's life during the period of the first volume of the diary. He began analyzing them as part of his introspective program. He viewed them as channels through which new insights might be gained, especially about the future.

This sort of fascination with dreams was widespread among the New England Romantics, as it had been with their European counterparts. The novels of Richter that Hecker read are filled with dream sequences in which the dreamer experiences deep revelations about his future destiny. As we will see, Hecker modeled some of his own dream experiences around those presented by Richter. In addition to the fascination with dreams present in German Romantic literature, there was a sub-strata of more marginal, more wildly speculative thought about the nature of dreams and sleep-walking that went under the title of somnambulism.

The post-Kantian age with its emphasis on the role of the subject in the process of knowing was the ground in which the seeds of modern psychology were sown. An examination of sleep was part of a larger study of human consciousness. True to form, the Romantics were fascinated by the more unusual phenomena like som-nambulism. The examinations of it ranged from the coolly rational discussions of a respected medical man like John Addington Symonds of England's Bristol Hospital, to the occult and bizarre. There was *The Account of Jane C. Rider, The Springfield Somnambulist* (Springfield, MA: Merriam, 1834) that was the strange story of how a young Massachusetts girl was stricken with attacks of somnambulism that drove her into the insane asylum. Then, for the more exotic imaginations, there was the 1837 Philadelphia edition of *Journeys into the Moon. Several Planets and the Sun,* which was the history of a female somnambulist from Württemberg who journeyed into astral regions and returned with new revelations. Hecker himself for sure read one such work of this genre, Justinus Kerner's *The Seeress of Prevost,* an account of a young woman's extraordinary experiences of the spirit world. See note 121.

20. What Hecker means here is hard to tell, since what he has written is not a word. He may mean anthropomorphidae, a type; or anthropomorphisms.

21. Arthur T. Christy sought to explain the appeal of Confucius to the Tran-scendentalists by pointing out that he was the philosopher of practicality whose max-ims resonated with Yankee common sense. See *The Orient in American Transcendentalism* (reprint, New York: Octagon, 1963), pp. 30–31.

22. Emanuel Swedenborg (1688–1772) was a Swedish scientist whose work in geology as his country's assessor of mines was coupled with some important achievements in the field of anatomy. His greatest notoriety, however, came from his spiritual writings which told of fantastic visions of the spirit world. His Doctrine of Correspondences argued that all material things corresponded in some precise fashion to things in the spiritual world. In the greatest detail he told of the nature of the spiritual realm, explicating it with the same cool, empirical tone that he used in his scientific writings.

As Ahlstrom has noted, the influence of Swedenborg in antebellum America was tremendously widespread. Certainly the Transcendentalists were among his greatest fans. The New Church, founded by his followers in 1787, flourished in America. See Marguerite Beck Block, *The New Church in the New World* (1932; reprint, New York: Octagon, 1968); Clarence P. Hotson, "Emerson and the Swedenborgians," *Studies in Philology* 27 (July 1930): 517–45; and note 1.

23. Charles Fourier (1772–1837) was a French social theorist whose rather frustrated career centered on attempts to interest the world in his utopian vision of a new social order, the theory of which he had claimed to discover. Educated at the Jesuit Collège de Besançon, he published *Théorie des quatre mouvements et des destinées générales* in 1808. During the 1820s he worked in Paris trying to interest people in his theories and produced the most accessible of his works, *Le Nouveau Monde industriel et sociétaire.* In 1832 he founded the first *Phalanstere,* which failed after two years.

His popularity in America of the 1840s was out of proportion with the relatively small impact that he had had in France. This was due in large part to the tireless efforts of his American disciples, the foremost of whom was Albert Brisbane. Brisbane's *The Social Destiny of Man* was a very popular presentation of the abstruse theories of Fourier. Brisbane was able to interest publisher Horace Greeley in the cause and get a running front page column in the *New York Tribune.* Eighteen forty-four was the height of interest in Fourierism, with thirteen of the twenty-eight Fourierist communities ever established in the U.S. being formed.

Fourier had developed a rather elaborate theory of Passional Attraction, to which Hecker refers here. For Fourier the theory of Passional Attraction was a scientific discovery akin to those made by Leibniz or Newton and of even greater significance. The theory, in the words of the editors of the New York publication of the Fourierist movement, meant simply "the attraction of the passions. Ambition, for example attracts or impels a Napoleon. . . . The Passions are governed in their action by fixed and invariable laws, which is a way one can make theories about their behavior. Men at present have either passions in a state of confusion and discord, and the key to a better society is to bring them into the proper order so that the energies of individuals may be directed to the areas to which they are naturally attracted." See "Theory of The Four Movements and General Destinies of Passional Attraction and Its Relation to the Fixed Sciences," *The Phalanx* 1 (November 4, 1843): 25–29.

24. Pierre Leroux (1797–1871), French utopian socialist writer and philosopher, had a significant impact on Hecker. Leroux blended St. Simonian social theory

with his own imaginative use of religious themes from Christianity and, to a lesser degree, Hinduism and Neo-Platonism. Hecker learned of him through Brownson, whose July 1842 article in the *Boston Quarterly Review*, "Leroux on Humanity," was one of the earliest presentations of the Frenchman's thought to America. His seminal work, *L'Humanité* (Paris, 1840), had the agenda of presenting a new philosophy that would make clear how "resting in Nature and in life, we can elevate ourselves to our spiritual center." He argued for a unified vision of humanity and for the reality of the perfection of the race through the progress of the whole race: "Life is a communion: communion with God, with one another, with the universe; but man is not able to commune directly with God, nor with creatures other than man. . . . by communion with man he is able to commune legitimately and normally with God and the universe" (p. 191).

It was that idea that captivated Brownson. He saw in Leroux's ideas the ultimate rebuttal to the selfish individualism of the industrial age with its illusion of individual progress. All of humanity is a corporate being and only as such can it be elevated. Individuals, as part of the race, can commune with God and be saved, but not as isolated persons. This was the seed that between 1842 and 1844 grew into a conviction that the Catholic doctrine of Apostolic Succession was correct and that membership in the church was necessary for salvation.

Hecker was caught up in Brownson's movement (see "Dr. Brownson's Road to the Church," *The Catholic World* 46 [November 1887]: 222–25 and "Dr. Brownson and Catholicity," *The Catholic World* 46 [November 1887]: 222–35). Neither Hecker nor Brownson were bothered by Leroux's rejection of the historical church or his dismissal of traditional views on Christ and the afterlife. They both were captivated by his synthetic vision.

In *L'Humanité* Leroux in fact says that man is "sensation-sentiment-knowledge indivisibly one" (p. 157). That Hecker would render *sensation* as "action" is odd and may reflect a popular translation-reinterpretation that made the three categories more distinct than does the original. It was not, however, the translation Brownson used in "Leroux on Humanity." There he rendered it "sensation."

25. For an amusing Jungian interpretation of these demons of Hecker's imagination see Robert Baer, "A Jungian Analysis of Isaac Hecker" in Farina, ed., *Hecker Studies* (New York: Paulist Press, 1983).

26. The May 9, 1843 letter to his family that he refers to contained some rather critical statements about Brownson's attempts to preach a Catholic-style Christianity without the Catholic church: "I confess that the sermon was wholly unsatisfactory to me. It was un-Catholic in its premises, and many of his arguments and facts were chimerical and illusive. If you grant that the Roman Catholic church is the true Church, there is, in my thought, no stopping-place short of its bosom. . . . I never shall join a Protestant church."

27. It is evident from the diary and the letters that Hecker's interest in Catholicism was more a product of his life in New York than it was a result of his associations at Brook Farm. At the opening of the diary, he is praying that God lead him into his "holy Church." Around the same time, while at Brownson's home in Chelsea, he is beginning to read "the Apostles of the Newness." As he says to his

mother, at times they make him laugh and at other times make him cry (Isaac Thomas Hecker, hereafter ITH, to Mother, December 24, 1844). The more he becomes familiar with the Transcendentalist writings, the more he has to take seriously their no-church philosophy. His struggle with it intensifies for the next twelve months.

28. Cf. note 13, above.

29. Lawrence McDonnell was the first to point out that this vision was probably inspired by the young man's reading of Richter (see Lawrence McDonnell, "Isaac Hecker, Man of Letters" [typewritten]). Consider the similarities between it and the scene in *Titan,* volume 1, cycle 7. Albano Cesara (Zesara), the young titan who is presented in the opening of the work visiting his father from whom he receives cryptic guidance in his search for his destiny, hears, as he walks near the water with a monk, a voice from heaven saying: "Love the beautiful one whom I will show thee—I will help thee." Looking about he sees "a female form, with long, chestnut-brown hair, and dark eyes, and a shining, swan-like neck . . . rise, like a noble Aphrodite, revealed down to her bosom, from out of the deepest waves."

30. Here is Hecker's version of the Transcendentalists' self-culture. Like Emerson he had a deep sense of what the Concord sage called "the sacredness of private integrity." He believed, as did Alcott, that it was in the "temple which the soul builds to herself" that his ultimate identity would be found, that his "I" would be established in the midst of a changing and perplexing world. Yet he lacked the ultimate commitment to the sufficiency of such self-culture that the pure Transcendentalists had. "Humanity *and* myself are first," he writes; the relation of his self to the whole of humanity was crucial. The "Me" in relation to the "Not-Me" was his starting point. For Emerson on self-culture, see C. Albanese, *Corresponding Motion* (Philadelphia: Temple University Press, 1977), pp. 121–22.

31. The June 5 entry marks the beginning of an eleven-day period of unusual perplexity for Hecker. It coincides, not without reason, with a movement toward the no-church philosophy that he had begun struggling with when leaving home. A May 30, 1843 letter home gives evidence of his dissatisfaction with all institutional religion. All sects "narrow and hamper" his sensitivities, he says. The Roman church also leaves him cold, he writes, because of "a want of genuine sympathy for the laboring and poorer classes." That perception of the ineffectiveness of existing religious structures resulted from a growing interest in more radical social experiments. It was at this time that he was seriously considering moving to Fruitlands. Also on May 30 after writing his letter he attended an Abolitionist meeting in Boston.

The intensity of the statements of anguish and doubt that dominate the next week and one-half of the diary should be set in the context of the far more sober and upbeat statements to his family during the same time. He writes to them on June 12: "One hates to be lost in perplexities or in ceaseless struggles. . . . What need is there of this waste of my own or others' time on the very simple experience of a young man in the year of our Lord 1843 named Hecker?" (Hecker to Family, May 30, 1843; June 12, 1843).

32. The short visit to Fruitlands that began on June 19 ended on the twenty-third and included a stopover on the way back to West Roxbury at the Shaker community in Harvard, Massachusetts. The brief stay had significant effects on Hecker. It got him interested more than ever in what we would call today alternative lifestyles. He also got a dose of the asceticism of the Fruitlanders and Shakers which he liked very much and which fed his enthusiastic disposition. He told his family the day he returned from Alcott's that he thought he would leave Brook Farm, for their life there "is not deep, holy, self-denying enough for, perhaps, me" (ITH to family, June 24, 1843). The more heavily he involved himself with those currents the more he found himself being swept away from old values—and with that, from old places and friends. That in turn caused more confusion, frustration, and soul-searching.

33. On Hecker's penchant for action in the spiritual life see *An American Experience of God,* pp. 52–55.

34. The advice that Hecker received was that he should get married and settle down (cf. John Hecker to Brownson, January 7, 1843). That council was particularly unappealing to him after recently visiting the celibate Shakers and the bane of Mrs. Alcott's existence: Charles Lane. Lane wrote an article for William Henry Channing's *The Present* in which he described marriage as the most selfish and unprogressive of institutions: "We must either serve the Universal (God) or the Individual (Mammon.) Both we cannot serve. Now, marriage, as at present constituted, is most decidedly an individual, and not a universal act. It is an individual act too, of a depreciated and selfish kind. The spouse is an expansion and enlargement of one's self, and the children participate of the same nature" ("The True Life," *The Present* 1 (March 1844): 315–16).

35. This quote is from book IV, chapter VIII, the final page. That section includes Carlyle's remarks on the Mammonism of the new industrial order: "But truly it is beautiful to see the brutish empire of Mammon cracking everywhere. . . . A strange chill, almost ghastly dayspring strikes up in Yankeeland itself: my Transcendentalist friends announce there, in a distinct, though somewhat lankhaired, ungainly manner, that the Demiurgus Dollar is dethroned. . . . " He then goes on to celebrate the triumph of the worker over the idle rich and the capitalist. The line after the one Hecker quotes reads: "Sooty Hell of mutiny and savagery and despair can by man's energy be made a kind of Heaven." Really then Carlyle is calling for Workers to arise and stop the dehumanizing progress of the Mammonists and free humanity from the soot and enslavement of the new industrial order. This is why Hecker launches into a reflection upon the need to reorganize Hecker Brothers Company after the Carlyle quote.

36. Is this another Richter-inspired fantasy? In volume 1, cycle 7, Albano Cesara meets a member of the order of St. Paul or *memento mori* (father of death) who tells him that his sister is about to die. This sounds plausible except for the fact that Hecker's sister Elizabeth was, in fact, soon to suffer an untimely death at the age of twenty-nine.

37. George Hecker, born in 1818, was the sibling closest to Isaac in age and in disposition. At the time of his visit he was reading the Oxford Tracts and

seriously considering Catholicism. He converted in 1845, approximately one year after Isaac.

38. The guiding spirits of the community were Bronson Alcott and Charles Lane. At the time they began the community, Alcott was forty-five and Lane was forty-three. For the last decade Alcott had been involved with his Temple School in Boston and with writing and musing. In 1842 he was invited by Lane and a group of English apostles of the Newness as preached by James P. Greaves to come to England to see the school that they had named in his honor. That trip led to an association with Lane. Lane was one of an unusual group of English reformers consisting of John Heraud, J. Westland Marston, Francis Barham, and the English Fourierist Godwyn Barmby. Its leader was James P. Greaves, whose *Affirmations* became a favorite in Transcendentalist periodicals like *The Present*. After Greaves's death, Lane became his literary executor. Lane was noted for his asceticism and his rigorous, radical application of principles. When Alcott returned from England in 1843, Lane came with him, bringing the cash for a new social experiment and Greaves's library on mysticism. Together they were easily the most transcendental of the Transcendentalists, which in fact accounted for their popularity among the younger members and visitors of Brook Farm.

Samuel Bower was an English reformer who was part of Lane's group and made the trip to America with him to start a community. Bower's great passion in life seemed to be to take his clothes off. After leaving Fruitlands, he told his friend Joseph Palmer of his plans: "I shall most assuredly, if the infinite Spirit will, make my home in the open heavens and resume the right so long in abeyance of being naturally and therefore sufficiently clothed." See Clara Endicott Sears, *Bronson Alcott's Fruitlands* (Boston: Houghton Mifflin, 1915), p. 142.

Sam Larned of Providence was only in his late teens at the time Hecker met him at Fruitlands. In Lindsay Swift's words: "He was given to all manner of ultra-isms," one of which was traveling throughout New England swearing at everyone he met in the belief that even profanity uttered in a pure spirit could be good. Another story tells that he refused to drink cow's milk in order not to oppress the animals and even considered giving up wearing leather shoes for the same reason. After the Newness got a bit old, he became a Unitarian minister in Mobile, where he married a slave-holding wife. Despite his new-found taste for a life of comfort, his earlier habits caught up with him when he died at age twenty-eight.

The other residents of Fruitlands were Abraham Everett, a cooper; Christopher Greene, a friend of Larned from Providence; Abram Wood, who for the sake of protest against conformity called himself Wood Abram; Anna Page, a teacher; and Joseph Palmer, a butcher from Fitchburg, renowned for his rebellious beard-wearing. See Anne Rose, *Transcendentalism as a Social Movement* [New Haven: Yale University Press, 1981], pp. 128–30.

39. In the entries of July 13 and 18 Hecker begins to evidence a new willingness to accept a nonmanipulative, passive view toward life in general and toward his own situation. This is a crucial development and can best be described as the birth of the contemplative in him. He proclaims in the July 13 entry, "Being is incomprehensible." Being: not merely his own situation, but the very stuff of the

universe. He was beginning to look with wonder on the mysterious side of life and to learn to revel in that gaze. With this came a new peace about his own state of undecidedness. There is no doubt that the influence of Fruitlands played the main role in the development of this new attitude. The tableside conversations on philosophy and religion left their mark, for there Alcott was at his best, musing about the Universal Love Spirit and the need for Harmony. Lane too excelled when it came to the cosmic, grand vision of life.

40. Between July 19 and 21 Hecker soured on Fruitlands. His earlier impressions, as conveyed to his family on July 13, are telling. He wrote then: "If these people are what they seem to be, they will be the means of bringing out and fixing that which has led me of late and been dimly foreshadowed in my speech and action." He had intended, as recently as the nineteenth, to stay at Fruitlands "until something further happens," and was assuring his brother John that his negative impressions of Alcott and Lane were wholly erroneous. From the reference Isaac makes to a letter that he received from John, it sounds as if John may have been worried that Alcott would try to fleece his younger brother (ITH to Family, July 19, 1843). Apparently that fear was born out when the celestial peddler tried to get a commitment out of the youngest member of a thriving New York business. Alcott was aware of the potential source of income for the thinly-financed social experiment and was anxious to see Hecker become a member, hoping that he would follow Lane's example of selflessness and contribute material assets to the cause. Hecker was put off by all this. He blurted out, at least to his diary, a list of his frustrations with the place, all of which were mainly complaints about Alcott, whom he perceived to be a rather lazy fellow anxious to live off of others. He also adopted Lane's complaint about Alcott's family getting in the way. Writing in the 1880s on the occasion of Alcott's death, Hecker said that Alcott had received him very kindly, "but from mixed and selfish motives." "I suspect," he continued, "he wanted me because he thought I would bring money to the Community" (in Sears, p. 84).

Hecker at that time also gave this assessment of why he left Fruitlands: "Their idea was human perfection. They set out to demonstrate what man can do in the way of the supremacy of the spiritual over the animal. All right, I said, I agree with you fully. I admire your asceticism; it is nothing new to me; I have practiced it a long time myself. If you can get the Everlasting out of my mind, I'm yours. But I know that I am going to live forever." Alcott, Hecker continued, then went to Lane and said: "Well, Hecker has flunked out. He hadn't the courage to persevere. He's a coward." But Lane said: "No; you're mistaken. Hecker is right. He wanted more
. than we had to give him" (Sears, p. 85, from Elliott).

41. Isaac wrote a letter expressing some of these concerns on July 19.

42. Barbara Welter's seminal article, "The Cult of True Womanhood," (*American Quarterly* [Summer 1966]: 151–74) pointed to three characteristics of the ideal antebellum American woman: piety, purity, and submission. Certainly Hecker's whole process of spiritual sensitization did in fact involve him in the acquisition of those three "feminine" traits. He was of course pious, that is, focused on religious questions. He had a great concern for purity, which his ascetic practices of fasting and abstinence, detachment from unprofitable social contacts, and reluc-

tance to work in commerce illustrate. In a letter written on August 14, 1843, he goes on at length about the different attributes of the sexes and suggests that he believes a true spiritual growth means combining in oneself both masculine and feminine traits. Thus he seems to have adopted that way of thinking, which was quite different from his attitude in the first fragment of the diary, written sometime before January 10, 1843, when he complained about his spiritual unrest as "unmanly despicable weakness of an effeminate nature." For more on conceptions of women in antebellum American religion, see Colleen McDannell, *The Christian Home in Victorian America, 1840–1900* (Bloomington, Ind.: Indiana University Press, 1986). For a discussion of "female manhood" and its relation to the New Thought movement, see Gail Thain Parker, *Mind Cure in New England* (Hanover, N.H.: University Press of New England, 1971), chapter 4.

43. Part of the problem Isaac faces is caused by the common experience of the adolescent who wishes to assert his independence but still wants to be loyal to a loving family. At this point the pull homeward is strong enough to move him, even though he still insists on holding on to his new sense of autonomy.

44. Hecker's devotion to the spirit was something that was present from the earliest pages of the diary. As this entry makes clear, the "spirit" for him is an amalgam of his own sense of self and his experience of God. The double nature of the symbol captures his commitment to his own development and integrity—the Me—and his effort to relate to others in the society—the Not-Me. God as Spirit is, for Hecker, part of both sides of the picture. He is both immanent and transcendent. See Joseph P. Chinnici, *Devotion to the Holy Ghost in American Catholicism* (New York: Paulist Press, *Sources of American Spirituality,* 1985); and my "Isaac Hecker and the Holy Spirit" (Ph.D. dissertation, Columbia University, New York, 1979).

His willingness to accept the Spirit's leadings as valid by this time is growing, as is his willingness to wait peacefully for God's help. He has embraced more fully than at anytime before the passive dimension of the spiritual life. He is content to commune with the Spirit within his soul and to trust God for assistance and light concerning the direction of his life.

Also notable is his remark that he was "never completely without the Spirit." This acknowledgment of the "small stream" having always run through his being stands in contrast to his later declarations made before his Redemptorist confessors in which he tried to down play his pre-Catholic experience. Nevertheless, it was that experience that put him in touch with fundamental theological issues and with the basic human needs and wants that factor into a religious experience. The apologetic that he was later to adopt as a Catholic missionary was based on the premise that, as St. Paul said, God "is not far from any one of us." Within the soul of every person are placed certain aspirations for divinity. Those along with the questions that the intellect asks us about the meaning of life can and must be explored and probed, if one is to come to a fuller experience of grace. He took Kant seriously and began with the subject's perceptions, but he would wish *not* to end there but in the synthesis of subjective religious feeling and objective truth, in the individual and the church. See Joseph Gower, "The New Apologetics of Isaac Thomas Hecker" (Ph.D. dissertation, University of Notre Dame, 1978).

45. Hecker's claim that he has learned much and has come into contact with the school of the mystics has a major significance in his own early development. As we have seen, it was while at Fruitlands that he learned to begin to walk in the contemplative way. The Fruitlands library was unquestionably the finest collection of mystical literature in Protestant New England during the 1840s. It contained works by Julian of Norwich, Bridget of Sweden, Michael de Molinos, Francis de Sales, Madame Guyon, François Fénelon, Thomas a Kempis, William Law, Henry More, and Emmanuel Swedenborg, to name some. Alcott and Lane were certainly the ones who, more than any of the other Transcendentalists with perhaps the exception of Thoreau, possessed a speculative, mystical spirituality that combined in the free-form New England fashion of the day the Platonic idealism made accessible by Thomas Taylor's 1833 English translations of Plato and Plotinus and popularized by Coleridge and Schilling, with ascetical practice. It was that combination of theory and practice that attracted Isaac to Fruitlands in the first place, and the failure of a rigorous and viable living out of that combination that disenchanted him. He was not content, as was an Emerson, to merely speak of these things and he lacked the literary skill to portray them artfully in a way that would satisfy him, though he was to try his hand at that with two apologetical works, *Questions of the Soul* (1855) and *Aspirations of Nature* (1857).

46. Metapsychosis refers to any interaction or influence between minds that happens without any physical medium. Interest in it was part of the fascination with occult, pseudoscientific subjects like phrenology and somnambulism. See note on somnambulism, below.

47. "Metamorphosis is another word for progress." This is a succinct statement of Hecker's view of progress—it is an inner transformation that has outward significance. This idea was not only at the heart of his theory of personal growth but also formed the basis for his views on social change. It must, he thought even in later years, begin inside the person and thoroughly transform him before it can change the society.

48. Hecker's anthropology was indeed optimistic, as was that of his Transcendentalist friends. The essential elements of it appear in this entry. Man is a spiritual being. This was an important point for one who had become so keenly aware of the tyranny of the material that threatened the real life of humanity in the new industrial age. Second, man participates in the process of revelation. He gives "utterance to God." More than that he does so "unconsciously." That signified that humanity by its very nature was bound up with the God-event. Its being in some sense was the being of God, its life, his life. Through its actions God was made manifest. Yet—and this is the third element of his anthropology—man is "an imprisoned God." As such he must struggle to realize his destiny; he must suffer to allow God to be manifest through him. For this reason, asceticism was acceptable, and even called for. It could train man to follow his higher passions and to contain the negative ones.

All of this he continued to believe as a Catholic. He would never accept the vision of a fallen humanity portrayed by Catholics like John Hughes. But, on the other hand, he would, as we shall see, come to understand the need for grace in the development of humanity.

49. The letter of July 31 from Isaac to John exudes with excitement over John's positive response to Isaac's big ideas. He tells John: "Family should be only another word for Concordia. . . . we will, with God's blessing, do our uttermost to bring about such a divine result." Such a restoration of the family would play a part in the grand scheme of societal renewal; it would be a light to "radiate in distance and brightness," just like Alcott thought Fruitlands would be. John, no doubt, was sincere in pledging to do all that he could to help his brother, and there is even some suggestion that he did improve the lot of their employees a bit. But largely, John was being sensitive to his brother's fragile sensitivities, which he did not want to wound. In the final analysis, he was far too practical a German-American businessman to embrace the quixotic. In a letter of August 20 to Brownson, John says that Isaac has somewhat of a mind to work again and is in good health, but he adds: "I think your Boston Transcendentalists have had too much influence on his mind, which I am in hopes will wear off."

50. Providence assumes an increasingly important role in his spirituality as he matures. Doubtless Providence and the related notion of destiny were favorite themes among the Romantics, as they had been with the Methodists who felt themselves raised up by God for the special purpose of spreading the doctrine of holiness and winning the United States to walk in the holiness of the Lord. By 1857, when he wrote his first book, the question Has man a destiny? had become the foundation of Hecker's apologetic. During the 1870s he wrote a preface to McMahn's English edition of J.P. de Caussade's *Abandonment to Divine Providence* and increasingly attempted to see the events of his day as fitting into a larger divine plan that he gave expression to in his most visionary piece, "An Exposition on the Needs of the Church and the Age" (1875).

51. This reflects the Romantic fascination with *Volksgeist,* the spirit of the people. Each society, it was thought, has a unique set of characteristics that distinguish it from the rest of humanity. The individual elements that made one society different from another were praised by the Romantics who looked to the infinite varieties of human experience as a symbol of its organic nature. Where the denizen of the Enlightenment stressed the universal laws that governed all of creation alike, the Romantic looked for the differences, the aberrations, the uniquely individual moments that spoke of boundless potential, change and development. The *Volksgeist* was the spirit that animated the whole of a people and was manifested in them in various ways.

While talk of national characteristics might strike many today as totally unscientific, it was, in fact, motivated by many of the developments in the science of biology during the nineteenth century. Forms of human life, from the family to a whole nation, were thought of in terms of the biological concept of organism. Human groups were treated as zoological objects, categorized and grouped according to their different characteristics and behaviors. As Hecker developed his ideas about racial and national characteristics he did so in a manner distinct from that of the deterministic social Darwinism of Spencer and Sumner that did not emerge until the 1870s.

52. Again there is no doubt that Hecker was influenced by Brownson in his ideas about providential men. In the May 1843 issue of the *Democratic Review*, Brownson offered an essay on "The Philosophy of History." In it he defined just what providential men are. They are those who come at long intervals of time and space and by their "superhuman virtue, intelligence, wisdom, love, and power of sacrifice, found systems and eras, redeem and advance their race" (in Henry Brownson, ed., *The Works of O. A. Brownson*. 4:399). Brownson in his discussion of the doctrine of providence was careful to insist that providential men were the result of special providence, but that there was a link between that and ordinary providence. In like manner, Hecker sees providential men as essentially exemplars of what ordinary men could be, were they to realize fully their godlike capacities.

53. The optimistic anthropology and the belief in providential men tie in closely with Hecker's faith in perfectibility. Humanity has a destiny to manifest God in his fulness. The world will be transformed by the spiritual transformation of humanity. Pefectibility, of course, was one of the great bywords of the age. The dawning of a new political-economic age brought with it the hope for a new, more perfect age that was expressed in religious terms by the millenarian Millerites or the Finneyites, or, in secular terms, by the St. Simonians and Fourierists, or even by the industrialists.

54. That Hecker should value the German mystic Jacob Boehme (1575–1624) above Reformers Martin Luther and John Calvin, Quakers George Fox and William Penn, and even Methodist founder John Wesley shows the influence of Alcott whose library was well stocked with Boehme's works and who was so impressed by Boehme that he once told Emerson that the German seer's works should be in the hands of anyone interested in the spiritual life (see Alcott's Journal, December 5, 1839, in Odell Shepherd, ed., *Journals of Bronson Alcott* [Boston: Little, Brown, 1938], p. 65).

55. John Frederick Denison Maurice (1805–1872) had published his most important book in 1837, just three years after his ordination by the Church of England. *The Kingdom of Christ* was written in the form of letters to a Quaker in which he critiques Protestantism as insufficient and defends a doctrine of the apostolic, catholic church, which he distinguishes from the Romish system.

Hecker refers to a long note in which Maurice discusses the ways in which human inspirations can join with the divine inspirations that are contained in the Scriptures and form a complementary whole. Cases in which this happened were Boehme, Fénelon, and Philo. What Hecker is objecting to is hard to tell. See F.D. Maurice, *The Kingdom of Christ*, volume 1, p. 305.

56. Charles Anderson Dana was born in New Hampshire in 1819, the same year as Hecker. He entered Harvard College in 1837, but poor health interrupted his studies and he was not awarded a degree until 1863, after he had become a renowned critic. At Brook Farm he taught Greek and German, which may be one of the reasons he was attracted to the German-speaking Hecker. They roomed together for a time and were fond of calling one another by German names. At West Roxbury, he was

known for his reserved, steady manner. After leaving Brook Farm he pursued a career in journalism, working as a correspondent for the *Herald Tribune* and later for the War Department covering the battles of the Civil War. His great fame, however, came from his efforts on behalf of the *New York Sun* which he wrote for from its inception in 1868 for nearly thirty years (see Sears, pp. 145–52).

William Bathchelder Greene (1819–1878) was the son of Nathaniel Greene of Haverill, Massachusetts, editor of the *Boston Statesman*. The early part of his life was spent in the army, where he served as a second lieutenant. In 1841 he left the army and began studies for the ministry which brought him to the Baptist Theological School at Newton and later to Harvard Divinity School, from which he was graduated in 1845. It was during this time that he visited Brook Farm and also met Brownson. He was a young disciple of Brownson's, but unlike his counterpart he did not follow his teacher's instructions so closely, never being seriously attracted to Brownson's Catholicism. In fact it was Brownson's social critique, articulated in his 1836 *New Views,* that attracted the wealthy young scion of a leading New England family that could trace its lineage back to the Revolutionary War hero, General Nathaniel Greene. Greene's own writings on social issues were insightful. In 1849 he published *Equality,* and in the same year a critique of the Newness entitled *Transcendentalism.* His later works included *the Sovereignty of the People* (1868) and *Socialistic, Communistic, Mutualistic, and Financial Fragments* (1875). In all likelihood Hecker met him through their mutual association with Brownson and Brook Farm (see *Transcendentalism* (1849) and *Equality* (1849), introduction by Martin Doudna [Delmar, NY: Scholar's Facsimiles and Reprints, 1981]).

57. The tenor of this conversation seems to have been set by William B. Greene. In his later writings, he was preoccupied with the the the problem of avoiding what he saw as the two great errors of the age: pantheism and materialism. Hegel he considered a pantheist. See Greene's *Transcendentalism* (West Brookfield, MA: Power Press of Oliver Cooke & Co., 1849).

58. This sounds a good deal like Emerson's appeal in his Divinity School Address to "become new-born bards of the Spirit." Despite the antipathy between the two men that grew up as soon as Hecker headed toward the Catholic church, Hecker was certainly well aware of the ideas of Transcendentalism's most famous spokesman.

59. John Sullivan Dwight (1813–1893) was one of the original members of Brook Farm who, along with Ripley, remained loyal to the experiment until the end. Dwight was a Harvard College and Divinity School graduate who after his graduation from the Divinity School in 1836 worked briefly as a Unitarian minister in Northampton. By 1841 he had decided to quit the ministry and give himself entirely to the Newness. At Brook Farm he made some worthwhile contributions as a translator of German literature, assisting Ripley in his *Specimens of German Literature* and writing poetry. Swift says that he was referred to as "the poet" more on account of his disposition than his literary production. Despite Hecker's prediction that his vocation was as a poet (see entry for June 5, 1844), he was to have the most impact as a music critic. His 1840 *Dial* essay, "The Religion of Beauty," and his piece on music in the *Aesthetic Papers* of Elizabeth Palmer Peabody played an important role

in the shaping of Transcendentalist aesthetic sensibilities. He more than any other
figure in New England was responsible for the growing popularity of Beethoven.
After the breakup of Brook Farm, he founded in 1851 *Dwight's Journal of Music,*
which he published for over thirty years.

60. Asceticism of the type Hecker describes here had become his habit by this
time. At Brook Farm meals were simple, yet most ate meat when it was available.
A few sat at a meatless Graham table. When Isaac came to Fruitlands he was in the
midst of those who shared his preference for self-denial. Alcott wrote in his diary
of his philosophy of eating: "I would abstain from the fruits of oppression and
blood, and am seeking means of entire independence. . . . Our wine is water, flesh,
bread—drugs, fruits. . . . This Beast named Man has yet most costly tastes, and
must first be transformed into a very Man, regenerate in appetite and desire, before
the earth shall be restored to fruitfulness, and redeemed from the curse of his cu-
pidity" (in Sears, p. 72).

This passage shows the development of Hecker's attitude toward asceticism.
It is aimed, as it has been from first appearance, at taming his negative desires in
order to free himself for growth toward perfection. What has come into clearer focus
by this time is that thing for which one frees one's self is, at least in part, contemplation. Purification enables one to "hear . . . the sweetest, the stillest sounds . . .
of angels." This stilling of the passions and calming of the soul to hear, in the inner
spirit, the small, still voice of God is basic to the contemplative experience. In the
passages that follow, Hecker shows that this practice of quieting his passions and
listening in stillness is yielding fruits. In what is one of the most lucid entries to
date, he speaks eloquently of the need to guard the senses in classical fashion. He
then moves spontaneously into a prayer for grace—no longer with the confessed
passion of some of the earlier cries for divine aid but with a calm sensibility, a certain gentle confidence. His longing is now focused on God. His pain is that of the
lover separated from his beloved. This is all much in keeping with the mystical experiences of many Western Christian writers. Certainly it is present in Julian of Norwich, whom he read at Fruitlands; but again it is more likely Boehme whose
Christocentric mysticism is reflected in Hecker's own emphasis on obedience to the
Father, on Jesus the Redeemer, and in the description of self-denial as "crucifixion."

61. The extent to which Hecker retained a Trinitarian conception of God and
a devotion to all three Persons of the Godhead is evident in this prayer. Even though
he was at this time in his most Transcendental period, the most intrigued by the no-
church philosophy and the belief in the perfectibility of man as he would ever be,
in the final analysis he was no radical Transcendentalist. He was too firmly set in
his belief in the necessity of the grace of God in Christ, a belief that he had grown
up with as the son of a fervent Methodist mother and had had reinforced by the
Oxford movement writings.

62. A belief that humanity contained both animal and divine capacities was
one that Hecker held since his earliest writings. Certainly William Ellery Channing
was one of the most eloquent prophets of man's "likeness to God" in New England
during the first half of the nineteenth century. It was a commitment to that reality

that was the basis for the Transcendentalist revolt against what Emerson so memorably called the ''corpse old'' Unitarianism of the day on the one hand, and the Orthodox Calvinism of the Synod of Dort on the other, as it still existed in Congregationalism, with the insistence on absolute depravity.

The attempts of thinkers like Auguste Comte to view humanity and the rest of creation in rationalistic terms were unacceptable to Hecker as were the proponents of the new biology who understood the origin of humanity in purely naturalistic terms, continuous with the rest of creation. Later in life, Hecker rejected Darwin's thesis in the 1859 *Origin of the Species* as nonsense. He was quite willing to embrace the concept of evolution if that meant the development of humanity's godlike capabilities. But Darwin's rejection of the Aristotelian doctrine of the uniqueness of man in creation was unacceptable.

63. The concept of a transcendent self reaches back in the history of Western mysticism to at least St. Augustine whose image of finding God by returning to the depths of one's true being became a classical type of the spiritual life. Hecker, of course, was moving toward this position via the manifold sources he encountered among New England Romantics. That this idea was part of Catholic tradition no doubt was one of the reasons why he could later feel comfortable with Catholic anthropology.

64. For a thorough analysis of the effects of his encounter with the Transcendentalists, see *An American Experience of God,* chapter 5.

65. George William Curtis (1824–1892) was at Brook Farm as a student with his brother Burrill from 1842 to 1843. He had come from his native Providence after failing to gain admission to Brown University. During his time at the Farm, he and his brother were among the most popular young men, known for their good looks and charming ways—''young Greek gods'' as Ida Russell called them. Judging from the many affectionate letters that passed between him and Isaac, it is clear that George and Burrill were, together with Charles Dana, Isaac's closest friends at West Roxbury. George left Brook Farm shortly after Hecker did and went with his brother to Concord where they worked on a farm and pursued their literary interests through associations with Emerson, Bradford, and Thoreau. In later life George became a founder of *Putnam's Monthly* and developed a successful career as an editor and columnist in New York. See George Milne, *George William Curtis and the Genteel Tradition* (Bloomington: Indiana University Press, 1956).

66. The kind of musical frolics that Hecker recounts here were common at Brook Farm as was the effort to blend art forms. Synaesthesia, as it was called, captured the interest in color-hearing and tone-painting that Romantics like A. W. Schlegel and Louis-Bertrand Castel delighted in. The popularity of Platonic philosophy, with its emphasis on the relation among pure ideas, tones, and numbers, played a role in the development of synaesthesia. See Charmenz S. Lenhart, *Musical Influence on American Poetry* (Athens, GA: University of Georgia Press, 1956), pp. 84–124.

67. George Ripley (1801–1880) founded Brook Farm in 1841. A graduate of Harvard College and Divinity School, he had had a successful career as a pastor of the Boston Unitarian Purchase Street Church for fifteen years before moving to West

Roxbury. During that time, he had been at the center of Boston intellectual life, contributing frequently to the *Christian Register* and the *Christian Examiner*. A founder of the Transcendentalist Club, his debates with Andrews Norton on the subject of miracles set the scene for the rise of the Transcendentalist movement in New England. During his time at Brook Farm he was greatly affected by the need for Associationist remedies to the problems of social reform. He became one of the leading advocates of Fourierism after 1843 and turned the *Harbinger* into the foremost Fourierist journal of its time. After the demise of the movement in the late forties, he went to New York where he began at age forty-five a career as a literary critic that eventually lifted him out of poverty and won him wealth and fame through his contributions to the *New York Tribune*.

68. George and Burrill Curtis were in very much the same situation that Isaac was in having recently gone home after a period of study at Brook Farm. In a letter written to Hecker on August 18, George Curtis complains to him: " . . . there is scarcely a person whom I care to see. No heroism, no beauty has yet made me bow." Hecker's letters to George Curtis and to Almira Barlow referred to here are not extant.

69. Around this time brother John, the most politically active of the Heckers, was getting involved in the candidacy of John C. Calhoun. John was organizing the wards in New York and invited Brownson to come to town to give a speech in Calhoun's support. Brownson, of course, was a great admirer of Calhoun and was deeply troubled by his subsequent defeat in the 1844 election. See John Hecker to Brownson, August 20, 1843, and ITH to Brownson, September 6, 1843.

The entry also shows that Isaac's interest in Methodism had not entirely waned, though when put in context it appears that his visit was more of a social call to see old friends than it was a mission of the earnest seeker.

70. Edward Palmer (1802–1886) was one of the shrillest critics of the current social and economic order in New England of the 1840s. Born in Belfast, Maine, he was well known by the prophets of the Newness, including Emerson, who admired the steadfastness with which he lived out his principles. His convictions about the evil nature of money led him to refuse its use, a policy that gained him no little notoriety in his travels throughout the region. By the time Hecker met him, he had already authored two major books, *An Address on the Origin and Evil Influences of Money* (Boston, 1839) and *A Letter to Those Who Think* (Worcester, 1840).

In fact he and Hecker never did come any nearer. Palmer met him at his most radical moment. Although he would find in the concept of voluntary poverty a remedy to the evils of Mammonism, Hecker as a Catholic never developed any serious critique of the economic system, the makings of which were clearly present at this time.

71. In this passage Hecker's use of terms like "holy quiet" and "peaceful stillness" are reminiscent of the Quietist tradition, and in all likelihood derive from it, since, as we shall learn in the entry from September 16, 1843, he was familiar with it.

72. Bernard Rosenthal in *City of Nature* (Newark: University of Delaware, 1980) argues that a common idea of nature held by Americans during this time

viewed nature as participating in a teleological process shaped in part by man and culminating in civilization. Nature connoted not the values of a wild, unordered realm, but of civilization. The journey into nature then was a journey to the city. For the Romantics that journey was an inner one, a journey to a spiritual city. In the eyes of some nature represented a commodity being transformed into civilization; for others it became the metaphor for a new spiritual mythology (pp. 44–45).

Clearly for Hecker the journey into nature was a spiritual one to a place of enlightenment, peace, and stillness. If these are considered values of civilization, then the Rosenthal thesis applies. Yet there was one sense in which the journey within, inspired by nature as it often was, was anything but a journey to the values of civilization. In fact it was in the case of Hecker often a movement away from the disorder of the civilization that surrounded him to a transcendent realm of eternal order, a move beyond the world of changing forms to the unchanging essence. I would argue further that such a use of nature was not unique to Hecker but was in fact shared by others, certainly by Thoreau.

73. We know little of J. W. Vethake. The State of New York Census lists him as a resident of New York in 1830, and 1840, but not in 1850. He corresponded with Hecker and was fond of developing long lists of correspondences that related masculine and feminine traits. Hecker's view is more in keeping with his earlier statement that man requires the "birth of the feminine in him" than it is with Vethake's view.

74. Antonia Bourignon was born in Lisle, France, in 1616. A Catholic, she grew up with strong religious leanings. After a series of mystical experiences as a young woman, she became an advocate of prophetic spiritual reform through reliance on the direct action of the Holy Spirit on the soul. She denounced both the infidelity of Rome and the waywardness of Protestantism and proclaimed a pure revelation of the heart of the Gospel, based on her mystical experiences.

Her major work, *The Light of the World: A Most True Revelation of a Pilgrimess, M. Antonia Bourignon, Travelling towards Eternity,* was first published in French in 1679, the year Hecker gives. The first English translation was completed in London in 1696. Its appeal to the Spirit's inner workings, its advocacy of true Christianity free from sectarianism, and its emphasis on radical discipleship all appealed to Hecker. Her ideas on the sexes are very much a sidelight, but he, nevertheless, was fascinated by them, because they reinforced his own idea of spiritual androgyny.

75. There are no extant letters by Hecker between August 1 and 30.

76. During the period covered by the diary, Hecker was a devoted vegetarian even before visiting Fruitlands. Certainly his abstinence from meat got a boost when he visited Fruitlands later in the year in July. Fruitlands, as the name implies, had as one of its basic tenets the avoidance of all animal products. Abstinence from flesh foods also was in vogue among many of his new associates who were not part of Alcott's commune. Thoreau, at least during his Walden period, was a vegetarian, as was Associationist and publisher Horace Greeley.

The vegetarian movement took impetus from the fact that many of the literary inspirations of the Newness were vegetarians. The Neo-Platonists had advocated a fleshless diet, as did the Hindu Brahmins. In Hecker's own time, Dr. William Alcott, cousin of Bronson, was a leader in the American vegetarian movement as was the creator of Granola, Dr. James Caleb Jackson of New York City, who appears to be the "Caleb" Hecker refers to as a family friend. Jackson, interestingly enough, founded in 1858 a "health sanitarium" in Dansville, New York, which Hecker frequented during the 1880s when he was enfeebled by chronic leukemia.

The best-known proponent of vegetarianism in the antebellum period was Sylvester Graham whose insistence on abstinence from flesh food was linked to a comprehensive program for the reform of the American diet and for healthful ways of living. Indeed Graham, like many vegetarians, was a friend of universal reform and saw dietary reform as part of a larger program. See Gerald Carson, *Cornflakes Crusade* (New York, 1957); Richard H. Shyrock "Sylvester Graham and the Popular Health Movement," *Mississippi Valley Historical Review* 28 (December 1931): 172–84, and Russell Blaine Nye, *Society and Culture in America* (New York: Harper and Row, 1974), pp. 350–53.

77. Their sensibility to the oppression of workers and slaves was part of the Brook Farm's, and even more, the Fruitland's environment. See George M. Fredrickson, *The Inner Civil War: Northern Intellectuals and the Crisis of the Union* (New York: Harper and Row, 1965).

78. The ambivalence that he feels about the prospect of leaving the city for an idyllic life at an agrarian reform community of his own creation is both an indication of the fanciful, unrealistic nature of his notion of forming such a community and of his own quite real affections for the city. When in 1857 he was offered the opportunity to locate the Paulist community in New York or the Ohio frontier, he chose New York, even though it meant compromising his desire not to involve the new group with parish work. See my essay in *Hecker Studies* (New York: Paulist Press, 1983).

79. The one letter is from Charles Dana and tells of the big news at Brook Farm since Hecker's departure—the coming of Albert Brisbane and Ripley's enthusiasm for Fourier. The other letter is from Almira Barlow and like many of the traces of the Brookline beauty in Hecker's life, it is not extant. It is, however, another indication that his affection for her did not end with the angelic dream vision of chastity, as Elliott and Holden suggest.

80. Cf. note 15.

81. Hecker records meeting Margaret Fuller on September 13, 1843 (see note for that date, below). Whether or not he met her sooner is not known, but he would have been sympathetic to some of her ideas. Equality of women as preached by Fuller was seen in the broader context of the equality of all human beings as free and creative. The relation of it to the spiritual questions that exercised the minds of the Transcendentalists was obvious: Men and women were of equal value because they had been created by God and endowed with a godlike capacity. At this time, he favored an androgynous view of human nature stressing the presence of masculine and feminine elements in each person. This did not mean that he wished to obliterate all distinctions between the sexes or to disassociate certain personality traits which eliminate gender considerations. He often talked, for instance, of the

need for "manly" action and "feminine" sensitivity, even though such action and sensitivity might be part of a given individual's personality.

82. Hecker's statement that he had seen "Prometheus Bound" is curious. Prometheus was the subject of numerous works of sculpture during the 1800s, such as those by John Quincy Adams Ward, Horatio Greenhough, and Robert Palmer. Yet an intensive search of the *Index of American Sculpture* at the University of Delaware, as well as a search of the indexes at the Archive of American Art at the Smithsonian in Washington, revealed no mention of any piece of sculpture entitled "Prometheus Bound." It was then a sketch of a painting that he saw. Americans of the 1840s had little choice but to look in sketch books for works of fine art, since the first public gallery did not open until 1852 in Philadelphia. (I am indebted to Dr. James Hartsoe of the National Gallery of Art and the University of Maryland for the research for this note.)

83. "The Black Domino" (*Le domino noir*) was an 1837 opera by Daniel François-Esprit Auber (1782–1871), the foremost representative of the *opéras comiques* in nineteenth-century France. The production had been playing in New York since July.

84. In this passage Hecker expresses—in language that is not dissimilar to his mature expression—his ideas on Providence, the value of the individual, and the place of self-denial. These were to become frequently repeated themes of the Catholic missionary. Cf. Hecker's musings as a Paulist, "Notes on the Spiritual Life," n.d., PFA.

85. It is not surprising to learn from the next entry that Alcott and Lane were with ITH on the day of this entry. The emphasis on the Spirit and the identification of the Spirit with love is a theme that Alcott liked to stress. The emphasis on the mnemonic method of education was responsible for Alcott's most successful moments as headmaster of his Temple School in Boston. His work gained him the accolade, bestowed by admirers like Lane, "the American Pestalozzi."

86. From September 9–13 Hecker hosted Alcott and Lane in the family home. During those days they spent their time visiting some of the friends of the Newness that were in the city including Thoreau and William Henry Channing. Channing was then editing the magazine *The Present,* which was just commencing publication. In a stimulating, effusive style he proclaimed the purpose of his enterprise, "to teach that all earnest seekers of holiness, truth, humanity, are co-laborers, under the leading of one heavenly hand, and that our Nation has a plain and urgent duty in common with the Grand Fraternity of Christendom, to advance the Reign of Heaven on Earth." Channing blended a keen theological mind with a burning sense of the need for social reform and a dedication to the theories of Fourier. That combination made *The Present,* like Ripley's *Harbinger,* a skillful blend of religious and secular reform sentiments. Channing (1810–1884) was the nephew of William Ellery Channing and was greatly influenced by and dedicated to him. He had a rich background that included Harvard College and Divinity School and extensive travel in Europe and the American West. He was one of the most skilled and vocal advocates of reform that antebellum America knew. He had a great sympathy for Catholicism and in fact came close to converting. Hecker told Brownson after visiting him that

Channing's heart was Catholic, but his head, unfortunately, was still Protestant (see *The Present* 1 (September 1843):1, and ITH to Brownson, September 6, 1843).

Margaret Fuller (1810–1850) with her prodigious linguistic and literary skills had become a player in the Transcendental circle through her editing of the *Dial* from 1839–41. When Hecker saw her she was in New York working for Horace Greeley and his *New York Tribune* as a literary critic. In September she was in the final stages of work on her most important book, *Woman in the Nineteenth Century,* a milestone in the women's rights movement. She was soon to journey to Italy where she became the wife of an Italian count, Giovanni Ossoli. Together they labored in vain in the cause of the Roman Revolution of 1847.

The Mrs. Green Hecker lists may in fact have been Mrs. William B. Greene whose husband was greatly involved in the Newness at this time. See note 56.

87. It is interesting to note that in the Byzantine mystical tradition, especially in the writings of Symeon the New Theologian, the "gift of tears" is presented as a grace that God gives to the enlightened to help them "clean the house of the soul" through true contrition. Later in the diary, Hecker becomes, if he is not yet, aware of the concept of the gift of tears and seems to assume that it applies to him. Certainly his feeling like crying that he reported on September 15 was not simple melancholia. That becomes clear from a glance at his correspondence from that time which is animated and much concerned with external events. Also he has just had a very stimulating few days with his Transcendentalist friends during which they had a number of discussions on social reform. It is likely that those discussions centered him more on the need for social reform and human salvation. That kind of experience of the need for redemption that grows out of a keen sense of what is wrong with the world and burns for the more perfect is at the heart of what Symeon meant by the gift of tears. See *The Discourses* in *Symeon the New Theologian: Selected Writings* (New York: Paulist Press, 1980), pp. 80 f.

88. Hecker's use of the term "Quietism" is curious (cf. May 28, 1843 entry, below, and note 71, above). He most likely acquired it through his contact with the Fruitlands mystics, especially Lane and Bower. Of course, the Fruitlands library had no shortage of Quietist literature. Molinos' *Spiritual Guide* in the 1789 Dublin edition was present as were six works by or on Madame Guyon and six by Fénelon. There is little doubt that Hecker uses the term Quietism loosely and does not attempt, even during one of his musing moments, to portray himself as the disciple of a true Quietist like Molinos or even to pose as a follower of the far more popular Fénelon. What appeals to Hecker are two notions that were in fact part of the Quietist legacy. The first is the notion of stillness. The response to the inner sanctuary where in quiet his soul contemplates the Beloved is very appealing to Hecker and emerges only after his visit to Fruitlands. But it is not accompanied by a claim that such contemplation is unbroken and nor was there an attempt to remove all mental images on which meditation and contemplation may be based. Whereas the Quietist Malaval attempted to disregard the humanity of Christ as a distraction, Hecker was committed to an optimistic anthropology that rejoiced in perfecting human nature. His meditation never becomes very abstract.

The second notion that attracted Hecker to Quietism was its emphasis on selflessness. The new industrial society, epitomized by the town of Lynn, was, in the eyes of the reformers, a symbol of human greed and selfishness. Unselfishness, sharing of one's life and resources in community, was the way to unity, harmony, and love. Hence there was the appeal of the Quietists' emphasis on selflessness. But the true Quietist took the notion of abnegation of the self to another extreme. The soul should require no consolations, have no care for perfect happiness, and despise any reflection on self as an infidelity to grace. As a result, acts of virtue were downplayed as unnecessary. In the extreme, such a view was taken to mean that the soul resting in perfect quiet could commit no sin, even though performing acts that might be considered sinful. Although one might pick up an echo of this in the practices of Sam Larned who went around swearing at people in the belief that even an impure act when done with a pure motive is good, the Fruitlanders, and Hecker included, were far too moralistic to ever have been real Quietists. They were deeply concerned with social reform and committed to action—personal and communal—to remedy the evils they saw around them. In the final analysis, they were activists.

All this becomes interesting in the case of Hecker because Charles Maignen in his infamous critique, *Père Hecker, Est-il un Saint,* suggests rather strongly that Hecker was tainted by Quietism and Illuminism. He supports his accusations with quotes from the diary that he took from Elliott's *Life of Father Hecker.* See "Uses of the Diary" in the general introduction.

89. See note 76 and entry for December 6, 1843.

90. See note 2.

91. This passage appears as a kind of relief from what in the previous few entries came close to being too great an emphasis on passivity. That we should be relieved to find such a balanced statement on the need for active as well as passive virtues is ironic if we take into account the warning made by Leo XIII in *Testem Benevolentiae* against the doctrines associated with Hecker known as Americanism. According to the pope, that teaching put too much value on "active" virtues. Were the mystical dimensions of his life known better, no one would associate Hecker with a neglect of the "passive virtues," unless of course one means only obedience. See Chinnici, chapter 5, and Portier, in *Hecker Studies.*

92. In this entry Hecker has again attempted to efface all traces of his affection for Almira. The name has been crossed out and the feminine third person pronouns have been changed to masculine! This manipulation of the text shows again that Hecker was ambivalent about leaving a record of their affection and that that affection had not simply died out after his angelic vision. See entry for October 18, in which he tries to respond to her letter.

93. The offending letter opens: "Your letters, so sincere and hearty, are precious, like these significant gusts of Autumn wind that indicate strong stirring life at the centre of things. Yet they are not free from the wail of these Fall Tempests—but breathe a despair, almost—let me not say quite. What are these fearful messengers . . . ? Why seems the hope for men almost hopeless, because neither Church—not Society hang out any beacon of Success? In the man, where the seed is sown, let us look for the harvest" (October 8, 1843). He proceeds to give him a good course in self-reliance.

94. This diagram shows Hecker's conception of the essential relationship among personal, social, and political reforms. It also illustrates the central place of religion, and specifically Catholicism, within the reform process. This view contributed to his conversion to Catholicism. This was to become one of his favorite themes as a Catholic. He judged that without a true religion, there could be no true social or political reform. Helped by Brownson, who had already established the need for the Church in the reform process, he was ready to affirm this himself and hold it throughout his life. Cf. his unpublished "last word to the public," "God and Man," PFA.

95. William Macready was a well-known British Shakespearean actor who thrilled large American audiences in the 1840s.

96. Apparently Macready's stirring rendition of Hamlet had quite an effect on Isaac, who takes the play's most memorable lines as the basis for this meditation. As Ninian Smart observed, "Brahman" was described so differently by various interpreters in the later vedantic tradition, it in effect becomes a number of different concepts with varying theologies. It appears, nevertheless, that Hecker is using the term for the Absolute in the sense of the unconditional (asankhata), the not born (ajatam), the not-become (abhutam), the not-made (akatam) as the goal of life as it is defined in Poli Buddhism. It is highly unlikely that he was aware of any such nuances; he only had picked up a superficial knowledge of the doctrine of Brahmin from readings in the *Dial* and conversations with Alcott. See Arthur Christy, *The Orient in American Transcendentalism* (New York: Octagon, 1963) and L. Goren, *Elements of Brahmanism in Emerson* (Hartford, CT: Transcendental Books, 1977).

97. On the religious dimensions of the Transcendentalists' notion of self-culture see Catherine Albanese, *Corresponding Motion* (Philadelphia: Temple University Press, 1977).

98. See note 110.

99. This strong, clear declaration of his devotion to Christ as Redeemer makes apparent how he, even in the midst of his fascination with the Newness, was struggling more with the question of which church, if any, should he join than with Christological questions. Christ was seen as model of a new creation—fully God and fully man, the synthesis of human and divine. The picture of Christ as suffering, persecuted, victorious savior that appears in Martin John Spalding and that was a cornerstone of the immigrant church is very different.

100. Sophia Willard Dana of Cambridge married George Ripley in 1827. She was, as Hecker sensed, close to him in that she shared his convictions about the church. Before her untimely death in 1861, she became a Catholic and translated the *Vita e Dottrina* of St. Catherine of Genoa, a book that Hecker was to publish through his Catholic Publication Society in the 1870s. See "Converts" in general introduction.

101. This paragraph is quoted by Maignen in *Père Hecker* to bolster his case that Hecker was an imbalanced enthusiast. The indivisible beings Hecker refers to in this context are most likely folks like Mrs. Ripley and William Henry Channing. Had Maignen known the context of the quote that he took from El-

liott's *Life of Father Hecker,* he probably would have been even more certain of Hecker's alleged heretical ways! See general introduction, "Uses of the Diary."

102. The Laocoön referred to here must be the ancient Hellenistic sculpture of the priest Laocoön and his sons as they are about to be killed by the serpents that hold them entwined. The piece was popular among the Romantics. Gotthold Ephraim Lessing used it in his famous discussion of aesthetic theory, *Laokoön: oder über die Grenzen der Malerei und Poesie* (1766). For information on Prometheus, see note 82.

103. Benjamin Isaac Haight (1809–1879) was the rector of All Saints' Church in New York. A graduate of Columbia College and General Theological Seminary, he was a professor of pastoral theology at General when Hecker met him. He was a moderate Puseyite who authored eight books, one of which was an explanation of the Arthur Carey affair. See *A Letter to a Parishioner, relative to the recent ordination of Mr. Arthur Carey* (New York: 1843). See note 167.

104. The comparison between Catholics and Quakers was based on Moehler's discussion in book 2, chapter 2 of *Symbolism.* Also Maurice's *Kingdom of Christ,* which Hecker also read, deals specifically with a comparison between Quakerism and Catholicism.

105. We see that Hecker's interest in the church question begins to accelerate in this section of the diary. The visit of Alcott and Lane—the Fruitlands mystics and symbols of the no-church reform position—put the great symbols of the reform-without-the-church party in juxtaposition with the symbols that had piqued his interest in the Oxford movement in New York. The contrast was fruitful and elicited in him a decision to move toward the church. He told Brownson in an October 15 letter of his relationship with the Transcendentalists: "It was necessary to have this susceptibility to their influence to be able to understand and appreciate their movement and spirit. I have gained in the period I was from New York a very fruitful experience. Underlying, and of infinite more importance, seems to me the Church movement than their personal, social and political reform, it being the soul centre of all life. . . . "

Of course Brownson himself was moving quickly toward the church at this time. On October 3, he wrote to Hecker declining a chance to edit a pro-Calhoun political newspaper in New York. Isaac was brokering an arrangement with Brownson on behalf of the New York Calhoun party, with which he and his brothers were heavily involved at the time. In November, he expressed his position on Christ clearly to Hecker. He criticized the Transcendental reformers, in this case William Henry Channing, as men of the highest principles and abilities who, nevertheless, did not believe in the Mediator and hence looked only to human resources to produce reform. But Brownson, who before had tried to establish his own universal reform society, had come to the conviction: "No man can be a reformer."

Hecker himself had always believed this, but now his realization of that belief became clearer. He wrote to Brownson on December 14: "The necessity for a medium through which the spirit can act—that man as man can be no reformer, and that the church is the only institution which has for its object the bettering of men's

souls, by giving to them a diviner love . . . are clear and important truths to me.''
Yet for both Brownson and Hecker the question of which church to join was still up
for grabs. Brownson on November 8 tended to think that the Episcopal church was
the most acceptable. But by January, when he wrote the first number of the *Brown-*
son Quarterly Review, he denied the claims of the Anglican church and argued for
a universal Catholicism that would gather together all denominations.

106. How literally can we take a statement like this? The accounts of Hecker
that others offered tend not to support a literal interpretation. He may have been
agonizing inside, but externally he maintained an ability to affect people as an af-
fable, energetic young man, sensitive, but not crippled by his sensitivity, and by no
means morbid.

107. This most likely was his maternal grandfather, Frederick Friend, who
lived in New York on Hester Street.

108. Hecker's instincts here, as in the entry of November 1, 1843, are Trinitarian and orthodox. His ecstasy is centered on Christ, the loving kindness of God.
He is both Brother and Redeemer, whose sacrifice should win the hardest of human
hearts and fill it with gratitude. The Spirit is the Spirit of Jesus, in which he longs
to be baptized. Fittingly the rapture ends with an invocation of the Father. The tone
and style of the meditation reflect a Romantic stress on sentiment. Christ's sacrifice
is viewed as full of morally persuasive value. That, more than a juridical view of
the Atonement, is the controlling orientation.

109. The man really had a way with numbers! Yet again, he is off by one year,
having been born in 1819. Perhaps this is the real reason why Isaac wanted to stop
keeping accounts among the partners in the family business.

110. This passage gives us another insight into Hecker's practice of prayer at
this time. His specific mention of a state of stillness, beyond reading, even beyond
speech itself, which was rich and constantly attractive, the source of continuing ed-
ification and enlightenment, indicates that he was in fact in the contemplative way
at this time. He struggles, however, to balance the demands of active life with his
own *attrait*. At the same time that he develops his contemplative powers he retains
an interest in politics as his efforts on behalf of Calhoun and Dorr indicate.

111. It is interesting to try to fit Hecker's notion of union into the larger Western Christian mystical tradition. One way of understanding the various approaches
to the question of union that existed between the twelfth and sixteenth centuries has
been suggested by Bernard McGinn. He notes that two views about the nature of
union with God were prevalent during that era. The first was well expressed in the
doctrines of Bernard of Clairvaux, the Victorines, and at the end of the era by John
of the Cross. Bernard was the first major figure in the West to present a clear notion
of union as the basic category for the description of the immediate experience of
God. His doctrine essentially follows that of Paul in 1 Corinthians 6:17: ''He who
is joined to the Lord is one spirit (*unus spiritus*) with him.'' It is a union of the wills
in love. The second conceptualization of union is best represented by Meister Eckhart. In his view union between the person and God is a unity without distinction
(*unitas indistinctionis*) in which the soul dwells with God in the ground of its being,
beyond all distinctions, ''the quiet desert into which distinction never gazed, not the

Father, nor the Son, nor the Holy Spirit'' (Bernard McGinn, *Meister Eckhart, The Essential Sermons* [New York: Paulist Press, 1981], p. 48). Another distinction may be made on the basis of how the relation of the goal of mystical union to the lower stages of human knowing is defined. It is here that the respective roles of love and knowledge are set forth in distinct ways by various mystics. Three tendencies are present. The first, expressed in the *unus spiritus* doctrine of union as defined in the classic Cisterian and Victorine theory and also later by John of the Cross, stresses the continuous, dynamic activity by which Divine Love subsumes all human activities under a transcendent union in which loving and knowing God are essentially one. A second, represented in the *Cloud of Unknowing,* placed a clear dividing line between knowing and loving, emphasizing the efficacy of love alone in piercing through to union. The third, as seen in Eckhart, claimed that all knowledge and love were negated in the union without distinction (Bernard McGinn, ''Love, Knowledge, and Mystical Union in Western Christianity: Twelfth to Sixteenth Centuries, ''*Church History* 56 [March 1987]: 7–24).

In the first volume of the diary there are passages that in the models suggested by McGinn would be union without distinction. For example, he writes on August 13, 1843 ''When the spirit begets us we are no more. The Spirit is all, and there is nothing else.''

We know that in fact Hecker read Eckhart and mentions briefly his reading in a letter to Brownson, simply listing Eckhart's name with no comment or indication of what exactly he was reading. The Fruitlands library contained books by Eckhart.

But there is another relation, crucial to both the Western tradition and the thought of Hecker, which is not included in the discussion of longing and knowing, namely the role of seeing. In the Johannine corpus this is clearly put forth: ''We shall be like him, for we shall see him as he is'' (1 Jn 3:2). The other source for this mysticism of seeing is the Neo-Platonic tradition, of which we have said much in the introduction, but which is certainly relevant here. Through the Alcott-Lane-Fruitlands connection Hecker would have received a good dose of Neo-Platonic mystical theories, as he would also from reading the works of Emerson. In that tradition, especially as represented by Platonism, union between the soul and the infinite fountain of Goodness is a union in which there is a sharing of substances between the soul and the Good; but certainly it is not one which is beyond knowing. Rather it is described as an experience of enlightenment of the intellect in which it comes to realize its essential nature to be redolent with Goodness. In glimpsing itself in a pure and unclouded fashion it in effect sees the Absolute. When that moment of enlightenment occurs, that vision itself transforms the person.

There are a number of entries in the diary that approach this. As he grows in his conviction of Catholic truth, he becomes more sure that the Transcendentalist doctrine, best summed up by Emerson's transparent eyeball, is too facile in assuming that the union between God and the soul can merely be recalled as easily as Emerson suggests, merely by ''looking up.'' Grace, the grace of Christ as it finds its fullness in the ministry of the Church, is the ultimate means of assistance for humanity on its journey back to unity with its Creator. Yet even while insisting this and developing a notion of unity that stressed the intermediary role of the spirit in a way that more closely resembles *unus spiritus* than *unitas indistinctionis,* he continued to stress the role of sight. Consider the passage from December 14, 1844: "Lord let me see more of thee. Open thou more of my vision. . . . Thy beauty, thy loveliness oh God is beyond our finite vision far above our expression and Lord all I can utter is, help my weakness." All the essential elements are here: his stress on seeing, his linking of union of God with an experience of beauty, and his expression of the need for grace.

It is the linking of union with an experience of beauty that is particularly intriguing. He did much to develop this mystical aesthetic, if you will, and much of that comes out in his series of letters with George Curtis of Brook Farm. The extended discussion of the nature of genius is the heart of the exchange. Curtis wishes to, in more traditional Transcendentalist fashion, claim that the genius is the larger category under which religion is best placed, along with painting, literature, music, philosophy, etc. Hecker rejects this and argues that the essence of genius is the inspiration of the Holy Spirit. In an entry for June 6, 1844, he says: "The genius in every work of art is religious"; and earlier in the same entry he wrote: "Art will reproduce itself so soon as Men are unioned with the great artists." Like Curtis he believed that genius was universal and could display itself in the work of a painter, a saint, or a merchant, but the source was always God. Holiness was presented as the essence of this inspiration, as both an attribute of God and of the purified soul. But again it was the vision of the holy to which the enlightened were privileged. As he wrote on July 22, 1844: "The good, the true, and the beautiful are worshipped in mystic unity under the form of the HOLY in the Catholic religion, in the *a priori* synthetic intuition of faith which is a more elevated and purer mode of activity of the faculty of Reason."

112. This is another perplexing dating. Thanksgiving Day was November 30, 1843; his birthday was December 19. Perhaps he does not mean the holiday of Thanksgiving, but merely a day of thanksgiving. But how could he continue to write the wrong date for his birthday?

113. Georgia is Georgiana Bruce, later Kirby, an English immigrant, born in 1818. She was of rather humble means and originally came to Brook Farm as a worker-pupil. Her book, *Years of Experience,* is an autobiographical memoir that contains many interesting anecdotes on Brook Farm life. In that work she mentions that Mrs. Hecker invited her to spend a month at her home in New York, without noting the date of the invitation (p. 183). She did in fact make a prolonged visit to the Hecker household, after having been driven out of Brook Farm early in 1844 (see Hecker to Brownson, March 9, 1844).

Orson Smith Murray was born in 1806 in Vermont. He was a Scotch-Irish Baptist who was one of the most vigorous reformers of the 1840s. He was a strong supporter of the Abolitionist movement, having secured the passage in Vermont of what was the first resolution by a state government against the slave trade. When Hecker saw him in 1843, he was in New York starting a weekly journal, *The Regenerator.* In that publication he advocated Owenite communitarianism, vegetarianism, abstinence, and women's rights.

114. Actually he spent eight months at Brook Farm, counting the two weeks-plus he was at Fruitlands.

115. Hecker here seems to be mimicking Alcott's views on Christ and Epicurus. In the light of what precedes (see notes 99 and 108), it must be judged as little more than that—certainly it is no serious departure from his earlier Christology.

116. Johann Wolfgang von Goethe (1749–1832) published *Die Leiden des jungen Werthers* in 1774. It quickly became popular all throughout Europe and was one of the principle works of the *Sturm und Drang* movement. Goethe's story mimics reality in its depiction of a young man whose despair over the realization that he can never consummate his love for a betrothed woman drives him to suicide. The novella took its inspiration from Goethe's infatuation with the fiancée of a friend and the widely reported suicide of a young German jilted in love. That the book which August Wilhelm Schlegel called "a declaration of the rights of feeling in opposition to the tyranny of social relations" should influence Hecker is no surprise. His first reading of the book at Brook Farm was accompanied by attempts in the diary to recreate the style and copy the emotions of the novella. Of course he lacked the skill of Goethe, which is evident from the uneven, immature style of those early pages of the diary. In light of this, much of the talk about suicide can be understood for what it was: a rather unsuccessful attempt to express in the most dramatic, evocative terms the agony of unfulfilled affection and the unwillingness to accept the realities of life that would interfere with the idyllic expression of love. Doubtless, Isaac's infatuation with Almira Barlow played a role in this. By January 1844, he had decided not to get further involved with her, although he was willing to carry on a platonic relationship. With that much critical distance, he was able to view *Werther* more objectively.

Around the time of his second reading of *Werther*, he wrote a crestfallen letter to Ida Russell, who responded with the advice: "Burn *Werther!*" (Russell to Hecker, November 7, 1843).

Die Wahlverwandtschaften (Elective Affinities) was Goethe's 1809 novel that employed some of the emphasis on the psychological states of the individual that characterized the works of Richter. Margaret Fuller, writing in the *Dial* in 1841, testified to the "storm of indignation that this book stirred up on account of its allegedly gross immorality." Yet she herself took a far more favorable attitude toward the work referring to it as "deeply moral and religious, even mystical, work." Hecker's comments indicate that he was aware of the controversies surrounding the book but, like Fuller, was nevertheless enthusiastic about it. The plot centers on the story of Edward, a wealthy nobleman, and his devoted wife Charlotte, whose idyllic serenity and happiness is shattered by the presence of two dear friends whom they invite to live with them on their estate.

Aus meinen Leben: Dichtung und Wahrheit was Goethe's massive autobiography, which he completed in 1822. Unlike the autobiography of Richter, which Hecker also read, Goethe's work was not merely the story of an individual, but the saga of an age and a nation. He masterfully wove the narrative of his own personality development in with an account of the times of his life that in its at-

tention to detail was remarkable. When Hecker later speaks about writing an autobiography he, not surprisingly, takes Richter's work as a model. Richter's
emphasis on the psychology of the individual was still more appealing than
Goethe's balanced style of blending the internal and the external. Although
Hecker never did write his autobiography his diary-keeping during his early years
certainly evidences his preference for recounting internal states almost exclusively. When in his fifties, he again began keeping a diary for a few years.
Though more interested in the sights and sounds around him than he had been in
the 1840s, he still chose to emphasize his interior machinations. When he did turn
his attention to the exterior, as he did during his Nile River trip in the winter of
1873–74, he kept two separate journals: one an account of the sights, the other
"Notes on Interior States."

117. James Pierpoint Greaves (1777–1842) was an English merchant who had
been ruined by the French Revolution and spent several years in Switzerland as an
associate of Pestalozzi before becoming the leader of the group of British reformers
whose center of operations was at Alcott House in London. Two articles about him
were published in the *Dial* for October 1842 and January 1843, and his book *Affirmations* was popular among the Transcendentalists. William Henry Channing ran
many short excerpts from it in *The Present*. This quote is from *The Present* 1 (December 15, 1843):155. The complete text reads: "The grand change which it is the
design of Love to accomplish is to bring the human mind to submit to be refined in
essence, instead of a reformation in existence, to be made new rather than to have
its results amended. Man is looking for a reformation in existence, while Love is
preparing a reformation in essence. Man can only be elevated by receiving the portion of being which was not generated as earth-born being, or, in other words, by
becoming heaven born in the love-sphere. To an Earth-born-nature a heaven-born
nature must be added to constitute happiness in essence."

118. George Fox (1624–1691), the founder of Quakerism. Hecker was made
aware of the teachings of Joseph Smith by Mormon Evangelist Parley Parker Pratt
whom he had met in New York sometime around 1837. See *An American Experience of God*, pp. 33–35. He had no direct contact with the Quakers, though they
were the subject of books on comparative dogmatics that he read like F.D. Maurice's *Kingdom of Christ* and J.A. Moehler's *Symbolism*.

119. In this entry Hecker considers two solutions to the problem of social
disorder: the church and the phalanx. He firmly believes that the church, not the
utopianism of Fourier, is the only road to the reformation of society into a new
universal, harmonious order. In this regard he is following Brownson, who in the
January and April 1844 numbers of his *Review* was to come out strongly against
Fourierism in favor of the church (see "No Church, No Reform," *Brownson
Quarterly Review* 1 [April 1844]:175–94, and Hecker's reaction to that article in
a March 23, 1844 letter to Brownson). Interestingly, Hecker sees Protestantism
as part of the disunited order of society that must be rejuvenated by a new call
to synthetic social structures. The Fourierists, as well as Hecker, saw the Catholic
church as a positive force for unity, but of course vehemently disagreed with
Brownson's criticism of their system as un-Christian. See "Mr. Brownson's No-

tions of Fourier's Doctrine,'' *The Phalanx* 1 (July 13, 1844):197–204. Also see general introduction, chapter 5.

120. Hecker may be thinking here of his meeting with Bishop John Hughes that he described in a December 14, 1843 letter to Brownson: "I asked Hughes his views of individual social and political. Alas! that I had not asked the latter."

121. *Die Seherin von Prevorst. Eröffnungen über das innere Leben der Menschen und über das Hereinragen einer Geisterwelt in die unsere (The Seeress of Prevorst. Revelations Concerning the Inner-Life of Man and the Inter-Diffusion of a World of Spirits in the One We Inhabit)* was published by Justinus Andreas Christian Kerner in 1829. Since the first English edition was done in London in 1845, Hecker must have read the original German text. Kerner was a member of the Swabian school of late Romantic poets. As a physician, he became interested in Spiritualism and somnambulism. *Die Seherin von Prevorst* is an account of the experiences of Friedrich Hauffe, a somnambulist and clairvoyant. The fact that Hecker read this work while at Brook Farm was yet another reason for his fascination with dreams during that period, and sheds light on his dreams about the deaths of his sister and mother.

122. On Spiritualism in antebellum America see Russell M. and Clare R. Goldfarb, *Spiritualism and Nineteenth-Century America* (Cranbury, NJ: Associated University Press, 1978). Georgiana Bruce Kirby makes mention of the fascination with Spiritualism in her *Years of Experience* (see note 113).

123. The letter, postmarked March 9, 1844, reveals a good bit about Hecker's intentions of entering the ministry. He asks for Brownson's frank advice as his "spiritual parent." He says that his spiritual growth has come to a standstill under the present arrangement of living at home and spending long hours of work at the business. To devote his whole energy and time to "becoming a laborer in the cause of the Church" is what he feels compelled to do, but he wonders about the amount of study that would be necessary, convinced that he is too old to master the classical languages. He presents two options—going to college or entering the tutelage of a divine. He strongly prefers the latter.

Brownson writes back that he believes the priesthood is Hecker's vocation. He urges him to decide whether he will become a Catholic or an Episcopalian and informs him of his decision to become a Catholic, a decision he has reached despite leonine struggles to the contrary. But he does not like the idea of a tutor and counsels instead a thorough preparation (Brownson to Hecker, March 11, 1844).

124. The Reverend William Herbert Norris was an Episcopal priest who authored a letter that appeared in *The Churchman* and elicited a sympathetic response from Hecker. He obtained his address from Benjamin I. Haight, the rector of All Saints' Church (see note 105).

On March 25, Norris wrote back to Hecker, declining to undertake the tutelage, claiming that he in fact was no great scholar and that his resources were so limited that he hardly had enough books for his own sermon preparation. It is odd that Hecker would have chosen such an obscure individual, when the resources of the High Church party at General Theological Seminary were at his disposal. His brother John, at the time Isaac is writing to Norris, is meeting with one of the leaders of the American Puseyites, Bishop Benjamin Onderdonk, president of the seminary and bishop of New York. John was on his way to joining the Episcopal church.

125. After visiting Hughes he told Brownson that he would probably be led to the church later, though not at the present (Hecker to Brownson, March 28, 1844). Doubtless he liked the ideal of Catholicism more than he liked the members of the church.

126. Samuel Seabury (1801–1872), was a Connecticut-born Episcopal priest whose career was centered in New York. Under the influence of Henry Hobart he became interested in the High Church tradition after his ordination in 1828. During the thirties he was editor of *The Churchman* and professor at General. In the 1840s he became one of the most loyal supporters of the Oxford movement. Around the time of Hecker's meeting with him he was a leader of the movement, supporting through his columns in *The Churchman* the ordination of his future assistant at the Church of the Annunciation, Arthur Carey, and the stand of Bishop Benjamin Onderdonk.

127. George Partridge Bradford (1807–1890) was a graduate of Harvard College and Divinity School. As an original member of Brook Farm, he taught languages there until his departure after the community became a phalanx (see Swift, *Brook Farm,* pp. 187–94). Hecker had discussed the arrangement with Brownson in a March 28, 1844 letter in which he felt certain that Bradford would be ''personally interested'' in him instead of merely an auditor of his recitations. Most importantly, he would be near Brownson, whose influence would more than offset the Transcendental breezes of Concord.

128. Here we have yet another instance of the silly attempts to change the gender of the pronouns referring to Almira. See note 88.

129. Hecker attended the Fourier Convention that was held in New York to commemorate the birthday of Charles Fourier on April 4–7, 1844. The convention brought to town some of his Brook Farm friends, who were now leaders in the Associationist movement. From the accounts in the pro-Fourier New York *Tribune,* we learn that the purpose of the meeting was ''to give coherence and system to the experiential efforts at Association now marking in various parts of the Country.'' The president of the convention was George Ripley, and he and Charles Dana addressed the congress on April 6. The convention issued a Preamble and Resolutions, which were largely the work of William Henry Channing. Parke Godwin was the author of the ''Address to the American People'' that ran on the front page of the *Tribune* for April 6 and decried the ''organic defects of society'' and proposed the Fourierist cure: reorganization of all of society according to the Frenchman's theories.

Although Hecker differed with the theories of Fourier for many of the same reasons Brownson did, he was far more sympathetic with the basic motivation and direction of the movement. For him it was an extremely positive sign that men like Ripley were turning to Fourier. ''It [Fourierism] has rid them of their transcendentalism, of their Protestantism, and most of their pernicious results.'' It would open their eyes to the Catholic principles. For Ripley, Fourierism was his ''apprenticeship for the priesthood'' (Hecker to Brownson, April 6, 1844). See general introduction.

130. This is the first entry from his new residence in Concord in the home of Henry David Thoreau, whose mother took in boarders for Bradford's language school.

131. From here until May 11, there is a long stretch in the diary of mystical rapture in which Hecker's attempts to express his contemplative experiences are particularly intense and more successful than ever before. We know that during this time he was reading many Catholic mystics: Pseudo-Dionysius, Meister Eckhart, Hugh and Richard of St. Victor, and Eriugena (see Hecker to Brownson, April 6, 1844). Although there is a hint of the influence of the love mysticism of the Victorines, by and large Hecker's vocabulary is that of the Romantic American, not that of the classical contemplative tradition. His focus on love is most often expressed by reference to the Love Spirit, which in its choice of words and images more closely resembles the Fruitlands mystics than anything else. Yet he goes well beyond the musings of Lane and Alcott and adds a clear Christocentric element to his meditations, one that realizes the necessity of the mediator and of the Church. The influence of his readings of the mystics was subtle. It essentially gave him confidence to pursue his own creative expression of his contemplative experiences. That confidence is evident throughout this last section of this volume.

132. See note 111.

133. George P. Bradford. See note 127.

134. The distinction between democracy in the church and democracy in the society is interesting and reflects some of the dissatisfaction with the political scene that affected Brownson as well after the demise of John C. Calhoun's candidacy.

135. It appears as if these poetical gems in the entry for the 9th are Hecker's own work. Would anyone actually bother to copy such unmemorable verse from the book of another?

136. There is no doubt about Hecker's ongoing commitment to interiority as a philosophical principle and as a way of life. As the juxtaposition of this entry with the one that follows shows, interiority and faith in the Church were not things that he saw as being in tension. The Transcendentalists' self-reliance was always distinguished in his mind from interiority.

137. Although he mentions four traditions—Roman Catholic, Anglican, Presbyterian, and Baptist—it is clear that during the writing of the diary only the first two command his serious consideration. During the 1830s he was involved with examining the Mormons, Deweyite Unitarians, and Methodists, but we have no record of any explicit discussion of either Presbyterians or Baptists and, therefore, one must conclude that this reference is merely random.

138. Ora Gannett Segwick. Swift recounts in *Brook Farm* that she was notable for having dared to tease Nathaniel Hawthorne, though she was just a girl of sixteen. She married Charles B. Segwick of Syracuse. Her autobiographical article "A Girl of Sixteen at Brook Farm" (*Atlantic Monthly Magazine* 85 [March 1900]: 394–404) is a well-known portrait of her experiences as a student. The letter of May 10, 1844, Isaac refers to opens: "You ask me to write freely and openly and so I will do, for although I cannot feel that I know you, there is somewhat within you that tells me

it were easy to be perfectly true and open and that you are one of those who possess a key that will unlock the way to my heart.''

139. These allusions to the Abolitionist movement reveal both Hecker's conviction about the priority of inner reform and his antipathy toward the Abolitionists. In other places he expresses his disdain for the institution of slavery; indeed his whole conception of the person as image of God makes his attitude toward slavery predictable.

A dislike of the motives and tactics of the Abolitionists was not uncommon among northern intellectuals. William Ellery Channing's 1835 *Slavery* had argued that the South's peculiar institution was contrary to Christian principles and would be abolished gradually. But the response to his plea was mixed with people like the attorney general of Massachusetts James T. Austin attacking him for his presumptuous judgmental tone and in fact branding him an insurrectionist. Doubtless the Massachusetts textile industry's dependence on slave-produced cotton did much to dull the consciences of many. New York, similarly, as the major port through which southern cotton was exported abroad benefitted greatly from slavery. Even many intellectuals less directly tied to the economic order than men like Austin were hesitant to resist slave holding. George Ripley, thoroughly aware of the need to reform society in other regards, was by and large silent on the Abolitionist movement. Orestes Brownson, though opposed to slavery, denounced the tactics of men like William Lloyd Garrison as a threat to the Constitution. Brownson admired John C. Calhoun more than any other politician of the time and accordingly was sympathetic to Calhoun's position on slavery. Emerson likewise shunned the radical methods of the Abolitionist, preferring instead to rely on appeals to the moral character of slave holders. Even Alcott, a man not given to caution, found himself preferring appeals to small groups and individuals rather than the mass meetings and pamphlets used by *The Liberator*. There of course were exceptions to this, the two most prominent being Theodore Parker and Thoreau. Parker engaged in a protracted public campaign that included speeches, writing, and direct legal and illegal actions like the Underground Railroad and the Boston Vigilance Committee. Thoreau was less pyrotechnic but, as his ''Plea for John Brown'' made clear, no less intense in his opposition and in his justification of civil disobedience as a response to the unjust laws of the country. See Rose, pp. 217–25.

140. See note 111 and general introduction.

141. All through his formative years Hecker struggled with the relationship between inspiration and study. Gifted with keen insights and a fertile imagination he was not dispositionally suited for scholarship. During his younger days he attended public school in New York only sporadically; but even more importantly he was part of a culture that put great stress on the practical and the immediate rather than on the theoretical and abstract. Whether it was the American preoccupation with ''know-how'' or the rejection of tradition as a basis for behavior, Americans were concerned with what their own senses told them about the present moment in which they found themselves. They were committed to action, and such action could not await the outcome of long speculative inquiries. There was a sense of urgency about building a new civilization and transforming a continent that pervaded Amer-

ican intellectual life, even the thought of those that prided themselves in their idealism. Alcott, for instance, was, judging by the accounts of his contemporaries, the most transcendental of the Transcendentalists. Yet he was compelled to put his ideas into practice whether it was in his Boston school or in his short-lived community. Brook Farm was another example of the urgency of action. Even though it was to be an educational and agricultural institute and was to promote a more harmonious style of life, it was a very busy place where the sons and daughters of Yankee farmers, artisans, and ministers worked hard at trying to raise crops on the stony soil of West Roxbury and at the same time grow in the discipline of self-culture. The culture's demands for urgency and immediacy were well-served by the Transcendentalists' intuitive method. Frederick Ives Carpenter has pointed out that in the case of Emerson his Transcendentalism was essentially religious, inspired more by the religious sentiment than by the Kantian reason. But for Carpenter, a problem arose when Emerson adopted Kant's distinction between transcendental reason and empirical understanding without heeding his warning that transcendental, intuitive reasoning cannot be applied to the world of senses. In failing to take this caution seriously Emerson wound up equating in naturalistic fashion, intuition with instinct. This confusion, as Carpenter saw it, "opened a Pandora's box of primitivistic and romantic delusions." The one safeguard to this, which Emerson did not always heed, was to test the intuitions by observing how they coincided with the information of the senses. In this fashion Transcendental method is close to the critical logic of science, as Santayana observed.

By giving such importance to his intuitions Hecker made a similar move, fraught as was Emerson's with dangers of subjectivism and self-delusion. Hecker tried to escape danger by applying a critical method of checking his intuitions. He checked them against what he called the will of God or the leading of the Holy Spirit that was manifested through the community of believers and through Providence. It functioned as a source of objective reality by which he could test the veracity of his intuitions.

It was that process of discernment or at least Hecker's interest in pursuing it that made him aware of the need for education and guidance. At times of confusion he was made clearly aware of that need. At other times, such as in the passage under discussion, he fears that he is inhibiting the work of his intuition by too much attention to outward matters. What he is after is inspiration, not information, and he fears that too much time spent seeking the latter will quench the former. The tension is acute enough to leave its mark on his development and later character.

142. Hecker skipped some leaves of his notebook, which he discovered on May 20, the day after the entry on the last regular page of the notebook from May 19. The entries from May 20–23, then, did in fact postdate that of May 19, but I have retained the order of the original. After the May 19 entry, Hecker copied a series of quotations from his readings on the end sheets of his notebook. These quotes were done at different times and written anywhere where there was space. It is impossible to determine the original order in which they were copied.

143. This tripartite division of the human person is similar to the one Hecker gives in the January 28, 1844 entry, above.

144. As the first volume draws to a close, Hecker demonstrates the new confidence he has acquired in being able to trust the leading of his interior muse. Although his troubles are by no means over, there is a new sense of peace and maturity emerging.

145. The quotes are from Goethe's *Iphigenie Auf Tauris* (1787). The three quotes are all from two different speeches of Pylades in *Zweiter Aufzug, Erster Auftritt, Orest Pylades.*

"Endless is the task that we must fulfill
Yet the soul pushes on.

You alone, O little one, should thank the gods
that so early they could do so much through you.

To a difficult task God calls the noble man,
who sinned greatly, and placed on his shoulder what seems
to us impossible and endless."

146. The last hard-to-decipher word may be "Eckermann," in which case the quote would be from *J.P. Eckermann Gespräche mit Goethe* (*Eckermann's Conversations with Goethe*), which had been a popular work since its publication in 1830. The passage is difficult to translate, since Hecker seems to have left out words: "Speak or be quiet, you cannot always know what is in my heart and remains there. Doing good does not require reflection. It is doubt that turns good deeds into evil. The one who understands is always higher than that which is understood. In faith this is reversed. The believer is lower than that which is believed. No being in creation can develop from a lower to a higher state unless endowed with the principle of development."

147. Jane Lead (1624–1704) was a British mystic who was one of the chief interpreters of the work of the German seer Jacob Boehme in English. In 1633 she became associated with Anglican clergyman John Pordage and founded a small group of devotees of Boehme. Her own imaginative talents soon proved a fertile ground for mystical writings of her own.

The work that Hecker quotes from is *Divine Revelations and Prophecies,* first published in London in 1700 and reprinted in Nottingham by H. Wild in 1830. The quote is taken from pp. 14–15 where it is part of a cryptic discussion entitled "An Answer to an Objection against the Translated State." In it Lead argues that some "specially elected" can experience a state of perfection prior to the visible return of Christ to redeem our bodies. The Second Coming has occurred in Spirit already with the giving of the Holy Ghost.

Hecker seems little interested in Lead's rather prolix theory and completely uninterested in her tortuous scriptural exegesis. He is attracted to a notion of spiritual perfection that fits into the understanding of the present nature of salvation, of the inner, hidden dimension of the perfect life, and of the stress on the potential for unlimited growth that were so much a part of the Transcendentalists' religion.

148. The quote is taken from *The Kingdom of Christ,* chapter II, section IV, "The Practical Workings of the Protestant Systems," and is quoted exactly as it appears in the book. The passage continues: "Romanists . . . have said that but one inference can be drawn from such a fact: he felt a bitter sense of disappointment in the result of his labours; if pride had permitted him, he would have confessed that he had rashly and sinfully entered upon them." But to judge Luther that way, Maurice argues, is to miss the point that his motivation was valid and godly, even though his methods were faulty. That Hecker copied only the first part of Maurice's comments indicates his primary interest in Catholic critiques of Lutheranism rather than in Maurice's sympathetic remarks. During the 1860s and seventies one of Hecker's favorite lecture topics was Martin Luther. He incorporated some of Maurice's telling criticisms of Luther's theology. Cf. note 55, above.

149. There is no indication that Hecker actually read the *Gathas* of Zoroaster. This quote was probably taken from a secondary source.

150. "Johann Picus" is the latinized name of Giovanni Pico della Mirandola (1463–1494), Italian Renaissance scholar and Platonic philosopher whose works included a commentary on Genesis entitled *Heptaplus* and a synoptic treatment of Plato and Aristotle, *De ente et uno.* The quote is from *On the Dignity of Man.*

151. *Festus* is the 1839 epic poem of James Philip Bailey (1816–1902). Bailey's Festus is a Romantic searcher after truth, a Faust figure, who caught the imagination of countless readers during the 1840s. The work was enormously popular, and Bailey was hailed as a great poet of rank with Wordsworth and Shelley.

152. This is a curious list of the ten precepts of Buddhism (*dasa-' sila*). It follows the traditional listing of the first five (*panca-sila*), but then lists five additional obligations that are entirely different from the five precepts for monastic novices that are usually cited as part of the ten precepts. The last five on Hecker's list make the *dasa-sila* read more like the Ten Commandments. Where he got the list is not known, but it is likely that it is copied verbatim from some source, since it occurs in the commonplace book section of the diary.

153. Ole Bull was a Norwegian violin virtuoso who made his first tour of the U.S. in late 1843. His November 26 concert in New York was typical in its ability to elicit wild praise from American audiences. The New York *Herald* wrote: "One of the most extraordinary excitements that we ever saw in the musical world in this country took place last evening at the Park Theater. The celebrated Ole Bull, the greatest artist on the violin in the world, made his first appearance before an American audience. It was a tempest—a torrent—a very Niagara of applause, tumult, and approbation throughout his whole performance." See Carl Bode, ed., *American Life in the 1840s* (Garden City: Doubleday, 1967), pp. 240–41.

154. Parley Parker Pratt (1805–1857) was a famed Mormon evangelist. He had met Hecker sometime between 1837 and 1839 when he was in New York City conducting missionary work and pursuing plans to publish a defense of Joseph Smith's doctrines. Hecker's interest in Mormonism was sincere and tied in intimately with his larger concerns for social reform, personal piety, and the primacy of the spiritual in human affairs. See *An American Experience of God,* pp. 33–37

and Parley P. Pratt, *Voice of Warning,* 13th ed. (Salt Lake City: George Cannon, 1891; 1st edition 1837).

155. The ambiguous nature of Hecker's commitment to study was heightened by his awareness that his brothers were home in New York working hard at their baking business and he was receiving money they earned to support him at Bradford's Concord school, as he had at Brook Farm. He was perplexed that although others were sacrificing to make his education possible, he was often unable to apply himself diligently to studies. There is no evidence that he ever became proficient in either Greek or Latin.

There runs through the diary and correspondence of this time a tentativeness about his present course of study. He tells his family in a May 27 letter that he would be willing to come home to work, were an emergency to occur, and that they should not worry about interrupting his studies. He also was keen to help out by suggesting new business opportunities for Hecker Flour. George had recently purchased a new machine to produce pearled flour. Isaac was sure that there would be a big market for that new product in Boston and urged his brother to run ads in the *Boston Post.* He also sent a gift of pearled wheat to George Ripley at Brook Farm. See Hecker to Family, May 23 and 27, 1844.

156. The two letters referred to are one of June 4, 1844, and another of May 16, 1844. The dating on the June 4 letter, as well as that of the June 5 diary entry, is wrong; Isaac apparently was able to transmit himself back in time two months, hence dating both pieces April instead of June. (This confusion was temporary, doubtless the result of eating some rotten apples provided by that scoundrel Alcott who never could grow fruit anyway.) By the time that Hecker wrote his next letter on June 11 he had caught up with the rest of the world.

In both of the letters to Brownson, he expresses the difficulty he is having studying and his predilection to attend to the inner flow of thoughts and inspirations instead of to the books. Brownson hastened to respond to his young friend in a letter of June 6. In the most tender and affectionate manner of a father chastising a son he scolded him for indulging emotional luxuries and reminded him that the power to control one's thoughts and feelings and fix them on whatever object one chooses is the highest aim of spiritual culture. "Be careful that you do not mistake a mental habit into which you have fallen for the guidance of the All-Wise." He then tells him that he cannot attain any progress without the help of the church: "You are wrong. You do not begin right. Do you really believe the Gospel? If so you must put yourself under the direction of the Church." He then says that he has begun the process of joining the church. "You must be a Catholic or a Mystic." See Hecker to Brownson, May 16, 1844 and June 4, 1844; Hecker to Brownson, June 6, 1844.

157. Alexandre Dumas Père (1802–1870) was a French playwright whose first major work, *Henry II et sa cour,* was performed at the Théâtre Français in Paris when he was just twenty-seven. During the 1840s he was hailed by some as "the French Shakespeare." Apparently the story Hecker recounts has a basis in fact.

158. See note 127.

159. Anna Q.T. Parsons was a Bostonian who visited Brook Farm and later in 1847 became the head of the Women's Associative Union in Boston. During her

younger days, she was know for her psychic powers that enabled her to read a person's character by pressing paper containing his handwriting against her forehead. See Johnson, *Charles King Newcomb*, p. 24; Rose, *Transcendentalism*, p. 187.

160. John Sullivan Dwight. See note 59. W.H.C. is William Henry Channing.

161. This quote is from Swedenborg's *Divine Providence*, p. 5228. See note 22.

162. The first of these two Wordsworth quotes is from *Ecclesiastical Sonnets* 3 (1822). The second is from *The Prelude* (c. 1789–1802).

163. Friedrich von Schiller (1759–1805), German poet, dramatist, historian, and philosopher. What works of Schiller Hecker read is not known, but from his comments it is likely that he had in mind his fiction, perhaps *Don Carlos* or *Freigeisterei der Leidenschaft*.

164. This rather standard account of the wounding and wooing dialectic of divine love is typical of the doctrine as put forth in Fénelon's *Dissertation on Divine Love*, the 1759 London edition of which was part of the Fruitlands Library. Fénelon took his notion of pure love from Catherine of Genoa whose *Dialogia* is the classical statement of the doctrine. Later in his life when ravished by chronic leukemia during the 1870s, Hecker often would turn to Catherine's masterpiece for comfort.

165. Source in Novalis unknown.

166. Lane wrote to Hecker June 3, 1844, from the United Society in Harvard, Massachusetts. See introduction to volume 2 for discussion of this letter.

167. On Benjamin F. Haight, see note 103. Later in this same entry he refers to him as "B.F.H."

168. The letter from Brownson encouraging him to enter the ministry is from May 23, 1844.

169. The entries from June 7 and 11 are crucial to understanding Hecker's conversion. The news that Brownson had himself decided to become a Catholic was the catalyst that set off an instantaneous reaction of assent. See introduction to volume 2.

170. The entry for the 14th contains one of the most famous passages from the diary that, like others, found its way into currency via Elliott's *Life*. Hecker's oft-quoted critique of the Transcendentalists occurs between the statement of his decision to convert and a note that he will travel with Emerson to Harvard the next day to see Alcott and Lane. Doubtless the substance of his critique is revealed in its form. Having become more aware than ever of his need for the grace of Christ as it flows from the ministry of the Church, he is ready to turn an unsympathetic eye on the system that shared all his Romantic sensibilities yet denied the essence of the Christian message. Alcott and Emerson epitomized this radical Transcendentalism, and for the latter Hecker had always had an antipathy. Emerson is in all likelihood the inspiration for the portrait of the tense, miserlike figure Hecker paints. Certainly either Alcott or Emerson would have fit the picture of one who "prefers Socrates to Jesus." It was Alcott himself who was to say: "My debt to Plato is greater, perhaps, than to any mind—greater than to Christ, I sometimes think" (*Journals*, p. 23, entry for March 28, 1850). Yet Hecker had a certain affection for Alcott who, of course, compared to Emerson, was far more mystically inclined.

171. Francis Quarles (1592–1644), British poet, essayist, and aphorist. One of his works was in the Fruitlands library and five were in Alcott's own library. This quote is from his 1646 *Judgment and Mercy for Afflicted Souls*.

172. This quote is from Christopher Marlowe's (1564–1593) *Hero and Leander* (1598).

173. Ben Jonson (1572–1637), British playwright and poet.

174. This is in all likelihood Abraham Cowley (1618–1667), British poet. He was enormously popular in his own day as a metaphysical poet in the school of John Donne. In our day he is little esteemed and regarded as the author of what one critic called "artificial, affected poetry, full of far-fetched conceits and extravagant similes" (see James Vinson, ed., *Great Writers of the English Language* [New York: Macmillan, 1979], pp. 122–23).

175. The Catholic College at Worcester was in fact the College of the Holy Cross. What Hecker saw was a fledgling institution that had been started by Bishop Fenwick in the fall of 1843. It was staffed by Fenwick's fellow Jesuits among whom was Thomas F. Melledy. It instructed mostly youngsters between the ages of eight and fifteen, though apparently Fenwick had thought that some arrangements might be made for Hecker to study there.

In his oft-quoted letter of June 24 to Brownson, he described how he felt that the Jesuits there, though adequately trained in understandings of the Scripture and the church, were completely in the dark regarding any philosophical understanding of their faith. Furthermore they are wanting "that vital consciousness of divine eternal life and high spiritual aspirations which have animated so many of the children of this true church." Instead they seemed content to base their religion on the lowest common denominator. What is more, they were wont to use too much snuff, even during Mass! (see R. Emmett Curran, *American Jesuit Spirituality: The Maryland Tradition* [New York: Paulist Press, 1988]).

Yet none of this seriously scandalized Hecker, for he had had to deal with the fact that becoming a Catholic would mean associating himself with the lower classes of American society, most of whom had little awareness of the richness of their faith. His conviction rested on an internal assurance of the truth of the church, and hence we see in the diary virtually no discussion of Worcester but a declaration: "I still (even after meeting the Jesuits with the right snuff) feel that my consciousness is interior to all life."

He likewise has nothing to say about a brief visit to the North American Phalanx, which probably occurred on June 23. The North American Phalanx was the premier Fourierist community in American during the 1840s. It was founded about forty miles south of New York in Monmouth County, New Jersey, and included among its founders and associates the country's most famous advocates of Associationism: Horace Greeley and Albert Brisbane. Founded in 1843 it outlasted all other phalanxes, carrying on until 1854. During 1844 it had about ninety members living on a 673-acre preserve. George Ripley commented upon visiting the place: "I had often heard it spoken of in terms of high commendation; but I must confess, I was not prepared to find an estate combining so many picturesque attractions with such rare agricultural capabilities." See John Humphrey Noyes, *A History of American Socialisms* (New York: Dover, 1966), chapters xxxvi and xxxvii.

It is curious that Hecker would visit the Phalanx when he did. It was not on his way and required a round trip of eighty miles, which he sandwiched in between his visit to Worcester and his meeting with Bishop McCloskey in New York. At a high point of his enthusiastic pursuit of membership in the church, why should he go out of his way to visit an Associationist community? Since there is no record of the visit causing him any consternation, the reason was probably purely practical. He had a fondness for old friends and an interest in reform communities and knew that his return home might mean, at least temporarily, the end of his leisurely life. Brother John would have plenty of work for him to do, so he had better see the sights while he could. For the same reason he had visited Lane at the Shaker community on June 15 at the start of his journey home from Concord.

176. John McCloskey (1810–1885) was indeed, as Hecker noted, of "broader education" than most Catholic clergy in the 1840s. After being educated at Mt. St. Mary's College and Seminary in Emmitsburg, Maryland, he spent three years at the Gregorian University at Rome. Before becoming coadjutor to Hughes in March of 1844, he had taught philosophy at the seminary at Nyack, New York, and had been the first president of St. John's (later Fordham) College. His openness to converts had enabled him to be instrumental in the conversion of James R. Bayley, later archbishop of Baltimore and friend of Fr. Hecker's. In a letter of July 15 to Brownson, Hecker portrayed McCloskey in tones similar to those of the diary, calling him "a man of wide information, mild and affectionate."

177. That Hecker was willing to use the term "mystic" with unqualified approbation is significant. In the 1840s the Puritan ethos with its avowedly antimystical brand of Reformed piety was still a potent force in the culture. No doubt, as Frederick Carpenter has observed, the Transcendentalist movement sought to "reestablish the mystical basis of all religion." But the term "mystic" carried with it a unique history that set it apart as an emblem of reprobation. For the Reformed tradition it was a sign of superstition and Romanism. For John Wesley, who had himself read the Quietists and come dangerously close to falling into what he called "the trap of the mystics," it was the symbol of a self-absorbed form of religious enthusiasm that kept believers from doing the work of saving souls and spreading the kingdom of God. Yet, against this background, some in New England of the 1840s used the term to designate not a false brand of religious experience but the essence of true religious sensibilities. Certainly Alcott and Lane were in that number, as we have shown in the general introduction, and in that regard Hecker felt more affinity toward them than he did toward Emerson.

In using the term "mystic," Hecker was joining the revolt against the Protestant religious establishment of the day. But to speak of mysticism in such glowing terms was to do more than that; it was to make a radical social statement as well. Hecker's line "Man is a mystic fact" stood in stark contrast to the claim of the dominant industrial order: "Man is a machine." By aligning himself with such a position Hecker was opting out of the life that his elder brothers had chosen, about as far out as he could get. Not only was he becoming religious, he was becoming a mystic as well. Even for someone as astute as Brownson, "mystic" meant a religiously unbalanced person. Hence, he would write to Hecker before Isaac joined the church, warning him: "You must either become a Catholic or a mystic." That he was intent on doing both was a sign of the degree to which he wished to leave behind the life of his middle-class German-American entrepreneurial family and issue an indictment against the values they held. That never came through in direct confrontation with them, but the substance of his actions was clear. Despite his deep affection for his family, he could not live by their values, and by the time of this entry, he had come to the point where he was content with the consequences of that stance and more determined than ever to live it out.

In light of this, Mary Lyons's statement that Hecker was "definitely not a mystic," is hard to substantiate. See "A Rhetoric for American Catholicism" (Ph.D. dissertation, University of California, Berkeley, 1983).

178. Hecker, like many of his contemporaries, was fascinated with the concept of genius. He carried on a long correspondence on that topic with George Curtis that began in 1844 and lasted until 1849. In it Hecker repeatedly spoke of the relation between religious inspiration and genius, arguing that they were one and the same. Curtis, on the other hand, while acknowledging the relation, maintained that there was a distinction—the artist's inspiration was not necessarily a special grace of God, but merely a talent of his own artistic nature. At the heart of their disagreement was the question of nature and grace that separated Hecker, the Catholic, from Curtis, the Transcendentalist.

179. Hecker may well have picked this up from Brownson. Cf. Brownson's 1839 *New Views of Christianity, Society, and the Church,* chapter III.

180. Hecker never did follow through with his plans to write an autobiography. Yet this inspiration did motivate him to seriously consider writing a book, which he did in 1857. No doubt much of that first work, *Aspirations of Nature,* was autobiographical. By that time he had a different intention—to convince non-Catholics of the truth of Catholicism—but he draws heavily on his own experience, especially in a section subtitled "Earnest the Seeker." Hecker had been known at Brook Farm as the Earnest Seeker, which is a clue to the autobiographical nature of this section. Also the text of that section is all written in quotation marks, as to suggest the actual words of Ernest. At points it had the look and feel of actual entries from the diary that have been reworked, polished and put to new uses.

His musings about writing an autobiography are important also because they reveal that he was paying close attention to organizing his diary, or "day book," as he calls it, and letters for further use in his writing, a practice that contemporaries like Thoreau and Emerson used often. This is a strong argument for attributing to Hecker the pencil annotations in the diary, as we have in determining the copy text.

Hecker read the autobiography of Goethe, *Aus meinem Leben: Dichtung und Wahrheit* and the 1842 autobiography of Richter (see G. Thomas Couser, *American Autobiography* [Amherst: University of Massachusetts Press, 1979]).

181. Here is one of the first intimations Hecker gives of an interest in a vocation as a religious (cf. entry for the 15th, below). It is linked with speculation

about starting a community of his own. That linkage was natural for him and led at length to the founding of the Paulists. It was also a linkage that members of the Associationist movement were not unaware of. See general introduction, "Catholicism and Associationism."

182. Hecker extends the indictment of the sensism of the Enlightenment to an indictment of the materialistic culture of antebellum America. Dissatisfaction with the dominant materialism of American culture was widespread among intellectuals. Michael Chevalier, writing in 1839, observed of the American: "His only means, and the object of his whole thought, is to subdue the material world, or, in other words, it is industry in its various branches, business, speculation, work, action" (*Society, Manners and Politics in the United States* [Boston: Weeks, Jordan, 1839], p. 224). More to the point, a rejection of the trend of the new industrial order that was transforming the Massachusetts countryside and causing New York City to burgeon was central to the Fourierist and to Brownson. It filled the pages of *The Phalanx* and *The Present,* and had been given full vent by Brownson in 1836 in his *New Views.* Hecker's articulation of the problems caused by the new order was never extensive. In the diary it most often takes the form of personal rejection of a life given to seeking material gain.

Yet he is as clear as anyone in presenting religion as a total intellectual, moral, and social alternative to the values of industrial America. As his commitment to Catholicism grows, so does the clarity of his critique, for Catholicism, especially in medieval European form, provides a model of pre-industrial society in which the values of the mind and soul play the dominant role. Unlike the Associationists who were groping after a life that was only, in the final analysis, a high-sounding series of speculations by a French visionary, Hecker had found in Catholicism a real, living example of what he and his Transcendentalist communitarian friends were seeking. No surprise then that shortly after his conversion he wanted to go to Europe on a pilgrimage and, appropriately enough, take Thoreau with him!

183. Hecker is becoming more familiar with Catholic apologetics as the above discussion illustrates. He was no doubt being instructed by Bishop McCloskey, who was himself a convert. Furthermore we know that he possessed at this time a Boston edition of *The Catechism of the Council of Trent* and a copy of J.A. Moehler's *Symbolism.* He is beginning to sound more orthodox with his use of phrases from the *Catechism.* He is finally clear in his trinitarian formulations: the Spirit is now unambiguously the Holy Spirit and is related to Jesus and to God the Father in traditional ways, though he is not beyond inserting some appropriately vague, Romantic effusions.

184. The concept of the hero intrigued the Romantic mind. One of the most influential treatments of the topic was Thomas Carlyle's 1841 *On Heroes, Hero-Worship, and the Heroic in History.* Following a similar tack, Hecker mused over the heroic nature of the artist and the religious prophet through the 1870s. See, for example, his "Theological Notes," PFA.

185. When Hecker visited McCloskey, the bishop gave him some books to read, the most remarkable of which was, he thought, Abbé Philippe Gerbet's *Considerations on the Eucharist* in the English translation (London: C. Dolman, 1840).

The work was an attempt to look at the Eucharist as "the generative dogma of Catholic piety" and followed an approach more like that of fundamental than dogmatic theology. It strove to place the notion of Eucharist in the broad context of the human experience of God, quoting not only from Old and New Testaments and church fathers, but also from the Vedas, Voltaire, and Hume. See Hecker to Brownson, July 15, 1844.

186. Isaac's idea to make a pilgrimage to Europe grew out of his fascination with the Middle Ages, a fascination that, as we have seen, was shared by his friends William Henry Channing and Burrill Curtis. It also was nourished by his desire to take on Catholic devotional forms. He even describes the pilgrimage to Brownson as penance (Hecker to Brownson, August 2, 1844). He asked his spiritual director Bishop McCloskey about it. The bishop seemed to have been cool toward the idea.

In a letter of July 31 that he writes to Thoreau, he credits him with supplying part of the inspiration. Hecker lived at the Thoreau family home in the west end of Concord as a boarder from April 25 to June 16, during his time of study with George Bradford. Hecker felt that he and Henry had "a higher affinity, that inclined us to commune with each other," and made him a most enthusiastic offer: "We desire to go without purse or staff, depending upon the all-embracing love of God, Humanity, and the spark of courage imprisoned in us. Have we the will, we have the strong arms, hard hands to work with, and sound feet to stand upon and walk with. The heavens shall be our vaulted roof, and the green earth beneath our bed. . . . "

Thoreau responded on August 14, after just returning from a hike to the Catskills and back that he was strongly tempted by the proposal but felt a desire to explore "the Farther Indies" through the pursuit of "a kind of Brahmanical, Artesian, Inner Temple life." That he found on the outskirts of Concord in a place called Walden Pond. Since Hecker knew of no one else who would possibly make such a trip, he dropped the idea.

187. The lack of commentary at the momentous occasions of receiving a sacrament for the first time is curious. It is absent from his letters and from the diary for this time when he was baptized and for the period around August 10 when he received first Eucharist. (An August 17 letter to Brownson contains one expression of exaltation, which seems to have been caused more by the news of Brownson's reception into the church than by Isaac's own joy.) But commentary is present in the August 2 entry describing his first reception of Penance. Perhaps the answer to this riddle lies in the August 11 entry in which he complains of a spiritual aridity since moving from Concord, but it seems to go deeper than that. Interior mystical communion with God was nothing new for Hecker who was gifted with a talent for contemplation that is present from his earliest writing. What was new was having an assurance that his sins were forgiven, that his own inadequacies were supplied, and a knowledge that his own subjective experience fit in with the experience of others. It was that that gave him most cause for rejoicing.

188. This change in style aptly symbolizes his transformation from an isolated individual to a member of the church.

189. A July 28 letter from Debora Gannett proclaimed to Isaac the type of strange dream experience that Romantics loved to revel in: "If ever it were possible

for the soul to disengage itself from the body, I shall believe mine did for a part went to you, for I seemed so distinctly to be with you the other night that I can not help its making me feel nearer to you ever since." For more on Hecker and dreams and somnambulism, see note 19.

190. The connection that Hecker makes between astrology and mathematics was based in part on the fact that in antebellum America mathematics was closely associated with astronomy, so much so that in many universities it existed only in conjunction with it. The mystical connection found its way into currency through the popularization of Neo-Platonist writings, including those of Pythagoras, and especially Proclus, whom Emerson and Alcott read intensely. Thomas Taylor in his *Commentaries of Proclus* suggested the mystical relationship of soul and number: "The essential number they [the Platonic philosophers] considered as first subsisting in the intelligible world, together with being. . . . the soul, by herself-moving energies, procreates number, while she numerates, and by this energy, causes the existence of quantity" (book I, xiv, xv, in Raine, *Thomas Taylor in America,* p. 34). See also Nye, *Society and Culture in America,* pp. 248–49.

191. This juxtaposition of study and reading illuminates further Hecker's complaints about not being able to study. Thus far, "study" has meant the study of languages, which was a rote process of memorization and recitation. That he had no mind for; but, on the other hand, as he says here and as we know from his writings, he was reading voraciously during the entire time of the diary. At one point he even wonders whether he reads too much.

192. Antonio Canova (1757–1822) was an Italian sculptor who became a dominant force in the development of Neo-Classicism in Europe in the nineteenth century.

193. Hecker's rather prudish reaction to Dante was not shared by many of his contemporaries. Emerson thought highly of him (see his *Journal* for 1844, entry 154), and even a review in *Graham's Magazine* thought to extol the art of Thomas Cole by comparing him to the Italian master. Hecker apparently wrote to Burrill Curtis sharing his disgust, to which Curtis replied that he found nothing offensive in the *Divina Commedia.* Perhaps reactions like that helped change his mind. By the end of volume 3 he is quoting Dante with no signs of displeasure and by October he is referring to him as "that great Christian poet." See Curtis to Hecker, August 15, 1844; Hecker to Brownson, October 23, 1844.

194. This is a succinct statement of the conviction that enabled the young mystic to put his faith in the Catholic church. *The Catechism of the Council of Trent,* which he was reading at this time, says: "Under the word 'Church' are comprehended no unimportant mysteries, for, in this 'calling forth,' which the word *Ecclesia* signifies, we at once recognize the benignity and splendour of divine grace. . . . For he called us by the interior inspiration of the Holy Ghost . . . " (*The Catechism of the Council of Trent* [Baltimore: James Myres, 1833], p. 91).

195. Literally, "life is to suffer."

196. Henry Thoreau. See note 186.

197. Bishop McCloskey. See note 185.

198. This may be from Richter's autobiography, *Wahrheit aus Jean Pauls Leben* (1833), which Hecker mentioned reading in volume 1.

199. On James P. Greaves, see note 117.

200. The concept of the masculine-feminine nature of the true self had been part of Hecker's anthropology for some time. Cf. entry for July 22, 1843.

201. It was during the 1820s that Jean-François Champollion was deciphering the Egyptian hieroglyphic writing with the aid of the recently discovered Rosetta stone. His work and the entrepreneurial exploits of an Egyptian soldier Mohammed Ali, who began a successful business of exporting Egyptian artifacts throughout Europe and America, set the stage for the major interest in Egyptian culture that was widespread during the 1840s. Swedenborgian Sampson Reed had latched onto Champollion's work and began publishing articles on Egypt as early as 1830 in his *New Jerusalem* magazine. In that same year, an English translation of J.G.H. Greppo's interpretation of Champollion's work was published in Boston. Emerson became a devotee of Egyptian culture and reflected his new affection in *Nature* and *Self-Reliance*. Thoreau's *Walden,* according to one interpreter, owes its emblematic style to contemporary theories of hieroglyphic emblems. See John T. Irwin, *American Hieroglyphics* (New Haven: Yale University Press, 1980).

202. Hecker's devotion to Mary began after his conversion and grew throughout his Redemptorist period during which time he would lead Novenas to the Blessed Mother during missions in Catholic parishes. After founding the Paulists, it fades into the background and is eclipsed by a return of devotion to the Spirit, which, of course, is the salient feature of his early piety. Marian devotion, then, functioned as part of a Catholicizing process that he wished to go through as part of his conversion. As Susan Perschbacher has shown in her dissertation, his conversion had a certain ongoing, progressive quality about it. See Susan Perschbacher, "Journey of Faith" (Ph.D. dissertation, University of Chicago, 1981).

203. Hecker is much less taken with Carlyle than he was earlier in the diary. See note 35. The allusion to Jean-François Retz, seventeenth-century French writer, is interesting.

204. Darien, CT.

205. The quotes in this section are from Dante's *Purgatorio.* Cf. note 193, and also see sections of general introduction on Sophia Ripley whose translation work on the *Divine Comedy* was known to Hecker.

206. Cf. note 178.

207. Henry Thoreau.

208. Hecker's progressive anthropology blended with a use of the idea of angels in both figurative and literal senses. Cf. entries for June 5, 1844, and April 24, 1845.

209. This entry indicates that Hecker was beginning to discover the mainstay of Catholic antebellum piety, the devotional manual. Just which one he was using is difficult to tell. As Ann Taves has pointed out, the devotional revival of the 1840s was aided by the proliferation of printed manuals. See her appendix for a list of manuals in use during this time.

The reference to Francis de Sales in one sense comes as no surprise. The positive, humanistic piety of the Salesian saint fits well in to Hecker's own upbeat anthropology. Although Hecker does not name the text he is using, it could have been an 1833 English edition of *Introduction to the Devout Life,* published in Baltimore.

210. On October 13, 1844, Curtis wrote: "I value your character so much and our personal intercourse so much. . . . " The statement was by way of warning Hecker that Georgiana Bruce was having a negative effect on their relationship because of her misunderstanding of Curtis.

211. Hecker was actually born on December 19, 1819, so he was commencing his twenty-sixth year. The confusion on the day might simply be the result of his writing in the evening and regarding the eve as the start of the next day; but given his frequent confusion over dates, the explanation might be that it was simply an error.

212. The relative lengths of his comments on the reception of Penance and the Eucharist are another indication that Hecker found the greatest consolation in the sacrament of Penance, even though he does revel in the wonders of eating the spiritual food of the Eucharist. At this point he was attending confession about once every two weeks.

213. During this time Hecker was reading and rereading Brownson's essays. This critique of reform movements as unable to effect any real change apart from the grace of Christ is a major part of Brownson's April 1844 *Review* essay, "No Church, No Reform," and his July 1844 essay in the same place, "Church Unity and Social Amelioration," in which Brownson takes on the Fourierists. See Hecker to Brownson, November 27, 1844.

214. In this fascinating section Hecker reveals his belief that the truth of Catholicism is grounded in the very nature of being. We see that his earlier efforts to relate the aesthetic, ethical, and religious moments come together now in his newfound faith. "Catholicism means the Universal Good, True and Beautiful." Furthermore, his belief in the universal nature of the religious inspiration, which in the past was symbolized in his odes to the Universal Love Spirit, lives on in his Catholic experience. What constitutes the church is the fact that it is one with God, "the Universal Love, Light, and Life. "This shows how the transition into the Catholic fold was, on the metaphysical level, an easy one. His dedication to the universal, real nature of truth and religious inspiration found its way into his Catholic thought.

215. In these two paragraphs on Adam, Hecker evokes two antithetical concepts of the Adam myth. In the first reference to "the new Man, the eternal youth" he plunges into what R.W.B. Lewis so aptly identified as the myth of the American Adam. That myth was very much alive in the 1840s and was a secularized version of the Pauline concept of the eschatological man, the second Adam. In it, the American was seen as a new man, emancipated from the past, standing heroically on the brink of the future. His experience was pristine, innocent, and childlike. He was, above all things, a type of the creator, a poet *par excellence,* whose words formed reality like the first Adam's did in the naming of the animals.

That myth doubtless shaped Hecker's conception of the Spirit-born Adam that we see here. In fact his larger concern with human potential, his constant evocation of the most exalted, godlike capacities of a human being is a corollary of that myth, and it is to those many statements that this short naming of the eternal youth should be linked.

Yet immediately after this comes a reference to Adam that evokes a very different myth, that of the first Adam, the parent of the human race and the victim of the Fall. "He that is made alive in Christ knows that he has sinned in Adam." It would be beyond credulity to think that Hecker was consciously aware of any subtle dialectic when he penned these two statements so close and in such distinction. Rather, they illustrate, not so much by his intention but by their mere presence, the ambiguity of the myth of the American Adam—an ambiguity that came through constantly. The image of an innocent, new creation, as compelling as it was, ignored the reality of evil and imperfection that accompanied the new American as it has all human beings. A sense that that reality was being neglected led on one level to what Lewis has described as the Party of Irony among American nineteenth-century writers—figures like James Russell Lowell and Orestes Brownson. Those writers would not forget the past and believe that the American Adam was really entirely new. They also had a sense of the tragic loss of America's innocence and of the betrayal of the American promise in the greed and selfishness of antebellum society. They were different from the consistently hopeful voices of Thoreau or Whitman whose *Leaves of Grass* stands as the fullest portrayal of the myth of the American Adam that the century produced.

In this context, Hecker appears to embody elements of both the Party of Hope and the Party of Irony, with a decidedly larger portion of the Hopeful than the Ironic. See R.W.G. Lewis, *The American Adam: Innocence, Tragedy and Tradition in the Nineteenth Century* (Chicago: University of Chicago Press, 1955).

216. The idea that Protestantism embodied the selfishness and individualism that was a barrier to true social progress was widespread. Hecker heard it from Associationists like William Henry Channing and Albert Brisbane who were decrying selfishness as the root of social evils. He followed Brownson's lead in linking Protestantism, individualism, and selfishness. As early as 1836 Brownson had begun criticizing Protestantism along these lines in *New Views*. He did it again and with more clarity in his January 1844 *Review* piece, "The Church Question."

217. Cf. note 11.

218. Manuscripts.

219. Friedrich von Hardenberg (1772–1801), wrote under the pseudonym "Novalis." His works had a major impact on German Romanticism and were popular among the New England Romantics, thanks to the efforts of John Weiss.

220. Shakespeare was enormously popular in antebellum America, largely through his plays which were widely presented. During 1835 in Philadelphia alone there were sixty-five performances. During the 1840s the number of inexpensive editions of his works grew rapidly to feed the public hunger. Emerson put forth his views on him in his famous *English Traits*. The English bard had a major effect on another Transcendentalist lover of Catholicism, Charles King Newcomb. See Charles Lee Francis, "Transcendental Hamlet," *Emerson Quarterly Review* 57 (Fourth Quarter 1969): 46–52.

We know from a letter to Brownson that Hecker was reading Torquato Tasso's

(1544–1595) *Gerusalemme Liberata* (*Jerusalem Delivered*) in English translation, probably the 1825 London, Hurst and Robinson edition. This work, considered to be his masterpiece, is highly attuned to the paradox between the lust for human aggrandizement and the search for spiritual growth. Tasso was himself tortured by scruples to the point of madness. Hecker at this time, as is far more evident in volume 6 than it is here, was also having his battles with a scrupulous conscience.

On Dante, see note 193.

221. Haydn's Symphony number 46 in B was composed in 1772. "Beethoven's Geister Waltz" is more problematic. No "Geister Waltz" is listed in his complete works. Hecker may have had in mind his piano trio Opus 70, number 1, known as the "Ghost Trio." Mendelssohn's work must be his "Lobgesang" (Symphony number 2 in B flat, opus 52, composed in 1840). Hecker's love of music was due in no small part to John S. Dwight. See note 59.

222. Heinrich Heine (1797–1856) was a German poet whose *Buch der Lieden der Lieder* (1827) won for him an international reputation. A spokesman of the post-Romantic school, he embraced much of the mood that had shaped the literature of the first quarter century but was keenly aware of its inadequacies, hence his criticism of Schlegel as overly sentimental.

August Wilhelm von Schlegel's (1767–1845) *A Course of Lectures on Dramatic Art and Literature* had wide currency in three English editions (London, 1815; Philadelphia, 1833; London, 1840).

223. Alexander Pope (1688–1744). There is no indication in any of the sources of what works of Pope's Hecker was reading.

224. On Hecker's mystical aesthetic, see note 111 and general introduction, "Conclusion."

225. Source unknown.

226. On the concept of synaestheticism, see note 66.

227. Although the pew rental system was a widespread Protestant tradition which was not part of Irish or German Catholicism, it had become popular in U.S. Catholic parishes by the 1840s. In New York parishes between 1836 and 1842 the income from pew rents almost equalled that from Sunday collections. In the parishes of New York that Dolan studied, only approximately 25 percent of parishioners could afford to rent pews. See Jay Dolan, *The Immigrant Church* (South Bend: University of Notre Dame Press, 1983), pp. 49–52.

Hecker wrote to Brownson on January 21 that in his desire to realize the Catholic church he had no eyes for its virtues, but only for its faults, meaning that he wished to see Catholics be all that they could be. The specific complaints about pew rents as well as Brownson's response are not extant.

228. No attempts at an autobiography are extant. The loose-leaf documents from around this time that we do have are clearly earlier products and are the beginnings of the diary. The continuing effect of Richter is evident. See general introduction on autobiography and note 2 on Richter.

229. Lent began that year on February 5. Hecker is concerned about keeping the fast prescribed by the church, although, ironically, he had before becoming a Catholic been more severe with himself.

230. Hecker was certainly taking to heart the words of *The Pius Guide:* "Contrition or sorrow must be such that the sinner sincerely and from his heart detest and hate the sin committed" (p. 105). He also follows them in his emphases on thankfulness for the sacrament of Penance and on the person of Christ as the one whose sacrifice makes possible the forgiveness of sins. Cf. pp. 105–06 of *The Pius Guide.*

231. Hecker throughout the diary often talks of the need for detachment. He continues to battle with the question here. Judging by his letter-writing, his later career, and the accounts that others have left of him, detachment from others was more something he talked about than practiced. In fact, what we have in the diary is probably a reaction against enjoying his friends too much and for some reason feeling guilty about it.

232. On the Cornelius Institute, see introduction to Volume 4.

233. Holy Week for 1845 began on March 16.

234. Bishop John Hughes had founded Fordham in the summer of 1841. Its first president was Hecker's confessor, Bishop John McCloskey. During Hecker's visit it was a humble place that did little to impress him after having lived at Brook Farm.

235. It is significant that Hecker mentions reading the lives of Ignatius and Francis Xavier. Throughout his life the Ignatian tradition influenced him at key points. Recall that the first Catholic bishop he met was Benedict Joseph Fenwick, of the Maryland Province of the Society of Jesus. His impression was very favorable, and he felt that Fenwick understood the process by which he was attracted to the church, something many Catholics did not. Here, when perplexed about vocation, he reads the lives of two Jesuit missionaries and will decide shortly to enter a missionary order and to define himself as a missionary to America. Later when in the Redemptorist novitiate, he reads the writings of the eighteenth-century Jesuit *spirituel,* Louis Lallemant, whose ideas on the internal guidance of the Spirit resonate deeply with his own. Finally when confronted with the greatest crisis of his life in his fifties—a case of chronic leukemia that took from him his active ministry—it is to a Jesuit author that he turns for help: J.P. de Caussade and his *Abandonment to Divine Providence.*

236. Holden believed, and he is almost certainly right, that this was yet another mistake by Hecker. The saint was Alphonsus Liguori, founder of the Redemptorists. The Redemptorists had charge of Holy Redeemer Church on Third Street in New York. Although Hecker was a bit put off by the unnamed pushy priest, his later visits proved fruitful and, of course, he wound up joining the order in August of the same year. See Holden, *Yankee Paul,* pp. 112 ff.

237. Hecker's study of Latin apparently hadn't gotten along too far. This is a corruption of the prayer from the Mass: "Agnus Dei qui tollis peccata mundi, dona nobis pacem."

238. Hecker at this point is in full swing in his conversion process. He is taking on more and more elements of Catholic piety—Mary, guardian angels, dependence on a confessor—and wants to become thoroughly remade. That desire motivates him to choose the Redemptorists, because of their Old World flavor and the opportunity

they represent of getting at last to Europe, a more thoroughly Catholic environment. See *An American Experience of God*, pp. 84–98.

239. Although formed as he was in the Neo-Platonic school of the Newness, Hecker had an admiration for St. Thomas. It is safe to say that he never saw the tensions between his own Platonic notions and the Aristotelian-Thomistic theology that was experiencing new popularity with theologians in Europe. Even later in life, he was attracted to Neo-Thomism for its cultural synthesis. He knew really only a little of Aquinas and appropriated bits and pieces of his thought over his career without ever being critical of the points at which his own thought differed. See "God and Man," PFA, and *The Church and the Age*.

240. Hecker's unmitigated trust in his spiritual director was to change after he entered the Redemptorists. After McCloskey, it was all downhill. His first director in the Redemptorists repeatedly frustrated him, failing to have a clue about where he was coming from. Although he had some good experiences with Redemptorists like Bernard Heilig, he returned to a sense of the importance of attending to one's interiority. It was there, he was to argue as a mature Catholic, that one could follow one's *attrait* and learn to discern the Spirit's leading. See "Notes on the Spiritual Life," PFA.

241. Orestes A. Brownson. See notes 6, 7, 26, 69, 94, 105, 119, 123, 156, 168, 213. This is Hecker's famous account of his mentor, which is one of the most poignant insights into the character of Brownson penned by one of his contemporaries.

242. Emerson. On Hecker's antipathy for Emerson, see note 170.

243. Baltimore.

244. Hecker later became quite familiar with the writings of the founder of the Sulpicians, Jean-Jacques Olier, but there is no indication that he knew much about the Sulpicians or their seminary in Paris at this point. (For later relationship between the Paulists and Sulpicians see Christopher Kauffman, *Tradition and Transformation in Catholic Culture* [New York: Macmillan, 1988].) One thing is evident, however, as the diary ends. Hecker has at this point nothing to share with his old Transcendentalist friends in New England. He is beginning the period of great enthusiasm for his new found conviction. During it many of the themes that have formed him seem to disappear behind standard Catholic apologetics and manual piety. But it is only temporary. The foundations laid during the years of the diary-writing in the final analysis hold fast. He builds on them what we have seen prefigured here: a Romantic, American, Catholic expression of his religious experience.

LIST OF EMENDATIONS EXPLAINED

A detailed list of emendations is given to allow the reconstruction of the original manuscript reading of any section in which an emendation has been made in this edition.

The first two columns indicate the location of a given emended text in this printed edition (**HP**) and in the original manuscript (**MS**). The page number is given, followed by the line number. Thus, for example, 1.13 indicates page one, line thirteen. Since there are no page numbers in the original, numbers have been assigned beginning with the earliest sections and moving on consecutively following the chronological order. The page of the diary volume (book) or the page of the lettered fragment (A-L) is given followed by a period and a line number.

The third and fourth columns indicate the nature of the emendations made. The **HP** column gives the reading as it has been rendered in this edition. The **MS** column gives the manuscript reading. The following abbreviations have been used:

↑↓ interlineated text.
⟨ ⟩ cancelled text. See Editorial Procedures #6.
Standard copy editor's marks are used to indicate dashes, capitalization, etc.

LIST OF EMENDATIONS

*Fragments (A–L)

HP	MS	HP	MS
87. 9	*A.15	it. It	it it
87.10	A.15–16	undeveloped. In	undeveloped in
87.11	A.18	life. But	life but
87.16	B. 2	understood. It	understood it
87.18	B. 6–7	Man. It	Man it
87.20	B.10	self. It	self it
87.21	B.10	out. It	out it
87.21	B.11–12	appearence. It	appearence it
87.23	B.12	object; it	object it
87.23	B.15	Ye	Ye ⟨a⟩
87.25	B.18–19	twaddle. It	twaddle it
87.29	B.25	AM. It	AM it
87.29	B.26	unknown. Many	unknown many
87.31	C. 1	by unmanly	by unman ↑l↓y
87.33	C. 5	Wertherism. It	Wertherism it
87.34	C. 6	spectre. It	spectre it
87.35	C. 8	Space. It	Space it
88. 2	C.12	spoken. Has	spoken has
88. 3	C.13	"Communion"?	"Communion" he
88. 3	C.14	Contemplated. He	Contemplated he
88. 4	C.16	Future. His	Future his
88. 6	C.19	times. Hence	times hence
88. 8	C.21	Change. But	Change but
88.11	C.26	as a great mind	↑ as a great mind ↓
88.11	C.26	as the father of a new light	↑ as the father of a new light ↓
88.13	D. 2	void. It	void it
88.14	D. 4	of. It	of it
88.15	D. 5	satisfy. It	satisfy it
88.16	D. 7	measure. It	measure it
88.17	D. 8	Men. It	Men it

HP	MS	HP	MS
88.18	D. 9	of an unknown	of ↑ an ↓ unknown
88.18	D.10	Man. It	Man it
88.22	E. 2	myself? What	myself what
88.22	E. 3	say? Is	say is
88.25	E. 6	love all	love ⟨them⟩ all
88.26	E. 7	too much	to much
88.26	E. 7–8	me. It	me it
88.28	E.10	life. My	life my
88.29	E.11–12	with. It	with it
88.30	E.13	unburthened. Riches	unburthened riches
88.30	E.13	up. What	up what
88.31	E.15	it. My	it my
88.32	E.16	speak? Who	speak who
88.33	E.17	Men. My	Men my
88.34	E.18	myself. Oh	myself oh
88.35	E.19	burthens. What	burthens what
88.35	E.20	home? When	home when
88.36	E.21	body. What	body what
88.36	E.22	do? How	do how
88.37	E.23	controls? And	controls and
88.38	E.24	task. How	task how
89. 2	E.26	spirit? Unto	spirit unto
89. 2	E.28	thee then do	the then do
89. 3	E.28	suffer; so	suffer so
89. 4	E.29	others. Why	others why
89. 4	E.29	so? Wherefore	so wherefore
89. 4	F. 1	here? If	here if
89. 8–9	F. 6	condition. My	condition my
89. 9	F. 7	gone. They	gone they
89. 9	F. 7	gratification. My	gratification my
89.13	F.12	do? Who	do who
89.13	F.12–13	Comforter? Will	Comforter? will
89.14	F.13	Christ? Alas	Christ alas
89.14	F.13	too deeply. And	to deeply and
89.15	F.14	utterance? If	utterance if
89.16	F.16	faith. Say	faith say
89.17	F.17	me. Why	me why
89.18	F.18	could. Neither	could neither
89.19	F.20	am. O	am o
89.21	F.23	in. Thy	in Thy
89.22	F.25	unto thee for	unto the for
89.26	G. 1	to an answer	⟨to⟩ an answer
89.27	G. 2	sent—which	sent which
89.28	G. 3	family—he	family he
89.28	G. 3	unbeknowingly	un⟨be⟩knowingly

HP	MS	HP	MS
89.34	G. 7–8	agreeable. It	agreeable it
89.35	G.13	than loose it	than lo⟨o⟩se it
89.40	G.19	upon me further	upon ↑ me ↓ further
90. 2	G.24–25	life. If	life if
90. 3	G.25	my guard I	my g ↑ u⟨a⟩ ↓ rd⟨..⟩ I
90. 7	H. 3–4	heart. Who	heart who
90. 8	H. 4	God? It	God it
90. 8	H. 5	kind. How	kind how
90.10	H. 7	Wisdom? Alas	Wisdom alas
90.11	H. 9	soul. The	soul the
90.12	H.9–10	understanding. Oh	understanding oh
90.14	H.13	again. This	again this
90.14	H.13	to itself	to its ↑ ⟨st⟩ ↓ self
90.15	H.14	suffering? Alone	suffering alone
90.17	H.17	spit upon and	spit ↑ upon ↓ and
90.17	H.17–18	Men. Oh	Men oh
90.19	H.20	which he came	which ↑ he ↓ came
90.19	H.21	bestow. Well	bestow well
90.20	H.22	do? He	do he
90.21	H.23	receive. He	receive he
90.21	H.24	him. He	him he
90.24	H.27	mercy are unbounded	mercy ↑ are ↓ un-bounded
90.25	H.28	closer communion	closer ⟨in⟩ commun-ion
90.29	I. 5	steps. The	steps the
90.32	I. 8	an ebb not	↑ an ↓ ebb not
90.34	I.12	commences. This	commences this
90.35	I.13	last? May	last may
90.36	I.14	peices. This	peices this
91. 1	I.19	I want is	I w⟨h⟩ant is
91. 2	I.19	direction. Not	direction not
91. 5	I.23	know not	no not
91. 6	I.26	spirits. The	spirits the
91. 9	I.27–28	Community. In	Community in
91.12	J. 4	with. It	with it
91.14–15	J. 5–6	had when I left home. If	↑ had when I ↓ left home if
91.17	J. 8	will. If	will if
91.19	J.11	sight. But	sight but
91.20	J.12	to do thy	to ↑ do ↓ thy
91.20	J.13	it. Give	it give
91.22	J.15	nothing. And	nothing and
91.27	J.20–21	Life. If	Life if
91.27	J.21	home in this	home ⟨and⟩ in this

HP	MS	HP	MS
91.29	J.23	suspense. Lead	suspense lead
91.29–30	J.24	to. Keep	to keep
91.30	J.25	life. It	life it
91.30	J.25	a temporary	a⟨n⟩ temporary
91.33	J.28–K.1	place. Leaving	place leaving
91.34	K. 3	unable. My	unable my
91.38	K. 8	off & on	of ⟨on⟩ ↑ & ↓ on
92. 2	K.13	Tabu. The	Tabu the
92. 5	K.19	cease. My	cease my
92. 6	K.20–21	gradually. There	gradually there
92. 7	K.22	go? When	go when
92. 8	K.23	place. A	place a
92. 9	K.24	time. My	time my
92.24	L.12	me? Oh	me Oh
92.25	L.13	bosom? It	bosom it
92.31	L.21	enter. it	enter it
92.36	L.25	see. Could	see could
92.37	L.27	life. The	life the
92.38	L.28	planet. Why	planet why
92.39	L.29	a sphere a	a⟨n⟩ sphere a⟨n⟩
92.40	L.30	and amidst the	an amidst the

VOLUME I

HP	MS	HP	MS
93. 6	I1. 9	thee? Unto	thee unto
93. 7	1.10	thee? Didst	thee didst
93.19	1.31	spirit. Do	spirit do
93.22–23	1.37	spirit. Willt	spirit willt
94. 2	2A.20	fire. He	fire he
94. 8	2A.27–28	I went with	I w⟨h⟩ent with
94. 9	2A.28	woods. My	woods my
94. 9	2A.29	pleasantly. The	pleasantly the
94. 9	2A.29	beautifull. The	beautifull the
94.10	2A.30	striking. The	striking the
94.19	2B. 1	Roxbury; it	Roxbury it
94.19–29	2B. 2	was Easter Sunday. The	was ⟨Good F⟩ Easter Sunday the
94.21	2B. 4	tomb. This	tomb this
94.22	2B. 5	sermon. In	sermon in
94.29–30	2B.16	head. It	head it
94.35	2B.25	senseless. A	senseless a
94.36	2B.26	were soaring	were ⟨—⟩soaring
94.39	2B.29	for? For	for for

HP	MS	HP	MS
94.39	2B.30	characters? Why	characters why
95. 1	2B.31	misspent? Are	misspent are
95. 2	2B.33	itself? Nay	itself nay
95. 4	2B.38	myself? What	myself what
95. 4-5	2B.38	hindrance? Nay	hindrance nay
95. 5	2B.39	any? So	any so
95. 6	2B.40	(Mrs. Barlow)	(—)
95. 7	3. 3-4	communion. Before	communion before
95.10	3. 9	vice-versa. Instead	vice-versa instead
95.17	3.21	Glory. The	Glory the
95.17	3.21	be. (What	be (what
95.20	3.26	it. Comprehend	it comprehend
95.25	3.34	world; out	world out
95.27-28	3.38	it? The Catholic	it the Catholic
95.31-32	4. 6	church. One	church one
95.32	4. 6	Pictures. Others	Pictures others
95.33	4. 7	emotions. In	emotions in
95.33	4. 9	us; another	us another
95.35	4.13	fact is	fact ⟨of⟩ is
96. 4	4.26	God? Is	God is
96. 4	4.26	here? Why	here why
96.15	5. 3	Time, Immensity	Time Immensity
96.20	5.10	phenomena	p↑h↓enomena
96.21	5.11	thought: There	thought There
96.28	5.23	support. The	support the
96.40	6. 4	back. Still after	back still for
97. 2	6. 8	changed. It	changed it
97. 4	6.12	that Thou dist	that Tho dist
97.17	6.39	Earth. None	Earth none
97.21	7. 8-9	character; they	character they
97.22-23	7.10	degree. Last	degree last
97.24	7.14	falling. Oh	falling Oh
97.25	7.16	am. It	am it
97.35	7.30-31	soul. It	soul it
97.36	7.31	sides. It	sides it
97.36	7.31-32	full. One	full one
97.37	7.34	changed. There	changed there
97.39	7.37	not, come and taste, try	not come and taste try
97.39	7.38-39	see; heaven	see heaven
98. 2	8. 6	good; it	good it
98. 9-10	8.17	body. At	body at
98.20	8.36	transgressions	tran⟨g⟩sgressions
98.31	9.17	affected me more	affected↑me↓more
98.33-34	9.22-23	Peter, Catholicism; Paul	Peter Catholicism Paul

HP	MS	HP	MS
98.34	9.24	Protestansm; John	Protestansm John
98.38–39	9.31	Individual, Infallibility	Individual Infallibility
98.39	9.34	Life. Neither	Life neither
99. 5	10. 2	knowledge. Of	knowledge of
99.22	10.30	difference: He	difference He
99.25	10.36	will and gives	will any gives
99.29	11. 4–5	Hope, "Future," Ideal	Hope "Future" Ideal
99.30	11. 6	and Object	and ⟨the⟩ Object
99.33	11.11–12	in. I	in I
100. 2	11.29	sights of all. We	si⟨i⟩ghts of all we
100. 3	11.30	centre. All	centre all
100. 5	11.35	attractions	attraction
100. 5	11.35	destiny: Fear	destiny Fear
100. 6	11.35–36	hope; Pain	hope Pain
100. 6	11.36	Pleasure; Strength	Pleasure Strength
100.12	12. 7	evil." "For	evill" "for
100.18	12.20	one; knowledge	one knowledge
100.20	12.21	If Adam	If ⟨the⟩ Adam
100.22	12.24	woman, which will	woman which will
100.22–23	12.24	union restored, is	union restored is
100.27	12.31	statement. Another	statement another
100.27	12.32	this; All	this All
100.31	13. 1	and more spiritual	and ⟨and⟩ more spiritual
100.37	13.10	feel that some one	feel tha some one
100.40	13.16	and oppressed me	and oppresse⟨s⟩ ↑ d ↓ me
101. 1	13.20	presence. If	presence if
101. 8–9	13.34–35	christian. Conversion	christian conversion
101. 9	13.35	immersion; the	immersion the
101. 9–10	13.36–37	state, atmosphere. He	state atmosphere he
101.10	13.37	life. He	life he
101.13–14	14. 7	meaning, The	meaning The
101.30	14.31	fiend. In	fiend in
101.32	14.36	saying the World	saying ⟨life⟩ ↑ the ↓ World
101.33	14.37	flowers; he	flowers he
102.10	15.26	fully, Who	fully Who
102.13	15.32	Christ never lived	Christ neve lived
102.14	15.33–34	life, The Father, as He said; and	life The Father as He said and
102.15	15.34	of the high	of the ↑ m ↓ high
102.21	16.11	a Conception an	a Conception⟨s⟩ an
102.23	16.13–14	Heart—a	Heart a
102.25–26	16.17–18	thought. This	thought this

HP	MS	HP	MS
102.27	16.19–20	accidents, because	accidents because
102.27–28	16.21	unexisting; but	unexisting but
102.31	16.27–28	his writing: the	↑ his ↓ writing the
102.37	16.36–37	They all have	The⟨re⟩ ↑ y ↓ all have
103. 1	17. 8	why he should	why ↑ he ↓ should
103. 2	17. 9	hence been founded	hence founded
103. 4	17.13	or can give	or can⟨.⟩ give
103. 4	17.14	through which his	⟨that⟩ ↑ through which ↓ his
103. 5–6	17.17	Church; have	Church have
103.10	17.26	historically true, for the Holy Divine men of the Past we find in the Church and	historically, true for the Holy Divine men of the Past we find in the Church, and
103.11	17.27	Church, and	Church and
103.13	17.31	believe: those	believe those
103.16	17.38	Christ. And even the	Christ and even: the
103.17–18	18. 3	the media of	the me⟨.⟩dia of
103.18	18. 5	them. Can	them can
103.24	18.17	This they appear	this the appear
103.30–31	18.31–32	Poverty? Ah	Poverty Ah
103.32	18.34–35	Bliss? Nay	Bliss nay
103.33	18.36	thy superiors	they superiors
103.33	18.36	Why talk	Why, talk
103.34	18.38	and blind	an blind
104. 1	19.15–16	desires. Would	desires would
104. 6	19.20–21	me. It	me it
104.22	20. 7	one. For	one for
104.27	20.15	not capable of	not ⟨susceptible⟩ ↑ capable ↓ of
104.33	20.28	life harmony	life ⟨and⟩ harmony
104.34	20.28	and union with	and uni⟨ty⟩ on with
104.37	20.35	superstition. How	superstition ⟨more or less as it may be⟩. How
104.38	20.37	to the past	⟨for⟩ to the past
105. 1	21. 4	desiring listfully	desiring list⟨ely⟩ ↑ fully ↓
105. 4	21. 9	Dead. Wish	Dead wish
105. 7	21.16	is now sorrow	is ↑ now ↓ sorrow
105.10	21.21	hear too delicate	her to delicate
105.10	21.22	Listen! Has	List has
105.11	21.24	moments a strain	moments a⟨s⟩ strain
105.13	21.25	music. The	music the
105.13	21.25	that the pleasure	⟨.⟩ that the pleasure

HP	MS	HP	MS
105.16	21.34	more pure	more ⟨beautiful & lovely⟩ ↑ pure ↓
105.17	21.35	thy senses	thy senses ⟨of soul⟩
105.19	22. 1	in that day	in th⟨e⟩ ↑ at ↓ day ↑ ⟨s⟩ ↓
105.22–23	22. 7	doubt! Hast	doubt hast
105.28	22.14	saw (I	saw ⟨for⟩ (I
105.31	22.19	was as if it were	was if it it were
105.37	22.30	image. It	image it
105.40	22.34	now at times that	now ⟨so⟩ ↑ at times ↓ that
106. 1	23. 1	mind. But	mind but
106.18	23.24	support myself	support ⟨..⟩ myself
106.20	23.28	sacrifice much of	sacrifice ⟨f⟩ much of
106.34	24.16	Love, Zeno	Love Zeno
107. 2	24.25	me; it	me it
107. 8	24.34	lovelier. On	lovelier on
107. 9	24.36	hor *rid*; it	hor *rid* it
107. 9	24.36	too horrid. Away	to horrid away
107.17	25.13	wailings; wherefore	wailings wherefore
107.18–19	25.15	these? Is	these is
107.20	25.18	or my soul would	or my ↑ soul ↓ would
107.21	25.18–19	in. To	in to
107.28	25.31	ha aha! why	aha why
107.34	26. 4	few. Those	few those
107.35	26. 6	me. What	me what
107.36	26. 7	go? What	go what
107.37	26. 9–10	go? Come	go come
107.38	26.11	hurrah, let	hurrah let
108. 1	26.14	Lies are	⟨They⟩ ↑ Lies ↓ are
108.14	26.34	do. Do these	do. Does these
108.14	26.34	not in a	not ↑ in ↓ a
108.16	26.37	Mark. Either	Mark either
108.22	27. 8	is; when	is ⟨.⟩ when
108.23	27. 9	religious, truth	religious truth
108.25	27.13	soulless; the	soulless the
108.29	27.19	a inperception	a in perception
108.34	27.27	this? Ah	this ah
108.38	27.33	*ex*plained	*ex* plained
109.18	28.23	inclination. Sometimes	inclination sometimes
109.24	28.32	do? This	do this
109.26–27	28.37	would. Others	would others
109.28	28.39–29.1	friends. What	friends what
109.31	29. 4	peace. He	peace he
109.32	29. 7	me. There	me there

HP	MS	HP	MS
109.38	29.15	children; thou	children thou
110. 1	29.18	love. Let	love let
110.10	29.29	morning. The	morning the
110.10	29.30	answered; for	answered for
110.15	30. 4	possible; accept	possible accept
110.20–21	30.14	Prayer and Doubt	Pr↑a↓yer and Doubt
110.22	30.15–16	face. What	face what
110.22	30.16	all? After	all after
110.23	30.17	you have did	you ha⟨d⟩↑ve↓ did
110.23	30.18	this: get	this get
110.27	30.25	be still; work	be still work
110.29	30.28–29	know what I	know would write at home what
110.34	30.38	too daily	to daily
110.41	31.10	immediately; there	immediately there
111. 7	31.21	shadows; beneath	shadows beneath
111. 8	31.21	nothing; they	nothing they
111.23	32. 5	others? But	others but
111.23	32. 5	me; it	me it
111.23	32. 5	death; it	death it
111.23	32. 5–6	work; nay	work nay
111.27–28	32.11	Your work gives	You work gives
111.39	32.28	one; they	one they
112.13	33.17	Unholy things must	Unholy thins must
112.14	33.17–18	unchristian in action	unchri↑s↓⟨s⟩t⟨ai⟩↑ia↓n
112.15	33.19	be unchristian in	be ⟨one⟩ unchristian in
112.15	33.19	words. It	words it
112.22	33.29	name, for	name ⟨and⟩ for
112.35	34. 9	God. Be	God be
112.35	34.10	speak. For	speak for
113.11	34.33–34	means. If	means if
113.11	34.34	the only remedy	the ⟨..⟩↑only↓ remedy
113.13	34.36–37	mind. It	mind it
113.14	34.38	is. Willt	is willt
113.17	35. 6	ground to live	ground and to live
113.19	35. 9	in them; they	in them they
113.20	35.10	future; they	future they
113.21	35.13	prophecies still	p⟨h⟩rophecies still
113.23	35.16	some nook	some ⟨little⟩ nook
113.27	35.21–22	me prophecy.	me p⟨h⟩rophecy
113.27	35.22	I now am; in it	I now am in it
113.28	35.24	life. How	life how
113.30	35.29	place; it	place it
113.30	35.31	me; it does	me it does

HP	MS	HP	MS
113.31	35.29	too much	to much
113.31	35.32	me; it is	me it is
113.34	35.38	to try it	to ⟨.⟩try it
113.35	35.40	soon. If	soon if
114. 5	35.11	past; now	past now
114.15	36.28	despond. It	despond it
114.24	37. 3	say. Am	say am
114.25	37. 5	is most proper	is ⟨..⟩ most proper
114.28	37.10	happy I would accept	happy accept
114.32	37.17	bed; farther	bed father
114.35	37.20	the difficulty	the difficult
114.36	37.23	unnaturel; how	unnaturel how
114.38	37.26	you; you are	you you are
115. 3	37.35	But alas I	But ⟨A⟩↑a↓las I
115. 6	38. 1	here. He	here he
115. 6	38. 1	days. He	days he
115.29	38.28	Mr Alcott's next	Mr Alcott's ⟨to-morrow⟩ next
116. 5	39.22	too much to	to much to
116. 6	39.24	Alas him I	Alas h⟨e⟩↑i↓⟨r⟩↑m↓I
116.16	40. 6	coincide; nay	coincide nay
116.22	40.12–13	Larned, thoughtfulness; I,	Larned thoughtfulness I,
116.22	40.13	I, Seriousness;	I, Seriousness
116.22	40.13	Lane, Fidelity	Lane Fidelity
116.24	40.14	This morning after	This morning This morning
116.25	40.16	Integrity; I,	Integrity I
116.25	40.16–17	I, Harmonic Being;	I Harmonic Being
116.25–26	40.17	Lane, Progressive	Lane Progressive
116.26	40.17	being; Larned	being Larned
116.26	40.17–18	Annihilation of Self; Bower,	Annihilation of Self Bower
116.35	40.32	Sunday last, and	Sunday ⟨ni⟩↑last↓, and
116.39	41. 4	too near	to near
116.39	41. 5	me; they	me they
117. 7	41.17	feel; if	feel if
117.15–16	41.32	too great or too much	to great or to much
117.32	42.26	compare; there	compare there
118.21	43.34	question of	question ⟨–⟩ of
118.29	44. 6	receive a answer	receive ⟨my⟩ a answer
119. 6	44.31	do. Man	do. The q Man
119.15	45.13	been; in	been in
119.27	45.30	to the benefit	to⟨o⟩ the benefit

HP	MS	HP	MS
119.34	46. 5	home. What	home what
119.35	46. 7	home; whether	home whether
120. 2	46.22	it; the influence	it the influence
120.14	47.12	me; one	me one
120.23	47.27	that leads; whatsoever	that leads whatsoever
120.23	47.27	me. It	me it
120.25–26	47.32	temptations. Willt	temptations willt
120.26–27	47.33	and the strength to	and ↑ the strength ↓ to
120.28	48. 1	Abraham came	Abraham ⟨..⟩ came
120.29	48. 3	life. He	life he
120.37	48.18	All. I? There	All. I there
120.40	48.24	find a new	find A new
121. 9	49. 4	prominent Men of	prominent Men ⟨t⟩ of
121.27	49.34	realities; the	realities the
121.39	50.15	it? What	it what
122. 3–4	50.22–23	Christ and (not	Christ ⟨Lucifer⟩ and (not
122.16	51. 3	a Lamb	a⟨n⟩ ⟨Angel⟩ ↑ Lamb ↓
122.20	51. 9	Soul, the Unknown	Soul, ↑ the ↓ Unknown
122.36	52. 7	exertions; we	exertions we
122.37	52. 8	it; it	it it
123. 2	52.18	place. And	place and
123. 3	52.20	give the opportunity	give ⟨an⟩ ↑ the ↓ opportunity
123. 5	52.23	others; nay	others nay
123. 8	52.29	what have we	what ↑ have ↓ we
123. 9	52.30	as unconscious of	as ⟨not⟩ unconscious of
123.12–13	53. 1	in the pious	in the ⟨in the⟩ pious
123.20	53.12	stated. But	stated but
123.24	53.20	week. With	week with
123.33	53.35	that they are	that ↑ they ↓ are
124. 8	54.20	the opinion	the the opinion
124.14–15		know now—all things	know now at is all things
124.23–24	55. 8–9	still increase dependest	⟨be a the⟩ increase ⟨is⟩
124.29	55.19	with her and	with her⟨e⟩ and
124.31–32		my highest I can	my highest and I can
124.33	55.26	to me I	to me ⟨-⟩ I
124.33	55.27	in that sense	in th⟨is⟩ ↑ at ↓ sense
124.34	55.29	fleshiness in	fleshiness ⟨about⟩ in
124.36–37	55.34	no one to	no ⟨.⟩ one to
125. 5–6	56.12	this link which	this li ↑ n ↓ k which
125. 8	56.16	and touches	and ⟨makes⟩ touches
125.13	56.26	greater degree the creature	greater ↑ degree the creature ↓

HP	MS	HP	MS
125.19	56.36	From all	from all
125.23	57. 3	becoming which is wrapt up in the dim approaching distance	becoming ↑ which is ↓ wrapt up in the ⟨distant⟩, dim approaching ⟨-⟩ ↑ distance ↓
125.29–31	57.11–12	the faculties which take cognizance of the inner....faculties which take cognizance of	the ↑ faculties which take cognizance of the ↓ inner...faculties ↑ which take cognizance ↓ of
125.31	57.13	which take	⟨of the⟩ which ⟨in⟩ ↑ take ↓
125.33	57.15	the human race	the ↑ human ↓ race
125.41	57.29	I care not; it	I care not it
126. 3	57.32	done, they are before us,	done they are before us
126. 6	57.37	the phrophecies of	the phrophec⟨y⟩ ↑ ies ↓ of
126.18	58.17	God. My	God my
126.18	58.18	this: it	this it
126.22	58.23–24	This; Instead	This Instead
126.27	58.33	In making	I making
126.28	58.34	So did	⟨such⟩ So did
126.31	59. 2	their individual	their indivi⟨a⟩ ↑ d ↓ ual
126.32	59. 3	state; but	state but
126.35	59. 9	view; selfism	view selfism
126.41	59.18	life. Out	life out
127.13	60.14	the intense.	the intense⟨s⟩.
127.14	60.15	With our	⟨mixed⟩ ⟨w⟩ ↑ W ↓ ith our
127.19	60.25	which can raise	which ⟨.⟩ can raise
127.19	60.27	vice versa. Christ	vice versa ⟨.⟩ . Christ
127.20	60.28	by a word; Peter	by a word Peter
127.20	60.29	by a word	by a⟨.⟩ word
127.24	60.35	proportionately; the	proportionately the
127.24	60.36	love; they	love they
127.25	60.37	love each give	love eac give
127.25	61. 1	loose but increase	loose but add increase
127.27	61. 4	have by their union their rapidity accelerated	have by ⟨-⟩ their ↑ union their ↓ rapidity accelerated ⟨by⟩
127.32	61.10	circumstance; it	circumstance it
127.33	61.13	Being as thought	Being ⟨i⟩ ↑ a ↓ s thought

HP	MS	HP	MS
127.38	61.19	those that have	those that have
128. 3	61.27	to the end of our	to ↑ the end of ↓ our
128. 6	62. 4	home. Heretofore	home heretofore
128. 8	62. 7	there. At	there at
128.18	62.27	acknowledge it	acknowledge ↑ it ↓
128.24	63. 3	me the smile	me th⟨y⟩ ↑ e ↓ smile
128.25–26	63. 7	unto me; what	⟨on⟩ unto me what
128.32	63.16	has been and	has ↑ been ↓ and
129. 2–3	63.29	was, one with God	was one with God
129. 7	64. 4	do. Continually	do continually
129.23	64.32	season? This	season this
129.25	65. 3	breadth. One	breadth one
129.26	65. 3–4	other. The present generation is added	other ⟨every⟩ ↑ the present ↓ generation is ⟨additio⟩ added
129.35	65.20	acts; these	acts these
130.14	65.21	endelibly the	↑ endelibly ↓ the
129.36	65.21–22	gasp. Sometimes	gasp sometimes
130.15	65.22	world. How	world ⟨upon⟩. How
130.16	65.23	what we smell feel	↑ what ↓ we smell ⟨or⟩ feel
129.39	65.29	discomfiture.	discomfiture. ⟨That⟩
130.21	66.33	increases life	increase life
130.21	66.34	quality. This	quality this
130. 1	65.36	eat too much	eat to much
130.28	67.12	when I go home	when I go ⟨away⟩ home
130.30	67.15	departed; there	departed there
130.32	67.19	more grown; and where my position, in what relation, this	more grown ⟨than⟩ and where my position in what relation this
130.33–34	67.22	is quite excited	is ↑ quite ↓ excited
130.42	68. 2	devout; inspire	devout inspire
130.42	68. 3	soul; raise	soul raise
131. 1	68. 5	help me to	help ⟨to⟩ me to
131. 8–9	68.19–20	spirit. Thou	spirit thou
131.10	68.22	spirit. Fill	spirit fill
131.12	68.26	Lord. Bless	Lord bless
131.16	69. 3	succession measured	succession ⟨is⟩ measured
131.17	69. 6	moving; hence	moving hence
131.28	69.25	life. Until	life until
131.28	69.26	because we	because ⟨.⟩ we
131.33	70. 3	we ourselves shut	we ⟨shut out⟩ ↑ ⟨our⟩ ↓ ourselves

HP	MS	HP	MS
131.39–40	70.15	a visible progress	a⟨s⟩ visible progress
132.12–13	71. 4	a celestine desert	a ⟨.⟩ celestine desert
132.26	71.25	Where will	Where ⟨.⟩ will
132.30–31	71.34	hands of one	hands o⟨n⟩ ↑ f ↓ one
133.17	73.32	Love-Feast. In	Love-Feast in
133.22	74. 6	feel sad. My	feel ⟨so⟩ sad. My
133.24	74. 9	please; life	please life
133.28	74.15	impossible).	impossible) ⟨for⟩.
133.28–29	74.15	Aspiration is as unfathomable as heavens	Aspiration is ↑ as unfathomable ↓ ⟨a bottomless⟩ as heavens
133.29	74.16	height is unreachable	⟨is⟩ he ↑ i ↓ ght ↑ is unreachable ↓
133.31	74.18	for stillness	for ↑ stillness ↓
134. 1	74.29	thee. Our	thee our
134. 3–4	74.33	a serene lovefullness	a ↑ serene ↓ lovefullness
134.11	75. 8	has occupied	has ⟨my⟩ occupied
134.16	75.15	not speak	not ⟨say so⟩ speak
134.18	75.18	two sexes	two ⟨.⟩ sexes
134.20	75.21	truth the same as Jesus Christ	truth ↑ the same as ↓ Jesus Christ
134.21	75.23	lovefullness and	lovef ↑ ull ↓ ness and
134.25	75.28	was without spot	was⟨a⟩ without spot
134.30	75.35	state wherein	state ⟨of⟩ wherein
134.31–32	76. 2	the unity of	the unity ⟨.⟩ of
134.34	76. 5	created by God as they are at	created ↑ by God ↓ as they ⟨were⟩ are
135. 9	77. 2	4 within a	4 within ⟨.⟩ a
135.12–13	77. 6	engages too much	engages to much
135.19	77.11	nuts. The	nuts The
135.29	77.32	until all that	until ⟨.⟩ all that
135.35	78. 8	questions not	questions ⟨.⟩not
135.35–36	78. 9	them; the	them the
136. 4	78.16	letters: one	letters one
136. 6	78.20	lieber Carl	lieber C⟨h⟩arl
136. 7	78.Margin	Sept. 1	↑ Sept. 1 ↓ ⟨Aug⟩
136.21	79. 8	that essentially	that ⟨is⟩ essentially
136.22	79.12	an Absolute	an ⟨a⟩ ↑ A ↓ bsolute
136.24	79.15	cause, absolute cause, of	cause absolute cause of
136.25	79.17	fall in with	fall in ↑ with ↓
136.28	79.23	Character; the	Character the
136.29	79.24	classification: the	classification the
136.29	79.25	Eastern, the	Eastern the

HP	MS	HP	MS
136.30	79.25	consolidation, the	consolidation the
136.33	79.30	One leads	One ⟨.⟩ leads
136.36	80. 2	not half aware	not ⟨a⟩ half aware
137. 2	80. 8	as dumb as a	as dumb⟨e⟩ as ⟨.⟩ a
137. 5	80.13	Why, what do you intend?	Why what do you intend
137. 8-9	80.21	One, We	One we
137.14	80.29-30	every other relation	every ↑ other ↓ relation ⟨at all⟩
137.15	80.32	can you	can ⟨.⟩you
137.18	81. 1	mysterious. Why	mysterious why
137.22	81. 9	the legitimacy	the ⟨present⟩ legitimacy
137.26	81.12	head speaks	head ⟨s⟩ speaks
137.31	81.19	sculptors. This	sculptors this
137.38	81.30	does not provide	d⟨id⟩ ↑ oes ↓ not provide
138. 3	82. 3	pennance Eucharist and	pennance ⟨e⟩ ↑ E ↓ ucharist and
138. 9	82.10	full far	full ⟨and⟩ far
138.11	82.12	being? Then	being then
138.19	82.23	Highest we	Highest ⟨more⟩ we
138.19	82.24	do; more	do more
138.25	83. 3	insane; we	insane we
139. 4	83.28	truth; it	truth it
139. 5	83.31	Death; to	Death to
139. 8	83a. 1-2	morning. They	morning they
139.20	83a.19	remembrance prospect	remembrance ⟨or⟩ prospect
139.25	83a.27	too sensitive	to sensitive
139.29	83a.33	melody. Where	melody where
140. 3	83b.12	Its odour	Its ⟨smell⟩ odour
140.22	84.17	too often	to often
141. 1	85.17	Instead of being	Instead of⟨e⟩ being
141. 8	85.27	God in	God ⟨.⟩ in
141.10	85.31	every thing;	every thing
141.29	86.21	darkness. It	darkness it
141.38	86.37	to solve them is	to ⟨be⟩ solve⟨d⟩ ↑ them ↓
141.42	87. 5	other. Our	other our
142. 3	87.10	perfect way than	perfect ↑ way ↓ than
142.14	87.25	God instead	God of in instead
142.17	87.29	by not coming	by ↑ not ↓ coming
142.21	88. 2	my spare time	my ↑ spare ↓ time
142.27	88.10	I have been in	I have been ⟨in some⟩ in
142.28	88.12	wished; this	wished this

HP	MS	HP	MS
142.30	88.14	Mrs Almira ⟨Bar⟩lowe	Mrs. ⟨A⟩↑G↓lmira ⟨Ba✗rl⟩↑d↓owe
142.31	88.16	him in which he	h⟨er⟩↑im↓in which ⟨s⟩he
142.31–32	88.17	to him and	to h⟨er⟩↑im↓and
142.32–33	88.18	towards him	towards h⟨er⟩↑im↓
142.34	88.21	for him to	for h⟨er⟩↑im↓
143. 1	88.30	been made with	been↑made↓with
143.17–18	89.16	labor. The	labor. ⟨The⟩ The
143.22	89.20	inspiration. Universal	inspiration⟨s⟩. Universal
143.28	90. 3	me last	me ⟨as⟩ last
144. 2	90. 7	the aching	the ⟨the⟩ aching
144. 9	90.15	it. Why	it why
144. 9	90.15	is. Since	is since
144.15	91. 1	stop; where	stop where
144.15	91. 2	Does it	Does⟨t⟩ it
144.18	91. 5	vicious; creation	vicious creation
144.21	91.10	sin. Therefore	sin therefore
144.29	91.25	God. To	God to
145. 6	92.18	resignation; what	resignation what
145. 8	92.20	me; its	me its
145.13	92.28	else time	else ⟨the⟩ time
145.18	93. 1	by it	by ⟨all⟩ it
145.24	93.10	the Christian should	the ⟨..⟩↑Ch↓ristian should
145.30	93.Margin	4th	⟨3⟩ 4th
146. 4	93.27	event disturb my	event disturb⟨e⟩ my
146. 5	93.30	I would live	I would li⟨f⟩↑v↓e
146. 7–8	93.33	a strenght of	a strenght⟨h⟩ of
146. 9	93.34	course. This	course this
146.13	94. 4	thank thee for	thank↑thee↓for
146.13–14	94. 4	me. It	me it
146.17	94. 9	them. Teach	them teach
146.21	94.19	Is he not	Is he ⟨.⟩ not
146.27	94.22	When a	When ⟨I⟩ a
147.10	95.24	am. I	am I
147.14	95.29	making me almost	making↑me↓almost
147.21	96. 3	I now know it	I ⟨k⟩now know it
147.22	96. 5	painfull	painfull⟨y⟩
147.28	96.13	prevented were circumstances	prevented w⟨h⟩ere circumstances
147.35–36	96.23	Anglicans have neglected	Anglicans ha⟨d⟩↑ve↓ neglected
147.42	96.32–33	not necessary	not necessary. ⟨.⟩

HP	MS	HP	MS
148. 2	97. 2	is on me.	is on⟨.⟩ me.
148. 4	97. 3	with Humanity	with ⟨with⟩ Humanity
148. 8	97. 9	disciples even unto	disciples event unto
148.10	97.12	holds that	holds ⟨.⟩ that
148.11	97.13	the visible	the ⟨.⟩ visible
148.22	98. 1	ambition; keep	ambition keep
148.24–25	98. 5	wavering; willt	wavering willt
149. 8	99. 2	progress. The	progress the
149. 9	99. 4	reading. Some	reading some
149.12	99. 7	can make	can ⟨be⟩ make
149.13	99. 9	A man	A ⟨.⟩ man
149.17	99.17	existence; the	existence the
149.19–20	99.21	not say I affirm. I	not ↑ say I ↓ affirm I
149.21	99.22	grumbling comes	grumbling ⟨is⟩ comes
149.27	100. 1	realization of the objects	realization of ↑ the ↓ objects
150.17	102. 1	destiny? what	destiny what
150.17	102. 1	we? Our	we our
150.18	102. 2	it? Have we an	it have have ↑ we ↓ an
150.19	102. 5–6	Earth? It	Earth it
150.21	102. 7	planet. Who	planet who
150.21	102. 8	it? How	it how
150.22	102.10	exist? Is	exist is
150.23–24	102.12	being. Do	being do
150.27	102.18	the present live	the ⟨future⟩ present live
150.27	102.18	future? Most	future most
150.38–39	103. 1	If all thats around	⟨If I am a portion⟩ If all thats around
150.40	103. 5	living. Therefore	living therefore
151.13	104. 3	myself. There	myself ⟨to⟩. There
151.15	104. 7	food. Is	food is
151.16	104. 9	impurity? By	impurity by
151.23	104.20	and oh God	and o⟨f⟩ ↑ h ↓ God
151.26	105. 3	bread. No	bread no
151.28	105. 6	Almira	⟨A⟩ ↑ d ↓ lm⟨i⟩ ↑ t ↓ r⟨a⟩ ↑ d ↓
151.29	105. 6	that is	⟨s⟩ ↑ t ↓ h⟨e⟩ ↑ a ↓ t is
151.33	105.14	is slow. Why? Because no	is slow why because no
151.35	105.17	sins; their	sins their
151.40	105.27	thee cry aloud. The	the cry aloud the
152. 1	105.28	heartful gratitude from	heartful grat⟨t⟩itude from
152. 9	106.10	thee; let	thee let

HP	MS	HP	MS
152.13	106.18	is too Great	is to Great
152.19	107. 4	existence. In ten days	existence in the⟨.⟩ days
152.23	107. 9	without a conscious	without a⟨n⟩ conscious
152.26	107.15	that the chronic	that ↑ the ↓ chronic
152.28	107.15	we see God	we ↑ see ↓ God
152.30	107.18	beautiful. Why	beautiful why
152.41	107.34	thee a hell	the a hell
153. 1	108. 2	have made some	have made⟨s⟩ some
153. 4	108. 6	truth have	truth ⟨are⟩ have
153. 4	108. 6	disappeared and given	disappeared an⟨g⟩ ↑ d ↓ given
153.12–13	108.20	English Grammar	Englis g Grammar
153.16	108.26	still. The	still the
153.18	108.28	sake; speak	sake speak
153.20	108.31	is around me.	is a⟨.⟩round me.
153.21	108.32	anything for to	anything for ⟨..⟩ to
153.24	108.37	directions. What	directions what
153.31	109.10	Heavenly Father as	Heavenly ⟨f⟩ ↑ F ↓ ather as
153.36	109.19	love. Therefore	love therefore
154.10–11	110.11	strength to Love	strength ⟨.⟩ ↑ t ↓ o Love
154.20–21	110.27	not; my heart	not my heart
154.23	110.31	loving-mercy. Willt	loving-mercy willt
154.27	110.37	am silenced with	am silen⟨t⟩ ↑ ced ↓ with
154.27–28	110.38	I now am	I ↑ now ↓ am
154.35	111.11	impossible. My	impossible my
155. 1	111.19	Almira; it	Almira it
155. 3	111.21	in the two	in ↑ the ↓ two
155.11	112. 8	an unknown spirit	an unknow⟨k⟩ ↑ n ↓ spirit
155.12	112. 9	not knowing who	not ↑ knowing ↓ who
155.16	112.15	there nine or	there nine⟨.⟩ or
155.21	112.21	nor so chaotic	not ↑ so ↓ chaotic
155.26	112.30	me active on	me a⟨.⟩ ↑ c ↓ tive on
155.38	113.12	Universe yet I	Universe ye⟨.⟩t I
156. 2	113.19	with. Man to	with. Man⟨y⟩ to
156. 5	113.24	repulsive. Those	repulsive those
156.38	115.13	with; he	with he
157. 2	115.16	tho too often	tho to often
157. 6	115.20	present impressions lead	present imp⟨p⟩ressions lead
157.16	116.11	we omit we	we omit ⟨.⟩ we
157.17	116.12	that strength which	that streng⟨h⟩th which
157.26	117. 2	it does to	it doe⟨.⟩s to

HP	MS	HP	MS
157.27	117. 5	spontaneous elements	spontaneous ⟨-⟩ elements
157.28	117. 7	humanity becoming	humanity ⟨developing⟩ becoming
157.38	117.23	etc. has destroyed	&c ha⟨ve⟩↑s↓ destroyed
158. 1	117.26	Community; and	Community and
158. 5	117.32	universal form	universal ⟨-⟩ form
158. 8	117.38	minds of all reformers	minds if all reformers
158. 8	117.38	and founders	an founders
158.11	118. 5	but what has prophecied	but ↑what↓ has prop↑h↓ecied
158.16	118.12	give the whole	give the ↑whole↓
159. 7	120. 4	man with bowed	man w⟨h⟩ith bowed
159.15	120.16	Gods, the	Gods the
159.16	120.18	Man, the	Man the
159.21	121. 3	birth, from	birth from
159.21	121. 4	the Spirit	the ⟨soul⟩ Spirit
159.26	121. 9	we most of us often	we ↑most of us↓ often
159.28	121.12	Spirit; not	Spirit not
159.28-29	121.13	the recollection	the ⟨the⟩ recollection
160. 1	121.17-18	soul. It	soul it
160.11	122. 5	she drew	she ⟨wrote⟩ drew
160.26-27	122.30-31	"pasttime of Shakerism." It	past⟨.⟩atine Shakerism" it
161.18	124. 9	where should..where will	Were should...were will
161.25	124.20	the consciousness of	the conscious↑ness↓ of
161.25-26	124.21	fleshy body? It	fleshy body↑?↓If
161.28	124.25	we were purified	we ↑were↓ purified
161.36	124.37	it is can	is is ⟨.⟩ can
161.36	124.37	be; therefore	be therefore
161.39	125. 3	Are our relations	Are our ⟨present⟩ relations
162. 3	125.10	can we not have	can we ↑not↓ have
162.18	125.34	time is occupied	time ⟨.⟩ is ⟨.⟩ occupied
162.25	126. 8	this: I	this I
162.35	126.21	the difficulties the	the difficul⟨.⟩ties the
163. 2	126.33	much advantage to	much advan⟨a⟩↑t↓age
163. 9	127. 7	Action perseverance	Act⟨.⟩↑i↓on perseverance
163.10	127. 9	than promises	than ⟨—⟩ promises
163.12	127.14	almost turns my	almost ↑turns↓ ⟨makes⟩

HP	MS	HP	MS
163.14	127.16	Anglican? To	Anglican to
163.22	127.29	whether he would	whether ⟨he had⟩ he would
163.23	127.31	gives me hearty	gives ↑ me ↓ hearty
163.37	128.13	of evil than	of evil⟨l⟩ than
163.40	128.18	We want	⟨w⟩ We want
164.12	129. 2	he can	he ⟨h.⟩ can
164.22	129.14	laws; and	laws and
164.25	129.21	elevating as	elevating ⟨only so far⟩ as
165. 7	130.26	Or is war	Or is ⟨it⟩ war
165.18	131.11	B.F. The	B.F. the
165.22	131.18	to be took.	to be ⟨taking⟩ took.
165.27	131.25	years a member	years a⟨n⟩ member
165.30–31	131.30	C Church	⟨R⟩ C Church
166. 1	132.37	of life which	of lif which
166.19–20	133. 4	Let us walk	Let us ↑ walk ↓
166.22	133. 8	acknowledge our	acknowledge ⟨of⟩ our
166.23	133. 9–10	gifts. Let	gifts let
166.39	134. 2	Humanity-Christ-as	Humanity-Chri⟨i⟩st-as
167.11	134.Margin	30	⟨29⟩
167.23–24	134.37	Anglican or Roman	Anglican o⟨f⟩ ↑ r ↓ Roman
167.26–27	135. 4	practice; they	practice they
167.30	135. 9	letter; it	letter it
168.10	135.33	become accquainted with	become ac ↑ c ↓ quainted with
168.19	136.14	he cannot	⟨s⟩ ↑ t ↓ he cannot
168.19–20	136.14	case he would	case ⟨s⟩ ↑ t ↓ he ⟨.⟩ would
168.20–21	136.16	him—it	h⟨e⟩ ↑ i ↓ ⟨r⟩ ↑ m ↓ —it
168.33	136.34	towards him but	towards h⟨e⟩ ↑ i ↓ ⟨r⟩ ↑ m ↓ but
169. 1	137.10	receive him as	receive ↑ him ↓ as
169.29	138.15	to realize its	to real⟨l⟩ize its
169.34	139. 4	break off above	break of above
169.39	139.12	Host, without	Host without
170. 5–6	139.21	Thine; do	Thine do
170. 7	139.24	heart; without	heart without
170.12	139.33	found me; leave me	found me leave me
170.24	140.10	work; all	work all
171. 1	140.32	a Greek sentence	a Greek⟨e⟩ sentence
171.11	141. 7–8	them but by the	them bu⟨t⟩t by ⟨through⟩ the
171.13	141. 9	shall know	shall ⟨no⟩ ↑ know ↓

HP	MS	HP	MS
171.22	141.21	As the fallen	As the ⟨—⟩ fallen
171.28	141.28	live; the soul, spirit	live the soul
171.28–29	141.29	spirit-truth; the spirit celestial love	spirit=truth, the spirit celestial love
171.38	142. 2	is a much	is ↑a↓ much
171.38	142. 2	of Wisdom	of ⟨—⟩ Wisdom
172. 3	142. 8	the dawn near	the dawn ⟨is⟩ near
172. 5	142.11	and it shall	and ⟨ye⟩ it shall
172.30	143. 9	who are around	who are⟨.⟩ around
172.30–31	143.11	are; if	are if
172.36	143.19	given us	given ⟨to⟩ us.
172.42	143.29	success; it	success it
173. 3	143.33	wilt they find	wilt the find
173. 5	143.36	revivy itself	revi ↑.↓ vy ⟨him⟩ ↑ it ↓ self
173.30	144.29	governments & laws	gover ↑n↓ ments & laws
173.31–32	144.31	governments & laws.	gover ↑n↓ ments & law⟨y⟩↑s.
174.15	145.27	be compared to	be compared ⟨th⟩ to
174.15	145.27	O Lord Thou	O⟨h⟩ Lord Thou
174.21–22	145.33	every mortal care."	every ↑ mortal ↓ care."
174.36	146.13	works, unconscious of	works, unconscious⟨.⟩ of
175. 4	146.21	When he calls	When ↑ he ↓ calls
175. 5	146.22	Man? Does	Man does
175.12	146.30	soul does not.	soul does⟨t⟩ not.
175.12–13	146.31	heaven, the	heaven the
175.31	147.19	winds filling	winds ⟨making⟩ filling
175.32	147.21	The water	The ⟨g⟩ water
175.34	147.23	home; this	home this
176. 2	147.23	How calm how	How⟨t⟩ calm how
176. 8	148. 3	The pure	The pure ⟨in—,⟩
177. 5	148. 5	reap our true	reap or true
177.10	148.10	I of my	I ⟨..⟩ ↑ of ↓ my
177.30	148.34	not too eager and	not to eager and
177.35	149. 6	life; the other	life th⟨is⟩ ↑ e ↓ other
178. 5–6	149.17	with God filled	with ↑ God ↓ filled
178. 8–9	149.22	State, hence	State, ⟨she⟩ hence
178.17	149.31	been too much for	been to much for
178.20–21	149.36	be too often repeated	be to often repeated
178.21	149.38	with too great an	with to great an
178.32	150.12	Man we should	Man w⟨h⟩e should
178.33	150.13	voice, when	voice when
178.36	150.17	should they be	should the be

HP	MS	HP	MS
179. 9	150.35	it can bear	it ↑ can ↓ bear
176.14	151. 8	places not to depart	places ⟨to⟩ not ↑ to ↓ depart
176.24	151.21	thee? What	thee what
176.26	151.27	wounds with the oil of gladness	wounds ⟨and⟩ ↑ with the ↓ ⟨—⟩ oil of gladness ⟨in it⟩.
176.29	151.31	trouble	trouble ⟨and⟩ and
176.32	151.35	every pore.	every⟨s⟩ po⟨.⟩ ↑ r ↓ e
177. 2	152. 4	be slain.	be ⟨free⟩ slain.
179.14	152. 9	to be but an	to ↑ be ↓ but an
179.20	152.18	like an empty	like ⟨—⟩ an empty
179.23	152.22	me but a blank	me ↑ but ↓ a blank
179.35	152.36	infinite alas such	infinite alas⟨.⟩ such
180. 3	153. 8	of yesterday is	of ⟨to day⟩ yesterday is
180.11	153.16	who we feel are	who ↑ we feel ↓ are
180.12–13	153.18	the spirit world	the spirit⟨ual⟩ world
180.15	153.21	natural Man even	natural ↑ Man ↓ even
180.16	153.22	the spirit world.	the spirit⟨ual⟩ world.
180.16–17	153.24	is within you."	in within⟨g⟩ you."
180.18	153.26	cannot ever	cannot ⟨.⟩ever
180.21	153.29	real; the	real the
181.23	153.Margin	11	1⟨0⟩ ↑ 1 ↓
180.25	153.33	cease; feed	cease feed
181.27	153.36	first must be led to deny	first ↑ must be led to ↓ deny
181.29	153.38	external; tho	external tho
181.32	154. 4	enquiry? Where	enquiry where
181.33	154. 4	of it so	of ↑ it ↓ so
181.34–35	154. 6	neglecting the invitation of Jesus	neglecting ↑ the invitation ↓ of Jesus
181.11	154.25	not now see	not ⟨k⟩now see
181.12	154.26	to the Church	to ↑ the ↓ Church
181.19	154.34	consistency too often	consistency to often
181.20–21	154.35	we are perfectly	we ⟨have been⟩ are
181.20–21	154.36	Love & Spirit	Love ⟨to the⟩ & Spirit
181.21–22	154.36	nothing but unitary	nothing ↑ but ↓ unitary
181.22	154.37	The nearer we	The neare we
181.24	155. 1	a letter in	a lette in
181.38–39	155.14	the feeling in	the feeling⟨s⟩ in
181.41	155.17	speak: we	speak we
182. 2	155.19	every one out	every ↑ one ↓ out
182. 4	155.22	in the chains of	in ↑ the ↓ chains ⟨by⟩ of
182. 5	155.22	Tis the Slavery	Tis the the Slavery

HP	MS	HP	MS
182. 8	155.25	are no greater	are no⟨t⟩ greater
182. 9	155.26	own wills	own ⟨self⟩ wills
182.10	155.28	of the freedom	of the⟨ir⟩ freedom
182.15	155.34	needed. Nay	needed nay
182.17	155.36	The wicked	The ⟨sp⟩wicked
182.21	156. 1	to wit," faith	to wit⟨l⟩," faith
182.39	157. 4	so frequent	so ⟨often⟩ frequent
183. 4	157.11	*sake* of *reading*	sake if reading
183. 9–10	157.18	that it is	that ↑ it ↓ is
183.10	157.19	in the pursuit	in th⟨is⟩ ↑ e ↓ pursuit
183.14	157.24	this self active	this ↑ self ↓ active
183.17–18	157.28	without to the conversation	without ⟨and⟩ to the ⟨sound⟩ ↑ conversation ↓
183.20	157.31	A good lesson	A god lesson
183.21	157.33	are as opposite	are ↑ as ↓ opposite
183.21	157.33	those for the	those ⟨f⟩for the
183.21	157.33	is above	is ⟨a⟩above
183.24	157.37	soul to	soul ⟨o.⟩ to
183.24–25	157.37	of Greek & Latin increase	of ↑ Greek & Latin ↓ increase
183.31	158. 3	Will not Jesus	Will ↑ not ↓ Jesus
183.31	158. 4	right hand of	right ha ↑ n ↓ d of
183.32	158. 4	who did promise	who ↑ did ↓ promise
183.34	158. 7	be prepared to	be ⟨able⟩ ↑ prepared ↓
183.35	158. 7	if we put	if ↑ we ↓ put
183.38	158.10	some serious consideration	some ↑ serious ↓ consideration
183.40	158.12	me? Was	me? ⟨what⟩ Was
184. 5	158.19	are; cease	are cease
184. 6	158.20	which will bear	which ↑ will ↓ bear
184.14	158.29	It was really	It ⟨is⟩ ↑ was ↓ really
184.15	158.30	such a hold	such ⟨depth⟩ a hold
184.16	158.31	Latin; is	Latin is
184.17	158.31–32	sanctions? The	sanctions the
184.18	158.33	eyes hear	eyes ⟨ears⟩ hear
184.19	158.35	we? Is	we⟨.⟩ ⟨.⟩Is
184.19–20	158.36	same Do not	same Do⟨.⟩ ⟨S⟩ not
184.20	158.36	then? Is	then is
184.20	158.37	Same? Are	Same are
184.21	158.38	their own feet.	their ↑ own ↓ feet.
184.22	158.38	we too but	we to but
184.25	159. 1	sight needs no	sight needs⟨s⟩ no
184.25	159. 1	drawn prosaical	drawn ⟨—⟩ prosaical
184.28–29	159. 5	the perennial life	the ↑ perrenial ↓ life

HP	MS	HP	MS
184.32	159. 8	what caused	what ⟨the⟩ caused
184.33	159. 9	satisfied with the	satisfied ⟨of⟩ ↑ with ↓ the
184.40	159.17	the very ground	the ↑ very ↓ ground
184.41	159.18	we are passive	we ↑ are ↓ passive
185. 2	159.18	for their l, l, l, purposes	↑ for their l, l, l, purposes ↓
185. 4	159.20	of the public	of ↑ the ↓ public
185. 9	159.26	overtaken; be	overtaken be
185.10	159.27	and they will	and the will
185.11	159.28	be taught by	be tau ↑ g ↓ ht ⟨from that⟩ by
185.14	159.31	God; he	God he
185.26	160. 7	show its *shame*fulness.	show ⟨.⟩ its shamefulness.
185.35	160.14	engage them	engage ⟨—⟩ them
185.37	160.15	perpetuity, they even did	perpetuity, ⟨th⟩they ↑ even ↓ did
186. 3	160.23	again. the	again ⟨s⟩. The
186. 8	160.28	conditions. No	conditions⟨.⟩ No
186.10	160.31	of opposition	of ⟨the⟩ opposition
186.16	160.40	forever; however	forever however
186.21	161. 2	the psychical spirits	the ps ↑ y ↓ chical spirits
186.22	161. 3	the love Spirit.	the ⟨—⟩ love Spirit.
186.22	161. 3	question. And	question. ⟨How far⟩ and
186.23	161. 4	nature are not	nature a⟨is⟩ ↑ re ↓ not
186.29	161.11	not the contrary	not the⟨s⟩ contrary
186.32	161.14	place us in	place ↑ us ↓ in
187. 7	161.29	"thanks, with	"thanks, ⟨to⟩ with
187. 9	161.31	us commune with	us commun⟨ion⟩ ↑ e ↓ with
187.11	161.33	love of Gods	love ⟨of the grace⟩ of Gods
187.14	161.37	Each note must	Each note ⟨chord⟩ must
187.17	161.39	makes me his Son.	makes ⟨us⟩ ↑ me ↓ his Son⟨s⟩.
187.22	162. 3	been so clearly	been so⟨.⟩ clearly
187.23	162. 4	the interior	the ⟨in⟩ interior
187.24	162. 5	body; but	body but
187.24	162. 6	this is attainable	this ↑ is ↓ attainable
187.26	162. 8	remarkable in fact	remarkable i⟨f⟩ ↑ n ↓ fact

HP	MS	HP	MS
187.28	162. 9	and even our best moments	↑ and even our best moments ↓
187.29	162.10	shut by the	shut ⟨from⟩ ↑ by ↓ the
187.29	162.10	This meeting through	Th⟨e⟩ ↑ is ↓ ⟨e⟩ meeting ⟨on the⟩ through
187.30	162.11	and most superficial	and ↑ most ↓ superficial
187.34	162.15	in the love	in ↑ the ↓ love
188. 6	162.25	How fruitful has	How fruitful⟨l⟩ has
188.10	162.30	side and from	side and and from
188.26	163. 8	world; and	world ⟨of⟩ and
190.24	163.14	4th	⟨3⟩ ↑ 4 ↓ th
190.24	163.14	Do not	Do⟨n⟩ not
188.33	164. 5	am; where	am where
189.38	164. 8	the spirit may	the ⟨very⟩ spirit Man
190.11	164.24	—the aspiration—	—⟨t⟩ ↑ T ↓ he⟨s⟩ aspiration—
190.11	164.25	as it was in	as i⟨f⟩ ↑ t ↓ was in
189.22	165.15	again *in spirit* to	again in ⟨th⟩ spirit to
189.28	165.24	looking out for	looking ⟨of⟩ ↑ out ↓ for

NOTE

After the last entry in Volume I, there are three pages (162–165) of quotations from various works written by ITH. The quotations start from the back of the book and are written upside down compared to the rest of the diary. They are included in the order in which they were apparently written, beginning with the last page of the diary moving toward the beginning.

VOLUME II

194. 6	1. 4	not be somewhat	not b⟨e⟩e somewhat
194.10	1.10	move in an	move ↑ in ↓ an
194.10	1.10	as different from	as diffe⟨r⟩ent from
194.15	1.18	town the next	town the⟨r⟩ next
194.19	1.23	feel a strong	feel ↑ a ↓ strong ↑ ⟨a⟩ ↓
195. 1	2.20	a delusion how	a d⟨.⟩elusion how
195. 1	2.20	from it is	from i⟨f⟩ ↑ t ↓ is
195. 4	2.25	to disobey it.	to disobe⟨.⟩y it.
195. 8	2.28	attributed to me with	attributed ↑ to me ↓ with
195.27	3.23	as spring from	as spring⟨s⟩ from
195.39	4. 5	in the material objective	in ↑ the material ↓ objective

HP	MS	HP	MS
195.41	4. 7	objective material world	objective ↑ material ↓ world
195.41	4. 7	to gain slowly	to gain⟨s⟩ slowly
196. 1	4. 8	a steady march	a st ↑ ea ↓ dy march
196. 8	4.18	so much more	so much ⟨the⟩ more
196.13	4.25	a going in a	a going in ⟨in⟩ a
196.30	5.20	and She has	and ↑ She ↓ has
196.39	5.32	Spirit would?	Spirit ⟨?⟩ ↑ would? ↓
197. 1	6. 4	self-conscousness?	se⟨f⟩ ↑ l ↓ f-conscious-ness?
197. 7	8. 1	off to OAB.	off to⟨.⟩ OAB.
197.15	8.11	purpose; but	purpose but
197.18	8.16	G.P.B.; it	G.P.B. it
197.24	8.24	outward cloak.	outward ⟨one⟩ cloak.
197.35	9.10	while to us	while ⟨we are⟩ to us
197.36	9.12	a little more	a ↑ little ↓ more
197.40	9.17	obscurity, the	ob⟨.⟩ ↑ s ↓ curity the
197.40	9.17	greater the better, whats	greater the better whats
197.41	9.18	this very moment	this ↑ very ↓ moment
198. 2	9.20	else but the	else ⟨than⟩ but the
198. 2	9.21	angels who are attendant	angels ↑ who are ↓ attendant
198. 2	9.22	Man." "a	Man." ⟨An⟩ "A
198.22–23	10.16	on any variety	⟨up⟩ on ⟨a⟩ ↑ any ↓ variety
198.30	10.29	much sensibility	much sensibil⟨.⟩ity
199. 3	11.12	growth; the	growth the
199. 8	11.21	nature decline	nature ⟨—⟩ decade
199.27	12.21	say good physical circumstances	say ↑ good ↓ physical ⟨are⟩ circumstances
199.28	12.23	to the spiritual	to the ⟨the⟩ spiritual
199.28	12.24	And it seems	And ↑ it ↓ seems
199.29	12.25	must take place	must⟨.⟩ take place
199.36	13. 5	physical or psychical	physical o⟨f⟩ ↑ r ↓ psychical
199.37	13. 7	to a higher	to ⟨.⟩ a higher
199.41	13.12	you may be	you ma⟨b⟩ ↑ y ↓ be
200. 2	13.16	better, then	better then
200. 8	13.26	life-is	life⟨?⟩-is
200.13	14. 1–2	life? Shall	life shall
200.14	14. 3	that foretaste of	that ⟨—⟩ ↑ foretaste ↓ of
200.16	14. 6	here after	here ⟨to enjoy⟩ after
200.17	14. 8	made with the	made ⟨by⟩ ↑ with ↓ the
200.19	14.10	P.M.	P.M.⟨.⟩

HP	MS	HP	MS
200.20–21	14.11	figs, & my drink water	figs, ↑ & my drink water ↓
200.24	14.16	heill-ouf,	h⟨o⟩ ↑ e ↓ ill-ouf
200.26	14.21	The condition of	The condition⟨s⟩ of
200.27	14.22	(Genius, fortune)	(Genius, fortun⟨a⟩ ↑ e ↓ ⟨te⟩)
201. 2	15.15	the effect of study	↑ the effect of ↓ study
201. 6–7	15.23	Lane's. As	Lane's as
201. 8–9	15.27	advanced higher	advanced ⟨tha⟩ higher
201.15	16. 7	at this period.	at⟨.⟩ this period.
201.16	16. 9–10	is all most	is ⟨not⟩ all most
201.21	16.16	the result of	the ↑ union ↓ result of
201.24	16.20	to say?	to say⟨s⟩?
201.26	16.24	now within me?	now ⟨for me?⟩ within me?
201.27	16.26	eternal affinities	et⟨.⟩ernal affinities
201.29	16.28	me ever inward	me ⟨r⟩ever inward
201.36	17. 7	as the origin	as ⟨our⟩ the origin
202. 9	17.27	our folly. In	our fo⟨o⟩ ↑ l ↓ ly. In
202.15	18. 2	discordant notes which	discordant ↑ notes ↓ which
202.20	18.10	reflects on	reflects ⟨from⟩ on
202.22	18.12	of life the deeper	of life ⟨of life⟩ the deeper
202.22	18.13	& richer becomes	↑ & richer⟨.⟩ ↓ becomes
202.24	18.15	poets hearts	poets ⟨souls⟩ hearts
202.28	18.21	shall create	shall ⟨produce⟩ create
202.33	18.28	mediums, Souls of Men	mediums, ⟨Mans⟩ Souls ↑ of Men ↓
203.34	21. 4	say? He	say he
203.37	21. 9	"I say frankly I	↑ "I say frankly ↓ I
204.12	22. 4	me wave	me wave⟨.⟩
204.25	22.25	finding it to	finding ↑ it ↓ to
204.32–33	23. 5	the involuntary will	the ⟨a⟩ ↑ i ↓ nvoluntary will
204.36	23. 8	up. Some	up. ⟨.⟩ Some
204.37–38	23.11	not have been	not ↑ have ↓ been
204.38	23.11	as to where	as ⟨..⟩ to where
204.41	23.16	this: should	this should
205. 1	23.19	etc. If	etc. if
205. 3	23.20	is am I	is ↑ ⟨'⟩ ↓ am I
205. 5	23.24	illumined with	illumined ⟨by⟩ with
205.11	24. 4	The latter	⟨ ↑ with ↓ ⟩ The latter
205.19	24.19	is a step	is ↑ a ↓ step

HP	MS	HP	MS
205.22	24.24	probably use	probably ⟨as⟩ use
205.30	25. 5	and no sooner	and⟨.⟩ no sooner
205.34	25.10	step, it	step it
205.35	25.13	Thou who hast lead me	Tho⟨..⟩ who hast lead⟨s⟩ me
205.39	25.18	speak freely the	speak freel the
206. 3	25.28	that on this	that ⟨I⟩ on this
206. 4	25.30	in my joining	in ⟨the⟩ my joining
206. 7	26. 4	the order	the ⟨character of⟩ order
206.13	26.13	I have consented	I have ⟨made⟩ consented
206.23	27. 1	is single.	is ⟨one⟩ single.
206.24	27. 3	is unity,.	is unity,. ⟨one⟩
206.30	27.10	with the single	with ⟨a⟩ ↑ the ↓ single
207. 5	28. 4	he his own God.	he his ↑ own ↓ God.
207.24	29. 4	than my union	than ⟨than⟩ my union
207.33–34	29.20	against thee I	against the I
208. 1	30. 5	happiness; it	happiness it
208. 2	30. 7	so with our	so with⟨.⟩ our
208.15	31. 1	Lord; is	Lord is
208.15	31. 3	any one nearer	any ↑ one ↓ nearer
208.21	31.16	We must be	We⟨.⟩ must be
208.25	31.18	when ever we	when ever⟨y⟩ we
208.31	32. 5	hates him, 'cause	hates hi⟨.⟩m, 'cause
209. 8	33. 3	to Serpent, doth	to Se ↑ r ↓ pent, doth
209.13	33.10	poorly live.	poorly li⟨f⟩ ↑ v ↓ e
209.16	34. 3	visited the Catholic	visited th Catholic
209.19	34. 7	my consciousness	my ⟨life⟩ consciousness
209.25	34.19	the superior standing	the ↑ su ↓ perior standing
210. 1	35.13	need. If	need if
210.13	36. 9	God. Let	God. ⟨in all⟩ Let
210.15	36.12	care and provide for us.	care an⟨.⟩d provide for⟨e⟩ us.
210.16	36.14	trouble. Come	trouble come
210.20	36.22	trouble was all	trouble ⟨.⟩was all
210.33	37.19	we should ever	we ⟨.⟩ should ever
210.35	37.22	actions thoughts	actions ⟨and⟩ thoughts.
210.37–38	37.27	& functions.	⟨of⟩ ↑ & ↓ functions.
210.38	37.29	the interior world	the inter ↑ i ↓ or world
211. 2	38. 7	time; the	time the
211. 3	38. 7	permit me; ever	permit me, ever
211. 4	38.11	all; ask	all ask
211.13	38.28	this suffices.	this ⟨.⟩ ↑ s ↓ uffices.
211.14	38.30	about; only	about only

HP	MS	HP	MS
211.15	38.30	do; follow	do follow
211.20	39.12	all; I	all I
211.21	39.13	me first and	me f⟨.⟩irst and
212. 5	40.24	I ponder.	I ⟨query⟩ ↑ ponder ↓ .
212. 8–9	41. 4	regenerated. This	regenerated this
212.18	42. 2	that which	that ⟨and that only⟩ which
212.19	42. 4	which is inconformable	which ↑ is ↓ inconform- able
212.20	42. 5	so far he	so ⟨ful⟩far he
212.20–21	42. 6	of his perfection	of ⟨that⟩ his perfection
212.31	42.16	the temptations which	the tempton which
212.37	43. 3	unable to perform	unable to ⟨to⟩ perform
213. 3	43.11	the desire of	the d⟨.⟩esire of
213. 4	43.12	thy Spirit	thy ⟨lov⟩ Spirit
213.18–19	44. 7	to encourage vice	to ↑ encourage ↓ vice
213.22	44.16	been diviner	been ⟨of.⟩ diviner
213.24–25	44.20	a divine life	a ⟨life⟩ divine life
213.26	44.23	of His immediate	of ⟨th⟩ His immediate
213.32	45. 7	him nor that	him no⟨t⟩ ↑ r ↓ that
213.33	45. 7	have left	have ⟨not⟩ left
213.33	45. 8	genius upon	genius ⟨th⟩ upon
214. 4	46. 3	may be to	may be ⟨not⟩ to
214. 5	46. 5	he can procure	he can ⟨produce⟩ procure
214. 6	46. 8	shall more	shall ⟨.⟩ more
214.18–19	46.28	within him but this that	within h⟨.⟩im but ↑ this ↓ that
214.30	47.23	new inward life.	new ↑ inward ↓ life.
214.31	47.25	unlike the	unlike ⟨we⟩ the
215.13	49. 2	Madona The	Ma⟨d⟩dona The
215.14	49. 4	his Paradise Lost	his Parad⟨t⟩ise Lost
215.19	49.13	encouraged Men	encouraged ⟨genius⟩ Men
215.21	49.17	made Men of	made ⟨of⟩ Men of
215.22	49.18	into geniuses but	into genius⟨'⟩es but
215.22	49.18	has given	has ⟨to⟩ given
215.23	49.20	inspiration and	inspiration ⟨as she⟩ and
215.24	49.22	been without	been ⟨under⟩ without
215.33	50. 9	the inner	the ⟨two years⟩ inner
216. 5	51. 8	first Period	first ⟨Chapter⟩ Period
216. 6	51.10	in Youth.	in Youth. ⟨They⟩
216. 8	51.12–13	actual The	actual ⟨and the supremacy of .⟩ The
216.25	52.15	I now think	I ⟨.⟩now think

HP	MS	HP	MS
216.28	52.19	period; the	period the
216.29	52.20	ideal; the	ideal the
217. 9	54. 1	Something in	Something ⟨of⟩ in
217.38–39	55.23	but embraces includes	but embrace⟨d⟩ ↑ s ↓ includes
218. 6	56.11	by a life	by ⟨at⟩ a life
218. 7	56.15	say: that	say that
218.19	57. 8	remarkable aptitude	remarkable ap⟨p⟩ ↑ t ↓ itude
218.26	57.22	every one should	every one sho ↑ u ↓ ld
218.30	57.30	possible; somewhat	possible somewhat
218.31	58. 2	expense. Otherwise	expense otherwise
219. 2	58.20	as I am.	as I ⟨now⟩ am.
219.11	59.15	would be willing	would be ⟨b⟩ willing
219.13	59.19	and influence of	and ⟨of⟩ influence of
219.19	60. 1	our, no God's, time.	our no Gods time.
219.21	60. 6	next one be.	next ⟨.⟩ one be.
219.32	60.28	It is for	It is ⟨that in⟩ for
219.37	61. 7	ourselves, to be Godlike, to	ourselves to be Godlike to
219.38	61. 9	may be, to	may be to
219.38	61. 9	nothing, is	nothing is
220. 3	61.18	life is one	life ⟨..⟩ ↑ is ↓ one
220. 6	61.23	Race, and	Race., ⟨who are and in next⟩ and
220. 6–7	61.24	in want of	in want⟨s⟩ of
220.14–15	62. 8	wood or iron	woo⟨o⟩d or iron
220.18	62.13	after a sensible	after a⟨.⟩ sensible
220.19	62.15	worse; we	worse we
220.28	63. 1	When the	When ⟨unity⟩ the
220.29	63. 3	death; when	death when
220.30	63. 4–5	fanaticism. It	fanaticism it
220.31	63. 6	progress liberty	progress l⟨.⟩iberty
220.34	63.10	True, Theology	True Theology
221. 3	63.23	as consequences	as ⟨a⟩ consequences
221. 3	63.24	generator; It	generator it
221. 3–4	63.25	regenerated by them	regenerated ⟨.⟩by them
221. 6–7	64. 2	to the introduction of	to ↑ the introduction of ↓
221. 8	64. 4	were uncivilized	were ⟨without⟩ uncivilized
221.12	64.10	He said	⟨H⟩ ↑ H ↓ e said
221.21	65. 1	what spirit	what ⟨my⟩ spirit
221.30	65.20	all; into	all into

HP	MS	HP	MS
221.30	65.22	if we	if ⟨he⟩ we
221.31–32	65.24	ways; what ever	ways what ever
221.32	65.26	us, let	us let
222. 8	66.25	deeper & deeper in	deeper ↑ & deeper ↓ in
222.18–19	67.16	lived in, and	lived ⟨a⟩ ↑ i ↓ n, and
222.20	67.19	was spontaneous	was ⟨the⟩ spontaneous
222.30	68. 8	through the instrumentality	through ↑ the ↓ instrumentality
222.32	68.10	manifestation; we	manifestation we
222.35	68.19	is given a new birth and saved	is ↑ given a new birth and ↓ saved
222.37	68.23	Light and an	Light ↑ and ↓ an
223. 7	69.10	herself to be	herself⟨t⟩ to be
223. 7	69.11	Sin; its	Sin its
224.14	70. 2	Fort Lee	F⟨r⟩ort Lee
224.27	70.28	intuition or faith	intuition o⟨f⟩ ↑ r ↓ faith
224.28	71. 1	controversy; it	controversy it
224.30	71. 5	Infinite in Man & Nature.	Infinite ⟨of⟩ ↑ in ↓ Man ⟨of⟩ ↑ & ↓ Nature.
224.32	71. 8	unseen the ideal in	unseen ⟨in⟩ the ideal⟨.⟩ in
223.23	72. 9	may enter	may e⟨t⟩nter
223.34	72.29	Gods kingdom upon	Gods kin⟨d⟩ ↑ g ↓ ⟨g⟩ ↑ d ↓ om upon
223.35	73. 1	All embracing Love	All embracing ⟨.⟩ Love
223.36	73. 3	infinite loveful manner.	infinite ↑ loveful ↓ manner.
223.37	73. 4	its loveful purposes	its ↑ loveful ↓ purposes
223.39	73. 9	work. We	work. ⟨H⟩ We
223.40	73.10	not to will	not ↑ to ↓ will
224. 9	73.27	fruit is permitted	fruit ⟨—⟩ ↑ is ↓ permitted
225. 4	74.10	affinities of	aff⟨i⟩inities of
225. 5	74.13	darkness; let	darkness let
225. 6	74.14	and the darkness	and ↑ the ↓ darkness
225.14	74.29	need; I	need I
225.18	75. 4	of a different	of ⟨som⟩ a different
225.19	75. 7	they add	they ⟨to⟩ add
225.24	75.14	greater crime than	greater ⟨sin⟩ ↑ crime ↓ than
225.24	75.15	committed sin.	committed ⟨crime⟩ ↑ sin. ↓
225.28–29	75.21	Manufacturer the	Manufacturer ⟨s⟩ the
225.30	75.24	Homer, Phidias	Homer ↑ Phidias ↓

HP	MS	HP	MS
225.32	76. 2	in mystic	in ⟨a higher⟩ mystic
225.34	76. 4	of faith which	of ⟨reason⟩ ↑ faith ↓ which
225.35	76. 6	of the faculty of Reason	of ↑ the faculty of ↓ Reason
225.37	76. 9	objective form	objective f⟨..⟩ ↑ or ↓ m
225.38	76.10	Holy incarnated in	Holy ⟨being⟩ ↑ incarnated ↓ in
225.39	76.13	be good; the	be good the
225.39	76.14	true; the	true the
225.40	76.15	beautiful; the	beautiful ⟨be⟩ the
225.41	76.18	they as consequences.	they⟨.⟩as consequences
226. 1	76.20	not sweetly seen	not ⟨divinely⟩ ↑ sweetly ↓ seen
226. 5	76.23	Race higher than it not	Race ↑ higher than it ↓ not
226. 7-8	76.27	would not be	would⟨—⟩not be
226. 8	77. 1	the object that	the ⟨s⟩object that
226. 9	77. 2	the subject, hence	the ⟨o⟩ ↑ su ↓ bject hence
226.10	77. 3	Ergo if	Ergo ⟨etc.⟩ if
226.17	77.14	Is it	Is ⟨.⟩ it
226.23	77.28	beleive in his	beleive ⟨at⟩ ↑ in ↓ his
226.28	78. 2	inspiration derived	inspiration deri⟨.⟩ved
226.31	78. 7	Same. In	Same. ⟨Th⟩ In
226.31	78. 8	the unknown	the ⟨invisible God the spirit⟩ unknown
226.36	78.18	for the Voice	for the the Voice
226.39	78.22	absolute universal	absolute ⟨..⟩ universal
227. 1	78.27	concentrate on whole	concentrate on⟨e⟩ whole
227.19	79.26	from which the	from ↑ which ↓ the
227.29	80.12	yield up	yield up⟨o⟩ on
227.40-41	80.30-31	be as few devils then as	be ⟨ ↑ then ↓ ⟩as few devils ↑ then ↓ as

VOLUME III

HP	MS	HP	MS
229.18	1. 4	is shame ful.	is shame ful⟨l⟩.
229.22	1. 9	ye are true	ye are ⟨but⟩ true
229.22	1.10	my own inner	my own ⟨life⟩ inner
229.23	1.11	in a moonlight night	in a moonlig⟨m⟩ ↑ ht ↓ night
229.35	2. 6	to equivocate.	to equivoc⟨.⟩ate
230.21	3.17	intellect; the	intellect the
231. 6	5. 8	Church through which	Church throug which

HP	MS	HP	MS
231.10	5.13	contrary in each case.	contrary ↑ in each case ↓.
231.12	5.15	first real	first ⟨external⟩ real
231.12	5.17	more—of an	more—of ↓ an
231.16	5.22–23	built. Whatever	built. ⟨upon.⟩ Whatever
231.16	5.23	may be I	may ↑ be ↓ I
231.16	5.23	care not; it	care not it
231.17	5.25	and I	and ⟨which⟩ I
231.18	6. 1	that the lack of it was	that ↑ the lack of it ↓ was
231.25	6.16	one, would	one, ⟨and⟩ would
232. 2	7.19	and through which	and ⟨by⟩ ↑ through ↓ which
232. 5	8. 4	humanity it follows	humanity i⟨f⟩ ↑ t ↓ follows
232.13	8.17	there, and	there and ⟨travel⟩
232.14	8.19	One true	One true ⟨a⟩ act
232.16	8.24	God, humanity	God, ⟨his own⟩ humanity
232.24	9.11	one link	one ⟨lik⟩ link
232.26	9.14	appetite. It	appetite⟨te⟩. It
232.30	9.19	of penance.	of pen⟨.⟩ance.
232.39	10.11	here; let	here let
233. 2	11. 5	go. We	go. ⟨W⟩We
233.12	11.13	is too strong	is to strong
233.28	12.16	or backward.	or backward⟨s⟩.
233.32	12.24	which the spiritual	which ⟨makes⟩ the spiritual
234.16	14.18	in the flesh	in ⟨h⟩ the flesh
234.33	15.22	asks, the	asks the
234.35	15.25	natures are	natures ⟨feed upon⟩ are
234.35	16. 1	ask; they	ask they
235. 1	16.10	that, we	that we
235. 4	16.16	dont know	don⟨k⟩ ↑ t ↓ know.
235. 5	16.19	we saw what	we ⟨saw see⟩ ↑ saw ↓ what
235. 7	16.22	to say therefore	to ⟨affirm⟩ ↑ say ⟨deny⟩ ↓
235.11	17. 3	distinctly. Now it	distinctly now ⟨for⟩ it
235.11	17. 5	many probably	many ⟨—⟩ probably
235.33	18. 6	astrology in	astrology ⟨and⟩ in
235.33	18. 7	the basis	⟨the mystical sciences in Latin⟩ The basis
236.17	20. 7	vague indefinite	vague⟨.⟩ indefinite
236.28	21. 1–2	satisfied, if the lord is, in	satisfied if the lord is in

HP	MS	HP	MS
236.30	21. 5	we might feel	we might ⟨hear⟩ feel
236.39	21.21	need thee therefore	need thee ↑ therefore ↓
237.11	22.13	beleive by Gods	beleive ⟨of⟩ ↑ by ↓ Gods
237.17	22.23	study; we	study we
237.21	23. 5	not with all	not ⟨by⟩ ↑ with ↓ all
237.25	23.10	The I is	The ↑ I ↓ is
237.26	23.10	not the We; it	not the We it
237.32	23.19	historical, the	historical the
237.32–34	23.21	The I is	The ↑ I ↓ is
237.35	23.24	is uneducable.	is un ↑ e ↓ ducable.
237.38	24. 3	through the silvery	throug the silvery
238. 3	24.13	Universal Law; but	Universal Law but
238.14	25. 3	the illimitable	the ⟨unlimited⟩ illimitable
238.15	25. 6	questions? We	questions we
238.21	25.16	or else	or ⟨.⟩ else
238.23–24	25.20	Like only responds	Like ⟨all⟩ ↑ only ↓ responds
238.29	26. 6	our everyday life	our ever day life
238.40–41	26.23	to all real & effectual	to all ↑ real & effectual ↓
239. 1	26.25	will reproduce	will ⟨but⟩ reproduce
239. 3–4	27. 5	association, no government	association ↑ no government ↓
239.13	27.16	the horrid	justify ↑ the ↓ horrid
239.14	27.18	as we understand	as we ⟨fe⟩ understand
239.16	27.22	its general influence	its ↑ general ↓ influence
239.25	28. 9	should be to	should ↑ be ↓ to
239.31	28.15	for the holy heroism	for ↑ the holy ↓ heroism
240.10	30. 1	the labourer all	the labo ↑ u ↓ er all
240.13	30. 5	God foreknew that	God fore ↑ k ↓ new that
240.17	30.11	trust in providence	trust ⟨o⟩ ↑ in ↓ providence
240.21	30.19	can profitably do outside of	can profitable do ou⟨r⟩tside of
240.23	30.21	Our real wishes	Our ↑ real ↓ wishes
240.25	30.24	all unconsciously educated	all ↑ unconsciously ↓ educated
240.30	31. 8	no particular talent	no ⟨decided⟩ ↑ particular ↓ talent
240.37	31.20	to accomplish	to ⟨the⟩ accomplish
240.41	32. 3	the whole world	the ↑ whole ↓ world
241. 4	32. 8	battlefield stake etc.	battlefield⟨s⟩ ↑ stake ↓ etc.
241.10	32.17	that great delight	that g ↑ r ↓ eat delight

HP	MS	HP	MS
241.10	32.18	this? Is	this is
241.12	32.22	Have I	Have ⟨.⟩ I
241.14	33. 1	grace I will live	grace ↑ I will ↓ live
241.21	33.14	the weight that	the w⟨h⟩eight that
241.22	33.17	ever before.	ever ⟨—⟩ before.
241.24	33.20	hold it ever	hold ⟨higher⟩ ↑ it ↓ ever
242.19	35.25	planned something	planned ↑ ⟨for⟩ ↓ something
242.27	36.14	crush those	crush⟨es⟩ those
242.28	36.17	18. Was	18 ⟨—⟩. Was
242.36	37. 7	magnetic sleep.	magnetic ⟨influence⟩ ↑ sleep ↓ .
242.38	37.11	same unfathomable	same ⟨life⟩ unfathomable
242.40	37.14	the preternatural	the ⟨super⟩ ↑ preter ↓ natural
243. 2–3	37.21	material industry	ma⟨a⟩terial industry
243. 7	38. 3	proclaimed him greater	proclaimed ↑ him ↓ greater
243. 8	38. 6	intellectual or physical	intellectual o⟨f⟩ ↑ r ↓ physical
243.16	38.22	purposes. Not	purposes. ⟨or⟩ Not
243.18–19	39. 2	Hence women are	Hence wom⟨a⟩ ↑ e ↓ n are
243.20	39. 4	Women believe, men	Wom⟨a⟩ ↑ e ↓ n believe men
243.21	39. 5	is mystical, man	⟨are⟩ ↑ is ↓ mystical man
243.22	39. 6	Women are	Wom⟨a⟩ ↑ e ↓ n are
243.22	39. 6	realists, men	realists men
243.26	39.13	each in themselves have	each ↑ in themselves ↓ have
243.28	39.17	sexes; woman	sexes woman
243.29	39.19	powers, restore	powers restore
243.30–31	39.22	higher being.	higher ⟨power⟩ ↑ being ↓ .
243.34–35	40. 3	fancie. As	fancie ⟨power⟩. As
243.40	40.14	by his	by ⟨sin⟩ his
244. 9	41. 7	compassion on him this	compassionate ↑ him ↓ this
244.13	41.14	strange; it	strange it
244.14	41.16	me, these	me, ⟨and⟩ these
244.23–24	42. 9	deep human longings.	deep ↑ human ↓ longings.

HP	MS	HP	MS
244.27	42.17	struggled for	struggled ⟨lik⟩ for
245. 7–8	44. 5	unknown influence	unknown ⟨of⟩ influence
245.10	44. 7	is the holy	is ↑ the ↓ holy
245.17	44.20	sufficient to pay the debt.	sufficient ↑ to pay the debt. ↓
245.18	44.21	thee; let	thee let
245.18	44.22	breathe praise	breathe ⟨be⟩ praise
245.31	45.23	quickening me with	quickening ↑ me ↓ with
246. 6	47. 4	done him.	done ⟨to⟩ him.
246. 9	47.11	His paintings	His ⟨sketches⟩ paintings
246.10	47.13	He has been, and	He has ↑ been, ↓ and
246.12	47.18	his own prophecy	his own ⟨philosophy⟩ prophecy
246.20–21	48.10	yet possible that	yet ⟨probable⟩ ↑ possible ↓ that
246.26	48.20–21	I attempt to do this	I ⟨attempt to do this⟩ attempt
246.39	49.19–20	grows, plants	grows plants
246.39	49.20	flower, and	flower and
247. 2	50. 1	with; let	with let
247. 4	50. 4	calmness nature	c⟨l⟩almness nature
247. 5	50. 7	pschical after birth	pschical ↑ after ↓ birth
247.29	51.20	world; we	world we
247.34	52. 5	and magnificent houses	and m ↑ a ↓ gnificent houses
247.35	52. 7	inconceivable object	inconceivable ⟨of⟩ object
248. 3–4	52.22	me strength that	me stren ↑ g ↓ th that
248.35	55. 6	are not Death	are ⟨.⟩ not ↑ Death ↓
248.39	55.13	union with a	union with ⟨.⟩ a
249. 3	55.21	truly seen	trul⟨l⟩y seen
249. 9	56. 4	is a mystery.	is a⟨n⟩ mystery.
249.14	56.16	advice ask	advic⟨c⟩e ask
249.14–15	56.16	know no other	know no⟨t⟩ other
249.39	58.15	becoming members	becoming ⟨—⟩ members
250.12	59.15	Thus would we	Thus would ⟨would⟩ we
250.17–18	59.21	individual; the	individual the
250.18–19	59.21	universal; the	universal the
250.35	60.25	is power.	is ⟨life⟩ power.
251. 5	61.19	affirmation in	affirmation ⟨of⟩ in
251.14–15	62. 9	relief. Alone	re⟨f⟩ ↑ l ↓ ief. Alone
251.19–20	62.16	All the	All ⟨around⟩ the

HP	MS	HP	MS
252. 8	64.18	too little	to little
252.18	65.14	Christ? I	Christ? ⟨Oh is this possible?⟩ I
252.26	66. 3	Twice have	⟨T⟩Twice have
256.30	66.10	because he is	because ⟨it⟩ ↑ he ↓ is

VOLUME IV

HP	MS	HP	MS
255. 9	1. 3	form a net to	f⟨r⟩orm a net ⟨un⟩to
255. 9	1. 4	And also	and al⟨.⟩so
255.19	1.19	without unpuring them.	↑ without unpuring them ↓ .
255.19–20	1.20	being so fleeting	being ⟨.⟩ ↑ s ↓ o fleeting
255.29–30	2.17	is a sin—	is a sin⟨.⟩—
256. 4	3. 6	see: ordinarily	see ordinarily
256.13	4. 1	Last night	Last ⟨.⟩ night
256.18	4.10	limit set	limit⟨s⟩ set
256.24	4.23	committing any	committing ⟨every⟩ any
256.27	5. 4	set. This	set this
256.27–28	5. 4	so. It ought	so it ⟨ou⟩ ought
256.28	5. 5	I must try	I must t⟨.⟩ry
256.35	5.17	got up some	got ↑ up ↓ some
257. 1	5.22	And if	And⟨y⟩ if
257. 3	6. 1	Our talk	Our talk⟨s⟩
257. 3	6. 2	character; how	character how
257. 4	6. 4	it were agreeable	it were a⟨g⟩greeable
257.13	6.20	city on	city ⟨.⟩ ↑ o ↓ n
257.16	7. 2	is sad and	is⟨s⟩ sad and
257.20	7. 8	the highest	the high⟨.⟩est
257.23	7.15	of uprightness	of u⟨.⟩prightness
257.34	8.11	seem so	seem s⟨.⟩ ↑ o ↓
257.35	8.13	have none	have ⟨no conpan⟩ ↑ none ↓
257.37	8.18	should not be	should ↑ not ↓ be
257.40	9. 3	which is not	which i⟨n⟩ ↑ s ↓ not
258. 2–3	9. 8	blame that we	blame ⟨.⟩ ↑ t ↓ hat we
258. 4	9.11	Oh Lord let	Oh Lord le⟨n⟩ ↑ t ↓
258. 4–5	9.12	be consumed	be ⟨oh.⟩ consumed
258.10	9.21	have at least broken	have at leas broken
258.11	10. 1	that I have that	that ⟨we⟩ ↑ I ↓ hast ↑ lost ↓ that
258.18	10.15	I do scarce	I d⟨.⟩ ↑ o ↓ scarce
258.22	10.24	me nor can	me n⟨.⟩or can

HP	MS	HP	MS
258.25	11. 7	Guardian Angel	Gu⟨..⟩↑a↓rdian Angel
258.30	11.18	Church of God	Church⟨.⟩ of God
258.33–34	12. 2	with its soft	with its ⟨..⟩ soft
259. 2	13. 1	some where—	some wh⟨.⟩ere—
259. 7	13.12	mind develope	mind dev⟨o⟩↑e↓lope
259. 7–8	13.13	an object	an⟨.⟩ object
259. 9	13.16	all its efferts	all ⟨..⟩↑it↓s efferts
259.12–13	13.24	time and energy	time ⟨with⟩ and energy
259.14	14. 4	purpose; we	purpose we
259.16	14. 6–7	interested, that is, self	interested that is self
259.17	14. 8	being. We	being. W⟨.⟩↑e↓
259.30	15.14	why oh Lord	wh⟨.⟩↑y↓ oh Lord
259.33	15.20	after its lost	after ⟨.⟩↑i↓ts lost
259.36	16. 6	kind; canst	kind canst
260. 4	16.21	are the lower world of	are ↑the lower world↓ of
260. 5	17. 1	shall we obtain	shall ↑we↓obtain
260.11–12	17.13	without to meet	without ⟨th⟩ to meet
260.12	17.14	talent genius	talent ⟨..⟩ genius
260.13	17.16	which would not	which ⟨does⟩ would not
260.14	17.19	mind; the	mind the
260.16	17.21	to, and	to and
260.19–20	18. 6	and employing it	and empl⟨y⟩↑o↓ying it
260.34	19. 5	care too much	care to much
261.11	20.19	Is it not a	Is it not it a
261.20	21.19	of increasing	of incre⟨.⟩↑a↓sing
261.25	22. 7	Creative-Being.	Creative ⟨..⟩ Being.
261.36–37	23.10	do; it may	do ↑it↓ may
262.10	24.21	were it in Hades	where it in Hades
262.13	25. 1	see; the	see the
262.14	25. 4	usual; shall	usual shall
262.28	26. 8	the substance	the ⟨.⟩ substance
263. 1	27. 8	design but from	design ⟨f⟩↑b↓ut from
263. 3	27.12	We rest on	We⟨.⟩ rest on
263.12	28.11	it; this	it this
263.36–37	30.21	The nervous shocks which	The ↑nervous shocks↓ which
264.37	30.23	subject to but	subject to⟨o⟩ but
264.38–39	31. 2	known of Spirits	known of ⟨.⟩↑S↓pirits
264. 1–2	31. 8	do not endeavor	do not e↑n↓deavor
264. 4	31.13	of some what.	of ⟨a⟩ some what.
264.17	32.18	perplexed us; then	perplexed us then
264.22	33.10	can I accuse	can I ⟨.⟩ accuse
265.23–24	33.15	I cannot accuse	I cannot a⟨..⟩↑cc↓use

HP	MS	HP	MS
265.24	33.16	and am so	and am⟨.⟩ so
265. 9–10	35.19	Students with	Students ⟨wh⟩ with
265.12	36. 1	in the topics	in the topic⟨.⟩ ↑ s ↓
265.15	36.10	Teacher of the	Teacher o⟨.⟩ ↑ f ↓ the
265.26	37.14	to express	to ⟨take⟩ express
265.38	38.19	the whole digestive	the who digestive
266. 2	39. 7	state. These	state these
266. 3	39. 8	us abstain	us ⟨.⟩ ↑ a ↓ bstain
266. 4	39.11	disadvantages; the	disadvantages the
266. 6–7	39.17	this salt	this ⟨—⟩ salt
266. 7	39.19	food that which	food ↑ that ↓ which
266. 8	39.20	can, its	can its
266.10	40. 1	These and many	These ⟨—⟩ ↑ and ↓ many
266.10	40. 2	cooking lead	cooking ⟨which⟩ lead
266.14	40. 9	time; they	time ⟨it⟩ they
266.15	40.13	weeks. This	weeks this ⟨.⟩
266.24	41. 7	without being angry	without ⟨.⟩ ↑ b ↓ eing angry
266.29	41.18	sinner; we	sinner we
266.29	41.19	help me	help ⟨to⟩ me
266.30	41.21	them to Thee.	them to ⟨t⟩ ↑ T ↓ ee.
266.32	42. 2	to the confessional.	to ⟨..⟩ ↑ the ↓ confessional.
266.33	42. 4	penitent for	penitent ⟨be⟩ for
267.13	43.18	cannot too often	cannot to often
267.15	43.23	and too much	and to much
267.23	44.17	repentant give me	repentant ⟨for⟩ give me
267.30–31	45.12	have erred on	have err⟨..⟩ ↑ ed ↓ on
267.33	45.20	Oh Lord what	Oh Lord ⟨.⟩ what
267.38	46. 7	day. If it	day. ⟨.⟩ ↑ I ↓ f it
268. 7–8	47. 8	and one on the	and ↑ one on ↓ the
268.11	47.14	day sky to	day ↑ sky ↓ to
268.12	47.17	and an azure	and ⟨displayed and at a⟩ an azure
268.14	47.22	again; yet	again yet
268.25	48.23	has so wounded	has so⟨.⟩ wounded
268.26–27	49. 3	art thou so	art tho so
268.27	49. 3	down. Oh	down. ⟨and⟩ Oh
268.33	49.15	my bosom is	my b⟨.⟩ ↑ o ↓ som is
268.38	50. 1	us; why	us why
269. 1	50. 4	hands, how	hands how
269. 5	50.10	heart; what	heart what
269.15	51.10	and my heart	and ⟨.⟩ my heart
269.20	51.20	me; it	me it
269.33	53. 4	It does my	It ⟨must⟩ ↑ does ↓ my

HP	MS	HP	MS
269.36	53.13	love. It	love. ⟨I⟩ It
270. 3	54. 6	Ah who	Ah ⟨—⟩ who
270.10	54.22	increases the	increases ⟨with⟩ the
270.11	54.24	more; does	more does
270.18	55.13	that is that	that is ↑⟨which⟩↓ that
270.20	55.18	not, eyes	not eyes
270.25	56. 6	by sins hideth their presence	by sin⟨.⟩s hideth their ↑⟨...⟩↓ presence
270.27	56.12	thee we ne'er	thee ↑we↓ ne'er
271. 6	58.13	embrace thee? Shall	embrace thee⟨.⟩? Shall
271.14	59.11	Lord; teach	Lord teach
271.19	59.24	eager; it	eager it
271.42	62. 9	This too shall	This to shall
272. 4	62.20	to me but	to me ⟨—⟩ but
272.12	63.14	thee O God	thee ⟨.⟩↑O↓God
272.17	64. 5	besides Thee nothing	besides ⟨.⟩↑T↓ee nothing
272.18	64. 7	wilt Thou	wil⟨l⟩t Thou
272.22	64.17	day; here	day here
272.24	64.24	thine, a	thine a
272.30	65.16	Thee: Doubt	Thee Doubt
272.36	66. 2	else the faith	else ⟨that⟩ the faith
272.39	66. 5	no interest	no ⟨—⟩ interest
273.18–19	68. 3	ear to hear	ear ⟨for⟩ to hear
273.35	69.14	have given away	have ⟨..⟩ given away
273.36	69.19	I have not	I ⟨do⟩ have not
273.37	69.20	up to Thee	up to⟨t⟩↑T↓ee
274.24–25	72. 8	myself everyday I	myself ever day I

VOLUME V

HP	MS	HP	MS
277.11	1. 9	grounds higher than	grounds ↑higher↓ than
277.15	1.17	are led to	are led⟨.⟩ to
277.16	1.18	of a garden of	of ⟨f⟩↑a↓garden⟨s⟩ of
277.23	2.14	with an extraordinary	wit⟨.⟩h an extraordinary
277.24	2.16	be beheld.	be beheld. ⟨M⟩
278. 8–9	4.17	Me and the not	Me—and the—not me
278.18–19	5.17	lowest in Man, the	lowest in Man the
278.21	6. 2	existence in God	existence ↑in↓God
278.24	6. 7	ground for	ground ⟨given⟩ for
278.28	6.16	of exhibitions flows	of e⟨.⟩↑x↓hibition flows
278.32	7. 3	act of our	act of ⟨of⟩ our

HP	MS	HP	MS
279.15	9.18	God & us. They	God us. They
279.19	10. 4	Only when the	O⟨.⟩nly when the
279.19–20	10. 5	Soul does Man	Soul ⟨can⟩ ↑ does ↓ Man
279.24	10.13	should add	should ⟨give⟩ add
280. 4	12.17	only he	only ⟨who⟩ he
280.23	15. 3	ever err, and	ever err⟨e⟩ and
280.33–34	16. 7	of the Pope	of ⟨.⟩ ↑ t ↓ he Pope
280.37–38	16.17	uncatholic being Catholic.	uncatholic ⟨as a⟩ ↑ being ↓ Catholic.
280.39	17. 3	error; he has left	error he ⟨.⟩ ↑ h ↓ as left
281. 6	18. 2	life; the	life the
281.22	19. 7	is born again	is born⟨a⟩ again
281.23	19.11	us is ever giving birth	us ↑ is ↓ ever⟨..⟩ given birth
281.30	20. 6	Man than he	Man than⟨.⟩ he
281.32	20. 8	Soul can only	Soul can ⟨only be⟩ ↑ only ↓
281.34	20.12	embrace? Why	embrace why
281.39	21. 7–8	love—perhaps	love ↑ — ↓ ⟨to⟩ perhaps
282. 5–6	22. 6	time he increases	time ↑ he ↓ increases
282. 7	22. 9	He who possesses	He who p⟨.⟩ ↑ o ↓ ssesses
282.11	22.18	earth, above the	earth, above ⟨..⟩ ↑ th ↓ e
282.15	23. 8	ah love unlocks	ah love⟨r⟩ unlocks
282.16	23.10	common life a	common li⟨.⟩ ↑ f ↓ e a
282.24	24.14	crime and increased	crime and increased⟨.⟩
283.22	28.20	religion superior	religion ⟨.⟩ ↑ s ↓ uperior
283.23	29. 2	Christ exhibiting	Christ ⟨chi⟩ exhibiting
283.26	29. 8	is a sect	⟨a⟩ is a sect
283.26	29. 9	Christianity; out	Christianity out
284.12	32.10	than the extinguishing	than ↑ the ↓ extinguish- ing
284.19	33. 4	not the unrealness	not ↑ the ↓ unrealness
284.25	33.16	affirmation is	affirmation ⟨and⟩ is
284.29	34. 6	saw were before	saw w⟨as⟩ ↑ ere ↓ before
284.38	34.21	to the heart	to the ⟨.⟩ heart
284.38	34.22	heart be granted	heart b⟨.⟩ ↑ e ↓ granted
285. 6	35.12	same God as	same ↑ God ↓ as
285. 8	35.16	to nonentity.	to ⟨nothingness⟩ ↑ nonentity. ↓
285.18	36.16–17	some other thing	some ⟨thing else⟩ ↑ other thing ↓
285.21	36.21	God is good?	Go⟨o⟩ ↑ d ↓ is good?
285.23	37. 3	is; And out of	is; ⟨a⟩ ↑ A ↓ nd out of
285.29	37.15	for were it	for ⟨.⟩ were it
285.30	37.18	lost; it	lost it

HP	MS	HP	MS
285.35	38. 8	are; the	are the
285.35	38. 8	carried higher	carried ⟨further⟩ higher
285.36	38.10	God, myself	God, ⟨nature⟩ myself
285.41	38.20	is, creatures	is, ⟨we⟩ creatures
286. 1–2	39. 3	is enough to	is enough⟨t⟩ to
286. 2	39. 4	hearts eternal	hearts etern⟨n⟩↑a↓l
286. 6	39.12	attributes: Eternity	attributes Eternity
286. 6–7	39.13	imaged forth in	imaged↑forth↓in
286. 8	39.17	Men know	Men ⟨who⟩ know
286. 9	39.19	and more having	and↑more↓having
286.10	40. 1	us. Man	us. ⟨In⟩ Man
286.18	40.17	utter oblivion.	utter oblivion⟨.⟩.
286.19	40.20	do immortal.	do ⟨are⟩ immortal.
286.22	41. 4	value; it	value it
286.23	41. 5	writes an essay	writes an⟨y⟩ essay
286.28	41.14	harmony, Music,	harmony, ⟨the⟩ Music,
286.31	41.19	Music. They	Music. ⟨except but⟩ They
286.31	41.20	to the same	to↑the↓same
286.36	42. 8	expression; it	expression it
286.39	42.13	that enjoyment	that ⟨.⟩ enjoyment
287. 2	42.19	is too late.	is to late.
287.17	44. 1	elsewhere as if	elsewhere↑as↓if
287.19	44. 3	All true	All ⟨—⟩ true
287.30	44.21	less now than	less ⟨k⟩now than
288. 4	46. 4	to be crucified	to ⟨—⟩ be crucified
288.16	47. 4	ages, wherefore	ages wherefore
288.26	48. 2	will not be	will↑not↓be
288.26	48. 4	position to	position ⟨th⟩ to
288.28	48. 9	past what	past ⟨how⟩ what
288.29	48.10	bosoms when	bosoms ⟨.⟩when
288.32	48.15	Back of all	Back of⟨.⟩ all
288.34	48.19	or unconsciously	or↑un↓consciously
288.34	48.20	formed. We	formed. ⟨which more or less⟩ We
288.39	49.13	possesses the	possesses ⟨all⟩ the
288.40	49.15	single branch	single ⟨of.⟩ branch
289.14	51.13	in Titan	in ⟨Alban⟩ Titan
289.16	51.17	his first I believe love	his↑first I believe↓ love
289.20	52. 3	that it be	that↑it↓be
289.24	52. 8	objectiveness And	objectiveness ⟨to me⟩ And
289.26	52.14	Tasso, were instincted	Tasso,↑were↓ instincted

HP	MS	HP	MS
289.31	53. 2	life in any	life ↑ in ↓ any
289.35	53.10	of Science	of ⟨the⟩ Science
289.36	53.11	youth this	youth ⟨of⟩ this
289.40	53.19	gained; what	gained what
289.40	54. 1	no science.	no⟨ne⟩ science.
289.41–42	54. 2	not for time	not f⟨.⟩or time
290. 3–4	54.12	If ye	If ⟨you⟩ ye
290. 4–5	54.14	with its hero, those	with ↑ its heros, ↓ those
290. 5	54.15	have been generously	have been ↑ generously ↓
290.12	55.11	thyself; labor	thyself labor
290.20	56. 8	Do thine own	Do thine ⟨.⟩ ↑ o ↓ own
290.21	56.12	call thee great	call the great
290.22	56.14	world. In	w⟨.⟩ ↑ o ↓ rld. In
290.23	56.15	wears off and	wears of and
290.26	57. 3	to the gaze	to the ⟨.⟩gaze
290.27–28	57. 6	fountain of inspiration	fountain ↑ of inspiration ↓
290.28	57. 6	for all ages.	⟨.⟩ ↑ f ↓ or all ages.
290.29	57.10	The martyr	The ⟨19⟩ mar⟨y⟩ ↑ t ↓ yr
290.32	57.17	act; heroism	act heroism
290.32	57.17	such stripe our	such ↑ stripe ↓ our
291. 6	59.10	therefore it is	therefore it⟨.⟩ is
291.14	60. 7	that he is	that ↑ he ↓ is
291.33	62. 8	faith; give	faith give
292.15–16	65. 6	beginning; excepting	beginning excepting
292.27	66.11	by the definite	by the d⟨i⟩ ↑ e ↓ finite
292.41	67.13	against. These	against. ⟨To do this⟩ These
292.42	67.16	Christ: Unitarians	Christ Unitarians
293. 1	67.18	See: the	See the
293. 3	67.21	Church: the	Church the
293.11	68.16	for a friend who	for a friend⟨s⟩ who
293.14	69. 4	and only at length when	and ⟨at⟩ only at lengt⟨.⟩ ↑ h ↓ when
293.15	69. 7	satisfy this	satisfy ⟨That⟩ this
293.16	69. 9	is too late.	is to late.
293.18	69.13	must find a	must ↑ find ↓ a
293.41	71.21	it; not	it not
293.41	71.22	till then	the⟨m⟩ ↑ n ↓.
294. 5	72.17	found in all	found ⟨o⟩ ↑ in ↓ all
294. 7–8	73. 2	with moments	with⟨in⟩ moments
294. 9	73. 7	he never falls	he never⟨s⟩ falls
294.10	73.10–11	There is a strength	There is a ⟨stre⟩ a strength
294.12	73.17	imagery; the	imagery the

HP	MS	HP	MS
294.14	74. 2	the 17 as that	the 1⟨6⟩ ↑ 7 ↓ as that
294.14–15	74. 4	a modern meeting	a ↑ modern ↓ meeting
294.16	74. 6	The great question	The⟨.⟩ great question
294.17	74. 7	to bring back	to ⟨back⟩ bring back
294.17	74. 9	to its original	to ⟨.⟩ ↑ its ↓ original
294.31	76. 3	art. The	art the
294.34	76.11	Men can do	Men ↑ can ↓ do
294.35	76.12	but it is	but i⟨s⟩ ↑ t ↓ is
294.39–40	76.24	power; it is a	power it a
294.40	76.25	supernatural degree.	s ↑ u ↓ pernatural degree.
295. 5	77.15	which were seperated	which w⟨as⟩ ↑ ere ↓ seperated
295.14	78.13–14	than is the gift	than ⟨it⟩ is ⟨to enjoy⟩ the gift
295.17	79. 1	I have never	I have ⟨I⟩ never
295.28	80. 9	all our labors	all ⟨all⟩ our labors
295.41	82. 4	the whole	the ⟨.⟩ whole
295.42	82. 5	into calculation Paganism	into calculation ⟨the⟩ Paganism
296. 2	82.11	beautifullest specimens	beautifullest ⟨lives⟩ specimens
296. 3	82.14	only this As	only ↑ this ↓ As
296. 3–4	82.14	civilization and	civilization ⟨is the—⟩ and
296.14	84. 1	reading Schlegls	reading ⟨Sch Schg⟩ Schlegls
296.15	84. 4	to The English	to ⟨.⟩ ↑ T ↓ he English
296.35–36	86.16	epitome of all	e⟨.⟩pitome of all
296.38	87. 3	essence, the	essence the
296.40	87. 6	with; he	with he
296.41	87. 9	midst of profound	midst ⟨.⟩ ↑ o ↓ f profound
297. 2	87.16	sand a universe	sand⟨&⟩ ↑ a ↓ universe
297.13	88.19	Are our optics	⟨I..⟩ ↑ Are ↓ our optics
297.16	89. 6	than God himself	than ⟨the⟩ God himself
297.20	89.16	the head or heart	the ↑ head or ↓ heart
297.25	90. 8	imagine. The	imagine the
297.26	90.12	we but place	we ↑ but ↓ place
297.27	90.14	with the infinite of	↑ with the infinite ↓ of
297.28	90.16	and had we	and ↑ had ↓ we
297.31.	91. 4	darkly; did	darkly did
297.32	91. 7	should be crushed	should ↑ be ↓ crushed
297.32–33	91. 9	Mans heart shortened	Mans ⟨purity⟩ ↑ heart ↓ shortened
297.34–35	91.14	is above us	is above⟨s⟩ us

HP	MS	HP	MS
297.38	92. 6	matter into tissues and	matter ⟨and to—⟩ ↑ into tissues ↓ and
298. 1	92. 8	—Religion a delusion the	— ↑ Religion a delusion ↓ the
298. 3	92.12	than of the	than ⟨a poem⟩ of the
298. 4	92.13	than Raffaellos	than ⟨the⟩ Raffaellos
298. 5	93. 3	months since	months ⟨in⟩ since
298. 6	93. 4	that the	that ⟨a man⟩ the
298. 6	93. 5	a man thinks	a man⟨s⟩ thinks
298. 6-7	93. 7	Because he	Because ⟨the⟩ he
298.10	93.18	two sheets.	two s⟨.⟩ ↑ h ↓ eets.

VOLUME VI

HP	MS	HP	MS
301. 8	1.22	but temporary	but ⟨a⟩ temporary
301. 8	1.23	not permanent	not ⟨an⟩ permanent
301. 9	1.26	eventually be abolished	eventually abolished
301.11	2. 2	principal: how	principal how
301.35	3.18	of it some	of some
301.35-36	3.20	plan I then	plan ⟨of it⟩ I then
302.22	5.24	this: that	this that
302.31-32	6.14	lent on one meal	lent ↑ on ↓ one ⟨a⟩ meal
303.13	8. 4	Responsibleness, Conscience,	Responsi⟨s⟩bleness, Conscience,
303.14	8. 6	Consciousness; these	Consc⟨ic⟩iousness these
303.23	8.27	I did do	I did ⟨but⟩ do
303.32	9.20	pleasure; give	pleasure give
304. 1	10.14	shall I express the	shall express the
304. 6-7	10.26	treated Him wicked,	treated ↑ Him ↓ wicked,
304.27	12.12	Thou oh Jesus	Tho oh Jesus
305. 5	13.22	to thoughts	to ⟨stu⟩ thoughts
306. 3	16.25	motto: All	motto All
306. 8	17.11	doubt of	doubt ⟨th⟩ of
306.13	17.23	older and	older ⟨than⟩ and
306.15	17.27	grace open	grace ⟨be⟩ open
306.18-19	18. 8	would have	would ⟨do⟩ have
306.24	18.21	make a perfect	make a⟨nd⟩ perfect
306.35	19.18	thine; do	thine do
307. 6	20.20	vitiates and	vitates and
307.13	21. 6	as he wills in	as wills in
307.19	21.19	light it stands	light ⟨they⟩ it stands
307.24	21.29	of self denial	of ↑ self denial ↓
307.30	22.11	we are in	we ⟨h⟩are in

HP	MS	HP	MS
307.34	22.21	that it	that ⟨I⟩ it
308. 6	23.25	cause of	cause ⟨for⟩ of
308.17	24.20	Christ and be	Chris⟨s⟩t and be
308.20	24.28	feel. I	feel. ⟨is⟩ I
308.27	25.16	see the inherent	see ↑ the ↓ inherent
309.18	28. 7	subdued. Verbum	subdued. ⟨it⟩ Verbum
309.20	28.10	litany of the	litany of⟨r⟩ the
309.22	28.15	may do it with	may⟨not⟩ do it ⟨as⟩with
309.27	28.25	practice the	practise ⟨thy⟩ the
309.30	29. 2	that it would	that ⟨I⟩ it would
310. 6	30.20	theme: my	theme my
310. 9	30.27	heaven; what	heaven what
310.14	31.10	the bosom of	the ⟨—⟩ ↑ bosom ↓ of
310.20	31.24	love; all	love all
310.41	33.16	that anything	that ⟨all⟩ anything
311.22	35. 8	tendencies: by	tendencies by
311.25	35.15	not occupy	not ⟨—⟩ occupy
311.27	35.20	me to some	me to ⟨.—⟩ some
312. 3	37.12	the order	the ⟨choice⟩ order
312.30	39.17	Thee; reject	Thee reject
312.36	40.Margin	25	2⟨6⟩ ↑ 5 ↓
313. 1	40.13	confession the	confession ⟨I will⟩ the
313. 4	40.21	and for which	and f⟨r⟩or which
313. 5	40.24	mind composed	mind ⟨as⟩ composed
313. 6	41. 1	If I look	If look
313. 9	41. 7	have me to	have ⟨.⟩ me to
313.31	43. 9	back at the	back ⟨and th⟩ at the
313.31	43.11	attempts that	attemp⟨.⟩ts that
313.33–34	43.17	Providence tho	Providence ⟨that⟩ tho
314.37	43.24	to know in	to now in
314.17	45.13	motive which	motive ⟨and⟩ which
314.27	46.10	—forever.	—⟨&⟩ forever.
314.37	47. 1	and weaknesses	and ⟨necessities⟩ weaknesses
315. 8	47.23	empty; let	empty let
315.14	48. 7	way too hard	way to hard
315.29	49.12	do and Thy	do ⟨with⟩ ↑ and ↓ Thy
315.36	49.25	a more	a ⟨more perfe⟩ more
315.39–40	50. 5	disadvantages: my	disadvantages my
316. 1	50.10	I did not	I ⟨had⟩ did not
316. 9	50.27	I selected	I ⟨took⟩ selected
316.10	51. 2	tormented and	tormented ⟨with⟩ and
316.18–19	51.20	give me strength	give me⟨.⟩ strength
316.23	51.28	keeps a	keeps ⟨one⟩ a
316.30–31	52.15–16	from attaining	from ⟨..— —⟩ attaining

HP	MS	HP	MS
316.37	53. 3	take persons	take ⟨scholars for⟩ persons
317.13	54. 4	not even one.	not ↑ even ↓ one.
317.17	54.13	our lives unprepared	our li⟨f⟩ ↑ v ↓ es unprepared
317.18	54.15	impending event.	impending ⟨danger⟩ event.
317.21	54.22	immortal? Can	immortal? ⟨?⟩ Can⟨t⟩
317.29	55.11	us either from	us ↑ either ↓ from
317.30	55.13	And with these,	And ↑ with ↓ these,
317.33–34	55.21	nature lower in	nature l⟨..⟩ ↑ ower ↓ in
317.34–35	55.23	moment perhaps his	moment ↑ perhaps ↓ his
317.39–40	56. 5	onflowing. It is tragic. It	onflowing. ↑ It is tragic ↓ It
317.41	56. 8	which changes the	which ⟨—⟩ ↑ changes the ↓
318. 2	56.15	All nature groans with the selfsame curse.	↑ All nature groans with the selfsame curse. ↓
318. 3–4	56.19	poison, and	poison, ⟨—⟩ and
318.28	59. 2	may be given	may given
319.11	61.10	Lord do for	Lord ⟨to⟩ do for
319.38	63.14	us; we	us we
319.39	63.16	us. Oh	us. ⟨and⟩ Oh
320. 2	63.25	Mans. How	Mans how
320. 3–4	64. 1	did not cling to	did ↑ not cling ↓ to
320.10	67.26	masters make new	masters ↑ make ↓ new
320.19	68.18	general—what	general what
320.27	69. 6	these dispositions when	these ↑ dispositions ↓ when
320.29	69.10	efforts is hard	efforts ⟨.⟩is hard
320.30–31	69.13	shall go in	shall go⟨.⟩ in
320.32	69.16	we to look	we ⟨and⟩ to look
321.32	69.17	an action of	an action⟨s⟩ on of
321.35	69.23	as Paul did	as Paul⟨d⟩ did
321.40–41	70. 5	him, and	him, ⟨yet⟩ and
322.10	71. 4	why we could	why ⟨.⟩ we could
322.17	71.20	from the head of Jupiter	↑ from the head of Jupiter ↓
322.30	72.24	it's borrowed.	its borrowed.
322.36	73. 9	genuine; we	genuine we
323.16	74.26	Hence we	Hence ⟨when⟩ we
323.24	75.14	dissipated our	dissipated ⟨and⟩ our
323.32–33	76. 3	their former positions	their f⟨.⟩ormer positions
323.38	76.17	study towards	study ⟨.⟩ towards
323.39	76.19	will; resistance	will resistance

HP	MS	HP	MS
324.15	78. 1	studied little	studi⟨.⟩ ↑ e ↓ d little
324.16	78. 4	or between	or ⟨what⟩ between
325.10	81. 5	pedestrian tour	pedestrian ⟨—⟩ ↑ tour ↓
325.24	82. 1	Our union and	Our union ⟨with⟩ and
325.28	82.12	God; how	God how
325.36	83. 5	energy to	energy ⟨towards⟩ to
326. 9	84. 3	prepare rather	prepare ⟨my⟩ rather
326.16	84.22	free, that	free, ⟨and⟩ that
326.29	85.28	go too far	go to far
326.29–30	86. 1	me and all	me and⟨f⟩ all

BIBLIOGRAPHY

Aaron, Daniel. *The Unwritten War: American Writers and the Civil War.* New York: Alfred A. Knopf, 1973.

Ahlstrom, Sydney. *A Religious History of the American People.* New Haven, Conn.: Yale University Press, 1972.

Albanese, Catherine C. *Corresponding Notion: Transcendental Religion and the New America.* Philadelphia: Temple University Press, 1977.

Alcott, Bronson. *Journals.* Edited by Odell Shephard. Boston: Little, Brown, and Company, 1938.

Alexander, Jon. *American Personal Religious Accounts: 1600–1980.* New York: Edwin Mellen, 1983.

Baer, Robert W. "Isaac Thomas Hecker: A Study in Individuation and the Collective." Diploma thesis, C. G. Jung Institute, Zurich, 1982.

Baird, Robert. *Religion in the United States of America.* New York: Harper and Brothers, 1856; reprint ed., New York: Arno Press and The New York Times, 1969.

Barbour, Brian M. *American Transcendentalism: An Anthology of Criticism.* Notre Dame, Ind.: University of Notre Dame Press, 1973.

Barrett, John Mandel. "The Autobiographer's Art." *Journal of Aesthetics and Art Criticism* 27 (1968): 217.

Barry, Canon William. "Father Hecker, Founder of the Paulists." *Dublin Review* 2 (July 1892): 63–95.

Bayley, J. R. *A Brief Sketch of the Early History of the Catholic Church on the Island of New York.* New York: The Catholic Publication Society, 1870; reprint ed., New York: U.S. Catholic Historical Society, 1973.

Belden, L. W. *An Account of Jane C. Rider, the Springfield Somnambulist.* Springfield, Mass.: G. & C. Merriam, 1834.

Bercovitch, Sacvan. *The Puritan Origins of the American Self.* New Haven, Conn.: Yale University Press, 1975.

Bestor, Arthur E., Jr. *Backwoods Utopias.* Philadelphia: University of Pennsylvania Press, 1950.

Block, Marguerite B. *The New Church in the New World.* New York: H. Holt and Company, 1932; reprint ed., New York: Octagon, 1968.

Bloom, Harold. *The Ringers in the Tower: Studies in Romantic Tradition.* Chicago: University of Chicago Press, 1971.

Blumenthal, Henry. *American and French Culture, 1800–1900.* Baton Rouge, La.: Louisiana State University Press, 1975.

Bode, Carl, ed. *American Life in the 1840s.* New York: Anchor Books, 1967.

Boller, Paul F., Jr. *American Transcendentalism 1830–1860: An Intellectual Inquiry.* New York: G. P. Putnam's Sons, 1974.

Bourignon, Antoinette. *The Light of the World.* London: Christian de Cort, 1696; reprint ed., London: Sampson Low, 1863.

Briancourt, Math. *The Organization of Labor and Association.* Translated by Francis Shaw. New York: William H. Graham, 1847.

Brisbane, Albert. *General Introduction to Social Science.* New York: Somerby, 1876; reprint ed., Westport, Conn.: Hyperion, 1976.

Brock, William R. *Conflict and Transformation 1844–1877.* Baltimore: Penguin Books, 1973.

Brown, Henry C. *The Story of Old New York.* New York: Dulten, 1934.

Brownlow, William G. *A Political Register: Principles of Whig and Locofoco Parties in United States.* Jonesborough, Tenn.: Jonesborough Whig Press, 1844; reprint ed., Spartanburg, S.C.: The Reprint Company, 1974.

Brownson, Orestes A. *Saint-Worship: The Worship of Mary.* Edited by Thomas R. Ryan. Paterson, N.J.: St. Anthony Guild, 1963.

——. *The Works of Orestes A. Brownson.* Edited by Henry F. Brownson. Detroit: Thorndike, 1882.

——. "Transcendental Road to Rome." *Brownson's Quarterly Review* 2 (Oct. 1857): 459–503.

——. *The Convert.* New York: Dunigan, 1857.

Brumm, Ursula. *American Thought and Religious Typology.* New Brunswick, N.J.: Rutgers University Press, 1970.

Buell, Lawrence. *Literary Transcendentalism: Style and Vision in the American Literature.* Ithaca, N.Y.: Cornell University Press, 1973.

Burton, Katherine. *In No Strange Land: Some American Catholic Converts.* David McKay Co., 1942; reprint ed., Freeport, N.Y.: Books for Libraries, 1970.

——. *Celestial Homespun.* New York: Longmans, Green, 1943.

Bushnell, Horace. *God in Christ*. Hartford, Conn.: Brown & Parsons, 1849.

Butler, Perry. *Gladstone: Church, State, and Tractarianism*. London: Oxford University Press, 1982.

Byrdsall, F. *The History of the Loco-Foco or Equal Rights Party*. New York: Clement and Packard, 1842; reprint ed., New York: Burt Franklin, 1967.

Cameron, Kenneth Walter. *Transcendental Curriculum of Bronson Alcott's Library*. Hartford, Conn.: Transcendental Books, 1984.

Carey, Patrick. *American Catholic Religious Thought*. New York: Paulist Press, 1987.

Carlyle, Thomas. *Past and Present*. London: Chapman and Hall, 1897; reprint ed., New York: Ams Press, 1969.

—. *Sartor Resartus*. Boston: James Munroe, 1837.

—. *On Heroes, Hero-Worship, and the Heroic in History*. Edited by Archibald MacMechan. Boston: Ginn, 1901.

Carpenter, Frederic I. *American Literature and the Dream*. New York: Philosophical Library, 1955; reprint ed., Freeport, N.Y.: Books for Libraries, 1968.

—. *Emerson Handbook*. New York: Hendrick's House, 1958.

Carson, Gerald. *Cornflakes Crusade*. New York: Rinehart, 1957.

Ceroke, Christian P. "The Scapular Devotion." *Mariology*. Vol. 3. Edited by Juniper B. Carol. Milwaukee: Bruce Publishing, 1961.

Certeau, Michel de. *La Fable Mystique*. Paris: Gallimard, 1982.

Challoner, Richard. *The Garden of the Soul: A Manual of Spiritual Exercises and Instruction*. Reprint ed., Westminster, Md.: The Newman Press, 1945.

Cheever, George B. *God's Hand in America*. New York: M. W. Dodd, 1841.

Chevalier, Michael. *Society, Manners and Politics in the United States*. Boston: Weeks and Jordan, 1839; reprint ed., New York: Augustus M. Kelley, 1966.

Chinnici, Joseph. *Devotion to the Holy Ghost in American Catholicism*. New York: Paulist Press, 1985.

Christy, Arthur. *The Orient in American Transcendentalism*. New York: Octagon Books, 1963.

Coleridge, Samuel Taylor. *Aids to Reflection*. Edited by Derwent Coleridge. London: Ward, Locke, and Co., 1854.

Cooper, James Fenimore. *The American Democrat: A Treatise on Jacksonian Democracy*. New York: Alfred A. Knopf; reprint ed., New York: Funk and Wagnalls, 1969.

Cross, Robert D. "Isaac Hecker's *The Church and the Age,* or, Was Hecker a Heretic?'' Paper delivered at Hecker Symposium, St. Paul College, Washington, D.C., 1974.

Couser, G. Thomas. *American Autobiography: The Prophetic Mode.* Amherst, Mass.: University of Massachusetts, 1979.

Crowe, Charles. *George Ripley, Transcendentalist and Utopian Socialist.* Athens, Ga.: University of Georgia, 1967.

Curran, R. Emmett. *American Jesuit Spirituality: The Maryland Tradition.* New York: Paulist Press, 1988.

Dawley, Alan. *Class and Community: The Industrial Revolution in Lynn.* Cambridge, Mass.: Harvard University Press, 1976.

Dawson, Christopher. *The Spirit of the Oxford Movement.* London: Sheed & Ward, 1934; reprint ed., New York: Ams Press, 1976.

De Caussade, J. P. *Abandonment; or Absolute Surrender to Divine Providence.* Translated by Ella McMahon. New York: Benziger, 1887.

De Goesbriand, L. *Catholic Memoirs of Vermont and New Hampshire.* Burlington, Vt.: 1886.

De Guibert, Joseph. *The Jesuits: Their Spiritual Doctrine and Practice.* Translated by William J. Young. Chicago: The Institute of Jesuit Sources, 1964.

Dehne, Carl. ''Roman Catholic Popular Devotions.'' *Worship* 49 (October 1975): 446–60.

Dolan, Jay P. *The Immigrant Church: New York's Irish and German Catholics, 1815–1865.* Baltimore: Johns Hopkins University Press, 1975.

—. *Catholic Revivalism: The American Experience 1830–1920* Notre Dame, Ind.: University of Notre Dame Press, 1978.

—. *The American Catholic Experience.* Garden City, N.Y.: Doubleday, 1985.

—. ''The Vision of the Early Paulists.'' Talk given at St. Paul's College, Washington, D.C., Jan. 26, 1976.

Donovan, J., trans. *The Catechism of the Council of Trent.* Baltimore: James Myres, 1833.

Duffy, John, ed. *Coleridge's American Disciples; The Selected Correspondence of James Marsh.* Amherst, Mass.: University of Massachusetts Press, 1973.

Edwards, Ram B. *A Return to Moral and Religious Philosophy in Early America.* Washington, D.C.: University Press of America, 1982.

Elliot, Walter. *Life of Father Hecker.* New York: Columbus Press, 1891.

—. *La Vie du Père Hecker.* Translated by Countess de Revillary. Paris, 1897.

Ellis, David M. *New York, State and City.* Ithaca, N.Y.: Cornell University Press, 1979.

Ellis, John Tracey and Robert Trisco. *A Guide to American Catholic History*. Santa Barbara, Cal.: ABC-Clio, 1982.

Emerson, Ralph Waldo. *Journals, 1841–1843*. Edited by Gilman Parsons. Cambridge, Mass.: Harvard University Press, 1970.

—. *Journals, 1843–1847*. Edited by Orth Ferguson. Cambridge, Mass.: Harvard University Press, 1971.

—. *Essays*. Boston: James R. Osgood, 1876.

Erikson, Erik. *Young Man Luther: A Study in Psychoanalysis and History*. New York: W. W. Norton, 1958.

Falk, Robert, ed. *Literature and Ideas in America*. Ohio University Press, 1975.

Farina, John. *An American Experience of God*. New York: Paulist Press, 1981.

—, ed. *Hecker Studies: Essays in the Thought of Isaac T. Hecker*. New York: Paulist Press, 1983.

—. "Hecker's Appeal for Today." *Paulist* (1982): 40–41.

—. "Isaac T. Hecker's American Spirituality." *New Catholic World* 225 (July/Aug. 1982): 166–69.

—. "Isaac Hecker: Spiritual Director." *Journal of Formative Spirituality* 4 (Feb. 1983): 109–116.

—. "The Use of the Early Diary of Isaac Hecker." *U.S. Catholic Historian* 3 (Spring 1984): 279–93.

Feidelson, Charles. *Symbolism and American Literature*. Chicago: University of Chicago Press, 1953.

Fenwick, Benedict Joseph. *Memoirs to Serve for the Future: Ecclesiastical History of the Diocese of Boston*. Edited by Joseph M. McCarthy. Yonkers, N.Y.: U.S. Catholic Historical Society, 1978.

Fredrickson, George. *The Inner Civil War: Northern Intellectuals and the Crisis of the Union*. New York: Harper and Row, 1965.

Gasquet, Abbot Francis A., ed. "Some Letters of Father Hecker." *Catholic World* 83 (May 1906): 233–45, 356–65, 456–65.

Gerbet, Olympe Philippe. *Consideration on the Eucharist*. London: C. Dolman, 1843.

Ghering, Harold A. III. "The Theology of Isaac Thomas Hecker and *Testem Benevolentiae*." M. A. thesis, Christ the King Seminary, East Aurora, N.Y., 1979.

Gilhooley, Leonard, ed. *No Divided Allegiance: Essays in Brownson's Thought*. New York: Fordham University Press, 1980.

Gilley, Sheridan. "Catholic Faith of the Irish Slum." *The Victorian City: Images and Reality*. Vol. 2. Edited by H. J. Dyos and Michael Wolff. Boston: Routledge and Kegan Paul, 1973.

Girgus, Sam B. *The Law of the Heart: Individualism and the Modern Self in the American Literature*. Austin, Tex.: University of Texas Press, 1979.

Gode-von Aesch, Alexander Gottfried. *Natural Science in German Romanticism*. New York: Columbia University Press, 1941.

Godwin, Parke. *A Popular View of the Doctrines of Charles Fourier*. New York: J. S. Redfield, 1844; reprint ed., New York: Ams Press, 1974.

Goethe, Johann Wolfgang. *Iphigenie auf Tauris*. Berlin: Aufbau-Verlag GmbH, 1946.

—. *Faust I & II*. Edited and translated by Stuart Atkins. Cambridge, Mass.: Suhrkamp/Insel, 1984.

—. *The Works, Vol. III: The Sorrows of Werther, The Elective Affinities, The Good Woman, A Tale*. Translated by Bayard Taylor. Philadelphia: J. H. Moore, 1882.

—. *J. P. Eckermann: Gespräche mit Goethe*. Leipzig: E. Diederichs, 1902.

Goldfarb, Russell M. and Clare R. *Spiritualism and Nineteenth-Century Letters*. Cranbury, N.J.: Associated University Press, 1978.

Goren, Leyla. *Elements of Brahmanism in the Transcendentalism of Emerson*. Hartford, Conn.: Transcendental Books, 1977.

Gower, Joseph. "The New Apologetics of Isaac Thomas Hecker (1819–1888): Catholicity and American Culture." Ph. D. dissertation, University of Notre Dame, 1978.

—. "A Test Question for Religious Liberty: Isaac Hecker on Education." *Notre Dame Journal of Education* (Spring 1976): 28–43.

—. "Democracy as a Theological Problem in Isaac Hecker's Apologetics." *America in Theological Perspective*. Edited by Thomas M. McFadden. New York: Seabury Press, 1976.

Gower, Joseph and Leliaret, Richard M., eds. *The Brownson-Hecker Correspondence*. Notre Dame, Ind.: University of Notre Dame Press, 1979.

Greene, William R. *Transcendentalism (1849) and Equality (1849)*. West Brookfield, Mass.: O. S. Cooke, 1849; reprint ed., Delmar, N.Y.: Scholar's Facsimiles and Reprints, 1981.

—. *Transcendentalism*. West Brookfield, Mass.: Power Press of Oliver Cooke, 1849.

Gura, Philip F. *The Wisdom of Words: Language, Theology, and Literature in the New England Renaissance*. Middletown, Conn.: Wesleyan University, 1981.

Haight, Benjamin Isaac. *A Letter to a Parishioner Relative to the Recent Ordination of Mr. Arthur Carey*. New York, 1843.

Handy, Robert T. "Father Hecker, A Bridge Between Catholic and Protestant Thought." *Catholic World* 202 (Dec. 1965): 158–59.

—. *Christian America: Protestant Hopes and Historic Realities*. New York: Oxford, 1971.

Haraszti, Zoltan. "Brook Farm Letters." *More Books* 12 (February 1937): 49–68.

—. "Brook Farm Letters." *More Books* 12 (March 1937): 93–114.

Harper, George Mills and Kathleen Raine, eds. *Thomas Taylor the Platonist: Selected Writings*. Princeton, N.J.: Princeton University Press, 1969.

Harris, Neil. *The Artist in American Society, the Formative Years 1790–1860*. New York: George Braziller, 1966.

Harris, Ronald Walter. *Romanticism and the Social Order 1780–1830*. London: Barnes and Noble, 1969.

Hawkins, Anne Humsaker. *Archetypes of Conversion*. Cranbury, N.J.: Associated University Press, 1985.

Hennesey, James. *American Catholics: A History of the Roman Catholic Community in the United States*. New York: Oxford University Press, 1981.

Herrnstadt, Richard L., ed. *The Letters of A. Bronson Alcott*. Ames, Iowa: Iowa State University Press, 1969.

Hess, M. Whitcomb. "Thoreau and Hecker, Freemen, Friends, Mystics." *Catholic World* 209 (1969): 265–67.

Hewit, Augustine F. "Tribute of *The Catholic World* to Its Founder, Father Hecker." *Catholic World* 68 (Jan. 1889): 571a–576a.

Hill, William Douglas, trans. *The Bhagavadgita*. London: Oxford University Press, 1928.

Hirn, Yrjö. *The Sacred Shrine: A Study of the Poetry and Art of the Catholic Church*. Boston: Beacon Press, 1957.

Hochfield, George, ed. *Selected Writings of the American Transcendentalists*. New York: The New American Library, 1966.

Hofstader, Richard, William Miller, Daniel Aaron, Winthrop Jordan, and Leon Litwack. *The United States*. Englewood Cliffs, N.J.: Prentice Hall, 1976.

Holden, Vincent. *The Yankee Paul: Isaac Thomas Hecker*. Milwaukee: The Bruce Publishing Co., 1958.

—. "The Early Years of Isaac Thomas Hecker, 1819–1844." Ph. D. dissertation, The Catholic University of America, 1939.

—. "An American Ahead of His Time." *Ave Maria* 97 (June 8, 1963): 5–8.

—. "Myth in *L'Américanisme*." *Catholic Historical Review* 31 (1945): 154–70.

—. "Father Hecker's Vision Vindicated." *Historical Records and Studies* 50 (1964): 40–52.

Hotson, Clarence P. "Emerson and the Swedenborgians." *Studies in Philosophy* 27 (July 1930): 517–45.

Ireland, John. *The Church and Modern Society*. Chicago: D. H. McBride, 1896.

Irwin, John T. *American Hieroglyphics: The Symbol of the Egyptian Hieroglyphics in the American Renaissance*. New Haven, Conn.: Yale University Press, 1980.

Jay, Elizabeth, ed. *The Evangelical and Oxford Movements*. London: Cambridge University Press, 1983.

Jones, Howard Mumford. *America and French Culture 1750–1848*. Chapel Hill, N.C.: University of North Carolina Press, 1927; reprint ed., Westport, Conn.: Greenwood Press, 1973.

Journeys into the Moon, Several Planets and the Sun. Philadelphia, 1837.

Kauffman, Christopher. *Tradition and Transformation in Catholic Culture*. New York: Macmillan, 1988.

Keble, John. *The Tracts for the Times #89: On the Mysticism Attributed to the Early Fathers of the Church*. London: James Parker, 1868.

Kehoe, Laurence, ed. *The Complete Works of John Hughes*. Vol. I. New York: The American News Company, 1864.

Kenrick, Francis Patrick. *The Catholic Doctrine on Justification*. Philadelphia: Eugene Cumminskey, 1841.

—. *The Validity of Anglican Orders Examined*. Philadelphia: Cumminskey, 1841.

—. *Letter on Christian Union Addressed to the Bishops of the Protestant Episcopal Church in the United States*. Philadelphia: Cumminskey, 1841.

Kerner, Justinus. *The Seeress of Prevorst*. Translated by Catherine Crow. London: J. C. Moore, 1845.

Kirby, Georgiana Bruce. *Years of Experience*. New York: G. P. Putnam's Sons, 1887.

Kirk, Martin J. "The Spirituality of Isaac Thomas Hecker: Reconciling the American Character and the Catholic Faith." Ph. D. dissertation, St. Louis University, 1980.

Knights, Peter R. *The Plain People of Boston, 1830–1860: A Study in City Growth*. New York: Oxford University Press, 1971.

Koster, Donald Nelson. *Transcendentalism in America*. Boston: Twayne Publishers, 1975.

Kurtz, Lester R. *The Politics of Heresy: The Modernist Crisis in Roman Catholicism*. Berkeley, Cal.: University of California Press, 1986.

Kwitchen, Mary Augustine. *James Alphonsus McMaster: A Study in American Thought*. Washington, D.C.: The Catholic University of America Press, 1949.

Langlois, Edward J. "The Formation of American Catholic Political Thought: Isaac Hecker's Political Theory." Ph. D. dissertation, Cornell University, 1977.

Larkin, Emmet. "The Devotional Revolution in Ireland, 1850–75." *The American Historical Review* 77 (June 1972): 625–52.

Le Brun, Jacques. "Political Spirituality: the Devotion to the Sacred Heart." *The Concrete Christian Life.* Edited by Christian Duquoc. New York: Herder and Herder, 1971.

Lead, Jane. *Divine Revelation and Prophesies.* Nottingham, England: H. Wild, 1830.

Lee, Eliza B., trans. *Life of Jean Paul Richter.* New York: D. Appleton, 1850.

Lenhart, Charmenz S. *Musical Influence on American Poetry.* Athens, Ga.: University of Georgia Press, 1956.

Leroux, Pierre. *De L'Humanité, Son Principe et de Son Avenir. Où se trouve exposée. La Vraie Définition De La Religion et où L'on explique Le Sens, La Suite et L'enchaînement du Mosaisme et du Christianisme.* Paris: Perrotin, 1840.

Lewis, R. W. B. *The American Adam. Innocence, Tragedy and Tradition in the Nineteenth Century.* Chicago: University of Chicago Press, 1955.

Locke, John. *An Essay Concerning Human Understanding.* Edited by Peter H. Nidditch. Oxford: Clarendon Press, 1975.

Louth, Andrew. *Westminster Dictionary of Spirituality.* Philadelphia: Westminster, 1984.

Lovejoy, Arthur O. *Essays in the History of Ideas.* Baltimore: Johns Hopkins University Press, 1948.

Lowance, Mason I., Jr. *The Language of Canaan: Metaphor and Symbol in New England from the Puritans to the Transcendentalists.* Cambridge, Mass.: Harvard University Press, 1980.

Lyons, Mary Ethel. "A Rhetoric for American Catholicism: The Transcendental Voice of Isaac T. Hecker." Ph. D. dissertation, University of California at Berkeley, 1982.

McCarthy, Harold E. "Aesthetics East and West." *Philosophy East and West* 3 (April 1953): 47–68.

McDannell, Colleen. *The Christian Home in Victorian America 1840–1900.* Bloomington, Ind.: Indiana University Press, 1986.

McGinn, Bernard. "Love, Knowledge, and Mystical Union in Western Christianity: Twelfth to Sixteenth Centuries." *Church History* 56 (March 1987): 7–24.

—, ed. *Meister Eckhart, the Essential Sermons.* New York: Paulist Press, 1981.

McSorley, Joseph. *Father Hecker and His Friends*. New York: B. Herder, 1952.

Maignen, Charles. *Études sur l' Américanisme. Le Père Hecker, Est-il un Saint?* Paris: V. Retaux, 1899. English trans. *Father Hecker, Is He a Saint?* London: Burns and Oates, 1898.

Mandel, John Barrett. "The Autobiographer's Art." *Journal of Aesthetics and Art Criticism* 27 (1968): 217.

Manuel, Frank. *The Prophets of Paris*. London: Cambridge University Press, 1962.

Marschall, John P. "Kenrick and the Paulists; a Conflict of Structures and Personalities." *Church History* 38 (1969): 88–105.

Martinet, Antoine. *Religion in Society*. New York: Sadlier, 1850.

Maurice, F. D. *The Kingdom of Christ*. London, 1837; reprint ed., New York: E. P. Dutton, 1937.

Maynard, Theodore. *Orestes Brownson: Yankee, Radical, Catholic*. New York: Hafner Publishing, 1971.

Meade, William. *Sermon on Confirmation*. Washington, D.C.: James C. Dunn, 1831.

Michelet, M. *Spiritual Direction and Auricular Confession; Their History, Theory, and Consequences*. Philadelphia: James M. Campbell, 1845.

Miller, Perry. *The Transcendentalists*. Cambridge, Mass.: Harvard University Press, 1950.

Milne, George. *George William Curtis and the Genteel Tradition*. Bloomington, Ind.: Indiana University Press, 1956.

Milner, John. *The Key of Heaven: A Manual of Prayer*. Baltimore: John Murphy, 1867.

Moehler, John Adam. *Symbolism*. Translated by James Robertson. London: Gibbings, 1906.

Moody, Joseph, ed. *Church and Society*. New York: Arts, 1953.

Myerson, Joel, ed. *The American Renaissance in New England*. Detroit: Gale Research, 1978.

—. *The Transcendentalists*. New York: The Modern Language Association, 1984.

—. *Brook Farm: An Annotated Bibliography and Resource Guide*. New York: Garland, 1978.

—. *The Brook Farm Book: A Collection of First-Hand Accounts of the Community*. New York: Garland, 1987.

—. *The New England Transcendentalists and the Dial*. Cranbury, N.J.: Associated University Press, 1980.

Neel, Ann. *Theory of Psychology*. New York: Schenkman, 1977.

Newcomb, Charles King. *The Journals*. Edited by Judith Kennedy Johnson. Providence, R.I.: Brown University Press, 1946.

Newman, John Henry. *Tracts for the Times #90: Remarks on Certain Passages in the Thirty-Nine Articles.* New York: H. B. Durand, 1868.

Nolan, Hugh J. *The Most Reverend Francis Patrick Kenrick, Third Bishop of Philadelphia 1830–1851.* Philadelphia: American Catholic Historical Society, 1948.

Noyes, John Humphrey. *History of American Socialisms.* Philadelphia: J.B. Lippincott, 1870; reprint ed., New York: Dover, 1966.

Nye, Russel Blaine. *Society and Culture in America 1830–1860.* New York: Harper and Row, 1974.

O'Meara, Thomas F. *Romantic Idealism and Roman Catholicism.* Notre Dame, Ind.: University of Notre Dame Press, 1982.

Ong, Walter F. "Man Between Two Worlds; St. Paul, the Paulists, and American Catholicism." *Catholic World* 186 (May 1958): 86–94.

Parker, Gail Thain. *Mind Cure in New England from the Civil War to World War I.* Hanover, N.H.: University Press of New England, 1973.

Parrington, Vernon Louis. *The Romantic Revolution in America 1800–1860.* New York: Harcourt and Brace, 1927.

Parsons, Wilfrid. "Brownson, Hecker, and Hewit." *Catholic World* 153 (1941): 396–408.

Paul, Sherman. *Emerson's Angle of Vision.* Cambridge, Mass.: Harvard University Press, 1952.

Perschbacher, Susan. "Journey of Faith." Ph. D. dissertation, University of Chicago, 1981.

Persons, Stow. *The Decline of American Gentility.* New York: Columbia University, 1973.

Pessen, Edward, ed. *Jacksonian Panorama.* Indianapolis, Ind.: Bobbs-Merrill, 1976.

The Pious Guide to Prayer and Devotion. Baltimore: Lucas Brothers, 1843.

Portier, William. "Providential Nation: An Historical-Theological Study of Isaac Hecker's Americanism." Ph. D. dissertation, University of St. Michael's College, 1980.

—. *Isaac Hecker and the First Vatican Council.* Babylon, N.Y.: Edwin Mellon Press, 1986.

—. "Isaac Hecker and Americanism." *Ecumenist* 19 (Nov./Dec. 1980): 9–12.

Pratt, Parley. *Voice of Warning.* Salt Lake City: George Cannon, 1891.

Preston, Thomas. *The Divine Paraclete.* New York: Robert Coddington, 1879.

Rahner, Karl. "Religious Enthusiasm and the Experience of Grace," *Theological Investigations.* Vol. 16. Baltimore: Helicon, 1967.

Raine, Kathleen and George M. Harper, eds. *Thomas Taylor the Platonist.* Princeton, N.J.: Princeton University Press, 1969.

Reardon, Bernard. *Liberalism and Tradition: Aspects of Catholic Thought in Nineteenth Century France.* Cambridge: Cambridge University Press, 1975.

Reed, Albert, ed. *The Romantic Period.* New York: Charles Scribner's Sons, 1929.

Reeves, Jesse. *American Diplomacy under Tyler and Polk.* Baltimore: Johns Hopkins University Press, 1907; reprint ed., Gloucester, Mass.: Peter Smith, 1967.

Reher, Margaret M. "Americanizing the Catholic Church." *Dialog* 14 (Fall 1975): 289–96.

Riasanovsky, Nicholas V. *The Teaching of Charles Fourier.* Berkeley, Cal.: University of California Press, 1969.

Richter, Jean Paul. *Horn of Oberon: Jean Paul Richter's School of Aesthetics.* Translated by Margaret R. Hale. Detroit: Wayne State University Press, 1973.

—. *Hesperus.* Translated by Charles T. Brooks. Boston: Ticknor and Fields, 1865.

—. *Flower, Fruit, and Thorn Pieces.* Translated by Edward Noel. London: William Smith, 1845.

—. *Titan.* Translated by Charles T. Brooks. Boston: Ticknor and Fields, 1864.

Ricoeur, Paul. *The Symbolism of Evil.* Translated by Emerson Buchanan. New York: Harper and Row, 1967.

Rose, Anne. *Transcendentalism as a Social Movement 1830–1850.* New Haven, Conn.: Yale University Press, 1981.

Rosenthal, Bernard. *City of Nature: Journeys to Nature in the Age of American Romanticism.* Newark, Del.: University of Delaware Press, 1980.

Rowell, Geoffrey, ed. *Tradition Renewed: The Oxford Movement Conference Papers.* Allison Park, Penn.: Pickwick, 1986.

Russell, E. H. "A Bit of Unpublished Correspondence Between Henry Thoreau and Isaac Hecker." *Atlantic Monthly* 90 (1902): 370–76.

Ryan, E. "The Oxford Movement in the United States." *Catholic Historical Review* 19 (April 1933): 33–39.

Sams, Henry W., ed. *Autobiography of Brook Farm.* Englewood Cliffs, N.J.: Prentice-Hall, 1958.

Santayana, George. *Wind of Doctrine and Platonism and the Spiritual Life.* New York: Harper and Brothers, 1957.

Schaff, Philip. *America: A Sketch of Its Political, Social, and Religious Character.* Edited by Perry Miller. Cambridge, Mass.: Harvard University Press, 1961.

Schimanski, Stefan and Henry Treece, eds. *A New Romantic Anthology.* London: The Grey Walls Press, 1949.

Schneider, Herbert W. *A History of American Philosophy.* New York: Columbia University Press, 1946.

Sears, Clara Endicott. *Bronson Alcott's Fruitlands.* Boston: Houghton Mifflin, 1915.

Sedgwick, Henry P., Jr. *Father Hecker.* Boston: Beacon, 1900.

Shephard, Odell. *Peddlar's Progress: The Life of Bronson Alcott.* Boston: Little, Brown, 1938.

Shyrock, Richard H. "Sylvester Graham and the Popular Health Movement." *Mississippi Valley Historical Review* 28 (December 1931): 172–183.

Spalding, Martin John. *Miscellanea: Comprising Reviews, Lectures, and Essays on Historical, Theological, and Miscellaneous Subjects.* Louisville, Ky.: Webb, Gill, and Levering, 1855.

Spalding, Thomas. *Martin John Spalding: American Churchman.* Washington, D.C.: The Catholic University of America Press, 1973.

Spencer, Michael Clifford. *Charles Fourier.* Boston: Twayne Publishers, 1981.

Sullivan, Robert and James O'Toole, eds. *Catholic Boston: Studies in Religion and Community, 1870–1970.* Boston: Northeastern University Press, 1986.

Symeon the New Theologian. *Symeon the New Theologian: The Discourses.* Translated by C.J. de Catanzaro. New York: Paulist Press, 1980.

Symonds, John A. *Sleep and Dreams.* London: John Murray, 1851.

Tackett, Timothy. *Priest and Parish in Eighteenth-Century France.* Princeton, N.J.: Princeton University Press, 1977.

Tanner, Tony. *The Reign of Wonder: Naivety and Reality in American Literature.* Cambridge: Cambridge University Press, 1965.

Tasso, Torquato. *Jerusalem Delivered.* Translated by J. H. Wiffen. London: Hurst and Robinson, 1825.

Taves, Ann. *Household of Faith.* South Bend, Ind.: University of Notre Dame Press, 1986.

Temin, Peter. *Causal Factors in American Economic Growth in the Nineteenth Century.* Essex, England: Anchor Press, 1975.

Temin, Peter. *The Jacksonian Economy.* New York: W. W. Norton, 1969.

Tennyson, Emile, ed. *Nineteenth Century Literary Criticism.* Vol. 7. Detroit: Gale, 1984.

Thoreau, Henry David. *The Writings of Henry D. Thoreau: Journal 1837–1844.* Edited by Elizabeth Witherell, William Howarth, Robert Sattelmeyer, and Thomas Blanding. Princeton, N.J.: Princeton University Press, 1981.

—. *The Writings of Henry D. Thoreau: Journal 1842–1848.* Edited by Robert Sattelmeyer. Princeton, N.J.: Princeton University Press, 1984.

—. *Translations*. Edited by K. P. Van Anglen. Princeton, N.J.: Princeton University Press, 1986.

—. *Walden and Civil Disobedience*. Edited by Owen Thomas. New York: W. W. Norton, 1966.

Tracts for the Times, Vol. IV for 1838–40. London: J. Rivington, 1840.

Tuke, D. Hack. *Sleep-walking and Hypnotism*. London: J & A. Churchill, 1884.

Turnbull, Grace, ed. *Essence of Plotinus*. New York: Oxford University Press, 1934.

Underhill, Evelyn. *Mysticism*. London: Mathuen, 1911.

Vinson, James. *Great Writers of the English Language: Dramatists*. London: Macmillan, 1979.

Vogel, Stanley. *German Literary Influences on the American Transcendentalists*. New York: Archon Books, 1970.

Waggoner, Hyatt H. *American Poets from the Puritans to the Present*. Baton Rouge, La.: Louisiana State University Press, 1984.

Walker, James. "Reaction in Favor to the Roman Catholics." *Christian Examiner* 23 (September 1837): 1 f.

Walworth, Clarence. *The Oxford Movement in America*. New York: The Catholic Book Exchange, 1895.

Weber, Eugene. *Europe since 1715*. New York: Norton, 1972.

Wells, Ronald V. *Three Christian Transcendentalists*. New York: Columbia University Press, 1943.

Welter, Barbara. "The Cult of True Womanhood: 1820–1860." *American Quarterly* 18 (Summer 1966): 151–74.

Wendell, Barrett. *A Literary History of America*. New York: Greenwood, 1968.

White, Morton. *Science and Sentiment in America: Philosophical Thought from Jonathan Edwards to John Dewey*. New York: Oxford University Press, 1972.

INDEX TO INTRODUCTIONS*

*General Introduction to the book and Introductions to each section of
The Diary.

"Address to the People of the
United States," 45; *see also*
Associationism; Fourierism
Aids to Reflection (Coleridge), 18,
66, 67
Agassiz, Louis, 37–38, 43
Agrippa, H.C., 30
Ahlstrom, Sydney, 17
Alcott, Bronson, 7, 8, 27–30, 42,
82, 299
Alexander, Edgar, 70–71
Angel, Guardian, 253
Anglican Orders, validity of, 57,
58; *see also* Oxford Movement
Associationism, 39, 42, 43–47,
60, 61, 83, 192; *see also*
Fourierism
Augustine, Saint, 44, 275
*Awful Disclosures of the Hotel
Dieu Nunnery in Montreal*
(Monk), 48

Ballou, Adin, 40
Baptism, 228

Barber, Virgil, 50
Barlow, Almira, 69, 82, 254
Bellarmine, Saint Robert, 30
Bernard of Clairvaux, Saint, 31
Bestor, Arthus, 33, 34
Bhagavadgita, 30
Blake, William, 21
Boehme, Jacob, 30
Bosco, Saint John, 71
Bower, Samuel, 82
Bradford, George, 83
Brigitta of Sweden, 30
Brisbane, Albert, 38–39, 42
Brook Farm, 5, 6, 8, 9, 17, 23–25,
31, 32, 81, 228; Fourierism, 40,
61; *The Harbinger,* 44; Catholic
converts, 61–66
Brownson, Orestes, 5, 8, 9, 15,
22, 25, 37, 44–47, 51, 64–66,
71, 73, 81, 82, 191, 192, 193,
228, 254, 275, 276, 277
Brownson Quarterly Review, 44,
254, 276
Bruce, Georgiana, 64, 82, 254

Bushnell, Horace, 72

Calhoun, John C., 15, 82
Campbell, Alexander, 16
Carey, Arthur, 20, 23
Carey, Patrick, 51
Carlyle, Thomas, 7, 18
Carpenter, Frederick Ives, 27
Carroll, Bishop John, 47, 50
*The Catholic Doctrine on
    Justification* (Kenrick,
    Francis P.), 57
"The Catholics and
    Associationists" (Channing,
    William Henry), 44, 63
Certeau, Michel de, 14
Channing, Julia, 63
Channing, William Ellery, 31, 39
Channing, William Ellery II, 43
Channing, William Henry, 8, 38–
    40, 41, 43, 44, 63, 64, 73, 228;
    Catholic sympathies, 63, 64;
    social consciousness, 73
Chateaubriand, François René de,
    19
Cheverus, Bishop Jean, 47, 50
Christ, 4, 16, 24, 25, 32;
    Brownson, 44–45, 65; grace of,
    46, 65, 192; suffering of, 53; as
    pure symbol, 67; need for, 72,
    82–83
Christian Advocate and Journal,
    59
The Christian Examiner, 31, 44
"Christian Song of the Middle
    Ages" (Channing, William
    Ellery II), 43
"Church Unity and Social
    Amelioration" (Brownson), 44
Church, Anglican, 254; *see also*
    Anglican Orders, validity of;
    Oxford Movement

Church, Catholic/Catholicism,
    general interest in, 44;
    Brownson's move toward, 46–
    47; alternative to
    Associationism, 46–47; 1840s,
    47–60; immigrants and
    foreignness, 47, 61, 65, 193;
    response to Romantic Mood,
    51–56; response to Oxford
    Movement, 56–60; Devotional
    Revival, 53–56;
    Ultramontanism, 55;
    Transcendentalism, 60, 61–66;
    as Newness, 64; Hecker, 66,
    70–73, 254
The Churchman, 23
Coleridge, Samuel Taylor, 18, 66,
    67, 73
Communion, life by, 22; Holy,
    228
Communitarian Movement, 32,
    33–38; *see also* Fourierism
Constant, Benjamin, 64
Contemplation, 27, 29, 30, 63, 65,
    228
*Conversations with Children on the
    Gospels* (Alcott), 27
Corinne (De Staël), 254
Cornelius Institute, 253, 275
Couser, G. Thomas, 9
Cratylus (Plato), 28
Critique of Pure Reason (Kant), 18
Curtis, Burrill, 69, 82, 228, 254,
    255, 275
Curtis, George, 69, 82, 228, 254,
    255, 275

Dana, Charles Anderson, 8, 24,
    69, 228; Fourierism, 40, 41;
    Hecker's roommate at Brook
    Farm, 41, 82
Dante, 44, 62

De Gammond, Madame Gatti, 42
DeMaistre, Joseph, 19, 71
DeSales, Saint Francis, 30
DeStaël, Germaine, 18, 254
Dewey, Orville, 5
Dial, 8, 25, 27, 29, 36, 63; first
  edition, 37; Associationists, 39
Dichtung und Wahrheit (Goethe),
  254
Die Leiden des jungen Werthers
  (Goethe), 8
Die Wahlverwandtschaften
  (Goethe), 8
Digbey, K, 30
"The Divine Presence in nature
  and in the Soul" (Parker), 37
Drey, Johann Sebastian, 71, 72

*The Early Years of Isaac Thomas
  Hecker* (Holden), 13
Eckhart, Meister, 83
Edwards, Jonathan, 28
Elliott, Walter, 6, 10–13
Emerson, Ralph Waldo, 6, 22, 30,
  31, 32, 36, 39, 48, 63, 82;
  Hecker's dislike of, 32–33
Emile (Rousseau), 18
End of Controversy (Milner), 24,
  57
Eriugena, 83
Everett, Abraham, 82

Faber, Frederick W., 71
Fenelon, François, 30, 31
Fenwick, Bishop Benedict Joseph,
  50, 55, 60, 254
Finney, Charles G., 15, 28, 41
Fitzpatrick, Bishop, 193, 254
*Foreign Conspiracy Against the
  Liberties of the United States*
  (Morese), 48

Fourierism, 38–43, 72, 254;
  Phalanxes, 32, 33, 38, 40, 61;
  The Phalanx, 41, 43, 60;
  Hecker, 82; no-churchism, 82
"Fourierism and the Socialists"
  (Emerson), 39
Francis DeSales, *see* DeSales,
  Saint Francis
Frank, Sebastian, 30
Fruitlands, 5, 13, 27, 32, 42, 68,
  81, 82, 83, 192; library, 30
Fuller, Margaret, 39, 63

Gannett, Debora, 228
God, 8, 9, 11, 12, 16, 23, 26, 27,
  28, 30, 33, 36, 69, 71;
  sovereignty of, 26, 28; living
  Spirit, 37; inward Spirit, 69;
  Brownson, 44; will of, 52
God in Christ (Bushnell), 67
Goethe, Johann Wolfgang, 8, 81,
  254
Gorres, Johann Joseph, 71, 72
Grace, 29, 192; of Christ, 46, 83
Greaves, James P., 29, 30
Greeley, Horace, and Fourierism,
  39, 41
Greene, William Betchelder, and
  Saint Augustine, 44
Gura, Philip, 67
Guyon, Madame, 30

Haight, Benjamin, 23
The Harbinger, 44
Harper, George Mills, 29
Hawthorne, Nathaniel, 63, 73
Hawthorne, Rose (Mother
  Alfonsa), 63
Hecker, Caroline Friend (mother),
  4, 81
Hecker, Elizabeth (sister), 4

Hecker, George (brother), 4, 5, 276
Hecker, Henry (brother), 4
Hecker, Isaac Thomas, biography, 4–6; Oxford Movement, 22–25; Brook Farm, 24, 25–27, 31, 61–64, 81–82; Fruitlands, 27–31; 42, 82; Catholicism, 33, 51, 62, 63, 65, 66, 70–73, 276, 277, 299, 300; influence of Hughes, 47; influence of Fenwick, 50; employed, 59; Sophia Ripley, 61–62, 64, 82; Dante, 62; Redemptorist, 62; Paulist, 62; George Ripley, 62–63, 82; immigrant Catholicism, 65; achievement, 66–73; Romantic impulse, 66; Quietism, 68; Almira Barlow, 69, 82; lasting influence of Transcendentalism, 70; Baptism, 70; most tumultuous period, 81; Fourier Convention, 82; movement for Suffrage Rights, 254; Confirmation, 276–277; religious vocation, 277, 300; scrupulosity, 299
Hecker, John (father), 4
Hecker, John, Jr. (brother), 4, 5, 23, 82
Hedge, Frederick Henry, 32
Henry, Caleb Sprague, 32, 33
Herbert, George, 30
Hesperus (Richter), 8
Heyne, Robert V., 14
History of American Socialisms (Noyes), 33
Hobart, John Henry, 19
Hochfield, George, 25–26
Hodge, Charles, 16
Holden, Vincent, 13
Hook, Walter F., 58

Hughes, Bishop John, 4, 16, 49, 50, 55, 56, 60, 62, 70, 300; social questions, 46–47, 58; influence on Brownson and Hecker, 47–50; difference from romanticism, 51–52; "resurgent Counter-Reformation Catholicism," 52; response to Oxford Movement, 58, 59

Infallibility, 24
"Influence of Catholicity on Civil Liberty" (Spalding), 52
Individualism, 71
Ireland, John, 11

Jackson, Andrew, 15
Jamblichus, 30
Jesuits, 34, 53
Julian of Norwich, 30

Kant, Immanuel, 18
Kay, James, Jr., 61
Keble, John, 19, 22, 56
Kenrick, Bishop Francis P., 56–58, 59
Kenrick, Bishop Peter R., 57
Kirby, Georgiana Bruce, *see* Bruce, Georgiana
Klein, Abbé Felix, 11

La Madonna di San Sista (Channing, William Henry), 43
Lacordaire, Jean-Baptiste, 19, 70
Lamennais, Félicité de, 19
Lane, Charles, 8, 27, 30, 32, 42, 82, 192, 299
Larned, Sam, 82
Law, William, 30
The Laws of Menu, 30
Le Père Hecker, Est-il un Saint? (Maignen), 6, 10

Leach, George, 61, 191
Lead, Jane, 30
Lectures on Dramatic Art and Literature (Schlegel), 275
Leroux, Pierre, 64, 81
Letter on Christian Union (Kenrick, Francis P.), 57
Liberty, 25, 27, 31, 60, 63
Life of Father Hecker (Holden), 6, 10–13
Lyons, Mary, 70
Locke, John, 28, 36, 66
Loco-Foco, 5, 46
Lowell, Francis Cabot, 34, 73
The Lowell Offering, 34

Maignen, Charles, 6, 10–13, 68
"Man, the Reformer" (Emerson), 36
Manning, Cardinal Henry Edward, 71
The Marble Faun (Hawthorne), 63
Marsh, James, 32, 33, 66–67, 72
Martinet, Antoine, 60
Mary, Blessed Virgin, 253
Mass, 253
Materialism, 36, 37
McCloskey, Bishop John, influence on Hecker, 60, 70, 193; spiritual director, 253, 254, 299, 300
McMaster, James, 20–21, 61
Meagher, James, 54–55
Memoirs to Serve for the Future (Fenwick), 50
Methodism, 4, 15, 23, 28, 35, 58, 68, 81
Middle Ages, 37, 43, 46, 47, 52, 53, 58, 70, 229
Millenialism, 41
Milner, 24, 57
Miscellanea (Spalding), 53, 60

Moehler, J.A., 23–24, 71, 73, 81
Molinos, Miguel de, 30
Monk, Maria, 48
Montalembert, Charles de, 19
Mormonism, 5, 16
Morse, Samuel F. B., 48
Mysticism, 27, 29, 30, 31, 63, 68, 69

Native American party, 48
Naturalism, 71
Nature (Emerson), 48
Nevin, John W., 16
New Views, 37
Newcomb, Charles King, 17, 63, 73
Newell, Benjamin Franklin, 35–36
Newman, John Henry, 19–21, 56, 71
Newness, 29, 32, 37, 81, 192; Catholicism as, 64
"No Church, No Reform" (Brownson), 44, 64, 82
Norton, Andrews, 29, 32
Noyes, John Humphrey, 16, 33, 34

O'Meara, Thomas F., 18, 71
On Germany (DeStaël), 18
Onderdonk, Benjamin T., 20, 23; *see also* Oxford Movement
Orders, Anglican; *see* Anglican orders, validity of; Oxford Movement
Orphic Sayings (Alcott), 27, 37
Owen, John J., 254
Owen, Robert, 34
Oxford Movement, 17, 19–25, 31, 61, 81, 82; Catholic response, 56–60; Hecker, 68

Palma, Johannes Baptist, 52
Palmer, Joseph, 82

"Pamphlet on Association, A Concise Exposition of the Doctrine of Association" (Brisbane), 39
Pantheism, 71
Papacy/Popes, 55, 57, 276
Parker, Theodore, 8, 26, 36, 37
Parmenides (Plato), 28
Paulist Church (Fifty-ninth Street), 62, 63
Paulists (Missionary Society of St. Paul the Apostle), 5, 10, 11
Penance, 229; sacrament of, 228, 229
The Permanent and Transient in Christianity (Parker), 26
Phaedo (Plato), 28
The Phalanx: Journal of Social Sciences, 41, 43, 44; *see also* Fourierism
Plato, 27, 28, 29, 30
Plotinus, 29, 30, 31; Plotinean mysticism differentiated from Christian, 29
Poeteri, Claudius de la, 50
Portier, William, 6
Praelectiones Historiae Ecclesiasticae (Palma), 52
Pratt, Parley Parker, 5, 191
Prayer, 228
Predestination, 15, 28
The Present, 39, 40, 42, 43
Proclus, 30
Providence, 37, 52, 53
Pseudo-Dionysius, 83
Pusey, 19, 56

Quietism, 68

Reason, 25, 54–55
Redemptorists, 5, 53, 62
Religion in Society, 60

"The Religion of Beauty" (Dwight), 37
Revivalists, 28, 41
Richter, Jean Paul, 8, 21, 63, 69, 81, 299
Ripley, George, 8, 24, 26, 32, 37, 62, 65, 81, 82; and Fourierism, 38, 41, 42; and Father Hecker, 62–63
Ripley, Sophia, 17, 63; and Dante, 44, 62; Brook Farm, 61–62, 82; conversion, 62, 64; Father Hecker her confessor, 62
Robert Bellarmine, Saint; *see* Bellarmine, Saint Robert
Romantic novelists, 69
Romanticism, 17–19, 21, 43; Catholic response to, 51–56; and Catholic piety, 53–56, 58; Hecker, 66–73; distinction between Reason and Understanding, 66–67
Rose, Ann, 13
Rosmini, 71
Rousseau, Jean-Jacques, 18; and Romanticism, 55
Russell, Ida, 82
Ryan, E., 19

Sacraments, 228
Sailer, J.M., 71
Schaff, Phillip, 16
Schelling, Friedrich, 69, 71
Schlegel, Friedrich, 71, 81, 275
Schleiermacher, Friedrich, 21, 72
Schwab, Christopher, 4
Seabury, Samuel, 23
Sears, Clara Endicott, 13
Seton, Saint Elizabeth Bayley, 19
Siebankas (Richter), 8
Shakers, 34, 82
Shakespeare, William, 275

Sin, 253
Smith, Joseph, 5, 16
Smucker, Samuel, S., 16
The Social Destiny of Man, or Association and Reorganization of Industry (Brisbane), 38–39
Spalding, Bishop Martin John, 4, 16, 52–53, 55; Hecker's friend, 52; interest in history, 52, 59; response to Oxford Movement, 59–60
Spirit, Holy, 4, 22, 24; Platonism, 28; God as, 37, 44; of Christ, 65; Romanticism, 66; inward, 69; Hecker's love of, 72
Stearns, Sarah, 17, 61
Suffrage Rights, Movement for, 254
Sullivan, John Dwight, 69
Swedenborg, Emanuel, 23, 43
Symbolism (Moehler), 23–24, 81
"Sympathy" (Thoreau), 37

Tanner, Toby, 7
Taylor, Edward, 30
Taylor, Nathaniel William, 28
Taylor, Thomas, 28
Teaching the Truth by Signs and Ceremonies (Meagher), 54–55
Teresa of Avila, Saint, 31
Thayer, John, 50
Thirty-nine Articles, 20–21; *see also* Oxford movement
Thomas à Kempis, 30
Thoreau, Henry David, 5, 7, 18, 30, 37, 82, 83, 229
"Thoughts on Labor" (Parker), 36
Timaeus (Plato), 28
Titan (Richter), 8
Tract 89: On the Mysticism Attributed to the Early Fathers of the Church (Keble), 22

Tract 90 (Newman), 20
Tractarianism/Tractarians, 37, 61, 65; *see also* Oxford Movement
Tracts for the Times, 23, 81
Tradition, 24
Transcendental Club, 27, 32, 66
Transcendentalism/Transcendentalists, 7, 9, 13, 17, 19, 25–33, 35; solitary, 31; social theory, 36; spirit, 42, 66; and Catholicism, 60–66; lasting influence on Hecker, 70; no-churchism, 82
Transcendentalism as a Social Movement (Rose), 13
Trent, Council of, 23; Catechism of, 23
"The Two Dolans" (Newcomb), 63

Ultramontanism, 55, 56
Unitarianism, 5, 26, 29, 36
United States Catholic Magazine, articles on Oxford Movement, 58–59
Unity, 61, 63
"Unity in Catholicity in the Church" (Channing, William Henry), 63
"The Unity and Catholicity of the Church Essential to Reform" (Brownson), 46

The Validity of Anglican Orders (Kenrick, Peter R.), 57
Victorines, 83
Vocation, 8, 81; religious, 277, 300

Wahrheit aus Jean Pauls Leben (Richter), 8
Walden (Thoreau), 30

Walker, James, 44
Walworth, Clarence, 20–22, 61
Ward, Samuel, 44
Webster, Daniel, 14

Whitman, Walt, 18

Xenophon, 30

INDEX TO TEXT

Abolitionists, 182, 362n139
Adam, 134, 135, 167, 169, 243,
  274, 281, 287, 288, 289, 296,
  297, 375n215
Affirmations (Greaves), 157
Alcott, Bronson, 109, 110, 113,
  115, 116, 117, 118, 121, 139,
  207
Alcott, Mrs., 121
Angels, 105, 172, 175, 182, 187,
  201, 210, 222, 225, 230, 235,
  248, 249, 251, 261, 277, 291,
  292, 302, 305, 319; Guardian,
  258, 259, 269, 274, 303, 305,
  312, 315, 319
Aquinas, Saint Thomas, 323,
  379n239; Hecker's Confirmation
  name, 316
Association, 157, 169
Atheism, 108
Augustine, Saint, 309, 345n63

Baptism, 101, 234; conditional,
  221, 227, 229; Hecker's, 232;
  Baptismal promises, 281, 314
Barlow, Almira, 95, 133, 136,
  142, 155, 168, 330n15, 351n92

Beethoven, Ludwig van, 238
Bernard, Saint, 225, 238
Bible, 95, 108, 147, 187, 320, 321
Black, Mrs., 139
Boehme, Jacob, 126, 342n54
Bourignon, Antonia, 134, 374n74
Bower, Samuel, 116, 121
Bradford, George Partridge, 168,
  197, 360n127
Brook Farm, 89, 93, 104, 106,
  120, 121, 132, 135, 136, 155,
  156, 188, 194, 215, 330n10,
  330n13
Brownson, Orestes, 88, 89, 91,
  101, 116, 155, 162, 163, 167,
  197, 203, 204, 210, 215, 301,
  303, 321, 322, 324, 325,
  333n24
Brownson Quarterly Review, 197
Bruce, Georgiana, 154, 161
Buddha, 190, 202
Buddhism, 160
Byron, Lord, 113

Calvin, John, 126
Canova, Antonio, 238, 373n192
Carlyle, Thomas, 246

Catholicism, *see* Church, Catholic

Cato, 212, 218

Channing, William Henry, 139, 146, 210, 349n86

Chase, William, 139

Christ, communion with, 90; suffering, 90, 297; mediator, 99, 234, 315; redeemer, 114, 130, 132, 352n99, 354n108; Spirit of, 131, 323, 354n108; humanity, 155, 166, 169; three-fold coming of, 189; Church as body of, 205; grace of God, 212, 344n61; power of, 243; incarnation of God, 287; divinity, 292; mentioned *passim*

Church, 100, 102, 103, 112, 117, 137, 138, 141, 143, 148, 158, 159, 162, 165, 166, 174, 177, 178, 180, 181, 187, 199, 205, 207, 213, 231, 239, 245, 295; clergy, 158, 159; authority, 280; necessity, 281

Church, Anglican, 147, 163, 167, 181, 206, 293

Church, Catholic, 94, 95, 97, 98, 107, 108, 147, 155, 157, 160, 163, 165, 177, 181, 199, 204, 205, 206, 209, 215, 219, 221, 222, 223, 225, 226, 230, 231, 232, 244, 279, 283, 290, 292; solidarity, 98; unity of, 155, 220; as foreign, 165; universality, 177; as progressive, 282; as Christianity, 291; primacy of Rome, 293; pew-renting, 300–301, 377n227; as true Church, 321; infallibility of, 324; Hecker's interest in, 334n26, 334n27; unattractiveness of,

235n31; immigrant Church, 352n99; as lower class, 368n175

Coleridge, Samuel Taylor, 113

Communion, 88, 90, 92, 95, 103, 148, 151, 181, 187, 274, 333n24

Communism, 157, 158

Confucius, 98, 332n21

Contemplation, 221, 305, 372n187

Conversion, 89, 101, 309

Cornelius Institute, 268, 324, 325

Curtis, Burrill, 188, 263, 345n65

Curtis, George, 188, 197, 345n65

Dana, Charles Anderson, 94, 128, 136, 342n56

Dante, 225, 238, 239, 247, 294, 295

Death, 93, 121, 127, 138, 139, 179, 187, 200, 222, 223, 243, 248, 272, 278, 292, 297, 317, 318

Deists, 292

Democracy, 177–178

DeSales, Saint Francis, 238, 244, 255, 374n209

Devil, *see* Satan

Dichtung und Wahrheit (Goethe), 156, 357n116

Die Leiden des jungen Werthers (Goethe), 87, 156, 328n5, 357n116

Die Wahlverwandtschaften (Goethe), 156, 357n116

Divine Comedy (Dante), 247, 294, 298

Dryden, John, 198

Dumas, Alexander, 197

Dwight, John Sullivan, 129, 132, 197, 343n59

Elective Affinities (Goethe), *see*
Die Wahlverwandtschaften
Elli, Frances Auston, 132
Emerson, Ralph Waldo, 116, 207,
210, 282–283, 287, 367n170
Epicurus, 106, 155
Eucharist (Blessed Sacrament),
138, 274, 316
Eve, 212
Everett, Abraham, 120, 121

Faith, 109, 110, 111, 177, 250,
271, 279, 292, 305, 307, 317,
319, 324
Faust (Goethe), 294
Fenwick, Bishop Benedict Joseph,
205
Fitzpatrick, Bishop, 205, 209
Fourier, Charles, *see* Fourierism
Fourierism, 158, 333n23,
360n129; phalanx, 209,
368n175
Fox, George, 126, 158
Francis, Saint, 309, 323
Francis deSales, Saint, *see*
DeSales, Saint Francis
Francis Xavier, Saint, *see* Xavier,
Saint Francis
Fredericka, 229
Freedom, 164, 182, 243
Fruitlands, 110, 115, 116, 121,
135, 155, 215, 336n32, 337n38,
338n40; library, 340n45
Fuller, Margaret, 139, 348n81,
349n86

God, will of, 91, 112, 214,
362n141; Spirit, 91, 93, 141,
144, 166, 169, 171, 181, 183,
184, 219, 281; presence of, 91,
164; as Father, 93, 102, 108,
109, 112, 130, 131, 134, 135,
144, 153, 161, 169, 178, 187,
204, 217, 226, 236, 273, 274,
285, 307; wisdom of, 99, 288,
321; kingdom of, 101, 106, 111,
112, 123, 172, 182, 201, 243,
248, 281, 291, 323; union with,
104, 161, 176, 307, 325,
354n111; help of, 119, 120,
126, 217; as love, 133; as
Parent, 154, 161, 172, 217,
236, 247; trust in, 195, 259,
319; God-man, 196, 223, 245,
306, 326; as wife, 293;
knowledge of, 325; mentioned
passim
Goethe, Johann Wolfgang, 156,
157, 190, 201, 216, 289, 294,
328n5, 357n116
Grace, 134, 175, 178, 183, 212,
235, 238, 295, 305, 313, 320,
323, 344n61
Greaves, James Pierpoint, 157,
242, 358n117
Green, William Bathchelder, 128,
342n56
Green, Mrs. William B., 139

Haight, Benjamin Isaac, 147, 163,
167, 201, 353n103
Hamlet (Shakespeare), 143, 197
Hecker, Caroline Friend (mother),
93, 117, 329n8
Hecker, George (brother), 115,
120, 124, 156, 316; Oxford
Movement and conversion to
Catholicism, 331n16, 336n37
Hecker, Isaac Thomas, family, 92,
93, 109, 117, 118, 329n7;
family business, 109, 110, 113,
122, 156, 162, 330n11, 330n13,

336n35, 366n155; baptized, 232; confirmed, 316; Oxford Movement and conversion to Catholicism, 331n16; *see also* Church, Catholic

Hecker, John (brother), 93, 115, 124, 156, 329n8; Oxford Movement and conversion to Anglicanism, 331n16

Hegel, Georg Friedrich, 129

Heine, 98, 296

Hesperus (Richter), 87, 327n2

Holy Spirit/Holy Ghost, 200, 212, 213, 220, 222, 231, 274, 362n141; Church as channel of, 205; *see also* God, Spirit

Homer, 225

Hughes, Bishop John, 165, 316, 326

Immortality, 150, 278, 285, 317

Individualism, 136, 155, 282

Individuality, 98

Infallibility, 98; of the Church, 95, 293, 324

Jesuits, 312, 368n175, 378n235

Jesus, *see* Christ

John, Saint, 98, 101

John the Baptist, Saint, 296, 320

Kingdom of Christ (Maurice), 128, 342n55, 365n148

Lane, Charles, 109, 116, 117, 118, 121, 139, 201, 207

Larned, Sam, 116

Leroux, Pierre, 129, 333n24

Liberty, 220, 293

Loyola, Saint Ignatius, 311, 323, 378n235

Luther, Martin, 98, 126, 140, 190

Mark, Saint, 108

Martin, Mr., 101, 124

Mary, Blessed Virgin, 220, 222, 236, 245, 258, 296, 303, 309, 315, 318, 374n202

Mass, 256, 258, 260

Materialism, 136

Maurice, John Frederick Denison, 128, 190, 342n55, 365n148

McCloskey, Bishop John, 210, 221, 229, 233, 236, 242, 301, 311, 313, 369n176; confessor, 262, 317; spiritual director, 306, 310, 311, 315, 318, 372n186, 379n240

Methodism, 167, 329n8, 344n61, 346n69

Michelangelo, 225, 295

Middle Ages, 215, 221, 372n186

Milton, John, 294

Moses, 123

Murray, Orson Smith, 155, 356n113

Napoleon, 214, 225

Nationality, 124, 125, 341n51

Norris, Rev. Mr., 163, 166, 167

Novalis, 200, 284

Order, religious, 312, 313, 316, 321, 326; *see also* priest/ priesthood

Orders, Holy, 242; *see also* Order, religious; Priest/priesthood

Orpheus, 126

Owen, John J., 262

Palmer, Edward, 133, 346n70

Pantheism, 129

Papacy/Pope, 167, 280, 281; *see also* Church, Catholic

Paradise Lost (Milton), 294

Parsons, Anne, 197

Past and Present (Carlyle), 113, 246

Paul, Saint, 98, 185, 230, 320, 321

Penance, 138, 235, 372n186; Sacrament/Tribunal of (Confession), 262, 264, 266, 267, 273, 303, 310, 312, 313, 316, 372n187; *see also* McCloskey, Bishop John, confessor; McCloskey, Bishop John, spiritual director

Penn, 126

Peter, Saint, 98, 127

Phalanx, *see* Fourierism

Phidias, 225

Plato, 106, 155, 212, 218, 220, 283

Pope, Alexander, 296

Pratt, Parley Parker, 194, 358n118, 365n154

Prayer, 89, 92, 93, 106, 110, 111, 138, 169, 188, 222, 250

Priest/Priesthood, 158, 165, 177, 221, 259, 280, 295, 311, 312, 315, 316, 317, 359n123; *see also* Order, religious; Orders, Holy

Progress, 88, 122, 127

Prophet/Prophecy, 124, 125, 150, 175, 212, 320

Protestant/Protestantism, 98, 107, 155, 157, 158, 165, 205, 215, 244, 245, 280, 282, 324–325; ignorance about Catholics, 265, 283; and liberty, 293; Hecker as, 301

Providence, 121, 124, 138, 163, 172, 341n50, 349n84, 362n141; Providential Men, 125, 226

Pythagoras, 108, 123, 155, 185, 212, 218, 220, 283

Quaker, 148

Quietism, 139, 142, 159, 350n88

Raphael, 225, 238, 294, 295

Rationalism, 108, 109

Reason, 98, 226, 250, 295

Redeemer, 196, 220, 287, 303, 352n99; necessity 223; *see also* Christ

Redemptorists, 326, 378n238, 379n240

Reform, 143, 158, 352n94

Revelation, 278, 284

Richter, Jean Paul, 87, 140, 216, 217, 244, 268, 289, 327n2, 335n29

Ripley, George, 94, 113, 132, 169

Ripley, Sophia, 146

Sacraments, 138, 148, 167, 281; *see also* Baptism; Eucharist; Penance, Sacrament/Tribunal of (Confession); Order, Religious; Orders, Holy; Priest/Priesthood

Saints, 93, 94, 227, 236, 244, 289, 292, 305, 319, 323

Satan, 122, 184, 227, 286, 314

Schelling, Friedrich, 98

Schlegel, Friedrich, 296

Schiller, Friedrich von, 199

Science, 125, 149, 195

Scripture, *see* Bible

Seabury, Samuel, 167, 360n126

Sex, 134–135, 137, 348n81

Shakers, 160, 336n32

Shakespeare, William, 159, 185, 225, 238, 289

Shelley, Percy, 113

Siebankas (Richter), 87

Sin, 107, 114, 144, 196, 210, 212, 213, 223, 232, 237, 245, 250, 251, 255, 256, 262, 263, 273, 274, 292, 315, 324, 325, 326; habitual, 261; mortal, 266; venial, 266

Smith, Joseph, 158, 358n118, 365n154

Socialism, 293

Socrates, 123, 144, 155, 185, 207, 212, 218, 220, 283

Solitary (Fredericka), 229

Solomon, 111

Spirit, union with, 186; *see also* God, Spirit; Holy Spirit/Holy Ghost

Stephen, Saint, 277, 284

Succession (Apostolic), 95, 333n24

Swedenborg, Emanuel, 126, 134, 198, 200, 333n22

Teresa, Saint, 309

Thomas Aquinas, Saint; *see* Aquinas, Saint Thomas

Thoreau, Henry David, 139, 232, 233, 236, 242, 246, 272n186

Titan (Richter), 87, 289, 327n2

Tradition, 95, 147

Transcendentalist, 90, 168, 206, 335n30, 367n170; as Protestant, 283

Trent, Council of, 147; Catechism of, 95, 331n16, 371n183, 373n194

Unitarians, 292

Vethake, Dr., 134

Werther/Wertherism, see *Die Leiden des jungen Werthers* (Goethe)

Wesley, John, 126

Wilhelm Meister (Goethe), 289

Wordsworth, William, 198

Xavier, Saint Francis, 311, 378n235

Zeno, 106, 155, 212, 218, 220, 283

Zoroaster, 190, 212, 218, 283

Other Volumes in This Series

Walter Rauschenbusch: Selected Writings
William Ellery Channing: Selected Writings
Devotion to the Holy Spirit in American Catholicism
Horace Bushnell: Sermons
Alaskan Missionary Spirituality
Elizabeth Seton: Selected Writings
Eastern Spirituality in America
Charles Hodge: The Way of Life
Henry Alline: Selected Writings
William Porcher DuBose: Selected Writings
American Jesuit Spirituality
Phoebe Palmer: Selected Writings
Early American Meditative Poetry:
   Anne Bradstreet and Edward Taylor